EXPERIMENTAL SOCIAL PSYCHOLOGY

EXPERIMENTAL SOCIAL PSYCHOLOGY

TEXT WITH ILLUSTRATIVE READINGS

CHESTER A. INSKO and JOHN SCHOPLER

University North Carolina
Department of Psychology
Chapel Hill, North Carolina

ACADEMIC PRESS New York and London

ACADEMIC PRESS, INC.
111 Fifth Avenue, New York, New York 10003

United Kingdom Edition published by
ACADEMIC PRESS, INC. (LONDON) LTD.
24/28 Oval Road, London NW1

LIBRARY OF CONGRESS CATALOG CARD NUMBER: 70-187227

PRINTED IN THE UNITED STATES OF AMERICA

To our wives, Verla and Jan

CONTENTS

Chapter 3   Source Characteristics and Persistence Effects

Chapter 4   Dissonance in Free-Choice Situations

Chapter 5   Dissonance in Forced-Compliance Situations

Chapter 6   Communicator Discrepancy

Chapter 7   Resistance to Persuasion

Part II INTERPERSONAL PROCESSES

Chapter 8 Person Perception and Attribution Processes

Chapter 9 Interpersonal Attraction

Chapter 10 Conformity

Chapter 11 Norm Formation and Exchange Theory

Part III SMALL GROUPS

Chapter 12 Preinteraction Variables

Chapter 13 Group Processes—Structure

Chapter 14 Extremity Shifts

Chapter 15 Intergroup Relationships: Outgroup Rejection

References

PREFACE

In at least three respects this book grew out of our laborious and yet rewarding collaboration as associate editors of the *Journal of Experimental Social Psychology*. First, the requisite reading of large numbers of manuscripts impressed us with the importance of learning the field through exposure to primary-source literature. Hence the present book contains illustrative readings as well as more orthodox textbook discussion. Second, we were struck by the fact that the typical textbooks did not adequately represent the type of literature submitted to or published by the *Journal*. Third, the *Journal's* commitment to *experimental* social psychology reinforced our feeling that a textbook with a similar commitment was needed. Although we are aware that there are potential artifacts in laboratory experimental social psychology, we believe that substantive advances in the field are most likely to come through the application of this method.

This book, containing both text and readings, represents a new approach to undergraduate social psychology. We believe this approach has evident merit compared to books containing only text or only readings. A text can present a coherent and nontechnical overview of social psychology, but cannot readily convey the flavor of social psychological research. It is difficult for a book of readings to present a coherent overall picture, and the technical aspects of many readings transcend the skills which should be required of a typical undergraduate student. Readings are valuable, not so much for conveying facts, as for providing concrete and detailed illustrations of the professional social psychologist at work. It is thus our hope that this book combines the best of both approaches. We do recognize that a few of the readings are fairly difficult and will require background discussions. Alternatively, some of the readings could simply be omitted.

In the course of preparing this book we have been helped by a number of people. Chief among these is John Thibaut. The germinal conception of this book dates back to our close association with him as editor of the *Journal of Experimental Social Psychology*. We are deeply appreciative of his willingness to comment on the manuscript and for his encouragement, although it should not be assumed that he is in agreement with everything we have written. We would also like to mention our gratitude to a number of students in various classes who strove to improve our ability to communicate. Several other individuals helped sustain our efforts through their interest, especially Miss Dorothy McNeill. Finally, the patience and thoroughness of Mrs. Patricia Eichmann, who labored with the typing, is gratefully acknowledged.

INTRODUCTION

Although social psychological thought and writing have a long history of unknown origin, the discipline of social psychology was officially launched in 1908 by the publication of two books, *Social Psychology: An Outline and Source Book* by E. A. Ross and *Introduction to Social Psychology* by W. McDougall. It is interesting to note that Ross was a sociologist and McDougall a psychologist. To this day social psychology maintains its interdisciplinary connections, being neither exclusively sociological nor psychological.

But what is the subject matter of social psychology? This is not an easy question to answer. For many years social psychology textbooks were filled with material borrowed from general psychology (e.g., motivation, learning, and perception), sociology (e.g., social class, crowd behavior), and even anthropology (e.g., national character, cultural differences). Gradually, however, social psychologists began to evolve a subject matter more exclusively their own. It is such subject matter that is the focus of this book. Thus with tongue in cheek we can define social psychology as that discipline which people who call themselves social psychologists are interested in studying.

As represented by the contents of the major journals on social psychology we believe that the subject matter of social psychology falls into three overlapping categories: attitude and belief change, interpersonal processes, and small groups. These areas constitute the three major sections, or parts, of this book. Although there are many differences and similarities among these areas of social psychology, they roughly lie along dimensions relating to the number of people and the extent to which social interaction is studied. The investigation of attitude and belief change typically involves the persuasive impact produced by a written or orally presented communication when directed at a person. Thus we have two people, communicator and communicatee, between whom there is one direction of influence. Usually social interaction is not investigated, i.e., there is no attempt to see how the persuasive communication produces reverberating effects from the communicatee back to the communicator and, in turn, back to the communicatee, etc. The process is simplified (some would say oversimplified) for purposes of study. In still other instances there may be no social influence at all, since only one person is involved. This would be the case in a study of the alteration in attitude toward Chevrolets as a function of having chosen to purchase one. The area of attitude and belief change is in reality best defined by reference to certain effects, attitude and belief change, whatever the number of people and process involved.

The area of interpersonal processes typically involves two people, puts greater emphasis upon the interactive nature of social relations, and is not restricted to just certain effects such as attitude or belief change. The study of interpersonal processes includes person perception, interpersonal attraction, conformity, conflict resolution, norm formation, etc.

The area of small groups includes the study of groups varying in size between two and the number beyond which face-to-face interaction among all the members does not, or cannot easily, occur. Included within this category is the study of leadership, status, group decision-making, etc. Here social interaction is highly salient and typically quite complex.

By excluding from consideration various areas of psychology, sociology, and anthropology we do not mean to imply that these areas are unimportant or that ultimately all of the areas may not be theoretically related. At the present time, however, no generally accepted grand theoretical synthesis exists. We feel that this fact, together with the further fact that a sizeable body of "social psychological" material exists, justifies our exclusiveness.

Finally, we should mention that as the word "experimental" in the title of this book emphasizes, coverage of material will to a great extent be dic-

tated by a preference for experimental as opposed to observational or correlational research. By experimental research we mean research in which
the investigator *manipulates* the variables whose causal effects he is interested in assessing and randomly assigns subjects to conditions.

The general plan of the book is to document succinctly the important
theories and research relating to particular topics and then present one or
more original articles which illustrate the primary source material available
in journals and books. Thus each chapter has two main subdivisions, text
and readings.

Part I

ATTITUDE AND BELIEF CHANGE

Before beginning the discussion of theory and research related to attitude and belief change it is appropriate to define what is meant by "attitude" and "belief" and to describe the two more common experimental designs.

The Concepts of Attitude and Belief

Although social psychologists by no means completely agree on what is meant by the term "attitude," there is at least a common thread of agreement running through most contemporary definitions. Most contemporary usage involves some reference to attitudes as *dispositions to evaluate objects favorably or unfavorably*. We will take this evaluative disposition as the defining characteristic of attitudes. Thus reactions following along a favorable unfavorable, pro-con, for-against, or like-dislike dimension are attitudinal reactions. Attitudes are directed against "objects." Objects may be abstract, like democracy, or they may be concrete, like Aunt Mildred. Thus someone may feel favorably toward democracy and dislike Aunt Mildred.

Beliefs fall into two categories, beliefs in and beliefs about (Fishbein & Raven, 1962). Beliefs in are *acceptances of the existence of some object,* for example, acceptance of or belief in the existence of God. Beliefs in can be expressed in propositions, such as "God exists." Measurement of such beliefs can be accomplished through a subject's indication of his extent of agreement or disagreement with the proposition in question. Beliefs about are *accepted relationships between two objects,* for example, "God has a son," "America is a democratic country." "God," "son," "America," and "democratic country" are all objects. Beliefs about, like beliefs in, can be expressed in propositions with which a person can indicate his degree of agreement or disagreement. For example, a subject can indicate whether he strongly agrees, agrees, disagrees, or strongly disagrees with the proposition, "Aunt Mildred is a deceitful person." Most of the beliefs with which we are concerned are of this latter type.

Owing to the fact that both evaluative dispositions and beliefs about relate to objects, it is possible to define attitudes so that they involve both the belief (cognitive) and evaluative (affective) dispositions toward some object. Thus an individual's attitude toward Aunt Mildred would include both feelings toward and beliefs about Aunt Mildred. It is obvious that there is some sort of relationship between affect and cognition. If, for example, our individual in question believed that Aunt Mildred is a deceitful person he would be unlikely to feel very positively toward her. Our beliefs or cognitions tend to be supportive of or consistent with our evaluations or affect. This "packaging" of cognition and affect provides a rationale for using the term "attitude" so that it refers to the total unit. Some social psychologists (e.g., Krech & Crutchfield, 1948) have used the term "attitude" in this more general way. We prefer, however, to restrict attitudes to just evaluative or affective dispositions and make the exact relation between affect and cognition a theoretical and empirical problem. In Chapter 1 we will discuss some balance-related theories which attempt to state the nature of the consistent relationship that does obtain between cognition and affect, or belief and attitude.

Actually cognition and affect are only part of the picture. In addition we have behavior or conation, Our hypothetical person may dislike Aunt Mildred, believe that she is a deceitful person, *and in addition* avoid being in her immediate presence. Thus there is even a larger package consisting of cognition, affect, and some sort of behavioral or conative disposition. This means, of course, that it would be possible to use the term "attitude" so that it includes cognitive, affective, and conative dispositions toward some object. Once again, however, we would prefer not to gloss over relationships with verbal shellac, but rather make the nature of the relationships a theoretical and empirical problem.

The distinctions among affect (attitude), cognition (belief), and conation (behavior) is an old one, having its historical roots in Plato's similar trichotomy of the institutions of the mind. For Plato each of the three elements of the trichotomy was seated in a different part of the anatomy—affect or emotion in the abdomen, cognition or thought in the head, and conation or striving in the breast. Two of the elements of the trichotomy, affect and cognition, have been made much of by contemporary social psychology. Although this distinction frequently masquerades under different labels, the concept of feelings, pleasures, sentiments, etc., as distinct from beliefs, thoughts, knowledge, etc., is one that occurs over and over again.

From time to time the term "opinion" will occur in certain of the readings. Most commonly opinions are simply regarded as beliefs. An individual may hold the opinion that "God exists," or that "Aunt Mildred is a deceitful person." However, some writers (e.g., Thurstone, 1928) regard opinions as verbal expressions of underlying attitudes. Thus if an individual states that "Aunt Mildred is a deceitful person" this may be regarded as a verbal expression of an underlying disposition to evaluate Aunt Mildred negatively. Writers who regard the term "opinion" as verbal expressions of underlying attitudes may thus to some extent use "opinion" and "attitude" interchangeably in their discussion.

Two Experimental Designs

Most of the experimental research on attitude and belief change has used either a before-after design or an after-only design. Table A describes both of these designs. With a before-after design there are two groups, experimental and control, to which subjects are randomly assigned. The experimental group receives a pretest of attitudes or beliefs, an experimental manipulation (such as exposure to a persuasive communication), and a posttest of attitudes or beliefs. The control group receives the same pretest and posttest, but no experimental manipulation. By comparing the difference between the pretest and posttest scores in the experimental group with the comparable difference in the control group an investigator can obtain an indication of the effectiveness of the manipulation. If the pretest-posttest difference for the experimental group is significantly different from the pretest-posttest difference for the control group then the manipulation is judged to have had an effect.

TABLE A

Two Experimental Designs

Design	Group	Pretest	Manipulation	Posttest
Before-after	Experimental	Yes	Yes	Yes
	Control	Yes	No	Yes
After-only	Experimental	No	Yes	Yes
	Control	No	No	Yes

The after-only design also has experimental and control groups. The experimental group receives the experimental manipulation and then a posttest. The control group receives only the posttest. Neither group receives a pretest. If subjects were initially assigned to the two groups on a random basis, then the difference between the posttest scores for the experimental and control groups will reflect chance factors and the effect of the manipulation. If the test of significance tells the investigator that the posttest scores for the two groups differ significantly more than would be expected on the basis of chance, then the experimental manipulation is judged to have had an effect.

The relative advantages and disadvantages of the before-after and after-only designs have been discussed at length (e.g., Campbell, 1957), but there does not seem to be any clear reason for universally preferring one design to the other. Superficially the before-after design would seem to be more sensitive than the after-only design. By examining the pretest-posttest or before-after differences the investigator gets a direct assessment of change, while this is not possible with the after-only design. On the other hand, the presence of the pretest may interact in some unknown way with the experimental manipulation so as to contaminate the change that is assessed. The pretest may commit the subjects so that the effect of the manipulation is reduced, or the pretest may sensitize subjects so that the effect of the manipulation is increased. Certainly the presence of the pretest does provide the subject with an additional cue as to what the investigator is studying. If a pretest is used the best procedure is undoubtedly to make the assessment in a context that is removed in time and space from the experimental manipulation (for example, in a regular class meeting some time before the subject appears for the laboratory session).

As previously stated, most of the research on attitude and belief change has utilized either before-after or after-only designs. These designs, however, do not always involve just experimental and control groups as indicated in Table A. Table A describes the simplest illustrations of before-after and after-only designs. Chapter 2 contains a discussion of the effect of fear-arousing communications on attitude change. One way of investigating this problem would be to present a high fear-arousing communication on some issue (smoking and lung cancer, for example) to one group of subjects and a low fear-arousing communication on the same issue to another group of subjects. In this instance we have two groups, high fear and low fear, which are analogous to the experimental and control groups of Table A. If the experiment included a pretest, we would have a before-after design. Without a pretest we would have an after-only design. The situation, however, could be made even more complicated. Suppose that there were three groups: high fear, medium fear, and low fear. Once again, the presence or absence of a pretest would determine whether the experiment involved a before-after design or an after-only design.

Chapter 1

BALANCE AND BALANCE-RELATED THEORIES

Recent years have seen a proliferation of consistency theories of attitude change. These theories are of two basic types, balance or balance-related theories and dissonance theory. Dissonance theory will be discussed in subsequent chapters (4, 5, and 6). The present chapter is devoted to a consideration of balance and balance-related theories. First, we will discuss Heider's (1946, 1958) balance theory and then those theories which have more specifically applied balance theory principles to attitude change. These latter balance-related theories are Rosenberg's (1956, 1960) affective-cognitive consistency theory and Osgood and Tannenbaum's (1955) congruity theory.

Heider's Balance Theory

Elements, Relations, and Symbols

Heider is mainly concerned with three different types of elements: the person in whose experience or phenomenology balance processes are operating, some other perceived person, and a perceived event, idea, or thing. The person is symbolized as p, the other perceived person as o, and a perceived event, idea, or thing as x.

One or both of two types of relations may exist among the elements, a *sentiment relation* or a *unit relation*. A sentiment relation is an attitudinal relation that implies liking or disliking, loving or hating, feeling favorable toward or unfavorable toward, etc. When the affect is favorable Heider refers to the sentiment relation as positive and when the affect is unfavorable Heider refers to the sentiment relation as negative. Unit relations refer to the degree of perceived unity between elements. Examples of unit relations are similar or dissimilar, close or far, belongs or does not belong, owns or does not own, etc. When the degree of perceived unity is high Heider refers to the unit relation as positive and when the degree of perceived unity is low Heider refers to the unit relation as negative.

Heider symbolizes a positive sentiment relation as L, a negative sentiment relation as nL, a positive unit relation as U, and a negative unit relation as nU. Thus pLo means that the person has a positive sentiment relation with another person, $pnLx$ means that the person has a negative sentiment relation with an event, object, or idea, and oUx means that p perceives that another person has a positive unit relation with (is associated with) some event, object, or idea. The sentiment and unit relations are relations that exist according to the way that p perceives matters. Thus if p perceives that o owns some object x, there is a positive unit relation between o and x. This is true regardless of whether or not o actually owns x.[1]

GENERAL MEANING OF BALANCE

By a balanced state Heider means a state in which everything fits together "harmoniously" without stress. A sense of fit or harmony occurs, for example, when positively valued elements are perceived as being unified or associated in some sense. Balance is not a state that characterizes actual relations among elements but rather p's perception or experience of relations among elements. Balance or the lack of balance is a characteristic of p's phenomenology. Whenever p experiences a lack of balance there is an accompanying sense of stress or strain, and a tendency to change one or more of the sentiment or unit relations so as to restore balance.

The traditional Judeo-Christian conception of heaven and hell is descriptive of the ultimate in a balanced state. All of the good people are located (positively associated) together in a place of absolute perfection

---

[1] The negation of a positive unit relation does not produce a negative unit relation. Thus if "p is married to o" illustrates a positive unit relation, "p is not married to o" does not illustrate a negative unit relation. On the other hand, "p is divorced from o" does illustrate a negative unit relation. Negative unit relations occur when there is an actively perceived tendency toward *disunity* and not just the negation of an actively perceived tendency toward *unity*.

which is separated by an eternally fixed gulf from a place of torment and pain where all of the bad people are located. In such a state everything fits together and there is no feeling that things need to be rearranged. According to balance theory everyone has a tendency to perceive only good things about their friends and only bad things about their enemies. Someone who operated solely on balance principles would seemingly be closed-minded; reality is, after all, not that simple. Heider, on the other hand, would argue that we all have at least a *tendency toward* the perception of balanced relations.

Heider's more specific discussion of balance considers first the dyad and then the triad.

BALANCE IN THE DYAD

Dyadic relations may involve either p and x or p and o. The p and x dyad is balanced if either both the sentiment and unit relations are positive or both the sentiment and unit relations are negative. In symbols if either $pLx + pUx$ or $pnLo + pnUx$ obtains, the system is balanced. If, for example, p admires x and owns x the system is balanced, or if p dislikes x and goes far away from x the system is balanced.

The dyad involving p and o, like the dyad involving p and x, is balanced if the sentiment and unit relations have the same sign. In addition, however, the p and o dyad is balanced if o is perceived as reciprocating p's sentiment relation. Thus if pLo and oLp obtains or if $pnLo$ and $onLp$ obtains the system is balanced; that is, if p likes o and perceives that o likes him or if p dislikes o and perceives o dislikes him balance exists. Further examples of dyadic relations between p and o are: p likes o and p is similar to o, p dislikes o and p is dissimilar to o, p likes o and p interacts with o, p dislikes o and p avoids interacting with o.

Balance theory implies that if p perceives himself as similar to o, he should be attracted by o. But what about the proverb which states that "opposites attract"? Heider maintains that not all opposites attract, but if opposites do attract it is because of a complementary relation that allows for the realization of some related purpose or goal, as, for example, in a sadistic-masochistic relationship. Complementarity which is instrumental in the attainment of related goals produces a degree of perceived unity. Thus the oppositeness or dissimilarity of p and o, if it is complementary in nature, should, according to the theory, result in attraction.

Balance theory also implies that if p remains in the proximity of o and if p interacts with o, then p should be attracted to o. Once again, however, we are confronted with a contradictory proverb, "familiarity breeds contempt." Heider maintains that interaction will lead to the formation of a positive sentiment relation only if there is not too great a dissimilarity in attitudes. If the degree of dissimilarity is only moderate interaction will indeed lead to an increase in attraction, but if the dissimilarity is too great interaction will produce hostility.

Research data bearing on the effect of proximity and similarity will be discussed at length in Chapter 9, Interpersonal Attraction.

BALANCE IN THE TRIAD

According to Heider the triadic relationship among p, o, and x is balanced if all three of the signs are positive, or if two of the signs are negative and one is positive. If, for example, p likes o and x, and perceives that o likes x, the system is balanced. Also, if p likes o, dislikes x, and perceives that o dislikes x the system is balanced.

If two of the signs are positive and one is negative the triadic relationship is not balanced. For example, if p likes o and x, and perceives that o dislikes x the triad is not balanced; or, to use an illustration involving a unit relation, if p dislikes o, likes a book x, and perecives that o wrote x, the system is not balanced.

According to Heider a triad involving three people, p, o, and q, should be balanced if all three of the sentiment relations are positive. Problems arise, however, if the three individuals are of differing sexes. For example, if two male friends, p and o, fall in love with the same girl, q, the triad or "triangle" is notoriously unstable. Heider argues that the problem here is the potential imbalance in the dyad involving p and q. In order for balance to exist in the dyad, pLq and qLp must both obtain; that is, p must perceive q as reciprocating the positive sentiment relation. Thus if the female q should fall in love with p's rival o, there is a strong possibility that q would cease to reciprocate p's positive sentiment and p would be involved in an imbalanced dyad. It is thus because of the potential imbalance in the dyad that the triad creates uneasiness.

Heider maintains that the case of three negative signs is "somewhat ambiguous" (1958, p. 203). Heider does not say whether a triad with three negative relations (p dislikes o and x and perceives that o dislikes x) is balanced or not. He does say that if p perceives that he and o agree in their common negative attitude or sentiment toward x, a positive unit relation results. Furthermore, since pUo tends to induce pLo, the triad of three negative relations will tend to break down into a balanced system of one positive and two negative relations.

In view of the fact that a triadic system of three negative relations is an unstable one, there is reason to consider such a system imbalanced. Subsequent workers in the balance tradition (e.g., Cartwright & Harary, 1956) have tended to consider a system of three negative signs imbalanced. With this minor modification of Heider's formulation it is possible to state a simple rule for determining balance and imbalance in the triad. The rule is to multiply the three signs. If the result of the multiplication is a plus the system is balanced, and if the result is a minus the system is imbalanced.

This means that systems with an odd number of minus signs ($-++$, $---$) are imbalanced and systems with an even number of minus signs ($+++$, $+--$) are balanced. (The symbol "$+$" stands for either a positive sentiment relation or a positive unit relation. Likewise the symbol "$-$" stands for either a negative sentiment or a negative unit relation.)

RESOLUTION OF IMBALANCE

An imbalanced dyad or triad is in a tense, unstable state. In such a state there will be a tendency to make changes that will restore balance. Heider describes the imbalance-resolving changes by discussing a triad involving a positive sentiment relation, a negative sentiment relation, and a positive unit relation (*p* likes *o* who has done something, *x*, of which *p* does not approve). Balance may be restored by changing either of the sentiment relations. Thus *p* may decide that he dislikes *o* or that he approves of *x*. Balance may also be restored by changing the unit relation so that, for example, *p* may decide that *o* is not responsible for *x*. Finally, *p* may differentiate *o* so that he is conceived of as having both good and bad aspects or parts. The bad part of which *p* does not approve is responsible for *x* and the good part of which *p* does approve is not responsible for *x*. The differentiation thus creates two separate triads, both of which are balanced. The extent to which this is a satisfactory mode of imbalance resolution is dependent upon the degree to which *o* is convincingly differentiated into two separate parts that are, in fact, perceived as distinct and unrelated.

Differentiation of an *o* (or other person) may be fairly difficult. Except in the case of "split personalities," like Jekyll and Hyde, people possess, or are perceived as possessing, a high degree of unity. However, when the element is an *x*, rather than an *o*, differentiation can more likely be convincingly accomplished—even though some degree of creative thinking may be required. For example, if *p* and his friend *o* disagree in their evaluation of foreign aid (an *x*), they may discover that the differentiation of foreign aid into economic and military may produce agreement. They may both like economic foreign aid and both dislike military foreign aid.

Rosenberg's Affective-Cognitive Consistency Theory

Rosenberg's (1956, 1960) affective-cognitive consistency theory is an application of Heiderian principles to problems of attitude structure and change.

DEFINITION OF ATTITUDE

One of the more common definitions of attitude is in terms of pro-con affect toward some concrete or abstract object. According to this conception a doctor who feels negatively toward the object, socialized medicine, possesses a negative attitude toward socialized medicine. According to Rosenberg, however, specification of the pro-con affect only goes part of the way toward understanding the nature of attitudes. In addition to feeling a certain way toward socialized medicine, the doctor has certain beliefs about socialized medicine. For example, he may believe that socialized medicine will hurt or lower medical standards and interfere with professional freedom. Thus Rosenberg argues that it is preferable to conceive of attitudes as possessing both cognitive (belief) and affective (feeling) components. The cognitions of particular interest to Rosenberg are the perceived or believed instrumental (causal) relations such as, interferes with, hurts, harms, decreases, facilitates, helps, increases, etc. Rosenberg thus conceives of attitudes as affect toward objects (such as "socialized medicine") which are believed instrumentally related to other objects of affective significance (such as "professional freedom").

In Heiderian terms instrumental cognitions are a particular type of unit relation. Following Heider's example, Rosenberg divides instrumental cognitions into two types, positive (e.g., facilitates, helps) and negative (e.g., interferes with, harms).

ATTITUDE STRUCTURE AND HOMEOSTASIS

According to Rosenberg attitudes possess structures. A psychological structure is a set of functional relationships among components such that a change in one component will lead to a change in another component. Thus a change in the cognitive component of an attitude may lead to a change in the affective component and a change in the affective component may lead to a change in the cognitive component. For example, if the doctor changed his affect toward socialized medicine from negative to positive he would be inclined no longer to believe that socialized medicine leads to lower medical standards or interferes with professional freedom. Conversely a change in belief would tend to produce a change in affect.

An example of an attitude structure is presented in Fig. 1-1. Disliked socialized medicine is seen as facilitating disliked bureaucracy and disliked federal control, and as interfering with liked high medical standards and liked professional freedom. This attitude structure contains four *cognitive bands;* for example, socialized medicine (—) facilitates (+) bureaucracy (—). A cognitive band is simply two objects of affective significance connected by a cognition or belief. Note that the multiplication of signs within each of the four cognitive bands results in a plus, thus indicating that the entire attitude structure is consistent or balanced.

Rosenberg conceives of the attitude structure as a homeostatic system which strives to maintain consistency among the related components. When a change in one of the components produces inconsistency that is greater than the individual's tolerance limit, reorganizing activity will occur. This

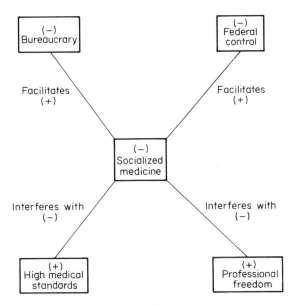

Fig. 1-1. An attitude structure. (Adapted from Insko, 1967, p. 181.)

activity may take any of *four forms. First,* the individual may reject the communication that produced the original inconsistency and thus restore the attitude structure to its original form. *Second,* the entire attitude structure may be fragmented or differentiated. For example, if someone were confronted with a very persuasive communication on the evils of education he might fragment his attitude structure by deciding that some forms of education are bad and some forms are good. *Third,* the induced cognitive change in the attitude structure might in turn produce affective change. If, for example, the doctor decided that socialized medicine would facilitate rather than interfere with high medical standards he would be inclined to change his affect toward socialized medicine from negative to positive. *Fourth* and finally, the induced affective change in the attitude structure might, in turn, produce cognitive change. If the doctor changed his affect toward socialized medicine from negative to positive he would be inclined to no longer believe that socialized medicine interfered with high medical standards and might possibly even believe that it facilitated high medical standards.

MATHEMATICAL INDEX

Owing to the tendency of attitude structures to maintain their homeostatic balance it is possible to compute a mathematical index which will predict the pro-con affect toward the attitude object on the basis of the pro-con affect toward the related objects of affective significance and the perceived or believed instrumental linkages. If, for example, we know the value the doctor places upon "professional freedom" and "medical standards" and the believed effect socialized medicine will have upon these objects of affective significance, it is not surprising that we can predict the doctor's pro-con affect toward socialized medicine. Rosenberg arrives at his mathematical index in four steps. We will illustrate these four steps with the attitude structure in Fig. 1-1. *First,* subjects rate the value placed upon the objects of affective significance. Thus suppose that some hypothetical subject, using a +3 (very favorable) to —3 (very unfavorable) scale, rates bureaucracy —3, federal control —3, high medical standards +3, professional freedom +3. *Second,* subjects rate the extent to which each object of affective significance (or value) is perceived as being instrumentally relevant to the attitude object. Suppose our hypothetical subject, using a scale ranging from +3 (strongly facilitates) to —3 (strongly interferes with), believes that socialized medicine strongly facilitates (+3) bureaucracy, strongly facilitates (+3) federal control, strongly interferes with (—3) high medical standards, and strongly interferes with (—3) professional freedom. *Third,* each subject's value rating is multiplied by his instrumentality rating for each band. Thus for the band socialized medicine strongly facilitates (+3) bureaucracy (—3) we would have +3 times —3 equals —9. For the band socialized medicine strongly interferes with (—3) high medical standards (+3) we would have —3 times +3 equals —9. For our particular hypothetical subject and attitude structure each of the four illustrative bands would have a product of —9. *Fourth* and finally, the value times instrumentality products are summed across bands to give an index of pro-con feeling toward the attitude object. In the example we would have —9 plus —9 plus —9 plus —9 equals —36. Across a number of subjects this sum of products should be predictive of, or correlate with, attitude toward socialized medicine. In our example the number —36 should be associated with a very negative attitude toward socialized medicine.

Rosenberg (1956) found that by using his mathematical index he could predict the pro-con feeling toward free speech for Communists and also toward segregated Negro housing. Other investigators (e.g., Fishbein, 1963) who have used analogous procedures have obtained similar results. Such results are evidence for the consistency of attitude structures. If attitude structures were not consistent such predictions could not be made.

TWO SEQUENCES OF ATTITUDE CHANGE

Some additional research has been devoted to demonstrating that one of two sequences of attitude change occurs: *cognitive change followed by affective change* or *affective change followed by cognitive change.* Carlson (1956) attempted to show that negative affective feeling toward integration could be changed by convincing subjects that allowing blacks to move into white neighborhoods would facilitate the attainment of four values: American prestige in other countries, protection of property values, equal opportunity for personal development, and being experienced, broad-minded, and worldly wise. The change procedure was carried out in two steps. First, as part of a regular classroom assignment students were given the task of supporting the proposition that integration would facilitate the attainment of the four values. Second, the instrumental linkage was further supported in a class discussion led by the instructor. An experimenter who was otherwise not associated with the class measured pro-con feelings toward integration, and the four values, as well as belief in the instrumental linkages. A control group was given the same before and after measures without the intervening experimental manipulation. The results indicated that, as expected, the change procedure produced an effect both in evaluation of integration and in acceptance of the instrumental linkages. Attitude toward integration became more positive and there was greater acceptance that integration would facilitate attainment of the four values. Furthermore, across subjects the change in attitude toward integration (affective change) was correlated with the change in acceptance of the instrumental linkages (cognitive change). Such a correlation gives greater assurance that at least some of the affective change was, in fact, produced by cognitive change rather than, for example, simple conformity to the instructor's point of view. Supportive results were also obtained by Di Vesta and Merwin (1960).

Rosenberg (1960) reports an investigation which obtained results consistent with the assertion that affective change leads to cognitive change. In the social environment much and possibly most affective change results from cognitive change. Persuasive communications, for example, produce affective change by first producing cognitive change. This is illustrated by a communication that attempts to produce a negative attitude toward some politician by first convincing the communicatee that the politician will facilitate the enactment of an undesirable policy. How, then, does one experimentally produce affective change without first producing cognitive change? Rosenberg used posthypnotic suggestion. Subjects were hypnotized and then given the suggestion that after coming out of the trance they would feel differently toward some attitude object, for example, federal medical insurance. The attitude structures associated with the manipulated attitude objects were measured before and after the manipulation. A control group received similar assessments before and after being told to fall asleep. The results indicated that the posthypnotic suggestions produced affective change as well as accompanying change in the perceived instrumental linkages (cognitive change) and values. If, for example, a subject, as a result of posthypnotic suggestion, changed his affect toward federal medical insurance from negative to positive, this change may have been associated with a greater acceptance that federal medical insurance would result in equal rights and increased evaluation of equal rights. This pattern of results was interpreted as indicating that affective change produced cognitive change which in turn led to more affective change. The initial affective change was in the attitude object and the final affective change was in the associated values.

Osgood and Tannenbaum's Congruity Theory

CONGRUITY AND INCONGRUITY

Although Osgood and Tannenbaum's (1955) congruity theory was apparently developed independently of Heider's work, the theory nonetheless belongs in the balance tradition. "Congruity" is Osgood and Tannenbaum's name for balance. Incongruity exists, for example, when a positively valued source makes a favorable remark about some unfavorable concept. If someone evaluated Senator Muskie quite highly and heard that Muskie praised the KKK, incongruity would result.

ASSOCIATIVE AND DISSOCIATIVE ASSERTIONS

In order for either congruity or incongruity to exist, sources and concepts, or more generally what are referred to as objects of judgment, must be associated by either an associative assertion (likes, goes with, praises) or a dissociative assertion (dislikes, avoids, criticizes). Associative assertions correspond to Heider's positive sentiment and unit relations and dissociative assertions correspond to Heider's negative sentiment and unit relations.

ATTITUDE CHANGE

When incongruity has been created by the linking of two objects of judgment with an assertion, pressure to restore congruity is created. This pressure is manifested in a change in evaluation of the associated objects of judgment. In the above example, there would be a tendency to lower the evaluation of Muskie and to raise the evaluation of the KKK. After the changes, congruity or equilibrium would be restored. The changes, however, are not necessarily the same for the two objects of judgment. The object of judgment which is more polarized or evaluated more extremely (in either the positive or the negative direction) will change less than the object of judgment which is less polarized or evaluated less extremely. Stated somewhat differently, change is inversely proportional to the degree of polarization. If the KKK is evaluated more extremely in the negative direction than Muskie is in the positive, the evaluation of Muskie will change to a greater extent than will the evaluation of the KKK. Muskie will lose more than the KKK will gain.

FORMULAS

As the above discussion makes evident, congruity theory differs from Heider's balance theory in making predictions about degree of evaluation and not just gross positive to negative or negative to positive changes. Osgood and Tannenbaum state mathematical formulas that exactly specify the amount of change in the two objects of judgment necessary to restore congruity. For the case of associative assertions these equations are

$$AC_{oj_1} = \frac{|d_{oj_2}|}{|d_{oj_1}| + |d_{oj_2}|} (d_{oj_2} - d_{oj_1}) \tag{1-1}$$

and

$$AC_{oj_2} = \frac{|d_{oj_1}|}{|d_{oj_1}| + |d_{oj_2}|} (d_{oj_1} - d_{oj_2}) \tag{1-2}$$

where AC_{oj_1} is attitude change in the first object of judgment, AC_{oj_2} is attitude change in the second object of judgment, d_{oj_1} is the degree of polarization of the first object of judgment, and d_{oj_2} is the degree of polarization of the second object of judgment. For dissociative assertions two slightly different equations are used:

$$AC_{oj_1} = \frac{|d_{oj_1}|}{|d_{oj_1}| + |d_{oj_2}|} (- d_{oj_2} - d_{oj_1}) \tag{1-3}$$

and

$$AC_{oj_2} = \frac{|d_{oj_2}|}{|d_{oj_1}| + |d_{oj_2}|} (- d_{oj_1} - d_{oj_2}) \tag{1-4}$$

The degrees of polarization are the mean ratings of a given object of judgment on a number of so-called semantic differential scales. Semantic differential scales are simply seven point bipolar scales with antonymous adjectives at either end. The following are examples:

```
     good _____:_____:_____:_____:_____:_____:_____: bad
beautiful _____:_____:_____:_____:_____:_____:_____: ugly
    clean _____:_____:_____:_____:_____:_____:_____: dirty
```

Subjects check each scale according to how some object, Nixon for example, is characterized by one of the two adjectives. The response categories are given numerical weights varying from $+3$ to -3 and the mean rating across a number of scales is taken as an index of the subject's attitude toward the object. Since the plus scores are given to the favorable adjectives and the minus scores to the unfavorable adjectives, a high plus mean signifies a favorable attitude toward the object and a high minus mean signifies an unfavorable attitude toward the object. In formulas (1-1) to (1-4) the degree of polarization for a given object of judgment refers to the mean rating for that object across a number of semantic differential scales.

As an example suppose that Nixon $(+1)$ praises (is linked by an associative assertion to) Kosygin (-2). The situation is schematically shown in graph A of Fig. 1-2. Arbitrarily designating Nixon as the first object of judgment and Kosygin as the second object of judgment, formulas $(1\text{-}1)$ and $(1\text{-}2)$ can be solved as follows:

$$AC_{oj_1} = \frac{|d_{oj_2}|}{|d_{oj_1}| + |d_{oj_2}|}\, (d_{oj_2} - d_{oj_1})$$

$$= \frac{2}{1+2}[-2-(+1)]$$

$$= -2$$

$$AC_{oj_2} = \frac{|d_{oj_1}|}{|d_{oj_1}| + |d_{oj_2}|}\, (d_{oj_1} - d_{oj_2})$$

$$= \frac{1}{1+2}[+1-(-2)]$$

$$= +1$$

Nixon loses 2 units and Kosygin gains 1, thus placing the point of congruity at -1. The situation is shown in graph B of Fig. 1-2. For dissociative assertions [formulas $(1\text{-}3)$ and $(1\text{-}4)$] the calculations are equally simple.

FORMULA CORRECTIONS

Osgood and Tannenbaum make two corrections in their congruity formulas. The first of these corrections involves the *assertion constant*. Common sense expects that the object of an assertion will change more than the source of an assertion. The above congruity formulas, however, do not differentiate between the source and object of an assertion. Osgood and Tannenbaum thus added an assertion constant to the predicted change in the object of the assertion or in the concept. This constant $(\pm A)$, which

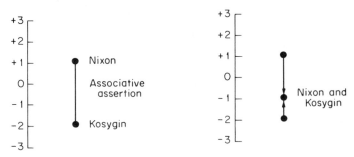

Fig. 1-2. *An associative link between Nixon and Kosygin* (A) *produces congruity* (B). (*From New Directions in Psychology, Roger Brown, Eugene Galanter, Eckhard H. Hess, and George Mandler, 1962. Adopted and reprinted by permission of Holt, Rinehart, and Winston, Inc.*)

is positive for positive assertions and negative for negative assertions, was empirically determined by Osgood and Tannenbaum to be 0.17 in units of the seven-step semantic differential scale.

The second correction is referred to by Osgood and Tannenbaum as the *correction for incredulity*. This correction is designed to handle the situation in which the subject disbelieves the assertion linking two objects of judgment. Such incredulity would obviously decrease the movement toward congruity. Osgood and Tannenbaum believe that incredulity is most likely to occur if the incongruity is quite large. This would be the case, for example, if Muskie (+3) praised Brezhnev (−3). Osgood and Tannenbaum thus correct the congruity formulas so that the amount of predicted change is reduced with increasing incongruity. The exact nature of this correction is based on conjecture and need not concern us here.

RESEARCH

The first research bearing on the accuracy of the congruity predictions was reported by Osgood and Tannenbaum (1955) themselves. Subjects were presented with reproductions of realistically written newspaper stories in which one of a number of sources (Labor Leaders, Chicago Tribune, Senator Robert Taft) made assertions about one of a number of concepts (Legalized Gambling, Abstract Art, Accelerated College Programs). Attitudes toward the sources and concepts were obtained five weeks before and immediately after reading the newspaper stories. The obtained data supported the congruity predictions to a very marked degree. The correlation between the obtained before-after change and the before-after change predicted on the basis of the congruity formulas was +.91. In general the predicted directions of change were obtained, but the predicted amounts of change were not. The formulas tended to predict more change than actually occurred.

Subsequent research has made it evident that the congruity predictions may be even less accurate than Osgood and Tannenbaum's data indicate. Kerrick (1959), for example, found that in some instances an associative assertion between two objects of judgment on the same side of the scale resulted in a shift to a more extreme or polarized judgment than had occurred before the linkage. Such a "summation effect" is directly contrary to the congruity predictions (although not contrary to balance theory in general). According to congruity theory an associative assertion between two positive objects of judgment should result in a kind of averaging, with the more polarized object being given more weight. The more positive object of judgment should lose slightly and the less positive object should gain a great deal.

Kerrick (1958) has also demonstrated that the congruity formulas predict better for relevant than nonrelevant source-concept pairings. Kerrick, for example, considered the Director of the Museum of Modern Art a relevant source for the concept, abstract art, but a nonrelevant source for the concept, protective tariffs for farm products. Although the congruity predictions for the relevant pairing were significantly better than those for the nonrelevant pairing, the predictions for the nonrelevant pairing were by no means poor. For the relevant pairings 83 percent of the source shift and 97.5 percent of the concept shift were predicted; for the nonrelevant pairing 70.5 percent of the source shift and 82.5 percent of the concept shift were predicted.

The more recent empirical investigations of congruity theory have tended to concentrate on the gross implications and to ignore the mathematical details. This is illustrated by a study of Tannenbaum's contained in the Readings section of this chapter. Tannenbaum (1966) found that a change in attitude toward a given concept will generalize so as to produce a change in attitude toward a source which previously made an assertion about that concept and also to an additional concept about which the source has made an assertion. Such generalized attitude change is, of course, consistent with general congruity theory implications, as well as all of the theories in the balance tradition.

Overview of the Three Theories

It should be apparent that despite differences in language Heider's balance theory, Rosenberg's affective-cognitive consistency theory, and Osgood and Tannenbaum's congruity theory all assume the same basic tendency to resolve inconsistency of affect among or between related objects. All three theories assume that the positive association of a positively evaluated object and a negatively evaluated object produce inconsistency, and the positive association of two positively evaluated objects produce consistency. Suppose that p perceives that o wrote the book, x. In balance language there is a positive unit relation between two objects. According to Heider balance exists if p likes (positive sentiment relation) o and x. On the other hand, imbalance exists if p likes o and dislikes x. From the perspective of Osgood and Tannenbaum if the subject perceives that o wrote x there is an associative assertion between o and x. Congruity exists if o and x are evaluated equally positive (by the subject, i.e., by p). On the other hand, incongruity exists if o is evaluated positively and x is evaluated negatively. Osgood and Tannenbaum do not explicitly refer to p, but obviously assume his existence in obtaining the degree of polarization values. From Rosenberg's perspective if the subject perceives that o wrote x there is a positive cognition between o and x. The statement "o wrote x" is referred to as a cognitive band and is only one of many bands in the attitude structure relating to x (or to o). If o and x are evaluated positively the band is consistent, and if o is evaluated negatively and x positively the band is inconsistent.

One clear difference between congruity theory and both balance theory and affective-cognitive consistency theory is that congruity theory does not allow for differentiation as a possible mode of incongruity resolution. Superficially it appears as if congruity theory allows for the resolution of incongruity only through a change in evaluation of the related objects. In balance terms this is a change in p's sentiment relations with o and x. However, insofar as Osgood and Tannenbaum make use of their correction for incredulity they do have another mode of incongruity resolution. In balance terms the incredulity reaction is analogous to p's disbelieving the sentiment or unit relation between o and x. To the extent that changes in evaluation and credulity (or incredulity) are not the only modes of incongruity resolution, and differentiation is, in fact, another mode, the congruity formulation is an oversimplification.

Heider's statement of balance theory differs from both congruity theory and affective-cognitive consistency theory in that sentiment relations are grossly categorized as positive or negative and there is thus no attempt to handle degree of positiveness or degree of negativeness. The more quantitative approach of Osgood and Tannenbaum and Rosenberg allows them to develop more precise, but nonetheless rather different, mathematical formulations.

Rosenberg's formulation requires that the quantitatively scaled plus to minus cognition be multiplied by the object of affective significance within each cognitive band and the resultant products *summed* across bands. The obtained sum is predictive of the evaluation of the attitude object common to all the bands (the attitude object at the "center" of the attitude structure). Osgood and Tannenbaum's formulas require that the two objects within a single cognitive band be *averaged*, with each object weighted according to its degree of polarization. Although the formulas were originally developed to handle only one cognitive band, they can be generalized so as to apply to any number of bands as does the Rosenberg formulation. Rosenberg thus assumes that summation is the appropriate combinational rule, while Osgood and Tannenbaum assume that averaging is.

Finally, a further difference in the mathematical details of congruity theory and affective-cognitive consistency theory relates to the treatment of the linking cognitions or assertions. Rosenberg makes use of the scaled value of the plus or minus cognition within each band, while Osgood and Tannenbaum simply categorize cognitions (assertions) as plus (associative) or minus (dissociative) and alter their formulas accordingly.

READINGS

Mediated Generalization of Attitude Change via the Principle of Congruity[1]

Percy H. Tannenbaum

Four sets of linkages with a single source and 2 concepts were first established—the source being for both concepts; for the 1st but against the 2nd; against the 1st and for the 2nd; and against both. Attitude toward the 1st concept was then manipulated —both favorably and unfavorably—without any mention of either the source or 2nd concept. It was reasoned from the principle of congruity that such manipulated change in the 1st concept would influence the source attitude (as a previous study had indeed demonstrated), and that this source change would in turn, produce appropriate modifications in the 2nd concept. The results provided strong confirmation of the theoretical expectations, the source-mediated change in the 2nd concept apparently occurring over and above any direct transfer from the 1st concept.

When attitude toward one of two objects in a cognitive relationship is modified, there often results a change in attitude toward the other object in order to maintain cognitive consistency. A particular instance of such a general consistency theory phenomenon is represented in applications of the principle of congruity (Osgood & Tannenbaum, 1955) where a persuasive communication directed at a given topic or concept also results in changes in attitude toward the message source.

Such generalization of attitude change from concept to source was more clearly indicated in a recent extension of the congruity model to a situation in which the two main cognitive operations involved—the establishment of an evaluative relationship between source and concept, and the manipulation of the concept attitude—were accomplished independently (Tannenbaum & Gengel, 1966). Three different source-concept linkages were first established—one source being for the concept, another against, and a third neutral. In a subsequent message, the concept was modified in either a favorable or unfavorable direction, but without any reference to the original sources. The resulting relative changes in attitude toward the sources were in accord with the theoretical predictions—evaluation of the

[1] From the *Journal of Personality and Social Psychology*, Volume 3, pages 493–499, 1966 (received November 10, 1964). Authors affiliation: University of Wisconsin. This research was supported under Grant G-23963 from the National Science Foundation. Gerard Leduc helped in the administration of the testing and in the data analysis. Reproduced by permission of the American Psychological Association.

sources changed in the direction establishing a congruent relationship with the altered concept position.

A further extension of the congruity principle as a model for generalization of persuasion is readily apparent. If attitude change toward a source results from manipulating the attitude toward an evaluatively linked concept, then *other* concepts with which that source has been associated should also be affected. That is, a given source may be linked to a number of different concepts, each such linkage constituting a particular cognitive relationship. Change in one concept affects the source attitude because it introduces an inconsistency, or incongruity, into one of those relationships. But now the change in the source creates a new incongruity with one or another of the remaining concepts, attitude toward which should change in order to resolve that incongruity. In this manner, generalization of attitude change from one concept to another may be accomplished—mediated through their initial association with a common source, and in the absence of any direct link between the concepts themselves.

The present experiment was designed to investigate such a phenomenon in terms of specific congruity principle predictions. Various directed relationships between a given source and two different concepts are first established, and then attitude toward one of the concepts is manipulated, either positively or negatively. This should result in favorable or unfavorable change in attitude toward the source, in accordance with congruity theory predictions. This source attitude change, in turn, should affect attitude toward the second concept, also in accord with specific congruity predictions. Thus, three critical variables are involved in such source-mediated generalization of persuasion from one concept to a second—the nature of the evaluative link between the source and the first concept, the direction of the manipulated attitude change toward the first concept, and the nature of the evaluative link between the source and the second concept.

METHOD

Subjects

A total of 218 male high-school students attending a summer military camp as Army cadets served as subjects in the experiment. They ranged between the ages of 16–18 years, and participated in the study as part of a series of tests they underwent during their stay in camp. Because of some incomplete participation, the data for 200 subjects were used.

Procedure

Materials similar to those employed in the previous Tannenbaum and Gengel (1966) study were used in the present investigation. On the basis of previous testing with undergraduate college students, two concepts—teaching machines (TM) and Spence learning theory (LT)—and a plausible but fictitious source (Prof. Walter E. Samuels of the University of California) were selected as the attitudinal objects for the study. The main criteria for selection were relative neutrality of initial attitude, and a relatively small variance.

Subjects were first tested on attitude toward the three objects (T_0) as part of a general inventory of attitudes and connotative meaning judgments, the objects of interest here being imbedded among a set of 20 different concepts. One week later, subjects were again assembled and were divided into four groups according to the intended source-concept linkages. One group had the source in favor of both the TM and LT concepts (the pp condition); for another, the source favored TM but disfavored LT (pn); for the third, the source was against TM but for LT (np); for the fourth, the source was against both concepts (nn).[2]

All subjects then participated in a totally separate task—completing several parts of the MMPI—for approximately one-half hour. After this interval of irrelevant activity, subjects were exposed to the TM concept manipulation message. Half the subjects in each linkage condition received a positive version designed to boost the TM attitude (the P treatment), and the other half received a belief attack (the N treatment). Attitudes toward the source and the two concepts were again assessed after the experimental messages (T_1). Thus, the basic design was a before-after 4×2 (Linkages $\times$ Manipulations) factorial design with independent cells ($n = 25$ per cell).

Experimental Materials

Linkage Messages. The various linkages were established in messages (of approximately 250 words each) reporting an ostensible symposium at the 1963 convention of the American Psychological Association dealing with "new educational procedures." To heighten interest somewhat, the message claimed the symposium was a widely discussed one which had "caused quite a stir . . . and considerable debate." Actually, the message only mentioned Prof. Samuels' position either for or against teaching machines or the Spence learning theory, without reference to other aspects of the alleged symposium. In order not to single out Prof. Samuels unduly the message also mentioned another individual, Prof. George L. Maclay of Cornell, as chairman of the symposium.

The main purpose of these messages was merely to establish the position of the source of both concepts. Accordingly, there was a minimum of further embellishment of information about either of the concepts or of further detail of the source's position. To establish the *favorable TM* connection, the message merely stated:

> Professor Samuels, a strong proponent of teaching machines, praised the use of teaching machines for instructional purposes in no uncertain terms. He hailed teaching machines as "the most significant single contribution of the behavioral sciences in the field of education."

The *unfavorable TM* version was almost identical in wording except that "opponent" was substituted for "proponent," and "attacked" for "praised." The direct quotation has Samuels hailing teaching machines as a "most pernicious influence on the entire educational system and a source of shame for behavioral sciences."

In either case, the connection with the second concept was made immediately after the paragraph dealing with teaching machines. The *favorable LT* version read:

> At the same time, Professor Samuels also expressed himself as strongly in favor

[2] Neutral linkage conditions were not included in the present design—partly because they were not absolutely essential to test the main theoretical predictions, and partly because the results of the Tannenbaum and Gengel (1966) study indicated a possibility of a contamination of the generalization data, as such, in a neutral linkage situation.

of the Spence Learning Theory. Known as a vigorous supporter of the Spence Theory, he called it "the most compelling explanation of the learning process yet presented."

The *unfavorable LT* connection was again highly similar. The word "against" was substituted for "in favor of," and "antagonist" for "supporter," with the quotation calling the theory "a veritable hodgepodge of unfounded notions with no meaningful basis."

Manipulation of Concept Attitude. Teaching machines was selected as the concept to be manipulated, with Spence learning theory as the secondary concept to which generalization would be investigated—largely because TM materials were already available. Both the positive and negative treatments of attitude toward TM were accomplished in messages purporting to be copies of an Associated Press article dealing with "a comprehensive report on teaching machines from the U. S. Office of Education," and were similar to those used in the Tannenbaum and Gengel (1966) study. The articles were about equal in length (approximately 475 words) and very similar in format, each stating their respective position on TM and citing a half-dozen more strongly worded arguments—with liberal quotation from the alleged report—in support of that position. In neither case was the source of the linkage message at all mentioned.[3]

Attitude Measure

Four semantic differential scales (cf. Osgood, Suci, & Tannenbaum, 1957), imbedded in a total set of 10 such scales, were used to assess attitude. These were selected on the basis of a factor analysis of the present data to be most representative of the evaluative factor on the particular attitudinal objects involved. They included: good-bad, worthless-valuable, successful-unsuccessful, and important-unimportant. The sum of ratings across all four scales, adjusted for consistency of attitudinal direction, constituted the attitude measure at both the T_0 and T_1 test sessions, with the $T_1 - T_0$ difference serving to index the dependent variable of attitude change.

RESULTS

The postulated mechanism for generalization involves a three-stage process. The TM attitude must first be altered by the experimental manipulations. This should affect the source attitude in accord with congruity principle predictions. Then, the critical third stage—change in the dependent LT concept—can be properly assessed. We will consider each in turn.

Change on Manipulated Concept (TM)

The primary intention of the manipulation messages was to change attitude toward the TM concept—in a favorable direction for the positive (P) treatment, and unfavorable for the negative (N) treatment. Table 1 reports the mean change scores for the different conditions and indicates a highly significant difference between the two experimental treatments. A

---

[3] Copies of the different experimental materials involved may be obtained from the Mass Communications Research Center, University of Wisconsin, Madison, Wisconsin 53706.

TABLE 1

Mean Attitude Change in Manipulated Concept (TM) and Results of Analysis of Variance

TM concept manipulation	Source-concept linkages				Marginals
	pp	pn	np	nn	
Positive (P)	$+8.56_a$	$+9.12_a$	$+7.32_a$	$+7.16_a$	$+8.04$
Negative (N)	-6.96_b	-7.12_b	-7.84_b	-8.24_b	-7.55
Marginals	$+.80$	$+1.00$	$-.26$	$-.54$	

Source	df	MS	F
Between linkages	3	23.15	—
Between manipulations	1	12,136.82	268.28*
Interaction	3	5.70	—
Within cells	192	45.24	

Note—Means with the same alphabetical subscript are not significantly different from one another at the .05 level by Newman-Keuls test (cf. Winer, 1962, pp. 80–85).
   $*p < .001$.

separate analysis showed a significant ($p < .001$, in each case, by sign test) shift *within* each treatment.

The lack of a significant difference between the linkage conditions, along with the insignificant interaction effect, are to be expected at this stage, since the linkage conditions should have little relevance to change on the TM concept, as such. Actually, some influence of the linkage message is apparent: The np and nn conditions, which involved some negative statement about the TM concept in the prior linkage messages, do not exhibit quite as much positive change in the P treatment as do the pp and pn linkages. Similarly, the latter conditions are not quite as negative in the N treatment. In all cases, however, these differences are short of statistical significance.

Source Attitude Change

This intermediate stage of the present study is similar to the main focus of the previous Tannenbaum and Gengel (1966) study, and accordingly the same predictions, derived from congruity theory, apply. For example, where there was a positive linkage between the source and TM and then TM was changed negatively, we would expect the source to change in a negative direction to maintain congruity. In this manner, favorable source attitude change is predicted for the pp and pn conditions under the P treatment, and in the np and nn conditions under the N treatment. The situation is reversed for prediction of negative source change—in the np and nn conditions for P, and the pp and pn conditions for N. It should be noted that change in source attitude is predicted solely on the basis of its

TABLE 2

Mean Attitude Change on Source (Samuels) and Results of Analysis of Variance

TM concept manipulation	Source-concept linkages				Marginals
	pp	pn	np	nn	
Positive (P)	$+4.96_a$	$+4.72_a$	-2.52_b	-2.96_b	$+1.05$
Negative (N)	-3.96_b	-3.00_b	$+3.76_a$	$+3.32_a$	$+.12$
Marginals	$+.50$	$+.86$	$+.62$	$+.18$	

Source	df	MS	F
Between linkages	3	4.00	—
Between manipulations	1	52.02	2.35
Interaction	3	891.17	40.25*
Within cells	192	22.14	

Note—Means with the same alphabetical subscript are not significantly different from one another at the .05 level by Newman-Keuls test.
*$p < .001$.

linkage with the initially manipulated TM concept, and is independent of its association with the second, nonmanipulated concept.

Table 2 clearly indicates that the various source changes occur as predicted. There is a highly significant interaction effect, but the overall main effects are not significant. It is obvious, however, that in both cases, this is due to a canceling-out of significant changes in opposing directions within a given row or column. These findings are in substantial accord with the results of the previous study.

Change on Nonmanipulated Concept (LT)

Given that the first two stages of the hypothesized process functioned as expected, the data on the main dependent variable may be analyzed. The relevant variables here are the new source attitude in each condition and the nature of the initial linkage between the source and the nonmanipulated concept. Where the source has become more favorable, its position vis-à-vis the LT concept should be reflected in the actual LT change— in a negative direction if the linkage was a negative one, and a favorable change if the linkage was a positive one. On the other hand, if the source attitude has altered in an unfavorable direction, then the LT change should be opposite to that advocated by the source—that is, a favorable change where the linkage was negative, and an unfavorable change where it was positive. By applying the congruity principle in this manner, we would thus predict favorable LT changes in the Ppp, Nnp, Npn, and Pnn conditions, and unfavorable LT changes in the Ppn, Nnn, Npp, and Pnp conditions.

The relevant LT change data are presented in Table 3, and indicate that

TABLE 3

Mean Attitude on Nonmanipulated Concept (LT) and Results of Analysis of Variance

TM concept manipulation	Source-concept linkages				Marginals
	pp	pn	np	nn	
Positive (P)	$+2.84_a$	-1.92_c	$-.76_{bc}$	$+1.56_a$	$+.43$
Negative (N)	-2.72_c	$+.60_{ab}$	$+2.12_a$	-2.52_c	$-.63$
Marginals	$+.06$	$-.66$	$+.68$	$-.48$	

Source	df	MS	F
Between linkages	3	18.20	1.48
Between manipulations	1	56.18	4.56*
Interaction	3	240.45	19.52**
Within cells	192	12.32	

Note—Means with the same alphabetical subscript are not significantly different from one another at the .05 level by Newman-Keuls test.

* $p < .05$.

** $p < .001$.

all changes are in the predicted directions. The four cells in which a positive change was anticipated on the basis of the congruity formulations all change in that direction, with the differences between them being not significant. Similarly, the predicted negative changes obtain, again without significant differences among them. However, the differences between matched pairs of positive and negative changes are always significant. Indeed, the only lack of significant difference between *any* pair of positive and negative means is between the least changing positive one, Npn, and the smallest negative one, Pnp. Comparing the two groups within a given linkage condition—for example, Ppp versus Npp, and so on—we find them to change, as anticipated, in opposite directions and to differ significantly from one another.

DISCUSSION

It is clear that the results confirm the theoretical predictions and hence provide support for the proposed theoretical model. It is important to note that within such a model, the change on the second concept may be in a direction opposite to that on the manipulated first concept—and, for that matter, the source attitude change may also be the reverse of that on the first concept. This is in distinction to other instances in which the mediated transfer of evaluation has been exhibited through conventional conditioning procedures. For example, Staats, Staats, and Heard (1939) used a semantic generalization paradigm, and found that the association of highly evaluated terms with stimulus words spread to synonyms of those stimulus words.

Even more to the point, Das and Nanda (1963), in a sensory preconditioning design, found that the association of the evaluative words "good" and "bad" with nonsense syllables influenced the judgment of tribal names which had been previously linked to the nonsense terms. In such cases, the judgment of the "conditioned stimulus" (e.g., the tribal names) was always the same, in attitudinal direction if not in degree, as the already established evaluation of the "unconditioned stimulus" (e.g., the words "good" and "bad").

That such a direct transfer of attitude change may be taking place in the present experimental situation is suggested by the difference in LT change as a function of the difference in manipulation of the TM concept, as indicated by the analysis of variance in Table 3. That is, where the initial TM change was positive (P manipulation) the overall LT change was also positive; there is a similar correspondence in the negative manipulation condition, the difference between the two manipulations being significant ($p < .05$). While this finding was not expected—the TM concept manipulation treatment, as such, was presumably not a relevant variable affecting LT change—it does not detract from the results in terms of the postulated congruity model, which can still function over and above any direct generalization from one concept to the other.

This is readily apparent when the means for selected individual cells are examined. If only direct transfer of change were operating, we would expect that in the P manipulation treatment, all four cells would change positively. This is clearly not the case here—the Ppn and Pnp actually change in a negative direction, and are significantly different from the positively changing Ppp and Pnn groups. The same is true for the N manipulation treatment of the first concept—the Npn and Nnp cells change positively rather than negatively and again are significantly different from the corresponding negatively changing Npp and Nnn cells. It is in these differential linkage conditions—the pn and np linkages under both the P and N manipulations—that the critical distinctions are to be found, with the results completely in accord with the congruity model predictions. Indeed, it is in these conditions that the postulated mediated generalization model had to operate *in contradiction* to the direct generalization effects —thus making the obtained findings all the more impressive.

Thus, though there is some evidence of direct generalization, the obtained results are best explained in terms of the congruity model which generated the study: Change in attitude toward an unmanipulated concept is a direct consequence of the tendency to maintain the various source-concept relationships involved in a psychologically harmonious or congruent state. At times, such change is in the same direction as that of the manipulated concepts, at times it is in the opposite direction—but it is always in that direction which makes for a congruent situation. Such a theoretical formulation might also be applied to explain the results obtained by Weiss (1957) in a study which had some similar properties to the present one. He found that the prior establishment of a negative source favoring a presumably highly valued concept facilitated the impact of a subsequent message in which that source attacked another concept. Uncertain as to "the nature of the facilitating psychological processes," Weiss dismissed an increase in source "trustworthiness" given the particular source employed (the *Daily Worker*), and tended to favor the apparent "opinion congruence" between the source and the subject created by the first message as the critical factor. This notion, not further developed by Weiss, appears highly similar to the theoretical rationale derived more explicitly from the congruity principle—which is probably the main reason why such similar labels were used, apparently independently.

The basic model, of course, also applies to the determination of changes noted in the intermediate stage of this investigation—change in the source attitude. As with the concept-to-concept change situation, the direction of the source change may or may not be in the same direction as the initial concept change, depending on the particular congruity conditions. In this sense, the results of the present experiment are even more impressive in their agreement with the basic theoretical predictions than were the findings in the earlier study (Tannenbaum & Gengel, 1966), where all the mean source-attitude changes were in a favorable direction. A number of possible reasons for this difference are suggested by some methodological differences between the two studies—for example, the use of somewhat different messages, deliberately rewritten for the entire passages to make them more persuasive, in the present study; use in the present study of perhaps more impressionable high-school, as opposed to college, subjects; a basic design change from the use of different sources within the same group to represent the different source-concept linkages, to the use of the same named source in different groups. Each of these alternatives may have allowed for a clearer manifestation of the generalization phenomenon under study, but these and others remain purely speculative for the present.

REFERENCES

Das, J. P., & Nanda, P. C. Mediated transfer of attitudes. *Journal of Abnormal and Social Psychology*, 1963, **66**, 12–16.

Osgood, C. E., Suci, G. J., & Tannenbaum, P. H. *The measurement of meaning.* Urbana, Illinois: University of Illinois Press, 1957.

Osgood, C. E., & Tannenbaum, P. H. The principle of congruity in the prediction of attitude change. *Psychological Review*, 1955, **62**, 42–55.

Staats, A. W., Staats, C. K., & Heard, W. G. Language conditioning of meaning to meaning using a semantic generalization paradigm. *Journal of Experimental Psychology*, 1959, **57**, 187–192.

Tannenbaum, P. H., & Gengel, R. W. Generalization of attitude change through congruity principle relationships. *Journal of Personality and Social Psychology*, 1966, **3**, 299–304.

Weiss, W. Opinion congruence with a negative source on one issue as a factor influencing
  agreement on another issue. *Journal of Abnormal and Social Psychology*, 1957, **54**,
  180–186.
Winer, B. J. *Statistical principles in experimental design.* New York: McGraw-Hill, 1962.

Chapter 2

REWARD AND FEAR: THE HEDONISTIC
ACCOUNT OF ATTITUDE CHANGE

Reward and fear are two variables that have traditionally been of interest to psychologists. Although frequently conceptualized in terms of drive reduction, learning psychologists have devoted a great deal of effort to the study of the effects of reward and fear upon both learning and performance. Clinical psychologists have also been concerned with the role of reward and fear, or pleasure and anxiety, in the creation of mental abnormality. It is thus quite reasonable that social psychologists should be concerned with the role of reward and fear in the production of attitude change. This chapter will be devoted to a discussion of this general problem.

Three Types of Psychological Hedonism

Research on reward and fear can be regarded as either a direct or indirect attempt to explore the adequacy of the hedonistic account of attitude

31

change. *Psychological hedonism is the view that individuals act so as to maximize exposure to rewarding, or pleasant, circumstances and so as to minimize exposure to unrewarding, or unpleasant, circumstances.* Psychological hedonism should be distinguished from ethical hedonism, or the view that actions which maximize pleasure and minimize pain are correct, moral, or good. Psychological hedonism is a perspective concerning the determinants of behavior and not the morality or immorality of such behavior.

For many purposes it is helpful to distinguish among three types of psychological hedonism: *hedonism of the past, hedonism of the present,* and *hedonism of the future.* The distinction among these three types of hedonism is necessitated by the fact that the responses which maximize reward in the present may not be the responses which maximized reward in the past or will maximize reward in the future. Hedonism of the past is the view that individuals make those responses which in the past maximized exposure to pleasant circumstances and minimized exposure to unpleasant circumstances. Hedonism of the past is associated with various theories of learning. When hedonism of the past is combined with a stimulus-response approach it results in a theory which maintains that when a stimulus-response sequence is followed by pleasant affect a learned association is formed between stimulus and response. Such an association guarantees that the reoccurrence of the stimulus will result in a tendency for the response to reoccur. According to this theory affective arousal is crucial to the formation of a learned stimulus-response association. It should parenthetically be noted that one of the more popular theories of learning, Hull's (1943) stimulus-response reinforcement theory, is not strictly speaking hedonistic. The reinforcement which is crucial to formation of a learned stimulus-response association is not affective arousal but drive reduction. Drive reduction may occur without affective arousal, as for example when someone is fed intravenously. Typically, however, drive reduction does occur in conjunction with affective arousal.

Hedonism of the present is the view that individuals act in the immediate situation so as to maximize exposure to pleasant circumstances and minimize exposure to unpleasant circumstances. This is the view that is most popularly associated with the general doctrine of hedonism. The doctrine is commonly associated with the epicurean glutton and sexual libertine. Although some psychologists may believe that individuals at times follow present hedonistic tendencies, no psychologist believes that such a doctrine is to be considered a serious general theory of human behavior.

Hedonism of the future is the view that individuals act so as to maximize the long-term exposure to pleasant circumstances and minimize the long-term exposure to unpleasant circumstances. Such a doctrine is associated with planfulness and rationality. In order to maximize long-term pleasure it is necessary that the individual assess the eventual consequences of present behavior. Thus someone may decide to be an apprentice or go to medical school, thereby "delaying gratification." Of course, the doctrine in no way dictates that the individual makes the right or correct decisions. It is just that the individual *attempts* to maximize eventual rewards.

But how much time must occur between response and reward in order for us to say that the individual's hedonistic orientation is toward the future rather than the present? There is no obvious answer to this question, but one solution is to use the individual's attention span as a demarcation. Thus if the time lag between response and reward is sufficiently long so that the individual's attention shifts to matters other than anticipated reward, we can speak of hedonism of the future rather than hedonism of the present.

Finally, it should be apparent that there is no reason why someone may not vacillate among the three types of hedonistic orientations, sometimes being directed by habitual responses rewarded in the past, sometimes acting so as to maximize present rewards, and sometimes acting so as to maximize future rewards.

Reward

Do individuals change their attitudes because they are rewarded for doing so? This is not an easy question to answer. Three specific situations in which this question arises relate to verbal reinforcement of attitudinally relevant responses, classical conditioning of attitude, and reward for counterattitudinal advocacy. These are three research areas in which some investigators have claimed support for the hypothesis that reward can change attitudes. As we shall see, however, alternative explanations are possible, and the issue is by no means resolved.

VERBAL REINFORCEMENT

The study of verbal reinforcement involves the investigation of various verbal stimuli which, when associated with certain verbal responses, increase the frequency of those responses. Greenspoon (1955) is responsible for calling our attention to the importance of verbal reinforcement. He found that if the experimenter said "mm-hmm" every time a subject uttered a plural noun the frequency of plural nouns increased. Subjects were initially instructed that their task was simply to say nouns. Subsequent investigators have more frequently used "good" rather than "mm-hmm" as the verbal reinforcer, and have tended to prefer an experimental task introduced by Taffel (1955). Taffel presented subjects with a series of cards each containing six pronouns ("I," "we," "you," "he," "she," "they") and a different past-tense verb. The verbs varied from card to card, but the pronouns always remained the same. The subjects were instructed to select one of the pronouns, put it with the verb, and make up a sentence. Every time the subject began a sentence with either "I" or "we" the experimenter said "good." Taffel found that the number of "I" and "we" sentences increased over trials.

Hildum and Brown (1956) were the first to demonstrate the importance of verbal reinforcement on attitudinally related responses. Harvard students were called on the telephone and asked to agree or disagree with each of 15 belief statements relating to the Harvard philosophy of general education. Half of the subjects were reinforced for responses indicating a positive attitude toward the Harvard philosophy of general education and half were reinforced for responses indicating a negative attitude toward the Harvard philosophy of general education. For some of the subjects "good" was the reinforcer and for some "mm-hmm" was the reinforcer. The results indicated that "mm-hmm" had no effect upon the belief responses but that "good" did. The subjects who were reinforced with "good" for responses indicating a positive attitude in fact made such responses to a greater extent than did subjects who were reinforced with "good" for responses indicating a negative attitude.

The fact that "good" has an effect on attitudinally related responses does not necessarily mean, however, that anything more than a temporary modification of interview responses has occurred. Does verbal reinforcement in fact produce enduring attitude change? Insko (1965) found that a delayed assessment of attitude approximately a week after verbal reinforcement produced evidence for enduring attitude change. Subjects from an introductory psychology class were called on the telephone and verbally reinforced. Approximately one week later the class instructor passed out a questionnaire assessing attitudes on a range of issues, including the one on which subjects had been reinforced. The questionnaire responses indicated that the subjects who had been reinforced in the pro direction were, in fact, more pro than the subjects who had been reinforced in the con direction.

Given that verbal reinforcement does in fact produce attitude change, it is of interest to ask why. What theoretical notions can be advanced to account for the successful verbal reinforcement of attitudinal responses? While there are undoubtedly many possibilities, we will just mention four.

The *first* of these theoretical possibilities is that verbal reinforcement is an artifact of the demand characteristics of the experimental situation. Orne (1962) has argued that laboratory experiments possess *demand characteristics,* or cues which provide subjects with hunches about the experimental hypothesis. He maintains that subjects engage in a type of problem solving in which they attempt to ascertain the experimental hypothesis and then act so as to confirm this hypothesis. Thus one theoretical possibility is that participants in a verbal reinforcement, following their wish to be "good subjects," guess the experimenter's hypothesis and act so as to confirm this hypothesis.

Suggestive support for the demand characteristics explanation comes from investigations of the relationship between awareness and verbal conditioning in the Taffel situation. The first investigators who used the Taffel situation typically assessed awareness with a single postexperimental question that enquired generally whether or not the subjects were aware of what was going on during the experiment. Such general questions would typically reveal that only a small percentage of the subjects were in fact aware that the experimenter had been saying "good" whenever a sentence was begun with "I" or "we." When these few subjects were eliminated from the sample the remaining subjects still manifested significant verbal conditioning. Such results were taken as indicating verbal conditioning can occur without awareness. Levin (1961), however, found that if awareness is assessed with a long probing interview somewhat different results are obtained. Subjects were first verbally reinforced in the Taffel situation and then given an extended postexperimental interview. The first questions in the interview enquired generally about what was going on during the experiment, and the final questions asked more pointedly whether the subjects were aware of any occurrences during the experiment and, if so, what such occurrences meant. On the basis of the responses to the first general questions 3 out of 60 subjects were classified as aware of the fact that "good" always followed sentences beginning with either "I" or "we." After elimination of these 3 subjects Levin found a significant increase in the number of "I" and "we" sentences, just as had previous investigators. On the basis of the extended interview 16 additional subjects were considered aware. When these subjects were eliminated Levin found no evidence for conditioning in the remaining sample. These results seemingly indicate that verbal conditioning does not occur without awareness.

Evidence, such as Levin's, for a relation between awareness and conditioning raises innumerable issues. One issue relates to whether or not reinforcement acts directly upon responses or is mediated by an expectancy of what response will produce reinforcement. This is one of the classic problems in the psychology of learning and is not of immediate concern to social psychologists. Another issue of more concern to social psychologists relates to the extent to which the awareness correlation indicates that the verbal reinforcement phenomenon is an artifact of the laboratory situation. Do the participants in the verbal reinforcement experiments, following their wish to be "good subjects," guess the experimenter's hypothesis and act so as to confirm this hypothesis?

Fortunately we are able to say whether or not the verbal reinforcement of attitudinally related responses is an artifact of the laboratory situation. The fact that verbal reinforcement of attitudinally related responses has been demonstrated many times in nonlaboratory contexts with subjects who do not know they are participating in an experiment resolves the issue. The use of subjects who are contacted over the telephone relieves the doubt about laboratory artifactuality. It has, in fact, been demonstrated for attitudinally related responses that telephone subjects manifest the verbal reinforcement effect to as great an extent as do laboratory subjects (Insko & Melson, 1969).

The *second* theoretical explanation of verbal reinforcement is that "good" has an effect due to hedonic satisfaction. In this situation, both hedonism of the past and hedonism of the present are potentially relevant. Subjects find the "good" rewarding or pleasant and thus make the attitudinal responses that in the past resulted in the receipt of this reward and in the present produce more reward. The most relevant information concerning this explanation comes from studies which have found a correlation between conditioning in the Taffel situation and postexperimental reports of the extent to which subjects wanted or did not want to hear the experimenter say "good" or "mm-hmm" (e.g., Spielberger, 1962).

The *third* explanation is in terms of the information value of verbal reinforcement. According to this explanation the "good" informs the subject of the interviewer's point of view and results in conformity to this point of view. From this perspective verbal reinforcement of attitude is a simple conformity or social influence effect.

The *fourth* theoretical explanation is the two-factor theory developed by Insko and Cialdini (1969). According to this notion the "good" provides information as to the interviewer attitude and creates positive rapport between the interviewers and subject. Thus one factor is information and the other is rapport. It is the positive rapport (or liking) which serves to motivate conformity consistent with the interviewer's attitude.

The reader should be aware of the fact that the two-factor theory of attitudinal verbal reinforcement can be regarded as a balance theory of attitudinal verbal reinforcement. This is true since balance theory implies, among other things, that individuals have a tendency to agree with liked persons and to disagree with disliked persons. According to the two-factor theory "good" produces liking for the experimenter and also provides information regarding the responses that are necessary for agreement with the experimenter. Thus in balance terms if the experimenter reinforces responses favorable toward some attitude object, x, the subject, or p, likes the experimenter, or o, and has information that o likes x. Thus in order to balance the triad p should also like x. In this case there is a balanced triad of three positive signs (p likes o, o likes x, and p likes x). On the other hand, if the experimenter reinforces responses unfavorable to x, the balance tendency would be toward a triad of one positive sign and two negative signs (p likes o, o dislikes x, and p dislikes x). In either case there is agreement between p and o.

Two experiments which support the two-factor account of attitudinal verbal reinforcement are those of Cialdini and Insko (1969) and Insko and Butzine (1967). The Cialdini and Insko study, which is contained in the

Readings section, provides evidence for the importance of information (the first factor) in producing attitudinal verbal reinforcement. In this experiment the attitude issue related to the relative importance of experimental and clinical psychology and the experimenter initially identified himself as either an experimental or a clinical psychologist. The intent of the experiment was to compare conditions in which the direction of reinforcement was consistent with the experimenter's affiliation (experimental reinforcement and experimental affiliation or clinical reinforcement and clinical affiliation) with situations in which the direction of reinforcement was inconsistent with the experimenter's affiliation (experimental reinforcement and clinical affiliation or clinical reinforcement and experimental affiliation). The results revealed significantly more influence in the informationally consistent than inconsistent conditions.

The Insko and Butzine (1967) study provides evidence that rapport (the second factor) is an important determinant of attitudinal verbal reinforcement. Before actually beginning the verbal reinforcement of responses to statements concerning pay-TV, subjects were asked some general questions relating to television. For example, one question asked what was the subject's favorite television program. In a positive-rapport condition subjects' answers to these general questions were complimented; in a negative-rapport condition subjects' answers were mildly ridiculed. The results indicated that the subjects in the positive-rapport condition subsequently conditioned better than the subjects in the negative-rapport condition.

Thus we are confronted with a situation in which the simple hedonistic position does not obviously do the best job of accounting for results which initially at least appeared to be a manifestation of the tendency to maximize exposure to rewarding stimuli. It is possible, however, that a more sophisticated version of the hedonistic hypothesis could account for the results of the above experiments. Such a more sophisticated version would argue that the experimenter's "good" is not always pleasant or rewarding. Rather "good" is only pleasant when it conveys unambiguous information from a liked other (experimenter with whom there is positive rapport). According to this position the two factors of rapport and information provide the boundary conditions which determine when "good" is rewarding. Thus both balance theory and this more sophisticated hedonistic position would both predict that individuals tend to agree with liked others. The important question here is whether or not the assumption that "good" is rewarding under certain conditions of information and rapport allows for the handling of results that could not otherwise be explained. To date research has not answered this question. One finding contrary to even this more sophisticated version of the hedonistic hypothesis comes from the Cialdini and Insko study, which is contained in the Readings. Cialdini and Insko found that postexperimental reports of the hedonistic satisfaction of "good" did not significantly correlate with amount of influence within any of the experimental conditions. Within the informationally consistent conditions greater hedonic satisfaction should have been associated with a greater amount of influence. One contrary finding, however, hardly ever rules out a theoretical point of view. Certainly the final word on this matter has not yet been said.

This shift in the conception of the rewardingness of "good" illustrates very clearly the major philosophical problem surrounding the hedonistic account of behavior. The problem is simply that the exact specification of what is and what is not rewarding has not been made. Until such specification occurs it is impossible to conduct an empirical test of the hedonistic notion. No matter what results occur, it can always be claimed that the subjects were "really" trying to maximize rewards; it is just that our initial conception of what was rewarding was incorrect. The problem is further compounded by the fact that the general hedonistic position has also not been elaborated so as to specify the circumstances determining when the subjects will shift their orientation from past to present to future maximization of reward. This problem of the slipperiness of the hedonistic approach will come up again in Chapter 11 when we discuss a hedonistic or "exchange" approach to social interaction.

The above discussion in no way implies that eventually an adequately specified hedonistic theory of human behavior may not be formulated. It is just that at present such a formulation does not exist. Hence for the present, at least, the hedonistic approach is simply a general orientation to human behavior and not a theory which makes definite predictions capable of being tested.

CLASSICAL CONDITIONING OF ATTITUDE

The investigation of classical conditioning of attitude involves a situation in which a relatively neutral stimulus is repeatedly paired with a second stimulus that is affectively arousing (such as electric shock). The affective stimulus can be either pleasant or unpleasant. Theoretically, however, the originally neutral stimulus acquires the same affective value as the stimulus with which it is paired. Thus an article of clothing, or souvenir, may provoke pleasant affect because of its association with an enjoyable vacation trip.

The animal literature abounds with convincing demonstrations of affective conditioning. Research with humans, however, has encountered a difficult methodological problem. If a subject is repeatedly given an electric shock paired with a neutral stimulus, such as a word, and later is asked how he feels about the word, the experimenter's conditioning hypothesis is transparently obvious. The problem then is one of demand characteristics. If the subject reports that he dislikes the word which was paired with the electric shock, is it because the word evokes genuine negative affect, or because the subject correctly perceives the experimenter's hypothesis and acts so as to confirm it?

One of the most convincing reports of the classical conditioning of attitudes is a study by Zanna, Kiesler, and Pilkonis (1970), which is contained in the Readings section of this chapter. Zanna *et al.* attempted to eliminate the demand characteristics possibility by divorcing the assessment of attitude toward neutral stimuli (the words "light" and "dark") from the experiment in which they were paired with the beginning or the ending of trials on which a "random" number of shocks occurred. The results indicated that the subjects who gave independent physiological evidence of conditioning (as evidenced by GSP response) significantly altered their affective ratings of the words. The words associated with shock offset were rated more positively than the words associated with shock onset.

What is the relevance of the hedonistic position to the classical conditioning of attitude? The answer to this question is somewhat complex. It is important to note that, unlike with attitudinal verbal reinforcement, hedonism of the present is not applicable to classical conditioning. In a verbal reinforcement study receipt of the reward (the experimenter's "good") is *contingent* upon the performance of a certain response. Hence, all such reward-contingent situations are frequently referred to as involving *instrumental* conditioning. In a classical conditioning study, on the other hand, receipt of the reward is not contingent upon the performance of a response. No response is instrumental to the elicitation of the reward. The experimenter always presents the reward together with the neutral stimulus regardless of what the subject does. Thus it is apparent that the hedonistic position that individuals act in the present situation so as to maximize exposure to reward is not a relevant explanatory possibility.

It should also be apparent that, as we have defined them, hedonism of the past and future are not relevant to the classical conditioning situation. The subject is not obviously acting in a manner that has maximized past rewards or in a manner that will maximize future rewards. After the subject makes the first conditioned response, it cannot be argued that he continues to make these responses on subsequent trials because such past actions *produced* reward. However, if hedonism of the past is restated so that the individual is assumed to make those responses which in the past were *associated* with the maximization of pleasant affect and the minimization of unpleasant affect, the doctrine becomes a relevant consideration. In the well known Pavlovian situation, for example, food was associated with, but not instrumentally dependent on, the conditioned salivation response. Likewise in the Zanna *et al.* experiment shock onset (or offset) was associated with, but not instrumentally dependent on, a conditioned affective response to the stimulus words. Performance of the conditioned response did not produce, but was associated with, a change in shock.

But is even this modified version of hedonism of the past consistent with the Zanna *et al.* results? The fact that the association of a word with shock offset resulted in affective conditioning is certainly consistent. Shock offset is a reduction in unpleasant stimulation. But why should the association of a word with shock onset result in affective conditioning? Here we seem to have an *increase* in unpleasant stimulation. Such a result appears inconsistent with the notion that the individual makes those responses which in the past were associated with the maximization of pleasant affect and the minimization of unpleasant affect.

How could a defender of the hedonistic doctrine account for the fact that the presumably unpleasant shock onset appeared to produce affective conditioning? It could possibly be argued that, since the subject knew he was to be shocked, the actual occurrence of a stimulus word followed by shock onset relieved the anxiety of uncertain waiting and thus, in fact, produced a net reduction in unpleasantness. Although such an argument is not very plausible, it does illustrate the previously developed point that the situation can always be redefined so as to make any behavior appear consistent with the hedonistic position.

Although typically not recognized, balance theory provides still a further perspective on the classical conditioning of attitude. In balance terms the repeated pairing of the neutral stimulus with a state of affective arousal creates a positive unit relation. The originally neutral stimulus and the state of affective arousal are perceived as belonging together. This positive bond should thus result in the neutral stimulus acquiring the same sign as the affective arousal. Thus if the affective arousal is pleasant, or evaluated positively, the neutral stimulus should acquire a positive evaluation. This would give a band of three positive signs. On the other hand, if the affective arousal is unpleasant, or evaluated negatively, the neutral stimulus should acquire a negative sign. This would give a band of two negative signs and one positive sign. Recall that bands of either three positive signs, or two negative signs and one positive sign, are balanced. From a balance perspective the classical conditioning of attitudes is just another illustration of the individual's general tendency to sort out his cognitive world in a consistent manner.

REWARD FOR COUNTERATTITUDINAL ADVOCACY

Counterattitudinal advocacy occurs when an individual argues for a point of view contrary to his own, as for example in a debate. Studies of the role of reward for counterattitudinal advocacy have arranged the situation so that subjects are led to believe that their counterattitudinal advocacy was of very superior or of mediocre quality. This differentially rewarding information always occurs after the counterattitudinal advocacy and is made to appear contingent upon the quality of the subject's counterattitudinal performance.

The first investigation of the role of reward for counterattitudinal advocacy was reported by Scott (1957). Scott found that subjects who were led to believe that they had won a debate changed their attitudes in the counterattitudinal direction more than subjects who were led to believe that they had lost. The debates took place in class and the judgment as to who had won and who had lost was supposedly a result of a class vote. In a further study Scott (1959) also demonstrated that the same effect can be produced when the rewarding information comes from three judges who listen to the debates.

In an interesting variation of Scott's procedure Bostrom, Vlandis, and Rosenbaum (1961) found that students who were given A's for their counterattitudinal essays showed more attitude change than students who were given D's. The assignment of grades was random and bore no relation to actual essay quality. Students wrote the essays on one of two topics, legalized gambling or socialized medicine, as part of their regular classroom assignment.

In Chapter 5 we will discuss evidence indicating that the simple counterattitudinal act, without any experimentally manipulated reward, can produce attitude change. In view of this fact it appears that in the Scott, and Bostrom *et al.* experiments the counterattitudinal arguments produced attitude change which was in turn strengthened or weakened depending upon the presence or absence of reward. From this perspective the mechanism producing attitude change was classical conditioning. Note that from the subjects' perspective receipt of the reward was not instrumentally dependent on attitude change. The subjects believed that the dependency was on a superior counterattitudinal performance. Attitude change produced by the counterattitudinal activity was, however, paired or associated with winning or losing the debate. Thus the changed attitude was associated with either pleasant affect (winning) or unpleasant affect (losing), and took on the evaluative sign of that affect.

Still a further explanation of attitude change following reward for counterattitudinal advocacy has been advanced by Wallace (1966). Wallace distinguishes between two types of reward for counterattitudinal advocacy, role reward and content reward. Role reward is reward for the manner and style in which the counterattitudinal advocacy is performed. Content reward is reward for the nature of the actual counterattitudinal arguments that are used. Wallace found that these two types of reward differentially affected attitude toward capital punishment. Subjects engaged in a counterattitudinal debate with an experimental accomplice in the presence of two other accomplices. Subjects who were for capital punishment argued against capital punishment, and subjects who were against capital punishment argued for capital punishment. At the conclusion of the debate, the two observer accomplices rated the debaters on both the role and content dimensions. In a role reward condition the naïve subject was told that the manner in which his speech was presented was quite superior but that the content of the speech was comparable to that expected from the average college student. In a content reward condition the naïve subject was told that the arguments he used were very powerful and persuasive but that the manner in which the speech was presented was comparable to that expected of the average college student. In a neutral condition subjects were told that both their arguments and delivery were average. Similar neutral feedback was given to the subject's opponent in all conditions. The results indicated that for the subjects arguing against capital punishment role reward was more effective than content reward but that for the subjects arguing for capital punishment neither type of reward produced any effect upon attitude change.

Wallace believes that the correct explanation of his results relates not to the direct effect of reward on attitude change but rather to an awareness of the dissonant (or inconsistent) relation between the counterattitudinal behavior and attitude. In later chapters we will discuss dissonance theory in somewhat greater detail. For now the reader can simply regard dissonance as an inconsistency between behavior and attitude. Thus from Wallace's perspective counterattitudinal advocacy creates dissonance. Dissonance is regarded as a tension state that the individual will attempt to reduce. One way the tension or dissonance produced by counterattitudinal advocacy can be reduced is for the individual to change his attitude in the direction of advocacy. Wallace thus interprets the superiority of role reward over content reward as being due to the fact that role reward produces a greater awareness of the dissonance between behavior and attitude. Supposedly role reward relative to content reward provided more information that the counterattitudinal behavior was inconsistent with the initial attitude toward capital punishment. Since the dissonance could be reduced through attitude change congruent with the direction of advocacy, such attitude change tended to occur.

Why is it that the subjects who argued for capital punishment were not influenced by either type of reward? Neither we nor Wallace have the answer to this question. It is possible that there was some sort of interference from the anti-capital punishment norm that exists in most academic subcultures, but there is no way of knowing for sure. This failure to find any effect for reward, however, does make it quite evident that our understanding of the effect of reward for counterattitudinal advocacy is far from complete. This conclusion is made even more compelling in view of the fact that a second investigator, Greenbaum (1966), also failed to find an effect for reward following counterattitudinal advocacy. We need to know more about the situations in which reward for counterattitudinal advocacy does and does not prove effective.

On the other hand, in view of the above interpretation of attitude change following reward for counterattitudinal advocacy in terms of classical conditioning, it is not surprising that the effect should not always be evident. In most conditioning situations the reward is presented repeatedly over a sizable number of trials. In the present counterattitudinal situation, however, there was only one trial, or one presentation of the reward. From this perspective it is certainly understandable why the effect should not always be present.

Fear

HEDONISM OF THE PRESENT AND FUTURE

The most common approach to the study of the relationship between fear and attitude change has been to compare persuasive communications which differ in level of fear arousal. In order to be able to make an unambiguous inference concerning the effect of fear upon attitude change it is necessary that the communications differ in amount of fear arousal but not in terms of other relevant variables such as amount of information conveyed.

Given that we have two communications, one strong fear arousing and one weak fear arousing, which is likely to produce greater attitude or belief change? Different answers are given to this question depending upon whether the subject is believed to have a present or future hedonistic orientation. From the perspective of hedonism of the present, the strong-fear communications should be less persuasive than the weak-fear communication. Since the strong-fear communication is unpleasant the subject should avoid attending to it or defensively avoid thinking about it. To the extent that the *weak-fear* communication is less unpleasant such avoidance should be less likely and the communication thus more likely to have a persuasive impact. On the other hand, if the subject adopts a future hedonistic orientation the strong-fear communication should be more persuasive. The assumption here is that the strong fear communication does the best job of informing the subject how he should change in order to avoid future unpleasantness. Thus from the perspective of hedonism of the present a strong-fear communication should be less persuasive than a weak-fear communication, and from the perspective of hedonism of the future a strong-fear communication should be more persuasive than a weak-fear communication.

RESEARCH

The first investigation of the effect of fear-arousing communications upon attitude change was reported by Janis and Feshbach (1953). Janis and Feshbach presented high school students with strong, moderate, or weak fear arousing communications on the cause and prevention of tooth decay. The strong fear communication emphasized the painful consequences of tooth decay and was accompanied by slides showing severe cases of oral pathology. The moderate fear communication was less personal, and the accompanying slides were of less severe cases of oral pathology. The weak fear communication replaced the fear arousing information with less threatening information and the accompanying slides were of healthy teeth and X rays. A questionnaire given immediately after exposure revealed that the three communications were differentially fear arousing, as expected. A second questionnaire administered one week later revealed that the strong appeal was less effective than the moderate appeal which in turn was less effective than the weak appeal in producing reported change in the frequency and manner of tooth brushing.

Janis and Feshbach interpreted their results as indicating that fear produced defensive avoidance reactions. They speculate that the evocation of emotional reactions might be an effective way of prompting immediate responses such as donating money, but when communication contains no reassurance or immediate way of obtaining reassurance, the emotional reaction may lead either to an avoidance of thinking about the content of the communication or to a minimization of the importance of the communication.

Janis and Terwilliger (1962) obtained evidence in support of the defensive-resistance hypothesis. Their weak-fear communication consisted of a series of 15 paragraph-statements by medical authorities which indicated that heavy smoking causes lung cancer. Their strong-fear communication consisted of the same 15 paragraphs plus 7 additional paragraphs which elaborated upon the seriousness of lung cancer. These latter 7 paragraphs were scattered among the 15 paragraph-statements by medical authorities. Volunteer subjects (student and adult) most of whom were smokers read either the strong-fear or the weak-fear communication one paragraph at a time. After reading each paragraph the subjects verbalized their reactions which were recorded by a concealed tape recorder. Before and again after exposure to the persuasive paragraphs the subjects were also asked to verbalize their ideas while they thought of themselves smoking a cigarette. A content analysis of this material revealed a marginal tendency for the strong-fear communication to be less influential than the weak-fear communication. A content analysis of the reactions verbalized to each communication indicated that the strong-fear communication was indeed more fear arousing than the weak-fear communication. Furthermore, it was found that the subjects in the strong-fear condition made more explicit rejection reactions to the 15 mildly threatening paragraphs than did subjects in the weak-fear condition. Janis and Terwilliger interpreted these results as indicating that a strong fear-arousing communication arouses defensive resistance to the arguments, conclusions, and recommendations contained in the communication.

Unfortunately, most of the subsequent research on fear arousal has obtained results which are not in agreement with those of Janis and Feshbach and Janis and Terwilliger. So many studies have in fact found that strong fear is more effective than weak fear in producing attitude change that it is probably safe to conclude that in most communication situations high fear will indeed be more effective.

In a 1969 review of this literature Higbee reports that 21 studies have found high-fear communications to produce more attitude or belief change than low-fear communications. These studies involved such diverse issues as dental hygiene practices, smoking, tetanus innoculations, safe-driving practices, fallout shelters, tuberculosis, roundworms, proper viewing of the sun during an eclipse, and the use of stairway handrails for safety. Furthermore, very diverse subject populations (ranging from Taiwan elementary school students to student nurses, to high-school students and college students) were studied. The bulk of the research thus supports hedonism of the future rather than hedonism of the past as the more appropriate theoretical perspective.

It should be noted, however, that this general tendency for strong-fear communications to be more persuasive than weak-fear communications relates entirely to attitude and belief change. Just because a high-fear communication produces a more favorable attitude toward a certain health practice than a low-fear communication does not mean that the actual behavioral follow-through will also be greater for the subjects exposed to the high-fear communication. The bulk of the research has not assessed behavioral as well as attitudinal change, but the research that has done so (e.g., Leventhal, Singer, & Jones, 1965) has typically found somewhat different results for the two dependent variables.

THE CURVILINEAR HYPOTHESIS

Focusing our attention on just attitude and belief change, what is the proper generalization to be drawn from the existing research data? In view of the fact that the bulk of the studies have found that increasing fear is associated with increasing attitude change, is the proper generalization simply that fear and attitude change are positively associated? Some theorists, for example, McGuire (1968) and Janis (1967), have proposed that there is a curvilinear relation between fear and attitude change. Increasing fear will produce increasing persuasion to a certain point beyond which further increasing fear will produce decreasing persuasion.

Janis (1967) has argued that as long as the level of arousal is not too great fear will have the effect of drawing the subject's attention to the communication and motivating the acceptance of the recommended point of view. Beyond a certain critical point, however, fear will produce defensive reactions (such as questioning of the alarmist intentions of the communicator) and will further produce marked constriction of cognitive processes, resulting in interference with attention and comprehension. Janis supports his argument by referring to some physiological evidence indicating that the ascending reticular system may deliver insufficient stimulation to the cortex at low levels of emotional arousal and too intense stimulation at high levels of arousal. The optimal level of arousal is an intermediate one in which the person is neither unalert and inattentive nor frozen with terror.

Janis further argues that in a persuasive situation various factors may raise or lower the optimal level of fear arousal. In general any factor that bolsters the argumentation or seals off obvious loopholes will raise the optimal level. For example, a communication coming from a highly credible source will have a higher optimal level of fear arousal than one coming from a moderately credible source. As Janis is aware, such a complex state of affairs makes hypothesis testing rather difficult.

Whatever the ultimate fate of the curvilinear hypothesis, it does have a common-sense appeal. As long as the level of fear is not too great the individual will be guided by hedonism of the future, with increasing fear producing increasing attitude change. As the level of fear passes a certain point, however, the individual will be guided by hedonism of the present, with increasing fear producing decreasing attitude change. From this perspective it is the level of fear which determines whether or not the individual shifts his orientation to minimize unpleasant affect from future to present. Actually such a hypothesis is reasonable if people are regarded as not being directed by hedonism of the present or hedonism of the future but by a total hedonistic orientation. If the individual attempts to maximize all rewards (present and future) and minimize all unpleasantness (present and future), the greater the fear-associated unpleasant affect during the present the greater the importance of this affect in the total picture. Thus from the standpoint of the total amount of affect (present and future), it is reasonable that beyond a certain intensity of fear-associated unpleasantness further increases in fear should produce avoidance tendencies and consequent decreasing attitude change. If the cure gets sufficiently unpleasant the individual may avoid it and resign himself to the disease.

Final Statement

As indicated at the beginning of this chapter, the ultimate status of the hedonistic approach to attitude change has, as yet, to be determined. It is nonetheless true that the hedonistic approach has explicitly or implicitly directed attention to some intriguing research problems.

The reader should be aware that the hedonistic orientation is not a testable theory. As previously mentioned, there are two main problems preventing hedonism from being a testable theory. First, exact specification of the circumstances determining when stimuli are rewarding or unrewarding has not been made. And second, the variables determining when the hedonistic orientation shifts from past to present to future have not been identified.

The above statement, however, in no way implies that it is impossible to state the hedonistic position so that it is a testable theory. In our opinion, however, such a theory will have to be rather sophisticated if it is to pass repeated empirical testing, to say nothing of accounting for already existing data.

READINGS

Attitudinal Verbal Reinforcement as A Function of Informational Consistency: A Further Test of the Two-Factor Theory[1]

Robert B. Cialdini and Chester A. Insko

Pro-clinical or pro-experimental attitudinal responses were reinforced with "good" by an experimenter who identified himself as either a clinical psychologist or as an experimental psychologist. Only in the condition in which the direction of reinforcement was consistent with the affiliation of the experimenter did influence occur. Since this manipulation of information consistency did effect awareness, but not rapport or other variables, the results were taken as supporting the hypothesis that conveying of information is one important factor in attitudinal verbal reinforcement. The further finding that experimental subjects who received a reinforcement liked the experimenter better than control subjects who did not receive a reinforcement was taken as indicating that the heightening of rapport is also an important factor in attitudinal verbal reinforcement. No support for a hedonic interpretation was found, nor was there any evidence for conditioning without awareness.

According to the two-factor theory developed by Insko and Cialdini (1969) attitudinal verbal reinforcement is a function of information and rapport. "Good" has an attitudinal effect because it conveys information about the interviewer's attitude and creates positive rapport. Since both factors are necessary in order for influence to occur, if one factor is held constant and the other varied there should be a variation in the attitudinal effect.[2] Insko and Butzine (1967) varied rapport and held information constant. The present experiment attempts to vary information and hold rapport constant.

The manipulation of information in the present study was suggested by the results of Krasner, Knowles, and Ullman (1965). Krasner *et al.* found that an interviewer identified with medical science could condition favorable, but not unfavorable, responses to medical science. If the consistency-inconsistency of information cues is responsible for these results, then an

---

[1] From the *Journal of Personality and Social Psychology*, Volume 12, pages 342–350, 1969 (received November 18, 1968). Authors' affiliation: University of North Carolina. Reproduced by permission of the American Psychological Association.

[2] This statement may appear superficially in disagreement with Insko and Butzine's (1967) finding of a significant attitudinal effect in the negative rapport condition. While the negative rapport condition may have been negative when the initial insults were delivered, the occurrence of positive reinforcements during the subsequent interview would theoretically have acted so as to counteract the negative rapport.

interviewer antagonistic to medical science should have been better able to condition unfavorable than favorable responses to medical science. In the present study there was a manipulation of the consistency-inconsistency of the direction of reinforcement and the affiliation of the experimenter. The interview question dealt with the relative merit of clinical and experimental psychology. By identifying the experimenter as a graduate student in either clinical or experimental psychology it was possible to manipulate the consistency of the direction of reinforcement (clinical or experimental) and the affiliation of the experimenter. If informational cues are important, verbal reinforcement should be significantly greater in the consistent condition than in the inconsistent condition. As a check on the consistency-inconsistency manipulation we used Dulany's (1962) assessment of reinforcement hypothesis. If, in fact, there is greater informational redundancy in the consistent condition, there should be a greater awareness of the reinforcement distribution (awareness of the reinforcement contingency) and significance (awareness of the interviewer's point of view) in the consistent than inconsistent condition. As a check on the possibility that the consistent and inconsistent conditions also differ in perception of an evaluation of the experimenter, we included a number of appropriate postexperimental questions. Finally, a number of appropriate postexperimental questions were also included in order to examine the correlation between the attitude effect and the hedonic evaluation of "good."

METHOD

Subjects

The subjects were 92 University of North Carolina students of both sexes who participated in the experiment as partial fulfillment of the requirements of an introductory psychology course. Sixteen subjects were randomly assigned to each of the four experimental conditions and 14 to each of the two control conditions.

Interview

During the interview subjects were asked to "strongly agree," "agree," "disagree," or "strongly disagree" with each of a series of 18 opinion statements regarding clinical and experimental psychology. The 18 interview statements were selected after extensive pilot testing. The last 14 of the statements were selected because they came closest to producing equal numbers of agreement and disagreement responses. The first four statements were selected because two of them typically produced pro-clinical responses and two of them pro-experimental responses. These statements assured an opportunity for reinforcement early in the interview. Half of the statements are pro-clinical and half are pro-experimental.

Procedure

When the subject arrived at the experimental room he was seated across a table from the experimenter, whose face was blocked by an opaque screen. A tape recorder was on the table at one end of the opaque screen. After obtaining the subject's name the experimenter (while seated behind the screen) gave the following instructions:

Well, first of all, I guess I can tell you something of what this experiment is about. Actually, it's not really an experiment in the strict sense of the word; it's more of an opinion survey concerning your attitudes toward psychology.

I'm going to let you read a description of each of two major areas of psychology—clinical psychology and experimental psychology. The descriptions come from an introductory psychology text and will serve to give you some information regarding the orientation and purposes of each of these areas over and above any information about them you may now have. After you've read the descriptions, I'm going to let you listen to some tape-recorded statements regarding the two areas and will ask you either to agree or disagree with each statement. I'll tell you more about that when we come to it, but now I'll tell you a little more about the purpose of the experiment. I'm a first-year graduate student in clinical [or experimental] psychology here at UNC, and I'm currently taking a public opinion course. One of the requirements for the course is that everyone must conduct an opinion poll of Psychology 26 students regarding some issue and then write a term paper on the outcome. The topic I've chosen has to do with the difference in the two major branches of psychology—clinical and experimental psychology. Do you have any questions so far? O.K., then, I guess I can tell you more specifically what you're going to have to do. As I said before, there are two main areas of psychology—clinical [or experimental] psychology, *the field I'm in, for example,* and experimental [or clinical] psychology. I'm going to let you read a textbook's description of clinical psychology and the same textbook's description of experimental psychology.

The subject was then handed two paragraph statements, one describing experimental psychology and one describing clinical psychology. After the subject finished reading the "textbook descriptions" the experimenter continued:

O.K., do you have any questions regarding the paragraphs themselves? Since I am a graduate student in clinical [or experimental] psychology and am most interested in clinical [or experimental] psychology, I could probably answer any question you have about that paragraph better than the other one.

All right then, if you have no questions we'll go on. I'm going to let you listen to a series of tape-recorded statements which have to do with clinical and experimental psychology. For each statement, I'd like you to indicate your reaction in one of four ways. With each statement, please tell me if you: (1) strongly agree, (2) agree, (3) disagree, or (4) strongly disagree. Do you have any questions? Then we will begin. Here is the first statement.

After each recorded statement the experimenter pushed a button, momentarily stopping the machine. The tape recorder and experimenter's hand were clearly visible to the subject. While the button was depressed the subject responded and the experimenter either said "good" or nothing. At the conclusion of the interview the experimenter continued:

O.K., that was the last statement. However, there's one more thing that I'd like you to do. Another student in my class has chosen as her topic "the attitude of Psychology 26 students toward being subjects in experiments." All the students in the class are also asking their subjects to fill out this form so that she can get some data on this question. It won't take long. You can do it right here and take it directly to her.

The first page of the postexperimental qeustionnaire contained the following statement:

This is an opinion survey regarding your feelings toward psychological experiments and your participation in them. You will not be asked to state your name, the name of the experiment you have just completed, nor the experimenter's name, so please be frank. After you have completed the questionnaire, *do not give it back to the experimenter;* rather, bring it to my office, Room 332. If I am not in my office, please slip it under the door.

After finishing the questionnaire the subjects orally answered additional questions designed to assess awareness, rapport, and hedonic evaluation of "good."

Independent Variables

Two independent variables were manipulated: direction of reinforcement (clinical versus experimental), and consistency of information (consistent affiliation and reinforcement versus inconsistent affiliation and reinforcement). These two independent variables generate four experimental conditions. In addition there were two control conditions in which there was no reinforcement. In one of these control conditions the experimenter had a clinical affiliation and in the other, an experimental affiliation.

Dependent Variables

Responses to the 18 opinion statements were scored 0, 1, 2, or 3, with high scores indicating a favorable attitude toward experimental psychology. This provided an assessment of attitude, the major dependent variable.

Items 8, 9, 10, 11, and 12 in the postexperimental questionnaire provided assessments of liking for the experiment, perceived truthfulness of the experimenter, perceived knowledgeableness of the experimenter, perceived trustworthiness of the experimenter, and liking for the experimenter, respectively. The items were responded to by checking a 4-point scale ranging from "very much" to "not at all." Question 12 regarding liking for the experimenter is a direct assessment of rapport. All of these questions were placed in the confidential postexperimental questionnaire (which the experimenter would supposedly never see) in order to encourage frankness in evaluating the experimenter.

After completing the postexperimental questionnaire, the experimental subjects only were given a postexperimental interview. The first three questions in the postexperimental interview assessed reinforcement hypothesis (Dulany, 1962). The percentage of perfect agreement between the two judges who coded the reinforcement responses was 94.

Question 4, "How much did you think that the 'good' that I would say meant that I approved of or liked you?" and Question 5, "How much did my saying 'good' make you like me?" were intended as further assessments of rapport. While these questions were not answered anonymously (as were those in the postexperimental questionnaire), they did have the advantage of inquiring directly about the effect of the reinforcement. This could not have been plausibly done in the postexperimental questionnaire.

Question 6, "How did you feel when I said 'good'?" and Question 7, "How hard were you trying to make me say 'good'?" were designed as assessments of the hedonic reaction to the reinforcement. Questions 4 and 7 were responded to with a 5-point scale ranging from "very much" to "not at all," and 5 and 6 were responded to with a 5-point scale ranging from "very pleased" to "very displeased."

RESULTS

Mean favorability-to-experimental-psychology attitude scores are presented in Table 1 and an analysis of variance of these scores in Table 2.

TABLE 1

Mean Attitude, Reinforcement Hypothesis, Evaluation of the Experiment, Perception of the Experimenter, Rapport, and Hedonism Scores in All Conditions

| Item | Reinforcement | | | | | |
| | Consistent information | | Inconsistent information | | No reinforcement | |
	Clinical reinforcement	Experimental reinforcement	Clinical reinforcement	Experimental reinforcement	Clinical affiliation	Experimental affiliation
Attitude[a]	23.69	29.56	29.06	28.50	28.07	28.57
Question 8[b]	2.31	2.63	2.38	2.31	1.93	1.71
Question 9[b]	2.56	2.38	2.56	2.75	2.64	2.57
Question 10[b]	2.50	2.62	2.44	2.56	2.43	2.21
Question 11[b]	2.62	2.62	2.62	2.75	2.79	2.36
Question 12[b]	2.50	2.62	2.62	2.62	2.39	2.29
RH[c]	3.13	3.38	1.94	2.13		
Interview 4[d]	4.12	4.56	4.69	4.50		
Interview 5[d]	4.19	4.19	4.38	4.06		
Interview 6[e]	2.62	2.62	2.44	2.19		
Interview 7[e]	4.75	4.56	4.69	4.06		

[a] The higher the attitude score the more favorable the reaction to experimental psychology.

[b] The higher the score the more positive the evaluation.

[c] The higher the score the greater the awareness.

[d] The lower the score the more positive the evaluation.

[e] The lower the score the more positive the evaluation of "good."

There is a significant main effect for reinforcement and a significant interaction between direction of reinforcement and consistency of information. The main effect indicates that there were more pro-clinical responses with clinical reinforcement than with experimental reinforcement. This effect,

TABLE 2

Analyses of Variance for Favorability-to-Experimental Psychology Attitude Scores and Reinforcement Hypothesis Scores

| Source | df | Attitude | | RH | |
		MS	F	MS	F
Consistency (C)	1	74.39	4.18*	23.77	17.35**
Reinforcement (R)	1	112.89	6.34*	0.76	
C × R	1	165.77	9.31**	0.02	
Within	60	17.80		1.37	

* $p < .05$.
** $p < .01$.

however, is only evident in the consistent-information condition. In the inconsistent-information condition there is, in fact, a slight reversal. This pattern of results produced the predicted interaction. There is, in addition, an unexpected main effect for consistency of information. Responses were more pro-clinical in the consistent-information condition than in the inconsistent-information condition.

A comparison of the two control conditions revealed no significant differences ($t = .38$). Affiliation alone did not significantly affect responses. Comparison of the clinical-affiliation control group with the consistent-clinical-affiliation experimental group revealed a significant difference ($t = 3.46$, $p < .01$), but a comparison of the experimental-affiliation control group with the consistent-experimental-affiliation experimental group did not ($t = 1.33$). Reinforcement was only significantly effective in the clinical direction.

Assessments of liking for the experiment, perception of the experimenter, and liking for the experimenter (Questionnaire Items 8, 9, 10, 11, and 12) are also reported in Table 1. These assessments were included in order to check into the possibility that the manipulation of consistency-inconsistency was a manipulation of other variables as well. Analyses of variance of the five assessments revealed no significant effect whatsoever. As the means in Table 1 make evident, the differences between the consistent and inconsistent conditions are remarkably small. The Fs for the consistency-inconsistency main effect are, in order, .67, 1.49, .24, .23, and .22.

Subjects in the control conditions also filled out the postexperimental questionnaire. The results are reported in Table 1. Comparison of the control subjects with all of the experimental subjects revealed significant differences on Questions 8 ($t = 3.28$, $p < .01$) and 12 ($t = 2.18$, $p < .05$). The experimental subjects who received reinforcements liked both the experiment (Question 8) and the experimenter (Question 12) better than the control subjects who did not receive reinforcements. We regard Question 12 as a fairly direct assessment of rapport, and thus interpret the significant difference between experimental and control groups as indicating that "good" does increase rapport with the experimenter. The fact that "good" also increased evaluation of the experiment is interesting, but was not expected.

If there is greater informational redundancy in the consistent condition than in the inconsistent condition the mean level of reinforcement hypothesis should differ between two conditions. Responses to Dulany's reinforcement hypothesis questions give us information regarding the subjects' awareness of the reinforcement contingency and awareness of the interviewer's point of view. Subjects who did not report the occurrence of "good" were given a 1. Subjects who reported the occurrence of "good" but not its distribution or significance were given a 2. Subjects who reported the distribution but not the significance of "good" were given a 3.

(Knowledge of the distribution is awareness either that pro-clinical responses are followed by "good" or that pro-experimental responses are followed by "good.") Subjects who reported both the distribution and the significance of "good" were given a 4. These were subjects who responded to the question, "Did you come to think there was or wasn't any purpose or significance to the 'good' in this experiment?" with a statement regarding the interviewer's attitude toward clinical or experimental psychology. In all previous research these categories have worked reasonably well. However, in the inconsistent-information condition of the present experiment there were five subjects who were aware of "good" but had the reinforcement contingency backwards, that is, reported that "good" was consistent with affiliation rather than actual direction of reinforcement. We decided to score these subjects with a 0. (Such a decision is consistent with Dulany's scoring of behavioral hypotheses and behavioral intentions that are contrary to the direction of reinforcement.) The mean level of reinforcement hypothesis in the four experimental conditions is reported in Table 1 and an analysis of variance of these scores in Table 2. The only significant F is the main effect for consistency of information. Awareness is significantly greater in the consistent condition that in the inconsistent condition.

Table 3 presents the frequency distribution for reinforcement hypothesis in the consistent and inconsistent conditions. A chi-square of these frequencies is significant ($\chi^2 = 48.7$, $df = 4$, $p < .01$). Of particular interest, however, are Categories 0 and 1. Subjects in Category 0 got the reinforcement contingency backwards and subjects in Category 1 did not report the occurrence of "good." The frequencies for both of these categories are markedly greater in the inconsistent-information condition. For Category 0 the difference is significant ($p = .03$ by binominal test), and for Category 1 the difference just misses being significant ($p = .055$ by binominal test). Combining Categories 0 and 1 the difference between the consistent and inconsistent conditions is clearly significant. These differences are intriguing because they suggest that there is a tendency for subjects in the inconsistent-information condition to react to the inconsistency either by not coding "good" at all or by coding it incorrectly.

Table 4 presents the mean attitude scores for unaware subjects (sub-

TABLE 3

Number of Subjects in Each Level of Reinforcement Hypothesis Awareness

	RH Level				
Condition	0	1	2	3	4
Consistent information	0	1	7	6	17
Inconsistent information	5	6	13	2	5

TABLE 4

Mean Attitude Scores for Reinforcement Hypothesis Unaware Subjects

	Consistent information		Inconsistent information	
Item	Clinical reinforcement	Experimental reinforcement	Clinical reinforcement	Experimental reinforcement
Attitude[a]	25.833	24.5000	29.000	31.333
n	6	2	11	6

[a] The higher the attitude score the more favorable the reaction to experimental psychology.

jects with reinforcement hypothesis scores of 2 or lower). An analysis of variance of these resulted in neither a significant main effect for reinforcement nor a significant Consistency $\times$ Reinforcement interaction. Thus we did not obtain evidence for conditioning without awareness.

Table 5 presents the within-cell correlation between reinforcement hypothesis and attitude. A positive relation between awareness and influence will produce a plus correlation when reinforcement is pro-experimental and a minus correlation when reinforcement is pro-clinical. Although none of the correlations are significant, all are in the right direction. After collapsing the consistency-inconsistency factor, however (Table 6), the within-cell correlations are significant.

Finally, mean results for Postexperimental Interview Questions 6 and 7 are presented in the last two rows of Table 1. These questions were designed to assess the hedonic evaluation of "good." Analyses of variance of responses to these questions resulted in no significant effects. Since a significant attitude effect occurred only in the consistent condition, a hedonic interpretation of reinforcement would predict a higher evaluation of

TABLE 5

Within-Cell Correlations between Attitude and Reinforcement Hypothesis and Attitude and Hedonic Evaluation of "Good"[a]

	Consistent information		Inconsistent information	
Item	Clinical reinforcement	Experimental reinforcement	Clinical reinforcement	Experimental reinforcement
RH	−.34	.49	−.32	.42
Interview 6	−.08	.05	.06	.13
Interview 7	.33	−.02	.28	.26

[a] A positive relation between RH and Attitude is indicated by a minus correlation in the clinical reinforcement condition and a plus correlation in the experimental reinforcement condition. The opposite is true for hedonic evaluation of "good."

TABLE 6

Within-Cell Correlations Ignoring Consistency-Inconsistency

Item	Clinical reinforcement	Experimental reinforcement
RH	− .50*	.43*
Interview 6	− .06	.14
Interview 7	.23	.19

* $p < .01$.

"good" in the consistent condition than in the inconsistent condition. The obtained differences are actually in the opposite direction.

Within-cell correlations between attitude and each of the two hedonic assessments are presented in Table 5. A positive relationship is indicated by plus correlation with clinical reinforcement and a minus correlation with experimental reinforcement. Only four of the eight correlations are in the positive direction predicted by the hedonic interpretation, and none of the correlations is significant. After collapsing the consistency-inconsistency factor (Table 6) only one of the four correlations is in the positive direction. None of the correlations is signficant.

DISCUSSION

The general pattern of results fits very nicely with the results obtained by Insko and Cialdini (1969). Verbal reinforcement had an effect upon attitude responses only when the informational cues were consistent with the direction of reinforcement. Furthermore, the awareness assessment provided validating information regarding the consistency-inconsistency manipulation, and the various perception and evaluation assessments failed to indicate that the consistency-inconsistency manipulation also had an effect on other relevant variables. These data provide fairly compelling evidence for the importance of information in attitudinal verbal reinforcement.

According to the two-factor interpretation, "good" has an effect both because it conveys information and because it creates positive rapport. That "good" does indeed create positive rapport is indicated by the fact that the control subjects, who were not reinforced, did not report that they liked the experimenter as well as the experimental subjects, who were reinforced. The fact, however, that a similar difference between experimental and control subjects occurred with regard to reported liking of the experiment suggests that something other than a simple effect of "good" upon rapport may have been operating. Conceivably the experimental subjects may have perceived that there was more to the experiment than a simple interview. They may have been intrigued by the reinforcement manipulation and thus found both the experiment and experimenter more interesting (or likeable) than did the control subjects. While such an alternative interpretation is plausible it, however, does not stand up under close scrutiny. If this interpretation is correct, then the subjects in the consistent-information condition who were more aware of what was going on should have liked both the experiment and experimenter more than the subjects in the inconsistent-information condition, who were less aware of what was going on. This, however, was not the case. Examination of the mean responses to Questions 8 and 12 (Table 1) reveals only trivial differences between the consistent- and inconsistent-information conditions. For Question 8 (liking of the experiment) the small difference is even in the wrong direction.

Several studies of verbal reinforcement in the Taffel (1955) situation have found a correlation between conditioning and subjects' rating of how much they wanted the experimenter to say "good" (Bryan & Lichenstein, 1966; Doherty & Walker, 1966; Spielberger, 1962; Spielberger, Berger, & Howard, 1963; Spielberger, Bernstein, & Ratliff, 1966; Spielberger, Levin, & Shephard, 1962). These studies provide some support for a hedonic interpretation of verbal reinforcement. We, however, failed to find a significant correlation between attitude and either of the assessments of hedonic evaluation of "good." Many of the within-cell correlations were, in fact, in the wrong direction. (This supports Insko & Melson's, 1969, argument that verbal reinforcement in the Taffel situation is fundamentally different from attitudinal verbal reinforcement.) Further evidence against the hedonic interpretation of attitudinal verbal reinforcement is the failure of either of the two hedonic assessments to differ between the consistent and inconsistent conditions. If hedonic considerations are responsible for the attitude effect then subjects should have strived harder to recieve reinforcements and should have regarded the reinforcements as more pleasant in the consistent condition or condition in which reinforcement had an effect. Judging from the responses to the postexperimental interview this did not occur. The results are, in fact, in the opposite direction, although nonsignificantly so.

Finally, reinforcement hypothesis was significantly correlated with attitude, and subjects unaware of the reinforcement contingency were not influenced by "good." These results disagree with those obtained in previous research (Insko & Butzine, 1967; Insko & Cialdini, 1969; Insko & Melson, 1969). Although previous research found some evidence for a correlation between awareness and attitude, the correlations were typically not as large as the ones in the present experiment, and, furthermore, "good" had a significant effect upon subjects unaware of the reinforcement contingency. Since the present experiment differs in so many respects from the previous ones it is impossible to specify with certainty the variable or variables accounting for the differing results. One possibility is the consistency-inconsistency manipulation. Conceivably this manipulation (which did not occur in previous research) may have increased the importance of awareness factors. In the consistent condition the large number of consistent cues may have guaranteed that any subject who was influenced would have noticed what was occurring. But what about the inconsistent condition? Here the significant awareness-attitude correlation may have resulted from the increased range of awareness scores. This was the first experiment in which some subjects got the reinforcement contingency backwards. When the five such subjects are eliminated the correlation is reduced from —.32 to —.15 in the clinical-reinforcement–inconsistent-information cell and from .42 to .04 in the experimental-reinforcement–inconsistent-information cell.

As previously indicated (Insko & Cialdini, 1969) the two-factor interpretation is basically a consistency or balance interpretation. Balance theory (Heider, 1958) has the common sense implication that in order to reduce imbalance p will tend to agree with a liked other, o. McGuire (1968) noted (in agreement with Smith) that attitude change research derives from four broad perspectives: information-processing theory, perceptual theory, consistency theory, and functional theory. He then stated that his approach was one of information processing or learning theory. McGuire conceived of the social influence process as a six-step Markov chain (communication delivery, attention to the communication, comprehension of the communication, acceptance of the communication, persistence of the acceptance, behavior consistent with the acceptance). From our perspective there is an interesting overlap between the two-factor interpretation and McGuire's information-processing theory. First of all, the information factor is roughly equivalent to the notion of information-processing. There is, however, some difference in emphasis. McGuire interpreted information processing as referring to the total message content while we more simply concentrate on information as to the major point of the message. This is, of course, a function of the fact that we are concerned with the simpler verbal reinforcement situation and not with the more orthodox persuasive-communication situation. Second, McGuire explicitly postulated that any personality characteristic or independent variable can affect attitude change by having an impact on any one of the mediational steps, and the two-factor notion implies or states that comprehension will result in acceptance if positive rapport exists. From McGuire's perspective, rapport can be regarded as one of the variables facilitating movement from Steps 3 to 4 in the Markov chain.

After conducting the above research it occurred to us that a third factor is possibly operating. For lack of a better name this third factor can be called behavioral commitment. The subject in the verbal reinforcement situation is not only receiving information from a liked communicator, he is also repeatedly agreeing with the communicator. If the reinforcement also has the effect of giving this behavior a positive sign, all three factors can be interpreted as providing the basis for triadic consistency (Insko & Schopler, 1967). Furthermore, Watts' (1967) and also Elms' (1966) results with regard to the superior persistence of attitude change following counterattitudinal advocacy provide some basis for speculating that the third factor may at least partially account for the persistence of verbally reinforced attitude change (Insko, 1965; Oakes, 1966).[3] From the perspective of McGuire's theory, behavioral commitment would thus be important in mediating the link between Steps 4 and 5 in the Markov chain.

REFERENCES

Bryan, J., & Lichtenstein, E. Effect of subject and experimenter attitudes in verbal conditioning. *Journal of Personality and Social Psychology,* 1966, **3,** 182–189.

Doherty, M. A., & Walker, R. E. The relationship of personality characteristics, awareness, and attitude in a verbal conditioning situation. *Journal of Personality,* 1966, **34,** 504–516.

Dulany, D. E. The place of hypotheses and intentions: An analysis of verbal control in verbal conditioning. *Journal of Personality, Suppl.,* 1962, **30,** 102–109.

Elms, A. C. Influence of fantasy ability on attitude change through role playing. *Journal of Personality and Social Psychology,* 1966, **4,** 36–43.

Heider, F. *The psychology of interpersonal relations.* New York: Wiley, 1958.

Insko, C. A. Verbal reinforcement of attitude. *Journal of Personality and Social Psychology,* 1965, **2,** 621–623.

Insko, C. A., & Butzine, K. W. Rapport, awareness, and verbal reinforcement of attitude. *Journal of Personality and Social Psychology,* 1967, **6,** 225–228.

Insko, C. A., & Cialdini, R. B. A test of three interpretations of attitudinal verbal reinforcement. *Journal of Personality and Social Psychology,* 1969, **12,** 333–341.

Insko, C. A., & Melson, W. H. Verbal reinforcement of attitude in laboratory and non-laboratory contexts. *Journal of Personality,* 1969, **37,** 24–50.

Insko, C. A., & Schopler, J. Triadic consistency: A statement of affective-cognitive-conative consistency. *Psychological Review,* 1967, **37,** 25–40. .

Krasner, L., Knowles, J. B., & Ullman, L. P. Effect of verbal conditioning of attitudes on subsequent motor performance. *Journal of Personality and Social Psychology,* 1965, **1,** 407–412.

McGuire, W. J. Personality and attitude change: An information-processing theory. In A. G. Greenwald, T. C. Brock, & T. M. Ostrom (Eds.), *Psychological foundations of attitudes.* New York: Academic Press, 1968.

Spielberger, C. D. The role of awareness in verbal conditioning. *Journal of Personality, Suppl.,* 1962, **30,** 73–101.

Spielberger, C. D., Berger, A., & Howard, K. Conditioning of verbal behavior as a function of awareness, need for social approval, and motivation to receive reinforcement. *Journal of Abnormal and Social Psychology,* 1963, **67,** 241–246.

Spielberger, C. D., Bernstein, I. H., & Ratliff, R. G. Information and incentive value of the reinforcing stimulus in verbal conditioning. *Journal of Experimental Psychology,* 1966, **71,** 26–31.

Spielberger, C. D., Levin, S. M., & Shepard, M. The effects of awareness and attitude toward reinforcement on the operant conditioning of verbal behavior. *Journal of Personality,* 1962, **30,** 106–121.

Taffel, C. Anxiety and the conditioning of verbal behavior. *Journal of Abnormal and Social Psychology,* 1955, **51,** 496–501.

Watts, W. A. Relative persistence of opinion change induced by active compared to passive participation. *Journal of Personality and Social Psychology,* 1967, **5,** 4–15.

[3] W. F. Oakes. Unpublished study, 1966.

Positive and Negative Attitudinal Affect Established by Classical Conditioning[1]

Mark P. Zanna, Charles A. Kiesler, and Paul A. Pilkonis

By pairing meaningful adjectives with the onset and offset of electric shock, an attempt was made to establish two attitudes, one based on negative affect and one based on positive affect, within each subject. Words paired with the onset of shock were evaluated more negatively; words paired with the offset of shock more positively. Conditioned affect also generalized to words similar in meaning. The results were much stronger for subjects who showed independent physiological evidence of conditioning and for the adjective which was initially more neutral in evaluation. The success of an elaborate cover story, including a disguised posttest given by a second experimenter, suggested that the demand characteristics of the experimental situation could not account for the data.

Attitudes are typically defined as predispositions to respond to some class of stimuli with certain classes of responses. Three major classes of responses are cognitive, affective, and behavioral (Rosenberg & Hovland, 1960). Thus when we refer to an individual's attitude, we refer to certain regularities of his thoughts, feelings, and actions toward some aspect of his environment (cf. Secord & Backman, 1964).

Traditionally, social psychology has been concerned both with the understanding of attitude change and with the understanding of attitude formation (cf. Allport, 1935). Research, however, has generally emphasized the study of attitude change rather than attitude formation. Research has also focused on changing the cognitive component of an attitude rather than its affective component. Although Rosenberg (e.g., 1960) has used the technique of hypnotic suggestion to change the affective component of

This research was supported in part by National Science Foundation Grant GS737 to Charles A. Kiesler. The research was conducted while Mark Zanna held a Predoctoral Fellowship from the National Science Foundation and Paul A. Pilkonis held an undergraduate fellowship from the National Science Foundation. The authors gratefully acknowledge the assistance of Irving Janis who permitted the use of his laboratory and his physiological recording equipment. A portion of this paper was presented at the meeting of the Eastern Psychological Association, April 1968.

an attitude, little information exists concerning the establishment of an attitude based primarily on affect.

[1] From the *Journal of Personality and Social Psychology*, Volume 14, pages 321–328, 1970 (received April 10, 1969). Authors' affiliation: Yale University. Reproduced by permission of the American Psychological Association.

The study of attitude formation, however, has not been entirely ne-
glected in psychology. Following Doob's (1947) assertion that attitudes
are learned mediating responses, investigators (e.g., Eisman, 1950; Das &
Nanda, 1963; Staats & Staats, 1958) have used a variety of classical conditioning paradigms to establish attitudes in the laboratory. Two procedures, which Staats (1967) has called "higher-order" and "first-order"
classical conditioning paradigms, have been used to establish attitudes
based on affect. Studies (e.g., Blasford & Sampson, 1964; Cohen, 1964;
Goots & Rankin, 1968; Staats & Staats, 1958) which use the "higher-order"
paradigm pair stimuli (usually neutral words or nonsense syllables) with
a series of words (usually adjectives) which have evaluative meaning.
Studies (e.g., Staats, Staats, & Crawford, 1962; Stagner & Britton, 1949)
which use the "first-order" paradigm pair a conditioned stimulus (CS) with
the onset of an aversive unconditioned stimulus (UCS—usually electric
shock). The typical finding in studies using both paradigms is that the
neutral stimulus, which was paired *either* with a series of unpleasant adjectives or with shock, comes to be evaluated more negatively. This finding
has supported the assumption that negative affect is associated with a series
of unpleasant adjectives and with shock and the hypothesis that attitudes
can be established by classical conditioning.

The data generated by these procedures, however, have a plausible
alternative explanation. There are a variety of ways by which a procedure
may obtain results spuriously. In the case of a simple conditioning paradigm, Kiesler, Collins, and Miller (1969) have suggested that because the
hypotheses are often direct and uncomplicated (especially to introductory
psychology students), subjects may easily be able to detect what they are
expected to do in the experiment and then simply comply with the experimenter's presumed wish. This possibility is increased when the same experimenter performs the conditioning phase of the experiment and then
administers the posttest in the same session. To the extent, then, that subjects become aware of the expected outcome of the experiment, an "experimenter demand" explanation can account for the results (Orne, 1962).
Rephrased, this alternative explanation suggests that the experimental
procedure has unwittingly given the subject an idea of what he "should
do." The subject then merely complies with this presumed demand of the
situation.

Page (1969) has recently suggested (and provided evidence) that the
results of the higher-order conditioning paradigm "are entirely artifacts of
demand characteristics [p. 185]." An internal analysis of his data revealed
that only those subjects who reported awareness of the CS-UCS contingencies, and before the posttest, awareness of how the experimenter expected them to evaluate the CSs, showed a conditioning effect. In contrast,
subjects either unaware of the contingencies or aware of the contingencies,

but unaware of the demands, did not show any evidence of conditioning. Although Staats (1969) has challenged the interpretation advanced by Page because postexperimental questionnaires may "*produce* varying levels of 'awareness' as well as measure it [p. 189]," these results remain, nevertheless, consistent with an "experimenter demand" explanation. In any case, all studies which have used a classical conditioning paradigm to establish attitudes are unable to rule out this alternative explanation. (For a more complete discussion of this problem, see Kiesler *et al.*, 1969.)

The major purpose of the present experiment was to establish an attitude based on negative affect in an experimental situation in which the demand characteristics could not account for the results. A first-order conditioning paradigm was employed. In the procedure a meaningful adjective was paired with the onset of shock. The main hypothesis was that this adjective would come to be evaluated negatively, thereby replicating the results of previous studies (e.g., Staats *et al.*, 1962).

In order to make the demand characteristics of the experimental situation irrelevant to the hypothesis, an elaborate cover story was created. Besides providing a plausible explanation for the experiment, the cover story fulfilled two other important functions: first, it allowed the contingencies of the pairings between the onset signal word and the shock to be made explicit to the subject from the beginning without arousing any suspicion as to the real purpose of the experiment; second, it allowed a second experimenter, blind to condition, to administer the posttest in a supposedly unrelated study.

In addition to establishing an attitude based on negative affect, an attempt was also made to establish an attitude based on positive affect within the same subject. Although past research on this problem has been rather limited, a behavior-therapy technique reported by Wolpe and Lazarus (1966) suggested a possible procedure.[2] These authors conditioned "anxiety-relief" responses in neurotic patients by pairing the word "calm" with the offset of shock. They suggested that "if an unpleasant stimulus is endured for several seconds and is then made to cease almost immediately after a specified signal, that signal may become conditioned to the changes that follow cessation of the uncomfortable stimulus [p. 149]." Wolpe and Lazarus reported that their patients appeared to experience these changes as a profound feeling of relief and therefore sug-

---

[2] Razran (1938, 1940) has used a so-called luncheon technique, in which he paired stimuli (e.g., political slogans) with the positive affect associated with eating a free lunch. Dabbs and Janis (1965), however, presented data which indicated that Razran's effect was not due to the conditioning of positive affect. Their alternative explanation is that "the consumption of proferred food induces a momentary mood of compliance toward the donor that is strongest at the time the food is being consumed but that decreases in strength rapidly after the food has been consumed [p. 141]."

gested that "anxiety-relief" conditioning "occurs in those patients who experience some degree of *emotional* disturbance (as opposed to mere sensory discomfort) in response to the electric shocks [p. 149]."

Animal research suggested another possible procedure for conditioning positive affect. For example, Rescorla and LoLordo (1965) found that a CS which informed their dogs that an expected shock would not occur came to inhibit fear when it was later introduced in an avoidance situation.

To test the possibility that positive affect is associated with the offset of pain and/or the offset of a danger period, a second signal word was incorporated in the procedure. This adjective signaled that shock would not follow. Two kinds of trials were actually employed. Following Wolpe and Lazarus (1966), on some trials this offset word signaled that shock was over. Thus the word was paired with the cessation of pain produced by shock. On other trials shock was not delivered. Following Rescorla and LoLordo (1965), on these trials the offset word signaled that shock would not occur. Thus the word was also paired with the cessation of danger aroused by the expectation of being shocked. The second hypothesis, then, was that a word paired with the cessation of pain and danger would come to be evaluated positively.[3] Together, the two hypotheses suggest that a classical conditioning paradigm could be used to establish two distinct attitudes based on affect within a single subject. One attitude would be associated with negative affect, the other with positive affect.

If affect could be conditioned, exploration of the power of the conditioning technique in terms of generalization effects seemed desirable. For this purpose, subjects evaluated concepts similar to the adjectives used as signal words as well as these adjectives modifying various nouns.

Finally, in order to have independent evidence of conditioning, a physiological response (galvanic skin potential or GSP) was continuously recorded. Since autonomic arousal is generally assumed to accompany affect arousal, it seemed reasonable to expect that attitudes would be established to the extent that autonomic arousal was conditioned (cf. Staats *et al.*, 1962).

METHOD

Subjects

Fifty female subjects,[4] ages 17–23, were recruited from sign-up sheets at Yale University and each was paid $2.50 for the hour and a half experiment. Three subjects were eliminated from the analysis because they failed to complete the posttest correctly.

[3] A test of the difference between the cessation of pain and the cessation of danger was not made in the present study. Instead it was assumed that the combination of the two kinds of trials would add to the power of the offset effect since both cessations may be associated with relief or anxiety reduction.

[4] Pretesting indicated that female subjects were made more anxious by the shock than male subjects.

Overview

Each subject was given an elaborate cover story. Subjects then received 25 shock trials arranged into four blocks. Each trial was initiated by the reading of an adjective (the onset signal word) and was terminated by the reading of a different adjective (the offset signal word). Next a second experimenter, blind to experimental condition, administered a semantic differential posttest in a supposedly unrelated study. Finally, subjects described the purpose of both experiments on an anonymous "departmental questionnaire" and were debriefed by the first experimenter.

Cover Story

Each subject was immediately seated in a chair, and as the experimenter placed various recording electrodes on her arms, he explained "our physiological equipment" (e.g., the heart-rate or EKG and GSP recording electrodes and the polygraph machine). After the electrodes were in place, the experimenter began by explaining the contrived purpose of the study.

> Our long range goal is to develop a more sensitive and instantaneous physiological measure than the old standard ones, like heart rate. . . .

The experimenter then explained that electric shock would increase heart rate, but that he was hoping that the shock's effect on GSP would be more consistent within and across persons, more instantaneous, and more resistant to adaptation effects. Finally, the experimenter justified the random contingencies of the conditioning procedure so that these contingencies would seem reasonable to the subject.

> In order to be precise in our physiological measurements, we have created blocks of shock trials with everything we could think of randomly determined. This, we hope, will ensure random physiological activity when you're not getting shocked and a precise response to shock when the shock is on.

Conditioning Procedure

Twenty-five conditioning trials were arranged into four blocks. Shock was delivered manually by the experimenter in 1-second bursts. The signal words were recorded on tape and the block of trials began by simply turning on the tape recorder. The instructions for the first block of trials were as follows:

> Each trial will begin with a signal word. There will be a short pause and then you will receive a few shocks. Actually, you will receive from 1 to 9 shocks. The number on any one trial has, of course, been randomly determined. You will know when you are receiving the last shock of the trial because a second word will indicate the end of each trial.

Subjects were then told what the signal words would be. Thus the instructions made the contingencies between the signal words and the shock explicit to each subject from the beginning. Moreover, these contingencies were completely justified within the context of the experimental situation. Each subject was told that she was supposed to relax between the shock trials (in order to get "a base-line measure of physiological responding"). Thus it was important for her to know when the shock was imminent and when the shock was completed. The signal words were supposedly introduced for this purpose.

The instructions for the remaining three blocks added three qualifications. First, each trial would "begin with the reading of a list of words." The onset signal word would be read only after a random number of words (1–11) had been read. These words were added to ensure that the subject paid close attention to the specific onset signal word. Second, there would be a random pause (1–9 seconds) between the onset signal word and the shock. The random pause was added to increase the anxiety-arousing potential of the onset signal word. Finally, the subjects were informed that there would be some trials, randomly determined, on which shock would not occur. On these trials, the offset signal word would simply be read after the random pause. As always, the offset signal word would indicate that the trial was over and that a rest period had begun. Six nonshock trials were included in the last 20 trials so that the offset signal word could be paired with the cessation of a danger period produced by the expectation of being shocked.

Independent Variables

Three experimental conditions were created. In one condition, the adjective "light" signaled the onset of shock and "dark" signaled shock offset (the light-on/dark-off condition). In the second condition these words were reversed (the light-off/dark-on condition). The onset and offset signal words in the control condition were "begin" and "end."

Physiological Conditioning

Although subjects did have EKG and GSP recording electrodes, only GSP was recorded (cf. O'Connell & Tursky, 1960). A reliable GSP response on the six nonshock trials was taken as independent evidence for conditioning. Learning curves over these six trials were not constructed for two reasons. First, subjects had received several trials before the first nonshock trial. Second, subjects were informed of the contingencies between the CSs and the UCS beforehand. The fact that subjects were able to verbalize the CS-UCS relations in advance suggests that any "conditioning" effect may not be due to a classical conditioning process, but due to these verbalizations per se. These possibilities are confounded in the present design. It must be noted, however, that previous studies using classical conditioning paradigms to establish attitudes allowed normal adult human subjects to verbalize the CS-UCS relations. This relational learning (as distinguished from classical conditioning) can never be entirely ruled out unless no effect is produced.

Posttest and Dependent Variables

After the fourth block of trials (or 25 trials), the experimenter explained that he wanted to give the subject an extra long rest period before the next block of trials. He explained:

> In order to see if your heart rate and GSP responses to shock have been adapting out, I'm going to give you a 15-minute rest period before the next block of trials. Hopefully, any adaptation will be eliminated by a rest period this long . . . . To take your mind off the situation during this period, I've been letting subjects either read a magazine or take part in another study a student down the hall is running . . . .

The experimenter left the room and returned within 2 minutes with the posttester, who appeared to be arranging his materials. After introducing the posttester to the subject and promising to return in 15 minutes to "finish up," the first experimenter left the room. The posttester gave an appearance of not knowing exactly what he should do to make the most of his 15 minutes. Finally, however, he collected his thoughts and told the subjects the following:

> I've got about half a dozen tasks here and I've been giving approximately three

or four of them, randomly, to each of the subjects I've been running, depending of course on the amount of time available. Let me check now [looking into his folder]. I think . . . with 15 minutes I'll give you some semantic differential material, an opinion questionnaire, and finally an aesthetic preference test.[5]

The posttester then explained semantic differential scales to the subject, indicated that he was "doing a replication of some earlier work," and that he would have to look up "20 words randomly from lists used in previous studies and published in this book." The book, which the subjects saw, was *The Measurement of Meaning* (Osgood, Suci, & Tannenbaum, 1957). Fourteen adjectives and six adjective-noun phrases were inserted in the book. Subjects rated these stimuli on evaluative scales taken from the semantic differential (Osgood *et al.*, 1957). Five scales were used: good-bad, beautiful-ugly, pleasant-unpleasant, sweet-sour, and painful-pleasurable. Three scales were labeled positive-negative while two scales were reversed. Evaluation of the signal words, "light" and "dark," constituted the main dependent variables of the study. As a test of generalization, subjects also evaluated the words "white" and "black" and the adjective-noun phrases "light car" and "dark car." Each of these stimuli received a score from 5 (most negative) through 20 (neutral) to 35 (most positive).

After the posttester had completed his third task, he thanked the subject and went to find the first experimenter. The first experimenter returned and completed a short fifth block of shock trials. He then asked the subject to fill out a questionnaire which the psychology department was supposedly using to evaluate some of its experiments. The experimenter explained that he was not allowed to see this anonymous "departmental questionnaire," and asked the subjects to place it in an envelope after completion. The real purpose of this questionnaire was to check for suspicion. Each subject was asked to describe "the purpose of each experiment in her own words." Finally subjects were debriefed.

RESULTS

Elimination of a Demand-Characteristic Explanation

The "departmental questionnaire" revealed that all subjects reported that they believed the contrived purpose of each experiment. Careful debriefing, during which the experimenter encouraged any questions or comments about either study, revealed that no subject reported that these two supposedly unrelated studies were associated. Taken at face validity, these verbal reports imply that any "demands," created by the conditioning procedure, could not influence behavior during the posttest. Thus the experimental design appears to have ruled out a demand-characteristic explanation of *any* potential result. It must be noted, however, that given

[5] Questions were embedded in the "opinion questionnaire" and the "aesthetic preference test" in order to test for generalization effects. One question on the opinion questionnaire asked the subject to advise "Mr. N., the chief curator of a large art museum," who had to make an important decision between displaying the "light, colorful but somewhat shallow works of Artist X" and the "dark, strong but somewhat sedate works of Artist Y." On the aesthetic preference test, subjects were asked: "How well do you like *light colors*?" and "How well do you like *dark colors*?" No differences between the experimental conditions obtained on these questions and the results will not be reported.

modern technology, a demand explanation can never be entirely ruled out, unless no experimental effect is produced.

Physiological Evidence of Conditioning

A consistent GSP response on the nonshock trials was taken as independent evidence for conditioning. A GSP response was defined as a deflection in the onset-offset interval which was greater than any deflection in the preceding 10 seconds. In almost all cases, either a clear change or no change in the GSP level obtained during this interval. Thirteen of the 47 subjects failed to respond during this interval on at least half of the trials. These subjects were considered not to have shown independent evidence of conditioning.

Conditioning of Positive and Negative Affect

The mean evaluation of each signal word and the mean preference of "light" over "dark" are presented in Table 1 for all subjects and for conditionable subjects. Since these data can be more easily viewed in terms of the preference of "light" over "dark," the results will mainly be discussed in terms of the mean preference (or difference) scores.[6]

It must be noted first, however, that a significant word effect obtained. In the present population of subjects the word light was evaluated more positively than the word dark (for all subjects, $F = 9.75$, $df = 1/44$, $p < .01$; for conditionable subjects, $F = 10.25$, $df = 1/33$, $p < .01$). Thus, compared to the control condition, the prediction is that the mean preference of light over dark will be larger when light is the offset signal (and dark is the onset signal) and smaller when light is the onset signal (and dark is the offset signal).

The pattern of mean preferences, presented in Table 1, conforms to this expectation. The mean preference of light over dark is largest in the light-off/dark-on condition, intermediate in the control condition, and

---

[6] Because the word-variable is a within-subject variable, there are two equivalent ways to analyze the results. The word-variable may be considered a repeated measure. In this case, the appropriate analysis is that of a two-factor experiment with a repeated measure on one factor (Winer, 1962, p. 302). Equivalently, each subject may be used as her own control and a difference or preference score between the two words can be calculated. In this case, the equivalent analysis is that of a single-factor experiment (Winer, 1962, p. 46).

To test the overall hypothesis that a stimulus will come to be evaluated positively if it is paired with the offset of pain and anxiety and negatively if it is paired with the onset of an aversive stimulus, a 1 df, a priori contrast was formed. In the repeated-measure analysis this contrast is orthogonal to both main effects and attempts to account for the systematic variance produced by the overall Word $\times$ Group interaction. In the single-factor analysis, the equivalent contrast is the linear trend comparison (Winer, 1962, p. 97). It should be noted that the Word $\times$ Group interaction is equivalent to the overall between-condition effect for the preference means.

TABLE 1

Mean Evaluation of the Signal Words, "Light" and "Dark," and the Mean Preference of "Light" over "Dark" (Light minus Dark) for All Subjects and for Conditionable Subjects[a]

Condition (or group)	Word		
	Light	Dark	Light minus dark
Light-on/dark-off, $n = 18$ (13)[b]	25.33 (25.08)[c]	24.00 (25.15)	1.33 ($-.08$)
Control, $n = 9$ (9)	26.22 (26.22)	22.00 (22.00)	4.22 (4.22)
Light-off/dark-on, $n = 20$ (14)	27.00 (27.21)	22.10 (19.57)	4.90 (7.64)

[a] The higher the mean, the more favorable the evaluation. The neutral point on the scale is 20.

[b] n's for conditionable subjects are in parentheses.

[c] Means for conditionable subjects are in parentheses.

smallest in the light-on/dark-off condition for all subjects and for conditionable subjects. Although, for all subjects, the a priori linear trend component accounts for 94.3% of the between-condition variation, this trend does not reach a conventional level of significance ($F = 2.16$, $df = 1/44$, $p < .20$).

However, when only those subjects who gave independent physiological evidence of conditioning (conditionable subjects) are considered, the results are much strengthened. For conditionable subjects, the predicted linear trend was significant ($F = 7.14$, $df = 1/33$, $p < .05$) and accounted for 99.6% of the systematic variation between the three experimental conditions. Thus both hypotheses are supported for those subjects who gave independent physiological evidence of conditioning—both positive and negative affect appear to have been conditioned.

Considering the signal words separately, it can be seen that the onset and offset conditioning effects occurred primarily with the word dark. For conditionable subjects, the a priori test for linear trend on dark is highly significant ($F = 9.18$, $df = 1/33$, $p < .01$) accounting for 99.9% of the systematic between-condition variation. Although the pattern of means conforms to expectation with the word light, the linear trend is not significant ($F = 1.25$, $df = 1/33$). The initial difference in affect associated with the two words is a probable reason for their differential susceptibility to conditioning. In the control condition, the mean evaluations of light and dark deviate from neutrality in the positive direction (6.22 and 2.00 units, respectively). The differential deviation from the neutral point of 4.22 units is significant at the 10% level ($t = 1.85$, $df = 8$). It seems reasonable to suggest that the greater the amount of affect initially associated with a CS, the more difficult it will be to condition affect to this CS.

TABLE 2

Mean Evaluation of the Related Words, "White" and "Black," and the Mean Preference of "White" over "Black" (White minus Black) for All Subjects, and for Conditionable Subjects[a]

Condition (or group)	Word		
	White	Black	White minus black
Light-on/dark-off, $n = 18$ (13)[b]	23.50 (24.23)[c]	21.33 (21.77)	2.17 (2.46)
Control, $n = 9$ (9)	25.78 (25.78)	19.00 (19.00)	6.78 (6.78)
Light-off/dark-on, $n = 20$ (14)	24.70 (25.50)	18.35 (16.21)	6.35 (9.29)

[a] The higher the mean, the more favorable the evaluation. The neutral point on the scale is 20.

[b] n's for conditionable subjects are in parentheses.

[c] Means for conditionable subjects are in parentheses.

GENERALIZATION OF CONDITIONED AFFECT

The mean evaluation of "white" and "black" and the mean preference of "white" over "black" are presented in Table 2 for all subjects and for conditionable subjects. Again, it must be noted first that a significant word effect obtained. In this case the word white was evaluated more positively than the word black (for all subjects, $F = 22.86$, $df = 1/44$, $p < .01$; for conditionable subjects, $F = 31.19$, $df = 1/33$, $p < .01$).

The pattern of mean preferences, presented in Table 2, conforms closely to the main dependent measure when all subjects are considered and exactly when only conditionable subjects are considered. For all subjects, the results are again of marginal significance. Significant at the 10% level ($F = 3.45$, $df = 1/44$), the linear trend accounts for only 79.6% of the between-condition variation. Just as was the case for the signal words, however, the results are much strengthened when only the conditionable subjects are considered. Now the predicted trend is significant at the 5% level ($F = 7.10$, $df = 1/33$) and accounts for 98.9% of the between-condition variation. Thus both positive and negative affect appear to have generalized to the related words, white and black.

Predictably, generalization occurred to a greater extent from the word that was most susceptible to conditioning. Thus the linear trend for black is significant ($F = 7.10$, $df = 1/33$, $p < .05$) and accounts for 99.6% of the between-condition variation. The linear trend is not significant for white ($F < 1$). In the control condition, white, just as light, deviated significantly more from neutrality than its opposite (mean differential deviation of 4.78 units; $t = 2.49$, $df = 8$, $p < .05$).

The adjective-noun phrases, "light car" and "dark car," did not show a generalization effect, even when only conditionable subjects are considered.

DISCUSSION

By pairing meaningful adjectives with the onset and offset of electric shock, two attitudes, one based on negative affect and one based on positive affect, were created within each subject. It was hypothesized that classical conditioning would establish these attitudes. However, the possibility that these attitudes were established by relational learning (or the ability to verbalize the contingencies) cannot be ruled out.

In any case, the present experiment attempted to rule out a demand-characteristic explanation of *any* possible result by divorcing the conditioning procedure from the posttest. Subjects did report that they believed the stated purpose of each experiment and that they did not feel the two studies were related.

Three aspects of the data are also inconsistent with a simple demand-characteristic explanation. First, the conditioning effect was stronger for subjects with independent physiological evidence of conditioning. Second, the conditioning effect was stronger for the more neutral or less extreme signal word (i.e., dark). Third, conditioned affect generalized from the specific signal words to a related concept (i.e., white and black), but not to various adjective-noun phrases (e.g., light car and dark car).

While these last three results suggest that a demand-characteristic explanation is unable to account for the overall results, they also contribute to the fact that the overall results appeared to be weaker than the results of other conditioning studies.

The fact that the overall results were not strong, however, leads to the troublesome problem that not all subjects conditioned. Two problems may be responsible for this fact. The first problem is that only 25 conditioning trials were employed. Clearly, more trials should increase the power of the conditioning technique. However, despite 30–60-second rest periods between trials and 2-minute rest periods between blocks of trials, subjects already appeared to be adapting to the shock by the end of the session. A solution to this problem would be to run each subject over several days (as is the practice in animal research). The second problem is that meaningful social stimuli already may have strong evaluative connotations. This problem has already been discussed.

Finally, it must be noted that Wolpe and Lazarus' (1966, p. 149) suggestion that positive affect is associated with the offset of shock seems to have received some empirical support. It must be stressed, however, that the present study did not specifically test the difference between the cessation of pain and the cessation of danger. The data do suggest, however, that if subjects were not aroused (i.e., did not show physiological evidence of conditioning) the conditioning effect was extremely weak. This fact may imply that the important theoretical contingency for the conditioning of positive affect was a pairing which occurred with anxiety-reduction (or relief). Anxiety-reduction may be associated with the cessation of pain (cf. Wolpe & Lazarus, 1966), with the cessation of danger (cf. Rescorla & LoLordo, 1965), or with both. Since the present experiment did not distinguish these possibilities, it would seem interesting to test the difference between the cessation of a painful stimulus and the cessation of a danger period in a future experiment.

REFERENCES

Allport, G. W. In C. Murchison (Ed.), *Handbook of social psychology*. Worcester, Massachusetts: Clark University Press, 1935.

Blasford, D., & Sampson, E. Induction of prestige suggestion through classical conditioning. *Journal of Abnormal and Social Psychology*, 1964, **69**, 332–337.

Cohen, B. Role of awareness in meaning established by classical conditioning. *Journal of Experimental Psychology*, 1964, **67**, 373–378.

Dabbs, J., & Janis, I. Why does eating while reading facilitate opinion change? An experimental inquiry. *Journal of Experimental Social Psychology*, 1965, **1**, 133–144.

Das, J., & Nanda, P. Mediated transfer of attitudes. *Journal of Abnormal and Social Psychology*, 1963, **66**, 12–16.

Doob, L. The behavior of attitudes. *Psychological Review*, 1947, **54**, 135–146.

Eisman, B. Attitude formation: The development of a color-preference response through mediated generalization. *Journal of Abnormal and Social Psychology*, 1955, **50**, 321–326.

Goots, S. W., & Rankin, R. E. Affective-cognitive consistency and the conditioning of social attitudes. Paper presented at the meeting of the Eastern Psychological Association, Washington, April 1968.

Kiesler, C. A., Collins, B., & Miller, N. *Attitude change: A critical analysis of theoretical approaches*. New York: Wiley, 1969.

O'Connell, D., & Tursky, B. Silver-silver chloride sponge electrodes for skin potential recording. *American Journal of Psychology*, 1960, **73**, 302–304.

Orne, M. On the social psychology of the psychological experiment: With particular reference to demand characteristics and their implications. *American Psychologist*, 1962, **17**, 776–783.

Osgood, C., Suci, G., & Tannenbaum, P. *The measurement of meaning*. Urbana, Illinois: University of Illinois Press, 1957.

Page, M. Social psychology of a classical conditioning of attitudes experiment. *Journal of Personality and Social Psychology*, 1969, **11**, 177–186.

Razran, G. Conditioning away social bias by the luncheon technique. *Psychological Bulletin*, 1938, **35**, 693.

Razran, G. Conditioning response changes in rating and appraising sociopolitical slogans. *Psychological Bulletin*, 1940, **37**, 481.

Rescorla, R., & LoLordo, V. Inhibition of avoidance behavior. *Journal of Comparative and Physiological Psychology*, 1965, **59**, 406–412.

Rosenberg, M. An analysis of affective-cognitive consistency. In M. Rosenberg *et al.*, *Attitude organization and change*. New Haven, Connecticut: Yale University Press, 1960.

Rosenberg, M., & Hovland, C. Cognitive, affective and behavioral components of attitudes. In M. Rosenberg *et al.*, *Attitude organization and change*. New Haven, Connecticut: Yale University Press, 1960.

Secord, P., & Backman, C. *Social psychology*. New York: McGraw-Hill, 1964.

Staats, A. An outline of an integrated learning theory of attitude formation and function. In M. Fishbein (Ed.), *Readings in attitude theory and measurement.* New York: Wiley, 1967.

Staats, A. Experimental demand characteristics and the classical conditioning of attitudes. *Journal of Personality and Social Psychology,* 1969, **11,** 187–192.

Staats, A., & Staats, C. Attitudes established by classical conditioning. *Journal of Abnormal and Social Psychology,* 1958, **57,** 37–40.

Staats, A., Staats, C., & Crawford, H. First-order conditioning of meaning and the parallel conditioning of a GSR. *Journal of General Psychology,* 1962, **67,** 159–167.

Stagner, R., & Britton, R. The conditioning technique applied to a public opinion problem. *Journal of Social Psychology,* 1949, **29,** 103–111.

Winer, B. *Statistical principles in experimental design.* New York: McGraw-Hill, 1962.

Wolpe, J., & Lazarus, A. *Behavior therapy techniques.* New York: Pergamon Press, 1966.

Chapter 3

SOURCE CHARACTERISTICS AND PERSISTENCE EFFECTS

The present chapter is concerned with two of the important research problems in attitude change, the effect of various communication source characteristics on persuasion and the persistence of influence effects. There is evidence that these two apparently different research problems are, in fact, closely related.

Source Characteristics

Communication sources have numerous characteristics that conceivably may modify their persuasive impact. The bulk of the research, however, has been concerned with source credibility.

SOURCE CREDIBILITY

A highly credible communication source is a person or agency that is perceived as being both expert and trustworthy. The typical experimental procedure is to compare the differential persuasive effects of a single communication when it is attributed to either a high-credibility or a low-credibility source. In a classic early study, which is contained in the Readings, Hovland and Weiss (1952) used this procedure to demonstrate the greater persuasive impact of high-credibility than low-credibility sources. Hovland and Weiss found, for example, that a communication concerned with the practicality of building an atomic-powered submarine was more influential when attributed to Oppenheimer (a well-known U. S. physicist in that decade) than to Pravda.

Subsequent research has by and large supported Hovland and Weiss' findings for the immediately greater persuasive impact of high- than low-credibility sources. As we shall see, however, the long-term, or persistence, effects of source credibility are more complicated.

So far we have been discussing source credibility as if it were a general characteristic, equally effective for all communication topics. Walster, Aronson, and Abrahams (1966) have pointed out, however, that even a communicator with very low credibility may be quite influential if he argues contrary to his own self-interest. They maintain that any communicator, regardless of his prestige, will increase his persuasiveness if he argues against his own self-interest. They report a study in which an imprisoned criminal is more influential if he argues that courts should have more power rather than less, while a prosecuting attorney is more influential if he argues that courts should have less power rather than more. For both the criminal and the attorney, argument contrary to self-interest produced more influence than argument consistent with self-interest. The difference, however, was much more marked for the criminal, possibly because his self-interests were more salient than the attorney's.

Koeske and Crano (1968) obtained results which were consistent with those of Walster *et al.* Koeske and Crano found, for example, that the statement, "Generally speaking the number of U. S. casualties in the Vietnamese conflict has far exceeded that reported in the U. S. press," was much more believable when attributed to General Westmoreland (the commanding general in Vietnam at that time) than when presented without any authorship at all. This was not true, however, for the statement, "U. S. bombing of North Vietnam has partially reduced the influx of men and military supplies to the South." The first statement is contrary to Westmoreland's self-interests, while the second is not. Findings such as those of Koeske and Crano and of Walster, Aronson, and Abrahams make it apparent that source credibility is not an absolute source characteristic, but is influenced by the nature of the communication topic.

SOURCE CREDIBILITY AND OTHER CHARACTERISTICS

There is little doubt that the credibility of a source affects a communication's persuasive impact. Can other source characteristics also have an effect? Aronson and Golden (1962) report an interesting experiment which varied both the credibility and the race of a communication source. Four different groups of sixth-grade children were exposed to four different communication sources: a white engineer, a black engineer, a white dishwasher, and a black dishwasher. For all four groups the communication consisted of the same tape-recorded talk, arguing for the value of arithmetic. The communication source was present in each group, but did not speak, supposedly because of hoarseness. Aronson and Golden conceived of the engineer-dishwasher variable as a manipulation of objectively relevant source characteristics (i.e., source credibility) and the black-white variable as a manipulation of objectively irrelevant source characteristics. This assumption was validated by postexperimental assessments indicating that the subjects rated the engineer source as more intelligent than the dishwasher source, but did not rate the white source as either more intelligent or more sincere (i.e., trustworthy) than the black source.

With regard to the main dependent variable the results indicated that the engineer source was more persuasive than the dishwasher source, but that there was no overall difference between the black and white sources. However, a breakdown of the subjects into "prejudiced" and "nonprejudiced," on the basis of questionnaire responses, indicated that race did indeed have an effect. The "prejudiced" subjects were more influenced by the white than the black source, and the "unprejudiced" subjects were more influenced by the black than the white source. This means that from at least some perspectives both groups of subjects were prejudiced, one against blacks and one against whites.

Aronson and Golden regard the engineer-dishwasher variable as a manipulation of objectively relevant source characteristics, that is, a manipulation of source credibility. From an objective standpoint of holding a correct attitude toward mathematics it was reasonable to agree with the more intelligent engineer. It was not reasonable, however, to agree more with the white source than the black source or the black source than the white source. Aronson and Golden report that their "prejudiced" and "unprejudiced" subjects rated the black and white sources equally intelligent and sincere. Those subjects then must have acted on the basis of objectively irrelevant source characteristics, characteristics whose persuasive impact could not be epistemologically justified.

Two source characteristics, other than credibility, relate to the source's ability to administer negative sanctions for nonconformity and the source's attractiveness. Kelman (1958) has argued that the influence of these latter two source characteristics is dependent on contextual variables which are unimportant for source credibility. Thus a source with the ability to administer negative sanctions, or a high means-control source, will be most influential when the communicatee believes that he is under surveillance by the source. Monitoring by a high means-control source will produce public conformity, but not necessarily private acceptance. An attractive source, on the other hand, will produce conformity whenever the communicatee is thinking about the source, that is, whenever the source is salient. If the source is not salient the amount of persisting influence will be less. For a highly credible source, however, the persistence of influence is not dependent upon either surveillance or salience. In this case public conformity and private acceptance are maximally correlated.

Kelman supported the above speculation with data from an experiment conducted at a black college just before the announcement of the Supreme Court decision on the desegregation of public schools. Freshmen subjects were presented with a taped communication represented as being part of a transcribed radio program and were told that the experimenter was interested in obtaining their reactions. The communication argued that even if the Supreme Court ruled that segregation was unconstitutional it would still be desirable to keep some of the private black colleges segregated in order to preserve black culture and tradition. Three different communication sources were used, each in a different condition. In the high means-control condition the communication source was introduced as the president of a foundation which supported black colleges. During the course of the program it became evident that he was primarily responsible for his foundation's decision to allocate funds to the subjects' college, and that he furthermore would not hesitate to withdraw support from any college if the students disagreed with him on the issue in question. In the high-attractiveness condition the communication source was introduced as a senior and the president of the student council in a leading black university and also as the chairman of his university's "Student Poll." The latter organization was represented as having recently done a survey of the attitudes of black college seniors on issues relating to the impending Supreme Court decision. During the course of the program the communication source made it clear that he was presenting not just his own attitude but the attitudes expressed by the overwhelming majority of seniors who had been surveyed. In the high-credibility condition the communication source was represented as a history professor from a leading university who was a highly respected authority on the history and problems of minority groups. He made it clear that he was concerned about blacks and that his position was based on research and historical evidence. Immediately after exposure to the taped communication the subjects filled out two attitude assessments, the first of which was signed by the subjects and the second of which was unsigned and anonymous. The subjects were told that the signed copy would be shown to the communication source. A third assessment was taken 1 to 2 weeks later in an unrelated context. Thus for the first assessment, but not the second and third assessments, there was surveillance by the communication source. Further, for the first and second assessments, but not the third assessment, the communication source was salient. Kelman had three predictions. First, the high means-control source would produce more influence on the first assessment (where there was surveillance) than on the second and third assessments (where there was no surveillance). This prediction was significantly supported. Second, the highly attractive source would produce more influence on the first and second assessments (where the source was salient) than on the third assessment (where the source was not salient). This prediction was significantly supported. Third and finally, the high-credibility source would not be influenced by either surveillance or salience of the source and thus would not produce more influence on the first two assessments than on the third. Consistent with this prediction there was no significant difference among the three assessments in the high-credibility condition. Thus all three of the predictions were supported.

Kelman's data do reveal a nonsignificant tendency for the influence by the high-credibility source to decline slightly from the two immediate assessments to the delayed, or third, assessment. If the time interval had been somewhat longer, this decreasing influence would undoubtedly have been larger and thus possibly significant. In a subsequent section we will describe some evidence indicating that the persuasive impacts of high-credibility sources decrease somewhat over time.

Source Credibility and Self-Credibility

The literature relating to source credibility is by and large very consistent. In most of the published studies high-credibility sources are more influential than low-credibility sources. There are occasional reports, however, of situations in which such a finding does not occur. Such was the case in the Hovland and Weiss (1952) study contained in the Readings. Averaging over all four of their communication topics, a significantly higher percentage of subjects were influenced by the high- than the low-credibility sources. However, for one of the topics, the future of the movie industry with the advent of television, this general pattern did not occur. In fact, there was a slight, and undoubtedly nonsignificant, tendency for the low-credibility source to be more influential than the high-credibility source. What is the reason for this? Possibly this is just a chance effect. Or possibly there is some as yet unspecified variable which has a modifying, or interactive, effect on the persuasiveness of high credibility sources.

What variable could modify the impact of source credibility? A tentative suggestion relates to the extent that the subject perceives himself as credible, or expert, on the communication topic. The greater the perceived self-credibility the less may be the impact of high source credibility. Hovland and Weiss' subjects were upperclass students in a history class at Yale. It is possible that these students perceived themselves to be as expert as the writer in Fortune magazine when it came to predicting the future of the movie industry. For the other communication issues, however, the students probably perceived themselves as less expert. This is particularly true for the issue relating to the practicality of building an atomic submarine, and this is the one issue for which source credibility had the greatest effect.

Persistence Effects

Although the bulk of the research on attitude change has concentrated on immediate effects, persistence effects are obviously of paramount importance. It is not enough to know that a given variable has a short-term effect; most applications of research findings require long-term effects.

THE PETERSON AND THURSTONE STUDY

The most extensive investigation of persistence effects is an early study by Peterson and Thurstone (1933). Approximately 2 weeks after filling out an attitude scale, groups of school children were exposed to one or more of a number of motion pictures. Each motion picture was oriented toward some attitude issue (such as prohibition, capital punishment, or race). If two or more films were shown to a given group, all of the films concerned the same attitude issue. The next morning the attitude scale was administered again. After a delay ranging between 2 months and 8 months the scale was administered a third time. For some groups the scale was administered a fourth time after a second delay. Peterson and Thurstone present their results in terms of the percentage of the immediate change that persisted after a given delay. These results are summarized in Table 3-1. Peterson and Thurstone interpret their data as indicating that, in general, some reduced percentage of the immediate change effect persisted over time. Note that in Table 3-1 most of the percentages are greater than 0 and less than 100. There are, however, some interesting exceptions to this general rule. Note that eight months after exposure to the film "All Quiet on the Western Front" there was change in the opposite direction to the immediate persuasive impact. Before exposure to the film, attitude toward war was 4.34 on an 11-point scale in which high numbers indicate a favorable attitude. Immediately after exposure to the antiwar film, attitude dropped to 3.74, but 8 months later increased to 4.64. There was just slightly more than a complete decay of the immediate effect. On the other hand, 6 months after exposure to the film "Four Sons" the persuasive impact had actually increased. Subjects were more in agreement with the film 6

TABLE 3-1

Persistence Effects in the Peterson and Thurstone Study[a]

Film	First delay		Second delay	
	Months since film	Percent of effect remaining	Months since film	Percent of effect remaining
"The Criminal Code"	$2\frac{1}{2}$	87	9	78
"Son of the Gods"	5	62	19	60
"The Birth of a Nation"	5	62	—	—
"Four Sons"	6	123	—	—
"All Quiet on the Western Front"	8	A change in the opposite direction	—	—
"All Quiet on the Western Front" and "Journey's End"	2	52	4	22
"The Big House," "Numbered Men," and "The Criminal Code"	2	100	4	111

[a] Adapted from Peterson and Thurstone, 1933, p. 63.

months after exposure than immediately after exposure. Such an occurrence is referred to as a *sleeper effect*.

It should be noted that Peterson and Thurstone did not have no-exposure control groups, or groups of children who were not exposed to films but did have their attitudes assessed at various time intervals. Thus we certainly cannot rule out the possibility of different environmental events having markedly affected the obtained results.

Most of the research conducted since Peterson and Thurstone's early study has not been explicitly concerned with persistence effects. However, in the course of investigating different attitude change variables many investigators have included delayed, as well as immediate, assessments. In agreement with Peterson and Thurstone most of these studies (cf., Cook and Insko, 1968) have found partial persistence effects at some reduced percentage of the immediate effects. In addition, however, there are some reports of sleeper effects, as well as reports of complete decay of the immediate effects.

A situation like the above, in which differing effects are routinely obtained, is an open invitation to specify the variables or circumstances accounting for the variation. The remainder of this chapter is concerned with suggestions as to what these circumstances might be.

DISSOCIATION OF SOURCE AND COMMUNICATION

Earlier we described the classic study by Hovland and Weiss (1952) which demonstrated the immediately greater persuasive impact of high-than low-credibility sources. In addition to the assessment of attitude immediately after exposure to a persuasive communication, attitude was also assessed 4 weeks after exposure. The delayed assessment revealed no difference between the high- and low-credibility sources. In the high-credibility condition the persuasive effect *decreased* over time. In the low-credibility condition, however, the persuasive effect actually *increased* over time; that is, a sleeper effect was obtained.

How could one account for this intriguing sleeper effect? One obvious possibility is that the subjects who showed the sleeper effect forgot the source of the communication. Although Hovland and Weiss' data are not entirely unambiguous on this matter, they can be most simply interpreted as indicating that subjects showing the sleeper effect did not differ from subjects not showing the sleeper effect in recall of the source. Hovland and Weiss speculated that the sleeper effect may be due to a failure of the subjects over time to *spontaneously* associate the source with the content of the communication. Such dissociation of source and content is not necessarily incompatible with the subjects' correct recall of the communication source in response to an explicit question. This hypothesis suggests that the important intervening variable relates to the nature of the subjects' thought processes rather than to their ability to recall when explicitly asked. In subsequent sections we will review some research which convincingly argues for the paramount importance of thought processes as opposed to simple recall.

How could Hovland and Weiss' hypothesis regarding dissociation of source and communication be experimentally investigated? One way would be to remind the subjects of the source for the previously presented communication and then measure attitude. In such a case the sleeper effect should not occur if the dissociation hypothesis is correct. Such a test was carried out by Kelman and Hovland (1953). Kelman and Hovland refer to the reminding of the subjects of the communication source as a *reinstatement* manipulation. A communication which advocated a more lenient treatment of juvenile delinquents was attributed to either a high-credibility source or a low-credibility source. The high-credibility source was a judge in a juvenile court who was also the author of several authoritative books on juvenile delinquency, and the low-credibility source was a dope peddler out on bail. The tape-recorded communication was presented to high-school students in the context of a supposedly real, educational radio program. An attitude assessment taken immediately after exposure to the communication revealed the expected results. Subjects for whom the communication was attributed to the high-credibility source were more influenced than subjects for whom the communication was attributed to the low-credibility source. Three weeks later half of the subjects exposed to the high-credibility source and half of the subjects exposed to the low-credibility source were reminded of the communication source and then asked again to indicate their attitude toward the treatment of juvenile delinquents. The other half of the subjects in the two credibility conditions simply indicated their attitudes without prior reinstatement of the communication source. These subjects for whom there was no reinstatement showed the same pattern of results that Hovland and Weiss had found; that is, over time the high-credibility source *decreased* in influence while the low-credibility source *increased* in influence. The net result was no difference in attitude between the groups which had previously been exposed to the high- and low-credibility sources. On the other hand, the subjects who had been reminded of the communication sources before indicating their attitudes maintained the same difference between high- and low-credibility conditions that were present immediately after exposure. Subjects who had been exposed to the high-credibility source were more influenced than subjects who had been exposed to the low-credibility source. Kelman and Hovland thus interpreted this general pattern of results as supporting the hypothesis that the decreasing influence of a high-credibility source over time and the increasing influence of a low-credibility source over time are due to a dissociation of source and communication.

It would doubtless be unwise to suppose that dissociation of source and communication and the accompanying sleeper effect will always occur. An important qualification may be the strength of the associative bond between communication and source. In any event, there is at least one reported instance in the literature (Watts & McGuire, 1964) in which a sleeper effect was not obtained. Investigators have not yet obtained an adequate understanding of the phenomenon.

LINKAGE TO IMPORTANT VALUES

Kelman (1958, 1960) has argued that a newly acquired attitude will persist to the extent that it is internalized. As Kelman uses the term "internalization" it refers to a process whereby the new attitude is linked to important values that the individual holds. In Chapter 1 we described Rosenberg's affective-cognitive consistency theory, which explicitly describes how attitudes are embedded in structures containing other attitudes or values. Kelman argues that a favorable attitude toward the UN, for example, should persist because of the belief that the UN averted war in a tense conflict situation. If the preservation of peace is an important value, the belief that the UN facilitated this value should, according to Kelman, lead to the persistence of the attitude. Cook and Insko (1968) have extended this idea somewhat by arguing that the greater the number of belief linkages to important values the greater the persistence of the attitude. Thus, following Kelman's example, if some individual placed a high value on the alleviation of starvation and the existence of an arena for the action of world public opinion, and in addition believed that the UN furthered both of these values, the positive attitude toward the UN might show even more persistence.

The above argument possesses a fair degree of common-sense plausibility. Unfortunately, the existing research evidence is as yet too scarce to have much certainty about the matter.

ADVOCACY VERSUS EXPOSURE

William Watts (1967) has investigated the relative persistence effects of written advocacy of a point of view versus simple exposure to written arguments for the same point of view. In the advocacy condition subjects were assigned the task of writing an essay supporting one of three positions: "Puerto Rico should be admitted to the Union as the 51st state"; "courts should deal more leniently with juvenile delinquents"; and "the Secretary of State should be elected by the people, not appointed by the President" (Watts, 1967, p. 7). Different subgroups of subjects wrote essays on each of the three issues. In the exposure condition different subgroups read persuasive communications on each of the three issues. The subjects, who were University of California education students, were initially told that the study was an attempt to develop a test of analytical thinking ability in future teachers. In the reading condition the subjects were to underline in each paragraph the shortest clause epitomizing the point being made. In the advocacy condition the subjects were asked to write a strong argument supporting the assigned issue, regardless of how they personally felt. After either writing an essay or reading one of the persuasive communications the subjects indicated their attitudes toward all three issues. Thus each subject provided control, or no-influence, assessments for two of the issues and experimental assessments for one issue. A comparison of the control assessments with the experimental assessments revealed that both advocacy and exposure had persuasive effects. Furthermore, the advocacy and reading effects did not differ from each other. Watts, in fact, had initially adjusted his persuasive communications so that they would approximately equal the advocacy manipulation in persuasive impact. Such an equating of immediate persuasive effects rules out an interpretation of differential persistence effects in terms of variables such as differential initial commitment.

Six weeks after the first session the subjects were contacted again and asked to fill out a questionnaire supposedly in order "to see whether the population's opinion on these issues is changing over time, or instead, is relatively stable, as well as to provide some additional information" (1967, p. 6). The questionnaire results indicated that the subjects in the advocacy condition showed a significantly greater persistence effect than the subjects in the exposure condition. In the exposure condition approximately half of the initially induced change had dissipated, while in the advocacy condition the amount of change actually increased, although not significantly so. In an experiment in which an antismoking advocacy was orally delivered, Elms (1966) obtained similar results. Elms' hired subjects were adult cigarette smokers who were applying for jobs at a state employment agency.

How can we account for a persistence effect produced by advocating a point of view? Watts reports that 63 percent of the subjects in the advocacy condition and 38 percent of the subjects in the exposure condition reported discussing the key issue with someone during the 6-week delay period. These significantly differing percentages suggest that at least part of the superior persistence effect in the advocacy condition is due to this variable.

DISCUSSION

Watts' finding that discussion of the attitude issue was associated with a greater persistence effect is reminiscent of an observation made by Peterson and Thurstone (1933). Recall that Peterson and Thurstone found that exposure to one movie, "Four Sons," resulted in a remarkable persistence effect. The film produced an immediate increase in favorability toward Germans. Six months later, however, the subjects' attitude had become even more favorable. Peterson and Thurstone speculated that perhaps this persistence effect is due to the fact that the film was shown to entertainment-deprived children who spent considerable time discussing the film.

Janis and Hoffman (1971) have presented evidence indicating that group discussion can produce remarkable persistence of reduced smoking behavior. They noted that "Proponents of Alcoholics Anonymous and Synanon have repeatedly described the buddy system as contributing to their members' success in 'staying on the wagon' or 'kicking the habit'" (1971, p. 25). The subjects were adult men and women who came to a smoking clinic at Yale University in response to a newspaper article and announcements offering free help to people who wanted to cut down on smoking in exchange for participation in a research program on smoking behavior. The only criterion used in selecting volunteers was that they smoked more than one pack of cigarettes per day. The actual mean number smoked per day was 32. Mean age of the subjects was 40 years.

In the experiment the subjects met two at a time for five weekly clinic sessions. At each of the meetings the clinic consultant functioned as a leader presenting tape-recorded or filmed antismoking information. Following exposure to the persuasive materials the consultant left the room while the two subjects engaged in spontaneous discussion. There were two basic conditions: high-contact and low-contact. In the high-contact condition the subjects were asked to telephone each other daily, in addition to attending the five clinic sessions. In the low-contact condition the subjects were explicitly asked not to telephone each other, but just to attend the five clinic sessions. Subjects reported how many cigarettes they were smoking per day immediately following the fifth clinic sessions and at delay intervals of six weeks, six months, and one year. The delayed assessments were obtained through a telephone interview conducted by the clinic secretary. She explained that some people had been helped and others had not, but that it would be helpful to know accurately how people were doing since such information would be valuable in evaluating treatment methods.

The results indicated that immediately following the fifth clinic the mean number of cigarettes smoked per day was approximately 4 in the high-contact condition and approximately 12 in the low-contact condition. These means are not significantly different from each other, but do compare favorably with the mean of 32 cigarettes per day for each group prior to the first clinic session. At the 6-week follow-up and at each of the succeeding delayed assessments the high- and low-contact groups *did* differ significantly from each other. One year after the last clinic session the high-contact mean was approximately 8 cigarettes per day and the low-contact mean was approximately 23 cigarettes per day. Obviously, the telephone discussions resulted in a greater degree of persistence over and above that produced by the five clinic sessions. This effect occurred in spite of the fact that in the high-contact condition the subjects stopped telephoning each other four weeks after the final clinic session.

Janis and Hoffman account for these results by arguing that "The most plausible mediating factor appears to be the increase in interpersonal attraction produced by daily contact, which makes for increased valuation of the clinic group and internalization of the norms conveyed by the consultant leader" (1971, p. 25). In support of this hypothesis Janis and Hoffman obtained data indicating that relative to the low-contact subjects the high-contact subjects reported greater attraction for their partners and greater satisfaction with the clinic sessions. Furthermore, the high-contact subjects reported less favorable attitudes toward smoking and made more explicit statements of their commitment to live up to the antismoking norm during the discussion sessions.

CONCLUSION REEXPOSURE

The Janis and Hoffman study dealt both with attitude change and with behavior change. Furthermore, the smoking behavior with which they were concerned is notoriously difficult to change in any permanent way. When we restrict our attention to just attitude change, group discussion may facilitate persistence even when there is no clear emergence of a norm. Group discussion, of course, is a very complex process, but one thing it does do is to remind the individuals of the attitude issue. Cook and Insko

(1968) demonstrated that just a simple reminder, which they refer to as conclusion reexposure, can facilitate persistence of attitude change.

In an experiment supposedly concerned with the evaluation of an unseen speaker, students from the University of North Carolina were exposed to two tape-recorded communications. One communication argued that having no sibling of the opposite sex has a slightly disadvantageous effect on marital adjustment during the first year of marriage, and the other argued for election of the President by Congress. After hearing the first communication the subjects rated the female speaker on a number of dimensions (knowledgeableness of the topic, modesty, warmth, etc.), and then were asked to indicate their number of brothers or sisters, supposedly since this might have affected their ratings of the speaker. The latter assessment and indeed the entire presentation of the first communication was intended as a cover for inquiring about influence by the second communication. After hearing the second communication the subjects rated the male speaker on the same dimensions mentioned above. Also subjects in the immediate-assessment condition indicated their agreement with the attitude issue, supposedly since this might have affected their ratings of the speaker. Subjects in the delay conditions were asked to return either 4, 7, or 11 days later for another experiment. All of these subjects were sent postcards reminding them of the time and place for the second experimental session. For half of the subjects in each delay condition the postcards explicitly mentioned the two advocated positions and for the other half of the subjects there was no mention of the advocated positions. The postcard reminder was thus a manipulation of conclusion reexposure. When the subjects returned they were told that the experimenter felt the necessity of ascertaining their attitude toward Congressional election of the President since this might have a bearing on their previous ratings of the speaker.

The results indicated that in the no-reexposure condition favorability toward Congressional election of the President progressively decayed over time. Eleven days after hearing the communication 43 percent of the initial change had dissipated. In the conclusion-reexposure condition, however, there was near complete persistence of the initial change. Apparently then, simple conclusion reexposure, even without group discussion, can facilitate persistence.

RETENTION OF COMMUNICATION CONTENT AND PRIMACY-RECENCY

Why should conclusion reexposure facilitate persistence? One obvious suggestion has to do with retention. Perhaps conclusion reexposure produces an increase in memory for communication content. For some time various social psychologists have been convinced that retention of communication content is an important factor mediating persistence effects. As we shall see, Miller and Campbell (1959) have made this assumption the cornerstone of a theory of primacy-recency in persuasion.

Primacy occurs when the first of two opposing communications has the greater persuasive impact, and recency occurs when the second of two opposing communications has the greater persuasive impact. Thus the primacy-recency issue relates to the old problem as to whether it is more advantageous "to get one's side of the argument in first" or "to have the last word." The typical experimental procedure used to investigate such order effects is one in which one group of subjects is exposed to two opposing communications in a pro-con order and another group is exposed to the two opposing communications in a con-pro order. In accordance with an after-only design, attitude is measured after, but not before, exposure to the second communication. A comparison between the mean assessments for the two groups then gives an indication of the order effect. Suppose, for example, that following exposure subjects marked a seven-point scale in which high scores indicated agreement with the pro communication and low scores indicated agreement with the con communication. If the pro-con mean was 3 and the con-pro mean 5, we would have evidence for recency. In this instance there is more agreement with the con communication when that communication is last rather than first. If the means were reversed, we would have evidence for primacy.

In their theory of primacy-recency Miller and Campbell began with the assumption that the persistence of attitude or belief change over time is a positive function of memory for communication content. Memory for, or retention of, communication content, on the other hand, is assumed to decay according to the Ebbinghaus curve. Two such curves are presented in Fig. 3–1. As described by the Ebbinghaus curve, retention decays very rapidly at first but progressively less rapidly as time increases.

Figure 3-1 graphically illustrates the basic order effect predictions that Miller and Campbell made. In session 1 the first of two opposing communications is presented to a group of subjects, and in session 2 the second opposing communication is presented. It is apparent that immediately after exposure to the second communication, memory for that communication is going to be greater than memory for the communication presented a week previously. Note that at session 2 the height of the dashed line representing retention of the second communication is greater than the height of the solid line representing retention of the first communication. This means that immediately after the second communication is presented in session 2 a recency effect is predicted.

Figure 3-1, however, also makes it evident that 1 week later (session 3) the difference in height of the two curves is markedly reduced. The two curves, in fact, have approximately the same height. Thus in session 3 the recency effect should be markedly less than in session 2 and may even be

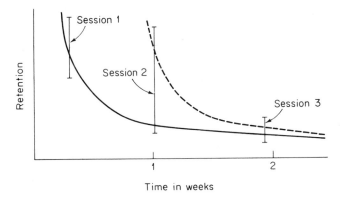

Fig. 3-1. *Forgetting curves for first (solid line) and second (dashed line) of two opposing communications. (Adapted from Miller and Campbell, 1959, p. 2.) Reproduced by permission of the American Psychological Association.*

nonexistent. Since Miller and Campbell weren't certain of the exact shapes of the curves their basic prediction was simply that there would be a smaller recency effect in session 3 than in session 2.

Miller and Campbell tested their theory with communications taken from an actual court case—a law suit in which a plaintiff sued a defendant for damages resulting from an accident. All of the material favoring the plaintiff was arranged in one block and all of the material favoring the defendant was arranged in another block. Subjects marked a scale indicating the degree to which they thought either the plaintiff or the defendant responsible for the accident and filled out a multiple-choice test assessing retention of the factual information contained in the communications (blocks of information).

Presentation of the communications one week apart with measurement of belief and retention either immediately after or one week after the second communication produced results in agreement with prediction. In session 2 there was a significant recency effect and in session 3 there was no order effect at all. The results are more puzzling, however, when the correlation between belief and the relative difference in recall of the two communications is examined. Since belief is hypothesized to be a function of the relative difference in recall of the two communications this correlation should be significantly positive. Across the various conditions, however, Miller and Campbell found that the average correlation was —.10.

Miller and Campbell's results leave the impression that the theory is right for the wrong reason or reasons. Similar agreement with order effect predictions, but low belief-recall correlations was found by Insko (1964). Actually the failure to find consistent relationships between recall of communication content and persuasion is a fairly common occurrence. Thus we are led to look for another explanation for the obtained order effects.

THOUGHTS

Anthony Greenwald (1968) has advanced the interesting hypothesis that persistence effects are mediated, not by memory for communication content, but by cognitive responses to the communication and its context. Such cognitive responses can be more simply referred to as thoughts. Greenwald's procedure for measuring such thoughts is very straightforward. Following exposure to a persuasive communication subjects are asked to list their thoughts, one thought per line, on ruled paper. They are explicitly told that,

> these thoughts may consist of (a) information favorable to one or the other viewpoint; (b) personal values of yours that are favorable to one or the other viewpoint; (c) features of either viewpoint that you perceive as good; (d) features of either viewpoint that you perceive as bad or harmful; and (e) any other thoughts you feel to be pertinent [Greenwald, 1968, p. 157].

After listing their thoughts subjects are asked to judge whether each thought is favorable or unfavorable to the position advocated in the communication. Thus it is possible to see whether the simple difference in number of favorable and unfavorable thoughts is in any way related to independently assessed attitude toward the communication issue.

For some purposes Greenwald distinguishes among three types of thoughts: *externally-originated, recipient-modified,* and *recipient-generated.* Externally-originated thoughts are thoughts that are directly traceable to communication content. Recipient-modified thoughts are thoughts that involve illustrations, qualifications, and reactions to the communication content. Recipient-generated thoughts are thoughts that involve own values and ideas not traceable to communication content. Greenwald (1968) describes some studies in which subjects themselves assign their listed thoughts to these three categories and some studies in which independent judges categorize the thoughts. For each category of thought an index was obtained by subtracting the number of favorable thoughts from the number of unfavorable thoughts. Greenwald found that the indices for each of the three types of thought were correlated with attitude. The correlation between recipient-generated thoughts and attitude, however, was somewhat greater than the correlations of the other two types of thought with attitude.

Why should recipient-generated thoughts be the most important of the three types of thoughts in mediating persuasion? Consider a communication defending initial American involvement in Vietnam. It is reasonable that the persuasive impact of this communication might indeed be greatly dependent upon the subject's own values as reflected in recipient-generated thoughts. Perhaps, on the other hand, if the communication were overpowerfully persuasive the externally-originated and recipient-modified thoughts might be relatively more important as mediators of attitude change. Such a hypothesis, however, has as yet not been experimentally tested.

The results described above relate entirely to the immediate or no-delay situation. Calder and Insko (1971), however, have found that thoughts correlate with and are predictive of persistence effects. Over time thoughts were found to change in a manner that closely paralleled the persistence in persuasion. Thus, there is reason to hope that the thought-listing procedure will provide a key to the unraveling of persistence effects. It is possible, for example, that order effects which Miller and Campbell found to result from the interval between opposing communications and the delay between the second communication and measurement could be a function of a declining number of thoughts. Calder and Insko found that number of thoughts do decrease over time in a manner that should produce the Miller and Campbell results. It is also possible that variables such as conclusion reexposure and discussion affect persistence through at least partial mediation by thoughts.

An interesting theoretical question concerns the exact causal connection between thoughts and attitudes. Research has revealed that thoughts and attitudes are correlated. Does this correlation, however, mean that thoughts cause attitudes or that attitudes cause thoughts? Greenwald's position is that thoughts cause attitudes. It may be, however, that people formulate their thoughts so as to be consistent with their attitudes. A good guess is that the causal sequence may go in both directions—sometimes thoughts causing attitudes and sometimes attitudes causing thoughts.

Summary of Variables Mediating Persistence Effects

The above described study by Peterson and Thurstone found three types of persistence effects: (1) partial persistence at some reduced percentage of the immediate effect, (2) sleeper effects, and (3) complete decay of the immediate effect. We have listed a number of variables, or circumstances, that have been suggested as possible mediators of such various persistence effects. These variables, or circumstances, include (1) dissociation of source and communication, (2) linkage to important values, (3) advocacy versus exposure, (4) discussion, (5) conclusion reexposure, (6) retention of communication content, and (7) thoughts.

READINGS

The Influence of Source Credibility on Communication Effectiveness[1]

Carl I. Hovland and Walter Weiss

An important but little-studied factor in the effectiveness of communication is the attitude of the audience toward the communicator. Indirect data on this problem come from studies of "prestige" in which subjects are asked to indicate their agreement or disagreement with statements which are attributed to different individuals (Sherif, 1935; Lewis, 1941; Asch, 1948). The extent of agreement is usually higher when the statements are attributed to "high prestige" sources. There are few studies in which an identical communication is presented by different communicators and the relative effects on opinion subsequently measured without explicit reference to the position taken by the communicator. Yet the latter research setting may be a closer approximation of the real-life situation to which the results of research are to be applied.

In one of the studies reported by Hovland, Lumsdaine, and Sheffield (1949), the effects of a communication were studied without reference to the source of the items comprising the opinion questionnaire. They found that opinion changes following the showing of an Army orientation film were smaller among the members of the audience who believed the purpose of the film was "propagandistic" than among those who believed its purpose "informational." But such a study does not rule out the possibility that the results could be explained by general predispositional factors; that is, individuals who are "suspicious" of mass-media sources may be generally less responsive to such communications. The present study was designed to minimize the aforementioned methodological difficulties by experimentally controlling the source and by checking the effects of the source in a situation in which the subject's own opinion was obtained without reference to the source.

A second objective of the present study was to investigate the extent to

[1] From the *Public Opinion Quarterly*, Volume 15, pages 635–650, 1952. Reprinted by permission of the authors and publisher. This study was done as part of a coordinated research project on factors influencing changes in attitude and opinion being conducted at Yale University under a grant from the Rockefeller Foundation. (See C. I. Hovland, "Changes in Attitude through Communication," *Journal of Abnormal and Social Psychology*, Vol. 46, 424–437, 1951.) The writers wish to thank Professor Ralph E. Turner for making his class available for the study.

which opinions derived from high and low credibility sources are maintained over a period of time. Hovland, Lumsdaine, and Sheffield showed that some opinion changes in the direction of the communicator's position are larger after a lapse of time than immediately after the communication. This they refer to as the "sleeper effect." One hypothesis which they advanced for their results is that individuals may be suspicious of the motives of the communicator and initially discount his position, and thus may evidence little or no immediate change in opinion. With the passage of time, however, they may remember and accept *what* was communicated but not remember *who* communicated it. As a result, they may then be more inclined to agree with the position which had been presented by the communicator. In the study referred to, only a single source was used, so no test was available of the differential effects when the source was suspected of having a propagandistic motive and when it was not. The present experiment was designed to test differences in the retention, as well as the acquisition, of identical communications when presented by "trustworthy" and by "untrustworthy" sources.

PROCEDURE

The overall design of the study was to present an identical communication to two groups, one in which a communicator of a generally "trustworthy" character was used, and the other in which the communicator was generally regarded as "untrustworthy." Opinion questionnaires were administered before the communication, immediately after the communication, and a month after the communication.

Because of the possibility of specific factors affecting the relationship between communicator and content on a single topic, four different topics (with eight different communicators) were used. On each topic two alternative versions were prepared, one presenting the "affirmative" and one the "negative" position on the issue. For each version one "trustworthy" and one "untrustworthy" source was used. The topics chosen were of current interest and of a controversial type so that a fairly even division of opinion among members of the audience was obtained.

The four topics and the communicators chosen to represent "high credibility" and "low credibility" sources were as follows: In some cases the sources were individual writers and in other periodical publications, and some were fictitious (but plausible) and others actual authors or publications.

The "affirmative" and "negative" versions of each article presented an equal number of facts on the topic and made use of essentially the same material. They differed in the emphasis given the material and in the conclusion drawn from the facts. Since there were two versions for each topic and these were prepared in such a way that either of the sources might have written either version, four possible combinations of content and source were available on each topic.

The communication consisted of a booklet containing one article on each of the four different topics, with the name of the author or periodical given at the end of each article. The order of the topics within the booklets

	"High credibility" source	"Low credibility" source
A. Anti-histamine Drugs: Should the anti-histamine drugs continue to be sold without a doctor's prescription?	*New England Journal of Biology and Medicine*	Magazine A[a] [A mass circulation monthly pictorial magazine]
B. Atomic Submarines: Can a practicable atomic-powered submarine be built at the present time?	Robert J. Oppenheimer	*Pravda*
C. The Steel Shortage: Is the steel industry to blame for the current shortage of steel?	*Bulletin of National Resources Planning Board*	Writer A[a] [A widely syndicated anti-labor, anti-New Deal, "rightist" newspaper columnist]
D. The Future of Movie Theaters: As a result of TV, will there be a decrease in the number of movie theaters in operation by 1955?	*Fortune* magazine	Writer B[a] [An extensively syndicated woman movie-gossip columnist]

[a] The names of one of the magazines and two of the writers used in the study have to be withheld to avoid any possible embarrassment to them. These sources will be referred to hereafter only by the later designations given.

was kept constant. Two trustworthy and two untrustworthy sources were included in each booklet. Twenty-four different booklets covered the various combinations used. An example of one such booklet-combination would be:

Topic	Version	Source
The Future of Movie Theaters	Affirmative	*Fortune*
Atomic Submarines	Negative	*Pravda*
The Steel Shortage	Affirmative	Writer A
Anti-histamine Drugs	Negative	*New England Journal of Biology and Medicine*

The questionnaires were designed to obtain data on the amount of factual information acquired from the communication and the extent to which opinion was changed in the direction of the position advocated by the communicator. Information was also obtained on the subject's evaluation of the general trustworthiness of each source, and, in the after-questionnaires, on the recall of the author of each article.

The subjects were college students in an advanced undergraduate course in History at Yale University. The first questionnaire, given five days before the communication, was represented to the students as a general opinion survey being conducted by a "National Opinion Survey Council." The key opinions bearing on the topics selected for the communication were scattered through many other unrelated ones. There were also questions asking for the subjects' evaluations of the general trustworthiness of a long list of sources, which included the critical ones used in the communications. This evaluation was based on a 5-point scale ranging from "very trustworthy" to "very untrustworthy."

Since it was desired that the subjects not associate the experiment with the "before" questionnaire, the following arrangement was devised: The senior experimenter was invited to give a guest lecture to the class during the absence of the regular instructor, five days after the initial questionnaire. His remarks constituted the instructions for the experiment:

> Several weeks ago Professor [the regular instructor] asked me to meet with you this morning to discuss some phase of Contemporary Problems. He suggested that one interesting topic would be The Psychology of Communications. This is certainly an important problem, since so many of our attitudes and opinions are based not on direct experience but on what we hear over the radio or read in the newspaper. I finally agreed to take this topic but on the condition that I have some interesting live data on which to base my comments. We therefore agreed to use this period to make a survey of the role of newspaper and magazine reading as a vehicle or communication and then to report on the results and discuss their implications at a later session.
>
> Today, therefore, I am asking you to read a number of excerpts from recent magazine and newspaper articles on controversial topics. The authors have attempted to summarize the best information available, duly taking into account the various sides of the issues. I have chosen up-to-date issues which are currently being widely discussed and ones which are being studied by Gallup, Roper and others interested in public opinion.
>
> Will you please read each article carefully the way you would if you were reading it in your favorite newspaper and magazine. When you finish each article write your name in the lower right hand corner to indicate that you have read it through and then go on to the next. When you finish there will be a short quiz on your reaction to the readings.
>
> Any questions before we begin?

The second questionnaire, handed out immediately after the booklets were collected, differed completely in format from the earlier one. It contained a series of general questions on the subjects' reactions to the articles, gradually moving toward opinion questions bearing on the content discussed in the articles. At the end of the questionnaire there was a series of fact-quiz items. Sixteen multiple choice questions, four on each content area, were used together with a question calling for the recall of the author of each of the articles.

An identical questionnaire was administered four weeks after the communication. At no prior time had the subjects been forewarned that they would be given this second posttest questionnaire.

A total of 223 subjects provided information which was used in some phase of the analysis. Attendance in the history course was not mandatory and there was considerable shrinkage in the number of students present at all three time periods. For the portions of the analysis requiring before-and-after information, the data derived from 61 students who were present on all three occasions were used. Thus for the main analysis a sample of 244 communications (four for each student) was available. Since different analyses permitted the use of differing numbers of cases, the exact number of instances used in each phase of the analysis is given in each table.

RESULTS

Before proceeding to the main analyses it is important to state the extent to which the sources selected on *a priori* grounds by the experimenters as being of differing credibility were actually reacted to in this manner by the subjects. One item on the questionnaire given before the communication asked the subjects to rate the trustworthiness of each of a series of authors and publications. Figure 1 gives the percentages of subjects who rated each of the sources "trustworthy."

The first source named under each topic had been picked by the experimenters as being of high credibility and the second of low. It will be observed that there is a clear differentiation of the credibility in the direction of the initial selection by the experimenters. The differences between members of each pair are all highly significant (t's range from 13 to 20). The results in Fig. 1 are based on all of the subjects present when the preliminary questionnaire was administered. The percentages for the smaller sample of subjects present at all three sessions do not differ significantly from those for the group as a whole.

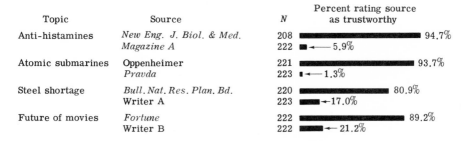

Topic	Source	N	Percent rating source as trustworthy
Anti-histamines	*New Eng. J. Biol. & Med.*	208	94.7%
	Magazine A	222	5.9%
Atomic submarines	Oppenheimer	221	93.7%
	Pravda	223	1.3%
Steel shortage	*Bull. Nat. Res. Plan. Bd.*	220	80.9%
	Writer A	223	17.0%
Future of movies	*Fortune*	222	89.2%
	Writer B	222	21.2%

Fig. 1. Credibility of sources.

*Differences in Perception of Communication of Various
Audience Sub-Groups*

Following the communication, subjects were asked their opinion about
the fairness of the presentation of each topic and the extent to which each
communicator was justified in his conclusion. Although the communications
being judged were *identical*, there was a marked difference in the way the
subjects responded to the "high credibility" and "low credibility" sources.
Their evaluations were also affected by their personal opinions on the topic
before the communication was ever presented. Audience evaluations of the
four communications are presented in Table 1. In 14 of the 16 possible com-

TABLE 1

*Evaluation of "Fairness" and "Justifiability" of Identical Communications When Presented
by "High Credibility" and "Low Credibility" Sources among Individuals Who Initially
Agreed and Individuals Who Initially Disagreed with Position Advocated by Communicator*

A. PERCENT CONSIDERING AUTHOR "FAIR" IN HIS PRESENTATION[a]

Topic	High credibility source		Low credibility source	
	Initially agree	Initially disagree (or don't know)	Initially agree	Initially disagree (or don't know)
Anti-histamines	76.5%	50.0%	64.3%	62.5%
Atomic Submarines	100.0	93.7	75.0	66.7
Steel Shortage	44.4	15.4	12.5	22.2
Future of Movies	90.9	90.0	77.8	52.4
Mean	78.3%	57.9%	60.5%	51.9%
N =	46	76	43	79

B. PERCENT CONSIDERING AUTHOR'S CONCLUSION "JUSTIFIED" BY THE FACTS[b]

Topic	High credibility source		Low credibility source	
	Initially agree	Initially disagree (or don't know)	Initially agree	Initially disagree (or don't know)
Anti-histamines	82.4%	57.1%	57.1%	50.0%
Atomic Submarines	77.8	81.2	50.0	41.2
Steel Shortage	55.6	23.1	37.5	22.2
Future of Movies	63.6	55.0	55.6	33.3
Mean	71.7%	50.0%	51.2%	36.7%
N =	46	76	43	79

[a] Question: Do you think that the author of each article was fair in his presentation of
the facts on both sides of the question or did he write a one-sided report?

[b] Question: Do you think that the opinion expressed by the author in his conclusion *was*
justified by the facts he presented or do you think his opinion *was not* justified by the facts?

parisons the "low credibility" sources are considered less fair or less justified than the corresponding high credibility sources. The differences for the low credibility sources for the individuals initially holding an opinion different from that advocated by the communicator and those for the high credibility sources for individuals who initially held the same position as that advocated by the communicator are significant at less than the .004 level.[2]

Effect of Credibility of Source on Acquisition of Information and on Change in Opinion

Information. There is no significant difference in the amount of factual information acquired by the subjects when the material is attributed to a high credibility source as compared to the amount learned when the same material is attributed to a low credibility source. Table 2 shows the mean number of items correct on the information quiz when material is presented by "high credibility" and "low credibility" sources.

Opinion. Significant differences were obtained in the extent to which opinion on an issue was changed by the attribution of the material to different sources. These results are presented in Table 3. Subjects changed their opinion in the direction advocated by the communicator in a significantly greater number of cases when the material was attributed to a "high

TABLE 2

Mean Number of Items Correct on Four-Item Information Quizzes on Each of Four Topics When Presented by "High Credibility" and "Low Credibility" Sources (Test Immediately After Communication)

	Mean number of items correct			
Topic	High credibility source		Low credibility source	
Anti-histamines	(N = 31)	3.42	(N = 30)	3.17
Atomic Submarines	(N = 25)	3.48	(N = 36)	3.72
Steel Shortage	(N = 35)	3.34	(N = 26)	2.73
Future of Movies	(N = 31)	3.23	(N = 30)	3.27
Average	(N = 122)	3.36	(N = 122)	3.26
Percent of items correct		84.0		81.5
$p$diff. M.			.35	

[2] The probability values given in the table, while adequately significant, are calculated conservatively. The two-tailed test of significance is used throughout, even though in the case of some of the tables it could be contended that the direction of the differences is in line with theoretical predictions, and hence might justify the use of the one-tail test. When analysis is made of *changes,* the significance test takes into account the internal correlation (Hovland, Lumsdaine, and Sheffield, 1949, pp. 318ff.), but the analyses of cases of postcommunication agreement and disagreement are calculated on the conservative assumption of independence of the separate communications.

TABLE 3

Net Changes of Opinion in Direction of Communication for Sources Classified by Experimenters as "High Credibility" or "Low Credibility" Sources[a]

Topic	Net percentage of cases in which subjects changed opinion in direction of communication			
	High credibility sources		Low credibility sources	
Anti-histamines	(N = 31)	22.6%	(N = 30)	13.3%
Atomic Submarines	(N = 25)	36.0	(N = 36)	0.0
Steel Shortage	(N = 35)	22.9	(N = 26)	−3.8
Future of Movies	(N = 31)	12.9	(N = 30)	16.7
Average	(N = 122)	23.0%	(N = 122)	6.6%
Diff.			16.4%	
pdiff.			<.01	

[a] Net changes = positive changes *minus* negative changes.

credibility" source than when attributed to a "low credibility" source. The difference is significant at less than the .01 level.

From Fig. 1 it will be recalled that less than 100 percent of the subjects were in agreement with the group consensus concerning the trustworthiness of each source. The results presented in Table 3 were reanalyzed using the individual subject's own evaluation of the source as the independent variable. The effects on opinion were studied for those instances where the source was rated as "very trustworthy" or "moderately trustworthy" and for those where it was rated as "untrustworthy" or "inconsistently trustworthy." Results from this analysis are given in Table 4. The results, using the subject's own evaluation of the trustworthiness of the source, are substantially the same as those obtained when analyzed in terms of the experimenters' *a priori* classification (presented in Table 3). Only minor shifts were ob-

TABLE 4

Net Changes of Opinion in Direction of Communication for Sources Judged "Trustworthy" or "Untrustworthy" by Individual Subjects

Topic	Net percentage of cases in which subjects changed opinion in direction of communication			
	"Trustworthy" sources		"Untrustworthy" sources	
Anti-histamines	(N = 31)	25.5%	(N = 27)	11.1%
Atomic Submarines	(N = 25)	36.0	(N = 36)	0.0
Steel Shortage	(N = 33)	18.2	(N = 27)	7.4
Future of Movies	(N = 31)	12.9	(N = 29)	17.2
Average	(N = 120)	22.5%	(N = 119)	8.4%
Diff.			14.1%	
pdiff.			<.03	

TABLE 5

Mean Number of Items Correct on Four-Item Information Quizzes on Each of Four Topics When Presented by "High Credibility" and "Low Credibility" Sources (Recall Four Weeks after Communication)

	Mean number of items correct			
Topic	High credibility source		Low credibility source	
Anti-histamines	(N = 31)	2.32	(N = 30)	2.90
Atomic Submarines	(N = 25)	3.08	(N = 36)	3.06
Steel Shortage	(N = 35)	2.51	(N = 26)	2.27
Future of Movies	(N = 31)	2.52	(N = 30)	2.33
Average	(N = 122)	2.58	(N = 122)	2.67
Percent of items correct		64.5		66.7
$p$diff.			.46	

tained. It appears that while the variable is made somewhat "purer" with this analysis this advantage is offset by possible increased variability attributable to unreliability in making individual judgments of the trustworthiness of the source.

Retention of Information and Opinion in Relation to Source

Information. As was the case with the immediate postcommunication results (Table 2), there is no difference between the retention of factual information after four weeks when presented by high credibility sources and low credibility sources. Results in Table 5 show the mean retention scores for each of the four topics four weeks after the communication.

Opinion. Extremely interesting results were obtained for the retention of opinion changes. Table 6 shows the changes in opinion from immediately after the communication to those obtained after the four-week interval. It will be seen that compared with the changes immediately after the communication, there is a *decrease* in the extent of agreement with the high

TABLE 6

Net Changes of Opinion from Immediately After Communication to Four Weeks Later in Direction of "High Credibility" and "Low Credibility" Sources

Topic	High credibility source (A)	Low credibility source (B)	Difference (B − A)
Anti-histamines	(N = 31) − 6.5%	(N = 30) + 6.7%	+13.2%
Atomic Submarines	(N = 25) − 16.0	(N = 36) + 13.9	+29.9
Steel Shortage	(N = 35) − 11.4	(N = 26) + 15.4	+26.8
Future of Movies	(N = 31) − 9.7	(N = 30) − 6.7	+ 3.0
Average	(N = 122) − 10.7%	(N = 122) + 7.4%	+18.1%
$p$diff.			.001

credibility source, but an *increase* in the case of the low credibility source. This result, then, is similar to the "sleeper effect" found by Hovland, Lumsdaine, and Sheffield (1949). The results derived from Tables 3 and 6 are compared in Fig. 2, which shows the changes in opinion from before the communication to immediately afterwards and from before to four weeks afterwards.

The loss with the "trustworthy" source and the gain with the "untrustworthy" source are clearly indicated. A parallel analysis using the individual's own evaluation of the source credibility (similar to the method of Table 4) showed substantially the same results.

Retention of Name of Source. One hypothesis advanced for the "sleeper effect" involved the assumption that forgetting of the source would be more rapid than that of the content. This is a most difficult point to test experimentally because it is almost impossible to equate retention tests for source and for content. It is, however, possible to make a comparison of the retention of the name of the source where the subjects initially agreed with the source's position and considered the communicator a "trustworthy" source, and those where they disagreed and considered the source "untrustworthy." Data on this point are presented in Table 7.

No clear differences are obtained immediately after the communication, indicating comparable initial learning of the names of the different sources. At the time of the delayed test, however, there appears to be a clear difference in the retention of the names of "untrustworthy" sources for the group initially agreeing with the communicator's position as compared with that for the group disagreeing with the communicator's position ($p = .02$). Since

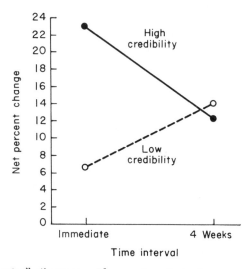

Fig. 2. "Retention" of opinion. Changes in extent of agreement with position advocated by "high credibility" and "low credibility" sources.

TABLE 7

Recall of Source Immediately after Communication and after Four Weeks

Recall	Trustworthy source		Untrustworthy source	
	Individuals initially holding posi-tion advocated by communicator	Individuals not initially holding posi-tion advocated by communicator	Individuals initially holding posi-tion advocated by communicator	Individuals not initially holding posi-tion advocated by communicator
Immediately after communication	93.0% (N = 43)	85.7% (N = 77)	93.0% (N = 43)	93.4% (N = 76)
Four weeks after communication	60.5 (N = 43)	63.6 (N = 77)	76.7 (N = 43)	55.3 (N = 76)

the "sleeper effect" occurs among the group which initially disagrees with an unreliable source (but subsequently comes to agree with it), it is interesting to note that among this group the retention of the source name is poorest of all. Too few subjects were available to check whether retention was poorer among the very subjects who showed the "sleeper effect," but no clear-cut difference could be seen from the analysis of the small sample.

Discussion

Under the conditions of this experiment, neither the acquisition nor the retention of factual information appears to be affected by the trustworthiness of the source. But changes in opinion are significantly related to the trustworthiness of the source used in the communication. This difference is in line with the results of Hovland, Lumsdaine, and Sheffield (1949), who found a clear distinction between the effects of films on information and opinion. In the case of factual information they found that differences in acquisition and retention were primarily related to differences in learning ability. But in the case of opinion, the most important factor was the degree of "acceptance" of the material. In the present experiment, this variable was probably involved as a consequent of the variation in source credibility.

The present results add considerable detail to the Hovland-Lumsdaine-Sheffield findings concerning the nature of the "sleeper effect." While they were forced to make inferences concerning possible suspicion of the source, this factor was under experimental control in the present experiment and was shown to be a significant determinant of subsequent changes in opinion. In terms of their distinction between "learning" and "acceptance," one could explain the present results by saying that the content of the communication (premises, arguments, etc.) is learned and forgotten to the same extent regardless of the communicator. But the extent of opinion change is influenced by both learning and acceptance, and the effect of an untrustworthy communicator is to interfere with the acceptance of the material ("I know what he is saying, but I don't believe it"). The afore-mentioned authors suggest that this interference is decreased with the passage of time, and at a more rapid rate than the forgetting of the content which provides the basis for the opinion. This could result in substantially the same extent of agreement with the position advocated by trustworthy and by untrustworthy sources at the time of the second posttest question-naire. In the case of the trustworthy source, the forgetting of the content would be the main factor in the decrease in the extent of opinion change. But with an untrustworthy source the reduction due to forgetting would be more than offset by the removal of the interference associated with "non-acceptance." The net effect would be an increase in the extent of agreement with the position advocated by the source at the time of the second post-communication questionnaire. The present results are in complete agree-ment with this hypothesis; there is a large difference in extent of agreement with trustworthy and untrustworthy sources immediately after the com-munication, but the extent of agreement with the two types of source is almost identical four weeks later.

The Hovland-Lumsdaine-Sheffield formulation makes forgetting of the source a critical condition for the "sleeper" phenomenon. In the present analysis the critical requirement is a decreased tendency over time to reject the material presented by an untrustworthy source.[3] This may or may not require that the source be forgotten. But the individual must be less likely with the passage of time to associate spontaneously the content with the source. Thus the passage of time serves to remove recall of the source as a mediating cue that leads to rejection.[4]

It is in this connection that the methodological distinction mentioned earlier between the procedure used in this experiment and that customarily employed in "prestige" studies becomes of significance. In the present analysis the untrustworthy source is regarded as a cue which is reacted to by rejection. When an individual is asked for his opinion at the later time he may not spontaneously remember the position held by the sources.

---

[3] In the present analysis the difference in effects of trustworthy and untrustworthy sources is attributed primarily to the *negative* effects of rejection of the untrustworthy source. On the other hand, in prestige studies the effects are usually attributed to the *positive* enhancement of effects by a high prestige source. In both types of study only a difference in effect of the two kinds of influence is obtained. Future research must establish an effective "neutral" base-line to answer the question as to the absolute direction of the effects.

[4] In rare instances there may also occur a change with time in the attitude toward the source, such that one remembers the source but no longer has such a strong tendency to discount and reject the material. No evidence for the operation of this factor in the present experiment was obtained, our data indicate no significant changes in the evaluation of the trustworthiness of the sources from before to after the communication.

Hence the source does not then constitute a one producing rejection of his position. In the usual "prestige" technique, the attachment of the name of the source to the statement would serve to reinstate the source as a cue; consequently the differential effects obtained with the present design would not be expected to obtain. An experiment is now under way to determine whether the "sleeper effect" disappears when the source cue is reinstated by the experimenter at the time of the delayed test of opinion change.

Finally, the question of the generalizability of the results should be discussed briefly. In the present study the subjects were all college students. Other groups of subjects varying in age and in education will be needed in future research. Four topics and eight different sources were used to increase the generality of the "source" variable. No attempt, however, was made to analyze the differences in effects for different topics. Throughout, the effects of the "Atomic Submarine" and "Steel Shortage" communications were larger and more closely related to the trustworthiness of source variable than those of the "Future of Movies" topic. An analysis of the factors responsible for the differential effects constitutes an interesting problem for future research. A repetition of the study with a single after-test for each time interval rather than double testing after the communication would be desirable although this variation is probably much less significant with opinion than with information questions. The generality of the present results is limited to the situation where individuals are experimentally exposed to the communication; i.e., a "captive audience" situation. An interesting further research problem would be a repetition of the experiment under naturalistic conditions where the individual himself controls his exposure to communications. Finally, for the present study it was important to use sources which could plausibly advocate either side of an issue. There are other combinations of position and source where the communicator and his stand are so intimately associated that one spontaneously recalls the source when he thinks about the issue. Under these conditions, the forgetting of the source may not occur and consequently no "sleeper effect" would be obtained.

SUMMARY

1. The effects of credibility of source on acquisition and retention of communication material were studied by presenting identical content but attributing the material to sources considered by the audience to be of "high trustworthiness" or of "low trustworthiness." The effects of source on factual information and on opinion were measured by the use of questionnaires administered before, immediately after, and four weeks after the communication.

2. The immediate reaction to the "fairness" of the presentation and the "justifiability" of the conclusions drawn by the communication is signifi-

cantly affected by both the subject's initial position on the issue and by his evaluation of the trustworthiness of the source. Identical communications were regarded as being "justified" in their conclusions in 71.7 percent of the cases when presented by a high credibility source to subjects who initially held the same opinion as advocated by the communicator, but were considered "justified" in only 36.7 percent of the cases when presented by a low credibility source to subjects who initially held an opinion at variance with that advocated by the communicator.

3. No difference was found in the amount of factual information learned from the "high credibility" and "low credibility" sources, and none in the amount retained over a four-week period.

4. Opinions were changed immediately after the communication in the direction advocated by the communicator to a significantly greater degree when the material was presented by a trustworthy source than when presented by an untrustworthy source.

5. There was a *decrease* after a time interval in the extent to which subjects agreed with the position advocated by the communication when the material was presented by trustworthy sources, but an *increase* when it was presented by untrustworthy sources.

6. Forgetting the name of the source is less rapid among individuals who initially agreed with the untrustworthy source than among those who disagreed with it.

7. Theoretical implications of the results are discussed. The data on post-communication changes in opinion (the "sleeper effect") can be explained by assuming equal *learning* of the content whether presented by a trustworthy or an untrustworthy source but an initial resistance to the *acceptance* of the material presented by an untrustworthy source. If this resistance to acceptance diminishes with time while the content which itself provides the basis for the opinion is forgotten more slowly, there will be an increase after the communication in the extent of agreement with an untrustworthy source.

REFERENCES

Asch, S. E. The doctrine of suggestion, prestige, and imitation in social psychology. *Psychology Review* 1948, **55**, 250–276.
Hovland, C. I., Lumsdaine, A. A., & Sheffield, F. D. *Experiments on mass communication*. Princeton, New Jersey: Princeton University Press, 1949.
Lewis, H. B. Studies in the principles of judgments and attitudes: IV. The operation of prestige suggestion. *Journal of Social Psychology* 1941, **14**, 229–256.
Sherif, M. An experimental study of stereotypes. *Journal of Abnormal Social Psychology* 1935, **29**, 371–375.

Chapter 4

DISSONANCE IN FREE-CHOICE SITUATIONS

Leon Festinger's (1957) theory of cognitive dissonance stimulated an extraordinary amount of research in the decade following its publication. The proportion of active social psychologists who did not conduct at least one dissonance experiment during this era was probably small. Dissonance theory is also a consistency theory of attitude change, but it is quite different from the various balance theories described in Chapter 1. The present chapter will present the general formulation and specific implications for what are referred to as free-choice situations.

General Formulation of Dissonance Theory

ELEMENTS AND RELATIONS

Cognitive elements are the basic units of dissonance theory. They are the things a person knows or believes about himself, his behavior, and his surroundings. The knowledge that one has just purchased a car is, for example, a cognitive element.

Some cognitive elements are perceived as related and some are not so perceived. Cognitive elements that are perceived as related may be in either a consonant relation or a dissonant relation. Festinger (1957) states that "two elements are in a dissonant relation if, considering these two alone, the obverse of one element would follow from the other" (p. 13). If, for example, someone who was in debt purchased a car dissonance would be created; not buying a car (the obverse of buying a car) follows from being in debt. Festinger elaborates several meanings that can be· attached to the phrase "follow from." Dissonance may require a logical inconsistency among elements, the violation of expectations as to what one should do, or the violation of expectations based on past experience. Apparently any kind of "unreasonable" relation among elements is sufficient to create dissonance.

Consonant relations occur when one cognitive element does follow from another. For example, the decision to stop smoking follows from the knowledge that smoking causes lung cancer. On the other hand, the decision to continue or to start smoking is dissonant with the knowledge that smoking causes lung cancer.

DISSONANCE MAGNITUDE AND REDUCTION

According to Festinger the magnitude of dissonance is dependent upon two things, the importance of the elements and the proportion of relevant elements that are dissonant. The greater the importance of the elements and the higher the proportion of elements that are dissonant the greater the dissonance. Due to a difference in the importance of the involved elements, deciding not to study for a final examination would create more dissonance than deciding not to study for a weekly quiz. Also the more reasons that one could state for studying for either exam the greater the dissonance created by the decision not to study. Such an increase in reasons for studying would alter the proportion of dissonant to relevant elements.

The greater the magnitude of dissonance the greater the pressure to reduce dissonance. In his general formulation of dissonance theory Festinger mentions three ways in which dissonance may be reduced: changing a behavioral cognitive element, changing an environmental cognitive element, and adding new cognitive elements. Changing a behavioral cognitive element is illustrated by the smoker who gives up smoking after learning of the harmful consequences of his habit; changing an environmental cognitive element is illustrated by the citizen who misperceives the political position of a candidate in order to justify supporting him; and adding new cognitive elements is illustrated by the smoker who reads literature critical of the research linking smoking and lung cancer.

Application to Specific Situations

Festinger elaborates upon his general formulation of dissonance theory by discussing its application to specific situations. Three of the most important of these are free-choice situations, forced-compliance situations, and involuntary-exposure situations. The last two of these topics will be discussed in Chapters 5 and 6. The remainder of the present chapter will deal exclusively with free-choice situations.

THEORY

Conflict occurs when a person has to make a choice among a number of alternatives. If the alternatives are desirable ones the situation is referred to as an approach-approach conflict (Lewin, 1935), or as a free-choice situation (Brehm & Cohen, 1962). According to Festinger once the choice has been made dissonance is created. Resolution of the conflict produces dissonance. In the present context dissonance is thus postdecisional conflict. Suppose that an individual has to choose which of two desirable automobiles to purchase. After making a decision the conflict is resolved, but dissonance is created. All of the desirable characteristics of the unchosen car are dissonant with the knowledge that the other car has been chosen.

Festinger maintains that the magnitude of dissonance in a free-choice situation is dependent upon three things: the relative attractiveness of the unchosen compared to the chosen alternative, the importance of the decision, and the degree of nonevaluative similarity between the alternatives. The greater the attractiveness of the unchosen alternative, the greater the importance of the decision, and the less the nonevaluative similarity between the alternatives the greater the magnitude of dissonance. These three functional relations can be illustrated as follows. The greater the attractiveness of an unchosen automobile relative to the attractiveness of the chosen automobile, the greater the dissonance resulting from a purchase. A choice between two automobiles will produce more dissonance than a choice between two brands of soap. And a choice between two books will create less dissonance than a choice between a book and a theater ticket.

Festinger states that the dissonance arising from a decision in a free-choice situation can be reduced in any of a number of ways: revoking the decision, increasing the attractiveness of the chosen alternative, decreasing the attractiveness of the unchosen alternative, perceiving greater similarity between the two alternatives. The first of these modes of dissonance reduction, revoking the decision, is likely to occur if the individual encounters information indicating that the decision was a poor one. Since revoking the decision puts the individual back in the choice conflict, however, this mode of dissonance reduction is not too satisfying or likely. The second and third modes of dissonance reduction, increasing the attractiveness of the chosen alternative and decreasing the attractiveness of the unchosen alternative, are much more likely to occur. Increasing the attractiveness of the chosen alternative and decreasing the attractiveness of the unchosen alternative are collectively referred to as a spreading apart of the alternatives. The final mode of dissonance reduction, perceiving greater similarity between the two alternatives, is illustrated by the boy who, having decided to go to a movie rather than the circus, decides that both are, after all, forms of entertainment. It should be noted that similarity here refers to similarity of attributes.

THE BREHM (1956) AND BROCK (1963) EXPERIMENTS

Apparently researchers have tended to regard the spreading apart of the alternatives as the most likely mode of dissonance reduction. In any event, published research has assessed revaluation of the alternatives rather than an increase in the perceived similarity between the alternatives. An early experiment in this area was conducted by Brehm (1956). Brehm asked female subjects to rate the desirability of a number of items, such as a portable radio, desk lamp, or an automatic coffee maker. The subjects were told that the manufacturers of these items were interested in obtaining consumers' reactions and that in return for their help they could have one of the items. Since, however, the items were in short supply it would be necessary to choose between two. Each subject was given a choice between one item she had previously rated highly desirable and another item rated somewhat less desirable. A few minutes after making a choice the subjects were asked to rate all of the items a second time. They were told that the manufacturers wished to know how the evaluation of items changed after customers had looked them over and left the store. The results, in general, indicate that the chosen item increased in desirability and the unchosen or rejected item decreased in desirability. This effect was particularly evident in a high-dissonance condition in which the initial rating of the two items differed by only ½ to 1½ points on an 8-point scale.

One problem with Brehm's experiment was that approximately 29 percent of the subjects chose the item that they initially rated as less desirable. These "choice-reversal" subjects were eliminated from the sample and the reported results based on the data for the remaining subjects (i.e., the subjects who chose the item initially rated most desirable). Brehm does state, however, that the changes in the desirability ratings for the eliminated subjects "were if anything, in the direction of reducing dissonance" (p. 385). Chapanis and Chapanis (1964) have pointed out that elimination of the choice-reversal subjects could artifactually produce the dissonance-reducing results that Brehm obtained. Assuming some unreliability in the initial ratings of the items, a given subject's second rating will not necessarily agree with the first rating. The second rating may be higher or lower. Random errors would guarantee such fluctuation. By elimination of the choice-reversal subjects, those subjects who decreased their evaluation of the initially preferred item and/or increased their evaluation of the initially less preferred item were eliminated from the sample. This leaves the subjects who increased their evaluation of the initially preferred item and/or decreased their evaluation of the initially less preferred item. Thus the remaining subjects will of necessity show increased evaluation of the chosen item and decreased evaluation of the unchosen item.

Brehm does report that his eliminated subjects did produce data in the predicted direction. He does not state, however, what the inclusion of the presumably weak data from his choice-reversal subjects would do to the significance of his findings. Subsequent investigators, though, have, by and large, been sensitive to the problem. A good example of this is a carefully conducted investigation by Brock (1963). Brock's report, which is contained in the Readings section of this chapter, indicates that inclusion or exclusion of the choice-reversal subjects makes no difference in the significance of the results. Brock also supported Festinger's (1957) prediction regarding the greater dissonance arousal of a choice between two dissimilar as opposed to two similar alternatives, as well as an interesting prediction that irrelevant tension or drive would facilitate increased evaluation of the chosen alternative and decreased evaluation of the unchosen alternative.

Pre- versus Postdecisional Spreading of the Alternatives

An overriding theoretical issue in this research area concerns whether spreading apart of the alternatives occurs before or after making the decision. It has been argued (e.g., by Jones & Gerard, 1967, Janis & Mann, 1968) that, in the case of alternatives initially evaluated quite similarly, spreading apart of the alternatives facilitates, and perhaps even makes possible, a conflict-resolving decision. In the conflict situation the individual attends to the alternatives and revaluates them as a prerequisite to making a hopefully wise decision. Jones and Gerard agree with Festinger that some spreading apart of the alternatives does occur after decision making, but disagree with Festinger in maintaining that some revaluation also occurs before decision making.

Jecker (1964) attempted to demonstrate the greater importance of postdecisional than predecisional processes in producing the spreading apart of alternatives. After female high-school students rated 15 records they were given a choice between two records, supposedly in payment for their help. Two variables were manipulated in the experiment, conflict and dissonance. Conflict was manipulated by information regarding the probability of receiving the unchosen record. All subjects would, of course, receive the chosen record. In a high-conflict condition subjects were told that the chances were 1 out of 20 that they would receive the unchosen record. In a low-conflict condition subjects were told that the chances were 19 out of 20 that they would receive the unchosen record. Information regarding the probability of obtaining the unchosen record was justified on the basis of the supposed supply of available records. Actually half of the subjects in both the high- and low-conflict conditions got only the chosen alternative (dissonance) and half got both the chosen and the unchosen alternative (no dissonance). The results indicated that significant spreading apart of the alternative occurred only with high dissonance (when the subjects received only the chosen alternative). Conflict produced no significant effect. Results supportive of Jecker's were obtained by Allen (1964).

Despite the apparent convincingness of Jecker's results, his experimental design has been criticized by a number of commentators. Zajonc (1968), for example, points out that Jecker confounded conflict and dissonance with disconfirmation of expectations. Disconfirmation of expectancies occurred for the subjects who received the unchosen record when the chances were 1 out of 20 that they would (high-conflict–no-dissonance), and for the subjects who did not get the unchosen record when the chances were 19 out of 20 that they would (low-conflict–dissonance).

Mann, Janis, and Chaplin (1969) report an experiment aimed at clarifying the nature of predecisional processes. They argue that as long as an individual expects more information he will remain open-minded and unbiased in his evaluation of alternatives. As soon as all of the information is in, however, the individual spreads apart the alternatives in order to resolve the conflict-produced tension and reach a decision. The elaborate experiment involved two predecisional ratings of supposedly unpleasant stimulation and then a choice. An information manipulation occurred between the two predecision ratings. Subjects were ushered by a white-coated experimenter into a "physiology" laboratory containing impressive electronic equipment, test tubes, etc. They were told that the experiment was concerned with the effects of physiological stimulations on the ability to carry out intellectual tasks. Accordingly they were to undergo three unpleasant forms of stimulation (movement, taste, and auditory) which might have temporary side effects such as nausea and headaches. Supposedly in order to help the experimenter understand performance on the intellectual task, subjects were asked to make their first (predecisional) rating of the three types of stimulation. Following a waiting period the subjects overheard the experimenter telephoning a senior investigator and reporting that there had been a breakdown in the movement apparatus. The subjects were then told that the movement apparatus had broken down and that, furthermore, there was only time for one type of stimulation. Thus the subjects were to be given a choice between taste and auditory stimulation. In an information condition subjects were informed that before they made their choice they would be given factual reports about the percentage of people suffering side effects from the different stimulations. In a no-information condition subjects were told that unfortunately nothing was known about the percentage of people suffering side effects as a result of the two types of stimulation. Subjects from both conditions were then informed that in view of the unexpected change in procedure it might be a good idea to get another rating of their subjective feelings toward the two types of stimulation. Thus the second predecisional rating was obtained. Finally, the experimenter told *all* subjects that after looking through his files it appeared that equal numbers of people suffered side effects as a result of the two types of stimulation. The subjects then made their choice.

The data were analyzed by examining the difference between the chosen and unchosen alternatives on the second predecisional rating compared to the comparable difference on the first predecisional rating. The results indicated that predecisional spreading apart of the alternatives at the time of the second rating occurred only in the no-information condition. This, of course, is consistent with the original hypothesis that the subject will remain open-minded as long as he thinks there is additional information bearing on the relative merits of the two alternatives.

Does this experiment, however, really demonstrate that spreading apart of the alternatives occurs predecisionally rather than postdecisionally? Certainly spreading apart of the alternatives did occur before the subjects made an *explicit* decision. On the other hand, as Mann, Janis, and Chaplin themselves admit, there is still the possibility that the spreading apart of the alternatives occurred after an *implicit* decision. Such a possibility makes it difficult to obtain definitive results regarding this issue.

REGRET

A final matter relates to the course of dissonance reduction over time. Assuming that making a decision activates processes that produce a spreading apart of the alternatives, how persistent through time is this dissonance-reducing effect? Do individuals ever *regret* their decisions as a result of or in conjunction with an increase in the evaluation of the unchosen alternative and a decrease in the evaluation of the chosen alternative? Walster (1964) reasoned that if regret ever occurs it will more likely appear when the two alternatives have both positive and negative attributes. Her subjects were army draftees from the reception center at Fort Ord. The draftees initially rated a series of occupational specialties, chose which of two they wanted to be assigned for the next 2 years, and then rated the occupational specialties for a second time. The occupational alternatives had been described to the draftees so as to have both desirable and undesirable characteristics. The major manipulation related to the time between the decision and the second rating. This time was systematically varied for different groups of subjects so as to be either 0, 4, 15, or 90 minutes. During the 4, 15, and 90 minute waiting periods the subjects were individually isolated in small cubicles. Mean dissonance reduction scores in the 0, 4, 15, and 90 minute periods were .71, −1.34, 2.14, and 0.31, respectively. A positive score indicates a revaluation of the alternatives so as to reduce dissonance and a negative score a revaluation of the alternatives so as to produce regret. The only indication of regret thus occurred in the 4-minute condition.

Final Statement

Despite some initial methodological reservations relating to the problem of choice reversals, there is no longer any doubt that from before to immediately after making a choice in a free-choice situation the chosen alternative increases in desirability and the unchosen alternative decreases in desirability. Beyond this, however, the issue as to whether this spreading of the alternatives occurs predecisionally, postdecisionally, or both predecisionally and postdecisionally is as yet unresolved. Also, the phenomenon of regret and the general problem of the course of dissonance reduction over time has only begun to be studied. As is typically the case with research, the answering of one question stimulates the asking of still further questions.

READINGS

Effects of Prior Dishonesty on Postdecision Dissonance[1]

Timothy C. Brock

One hundred and forty-five children (aged 3–12) indicated liking for 3 toys and 3 crackers. After being exposed to a temptation to be dishonest and given a choice of 1 of the objects, they gave liking ratings of their chosen and unchosen alternatives. Postdecision dissonance reduction (increased liking for the chosen, and decreased liking for the unchosen alternative) was greatest when choice from among dissimilar objects (toy and cracker) followed dishonesty; it was least when honesty preceded choosing from among similar objects (2 toys or 2 crackers). Results were consistent with formulations by Hull, on drive summation, and Lewin, on tension spread: irrelevant tension combines with relevant tension to produce greater response to the latter.

Cognitive dissonance is thought of as tension with drive character resulting from the juxtaposition of cognitions that do not fit with one another (Festinger, 1957). An interesting theoretical problem concerns the relation between dissonance and other cognitive tensions. The nature of this relation may be understood in terms of models by Hull (1943) and Lewin (1951).

Although exceptions exist (e.g., Grice & Davis, 1957), the bulk of experimental evidence (Amsel, 1950; Brandauer, 1953; Braun, Wedekind, & Smudski, 1957; Kendler, 1945; Siegel, 1946; Webb, 1949) has generally supported derivations from Hull's theory concerning summation effects of irrelevant drives on response strength to the relevant drive. The pertinent formula is $\bar{D} = 100(\dot{D} + D)/\dot{D} + 100$, where $\bar{D}$ means the total effective drive strength operating at a given moment; and D and $\dot{D}$ denote drive strengths ascribable to relevant and to irrelevant or quasi-drives, respectively. The highest value of $\bar{D}$ obtains when both $\dot{D}$ and D are high; the least value of $\bar{D}$, when both $\dot{D}$ and D are low; and intermediate values of $\bar{D}$ under other conditions, i.e., when either $\dot{D}$ or D is high.

Lewin's (1951) expression of the basic relation between neighboring tension systems, $t(S^1)$ and $t(S^2)$, is somewhat analogous to Hull's formula. In Lewin's statement, "b_{s^1} and b_{s^2} indicate the boundaries of the systems

[1] From the *Journal of Abnormal and Social Psychology*, Volume 66, pages 325–331, 1963 (received January 12, 1962). Reproduced by permission of the American Psychological Association. Author's affiliation: Iowa State University. The research was carried out while the author was at the University of Pittsburgh. The writer is greatly indebted to A. R. Cohen for his comments and suggestions.

115

S^1 and S^2, $b_{s^1} \cdot b_{s^2}$ their common part. If $t(S^1) \neq t(S^2)$ and $b_{s^1} \cdot b_{s^2} \neq 0$, a tendency exists to change so that $t(S^1) = t(S^2)$" (p. 11). Tension should be maximal in S^1 when both $t(S^1)$ and $t(S^2)$ are high; least, when both $t(S^1)$ and $t(S^2)$ are low; and intermediate under other conditions.

It is consistent with Hull's and Lewin's formulations to say that irrelevant tension, $\dot{D}$ or $t(S^2)$, may combine or summate with the relevant tension, D or $t(S^1)$, to produce greater response to the latter. The relevant tension in the present study, postdecision dissonance, was varied by manipulating the similarity of alternatives involved in a decision. Selection of the source of irrelevant tension, dishonesty, was based on pilot research which showed that manifest tension, as operationally defined below, was less in tempted subjects who were honest than in those who were dishonest. The relevant tension, postdecision dissonance, should be greater when the decision involves dissimilar rather than similar alternatives (Brehm & Cohen, 1959); it should also be greater when accompanied by tension from an irrelevant source, namely, prior dishonesty. Thus, it was predicted that postdecision dissonance reduction would be greatest for persons making a decision between dissimilar alternatives immediately following dishonest behavior; dissonance reduction would be least for persons making a decision between similar alternatives following honest behavior; dissonance reduction would be intermediate under other conditions (dissimilar-honest, similar-dishonest). Lewin's common boundary requirement was met by having the victim of dishonesty be the same person who provided the choice among alternatives.

METHOD

Children were asked to indicate how much they liked each of three kinds of small toys and each of three kinds of crackers. An attractive guessing contest was introduced in which a child could maximize his chances for winning by being dishonest. Then, about one-half the subjects was given a choice between similar objects (two bags of crackers or two toys) and the other half, a choice between dissimilar objects (a bag of crackers and a toy). It was assumed that postdecision dissonance would be reduced by increased liking of the chosen, and decreased liking of the unchosen alternative (Brehm, 1956; Brehm & Cohen, 1959). An index of the child's change in liking of the chosen and unchosen alternatives was the dependent variable.

Subjects

The original samples consisted of 141 pupils, aged 5–12, at Baldwin Township Highlands School[2] and 37 children, aged 3–4, present for diagnostic testing at Pittsburgh Children's Hospital Speech Clinic. More subjects were available in the two higher of four age categories: 10–12, 7–9, 5–6, 3–4. A selection procedure, to be described later, reduced the usable number in each of these categories to 45, 40, 29, and 31, respectively. In each category the number of boys and girls was approximately the same.

[2] Special thanks are due Thomas Burkhart for his cooperation in obtaining subjects and Richey Hale for her able assistance in collecting the data.

Procedure

The experimenter brought each subject to the experimental room and explained that she was a writer of children's stories and books and needed to have information on "what children liked and didn't like." The experimenter showed the subject six objects: saltine, graham, and cheese crackers, in transparent plastic bags; and three small plastic toys requiring manual manipulation (ring toss, spinning top, and yoyo). The children were allowed to taste a little of each of the crackers and to handle the toys. The experimenter said:

> So that I can have a record of how much you like or don't like each of these things I would like you to rate each one.

Each object was placed at the top of a separate rating sheet on which was printed the name (e.g., Yoyo Toy, Graham Crackers). The subject was asked to "check here on this sheet how you really feel about this [name of toy]." When the ratings were completed, the experimenter put the sheets and objects away in a drawer.

Then the experimenter called the subject's attention to a large (approximately $2' \times 2' \times 2'$) box at her side and said:

> Now I want to tell you about a special guessing contest that we are having here. The reward for winning this contest is two tickets to any movie you want to go to. You can bring your mother with you or anybody you want. Would you like to win those tickets? [All subjects were enthusiastic.] OK, in that box there are three things that most children like to play with and you can win the movie tickets if you can guess what they are. [The box actually contained three familiar playthings.]

While giving these instructions, the experimenter lifted the lid of the box just barely two or three times. Then, the experimenter gave the subject a sheet with clear line drawings of the following: doll, teddy bear, skates, whistle, bat and ball, dump truck, airplane, basketball, sailboat, air rifle, toy blocks, balloons. The experimenter explained that the contest involved guessing which 3 of the 12 objects were in the box; the subject was to check three of the drawings to represent his guess and the winner would be the one who guessed the most correctly. The subject was given a brown manila envelope with his name on it and asked to put his guessing sheet inside when he was finished. When the contest instructions were clearly understood, the experimenter excused herself, saying she had to see a teacher who was waiting for her, that she would be gone 5 minutes, and that the subject should go ahead and check his guesses. When the experimenter left, she took the previously obtained ratings of toys and crackers with her.

On her return, the experimenter put the manila envelope for the guessing contest aside and said:

> Now I would like to give you something for helping me. Here are two things you might have but since I don't have very many I would like you to choose whichever one of these you really want most.

About half the subjects were given a choice between dissimilar objects (a toy and a bag of crackers); half, a choice between similars (two toys or two bags of crackers). Following the subject's choice, the same rating procedure described above was employed for the chosen and unchosen objects. The subject was told to return before going home to pick up the object he had chosen. Finally, the experimenter glanced into the subject's guessing-contest envelope and said:

Well, you got at least one right so you might be the person who will win the movie tickets.

The experimenter enjoined the subject to secrecy to protect his chances of winning and so the contest would not have to be stopped. When the subjects returned for their chosen objects, they were again reminded to maintain secrecy; there was no evidence of contamination. After the completion of the experiment, an arrangement was made to show a movie to all subjects with the rationale being "so many of you made good guesses in the contest." Thus, dishonesty was not differentially rewarded and, of course, each subject was offered a gift he desired.

Measures

Rating Sheet. The rating sheet was a scale consisting of a horizontal line of 71 equally spaced dots with 8 equally spaced markers labeled: don't like it very much; don't like it a lot; don't like it; don't like it a little; like it a little; like it; like it a lot; like it very much. Values were given to these ratings by assigning the numbers 0 through 7.0 to these labels, respectively, and scoring each check to the nearest tenth of an interval (i.e., to the nearest dot on the scale). Subjects were instructed to make a pencil check anywhere along the dotted line.

Manifest Tension. On returning to the experimental room, the experimenter recorded the presence or not of the following behaviors: fidgeting, playing with hands, picking at hem of dress, refusal to look at the experimenter, fixated staring at contest box, startle, hurry to leave, spontaneous verbal confirmation or denial (e.g., saying "I didn't look"), and restlessness (Deutsch, 1954, p. 200; Lewin, 1938, p. 138). The reliability of the manifest tension rating, .87, was determined from scoring of 23 subjects by the experimenter and the writer (who observed the subject through a window in the door of the experimental room).

Dishonesty. After the subject returned to his previous activity, the experimenter compared his guesses with the objects in the box (these were changed frequently by the experimenter as a precaution). A subject with all three correct was considered to have peeked, to have been dishonest, since a blind correct selection of 3 target objects out of 12 is an extremely improbable event.

Control Condition and Modifications for Preschool Subjects

In the control condition, the experimenter remained seated in front of the subject while he guessed what playthings were in the contest box—there was no opportunity for peeking. Forty control subjects were available but the usable number was 15 in the 10–12 year old, and 16, in the 7–9 year old group.

For the preschool subjects, aged 3 and 4, certain modifications were necessary. A 24" × 24" plywood panel was used to conceal the contest objects instead of the box with the liftable lid. The rating sheet labels were slowly read to the subject by the experimenter and, although these subjects were capable of grasping a pencil and making some sort of mark, it was necessary for the experimenter to ask the subject to point to where he wanted his mark to go: the experimenter guided his hand and helped him make his mark. This admittedly crude procedure was only needed for the rating sheets; the drawings on the guessing sheet were so large and distinctive that they were easily marked by the preschool subjects.

Experimenter's Selection of Choice Alternatives and Usable Subjects

When the experimenter left the subject during the guessing period, she selected alternatives for the subjects (within random assignment to similar and dissimilar conditions) in terms of requirements that had to be met to permit an appropriate test of the hypotheses (Brehm & Cohen, 1959). One of the choice objects had to be liked more than the other so that its choice could be expected; but not liked so much that an increase in liking would be impossible. To insure that an initially less liked alternative was seriously considered as a possible choice, its initial rating could not be much lower than that of the more liked alternative. When one alternative is considerably less attractive, little post-decision dissonance is aroused (Brehm, 1956).

The criteria used were: the initially more liked alternative had to receive a rating between 3.8 and 6.5, or, in other words, a moderate to high Liking score; the other alternative could be no more than 1.5 scale points lower, but had to be at least .1 scale point lower (the least measurable difference). When, for 24 subjects it was impossible to satisfy these requirements, the experimenter did not complete the experiment (provide a choice and second ratings): instead, the subject was given the usual secrecy injunction and told he could return at the end of the day to pick up a reward for helping, whatever object he initially rated highest. Data from nine additional subjects were omitted because they did not choose the initially more liked alternative.[3]

RESULTS

The experimenter's recording of manifest tension was made before she knew whether peeking had occurred. One or more tension behaviors were noted in 82% of the Peekers, in 15% of the Nonpeekers, and in 8% of the Control subjects (where opportunity for peeking was ruled out). The difference between the values for the Nonpeekers and the Control subjects was

TABLE 1

Mean Changes in Liking of Chosen and Unchosen Alternatives[a]

Age group	Peeked Dissimilar	Similar	Did not peek Dissimilar	Similar	Control Dissimilar	Similar
10–12						
Chosen	1.11 (7)	0.81 (7)	0.60 (8)	0.46 (8)	0.79 (7)	0.39 (8)
Unchosen	−1.20	−0.80	−0.55	−0.38	−0.57	−0.40
7–9						
Chosen	1.17 (6)	0.70 (5)	0.99 (7)	0.68 (6)	0.75 (8)	0.43 (8)
Unchosen	−1.25	−0.66	−0.94	−0.63	−0.80	−0.43
5–6						
Chosen	1.20 (8)	0.66 (5)	0.75 (8)	0.60 (8)		
Unchosen	−1.24	−0.78	−0.71	−0.54		
3–4						
Chosen	1.39 (7)	0.88 (8)	0.84 (8)	0.61 (8)		
Unchosen	−1.24	−0.83	−0.70	−0.68		

[a] A positive number indicates increased liking, a negative, decreased liking. Cell Ns in parentheses.

[3] These subjects were discarded because their initial ratings were apparently not valid. While this procedure may be questionable, the inclusion or exclusion of these nine subjects made no difference in the results.

not statistically significant but both groups differed from the Peekers at beyond the .001 level.

Analysis of variance of initial ratings of the chosen and unchosen alternatives yielded no between-condition differences ($Fs < 1$). The principal dependent variable was dissonance reduction as measured by decrease in liking for the unchosen alternative and increase in liking for the chosen alternative. For both components (Table 1), results were consistent with predictions: dissonance reduction was greatest when dishonesty preceded a choice between dissimilar alternatives; it was least when subjects were honest before choosing between similar alternatives; and intermediate under other conditions. Subsequent comparisons were based on a dissonance reduction score obtained by adding amount of increase in liking for the chosen to decrease in liking for the unchosen alternative.

An analysis of variance (Table 2) showed a significant main effect ($p < .001$) of the dissimilar-similar variation (thus corroborating the same finding by Brehm & Cohen, 1959); and a main effect of the split into Peekers and Nonpeekers. Prior dishonesty led to greater dissonance reduction than prior honesty ($p < .001$). The significant interaction between similarity and peeking ($p < .05$) was attributed to the fact that the difference within Peekers between Dissimilar and Similar subjects was more than twice as great as the corresponding difference within Nonpeekers. A test of the simple effect of peeking versus nonpeeking under high dissonance (dissimilar alternatives) yielded a two-tailed t of 4.72 ($p < .001$). The direct effect of manifest tension on dissonance reduction was further evaluated by splitting Peekers approximately at their median in manifest tension scores and testing the difference in dissonance reduction between the Highs and Lows thus obtained. Peeking subjects high in manifest tension

TABLE 2

Analysis of Variance of Dissonance Reduction Scores[a]

Source	df	MS	F
Peeking versus No Peeking	1	172.33	20.81*
Dissimilar versus Similar	1	167.90	20.27*
Age group	3	8.02	<1
Peeking × Similarity	1	29.84	3.60**
Peeking × Age	3	8.68	1.05
Similarity × Age	3	1.95	<1
Peeking × Similarity × Age	3	0.58	<1
Error	98	8.283	

[a] Because subclass frequencies were unequal, an approximation by Walker and Lev (1953, p. 381) was employed.

Omits control groups data.

* $p < .05$.

** $p < .001$.

reduced dissonance more than the Lows but the two-tailed t (1.73) fell short of significance (.05 < p < .10).

There is the possibility that an appreciable amount of conflict was created in the Nonpeekers because their honesty was inconsistent with their desire to win a prize (Mills, 1958). If so, this might be reflected in their dissonance reduction scores. The likelihood of this effect in the present experiment was examined by testing the difference between the average dissonance reduction of the Control subjects (1.10, $N = 31$) and that of the 7–12 year old Nonpeekers (1.29, $N = 29$). Although the direction of this difference was consistent with Mills' argument, it was small enough to be attributable to chance variation ($t < 1$). Both of these groups, on the other hand, showed significantly less dissonance reduction than the corresponding group of 7–12 year old Peekers ($p < .01$, two-tailed).

Finally, in that age category had no effect, it was considered appropriate to regard the main predictions as being supported by three replications.[4]

DISCUSSION

The main finding of the present experiment concerned the effect of the arousal of irrelevant cognitive tension on magnitude of dissonance. The results were consistent with minor extensions of formulations by Hull (1943) and Lewin (1951). Temporally proximate tension from dishonesty increased postdecision dissonance beyond the magnitudes produced by choosing between dissimilar (or similar) alternatives. That the variable of irrelevant tension was not a true manipulation but a product of subject self-selection, is, of course, a general qualifier to the following conclusions.

The present results have significance for theories in psychology which recognize that, at a given moment, the individual's behavior is typically energized by *more than one* motive, drive, tension, etc. Some investigators using infrahuman subjects (Kendler, 1945; subsequent authors) have already explored this problem. A significant implication of the present experiment is that the same general formulation, Hull's, leads to confirmable deductions when the motives or tensions involved are cognitive rather than physical. Cognitive tensions "summated" to produce greater response to the relevant tension (dissonance). This result parallels the expectation, for example, that thirsty animals will respond more to hunger than nonthirsty animals. Theoretically, therefore, the present findings strongly reinforce the conceptualization of dissonance as a drive because, when "dissonance" was substituted for "drive" in an appropriate formula, the ensuing derivations were empirically supported.

A second implication concerns the adequacy of present compilations of

---

[4] Although there was a slight nonsignificant tendency for greater peeking among boys in the oldest age category, sex did not contribute to the variance, either in main or interaction effects.

antecedents of dissonance. It has been assumed that dissonance can only occur when inconsistent cognitions are based on relevant need satisfactions: choosing or commiting oneself to Cognition A means giving up the need satisfaction mapped by Cognition B. While this restriction is not being challenged—in fact, it was essential to the derivation that choice between dissimilar alternatives would produce more dissonance than a choice between similars—further elaboration of the theory may be required. Knowledge or manipulation of motives or cognitions irrelevant to the dissonance setting ones will enable the investigator to make more precise predictions. When the conditions for differential dissonance are produced, the introduction or presence of a temporally contiguous but irrelevant tension generates greater response to dissonance (its reduction) than when irrelevant tension is not present or has not been introduced. This proposition assumes that contiguous irrelevant tension will always summate with dissonance and it is unspecific as to the basis for the irrelevant tension. Whether summation (and not interference or canceling) will, in fact, always occur, and, whether the source of tension is immaterial (appetition, noxious stimulation, etc.), are problems for further research.

Lewinian Explanation

In Lewin's terms, tension spread from an innerpersonal system concerned with conflict between superego prescriptions and actual behavior to another system concerned with disparities between what was gained and what was relinquished by making a decision. Spread of tension was facilitated by overlap among the two systems: the victim of dishonesty was the same person who preferred the choice among alternatives. Given this framework, an explanation was sought by examining relations that can exist between neighboring systems. Two have been emphasized: intercommunication or spread of tension between innerpersonal systems corresponds to fluidity and/or level of reality-irreality (Lewin, 1951, pp. 11–29); a dominant system "uses" a subordinate system as its "tool" (Lewin, 1938, pp. 102–104). In terms of the first possibility, it might be assumed that each subject felt some tension merely from being left alone by the experimenter and exposed to a temptation. Subjects who peeked adopted a relatively more irreal level of functioning than those who did not peek. Thus, for peeking subjects, fluidity among innerpersonal systems was increased: any tension that was present would be communicated more readily to neighboring systems, specifically, that concerned with the decision. The honest subjects, on the other hand, although also experiencing tension, maintained relatively impermeable boundaries between innerpersonal systems: tension did not spread to motoric systems (significantly less was actually observed) or to the decision situation. The gist of this explanation is that dishonesty implies departure from reality functioning and thereby increases fluidity between innerpersonal systems and consequent intercommunication of tension.

A second possibility involves the notion that one innerpersonal region or system bears an instrumental relation to another. Lewin assumed force fields corresponding to relatively central and relatively peripheral innerpersonal systems. It is plausible to assume that concern with violating superego prescriptions mobilized a relatively central system; and the decision situation, a relatively peripheral system. The former is concerned with highly salient ethical standards, and the latter, with simple tastes and preferences; violation of an ethical rule is more consequential for the person than choosing between crackers and toys. According to Lewin, "the basic dynamical fact" is that tension in a field of forces corresponding to a peripheral system may be induced by tension in a field of forces corresponding to a central system. Reduction of tension in the peripheral serves tension reduction in the central system. If this explanation is correct, residual tension from dishonesty should be less for high than for low dissonance reducing subjects. Some indirect evidence concerning this implication was available by making a further assumption: subjects who felt considerable tension from dishonesty would be less likely to return to pick up their chosen object than subjects who felt little or none. When all subjects were split at the median into Highs and Lows according to their dissonance reduction scores, there was no difference in number of returning subjects within Nonpeekers (96% of the Highs and 100% of the Lows). Within Peekers, however, the values were 88% for the Highs and 56% for the Lows. These differences were consistent with the assumption that reduction of tension in a peripheral system (dissonance tension) *served* reduction of tension in a central system (dishonesty tension).

Dissonance Interpretations

Peeking might be said to have aroused dissonance since dishonesty does not follow from usual values and training (Mills, 1958). Thus, "dissonance" might be substituted for "irrelevant tension" and the argument recast in terms of cumulating dissonances. This view requires the assumption (Brehm, 1960, pp. 182–183) that restraining forces, values and training, and inducing forces, attractiveness of movie ticket prize, were roughly equivalent for both Peekers and Nonpeekers. However, to paraphrase Brehm, honest subjects presumably had a strong attitude against peeking prior to the experiment or they would have peeked when tempted. If this issue of self-selection can be ignored, a problem still remaining concerns how dissonance occasioned by peeking can be reduced by revaluation of choice alternatives. A possibility is that a person can reduce dissonance from dishonesty by increased liking for whatever he is subsequently given by the victim of his dishonesty. This hypothesis might suggest *increased* liking of the chosen but not obviously *decreased* liking of the unchosen alternative. The appropriate test was examination of differential change in liking of the chosen alternatives separately to see whether the chosen alternative contributed a greater difference between Peekers and Nonpeekers than did the unchosen. Contrary to this account, the difference between the means for Peekers and Nonpeekers on the chosen alternative (.32) was *less* than that on the unchosen alternative (.38). These values did not differ reliably $(t < 1)$.

A second dissonance formulation was suggested by research on the role of volition in determining magnitude of forced compliance dissonance. See Cohen's (1960) review. A person given a choice in the enactment of some behavior experiences dissonance when the behavior does not follow from some prior cognition or experience. It was assumed that acceptance of a gift from the experimenter did not follow from victimization of the experimenter by dishonesty. At least, gift acceptance was considered less inappropriate by a subject who behaved honestly when tempted. Thus, some overall dissonance may have been present for Peekers, but not for Nonpeekers, because they were accepting a gift from a person they victimized and volition was engaged in choosing the gift. Dissonance from these sources may have combined with that from the decision to produce heightened revaluation of the choice alternatives. In sum, it was difficult to prefer either Lewinian or dissonance interpretations because manifest tension was present in Peekers before the choice situation.

REFERENCES

Amsel, A. The combination of a primary appetitional need with primary and secondary emotionally derived needs. *Journal of Experimental Psychology,* 1950, **40**, 1–14.

Brandauer, C. M. A confirmation of Webb's data concerning the action of irrelevant drives. *Journal of Experimental Psychology,* 1953, **45**, 150–152.

Braun, H. W., Wedekind, C. E., & Smudski, J. F. The effect of an irrelevant drive on maze learning in the rat. *Journal of Experimental Psychology,* 1957, **54**, 148–152.

Brehm, J. W. Postdecision changes in the desirability of alternatives. *Journal of Abnormal & Social Psychology,* 1956, **52**, 384–389.

Brehm, J. W. A dissonance analysis of attitude-discrepant behavior. In M. J. Rosenberg & C. I. Hovland (Eds.), *Attitude organization and change.* Chapter 5. New Haven, Connecticut. Yale University Press, 1960.

Brehm, J. W., & Cohen, A. R. Re-evaluation of choice alternatives as a function of their number and qualitative similarity. *Journal of Abnormal & Social Psychology,* 1959, **58**, 373–378.

Cohen, A. R. Attitudinal consequences of induced discrepancies between cognitions and behavior. *Public Opinion Quarterly,* 1960, **24**, 297–318.

Deutsch, M. Field theory in social science. In G. Lindzey (Ed.), *Handbook of social psychology.* Vol. 1. *Theory and method.* Reading, Massachusetts: Addison-Wesley, 1954. Pp. 181–222.

Festinger, L. *A theory of cognitive dissonance.* Evanston, Illinois: Row, Peterson, 1957.

Grice, G. R., & Davis, J. D. Effect of an irrelevant thirst motivation on a response learned with food reward. *Journal of Experimental Psychology,* 1957, **53**, 347–352.

Hull, C. L. *Principles of behavior.* New York: Appleton-Century, 1943.

Kendler, H. H. Drive interaction: I. Learning as a function of the simultaneous presence of hunger and thirst drives. *Journal of Experimental Psychology,* 1945, **35,** 96–109.

Lewin, K. The conceptual representation and measurement of psychological forces. *Contract Psychology Theory,* 1938, 1, No. 4.

Lewin, K. *Field theory in social science.* New York: Harper, 1951.

Mills, J. Changes in moral attitudes following temptation. *Journal of Personality,* 1958, **26,** 517–531.

Siegel, P. S. Alien drive, habit strength, and resistance to extinction. *Journal of Comparative Psychology,* 1946, **39,** 307–317.

Walker, Helen M., & Lev, J. *Statistical inference.* New York: Holt, 1953.

Webb, W. B. The motivational aspect of an irrelevant drive in the behavior of the white rat. *Journal of Experimental Psychology,* 1949, **39,** 1–14.

Chapter 5

DISSONANCE IN FORCED-COMPLIANCE SITUATIONS

According to Festinger (1957) forced compliance exists when public pressure forces an individual to engage in behavior that is inconsistent or dissonant with his beliefs or attitudes. The compliant pressure may arise from threatened punishment or offered reward, but once the behavior has occurred dissonance results. If someone is offered a sizable bribe for betraying his country he is placed in an approach-avoidance conflict (Lewin, 1935). The bribe is attractive but the betrayal is not. Once the individual makes a choice for either of the alternatives, dissonance is created. Suppose, on the other hand, our hypothetical individual is told that unless he betrays his country his wife and children will be harmed. He is now in an avoidance-avoidance conflict (Lewin, 1935). Neither of the alternatives is attractive. In this avoidance-avoidance conflict, as in the previous approach-avoidance conflict, once a decision is made, dissonance is created. In both instances there are forced-compliant pressures to engage in behavior that is inconsistent with the individual's beliefs or attitudes.

127

In this chapter we will examine some of the factors that seem to be important in forced-compliance situations: reward, punishment (threatened or actual), effort, and choice. We will begin, however, with a discussion of the simple effect of counterattitudinal role-playing.

Counterattitudinal Role-Playing

Counterattitudinal role-playing occurs when an individual engages in behavior inconsistent with his beliefs and attitudes. Counterattitudinal role-playing is illustrated by the nonbeliever who attends and actively takes part in church activities. Dissonance results from the fact that the role behavior is inconsistent with existing attitudes and beliefs. Most of the research on counterattitudinal role-playing has been concerned with the special case of counterattitudinal advocacy. Counterattitudinal advocacy occurs when an individual argues for a point of view opposite from his own, as for example in a debate. Research on the simple effect of counterattitudinal advocacy has not been concerned with the factors producing the advocacy behavior (rewards, reasons or justifications, etc.) or with the amount of freedom the individual experienced when deciding to engage in the behavior, but rather with just the effect of the presence or absence of the advocacy upon attitude or belief change. The predecisional variables are presumably held constant. The requisite control condition for demonstrating an effect for counterattitudinal advocacy is a situation in which subjects are exposed to counterattitudinal arguments that they themselves did not produce. If experimental subjects who develop counterattitudinal arguments are more influenced than control subjects who are exposed to similar counterattitudinal arguments, evidence exists for the special persuasive power of counterattitudinal advocacy over and above the simple effect of exposure to information.

Janis and King (1954) did the pioneer investigation in this area. Four weeks before the experimental sessions an opinion or belief questionnaire was passed out in a large class. The questionnaire contained three key items concerning opinions about: the number of movie theaters that would be in existence three years hence, the total supply of meat available to the United States in 1953, and the number of years it would take to find a cure for the common cold. Upon arriving at the experimental session, groups of three subjects were told that they were taking part in a project designed to develop a test of oral-speaking ability. Accordingly, each subject was given a prepared outline relating to one of the above issues and asked to give an informal talk. The outlines presented arguments advocating a decrease below the opinion estimates previously given by any of the subjects. While each subject gave his counterattitudinal talk the other two subjects listened. After the final talk each subject filled out a questionnaire assessing both the performance of the other subjects and his opinion regarding the three key issues.

Janis and King analyzed their results by comparing the before-after changes for the speakers with the similar before-after changes for the nonspeakers. Such a comparison allows for a test of the special persuasive impact of advocacy over and above that of simple exposure to information. The results indicated that the speakers changed more than the nonspeakers on the movie theater and meat supply issues and nonsignificantly more on the common cold issue. Overall there is little doubt that counterattitudinal advocacy in fact had an effect. Subsequent research has overwhelmingly documented this fact (see Insko, 1967).

A dramatic illustration of the impact of counterattitudinal role-playing (which does not explicitly involve advocacy) is the Janis and Mann (1965) experiment, contained in the Readings section of this chapter. Janis and Mann found that role-playing a lung cancer patient produces both attitude change and a reported reduction in smoking.

Janis is not a dissonance theorist and prefers to interpret his results as simply demonstrating the effect of role behavior upon beliefs and attitudes. Festinger (1957), however, explicitly cites the Janis and King (1954) study as illustrating the general effect of forced compliance. From our present vantage point there does not seem to be any convincing way of deciding whether a dissonance orientation or a general role orientation provides the more appropriate way of interpreting the counterattitudinal role-playing literature.

Reward and Forced Compliance

According to Festinger (1957) the less the reward used to induce forced-compliant behavior the greater the resultant dissonance. If an adult accepted a million dollars to state publicly that he valued and liked comic books, he would suffer very little dissonance. On the other hand, if the reward were only $.10 the dissonance would be markedly greater. Festinger states that the dissonance resulting from forced-compliant behavior can be reduced in any of a number of ways: reducing the importance of the attitude or behavior involved, changing the private attitude so as to agree with the public behavior, or magnification of the reward used to induce the behavior. Such multiple consequences of dissonance make testing of the theory rather difficult. Most investigators, however, have focused upon attitude change as the most likely mode of dissonance reduction. Thus research has concentrated on testing the prediction that the less the reward used to induce forced-compliant behavior the greater the attitude change.

Festinger and Carlsmith (1959) report a well-known experiment on the effect of reward in a forced-compliant situation. After spending an hour at tasks designed to be boring (spool packing and peg turning) individual male subjects were informed that the experiment was over, but that their help was needed in introducing the next subject to the experiment. It was explained that the stooge who normally did this had failed to arrive. The stooge's job was to act like a subject who had just finished the experiment and to tell the waiting subject that the experiment was interesting and fun. As payment for deceiving the waiting subject and for being on call in case of future emergencies some of the subjects were offered $1 and some $20. After talking to the waiting subject (who was actually a female stooge) the subjects were taken to another office and introduced to an interviewer. It had earlier been announced in the class from which the subjects were obtained that a sample of subjects would be interviewed to provide the psychology department with information concerning reactions to research being conducted under its auspices. During the course of the interview the subjects were asked how enjoyable they considered the experimental tasks. This, of course, provided an assessment of the dependent variable of principal interest to Festinger and Carlsmith. The results indicated that the subjects receiving $1 as incentive for deceiving the waiting "subject" actually regarded the experimental tasks as more enjoyable than the subjects who received $20. The results thus conform to Festinger's nonobvious prediction. Theoretically the dissonance created by compliance for a low or insufficient reward was reduced through increased evaluation of the experimental tasks. Due to the fact that $1 was not sufficient incentive for falsely maintaining that dull tasks were in fact enjoyable, the dissonance was reduced through an increased evaluation of the tasks.

Superficially Festinger and Carlsmith's results appear to disagree with the results of the Scott (1957) experiment. Scott found that subjects who thought they won a debate were more influenced in the direction of (counterattitudinal) advocacy than subjects who thought they lost. There are at least two important differences between Scott's situation and Festinger and Carlsmith's situation. First, in Festinger and Carlsmith's situation the behavior was induced by a reward, while this was not the case in Scott's situation. Second, in Scott's situation the reward was supposedly contingent upon the quality of performance, while this was not the case in Festinger and Carlsmith's situation.

Unfortunately subsequent research has not always succeeded in replicating Festinger and Carlsmith's findings. Some investigators have obtained dissonance results (an inverse relation between reward and attitude change), some have obtained reinforcement results (a direct relation between reward and attitude change), and some have obtained neither dissonance nor reinforcement results. In such a situation it is necessary to identify the variables or circumstances accounting for the differing results, and social psychologists have devoted a considerable amount of time and effort to doing just that. Unfortunately, however, research has demonstrated that many of the suggested formulations are inadequate.

Nel, Helmreich, and Aronson (1969) have made one of the recent attempts at reconciliation. Their rather elaborate experiment was an attempt to test the general hypothesis that dissonance is created whenever the counterattitudinal act diminishes evaluation of the self. They reasoned that counterattitudinal advocacy will more likely violate the self-concept if the advocacy is expected to have a persuasive impact than if it is not expected to have a persuasive impact. Female college students who had previously filled out a questionnaire indicating they were strongly opposed to legalization of marijuana were called on the telephone and asked to take part in an experiment for required course credit. When they arrived individually at the experimental room it was explained by an experimenter (hereafter referred to as the first experimenter) that they were to fill out first a value survey and then an opinion poll. After about 10 minutes a second experimenter knocked on the door and asked if the subjects would be willing to help her make a video tape about marijuana. The second experimenter stated that the activity was not part of an experiment and she could not give class credit, but she did have money from a research grant which would enable her to pay the subjects. (All subjects agreed to make the video tape.) When the subjects finished the value survey and started the opinion poll it was noticed that the first page occurred twice and there was no second page. The first experimenter then explained that, since she would have to go to the next building to obtain the proper page, the subjects might as well go ahead and make the video before completing the opinion poll. (Unknown to the subjects, the missing page assessed attitude toward the legalization of marijuana.)

Upon arriving at the second experimental room, the second experimenter explained that she was preparing materials to be used in research on the attitudes of a large group of students about the use of marijuana. At this point the first manipulation concerning the attitudes of the intended audience was introduced. One group of subjects was told that a survey had indicated that the students were largely uninformed about marijuana and didn't really have strong opinions. A second group of subjects was told that the students were favorable toward marijuana, and a third group of subjects was told that the students were unfavorable toward marijuana. After informing them as to the nature of the intended audience, the subjects were given an outline containing five arguments for the legalization of marijuana and asked to elaborate on these arguments while a video tape was made of their advocacy. Some of the subjects were offered $.50 and some $5.00 for making the tape. All subjects were given the freedom to refuse and one, in fact, did. After making the tape it was played back and they made ratings of sincerity and persuasiveness. The subjects finally returned to the first experimental room where they filled out the previously missing page of the opinion poll, which assessed, among other things, attitude toward the legalization of marijuana.

Nel *et al.* predicted that a dissonance effect, or inverse relation between money and attitude change, would occur only when the audience was neutral and uncommitted. With the neutral audience there was more of a possibility that the advocacy would have a persuasive impact. Thus in this situation the consequences of the advocacy behavior were contrary to the subject's self-concept. The results supported this reasoning. Only with the neutral audience did the $.50 have a significantly greater effect than the $5.00 in producing favorable attitudes toward the legalization of marijuana.

Cooper and Worchel (1970) have approached this problem by using the original Festinger and Carlsmith procedure. Recall that Festinger and Carlsmith gave subjects different amounts of money for convincing the waiting "subject" (actually a stooge) that the boring task was actually interesting and fun. Cooper and Worchel's experiment differed from Festinger and Carlsmith's in two salient respects. First and most important, there was a manipulation of whether or not the waiting stooge appeared to be convinced by the subject's argument that the task was interesting and fun. For half of the subjects, the stooge appeared convinced and for half unconvinced. Second, rather than different amounts of money, Cooper and Worchel used different amounts of experimental credit. The subjects were drawn from the introductory psychology class at Duke University and needed to obtain a specified amount of credit for participating in psychological experiments.

The results indicated that when the stooge was unconvinced incentive had no effect on the subjects' rated enjoyment of the task, but when the stooge was convinced the expected dissonance effect occurred; that is, there was an inverse relation between reward and attitude change. The task was rated more enjoyable with low reward than with high.

These results nicely complement those of Nel et al. in which the nature of the intended audience (and hence the anticipated persuasive impact) was manipulated. Cooper and Worchel also claim that their condition in which the stooge appeared convinced roughly parallels what happened in the Festinger and Carlsmith experiment. Cooper and Worchel point out that after an initial disagreement the stooge "listened quietly, accepting and agreeing to everything the subject told her" (Festinger & Carlsmith, 1959, p. 206).

Punishment and Forced Compliance

Research on the role of punishment in a forced-compliance situation can be broken down into four types: compliance in an avoidance conflict, noncompliance in an avoidance-avoidance conflict, compliance in an approach-avoidance conflict, and noncompliance in an approach-avoidance conflict. An avoidance-avoidance conflict is illustrated by the situation in which an individual is threatened with physical harm if he does not engage in some disliked behavior such as lying. If the individual is forced by the threatened punishment into the disliked behavior he is complying; if not, he is said to show noncompliance. An approach-avoidance conflict is illustrated by a situation in which an individual has to tolerate punishing or unpleasant circumstances (e.g., initiation) in order to reach some desirable goal (e.g., membership in a fraternity). If the individual decides not to tolerate the punishment he is complying (with the implications of the punishment); if he decides to tolerate the punishment, he is said to show noncompliance. Compliance occurs when the individual's behavior is determined by the implications of the punishment. Thus deciding not to tolerate an initiation is an illustration of compliance, even though the fraternity may expect otherwise. While there is literature bearing on each of the four types of situations, somewhat more attention has been paid to the two types of approach-avoidance conflicts. Discussion will thus be limited to compliance in approach-avoidance conflicts and noncompliance in approach-avoidance conflicts.

Compliance in Approach-Avoidance Conflicts

Aronson and Carlsmith (1963) investigated the effect of severity of threat for playing with a desirable toy upon dissonance-reducing disparagement of this toy by compliant nursery school children. Theoretically avoidance of the toy following a mild threat should produce more dissonance than avoidance of the toy following a severe threat. Since the compliant-resultant dissonance can be reduced through disparagement of the avoided toy, Aronson and Carlsmith predicted a lesser valuation of the toy in a mild-threat condition than in a severe-threat condition. Each child's initial evaluation of five toys was assessed with a paired comparison technique. Then the children were individually left alone for 10 minutes after being told that they were not to play with one of the toys. The forbidden toy was always the one ranked second by each child. In the mild-threat condition the children were told that the experimenter would be annoyed if they played with the forbidden toy and in a severe-threat condition they were told that he would be extremely upset and take away all of the toys if they played with the forbidden toy. During the 10-minute period in which each child was alone he or she was observed through a one-way mirror. None of the children played with the forbidden toy. After returning to the room the experimenter had the children evaluate the toys a second time. The results indicated that the forbidden toy decreased in attractiveness in the mild-threat condition and unexpectedly increased in attractiveness in the severe-threat condition. The unexpected increase in the severe-threat condition was interpreted as being due to satiation with the other

toys. Subsequent research has, by and large, supported Aronson and Carlsmith's findings.

Noncompliance in Approach-Avoidance Conflicts

Aronson and Mills (1959) were the first investigators to study the dissonance effects of noncompliance in an approach-avoidance conflict. Their
results imply that the evaluation of a group by its members varies directly
with the severity of initiation. The more severe the initiation the greater
the dissonance in noncompliant individuals who are not deterred by the
obstacle. Since the resultant dissonance can be reduced by increased valuation of the group, Aronson and Mills predicted that subjects in a severe-
initiation condition should evaluate the group more highly than subjects
in a mild-initiation condition. The subjects were female college students
who had expressed an interest in joining a group concerned with the psychology of sex. When the subjects individually arrived they were told that
in order to avoid embarrassment it had been decided that the group members would not see each other but would communicate by microphones and
headphones. In order to join the group the subjects were required to take
an "embarrassment test." In the severe-initiation condition the test was
to read in the presence of a male experimenter 12 obscene words and two
vivid descriptions of sexual activity from contemporary novels. In the mild-
initiation condition the test was to read five sexual, but nonobscene, words
in the presence of the male experimenter. After completing the initiation,
the subjects were told that since they had not completed the required
preparation they could not participate in the group discussion that was
already in progress. They were, however, allowed to listen via headphones.
The group discussion, which was actually tape-recorded, was a purpose-
fully dull discussion of the secondary sexual activity of animals. At the
conclusion of the recording the subjects filled out a questionnaire which
asked for an evaluation of the discussion. The results indicate that, in
accordance with prediction, the discussion was evaluated more highly in
the severe-initiation condition than in the mild-initiation condition.

Although supportive of the dissonance prediction the Aronson and
Mills results are subject to a sizeable number of alternative explanations.
In an experiment contained in the Readings section of this chapter Gerard
and Mathewson (1966) utilized a complex experimental design in an attempt to rule out these alternative explanations. Their results are consistent
with the dissonance account of noncompliance in an approach-avoidance
situation.

Effort and Forced Compliance

Dissonance theory can be interpreted as indicating that the greater the
amount of effort expended on some task the greater the arousal of disso-

nance and consequent dissonance-reducing increased evaluation of the task (e.g., Aronson, 1961). If the task is to develop or to comprehend a counterattitudinal communication, the prediction is that effort expenditure will result in increased agreement with the communication. Wicklund, Cooper, and Linder (1967) report two experiments supporting this prediction. In both experiments Wicklund *et al.* found that the anticipation of effort *preliminary* to exposure to a counterattitudinal communication resulted in increased agreement with the announced topic of the communication. In the first experiment subjects at Duke University initially indicated on a classroom questionnaire their agreement-disagreement with a number of statements, including a key one, "The federal government is assuming too many of the responsibilities which should be left up to the states." Approximately 8 weeks later subjects who had initially agreed with this statement were recruited for the experiment. Upon individually arriving at the laboratory, subjects were told that the purpose of the study was to evaluate the effect of voice quality upon the comprehension and understanding of an orally presented communication. Accordingly the same communication had been tape-recorded by individuals having voices of differing qualities. All subjects were supposedly to hear the same communication, but different groups were to hear different speakers. A comprehension and recall test was to be administered following exposure to the communication. It was further explained that the standard message was a speech given at Duke University a few years ago by Luther Hodges, former Secretary of Commerce and governor of North Carolina. The speech supposedly consisted of a number of arguments supporting the position that ". . . the federal government should assume more of a role in matters that have traditionally been left to the states." At this point the manipulation of effort or delay was introduced. In the long-delay (or high-effort) condition the subjects were told that the experiment was being conducted simultaneously by another psychologist down the hall, and by an unfortunate coincidence he was running the same condition the subject was supposed to be in. Since the other experimenter was using the tape there would be a 15-minute delay before the experiment could proceed. Such a 15-minute wait would require that the subject wait 10 minutes more than the 30-minute period for which he or she had originally agreed to serve in the experiment. All subjects were given an explicit choice of waiting or leaving. In the short-delay (or low effort) condition subjects were informed that there would be a 1-minute delay before the experimenter down the hall finished with the tape. Subjects in this condition were also given the choice of waiting or leaving. All subjects in both delay conditions agreed to wait. Finally, the experimenter informed the subjects that while they were waiting they could fill out a questionnaire which might be relevant to their performance on the recall test. The questionnaire assessed attitude toward the communication topic. This assessment ended the experiment. Subjects thus neither heard the communication nor waited the requisite time. The experimental manipulation related entirely to anticipations of hearing a counterattitudinal communication and the length of preliminary delay. The results indicated significantly more agreement with the counterattitudinal communication in the long-delay condition than in the short-delay condition.

Wicklund's *et al.* second experiment was like the first except that the communication advocated elimination of draft deferments for college students, and the manipulation of effort was somewhat different. In the high-effort condition subjects anticipated having to run while standing in place for seven minutes prior to hearing the counterattitudinal communication, and in the low-effort condition subjects anticipated having to sit quietly for seven minutes prior to hearing the counterattitudinal communication. These anticipated activities were justified with a cover story explaining that the experiment was an investigation of the effect of heart rate on recall. As in the first experiment the subjects neither heard the communication nor exerted the requisite effort. The results indicated significantly more agreement with the counterattitudinal communication in the high-effort condition than in the low-effort condition.

In the two Wicklund *et al.* experiments the subjects were aware both of the effort and the point of view advocated in the communication before choosing to hear the communication. In a subsequent experiment Linder, Cooper, and Wicklund (1968) found that if subjects choose to listen to a communication before learning either of the preliminary effort or of the point of view advocated in the communication, the anticipation of high effort did not facilitate persuasion. High effort involved the anticipated memorization of nonsense syllables and low effort involved sitting quietly for seven minutes. The communication supposedly argued against expansion of the rehabilitation program of the state prison system. Subjects were told that the experimenter was interested in the effect of performing prior mental tasks on later ability to recall verbal material (like that contained in the communication). When the choice to hear the communication was made with full knowledge of the preliminary effort and the point of view advocated in the communication, high anticipated effort facilitated persuasion. When the choice to hear the communication was made prior to learning either of the preliminary effort or of the point of view advocated in the communication, anticipated effort did not facilitate persuasion. Such results argue for the importance of choice in the creation of dissonance.

Toward the Reinterpretation of Dissonance Theory

Since Festinger's (1957) original statement of dissonance theory there have been a number of attempts at revision or reinterpretation. We will look at three such attempts: Brehm and Cohen's (1962) choice, commitment, and volition interpretation; Aronson's (1968) expectancies interpretation; and Bem's (1965, 1967) attribution interpretation.

BREHM AND COHEN'S CHOICE, COMMITMENT, AND VOLITION INTERPRETATION

In their influential book on dissonance theory Brehm and Cohen (1962) argue for the crucial role of choice, commitment, and volition in the production of dissonance. Choice is involved in both free-choice and forced-compliance situations. When the individual makes a choice in some type of conflict he acquires a commitment to one alternative or course of action. It is the inconsistency between other cognitions and the commitment that produces dissonance. Volition, like commitment, is also involved when an individual makes a choice in a conflict situation. Volition implies control of and responsibility for the consequences of one's actions. Brehm and Cohen explicitly state that the greater the volition (control of and responsibility for a choice) the greater the dissonance. The implication of this line of reasoning is that the attractiveness of the alternatives, reward, punishment, and effort arouse dissonance only when they have an effect upon volition. Although it is by no means clear when it is that such variables will have an effect upon volition, it is not unreasonable to assume some sort of causal linkage. For example, it is reasonable to assume that insufficient reward for counterattitudinal advocacy will increase the control of and responsibility for the consequences of one's actions. The less the reward offered to induce counterattitudinal advocacy the more likely the individual will experience control of his actions and acknowledge responsibility for the consequences of his actions. The individual cannot argue that he had "no choice" because the reward was of such overwhelming magnitude.

Festinger (1957) maintains that involuntary exposure to information may create dissonance. In Chapter 6 we will discuss the literature that relates to one aspect of involuntary exposure—the discrepancy between the position of the communicator and the position of the communicatee. According to Brehm and Cohen it is equivocal whether or not involuntary exposure will create dissonance. Brehm and Cohen argue that only when some past volition could have prevented the communicatee from having the cognitions that are contrary to the point of view advocated in the communication will involuntary exposure create dissonance. From a research point of view tracking down the existence of past volitions may, of course, be an extremely difficult if not impossible task. In general, Brehm and Cohen prefer to limit dissonance theory to situations in which the subject makes an observed choice and thus is known to have a specific commitment.

ARONSON'S EXPECTANCIES INTERPRETATION

According to Festinger "two elements are in a dissonant relation if, considering these two alone, the obverse of one element would follow from the other" (1957, p. 13). This definition of dissonance sounds very precise. Festinger goes on, however, to elaborate various meanings of "follow from" and to point out that the phrase should not be interpreted literally. After confronting the above lack of conceptual clarity, Aronson (1968) states that dissonance can best be conceptualized as a violation of expectancies. Thus to walk in the rain and not get wet would create dissonance, not because getting wet "follows from" walking in the rain, but because walking in the rain leads to the expectancy of getting wet.

Aronson goes on to argue that in the clearest experimental tests of dissonance theory the expectancies have related to the self-concept. Given the subject's expectancy that he as a decent person should act in a decent manner, it is dissonant to have misled someone by misinforming him that a boring task is actually quite interesting. In the Festinger and Carlsmith (1959) experiment dissonance does not flow from the relation between believing that a task is boring and telling someone that it is interesting but from the violation of expectancies flowing from the self-concept. As Aronson points out, lying does not create dissonance in a psychopathic liar. Here there is no violation of expectancies. The fact, however, that most people conceive of themselves as basically moral and decent has led dissonance researchers to intuitively pick experimental situations in which expectancies regarding the self are involved.

It was such theoretical reasoning which led Nel et al. (1969) to design the previously referred to study on insufficient reward. Nel et al. make the interesting point that when the subject chooses to behave counterattitudinally, expectancies regarding the self are more likely to be violated. The implication of this statement is that Brehm and Cohen's emphasis on choice is justified only insofar as the presence of choice raises expectancies regarding the self.

Nel, Helmreich, and Aronson point out that an emphasis on the importance of the self has also been made by Collins (1969) and Bramel (1968). Actually, however, Brown (1965) anticipated everyone with a remarkably perceptive discussion of the meaning of dissonance. Like Aronson, Brown arrives at the conclusion that dissonance involves the violation of expectancies. Unlike Aronson, however, Brown makes the further point that ". . . if we seek out the sources of these various expectations we will find that some of them are ultimately logical" (1965, p. 596). The logical relations are produced by what Brown calls "suppressed premises." Thus dissonance exists between the propositions "Canada is north of the United States" and "Windsor is south of Detroit" because of the suppressed premises, or implicitly held beliefs, that "Windsor is a part of Canada" and "Detroit is a part of the United States." If someone did not believe the premises there would be no dissonance. This leads Brown to observe that the most obvious way of determining the dissonant effects of a combination of ideas would be to ask subjects about their beliefs (or suppressed premises). This procedure, however, has not been followed. Rather experimenters have worked with situations in which the suppressed premises are widely held. Such premises are complementary to the self. Brown lists a number of such premises which he believes to have formed the basis of dissonance effects: "(1) I say what I believe; (2) I do what I want to do; (3) If I willingly endure something unpleasant it always turns out to have been worth it; (4) What I choose is better than anything I reject" (1965, pp. 597–598). If a subject believed that he were ". . . a liar with bad luck, poor judgment, and no will power" the more typical attempts to create dissonance would fail.

BEM'S ATTRIBUTION INTERPRETATION

Daryl Bem (1965, 1967) has developed an alternative explanation of various dissonance effects in terms of self-perception. According to Bem self-descriptive attitude statements are mostly a function of the individual's observation of his own behavior and the external stimulus conditions in which the behavior occurs. The individual observes his own behavior and thus attributes himself with an attitude. According to Bem (1967), an individual's self-descriptive attitude statements

> . . . are functionally similar to those that any outside observer could make about him. When the answer to the question, "Do you like brown bread?" is "I guess I do, I'm always eating it," it seems unnecessary to invoke a fount of privileged self-knowledge to account for the reply. In such a case the reply is functionally equivalent to one his wife might give for him: "I guess he does, he is always eating it." Only to the extent that "brown bread" elicits strongly conditioned internal responses might he have additional evidence, not currently available to his wife, on which to base his self-descriptive attitude statement [p. 186].

Bem's "I must be afraid because I'm running" point of view initially strikes one as outlandish. Research on emotion (Schachter, 1964), however, has demonstrated that the self-attribution hypothesis has much to commend it. This literature will be discussed in Chapter 8. For now our only purpose is to discuss the relevance of self-attribution to various dissonance effects.

Bem (1967) attempts to show how his theoretical point of view can account for dissonance effects in forced-compliance and free-choice situations. He demonstrates that observer subjects who merely read summaries of the procedure in one condition of a dissonance experiment will attribute to actor subjects the same attitudes as were found in the original experiment. The first simulation that Bem reports is of the previously described experiment by Festinger and Carlsmith (1959). It will be recalled that Festinger and Carlsmith found that subjects who were paid $1.00 to argue counterattitudinally changed their attitudes to a greater extent than subjects who were paid $20.00. When Bem's observer subjects read the procedure in either the $1.00 condition or the $20.00 condition they attributed the actor subjects in the $1.00 condition with more advocacy-consistent attitudes than the actor subjects in the $20.00 condition, thus reproducing the Festinger and Carlsmith results. Similarly, in a simulated replication of a free-choice experiment Bem found that observer subjects believed that actor subjects who made a choice evaluated the chosen alternative more highly than actual control subjects who did not make a choice.

Why is it that Bem's observer subjects were able to attribute the same attitudes to actor subjects as actor subjects describe themselves as having? Consider the Festinger and Carlsmith study. When the observer subjects learned that an actor subject was induced to argue, for an insufficient reward ($1.00), that the experiment was interesting, they evidently concluded that the only way to account for this behavior was to believe that the actor subject did in fact consider the experiment interesting. Similarly in a free-choice situation the observer subjects evidently interpreted the choice as indicating that the experimental, actor subject relative to a control, actor subject valued the chosen alternative much more highly than the unchosen alternative.

Jones, Linder, Kiesler, Zanna, and Brehm (1968) argued that Bem is able to obtain his results only by giving his simulated subjects an incomplete description of the various dissonance experiments. They demonstrated that when observer subjects are told of the actor subject's initial attitudes the dissonance results are not reproduced. They argue that a complete description of the experimental setting should include information as to the actor subject's initial attitude. In the absence of this information the observer subjects assume that the actor subjects in the high-dissonance condition have atypical initial attitudes. For example, actor subjects who are willing, for an insufficient reward, to argue for a given point of view must not be opposed to that point of view. In the absence of correct information as to the actor subjects' initial attitudes the observer subjects assume that the actor subjects in the high-dissonance condition have atypical attitudes.

Bem (1968) replied to Jones et al. that they are correct that observer subjects attribute attitudes to the actor subjects on the basis of an implicit self-selection hypothesis. Bem argues that actor subjects in high-dissonance conditions make the same kind of self-attribution. Actor subjects assume that they are atypical or self-selected. Bem argues that when Jones et al. provided the observer subjects with information as to the initial attitudes of the actor subjects the situation was crucially altered. According to Bem (1968, p. 271),

> Engaging in the behavior may provide such strong cues for the experimental subject that any control exercised by the initial attitude may be swamped. As Heider (1958, p. 54) has said in this connection: "It seems that behavior in particular has such salient properties it tends to engulf the total field rather than

be confined to its proper position as a local stimulus whose interpretation requires the additional data of a surrounding field."

Bem's reply to Jones *et al.* rests on the assumption that the subject is so much impressed by his counterattitudinal behavior that his initial attitude is of little significance. In an interesting study Bem and McConnell (1970) found some evidence supportive of this assumption. The evidence specifically indicates that after subjects choose to engage in counterattitudinal advocacy they incorrectly recalled their premanipulation attitudes as being consistent with the subsequent advocacy. Students from Carnegie Mellon University wrote counterattitudinal essays advocating little or no student control over the kind of courses offered. There were two independent variables: choice versus no choice in writing the essay and final-attitude assessment versus recall-of-initial-attitude assessment. The final-attitude assessment was simply a measure of attitude toward student control of courses. The recall-of-initial-attitude assessment was a recall of attitude before writing the essay. Both assessments indicated that there was more influence in the direction of advocacy when the subjects were given a choice regarding essays than when they were not given a choice. Greater influence in the choice and no-choice conditions was apparent both for the final-attitude assessment and for the recall-of-initial-attitude assessment. Subjects recalled their initial attitudes as consistent with the chosen advocacy. Such results are consistent with Bem's assumption regarding the relative unimportance of initial attitude. Just how general such results are, however, is an open question.

Final Statement

The avalanche of research on forced-compliance situations has demonstrated some truly remarkable results. It is easy to understand why social psychologists have been fascinated by the nonobvious effects of variables such as reward, punishment, and effort. The results of such research have in turn stimulated theoretical statements that differ from Festinger's original statement of dissonance theory. It is, of course, obvious that the ultimate status of these newer theoretical statements is at present unknown. It is a reasonably safe assumption, however, that the existing theoretical controversy will stimulate continued work in this general area.

READINGS

Effectiveness of Emotional Role-Playing in Modifying Smoking Habits and Attitudes[1]

Irving L. Janis and Leon Mann

This experiment was designed to investigate the effectiveness of "emotional" role-playing in modifying smoking habits and attitudes toward cigarette smoking. Fourteen women were asked to play the role of a lung cancer patient who receives bad news from a physician. This role-playing group showed markedly greater changes in attitudes than an equivalent group of 12 control Ss, each of whom received identical information by listening to a tape recording of a role-play session. The high level of fear and vigilance aroused by the realistic quality of the experimental situation appears to be a factor responsible for the increased antismoking attitudes and the changes reported in smoking habits two weeks later.

The persistence of undesirable habits such as heavy smoking and over-eating, despite the desire of many people to modify their overindulgences, poses a major challenge for research on attitude change. The problem of smoking has attained prominence because of the incongruity between the average smoker's continuance of the habit and his knowledge that it might cause lung cancer. In general it appears that rational appeals, making use of cogent scientific evidence, have little sustained effect, if any, on the cigarette smoker. Even when influenced by persuasive messages that vividly convey the threatening consequences of the smoking habit, most smokers are affected only temporarily and usually return to the habit within a few days, bolstering their original attitude by minimizing, distorting, or denying the content of the message. It is a well-known fact that the cancer scare promoted by repeated publicity campaigns in the mass media during the past decade has had little residual effect on the American population and the consumption of cigarettes has continued to increase (Toch, Allen, and Lazer, 1961; Cannell and MacDonald, 1956; Greenberg, 1964).

A number of individual cases have been observed, nevertheless, in

[1] From the *Journal of Experimental Research in Personality*, Volume 1, pages 84–90, 1965. Authors' affiliation: Yale University. The experimental sessions were conducted during the summer of 1963, approximately 5 months before the release of the Surgeon General's report on *Smoking and Health*. The analysis of the data for this research was partly financed by a grant to Irving L. Janis, principal investigator, from the National Institute of Mental Health (MH08564-02) for research on factors influencing deprivation tolerance. This study was also partly financed by a grant from the Rockefeller Foundation for the Yale Studies in Attitude and Communication.

which dramatic conversions took place as a result of direct personal encounters with the threat, as in the case of physicians, cancer scientists, and
the relatives of cancer victims (Snegireff and Lombard, 1959; Lawton and
Goldman, 1961). It seems probable that when people stop smoking after
direct encounters with cancer victims, it is partly because of an empathic
reaction involving the realization that, if it can happen to others, it can
happen to themselves. A marked change in attitude and behavior is likely
to occur if a smoker can no longer relegate the feared consequences to the
category of remote or irrelevant dangers.

The present study was devised to investigate the possibility that the
technique of role-playing, which has been found to be effective in facilitating attitude change, might be used in a way that would provide an empathic "contact" experience similar to the type of direct contact that occasionally leads to a spectacular conversion. Several experiments (e.g.,
Culbertson, 1957; Janis and King, 1954, 1956; Kelman, 1953) have shown
that when a person verbalizes a belief or judgment to others he becomes
more inclined to accept it himself. The role-playing procedure in these experiments requires the person to take the part of a rational advocate of a
position contrary to his personal opinions, so that he is induced to scan the
opposing viewpoint and to improvise new arguments. Thus the person finds
himself examining belief systems that were formerly sealed off, as he con-
scientiously executes the task of examining the other side of the issue. It is
quite possible, however, for a person to carry out a cognitive role-playing
assignment in a defensive way with a minimum of emotional involvement
and with covert denial of the relevance of what he is saying to his personal
outlook. This type of defensiveness might explain why modest success was
attained in Horn's (1960) study, which was a unique attempt to use a role-
playing technique for the purpose of trying to influence smoking habits. In
Horn's experiment, high-school students took the role of providing information to their parents on the dangers of smoking and this led to only a small
decrease in the number of students who would have otherwise commenced
smoking.

When rational appeals fail, some degree of success in modifying deep-
seated habits may nevertheless be achieved by vivid emotional appeals that
personalize the threat, as in the case of audiences exposed to dramatic
"scare" films depicting the suffering and mutilation of cancer victims (Janis,
1968). It seems plausible, therefore, to expect that some comparable
degree of success in breaking through the defensive facade might be attained by using an "emotional" type of role-playing, which induces the
person to become empathically involved in a life-like situation. "Emotional"
role-playing in this case consists of a standardized psychodramatic procedure in which the E induces the S to give an improvised emotional performance by asking him to act out a fictitious calamity as though it were
really happening, using props and other staging devices to enhance the

illusion of reality. One of the unique features of this type of role-playing procedure is that the E enters directly into dramatic dialogues with the S, following a standardized script that he has memorized, and thus is able to focus the S's attention on the emotionally arousing features of the distressing episode that is being enacted.

In the present study, the form of emotional role-playing we devised requires the S to play the role of a medical patient who has just completed a series of intensive medical examinations and has asked the physician to tell the truth about the diagnosis. Enacting the role of the physician, the E informs the "patient" that the diagnosis is cancer of the lung, that a lung operation will have to be undergone as soon as possible, and that cigarette smoking must be given up immediately. The role-playing setting and the E's script were designed to facilitate the arousal of fantasies and personalized images of being victimized by lung cancer, with the expectation that when the threat cannot be readily denied or ignored the person may begin for the first time to experience some genuinely fearful anticipations that "it *could* happen to me."

In the literature on psychodrama, there are a few anecdotal accounts of the clinical use of similar role-playing procedures which appear to have been helpful in the treatment of delinquents and other types of "problem" cases (e.g., Moreno, 1957; Corsini, 1958); but so far as we know, the present study represents the first systematic attempt to investigate the effectiveness of emotional role-playing in modifying attitudes and habits.

Method

Subjects

The Ss were 26 women, 18–23 years of age, all of whom volunteered to participate in a research study under the auspices of their local State College. None of them knew that the purpose had anything to do with changing their smoking habits. They were screened by telephone to make sure they were moderate or heavy smokers (i.e., were consuming at least 15 cigarettes per day). The rationale given for asking about their smoking habits was simply that the study involved playing a role that required the person to be a smoker.

Subjects were randomly assigned to one of two conditions: 14 were placed in the experimental group (role-players) and 12 in the control group (non-role-playing "judges," exposed to the same instructions and information).

Experimental Procedures

The young women in both the experimental and control groups were told at the beginning of the session that role-playing is sometimes used as a research technique to create life-like situations when it is difficult to make direct observations of real-life behavior, such as the emotional reactions of patients in a doctor's office. The E then explained that the purpose of the research was to study two important problems concerning the human side of medical practice, namely how patients react to bad news and how they feel about a doctor's advice to quit an enjoyable habit like smoking.

On the pretext that E would best understand S's performance of the role of a patient if he knew her personal opinions on relevant topics, a premeasure of attitudes toward smoking was administered. The questionnaire contained 15 items which assessed S's beliefs about smoking and cancer, her feelings of concern about being a smoker, and her intention to modify or continue the habit.

The procedures up to this point were identical for both experimental and control Ss, but after the initial questionnaire only those assigned to the experimental condition were given the emotional role-playing instructions. Each S in the latter group was asked to imagine that E was a doctor who was treating her for a "bad cough that was not getting any better." She was to make believe that this was her third visit to his office, and that she had come this time to be informed of the results of Xrays and other medical tests. The E gave a brief sketch of five different scenes and S was asked to act out each one as realistically as possible:

Scene 1. Soliloquy in Waiting Room. The S is asked to give her thoughts out loud, expressing worry while awaiting the doctor's diagnosis and feeling conflicted about whether or not to smoke a cigarette.

Scene 2. Conversation with the Physician as He Gives the Diagnosis. In acting out the standard (memorized) script of the physician's role, E begins by informing the patient that he will tell her the whole truth, since this is what she had requested last time. He goes on to say that a definite diagnosis can now be made on the basis of the Xray and sputum tests and that, unfortunately, it is bad news. Pointing to an actual chest Xray obtained from the Pathology laboratory, he explains that there is a small malignant mass in the patient's right lung; an operation therefore is needed as soon as possible. He encourages the S to ask questions. In the course of this conversation, E again refers to S's former request for all the facts and then informs her of the fact that there is only a moderate chance for a successful outcome from surgery for this condition.

Scene 3. Soliloquy while Physician Phones for a Hospital Bed. The S is again asked to express aloud her thoughts and feelings about the bad news while E is telephoning in a distant part of the room.

Scene 4. Conversation with the Physician Concerning Arrangements for Hospitalization. Continuing to act on the basis of the standard script, E gives detailed information about reporting to the hospital the following morning and asks several questions about the patient's family and personal circumstances. He informs her that she should expect to be in the hospital at least six weeks because surgery of the chest takes a long time to heal.

Scene 5. Conversation with the Physician about the Causes of Lung Cancer. The E raises some questions about the patient's smoking history and asks her if she is aware of the connection between smoking and cancer. Then E discusses with the patient the urgent need to stop smoking immediately and encourages her to speak freely about the difficulties she expects to encounter in trying to give up the habit at this time, now that she knows it is essential.

Control Group

In this group Ss were given no opportunity to role-play, but were exposed to the very same information as the experimental group. This was done by asking each S to listen to an authentic tape recording of a role-playing session.

When the initial questionnaire about smoking was administered, these Ss were told that, since people's judgments are sometimes influenced by their personal habits and opinions, E wanted to find out how they felt about the various issues raised in the five scenes that were about to be heard. The control Ss were told that the recording was to be judged in terms of the quality of the role-player's performance and the intensity of her emotional involvement in the role. The particular tape that was played for this purpose was of 25 minutes' duration (the average amount of time for the role-playing activity) and was selected because of its exceptionally dramatic and emotional quality.

After hearing the tape, the control Ss were given a questionnaire containing some items requesting them to evaluate the role-player's performance and other items asking them to report their own reactions to the recording.

Follow-Up Interview

At the end of the session, Ss in both groups were again given the questionnaire containing items about attitudes toward smoking. Each S was told that the main purpose was to ask some additional questions about her reactions to the procedure she had just gone through, but that some of the questions would be the same as those asked earlier, all of which should be answered, "according to how you think and feel right now."

As each S was leaving, E mentioned that he would phone her when the results of the experiment became available in order to provide a summary report. Nothing whatsoever was said about a follow-up interview. Then, two weeks after the session, E telephoned S and reported briefly about various types of comments the Ss had made about different types of role-playing procedures that had been tried out, without suggesting that any changes in personal smoking habits had occurred or were to be expected. As an after-thought, E inquired whether S had thought about the experiment and—if modification in amount of smoking was not spontaneously mentioned—he asked whether her own smoking behavior had changed in any way during the past two weeks.

RESULTS AND DISCUSSION

Immediate Attitude Changes

Both groups were initially similar in attitudes toward smoking, the differences on all items in the initial questionnaire being very slight and nonsignificant. After playing the role of a cancer victim, however, the Ss in the experimental group showed marked changes in attitude as compared with the control group. The findings for the first four items in Table 1 indicate that the role players showed a significantly greater increase in antismoking attitudes than the controls on all four of the indicators used to assess the immediate effects of the experimental treatment: (a) personal belief that smoking leads to lung cancer ($p < .01$), (b) expectation that "much harm can come to me from my smoking" ($p < .01$), (c) willingness to try to give up smoking ($p < .01$), and (d) expressed intention to stop smoking immediately ($p < .05$).[2]

Changes in Smoking Habits Reported Two Weeks Later

One of the major aims of the study was to investigate whether emotional role-playing can produce a conversion-like experience that would lead to a marked and persistent change in actual smoking habits. The results for the

[2] All probability values are for a one-tailed test of significance, since the direction of the differences was predicted by the hypothesis that emotional role-playing is more effective in modifying attitudes and habits than passive exposure to the same information.

TABLE 1

Comparisons between Experimental (Role-Playing) Group and Control Group on Attitude Change and Habit Change

Items	Group[a]	Mean score before role play	Mean score after role play	Net change	t test
1. Belief that smoking causes lung cancer	Experimental	4.50	5.86	1.36	2.78**
	Control	4.17	4.17	0	
2. Fear of personal harm from smoking	Experimental	4.36	6.00	1.64	2.93**
	Control	4.25	4.33	0.08	
3. Willingness to attempt modification of smoking	Experimental	2.57	4.50	1.93	2.73**
	Control	2.42	3.00	0.58	
4. Intention to quit smoking	Experimental	2.79	5.08	2.29	2.05*
	Control	2.50	3.58	1.08	
5. Number of cigarettes smoked daily	Experimental	24.1	13.6[b]	−10.5	1.84*
	Control	21.7	16.9[b]	−4.8	

[a] $N = 14$ in experimental group, $N = 12$ in control group.

[b] This measure was obtained two weeks after the session, whereas the other four measures were obtained immediately after the role-playing performance (or control condition).

* $p < .05$.

** $p < .01$.

fifth item in Table 1 show that initially, before being exposed to the experimental treatments, there was a negligible difference in the amount of daily cigarette consumption reported by the two groups ($p > .40$). In the follow-up interview conducted two weeks after each experimental session, the role-players reported an average decrease of 10.5 in their daily cigarette consumption, whereas the controls reported an average decrease of only 4.8; this difference is statistically significant at beyond the 5% confidence level. The comparatively large drop found for the role-playing group is not attributable to a few extreme cases: The majority of the role-players (10 of the 14 women) reported a sizeable decrease, whereas the majority of the controls (7 of the 12 women) reported no change at all.

Although one must be somewhat skeptical about Ss' verbal reports about their current cigarette consumption, the findings supplement the attitude data in indicating that emotional role-playing was *differentially* more effective in producing manifestations of change than the control condition, which passively exposed the Ss to the same informational inputs and "demand" characteristics. That the Ss' verbal reports about the drop in their cigarette consumption were probably quite genuine is strongly suggested by additional comments they made about the difficulties they were having in avoiding the temptation to resume smoking, and the special efforts they were making to implement their decision to cut down on smoking. (E.g., "I made a pact with friends to put 30¢ in the bank for every day I don't smoke.")

Fear as the Mediating Source of Motivational Changes

The arousal of fear appears to have been a mediating factor in producing the observed changes in attitudes and reported behavior. This interpretation is strongly suggested by some additional evidence obtained during the role-playing and control sessions. In response to two additional items on the immediate post-treatment questionnaire, the role-players reported much more fear about their health than the controls ($t = 2.37$, $p < .05$) and also expressed much more worry about lung cancer ($t = 2.81$, $p < .01$).

The E's observational notes also indicate that the role-players displayed considerable affect arousal during their performance, including tremors, trembling, and flushing. These manifestations of fear impressed us as being far beyond the call of duty, even for whole-hearted adherents of the Stanislavski method of acting. The E's observational notes on the control group, on the other hand, indicated that these Ss showed considerable interest while listening to the dramatic tape recording, but with signs of only a very mild degree of emotional arousal as compared with the role-players, several of whom continued to show signs of being severely shaken long after the performance was over. Spontaneous comments made by almost every role-player at the end of the session indicated awareness of fear arousal: e.g., "You scared me to death"; "I was really getting scared"; "That just shook me up—it does scare me—it does!"

Further evidence of the plausibility of attributing the major motivational impact of the role-playing procedure to fear arousal is provided by correlational data indicating a positive association between reported level of fear about health (regardless of experimental condition) and subsequent reported modification of smoking habits ($\chi^2 = 4.53$, $df = 1$, $p < .05$).

For many Ss, the intense emotional experience that occurred while playing the role of the cancer victim appears to have functioned as a "last straw" which impelled them to transform their "good intentions" into action. One role-player put it this way: "This is the oomph I needed for giving up"; while another asserted, "I heard so much about the dangers of smoking, and then one more thing and that was it."

The passively exposed control group, in contrast, expressed more disbelief and affective detachment. On the posttreatment questionnaire, for example, the controls were much more likely than the role-players to agree with the following assertions: (a) that a causal relation between smoking and cancer has *not* been proven ($t = 2.19$, $p < .05$); (b) that the seriousness of lung cancer has been exaggerated ($t = 2.05$, $p < .05$); (c) that smoking is "just another one of those risks" ($t = 2.26$, $p < .05$); (d) that individual susceptibility rather than smoking is the important factor in lung cancer ($t = 3.66$, $p < .01$); and (e) that continuing to smoke does *not* imply any "lack of control and will power" ($t = 1.71$, $p < .10$). Along with their efforts to minimize the relevance of the well-publicized scientific evidence concerning the link between smoking and cancer, the control Ss were more likely to react negatively toward those who convey the unpleasant information, as indicated by their relatively strong endorsement of the statement "I feel very annoyed when people warn me about the dangers of smoking" ($t = 2.68$, $p < .01$).

In the follow-up interviews, there were also some indications that the emotional role-playing procedure had activated, over the two-week interval, an increase in vigilance as well as a heightened need for reassurance, in line with theoretical expectations concerning the nature of reflective fear (Janis, 1962). Specifically, three types of fear-related changes were spontaneously mentioned by the role-players while talking with E on the telephone:

1. Increased awareness of the literature on smoking and lung cancer: e.g., "After I saw you so many articles popped out at me"; "I'm more aware of the symptoms and I think about it . . . ; and [I would like to get a] book on the warning signs of cancer."

2. Active attempts to obtain reassurance: e.g., "I got scared—I'm glad I did—I went to a doctor for a check-up"; and "I'm planning to go and get an Xray."

3. Continued realization of personal vulnerability: e.g., "If I'd kept smoking I'm sure something would have happened to me, with my luck"; "Driving home afterwards I got scared—[I thought] what if it would be me—how would I actually react to getting lung cancer?"; "I've really thought about it—especially because Grandmother had cancer—there is a weak spot in the family."

The comments indicating awareness of personal vulnerability, made spontaneously by a few role-players during their follow-up interview, were very similar in content to those that had been made by many role-players immediately after their performance. For example, one girl reported, "I felt after a while I wasn't acting, it was really true"; another commented, "It makes it sound so near"; a third said, "I started to think, this could be me—really!"

Although the role-playing activity as a whole had an impressive emotional quality, certain parts of the psychodramatic sequence seemed to be particularly salient to the Ss as concrete representations of the threat. In response to the question, "Which part made the greatest impression on you?" several role-players mentioned the immediate threat of hospitalization, and a few spontaneously mentioned that the coughing symptoms described in the script were applicable to themselves. (E.g., "I really do have that cough and it's bad in the morning"; and "I felt I was in the part because I do cough.")

This phenomenon of becoming deeply impressed by specific disturbing details from enacting the fictional role of a cancer victim suggests that the procedure may entail more than merely a novel or dramatic way of eliciting attention to the relevant information. During the performance unpleasant outcomes such as pain, physical incapacity, hospitalization and death seem to acquire in fantasy a personal reality that is usually resisted when people are told about these same threatening outcomes in the usual types of warning communications.[3]

Thus, the qualitative observations supplement the quantitative data on attitude change in suggesting that the techniques of emotional role-playing may prove to be an exceptionally successful means for arousing potentially adaptive fear reactions, breaking through the defensive facade that normally prevents many people from taking account of their personal vulnerability to objective sources of danger. As yet we do not know how persistent the effects of emotional role-playing will prove to be, but this question is now being investigated by a follow-up study on the Ss in this experiment, which will provide information about their smoking habits over a two-year period.

REFERENCES

Cannell, C., & MacDonald, J. The impact of health news on attitudes and behavior. *Journalism Quarterly*, 1956, 33, 315–323.
Corsini, R. Psychodrama with a psychopath. *Group Psychotherapy*, 1958, 11, 33–39.
Culbertson, F. Modification of an emotionally held attitude through role-playing. *Journal of Abnormal and Social Psychology*, 1957, 54, 230–233.
Greenberg, D. S. Tobacco: After publicity surge, Surgeon General's Report seems to have little enduring effect. (News and Comment.) *Science*, 1964, 145, 1021–1022.
Horn, D. Modifying smoking habits in high school students. *Children*, 1960, 7, 63–65.
Janis, I. Psychological effects of warnings. In D. Chapman and G. Baker (Eds.), *Man and society in disaster*. New York: Basic Books, 1962.
Janis, I. *The contours of fear: Psychological studies of war, disaster, illness, and experimental stress*. New York: Wiley, 1968.
Janis, I., & King, B. The influence of role-playing on opinion-change. *Journal of Abnormal and Social Psychology*, 1954, 49, 211–218.
Kelman, H. Attitude change as a function of response restriction. *Human Relations*, 1953, 6, 185–214.

[3] The finding that the controls modified their attitudes and smoking habits to some extent indicates that listening to the information and dramatic presentation in the tape recording of a role-playing session may also have been quite effective with Ss of the type used in this experiment, even though it produced less change than the role-playing procedure. Pilot studies carried out with other types of Ss suggest that young college women may be especially receptive to antismoking communications. It is quite possible, therefore, that the results obtained from the role-playing may be partly dependent on the predispositions of the sample used in the investigation. For example, in an older sample, with more deeply ingrained habits and greater inhibitions about acting in a make-believe situation, less involvement and accordingly less change would be expected. Replications of the present study with different types of persons are obviously essential before any firm conclusions can be drawn as to how successful the emotional role-playing technique would be in smoking clinics or in any large-scale program to modify the smoking habits of various sectors of the population.

King, B., & Janis, I. Comparison of the effectiveness of improvised vs. non-improvised role-playing in producing opinion changes. *Human Relations,* 1956, **9,** 177–186.

Lawton, M., & Goldman, A. Cigarette smoking and attitude toward the etiology of lung cancer. *Journal of Social Psychology,* 1961, **54,** 235–248.

Moreno, J. The psychodrama. In J. F. Fairchild (Ed.), *Personal problems and psychological frontiers.* New York: Sheridan House, 1957.

Snegireff, K., & Lombard, O. Smoking habits of Massachusetts physicians. *New England Journal of Medicine,* 1959, **261,** 603.

Toch, H., Allen, T., & Lazer, W. Effects of cancer scares: the residue of the news impact. *Journalism Quarterly,* 1961, **38,** 25–34.

The Effects of Severity of Initiation on Liking for a Group: A Replication[1]

Harold B. Gerard and Grover C. Mathewson

This experiment represents an attempt to rule out a number of alternative explanations of an effect found in a previous experiment by Aronson and Mills. This effect, that the more a person suffers in order to obtain something, the greater will be the tendency for him to evaluate it positively, was predicted from dissonance theory. By modifying the original experiment in a number of ways, and applying additional treatment variations, these other hypotheses were effectively ruled out, thus lending considerable additional support to the original "suffering-leading-to-liking" hypothesis.

The experiment by Aronson and Mills (1959), in which a positive relationship was found between the severity of initiation into a group and subsequent liking for that group, is open to a variety of interpretations other than the one the authors give. The purpose of the experiment to be reported here was an attempt to rule out some of the more cogent of these alternative interpretations.

The observation that people often tend to value highly things for which they have suffered or expended a great deal of effort can be interpreted as having been due to dissonance reduction. The hypothesized process involved assumes that knowledge held by the person that he had suffered or expended a great deal of effort for a desired goal is inconsistent with knowledge that the goal or certain aspects of it are worthless. Such inconsistencies produce psychological dissonance which is unpleasant and the individual

[1] From the *Journal of Experimental Social Psychology,* Volume 2, pages 278–287, 1966 (received October 18, 1965). Authors' affiliation: University of California, Riverside. Mathewson subsequently at the University of Texas. This experiment was conducted by the junior author as part of an undergraduate senior tutorial. We gratefully acknowledge the financial support provided by grant No. MH 1181701 from the National Institute of Mental Health and grant No. GS 392 from the National Science Foundation.

will attempt to reduce this unpleasantness by cognitive work. In this case he can either distort his beliefs about the amount of suffering or effort he expended by coming to believe that it was less than he had previously thought or he can distort his belief about the worthlessness of aspects of the goal by coming to believe that these aspects were really not worthless. In their study, Aronson and Mills attempted to create a laboratory situation in which the latter hypothesized process could be examined. Let us review that experiment in some detail so that we may then point up the basis for the other interpretations of the data.

The subjects were college coeds who were willing to volunteer for a series of group discussions on the psychology of sex. The ostensible purpose of the study was presented to the subject as having to do with the investigation of group dynamics. Before any prospective member could join one of the discussion groups she was given a "screening test" to determine her suitability for the group. The severity of this screening test (or initiation) was varied; in the "severe" treatment the subject read obscene literature and a list of dirty words out loud to the experimenter (who was a male), whereas in the "mild" condition the subject read sexual material of an innocuous sort. The subject was told that the screening test had been necessary in order to weed out people who were too shy to discuss topics related to sex. After the initiation, each experimental subject was informed that she had passed the test and was therefore eligible for membership in the group. She was led to believe that the group she was to join had been formed several weeks ago and that she was to take the place of a girl who had to drop out. Her "participation" in her first meeting with the group was limited to "overhearing" via headphones what was presented to her as an ongoing discussion by the group on aspects of sexual behavior in animals. The reason she was given for not being able to participate actively in the discussion was that the other three girls had prepared for the discussion by reading a book on the sexual behavior of animals. It was also suggested to her that overhearing the discussion without participating in it would give her an opportunity to get acquainted with how the group operates. What she heard was not an ongoing discussion but was instead a standardized recorded discussion on the sexual behavior of animals that was extremely boring and banal. The discussion was contrived to be worthless in order to maximize the dissonance of the subject in the "severe" initiation group, since the knowledge that she had suffered to get into the group would be dissonant with finding out that the discussion was worthless.

After hearing the taped recording, the subject was asked to evaluate the discussion and the participants on a number of semantic differential-type scales. A control group was also run in which the subjects evaluated the discussion without having received any initiation whatsoever. The findings of the experiment supported the derivation from dissonance theory, namely that the subjects in the "severe" treatment evaluated the discussion more favorably than did the "mild" or control subjects. A dissonance theory interpretation conceives of the "severe" initiation as confronting the subject with the "problem" of having suffered for something that was later found to be worthless and the prediction is based upon how that problem is "solved." One of the reasons why the results are important and provocative is that they are exactly opposite to what a strict application of secondary reinforcement theory would predict, in which it would be expected that the unpleasantness of the initiation would "rub off" and generalize to the discussion.

While the results are consistent with dissonance theory, they lend themselves to a variety of other, quite plausible interpretations. For example, there is an entire *family* of interpretations that derives from the fact that the content of the initiation and the content of the discussion are so closely related, both having to do with sex. One could argue that the initiation aroused the girls sexually to a greater extent in the "severe" as compared with the "mild" treatment and they were therefore more anxious to get into the group in order to pursue the discussion of sex. Along similar lines, one could also argue that the girls in the "severe" treatment did not know the meaning of some of the dirty four-letter words and believed that they could find out their meaning by joining the discussion group. This is a variation of the uncertainty-affiliation hypothesis. Still another possibility is that the subjects in the "severe" treatment were intrigued by the obscene material and the dirty words and may have believed that, if not now, sometime in the future these things would be discussed by the group. One could continue to list related interpretations based upon the assumed arousal of one or another motive in the "severe" treatment that might be satisfied by joining the discussion group (thus making the group more attractive).

Another possible interpretation, a "relief" hypothesis, is that the reading of the obscene material built up anxiety which was subsequently reduced by the banal, innocuous material of the group discussion. Since the discussion was responsible for reducing the anxiety, it took on positive value for the subject in the "severe" treatment.

Schopler and Bateson (1962) find partial support for a "dependency" interpretation of the Aronson and Mills findings. Following Thibaut and Kelley (1959), Schopler and Bateson suggest that, as contrasted with the "mild" initiation, the "severe" initiation induced in the subject dependence upon the experimenter. This, according to them, occurred because the experimenter had "moved" the subject in the "severe" treatment through a "wide range of outcomes," consisting of the unpleasant shock and the pleasantness associated with the pride experienced by the "severe" subject upon learning that she had passed the test. Subjects in the "mild" condition had not experienced this range of pleasantness of outcome and hence were less dependent. Also, their argument continues, somehow the subject assumed that the experimenter expected her to like the discussion. Due to the assumed differential dependency induced by the initiation treatments, the subject in the "severe" treatment was more concerned with pleasing the experimenter than was the subject in the "mild" treatment and hence attempted to a greater extent to meet his expectations by indicating to him that she liked the discussion.

Chapanis and Chapanis (1964) suggest an "afterglow" hypothesis to explain the data. All subjects in the experiment were told that they had passed the embarrassment test. Presumably, subjects in the "severe" treatment perceived the test as being more difficult than did subjects in the "mild" treatment and, according to Chapanis and Chapanis, they therefore may have had a greater sense of accomplishment. This self-satisfaction somehow "rubbed off" onto other aspects of the task situation, including, presumably, the group discussion. This might then account for the "severe" subjects' more positive disposition toward the discussion.

Still another, even more plausible interpretation of quite a different sort, is that any experience following the "severe" initiation, which we assume was unpleasant, would by contrast seem more pleasant than it would following the "mild" initiation. It is important that this rather simple "contrast" hypothesis, which is a compelling explanation of the Aronson and Mills data, be ruled out, if possible.

A problem in the experiment related to the first set of interpretations concerns the nature of the initiation itself. Was the "severe" initiation really more unpleasant than the "mild" one? The authors do not report any check of the success of the experimental manipulation in producing differences in unpleasantness. Without the assurance that this all-important requirement was met, certain other interpretations of the data are quite plausible. It is not unlikely that many of the subjects in the "severe" treatment found the experience pleasant and exciting.

The experiment we shall report here is an attempt to replicate, not so much in fact but in spirit, the Aronson and Mills study, in order to counterpose the dissonance interpretation of the results against the other interpretations discussed above.

METHOD

An Overview of the Design

Two basic treatments were compared, one in which the subject received electrical shocks as part of an initiation procedure and one in which she received shocks as part of a psychological experiment, the "noninitiate" treatment. Within each of these treatments, half of the subjects received strong shocks and half received weak shocks. Half of the "severe" and half of the "mild" initiates were told that they had passed the screening test whereas the other half of each were not told whether they had passed. After the shocks, all subjects heard and then evaluated a boring and worthless group discussion about cheating in college. The "initiates" believed that this was a recording of a previous meeting of the group that they were slated to join, whereas the "noninitiates" evaluated the discussion as just one of a series of stimuli to which they were being exposed.

Procedure

The subjects were 48 female undergraduate volunteers contacted at random from the student body of the University of California at Riverside. All subjects were first contacted by telephone. During the telephone contact a subject selected to be an "initiate" was asked whether or not she would like to volunteer for a discussion club that was to discuss the problem of morals on university campuses. The "noninitiates" were asked, during the telephone contact, whether they would like to volunteer to be a subject in a psychological experiment. Thus, half of the subjects reported to the laboratory believing that they were going to be members of a discussion club whereas the other half believed that they were participating in a psychological experiment. The procedure followed during the experimental session was essentially the same for both "initiates" and "noninitiates." The "noninitiate" condition was introduced in an attempt to rule out the "contrast" and "relief" hypotheses. If the unpleasant experience represented by the initiation was not seen as instrumental to joining the discussion club and the same effect was found as in the Aronson and Mills experiment, both alternative explanations would receive support. If, however, the "initiates" showed the effect and the "noninitiates" did not, both the "contrast" and "relief" hypotheses would have been effectively ruled out. We might expect a secondary reinforcement effect in the "noninitiate" condition which would manifest as a negative relationship between the unpleasantness of the shocks and the evaluation of the discussion, the assumption being that the effect produced by the shocks would generalize to the discussion.

When the "initiate" arrived in the laboratory she was seated in an isolation booth and was told:

"In the past we have had considerable difficulty with some of the girls who have joined these discussion clubs. The problem is that some people cannot maintain an attitude of objectivity during the discussion. When this happens, naturally the discussion tends to deteriorate and emotions run very high. In order to avoid this difficulty in the future we have just instituted a screening test to weed out those girls who would tend to let their emotions run away with them during a discussion. You are the first person to whom we will be administering the test which is a very good one that has been used by psychologists for many years. It consists of determining your physiological reaction to a series of stimuli. We do this by hooking you up to these electrodes [the experimenter shows the subject a pair of dummy GSR electrodes] that detect changes in your skin resistance during the test which is done with the aid of this recorder [the experimenter shows the subject a small strip-chart recorder]. By your response on this chart we can tell how objective you are likely to be under conditions represented by the morals discussion."

The subject was told that she was the first one to take the test in order to eliminate the possibility that she would want to be in the group in order to compare her reactions to the test with those of the girls already in the discussion group.

The "noninitiate" was told when she arrived at the laboratory, "You are going to be a subject in a psychological experiment which involves your being exposed to a variety of different kinds of stimuli. We are going to determine your reaction to these stimuli with the aid of these electrodes [the experimenter shows the subject GSR electrodes] which are hooked up to this instrument [the experimenter shows the subject the strip chart recorder]."

All subjects were hooked up to the electrodes and received exactly the same sequence of stimuli which was designed to be a credible screening test for the "initiate." The sequence consisted of a spray of perfume from an atomizer placed in the ceiling of the subject's booth, a series of slides of paintings projected on the wall in front of the subject's booth [the paintings were: Roualt, *The Apprentice;* Picasso, *Madame Picasso, Portrait of A. Vollard, Figure by the Sea;* La Tour, *Self Portrait;* Matisse, *Landscape;* and Klee, *Girl Possessed*]. Each painting was presented for 15 seconds with a 15-second pause between presentations. After all of the paintings were shown, the subject was fitted with headphones and heard the shooting sequence in Copland's ballet, *Billy the Kid.* Finally, the subject received the critical stimuli which were a series of three shocks delivered 15 seconds apart by a Lafayette inductorium. In the "severe" treatment the shocks were quite strong whereas in the "mild" treatment they were barely supraliminal. This method of varying suffering would be more likely, on the face of it at least, to produce greater uniformity of psychological state within each of the two suffering levels than the method used by Aronson and Mills. Using electric shock this would rule out the family of interpretations that are all based upon the content of the discussion. If the Aronson and Mills effect were to be found by using shock this would rule out the family of interpretations that are all based upon the similarity of content of the two phases of the experiment.

Aronson and Mills informed all of their subjects that they had passed the screening test. The subject, thus, had acquired that for which she had suffered. It was inappropriate in the present experiment to inform the "noninitiates" as to how they had done in responding to the sequence of stimuli since they had not been told that they were taking a test. In order to control for this difficulty, half of the "initiates" were told, after receiving the shocks, that they had passed the screening test, whereas the other half were treated like the "noninitiates" by not receiving any feed-back concerning their performance on the screening test. This "told" vs. "not-told" factor was counterbalanced across the "severe" and "mild" initiates. More importantly, this treatment also enables us to test the Chapanis and Chapanis "afterglow" hypothesis, the plausibility of which is based on the assumption that the pleasure experienced in passing the severe initiation generalized to the group discussion. If those subjects who were told that they had passed showed the Aronson and Mills effect and those who were not given this information did not show the effect, the "afterglow" explanation would be supported. The Schopler and Bateson "dependence" hypothesis would also be supported if the Aronson and Mills effect replicated in the "told" but not in the "not-told" treatment, since the assumed broader range of outcomes experienced by the "severe" subject depends on the pleasure experienced by the subject upon learning that she had passed the test.

All subjects then listened to a five-minute tape recording of three girls having a discussion of cheating in college. This discussion was absolutely worthless, consisting mostly of hemming, hawing, clearing of throats, and pauses. The "initiate" was told that this was a recording of a previous discussion of the group that she was slated to join. The "noninitiate" was merely asked to listen to the discussion as one of the sequence of stimuli. Aronson and Mills presented the recording as an ongoing discussion. This difference in procedure in our "initiate" treatment did not seem to us to be critical.

In the final phase of the experiment, all subjects evaluated the discussion using semantic differential-type scales similar to those used by Aronson and Mills. Eight scales dealt with the qualities of the participants and eight with qualities of the discussion itself. Each scale was numbered from 0 to 15, the polarity of the scales being

TABLE 1

The Effects of Severity of Shock, Initiation, and Feedback on Evaluation of the Group Discussion[a]

	Initiate				Noninitiate	
	Mild shock		Severe shock		Mild shock	Severe shock
	Told	Not told	Told	Not told		
Participant rating	11.5	26.1	31.1	41.0	19.8	13.2
Discussion rating	11.0	15.6	27.0	28.2	9.1	5.8

[a] The larger the number, the more favorable the evaluation.

alternated in order to counteract any response bias. After this evaluation sheet was filled out, the subject was administered a post-experimental questionnaire which asked her to rate the pleasantness or unpleasantness of the various stimuli. The subject's evaluation of the shocks on this questionnaire was, of course, the check on the manipulation of suffering.

RESULTS

The two shock levels clearly induced different degrees of pleasantness. The post-questionnaire contained a 7-point scale on which the subject rated the pleasantness of the shocks. The difference between the two shock conditions was extremely large ($p < .001$ by chi-square[2]) with the majority of subjects in the "severe" condition indicating that the shocks were "extremely unpleasant." No subjects in the "mild" treatment found the shocks more than only "mildly unpleasant."

The discussion evaluation data are shown in Table 1. The figures in the table represent the means of the pleasantness ratings for both the par-

TABLE 2

Analysis of Variance of the Participant Evaluation

Source	SS	df	MS	F[b]
Initiation (I)	1276	1	1276	8.28
Severity (S)	1045	1	1045	6.78
I × S	1504	1	1504	9.77
Told (T)	1201	1	1201	7.80
S (I) × T[a]	45	1	45	
Error	6471	42	159	

[a] Interation of feedback (Told vs. Not-told within the initiate condition).

[b] $F .05 = 4.07$, $F .01 = 7.27$.

[2] Chi-square was used as a test of significance because the distribution in the "severe" treatment was skewed.

TABLE 3

Analysis of Variance of the Discussion Evaluation

Source	SS	df	MS	F
Initiation (I)	1811	1	1811	13.22
Severity (S)	850	1	850	6.20
I × S	835	1	835	6.09
Told (T)	69	1	69	
S (I) × T	23	1	23	
Error	5774	42	137	

ticipant and the discussion evaluation, summed over the eight scales used for each. Tables 2 and 3 present the analysis of variance for each of the two evaluations. We see a clear main effect of the initiation factor. When the subject anticipated joining the group whose discussion she had heard, she tended to evaluate both the discussion and the participants more highly than she did when there was no such expectation. This shows a general "effort effect" in line with dissonance theory. There was also a main effect of severity that is accounted for by the "initiates." The crucial degree of freedom that concerns us here is the interaction between initiation and severity which also yields a significant F-ratio. A t test applied within the "initiates" and within the "noninitiates" shows that both trends, which are opposite, are significant, the trend in the "initiate" treatment being stronger ($p < .01$) than the trend in the "noninitiate" treatment ($p < .05$). Whether or not the "initiate" received feedback about her performance on the screening test (the "told" vs. "not-told" variations) appears not to have interacted with severity of the shock. We do see, however, that for the participant evaluation there does seem to be a main effect of feedback. Informing the subject that she had passed the test appears to have reduced the evaluation of the participants.

Since there was some variation in both the "severe" and "mild" shock conditions in the perception of unpleasantness by the subject, we were in a position to do an internal analysis of the data by examining the correlation between *perceived* severity of the shock and liking for the group discussion. On the basis of dissonance theory we would expect a positive relationship only within the "initiate" condition. The overall correlation with the "initiate" treatment is .52 for the participant rating and .45 for the discussion rating ($p < .01$ for both correlation coefficients). The corresponding correlations in the "noninitiate" treatment are .03 and .07.

Discussion

The data from the experiment strongly support the "suffering-leading-to-liking" hypothesis and effectively rule out a number of other interpretations of the original experiment by Aronson and Mills. Our data for the "initiate" treatment are much stronger than those in the first experiment. This is probably attributable to the shock manipulation which undoubtedly produced more uniform within-treatment levels of suffering. The fact that the content of our suffering manipulation was divorced from the content of the group discussion eliminates the family of interpretations of the Aronson and Mills data that invoke some motive for wanting to affiliate that would be assumed to be greater in the "severe" than in the "mild" initiation treatment. The fact that there was an interaction between the initiate and severity factors eliminates the "contrast" and "relief" hypotheses. Both hypotheses predict the same difference under the "initiate" and the "noninitiate" treatments. We see instead an effect within the "non-initiate" treatment that supports a secondary reinforcement interpretation; the more severe the shock the *less* did the subject like the discussion. The internal correlational analysis adds further support for the "suffering-leading-to-liking" hypothesis and further weakens the "contrast" and "relief" hypotheses, since within the "initiate" treatment the greater was the perceived suffering the greater did the subject like the group discussion, whereas no such relationship was found within the "noninitiate" treatment.

Both the Chapanis and Chapanis "afterglow" and the Schopler and Bateson "dependence" hypotheses depend upon the subject having had a success experience after learning that she had passed the screening test. This success experience is presumed to have been greater in the "severe" than in the "mild" initiation treatment. Greater liking for the discussion under the "severe" initiation should therefore, according to both hypotheses, occur under the "told" but not under the "not-told" treatment. The lack of such an interaction effectively rules out both hypotheses.

Feedback did have a main effect on the evaluation of the participants. The high evaluation of the participants in the "not-told" as compared with the "told" condition may reflect a desire to be in the group. When informed that she had passed the screening test and would be in the group, the subject reduced her evaluation. Objects that a person is not sure he can have may appear more attractive to him under certain circumstances than similar objects that he already possesses. Having suffered or expended effort in order to acquire the object may be just such a circumstance. This effect was not predicted and our interpretation, therefore, must be considered as highly speculative.

REFERENCES

Aronson, E., & Mills, J. The effect of severity of initiation on liking for a group. *Journal of Abnormal and Social Psychology*, 1959, **59**, 177–181.
Chapanis, N. P., & Chapanis, A. Cognitive dissonance: five years later. *Psychological Bulletin*, 1964, **61**, 1–22.

Schopler, J., and Bateson, N. A dependence interpretation of the effects of a severe initiation. *Journal of Personality*, 1962, **30**, 633–649.

Thibaut, J., and Kelley, H. H. *The social psychology of groups*. New York: Wiley, 1959.

Chapter 6

COMMUNICATOR DISCREPANCY

Dissonance in Exposure Situations

According to Festinger (1957) involuntary exposure to information is potentially dissonance arousing. Social interaction and the mass media frequently result in exposure to new information. If this information implies the obverse of existing cognitions dissonance is aroused. In "exposure" situations, unlike free-choice and forced-compliance situations, Festinger makes no mention of choice or decision as being of crucial importance.

Brehm and Cohen (1962) prefer to explicitly limit dissonance theory to situations in which the individual exercises volition so as to make a choice and thus acquire a commitment. They argue that it is equivocal whether or not dissonance is created by exposure to new information. If past volition is responsible for the cognitions that imply the obverse of new information then exposure may indeed create dissonance. If past volition is not responsible for the cognitions then exposure will not create dissonance. Brehm and Cohen give the example of the farmer who decided to plant tobacco rather than corn and then later on in the season hears that tobacco causes a deadly disease. The unexpected disclosure would arouse dissonance since the farmer had really considered planting corn instead. Suppose, however, the farmer heard that land taxes were to be raised. Whether or not this unpleasant information would arouse dissonance depends upon whether ownership of the land is a result of some recent volition. If the land had been recently purchased dissonance would be created, but if the land had been inherited dissonance would not be created.

Since Brehm and Cohen, in disagreement with Festinger's original theoretical statement, believe that volition is a necessary prerequisite for dissonance arousal, they prefer to investigate situations in which the experimenter can be certain that a definite choice has been made. It is in these free-choice and forced-compliance situations that dissonance theory frequently makes nonobvious predictions that distinctively differ from the predictions flowing from other theoretical formulations. Not all dissonance theorists, however, have agreed with Brehm and Cohen's suggested revisions of the dissonance formulation. Some of this research on communicator discrepancy exemplifies this disagreement.

Dissonance Theory of Communicator Discrepancy

One of the variables that determines the magnitude of dissonance in an exposure situation is the discrepancy between the position of the communicator and the position of the communicatee (Festinger, 1957). Suppose an individual believes that for maximum health and well-being he should get eight hours' sleep per night and is exposed to a persuasive communication advocating six hours' sleep per night as optimal. In this instance there is a given degree of discrepancy between the positions of the communicator and the communicatee. This discrepancy would be increased if the communication advocated less than six hours' sleep per night. Communicator discrepancy thus refers to the extent of attitude or belief disagreement between communicator and communicatee regarding some issue.

Festinger and Aronson (1960) and Aronson, Turner, and Carlsmith (1963) have theorized about the interaction of communicator discrepancy and communicator credibility. Their argument is developed in the following way. When someone is exposed to a communication implying the obverse of existing cognitions dissonance is created. Furthermore, the more discrepant the communication the greater the dissonance. Dissonance from a discrepant communication can be reduced in any of four ways: (1) disparaging the communicator, (2) conforming to the communicator's belief or attitude, (3) convincing the communicator to change his belief or attitude, (4) seeking social support from other like-minded individuals. In the typical laboratory situation the last two modes of dissonance reduction are not available. Subjects are not allowed to interact with each other or the communicator (who, in the case of written or tape-recorded presentations may not even be present). This leaves the first two modes of dissonance reduction, disparagement and conformity, as the only two available means of dissonance reduction. (Disparagement occurs when the communicatee decides that the communicator is incompetent, insincere, untrustworthy, stupid, etc.) As long as the discrepancy is not too great it is argued that conformity will be the preferred mode of dissonance reduction. This means that in the low to moderate discrepancy ranges the increasing dissonance produced by increasing discrepancy will result in increasing influence or conformity. As the discrepancy continues to increase into the more extreme ranges, however, disparagement will become the preferred mode of dissonance reduction—particularly if the communicator is not "perfectly credible." Disparagement and conformity are regarded as alternative modes of dissonance reduction. A communicator who is disparaged will not be influential and a communicator who is influential will not be disparaged. Thus in the more extreme discrepancy ranges increasing discrepancy will result in decreasing influence. The net result is that over the entire discrepancy range there is a curvilinear relation between discrepancy and influence. Over the low ranges increasing discrepancy produces increasing influence and over the more extreme ranges increasing discrepancy produces decreasing influence. A crucial variable affecting the shape of the discrepancy-influence function is communicator credibility. Since a highly credible communicator is fairly difficult to disparage, the point at which the discrepancy-influence function levels off and ceases to rise may be at a fairly extreme position on the discrepancy dimension. In fact, if the communicator is "perfectly credible" disparagement may not occur at even the most extreme discrepancy levels and the influence function thus continues to increase uniformly (see Fig. 6-1). For a less credible communicator the function should level off at a less extreme position on the discrepancy dimension. In Fig. 6-1 (taken from Aronson *et al.*, 1963) the influence function increases uniformly for the "perfectly credible" communicator, increases and then levels off for the highly credible communicator, increases and then decreases for the mildly credible communicator.

Methodological and Quasi-Methodological Problems

Research on communicator discrepancy involves a number of methodological or quasi-methodological problems. The first of these problems has to do with the relation of the amount of attitude or belief change obtained to the amount of possible change. It is impossible for subjects slightly dis-

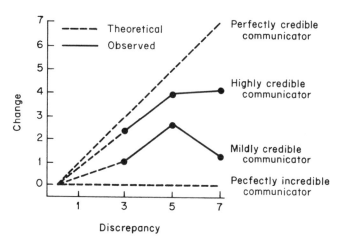

Fig. 6-1. Attitude change as a function of communicator discrepancy and credibility—theoretical and observed curves. (From Aronson et al., 1963, p. 34.) Reprinted by permission of the American Psychological Association.

crepant from a communicator to exhibit as much movement toward the advocated position as subjects who are more discrepant from the communicator. This means that any finding of increasing change with increasing discrepancy may be partially a function of the amount of change that is possible. If the discrepant communications are so powerful as to produce complete or almost complete conformity then increasing discrepancy will of necessity result in increasing change. This does not mean, of course, that slightly discrepant subjects cannot in some circumstances exhibit more change than more discrepant subjects. In the latter circumstance the results are less likely confounded by the amount of change possible.

The second problem has to do with the choice of experimental design. One possible design involves measuring subjects' initial positions along some dimension, presenting a single persuasive communication that argues for a single position, and then measuring the subjects' final positions. The further the distance between each subject's initial position and the persuasive communication the greater the discrepancy. After collecting the data it is, of course, possible to relate the amount of discrepancy for each subject with an amount of before-after change or influence. We can refer to this procedure as a between-subjects design. A second possible procedure, which we can refer to as a between-communications design, involves constructing a number of communications each arguing for a different position on the discrepancy dimension and presenting one of each of the communications to different groups of subjects with the same initial positions. The subjects' attitudes or beliefs can be measured before and after exposure, or just after exposure, to the communication. If an after-only procedure is used then the experimenter should pick a communication topic with regard to which there is considerable initial agreement in the population from which the subjects are drawn.

With the between-communications design the experimenter directly *manipulates* discrepancy through the construction of communications which differ in their advocated position. With the between-subjects design the experimenter *selects* subjects of varying discrepancies from the single communication. This latter design thus involves a confounding of discrepancy and the subjects' initial positions. If the communication should advocate a neutral position on some attitude dimension the subjects in the high-discrepancy conditions would of necessity be subjects whose initial positions were extremely pro or extremely con and the subjects in the moderate discrepancy conditions would be subjects with less extreme pro or con attitudes; that is, discrepancy would be confounded with initial position. Thus we will only discuss research which has used the between-communications design.

The third and final methodological or quasi-methodological difficulty relates to the nature of the discrepancy dimension itself and how thoroughly it should be explored. If an investigator is interested in describing the function relating attitude change with some particular discrepancy dimension it is obviously necessary to explore the dimension from one extreme to the other; that is, persuasive communications should be located at the slight, moderate, and extreme discrepancy levels. This poses a problem, however, for discrepancy dimensions that extend infinitely. Consider the issue of increasing tuition at some college or university. Tuition could be increased by $5.00, $50.00, $500.00, $5,000.00, and so on indefinitely. With such an issue what should be the dollar increase for the extreme level? In a paper contained in the Readings section Bochner and Insko (1966) attempted to get around this problem by working with an issue, how many hours' sleep the average young adult should get per night, which possesses a finite ceiling. Persuasive communications advocated 8, 7, 6, 5, 4, 3, 2, 1, and 0 hours' sleep per night. Since it is impossible to sleep less than 0 hours per night, the extreme end of the dimension was reached. Bochner and Insko also suggest a possible method of working with dimensions without finite ceilings. For such dimensions the psychological meaningfulness of objectively equal increments becomes less and less as the extremity of the values increases. For example, an increase in tuition from $50.00 to $1050.00 appears more extreme than an increase from $1050.00 to $2050.00. Thus it is theoretically possible to place the most extreme communication at a position beyond which any further increment would appear trivial. Ideally, research on the communicator discrepancy problem should be preceded by some sort of scaling of the dimension that would allow for the placement of communications at psychologically equal intervals from least extreme to most extreme. To date none of the reported research has used such an approach.

Research

One of the first studies to use a between-communications design was conducted by Hovland and Pritzker (1957). Subjects were initially given a questionnaire asking them to indicate on seven-point scales their beliefs regarding various uninvolving issues, such as whether married or single women are better teachers. One month later the questionnaires were re-administered with the beliefs of various authoritative groups indicated for each issue or item. These bogus authoritative beliefs were manipulated for each subject individually so that they differed from the previously indicated beliefs by one step for some items, two steps for some, and four steps for others. The bogus authoritative beliefs thus constituted persuasive "communications" which were placed at one of three discrepancies from each subject's initial position. For each of the obtained belief responses to each item, one-third of the subjects were given a bogus belief one step removed, one-third two steps removed, and one-third three steps removed. This assured the independence of discrepancy and initial position. The results indicated that the greater the discrepancy of the bogus belief the greater the amount of before-after change or influence.

Aronson, Turner, and Carlsmith (1963) performed an experiment designed to test the dissonance account of communicator discrepancy. Female subjects initially ranked nine stanzas from obscure poems, all of which contained alliteration. Following the ranking the subjects read a persuasive communication entitled "The Use of Alliteration in Poetry." The communication read by each subject was individually tailored so that it always evaluated the eighth ranked poem as an example of alliteration. For one-third of the subjects this poem was described as average, for one-third as superior to all but two of the nine examples, and for one-third as superior to all nine examples. Thus the experiment involved three levels of discrepancy. Half of the subjects in each discrepancy condition were told that the communication was written by T. S. Eliot (highly credible source) and half were told that it was written by a student at Mississippi State Teachers College who was studying to become a high-school English teacher (mildly credible source). After reading the communication the poems were ranked for a second time.

Figure 6-1 describes the before-after change in the poem that was initially ranked eighth by each subject. For the mildly credible communicator change or influence appears curvilinearly related to discrepancy. For the highly credible communicator change increases at each discrepancy level. The rate of change appears to fall off to some extent between the middle and most extreme discrepancy levels, but the amount of change still increases. This general pattern of results is consistent with the dissonance formulation. Theoretically the increasing dissonance produced by increasing discrepancy is resolved through either conformity to the communicator's position or disparagement of the communicator. Since disparagement of a mildly credible source is easier than disparagement of a highly credible source, the difference in conformity or influence between the two sources should increase with increasing discrepancy. This, in fact, occurred.

Aronson *et al.* included a measure of disparagement along with their after-assessment of attitude toward the crucial poem. The disparagement measure consisted of agreement-disagreement ratings of 14 evaluative statements regarding the communication and source. At every discrepancy level the highly credible source (T. S. Eliot) was disparaged less (evaluated more highly) than the mildly credible source (student at Mississippi State Teachers College), but disparagement was not affected by discrepancy. Theoretically disparagement should have increased with increasing discrepancy, particularly for the mildly credible source. Thus while the attitude results support the dissonance formulation the disparagement results do not.

An additional study relating communicator discrepancy and communicator credibility was performed by Bergin (1962). Subjects were exposed to information regarding their masculinity-femininity before and after rating themselves on a masculinity-femininity dimension. The information was orally delivered by either a high-credibility or a low-credibility source. The high-credibility source was a staff member of the Stanford Medical Center Psychiatry Department who based his interpretation upon a battery of test information. In the high-credibility condition the experiment was conducted in a hospital setting where the subject had reported to participate in a personality assessment project. In the low-credibility condition the experiment was conducted in the basement of a building housing the education department. Under the guise of a study of interpersonal perception the subject and "high-school freshman" (actually a stooge) rated each other on a masculinity-femininity scale and then exchanged ratings. For both the high-credibility and low-credibility conditions the masculinity-femininity information was at one of three discrepancy levels. Bergin labeled the levels moderate, high, and extreme.

The before-after belief change results for Bergin's experiment are graphically presented in Fig. 6-2. The results in the high-credibility condition are strikingly similar to the results for Aronson *et al.* (1963) analogous condition. Influence increased over the three levels, but the rate of increase between the second and third levels was less than between the first and second levels. In the low-credibility condition Bergin found that influence nonsignificantly decreased over the three discrepancy levels. How can we account for the difference between these results and Aronson, Turner, and Carl-

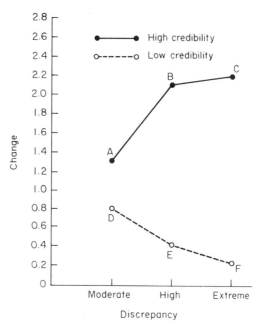

Fig. 6-2. *Belief change as a function of communicator discrepancy and credibility.* (*From Bergin, 1962, p. 433.*) *Reprinted by permission of Duke University Press.*

smith's results for their mildly credible communicator? One possible answer is in terms of the degree of source credibility. A high-school freshman is undoubtedly a less credible source than a college student.

Bergin also obtained some results from a postexperimental enquiry regarding the sources' perceived ability to evaluate personalities. The obtained data indicated that the high-credibility communicator was uniformly perceived as more expert (disparaged less) than the low-credibility communicator. Of greater interest, however, is the fact that the perceived expertness or credibility of the low-credibility source declined significantly over the three discrepancy levels. This is the type of effect which Aronson, Turner, and Carlsmith had expected to find. Since disparagement is regarded as an alternative to conformity, whenever conformity or influence starts decreasing disparagement should increase.

In a report contained in the Readings section Bochner and Insko (1966) describe a third investigation of communicator discrepancy and credibility. The results of the study are at least partially consistent with the dissonance formulation.

One possible difference between the Aronson *et al.* experiment and the Bergin experiment has to do with the involvement of the subjects with the communication issue. Freedman (1964) has reported an investigation dealing with involvement and communicator discrepancy. His procedure involved the use of a concept-formation task. Subjects were presented with eight rectangles each containing figures that varied in shape (circle, triangle, or square), size (large or small), number of a particular size or shape (one, two, or three), and position (any of three). Each of the eight rectangles was labeled as to whether it did or did not exemplify some concept. The subjects' task was to identify the concept which, for example, could be two small circles in the third position. After completing three of the concept-formation tasks, the subjects copied the concept for the first task on a separate sheet of paper and examined 16 instances which were supposedly labeled as to whether they did or did not exemplify the *same* concept. Actually five of the new instances were inconsistent with the initial concept, although all 16 instances were consistent with a new concept. Discrepancy was manipulated by the number of elements which the two concepts shared. In a high-discrepancy condition the two concepts shared no elements, in a moderate-discrepancy condition, two elements, and in a low-discrepancy condition, three elements. Involvement was manipulated by telling some of the subjects that the first part of this "intelligence test" was more important (high involvement) and some that the second part was more important (low involvement). Subjects were thus more committed to their initial positions in the high-involvement condition.

The results in terms of before-after change in the concept elements are shown in Fig. 6-3. In the low-involvement condition influence increased uniformly (or linearly) over the three discrepancy levels. In the high-involvement condition influence increased and then decreased (varied

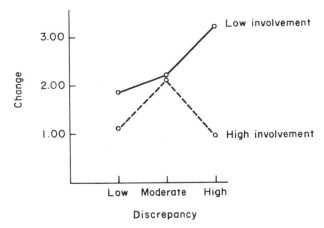

Fig. 6-3. Concept change as a function of communicator discrepancy and issue involvement. (From Freedman, 1964, p. 293.) Reproduced by permission of the American Psychological Association.

curvilinearly) over the three discrepancy levels. These results point very convincingly to the importance of involvement or commitment as a parameter affecting the relationship between influence and discrepancy.

Can dissonance theory account for Freedman's results? Although Aronson *et al.* (1963) did not include involvement in their theoretical statement, Festinger and Aronson (1960) did state that the magnitude of dissonance resulting from social disagreement increases as a positive function of "the importance and relevance to the individual of the issue concerning which the disagreement exists" (p. 222). Thus it is reasonable to speculate that in Freedman's high-involvement condition relative to his low-involvement condition a lesser amount of discrepancy would be required to raise the level of dissonance to a point at which disparagement rather than conformity would be the dominant mode of dissonance reduction. This, of course, would produce decreasing conformity or influence at the high-discrepancy levels of the high-involvement condition.

Finally, we should mention that Brock (1967) has presented some evidence indicating that the dissonance formulation of Festinger and Aronson (1960) and Aronson *et al.* (1963) may be somewhat oversimplified. Brock was interested in demonstrating the importance of anticipatory counterarguing in the mediation of communicator discrepancy effects. Subjects were asked to list their thoughts *prior* to reading a persuasive communication advocating either a $10.00, $125.00, or $275.00 increase in tuition. At the time the subjects listed their thoughts the subjects knew that they were to read a communication advocating either a $10.00, $125.00, or $275.00 increase in tuition. Coding of the data indicated that the greater the anticipated amount of advocated increase the greater the number of counterarguments. Counterarguing conceivably may be an important intervening link between discrepancy and influence. It should be pointed out, however, that Brock's data are not necessarily incompatible with the dissonance account of discrepancy. Counterarguing and disparagement may be closely related processes that produce similar effects.

Brock's emphasis upon counterarguing is similar to Greenwald's (1968) general position regarding the importance of thoughts. In Chapter 3 we described some of the intriguing research using Greenwald's listed thought technique. Counterarguing is, of course, a thought process. It is interesting to note that Greenwald had his subjects list their thoughts after exposure to a communication, and Brock had his subjects list their thoughts before exposure to the communication (but after learning of the communication topic). Common sense suggests that thoughts which occur before, during, and after exposure may be of considerable importance. An obvious methodological and theoretical problem arises, however, relating to the possible effect of assessing these thoughts on both subsequent thoughts and attitude change. There is good reason to suppose, though, that a thorough understanding of the effect of communicator discrepancy upon attitude change will be dependent upon adequate conceptualization of the relevant thought processes.

Final Statement

The research described above makes it fairly obvious that communicator discrepancy is an exceedingly important attitude change variable. Furthermore, there does not seem to be much doubt about the fact that the shape of the function relating discrepancy and attitude change is influenced by the credibility of the source and the subject's involvement with the issue. Future research may reveal the importance of still other variables. One likely candidate is the number of arguments contained in the communication. Another is the potency of the arguments.

At a more theoretical level there is at least some research evidence indicating that the function relating communicator discrepancy and attitude change is partially mediated by disparagement either of the source or of the communication, and by counterarguing. Still a further possible mediating process may be the subject's reaction against his threatened freedom. This is a matter that will be considered in the following chapter.

READINGS

Communicator Discrepancy, Source Credibility, and Opinion Change[1]

Stephen Bochner and Chester A. Insko

Utilizing an after-only design an experiment was carried out in which Ss were exposed to written communications advocating 8, 7, 6, 5, 4, 3, 2, 1 or 0 hr. sleep per night. Opinion change was found to be linearly related to communicator-communicatee discrepancy for a high credibility source, and curvilinearly related to communicator-communicatee discrepancy for a medium credibility source. Furthermore, the curve trends for the 2 sources interacted significantly. It had originally been expected that, since the discrepancy dimension was being explored completely to the extreme end, opinion change would be curvilinearly related to discrepancy for both high and medium credibility sources. Disparagement of the medium but not the high credibility source and of the communication in both source conditions was linearly related to discrepancy. The pattern of correlations between opinion change and discrepancy was only roughly as expected. These results were taken as giving some qualified support to the dissonance interpretation of the effect of communicator-communicatee discrepancy on opinion change.

Under appropriate circumstances both Sherif and Hovland's (1961) judgmental theory and Festinger's (1957) dissonance theory (particularly as interpreted by Aronson, Turner, & Carlsmith, 1963; Festinger & Aronson, 1960) predict a curvilinear relationship between communicator-communicatee discrepancy and influence. According to judgmental theory a communication is an external anchor that produces increasing positive influence (assimilation) with moderate discrepancy and decreasing influence (contrast) with extreme discrepancy. The assimilation and contrast regions are theoretically determined by the latitudes of acceptance and rejection as operationally defined in terms of the range of positions that the individual finds acceptable or objectionable. According to dissonance theory increasing communicator-communicatee discrepancy produces increasing dissonance that can theoretically be reduced in any of four ways: conformity to the communicator's point of view, disparagement of the communicator, persuasion of the communicator that he is incorrect,

[1] From the *Journal of Personality and Social Psychology,* Volume 4, pages 614–621, 1966 (received December 17, 1965). Authors' affiliations: Bochner, University of New South Wales; Insko, University of North Carolina. This paper is based on a master's thesis done by the first author under the direction of the second. Reproduced by permission of the American Psychological Association.

and obtained social support from other like-minded individuals. Since in most laboratory experiments subjects are not allowed to talk either to each other or to the communicator, the latter two modes of dissonance reduction are not available. This leaves only conformity and disparagement. Theoretically, increasing discrepancy should result in increasing conformity at the moderate discrepancies, and in increasing disparagement (if the communicator is not perfectly credible) at the extreme discrepancies. Since conformity and disparagement are regarded as alternative modes of dissonance reduction, the net result is that conformity is curvilinearly related to communicator discrepancy. This analysis, however, does not make clear why conformity is the preferred mode of dissonance reduction at the slight and moderate discrepancies or why conformity drops out at the extreme discrepancies. Insko, Murashima, and Saiyadain (1966) offer a suggestion for the latter problem in terms of extreme conformity producing too much inconsistency with already held cognitions.

The bulk of the studies which have experimentally manipulated communicator-communicatee discrepancy have found an increasing linear relation with influence (Aronson et al., 1963; Bergin, 1962; Fisher & Lubin, 1958; Freedman, 1964; Goldberg, 1954; Helson, Blake, & Mouton, 1958; Hovland & Pritzker, 1957; Rosenbaum & Franc, 1960; Tuddenham, 1958; Zimbardo, 1960). However, one study found a decreasing linear relation (Cohen, 1959), and several studies have found a curvilinear relation (Aronson et al., 1963; Freedman, 1964; Insko et al., 1966).

Various suggestions have been offered for the inconsistencies in the communicator-discrepancy literature. Hovland (1959) has argued that decreasing change with increasing discrepancy is more likely to occur with highly ego-involved issues and that increasing change with increasing discrepancy is more likely to occur with highly credible sources. Insko et al. (1966) have pointed to the obvious fact that differing results may be obtained simply by focusing upon differing segments of the communicator-communicatee discrepancy dimension. Many of the studies which found increasing linear relationships might have conceivably found curvilinear relationships if the discrepancy dimension had been explored into the more extreme regions.

If one attempts to experimentally explore a communicator-discrepancy dimension, an obvious practical and theoretical question concerns how far one should go in order to have satisfactorily manipulated the variable. Ideally, one should go clear to the extreme end. However, since many dimensions extend into infinity, this may not always be possible.[2] There are some dimensions, however, with finite ceilings. The present research was designed to pick one such dimension, number of hours sleep the average young adult should get per night, and explore it thoroughly from 8 down to

---

[2] Additional discussion of this problem occurs toward the end of the paper.

0. In addition, in order to extend the results of Aronson *et al.* (1963), a manipulation of source credibility was included.

It was predicted, first, that opinion would be curvilinearly related to discrepancy for both high and low credibility sources, and, second, that the hump of the influence curve would occur further out on the discrepancy dimension for the high than the low credibility source; that is, there would be an interaction between the curvilinear trends for the two communication sources. The first prediction is simply a common-sense hunch. The second prediction, however, flows from a dissonance orientation. The disparagement that supposedly produces decreasing influence at the extreme discrepancies should theoretically be more difficult with a high than with a low credibility source.

METHOD

Communication[3] and Issue

The communication consisted of a three-page essay arguing, on the grounds of health and efficiency, for a reduction in the number of hours spent in sleep per night. The issue was chosen for two reasons. First it possessed a finite ceiling. And second, individuals within our subject population of university students expressed a high degree of agreement with regard to how many hours sleep per night a person should get. For a sample of 202 subjects, responses to the question, "For maximum health and well being, how many hours sleep per night should a person get," had a mean of 7.89 and a standard deviation of 1.05.

Dependent Variables

Three dependent variables were measured: opinion regarding sleep, disparagement of the communication, and disparagement of the source. Opinion regarding sleep was assessed through the following question: "For maximum health and well being, how many hours of sleep per night do *you* think the average young adult should get?" The alternatives ranged from "no sleep at all" to "ten hours per night" in 11 steps of 1 hour each. References to communicator disparagement in the context of dissonance theory (e.g., Aronson *et al.*, 1963) usually involve both communication disparagement and source disparagement. In the present study these variables were assessed separately. The assessment of communication disparagement was obtained by summing the responses to six 7-point scales regarding the extent to which the communication "made sense," "covered all relevant aspects necessary for evaluating the need for sleep," and was "easy to read," "easy to understand," "reasonable," and "logical." The assessment of source disparagement was obtained by summing the responses to six 7-point scales regarding the extent to which the communicator was "sincere," "competent," "trustworthy," "intelligent," "credible," and "knowledgeable."

[3] An example of one of the experimental booklets containing the persuasive communication has been deposited with the American Documentation Institute. Order Document No. 9049 from ADI Auxiliary Publications Project, Photoduplication Service, Library of Congress, Washington, D. C. 20540. Remit in advance $1.75 for microfilm or $2.50 for photocopies and make checks payable to: Chief, Photoduplication Service, Library of Congress.

Independent Variables

Three independent variables were manipulated: discrepancy (nine levels), source credibility (high or medium), and order of dependent-variable measurement (opinion-disparagement or disparagement-opinion). Each of these variables involved between-subject comparisons. Discrepancy was manipulated by inserting the recommended hours of sleep into the persuasive communication. The communication was identical at all discrepancy levels except for the hours recommendation. Communicator credibility was manipulated by attributing the communication to either "Sir John Eccles, Nobel prize winning physiologist," or to "Mr. Harry J. Olsen, director of the Fort Worth YMCA." Data collected from 30 subjects indicated that these two sources did significantly differ in credibility relative to the hours of sleep issue. The mean rating on six 7-point scales (expertness, competence, trustworthiness, intelligence, credibility, and knowledgeableness) was 12.07 for a "Nobel prize winning physiologist" and 23.80 for "Director of the Fort Worth YMCA."

Procedure

Five-hundred and seventeen students from introductory psychology and education courses at the University of Hawaii served as subjects during their regular class periods. Each subject was given a booklet on the front page of which appeared the information that the experimenter was developing a new reading-comprehension test specifically applicable to Hawaii, and that subjects would act in the capacity of a normative population. The format of the booklet closely imitated the style of a widely used reading-comprehension test. On the second and third pages there appeared a practice passage and some practice items. The next pages contained the persuasive communication, immediately followed by a "comprehension test." The reading of the communication and completion of the comprehension test were timed with a stopwatch in order to reinforce the deception that this was a reading-comprehension task. The final pages of the booklet were concerned with "Evaluation of the Passage." In the initial instruction there had been mention of the fact that since this test was still in its early experimental stages, in addition to the usual reading-comprehension-type questions, the booklet also contained some questions concerning the reaction of readers to the topic, the author, and the passage. In fact, the final section of the booklet allowed for assessment of the three dependent variables.

In order to manipulate the three independent variables 36 different booklets were required. These booklets were passed out so that subjects who were sitting next to each other did not receive the same ones.

RESULTS

Of the 517 subjects tested 13 were eliminated, 9 because they did not completely fill out the questionnaires in the booklet and 4 in order to create an equal number of subjects (14) in each of the 36 cells ($N = 504$). The reading-comprehension test indicated that 21 subjects (4.06%) miscomprehended the source of the communication and that 31 subjects (5.9%) miscomprehended the number of hours advocated by the communicator. These subjects were distributed fairly evenly over the 36 conditions and were *not* eliminated from the analysis.

Mean opinion in each of the experimental conditions is presented in Table 1 and an analysis of variance of the opinion data in Table 2. The two significant effects are for discrepancy and the Discrepancy × Source inter-

TABLE 1

Mean Opinion, Source Disparagement, and Communication Disparagement in Each Experimental Condition

Hrs.	Opinion Nobel O-D	Nobel D-O	YMCA O-D	YMCA D-O	Source disparagement Nobel O-D	Nobel D-O	YMCA O-D	YMCA D-O	Communication disparagement Nobel O-D	Nobel D-O	YMCA O-D	YMCA D-O
8	7.71	7.21	7.50	7.57	13.36	11.64	17.07	15.00	13.71	12.50	16.00	12.64
7	7.14	7.79	7.57	7.36	12.93	14.64	14.00	14.50	12.86	15.93	15.29	12.43
6	7.29	7.50	7.14	7.14	13.93	12.00	15.57	13.43	12.00	12.79	15.14	11.71
5	7.00	7.07	6.50	7.29	9.79	13.70	13.21	15.79	14.50	11.79	12.57	14.00
4	7.21	7.14	7.14	6.50	11.36	14.36	16.50	15.71	14.57	15.64	16.64	13.50
3	6.64	6.79	6.50	6.29	17.50	11.57	17.93	14.36	16.50	14.14	15.79	14.86
2	5.86	6.71	6.93	6.86	16.14	14.00	16.86	16.93	17.57	14.07	19.57	14.86
1	5.71	6.21	6.86	6.57	12.79	13.50	15.29	17.00	15.79	14.36	16.64	14.36
0	6.79	6.93	7.29	7.00	14.50	13.36	20.00	16.64	16.86	16.79	16.86	18.00

action. The discrepancy F indicates that there was significantly more overall opinion change at the moderately extreme discrepancy levels, and the interaction indicates that the high credibility or Nobel source was somewhat more persuasive at the extreme discrepancies and somewhat less persuasive at the slight discrepancies. The data are graphically presented in Fig. 1 and trend analyses for these data in Table 3. The trend analyses indicate that the discrepancy effect for the Nobel source is significantly linear. Although the deviation from linearity is significant and the curve has a marked drop at the extreme discrepancy level, the curvilinear or quadratic

TABLE 2

Analyses of Variance of the Three Dependent Variables

Source	Opinion MS	Opinion F	Source disparagement MS	Source disparagement F	Communication disparagement MS	Communication disparagement F
Order (O)	0.51		42.88	1.00	233.43	8.78**
Source (S)	0.64		775.05	18.21**	28.10	1.06**
Discrepancy (D)	9.32	8.38**	56.78	1.33	116.66	4.39**
O × S	3.18	2.85	5.16		54.02	2.03
O × D	0.96		84.15	1.98*	26.42	
S × D	2.25	2.02*	20.72		5.85	
O × S × D	1.24	1.11	14.40		36.19	1.36
Within	1.11		42.57		26.58	

* $p < .05$, $df = 8$.
** $p < .01$, $df = 1, 8$.

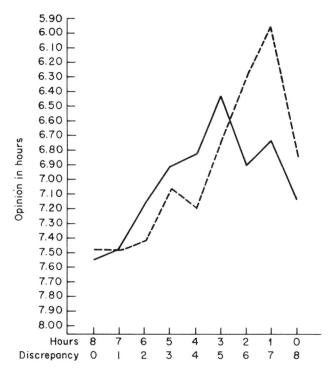

Fig. 1. *Opinion as a function of discrepancy in both the Nobel (dashed line) and YMCA (solid line) conditions.*

F is not significant. The YMCA source has both a significant linear and curvilinear trend. The quadratic F is larger than the linear F, but the difference is relatively trivial. Further analysis indicates that there is a significant interaction between the linear components ($F = 4.72$, $p < .01$) and the quadratic components ($F = 3.45$, $p < .05$) of the two source curves. Both of these interactions, as well as the previous Source × Discrepancy

TABLE 3

Trend Analyses for the Three Dependent Variables

	Opinion		Source disparagement		Communication disparagement
	Nobel	YMCA	Nobel	YMCA	Nobel & YMCA
Linear	29.58**	13.28**	1.24	4.92*	24.29**
Linear deviation	2.16*	3.24**	0.60	0.57	1.49
Quadratic	0.49	15.74**	0.00	1.53	1.66
Quadratic deviation	6.33**	2.88*	0.78	1.06	4.72**

*$p < .05$.
**$p < .01$.

interaction in the analysis of variance, are contributed to by the greater persuasive effect of the Nobel source at the high discrepancies and the lesser persuasive effect at the moderate discrepancies. However, a t test for the differences between the sources at the 1- and 2-hour positions (high discrepancies) is significant ($t = 1.83$, $p < .05$, one-tailed), while a t test for the difference between the sources at the 3- and 4-hour positions (moderate discrepancies) is not significant ($t = 1.28$).

The mean source-disparagement scores in each of the 36 cells are presented in Table 1, and an analysis of variance of the source-disparagement data is presented in Table 2. The only significant Fs in the analysis of variance are the ones for source and the Order $\times$ Discrepancy interaction. The source F indicates that the Nobel prize winner was regarded as significantly more credible than the YMCA director, and the interaction F indicates that at some discrepancy levels there was greater disparagement of the sources when disparagement was measured before rather than after opinion, and at some discrepancy levels greater disparagement of the sources when disparagement was measured after rather than before opinion. The data are graphically presented in Fig. 2 and trend analyses for the two sources over the nine discrepancy levels in Table 3. The YMCA curve shows a significant increasing linear trend, but the Nobel curve does not show either a significant linear or curvilinear trend.[4]

The mean communication-disparagement scores are presented in Table 1, and an analysis of variance of the communication-disparagement data in Table 2. The Fs for order and discrepancy, but not for source, are significant. The order effect indicates that communication disparagement was

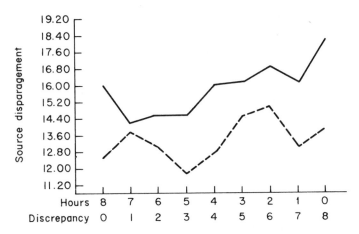

Fig. 2. *Source disparagement as a function of discrepancy in both the Nobel (dashed line) and YMCA (solid line) conditions.*

[4] Further analyses reveal that the curve is not cubic ($F = .50$), or quartic ($F = .41$), but may be quintic ($F = 2.90$, $p < .10$).

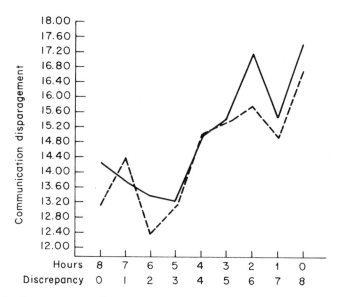

Fig. 3. *Communication disparagement as a function of discrepancy in both the Nobel (dashed line) and YMCA (solid line) conditions.*

greater when disparagement was measured after rather than before opinion, and the discrepancy effect indicates a tendency for communication disparagement to increase with increasing discrepancy. The data are graphically presented in Fig. 3, and a trend analysis of the combined data for both sources is presented in Table 3. Due to the similarity of the curves for the two sources and the lack of a significant difference between them the trend analysis was performed on the combined data for both sources. The results indicate a highly significant overall linear trend.

The matrix of zero-order correlations among the three dependent variables is presented in Table 4. The only significant correlation is the one between source and communication disparagement (.62). By Fisher's z transformation the average within-cell correlation between opinion and source disparagement is .10 ($p < .05$), and the average within-cell correlation between opinion and communication disparagement is .11 ($p < .05$).

TABLE 4

Zero-Order Correlations among Three Dependent Variables

	Opinion	Source disparagement	Communication disparagement
Opinion	+1.00	+.08	+.08
Source disparagement		+1.00	+.62*
Communication disparagement			+1.00

*$p < .01$.

TABLE 5

Within-Cell Correlations between Opinion and Disparagement[a]

		\multicolumn{9}{c}{Recommended hours}								
		8	7	6	5	4	3	2	1	0
Opinion and source	Nobel	+.03	+.13	+.17	+.44	+.17	+.26	+.09	+.23	+.01
disparagement	YMCA	−.34	−.12	−.34	−.24	+.30	+.42	+.07	+.33	+.17
Opinion and com-	Nobel	+.06	+.07	+.20	+.32	+.12	+.27	−.03	+.25	+.14
munication dis-	YMCA	−.40	+.09	−.46	+.06	+.26	+.47	+.07	+.37	+.17
paragement										

[a] A positive correlation indicates a negative relation between disparagement and attitude change.

In view of the way in which the variables are scored a positive correlation indicates a negative relationship between disparagement and opinion change. Averaging the within-cell correlation across the two orders of measurement gives the values presented in Table 5. As can be seen from this table it is mainly in the Nobel condition that the correlations are uniformly positive. For the relationship with source disparagement the average within-cell Nobel correlation is .17 ($p < .05$), and the average within-cell YMCA correlation is .03 (ns); the similar correlations with communication disparagement are .16 ($p < .05$) and .07 (ns), respectively.

DISCUSSION

The prediction with regard to significant curvilinearity for the high and medium credibility sources was confirmed only for the medium credibility (YMCA) source. Furthermore, the medium credibility source manifests significant linearity as well as significant curvilinearity. The high credibility (Nobel) curve does drop markedly at the end, but the entire curve is nonetheless significantly linear and not significantly curvilinear. It had been originally thought that a thorough manipulation of the entire discrepancy dimension would almost certainly produce a curvilinear trend, even for a very high credibility source. This expectation, obviously, is not supported by the data.

The expectation, however, that the curve trends would interact is supported by the data. The interactions for the linear and curvilinear components, as well as from the analysis of variance, are all significant. The embarrassing thing about these interactions, though, is the fact that they are contributed to both by superiority of the high credibility source at the extreme discrepancies and by inferiority of the high credibility source at the moderate discrepancies. Theoretically the high credibility source should have been equal to or slightly superior to the medium credibility source at the moderate discrepancies and greatly superior at the extreme discrepancies. In agreement with this expectation, however, it is only at the extreme discrepancies that t tests reveal a significant difference between the two sources. For purposes of generalization, therefore, we are willing to conclude that the medium and high credibility sources do not differ at the moderate discrepancy levels, but that the high credibility source is superior at the extreme discrepancies. This interaction between communicator-communicatee discrepancy and source credibility warns against any further study of source credibility that does not incorporate a manipulation of discrepancy.

As Aronson *et al.* (1963) have developed the dissonance interpretation of communicator-communicatee discrepancy, communicator disparagement is assumed to increase with increasing discrepancy. They, however, failed to obtain results supporting this assumption. Although not interpreted in the context of dissonance theory, Bergin (1962) did find evidence for increasing disparagement of a low but not a high credibility source. For purposes of the present study communicator disparagement was divided into two parts or aspects, source disparagement and communication disparagement. The results indicated an increasing, significant linear trend in source disparagement for the medium credibility source condition, but not for the high credibility source condition, and an increasing, highly significant linear trend in communication disparagement for both the high and medium sources conditions combined. These results, then, partially support the dissonance expectation.

The theoretical expectations with regard to the correlation between disparagement and attitude change are fairly complex. In general the theory implies a negative relationship between disparagement and attitude change, and the average within-cell correlations in fact support this expectation. A closer examination of the theory, however, reveals that the negative relationship between attitude change and disparagement should become most or only apparent at the moderate and extreme discrepancies where disparagement has increased to such a level of potency that it starts becoming associated with decreasing opinion change. Therefore, within any one moderate or extreme discrepancy level the disparagement measure should order individuals negatively with regard to opinion change, but within any one slight discrepancy level the disparagement measure should bear little relation to opinion change. An examination of the pattern of within-cell correlations presented in Table 5 reveals some very rough tendency for the correlations to change across discrepancy levels in the expected manner for the moderate credibility or YMCA source. Since it was only the moderate credibility source that produced a significant curvilinear trend, this makes at least some degree of sense. The high credibility source, however, does not show an increased negative relationship (as manifested by an increased positive correlation) even at the extreme discrepancy levels where the opinion curve leveled off and dropped.

Theoretical expectations with regard to the zero-order correlations are fairly ambiguous. Zero-order correlations include the variation within as well as among cells, and it is the latter source of variation which is mainly responsible for the ambiguity. In the slight discrepancies opinion change theoretically increases rapidly and disparagement considerably less rapidly. Eventually, however, disparagement may increase to such a level of potency that it becomes associated with or causes a leveling off and dropping of opinion change. The net result of all this is that the cell means for opinion change and disparagement may be positively associated over the slight discrepancies and negatively associated over the extreme discrepancies. With each type of disparagement the empirically obtained zero-order correlations are, in fact, practically zero (both .08).

How can we make sense of these data? In the high credibility or Nobel condition, opinion increased linearly, source disparagement varied complexly, and communication disparagement increased linearly. In the medium credibility or YMCA condition, opinion varied curvilinearly, source disparagement increased linearly, and communication disparagement increased linearly. Furthermore, there was no significant main-order difference between the high credibility and medium credibility sources in communication disparagement, but there was a significant difference in source disparagement. This general pattern of results makes it appear as if source disparagement is a more important determiner of the opinion curves than is communication disparagement. The data imply that if the discrepancy manipulation is not potent enough to produce increasing source disparagement, then the opinion curve will be linear.

In general the results agree only approximately with theoretical expectations. There are two main difficulties. First, the relationship between opinion change and disparagement did not become increasingly negative for the high credibility source at the point at which the opinion curve leveled off and dropped. And second, communication disparagement and source disparagement manifested different trends across discrepancy levels in the high credibility condition. The former difficulty makes it appear as if disparagement is not a complete explanation for a decreasing opinion curve, and the latter difficulty makes it appear as if disparagement is not one unitary mode of dissonance reduction.

One final matter has to do with the type of scale that is used to measure communicator-communicatee discrepancy. This is a problem that has not at all been discussed in the literature. In the present research the communications were placed at supposedly equal positions along an assumed ratio scale relating to number of hours. In retrospect, however, we realized that in terms of psychological meaningfulness our scale is probably neither ratio nor interval. We specifically suspect that discrimination among the differences between the middle hours, 6, 5, 4, 3, and 2, is much less sharp than discrimination among the high hours, 8 and 7, or the low hours, 1 and 0. This supposition is reinforced by the fact that, for the opinion data at least, a plot in terms of 8, 7, 5, 3, 1, and 0 hours yields smooth curves for both high and medium credibility sources.

Our dimension of number of hours sleep per night has a finite ceiling and therefore an anchor at both ends to aid in discrimination. What about a dimension without a finite ceiling, such as the amount by which tuition should be increased? Since this dimension has no anchor at the upper end, we suspect that discrimination will get progressively poorer as the values become more and more extreme. For example, an increase in tuition from $50 to $1,050 should appear much more extreme than an increase from $1,050 to $2,050. If this is, in fact, the case, then there is a possible solution to the problem relating to the placement of sufficiently extreme communications on discrepancy dimensions without finite ceilings. The most extreme communication should be far enough along the dimension so that any possible further extreme communication would appear only trivially different.

REFERENCES

Aronson, E., Turner, J. A., & Carlsmith, J. M. Communicator credibility and communication discrepancy as determinants of opinion change. *Journal of Abnormal and Social Psychology*, 1963, **67**, 31–36.

Bergin, A. E. The effect of dissonant persuasive communications upon changes in a self-referring attitude. *Journal of Personality*, 1962, **30**, 423–438.

Cohen, A. R. Communication discrepancy and attitude change. *Journal of Personality*, 1959, **27**, 386–396.

Festinger, L. *A theory of cognitive dissonance*. Evanston, Illinois: Row, Peterson, 1957.

Festinger, L., & Aronson, E. The arousal and reduction of dissonance in social contexts. In D. Cartwright & A. Zander (Eds.), *Group dynamics: Research and theory*. (2nd ed.) Evanston, Illinois: Row, Peterson, 1960. Pp. 214–231.

Fisher, S., & Lubin, A. Distance as a determinant of influence in a two-person serial interaction situation. *Journal of Abnormal and Social Psychology*, 1958, **56**, 230–238.

Freedman, J. L. Involvement, discrepancy, and change. *Journal of Abnormal and Social Psychology*, 1964, **69**, 290–295.

Goldberg, S. C. Three situational determinants of conformity to social norms. *Journal of Abnormal and Social Psychology*, 1954, **49**, 325–329.

Helson, H., Blake, R. R., & Mouton, J. S. An experimental investigation of the effectiveness of the "big lie" in shifting attitudes. *Journal of Social Psychology*, 1958, **48**, 51–60.

Hovland, C. I. Reconciling conflicting results derived from experimental and survey studies of attitude change. *American Psychologist*, 1959, **14**, 8–17.

Hovland, C. I., & Pritzker, H. A. Extent of opinion change as a function of amount of change advocated. *Journal of Abnormal and Social Psychology*, 1957, **54**, 257–261.

Insko, C. A., Murashima, F., & Saiyadain, M. Communicator discrepancy, stimulus ambiguity, and influence. *Journal of Personality*, 1966, **34**, 262–274.

Rosenbaum, M. E., & Franc, D. E. Opinion change as a function of external commitment and amount of discrepancy from the opinion of another. *Journal of Abnormal and Social Psychology,* 1960, **61,** 15–20.

Sherif, M., & Hovland, C. I. *Social judgment.* New Haven: Yale University Press, 1961.

Tuddenham, R. D. The influence of a distorted group norm upon individual judgment. *Journal of Psychology,* 1958, **46,** 227–241.

Zimbardo, P. G. Involvement and communication discrepancy as determinants of opinion conformity. *Journal of Abnormal and Social Psychology,* 1960, **60,** 86–94.

Chapter 7

RESISTANCE TO PERSUASION

Most of theory and research in the previous chapters was directed at understanding why attitude and belief change occur, or why it is that people are persuaded. The present chapter, however, takes a different approach. The concern here is with theory and research directed at understanding why attitude and belief change do not occur, or why it is that people resist persuasion. Everyday observation certainly indicates that resistance to persuasion does occur. It is only natural then that attitude theorists should confront this matter directly and pose possible explanations for the occurrence of resistance to persuasion. In this chapter we will consider the two best known theories of resistance to persuasion, McGuire's inoculation theory and Brehm's reactance theory.

Inoculation Theory

A RESISTANCE TO DISEASE ANALOGY

As developed by McGuire (1964), inoculation theory is based on an anology with biological resistance to disease. There are two main ways of creating resistance to disease, supportive therapy and inoculation. Supportive therapy involves exercising, going on a special diet, and taking vitamins. Inoculation, on the other hand, involves injecting a weakened form of the disease-producing bacteria and thereby stimulating the body to develop defenses capable of handling stronger bacteria. If someone has been living in a germ-free environment inoculation is the best procedure for producing resistance to disease.

Suppose that someone is going to be exposed to a counterattitudinal communication. How can resistance to this communication be created? Following the biological analogy there are two possible procedures. The first is to make the to-be-attacked attitude or belief "healthier" through the use of supportive arguments. This is, of course, analogous to supportive therapy. The second is to inoculate the to-be-attacked attitude or belief by exposing the subject to refuted counterattitudinal arguments. This is, of course, analogous to biological inoculation. Thus if the individual has been living in an environment in which his attitudes or beliefs have not been threatened, inoculation should be superior to supportive arguments in producing resistance to counterattitudinal arguments.

CULTURAL TRUISMS

In order to test his theory McGuire needed to find attitudes or beliefs that had never been attacked. By analogy such attitudes or beliefs exist in a germ-free environment. He selected "cultural truisms," or widely shared beliefs that are seldom questioned. McGuire discovered that the area of health abounds with beliefs for which the majority of subjects would check 15 on a 15-point agreement scale. Some of these beliefs, or cultural truisms, are the following: "It's a good idea to brush your teeth after every meal if at all possible." "The effects of penicillin have been, almost without exception, of great benefit to mankind." "Everyone should get a yearly chest X-ray to detect any signs of TB at an early stage" (McGuire, 1964, p. 201).

MOTIVATION AND PRACTICE

Following the biological analogy, a belief that has existed in a non-threatening environment should be susceptible to attacking counterarguments. Aside from the analogy, however, why should this be the case? McGuire argues that there are two purely psychological reasons for this vulnerability: lack of practice in defending the belief and lack of motivation to defend the belief. The individual is unpracticed because he has never had to defend the belief, and he is unmotivated to start practicing because he regards the belief as unassailable.

As indicated above McGuire maintains that presentation of refuted counterarguments produces resistance to subsequent stronger counterarguments. The refuted counterarguments are analogous to a vaccine containing weakened virus or bacteria. From a psychological perspective, however, why should the presentation of refuted counterarguments produce resistance to subsequent attacking arguments? McGuire's answer is, again, in terms of motivation and practice. Inoculation, or the presentation of refuted counterarguments, motivates the individual to develop bolstering arguments for his somewhat weakened belief. This leads to practice, or skill, in defending the belief.

Inoculation theory was developed prior to Greenwald's work (1968) demonstrating the importance of various types of thoughts in mediating the persuasive impact of persuasive communications. In Chapter 3 we described Greenwald's thought-listing technique, and his general argument that relevant thought and not learning of communication content is the crucial mediator of attitude change. Such a perspective is, of course, quite compatible with McGuire's position regarding the development of bolstering arguments subsequent to inoculation, or exposure to refuted counterarguments.

Research Comparing Supportive and Refutational Defenses

A supportive defense is a communication that lists and elaborates a number of arguments favorable to a cultural truism. For example, a supportive defense for the importance of annual X-ray examinations to detect TB might include an argument linking the decline of TB in this country to the use of annual X-ray examinations, and an argument concerning the ease and convenience of obtaining X-ray examinations from either permanent or mobile centers. A refutational defense, on the other hand, lists and then refutes arguments against a cultural truism. For example, a refutational defense for the X-ray truism might list arguments that X-rays can cause cancer and sterility and then attempt to refute these charges by arguing that the amount of radiation from annual X-rays is insignificantly small (equivalent to the amount obtained from wearing a wrist watch with a luminous dial during the same period), and that a chest X-ray does not expose the reproductive tissues to radiation.

According to inoculation theory a refutational defense should be more effective than a supportive defense in providing resistance to subsequent attacking arguments. In accordance with the biological analogy the refutational defense immunizes the subject against the subsequent attack. An initial test of the hypothesized superiority of refutational to supportive defenses in conferring resistance to attacks was conducted by McGuire and Papageorgis (1961). The experiment involved four different conditions: supportive-defense-then-attack, refutational-defense-then-attack, attack-only, and neither-attack-nor-defense. In the supportive-defense-then-attack condition the subjects were exposed to a supportive defense and then 2 days later were exposed to an attack on the previously defended truism. In the refutational-defense-then-attack condition the subjects were exposed to a refutational defense followed 2 days later by an attack on the previously defended truism. In the attack-only condition the subjects were exposed to an attack on a truism that had not been defended, and in the neither-attack-nor-defense condition the subjects simply indicated their acceptance of a truism that had neither been attacked nor defended. Similar agreement ratings on a 15-point scale were made by the subjects in all conditions.

McGuire and Papageorgis used four different truisms in each condition and the reported results were thus averaged across truisms. Mean acceptance was 12.62 in the neither-attack-nor-defense condition and 6.64 in the attack-only condition. These significantly differing means indicate that in the absence of any defense an attack is quite successful in reducing acceptance of the truisms. Mean acceptance was 11.51 in the refutational-defense-then-attack condition and 7.47 in the supportive-defense-then-attack condition. These significantly differing means indicate that the refutational defense was superior to the supportive defense in conferring resistance to the subsequent attack. Mean belief in the supportive-defense-then-attack condition, 7.47, is not even significantly greater than mean acceptance in the attack-only condition, 6.64.

Although the results of McGuire and Papageorgis agree with theoretical prediction, they are not as unexpected as one might initially believe. The reason for this is that the attacks utilized exactly the same arguments that the refutational defense had previously "refuted." It is, of course, not hard to believe that refuted arguments are going to lose a good deal of their potency. What would happen, however, if the attacks contained arguments that were different from the ones which the refutational defense had previously refuted? This question was answered in an experiment by Papageorgis and McGuire (1961).

The main purpose of the Papageorgis and McGuire experiment was to compare a refutational defense refuting the same arguments that are contained in a subsequent attack with a refutational defense refuting different arguments than are contained in a subsequent attack. Papageorgis and McGuire refer to these as refutational-same and refutational-different defenses. With a refutational-different defense the attacks concentrated on things like the use of skin tests as both safer and cheaper than chest X-rays. With a one-week interval between sessions Papageorgis and McGuire found that the refutational-same defense was as effective as the refutational-different defense in conferring resistance to subsequent attack. These results are thus in good agreement with inoculation theory.

McGuire argues that refutational defenses, and particularly refutational-different defenses, are effective in conferring resistance to subsequent attack because they motivate the individual to develop bolstering arguments for belief. If this assertion is correct, one would only expect refutational-different defenses to be superior to supportive defense if there were some time interval between defense and attack. In one of the two above studies there was a 2-day interval between defense and attack and in the other there was a 1-week interval. McGuire (1962, 1964), in fact, found in two different studies that as time between defense and attack increased up to 7 days the superiority of refutational (and in particular refutational-different) over supportive defenses became more marked. With short (2 to 7 day) time intervals the effectiveness of supportive defenses declined and the effectiveness of refutational defenses actually increased. Such results, of course, are in striking agreement with McGuire's expectations.

Reactance Theory

Like McGuire's inoculation theory, Brehm's (1966) reactance theory is a theory of resistance to persuasion. In most other respects, however, reactance theory is distinctly different from inoculation theory.

FREE BEHAVIORS AND REACTANCE

Brehm assumes that for any given person at a given time, there is a set of behaviors which could be engaged in either at that time or at some time in the future. These behaviors are termed free behaviors. According to Brehm, "for specified behaviors to be free, the individual must have the relevant physical and psychological abilities to engage in them, and he must know, by experience, by general custom, or by formal agreement, that he may engage in them" (1966, p. 4). Brehm admits that when relevant knowledge and experience is lacking neither the individual himself nor an observer may know which behaviors are in fact possible. In a laboratory setting, though, situations can be constructed in which there are obvious behavioral freedoms.

According to Brehm, "*Given that a person has a set of free behaviors, he will experience reactance whenever any of those behaviors is eliminated or threatened with elimination*" (1966, p. 4). Reactance is produced when a free behavior is either eliminated or simply threatened with elimination. Furthermore, the elimination, or threat of elimination, can be either impersonal or personal. The significant aspect of impersonal elimination (or threat of elimination) is that the individual cannot easily perceive the elimination as having been directed at him. (For example, the individual may notice that the supermarket is out of the brand of coffee that he sometimes buys.) The significant aspect of personal elimination (or threat of elimination) is that the individual can easily perceive the elimination as having been intentionally directed at him.

REACTANCE AND SIMPLE FRUSTRATION

Brehm gives two hypothetical examples which serve to distinguish reactance from "simple frustration," defined as "blocking of the person from his preferred goal" (1966, p. 3). The first example relates to a man, Mr. John Smith, who normally plays golf on Sunday afternoons, but occasionally spends Sunday afternoons puttering around his workshop or watching television. On one particular Sunday, however, Smith's wife informed him that he would have to play golf (as he normally does) since she had invited some of her female friends in for a party. This, of course, threatens Smith's freedom to watch television, and putter around his workshop, as well as his freedom not to play golf. In attempting to reestablish these freedoms Smith might be expected to protest that there was an important television show he wanted to watch, that he had planned to work in his workshop, or that the golf course is not in good condition. If the amount of reactance were great enough he might spend the afternoon watching television with the volume turned up.

The second example relates to a man who normally smokes Camels but occasionally smokes Kools. On one particular occasion, after locating a vending machine dispensing both Camels and Kools, he decides to purchase his preferred brand, Camels. After inserting his money, but before pulling the lever indicating his choice, the machine releases a pack of Camels. In this instance his freedom to have Kools has been eliminated. The individual would then experience an increased desire for Kools, and might even insert more money into the machine in order to buy a pack.

The first of these examples involves a personal threat to freedom and the second an impersonal elimination of freedom. In both instances, however, the threatened or eliminated freedom does not relate to the preferred choice. Reactance occurs whenever any choices or freedoms are eliminated, while simple frustration occurs when only the preferred choice or freedom is eliminated. The definition of simple frustration is thus less broad than the definition of reactance. A comprehensive discussion of frustration will be deferred until Chapter 9.

MAGNITUDE OF REACTANCE

According to Brehm the magnitude of reactance is a direct function of three determinants: (1) importance of the threatened or eliminated free behaviors, (2) proportion of free behaviors that are threatened or eliminated, (3) and, only in the case of threatened free behaviors, the magnitude of the threat.

The direction of these determinants of the magnitude of reactance agrees with common sense. With regard to the first determinant, *"the more important is that free behavior to the individual, the greater will be the magnitude of reactance"* (1966, p. 4). The importance of free behaviors is a function of the necessity of these behaviors for the satisfaction of *potentially* important needs. As long as the individual believes that he might have certain important needs at some time, the free behaviors necessary for the satisfaction of these needs are important.

With regard to the second determinant, "Given the individual's set of free behaviors, *the greater is the proportion eliminated or threatened with elimination, the greater will be the magnitude of reactance"* (1966, p. 6). And finally with regard to the third determinant, *"the greater is the threat, the greater will be the magnitude of reactance"* (1966, p. 6). A threat increases with an increasing probability that it will be carried out. Brehm makes two further points regarding threats. First, when a given free behavior is threatened or eliminated, there may be an implication that additional free behaviors will also be eliminated. For example, forbidding a secretary to chew gum possibly carries with it the additional implication that she is also forbidden to drink coffee or eat candy. Second, when an individual perceives that someone else's free behaviors are threatened or eliminated he may feel that his own free behaviors are by implication also threatened.

Effects of Reactance

Brehm mentions four effects of reactance. First, there is the *increased desirability of the threatened or eliminated free behavior.* This effect occurs in situations in which the individual is aware of reactance. Such awareness in turn occurs in situations in which reactance does not motivate antisocial behavior that is defensively denied.

Second, there is the *increased importance of the threatened or eliminated free behavior.* Reactance is not simply an unpleasant state which the individual can reduce through defensive tactics such as lowering the importance of the freedom. Rather, reactance is a motivational state with a specific direction, the recovery of freedom. Thus the threatened or eliminated free behavior would increase in importance, as well as in desirability.

Third, there is the *direct reestablishment of the free behavior.* If free behavior A is forbidden there will be a tendency for the individual to do A. Or if in a set of free behaviors A and B, the individual is told to do B, there will be a tendency to do A. Such reestablishment of free behavior is, of course, not possible in situations in which the behavior has been unequivocally eliminated.

Fourth and finally, there is the *reestablishment of free behavior by implication*. For example, if a secretary is forbidden to chew gum on the job, she may start engaging in other behaviors, such as eating candy bars or smoking, while still at work. According to Brehm, reestablishment of free behavior by implication tends to occur when there are restraints against the direct reestablishment of free behavior.

REACTANCE AND ATTITUDE CHANGE

Consider an individual holding an attitude at position A on a pro-con continuum. Suppose, further, that the individual is exposed to a persuasive communication advocating position B on the same pro-con continuum. In such a situation there are two salient freedoms, the freedom to adopt the attitude at position B and the freedom not to adopt the attitude at position B. According to Brehm, the importance of the freedom to adopt the attitude at position B is a monotonically decreasing function of the distance between A and B. The greater the distance between A and B the less the importance of the freedom to adopt the attitude at position B. The importance of the freedom *not* to adopt the attitude at position B, on the other hand, is a monotonically increasing function of the distance between A and B. The greater the distance between A and B the more the importance of the freedom not to adopt the attitude at position B.

Although Brehm does not directly discuss the implications of the two above functions, they could possibly be interpreted as implying that increasing communicator-communicatee discrepancy produces forces toward decreasing attitude change. The importance of the freedom to adopt the attitude at position B should facilitate attitude change, and such importance decreases with increasing discrepancy. The importance of the freedom not to adopt the attitude at position B should hinder attitude change, and such importance increases with increasing discrepancy. Brehm points out, however, that neither the freedom to adopt the attitude at position B nor the freedom not to adopt the attitude at position B may have too much importance to the individual. Whether or not these freedoms are important is dependent upon the extent to which they are related to values that the individual regards as important. Thus only when the two relevant freedoms are extremely important does reactance theory imply that increasing communicator-communicatee discrepancy produces decreasing conformity to the position advocated by the communicator.

When an individual is exposed to a persuasive communication advocating an attitude-discrepant position his freedom not to adopt this position is threatened and reactance results. Reactance, in turn, produces attempts to reestablish the freedom. Such reestablishment may occur through refusal to adopt the advocated position with a possible increase in confidence regarding the individual's own position. Or the individual may move his own position in the opposite direction from that advocated in the communication. Descriptively, such an occurrence is usually referred to as a *boomerang effect*.

Such pure reactance effects, however, are typically not manifested in uncontaminated form. The reason for this, according to Brehm, is that the content of the communication may contain facts and arguments which are in themselves convincing and conducive to change. Brehm makes a crucial distinction between communication content designed to help the individual decide upon the correct position and communication content designed to force the individual to adopt a particular position. There are numerous factors that may contribute toward perceiving the communicator as a source of influence. These include communicator characteristics such as untrustworthiness or having something to gain, and communicator acts such as drawing a strong conclusion, and giving a one-sided, emotional, or extreme message.

RESEARCH

In his 1966 book, *A Theory of Psychological Reactance*, Brehm describes a number of experiments conducted by him and his students. Most of these experiments, however, are of a very preliminary nature and do not warrant detailed description. Since 1966, however, more convincing evidence has been presented. Of the studies published since 1966, perhaps the most compelling is the one conducted by Sensenig and Brehm (1968). This latter study, which is an investigation of the effect of implied threat on attitude change, is contained in the Readings of this chapter.

Final Statement

Inoculation theory is a theory specifically focused on resistance to persuasive attacks against cultural truisms. Reactance theory, on the other hand, is a more general theory of resistance to influence. As such, reactance theory meets an obvious need for a more general theory. It is quite apparent both that resistance to influence does occur and that freedom is an important value. In the preface to this 1966 book Brehm makes an interesting observation about reactance.

> If there is anything surprising about a theory concerning how people respond to elimination of freedom it is that such a theory has not been proposed earlier. For given the historical concern of our culture for freedoms of one kind or another, and given the current plethora of freedom demonstrations, it seems obvious that concern for freedom should have some general psychological implications.

Brehm's point is well taken.

READINGS

Attitude Change from an Implied Threat to Attitudinal Freedom[1]

John Sensenig and Jack W. Brehm

College students were told they were to write an essay supporting 1 or the other side of each of 5 issues, and were led to believe they might be able to influence the decision about which side of an attitudinal issue they were to support. In all cases they were then told to support the side (either pro or con) they initially preferred, and post-measures were then obtained before the actual writing. Those who were given the impression that their preference was taken into account in the decision regarding which side they would support on the 1st issue showed attitude change favoring the preferred position (i.e., moving toward greater extremity, while retaining their initial polarity). Others, who were given the impression the decision was made without regard to their preference, tended to show attitude change away from the preferred position they were told to support. Within this latter group, those who expected to be told on which side to write on all 5 issues showed significantly greater change away than did those who expected to be told which side to support on only the 1st of the 5 issues.

The existing literature on social influence and attitude change has been primarily concerned with accounting for varying degrees of positive change. There has been some discussion of factors which might lead to resistance the persuasion and to boomerang effects (e.g., Cohen, 1962; Hovland, Janis, & Kelley, 1953; McGuire, 1964), but one can find surprisingly little systematic experimental investigation in this area, recent exceptions being studied by Berscheid (1966) and Abelson and Miller (1967). Indeed, in traditional attitude-change studies the subject's resistance to a persuasive communication is often interpreted as evidence of a weak manipulation, and a boomerang effect would generally be considered an experimental disaster. These interpretations are, of course, usually correct in that the investigators are primarily attempting to operationalize theories which predict differential amounts of positive influence, and they must therefore be able to show reliable amounts of positive attitude change. The purpose of the present study is to test a theory (Brehm, 1966) which predicts active resistance to persuasion and boomerang attitude change.

The theory assumes that a person generally feels free to select his own

[1] From the *Journal of Personality and Social Psychology*, Volume 8, pages 324–330, 1968 (received April 6, 1967). Authors' affiliation: Duke University. This research was supported in whole by National Institute of Mental Health Grant MH11228-02 under the direction of the junior author. Reproduced by permission of the American Psychological Association.

position in regard to attitudinal or opinion issues. To the extent that this is true, the person will experience a motivational state called "psychological reactance" whenever his attitudinal freedom is threatened by attempts to influence or change his attitude. Reactance motivation will oppose those forces which lead to compliance with the influence attempt, and if this motivation is sufficiently large a boomerang effect will occur. Evidence in support of this analysis has recently been obtained by Wicklund and Brehm (1968).

There are, of course, a number of reasons why influence attempts generally do not produce boomerang effects. The influence communication may contain persuasive information, the communication may appear to be an expert, and the issue or the person's position on it may be of low importance, leading to the individual's placing low value on his freedom to hold any attitudinal positions. For these reasons reactance forces presumably often serve more to weaken positive influence than to produce outright movement away from the advocated position.

The theory states that a threat to several freedoms should arouse more reactance than a threat to a single freedom. Thus, when a threat to a given freedom *implies* threats to further freedoms, the individual should experience more reactance than if the same threat led to no such implications. A study by Brehm and Sensenig (1966) attempted to test this prediction in a situation where subjects made a series of two-alternative choices and another (fictitious) person sent them a note telling them which alternative to select on the first set of alternatives. It was predicted that in a condition where subjects expected to receive later notes (implying the possibility of further suggestions) they would be less likely to choose the suggested alternative than in a condition where they would receive only one such note. It was found that subjects who were told which alternative to choose were significantly less likely to select the suggested alternative, but contrary to the prediction the expectation of later messages made no significant difference. Since the manipulation of implied threat in this study was thought to be weak, it was felt that the implication hypothesis had not been adequately tested. The present study was designed to strengthen the manipulation of implied threats to the subject's freedom and to extend the hypothesis to the area of attitude change. In the original study the restriction to the subject's freedom involved a series of simple choices between different sets of pictures, one of which the subject would then "work with." The present study attempted to establish the reactance effect in terms of change on an already existing attitude, and utilized a pre- and postmeasure design.

METHOD

The plan was to have two subjects fill out an attitude questionnaire concerning several issues, to lead them to believe that they would have to write essays supporting one side or the other on some of the issues, and that the other member of the pair would decide which side they would both support. Subjects were further to believe the other person could solicit their preference before deciding which side they would support on each issue. For one-third of the subjects this preference was actually solicited on the first issue (control condition) while the remaining subjects were arbitrarily told which side to support. One-half of these remaining subjects expected to be told which side to support on only the first issue (low implied threat to freedom) while others expected to be told in regard to all five issues (high implied threat to freedom). Subjects' attitudes on the first issue were again measured before they wrote their essay.

Subjects

Ninety-nine female students from introductory psychology classes at Duke University participated in the study as part of the course requirement. Subjects were randomly assigned with the exception that they would be equally distributed among three experimental conditions, two subjects being run at each experimental session. Nine subjects were eliminated from the analysis; seven because they checked an end point on the premeasure item, thus allowing attitude change in only one direction; one because she apparently misused the premeasure scale; and one because of extreme suspicion. It should be noted that if the deleted subjects had been included in the analysis the obtained differences would have been slightly greater in the predicted direction.

Procedure

Two subjects were run at each experimental session.[2] After a brief introduction they were asked to fill out a 15-item questionnaire containing such opinion statements as "The United States is justified in fighting in Viet Nam." Below each statement was a 31-point scale labeled "strongly agree" at one end and "strongly disagree" at the other end. Below each opinion statement were two similar 31-point scales on which subjects were to indicate their "confidence" and the "importance" of the issue. After the questionnaires were completed the experimenter explained that he was interested in why people felt the way they did on these issues, and the remainder of the study would require that they write a short essay on each of 5 different issues which had been selected from the 15 issues on the questionnaire they had just completed.

In both the high-implied-threat and control conditions it was explained that the experimenter was also interested in "comparing the essays that are written by the two people who are in the study together," and so they would be required to write from the same point of view *on each of the five essays.* In the low-implied-threat condition the same instructions were given with the exception that *only on the first essay* would they be required to write from the same point of view. On the four later essays these subjects would each be able to select the side which they preferred.

The procedure to this point laid the groundwork for restricting the subject to write on a given side of the issue. However, the arousal of psychological reactance theoretically requires a real or implied reduction in freedom, not just a restriction. For this reason it was necessary to give the subjects the impression they had some freedom to influence the decision as to which side they would support. At the same time, in order to insure that the decision maker would appear to be acting in a credible fashion, and not inconsistently with the experimental instructions, the freedom given to the subject could only be partial. The remaining instructions, then, were designed to give the subjects the impression they had some limited amount of freedom to determine which side they would support on their essay(s). They were told that some of the previous

[2] In the early stages of the experiment, five subjects were run using a confederate as the second person. This was done when either of the two regularly scheduled subjects failed to keep her appointment. This procedure was discontinued when it was determined that there was a relatively low number of subjects who failed to appear.

subjects who had been appointed to make the choice(s) had wanted to know how the other subject felt on the issue(s). Because of this, it was explained, subjects doing the choosing would be able to ask the other subject about her preference. In any case, the person making the choice would have the final say as to which side both of them would support on the essay(s).

Subjects were told they would be in separate rooms while writing their essays, and their questions about procedure were answered. Each was asked to draw a slip of paper to determine which one would make the decision(s), and they were immediately placed in separate experimental rooms. The two slips were actually identical and each subject was informed by the note that "The other person will make the choice on the first essay," in the low-implied-threat condition or "The other person will make the choice on each of the five essays," in the high-implied-threat and control conditions.

Premeasure questionnaires were collected and each subject was given a list of five items taken from the questionnaire. These were the items on which they expected to write their essays. The first, and critical, attitude statement was: "Federal aid to church-run schools should be discontinued." This issue was one on which pretest subjects had not generally been extreme, and would therefore allow attitude change in either direction. The four additional items were selected to strengthen the implied-threat manipulation. They were of general high importance and the freedom to support one side or the other should have been of correspondingly high importance.

While the subjects thought about their essays the experimenter went into another room, scored the critical item on the premeasure (Number 8 of the 15), and assigned each of the subjects a bogus note which the subject was to believe came from the other person. The note always assigned the subject to write her essay in support of the side of the issue she had favored on the premeasure. The high-implied-threat condition and the control condition contained exactly the same instructions and procedure with the exception of the type of note that the subject received. This made it possible to run a high-implied-threat subject and a control subject at the same experimental session with the experimenter remaining blind through all instructions up to the actual assignment of notes. At this time the experimenter flipped a coin determining which condition each subject would be in and each was assigned the appropriate note. Since the instructions in the low-implied-threat condition differed from those of the other two conditions, it was not possible for the experimenter to remain blind in this condition.

The Threat. The note constituted the manipulation of threat to the subject's freedom and was identical in the high- and low-implied-threat conditions. It consisted of the issue printed on it and the handwritten statement, "I've decided we will both agree [disagree] with this." The control condition received a note which said, "I'd prefer to agree [disagree] with this if it's all right with you." It can be seen that on both of these notes the other person stated a definite preference, but with the note given in the control condition, the person appeared to allow the subject the freedom of disagreeing with her if the subject wished.

The experimenter returned to each room in turn and gave the subject the appropriate note and the essay form for the first issue. At the top of this form were three scales on which the subject was to indicate her "actual feelings" on this issue. These scales were repeat measures of agreement, confidence, and importance as contained on the premeasure questionnaire, and they constituted the main dependent measures. After checking these three items the subject was to write her essay on the lower part of this form. Subjects in the high-implied-threat condition and control condition were reminded that, "You will also receive a note before each of the four later essays." Subjects in the low-implied-threat condition were reminded that, "This is the only note you will receive." All subjects in the control condition agreed to write from the point of view expressed in the note. The experimenter left the subjects and returned after approximately 5 minutes with a short questionnaire to fill out "before we go on to the second essay." The questionnaire was rationalized as being a check on impressions they might have formed of the other person during the experiment. It contained eight questions about such impressions, the perceived likelihood that the other person had affected their attitude, and their perceptions of the manipulations. This completed the formal procedure, and the subjects were brought together, asked about suspicions they might have had, and finally informed as to the deceptions employed and the true purpose of the experiment.

Results

To check on the success of the implied-threat manipulation the following question was included in the postexperimental questionnaire: "How likely do you think it is that she will ask for your opinion on later choices?" Responses were on a 31-point scale labeled "not at all likely" at one end, and "very likely" at the other, scored with a higher number indicating greater perceived likelihood. Responses are available only for subjects in the control and high-implied-threat conditions since those in the low-implied-threat condition expected to receive no further notes and could not reasonably be asked to respond. The mean response in the high-implied-threat condition, 12.2, was clearly less than that in the control, 18.8 ($t = 4.35$, $df = 58$, $p < .001$), indicating that there should indeed have been a differential perception of threat between the high- and low-implied-threat conditions.

Attitude Change. Since subjects in the control condition received a note that suggested that the essay be written from the point of view which they originally favored, and since the other person asked the subject's opinion on that issue, the note would likely be seen as positive social support for the subject's existing attitude. It was expected, therefore, that the subjects in this condition would be positively influenced, that is, they would move in the direction advocated by the note and more toward the extreme on the dependent measure item than they had been on the same

TABLE 1

Premeasure and Change Scores on the Attitude Issue[a]

Condition	Premeasure		Change	
	M	s^2	M	s^2
Control	14.53	45.15	1.37	8.80
Low implied threat	14.10	43.88	−.27	16.62
High implied threat	14.37	58.03	−4.17	68.83

[a] Significance of differences using a pooled error term ($df = 58$): low versus control, $t = 1.13$, $p > .10$; high versus control, $t = 3.83$, $p < .01$; high versus low, $t = 2.70$, $p < .01$.

item on the premeasure questionnaire. In Table 1 it can be seen that only in the control condition are the subjects' attitudes positively influenced.

Since subjects in the low-implied-threat and high-implied-threat conditions also received notes which agreed with the point of view they originally favored, there would have been some social support in these conditions as well. However, it was predicted that reactance aroused by the threat to freedom would tend to produce attitude change away from the supported position, and that the magnitude of reactance and consequent tendency to change away would be greater in the high-implied-threat condition than in the low. Thus, if reactance effects were great enough, negative attitude change would occur despite social support for initial position. Table 1 shows that these predictions were confirmed.[3] The low-implied-threat condition subjects showed a slight negative attitude change which is not significant when compared to the positive change shown by control subjects ($t = 1.13$, $df = 58$, $p > .10$). The high-implied-threat condition subjects showed a clearly significant negative attitude change when compared to the control subjects ($t = 3.83$, $df = 58$, $p < .01$), and also showed significantly greater negative change than the low-implied-threat-condition subjects ($t = 2.70$, $df = 58$, $p < .01$). There are no significant differences between conditions on the items measuring either confidence or importance, although there is a trend for confidence to increase with increasing threat.

Perceived Characteristics of Note Sender. It might be argued that there are at least two factors which would affect a person's power to influence the attitudes of another. These are: (a) his personal attractiveness, and (b) his perceived competence on the issue. The power of the note sender in this experiment may have been differentially affected by the content of the notes, which might have caused him to be seen, in the reactance conditions, as (a) personally unattractive, on the basis of a rude note which did not ask the subject's opinion, or (b) incompetent on such issues, perhaps related to the note sender's general social insensitivity as indicated by the restricting note. It is not exactly clear how these arguments would predict the differential attitude change related to implication, and the differential attitude change which exists between the high-implied-threat and low-implied-threat conditions, which used the same note. It is possible, however, that some such differences might have developed even between these conditions as a function of the implication manipulation. Since an explanation of this attitude change based on reactance theory requires that these

---

[3] It will be noted that the variance of change scores are much greater in the high-implied-threat condition than in the low and control conditions. This difference is reasonable since subjects in the high condition are theoretically placed under conflicting pressures to change positively and negatively. A pooled error term was used for the *t* tests. It may also be noted that the proportion of negative changers increases directly with threat to freedom: 30% in control, 43% in low, and 63% in high.

TABLE 2

Mean Ratings of Likability and Competence of the Note Sender

Condition	Likability		Competence	
	M	s^2	M	s^2
Control	22.93[a]	15.86	22.13[a]	15.50
Low implied threat	21.97	16.10	21.77	11.01
High implied threat	21.37	28.62	20.87	8.36

[a] Higher score indicates greater likability and competence.

effects not be primarily mediated by negative impressions of the restricting agent, it was thought valuable to have some check on these impressions. Several such measures of the subject's perception of the other person were obtained a few minutes after the dependent measure. The crucial ratings in this regard were two 31-point scales on which the subject was asked to rate the other person on likability and competence. The first question was: "How much do you like the other person?" and the scale was labeled "very likable" at one extreme, and "not at all likable" at the other extreme. The second question was "How competent do you feel the other person is on tasks such as you are doing?" and the scale was labeled "not at all competent" at one extreme and "highly competent" at the other extreme. The mean ratings on these measures for the three experimental groups are shown in Table 2. It would seem that the other person is seen as moderately likable and competent in all conditions. None of the differences approaches significance and it is improbable that they account for the observed attitude change effects.

Displacement of Hostility

An alternative explanation of the attitude-change data might be based on the concept of displaced hostility. It might be argued that the restricting note aroused hostile feelings in the subject, and that these feelings would be more extreme when the subject expected further notes. Since the experimental procedure did not allow the subject to retaliate by doing something hostile to the note sender, some subjects might find that they could displace this hostility in one of the only ways available to them, changing their attitude. This would seem to be true of those subjects who *originally disagreed* with the statement that federal aid to church-run schools should be discontinued. By moving away from their original position they would, in effect, be displacing their hostility by agreeing that money should be taken away from these schools.

The attitude premeasure and change scores were broken down and analyzed separately according to initial position. The results of this analysis show that, in the crucial high-implied-threat condition, there is in fact somewhat more negative change shown by those who initially disagreed ($n = 16$, initial $M = 8.44$, mean change $= -5.38$)[4] than in those who initially agreed ($n = 14$, initial $M = 22.57$, mean change $= -2.79$). This trend, however, does not even approach statistical significance ($t = .85$, $df = 28$, $p > .10$). Furthermore, it can be noted that no matter which side of the issue a subject originally favored, he does show negative change, that is, he changes away from the position taken in the note. The displacement of hostility argument would not predict this change on the part of those who initially agreed with the statement. If these subjects feel hostile why should they change toward giving money to church schools? These factors would seem to severely weaken, if not eliminate, an alternative explanation of the attitude-change data based on the notion of displacement of hostility.

Self-esteem

Having the other person not ask the subject's opinion and, instead, order her around might have had the effect of lowering the self-esteem of the subjects. To the extent that the subjects felt lowered self-esteem they might have tended to express more moderate attitudes after receiving the note from the other. The attitude-change results would, then, be the same if the experimenters had inadvertently manipulated self-esteem rather than the hypothesized reactance motivation.

It will be remembered that both on the initial premeasure questionnaire and on the dependent measure the subjects were asked to indicate not only their attitude but also the importance of the issue and the confidence they had in their opinion. It would seem that any changes in self-esteem might best be revealed by changes in this latter item, that is *confidence*. These data reveal that the high-implied-threat condition showed the greatest increase in confidence (mean change $= 3.63$), the low-implied-threat condition showed a moderate increase in confidence (mean change $= 2.46$), and the control condition showed the least amount of increase in confidence (mean change $= 1.90$). Although none of these changes reaches an adequate level of statistical reliability, it is obvious that the trend revealed in these confidence change scores is in the opposite direction of what would be predicted by the self-esteem explanation. There is, then, evidence that it was not lowered self-esteem which mediated the observed attitude-change results.

Results have been reported on three of the eight questions asked after the dependent measure (perceived competence and likability of the note sender, and likelihood of being consulted on later decisions). The remaining five items were attempts to obtain self-reports from subjects on their general reactions to the note (for example: "How likely do you think it is

---

[4] Higher numbers indicate greater agreement with the statement that federal aid should be discontinued.

that she affected your opinion?"). The trend of the data on these questions indicates a slight tendency toward greater awareness of possible attitude change in those groups which actually did show more change (i.e., the high-implied-threat and control conditions). However, these differences do not approach statistical reliability and they will not be discussed further.

DISCUSSION

The present findings indicate that when a person's freedom to support a position on an attitude issue is eliminated, psychological reactance is aroused in him, and he consequently tends to change his attitude in such a way as to restore the lost freedom. The results also indicate that the magnitude of reactance and consequent attitude change increases with the number of freedoms implicitly threatened with elimination.

It is interesting to note that attitude change takes place even though there is no seeming external instrumental value to the change. The subjects in the threat conditions had no choice but to write on the side of the issue stated in the note, and they had no reason to expect that the note sender would know how they felt. Thus, moving away from a position which they had originally favored could in no way change their fate, and indeed it might make it somewhat more difficult to write an essay from the required point of view. We would contend, however, that within the experimental situation it was difficult for subjects to reestablish their freedoms in any fashion other than negative attitude change. When the subjects received the restricting note, and particularly when they expected later similar notes, one of the easiest ways for them to establish their freedom phenomenally was to move their attitude away from the position which the note sender was demanding they support. This shift in attitude would serve to indicate that, although they might have to write from the required point of view, they were still free to take different positions in regard to their actual beliefs or attitudes.

Regarding their somewhat similar experiment, Brehm and Sensenig (1966) presented an alternative explanation which they were unable to rule out effectively. It centered around the idea that in this type of experiment the note sender may be perceived as transgressing the rules of the experiment. Thus, if the note is unexpected and seemingly not in keeping with the experimental instructions, the subject may attempt to cover up for the other person's transgressions by simply ignoring the note as much as possible. This tendency to ignore the note rather than to oppose it actively is a tenable explanation when a clear and significant boomerang is not produced. In an attempt to lower the likelihood of this type of reaction to the note in the present experiment the experimenter tried to make clear that it was acceptable for the note sender either to ask the other's opinion or not. It was mentioned, however, that some of the subjects had wished to know how the other person felt on the issue(s) and that this was why they were to receive notes. It was assumed that most subjects would anticipate being consulted on at least the first choice (on which most subjects were less extreme and perhaps more flexible). Thus, subjects would have a normative expectation of being consulted on the first decision, but if the note sender did not ask their opinion it could not be perceived as an open transgression of experimental requirements. In the present experiment these safeguards may have been less necessary since there is a clear and significant boomerang effect shown in the high-implied-threat conditions. This negative change could hardly be explained by a mere tendency to ignore the note and rather requires positing an active force operating to move the person away from the suggestion.

The differences between experimental conditions do not seem to be based simply on negative attributions associated with the note sender, or on the displacement of hostility, or on lowered self-esteem, or the subjects' simply ignoring the note because of perceived experimental transgression by the note sender. The present authors would contend that the differences are related to differential threats to the subject's attitudinal freedom and concomitant reactance forces. Therefore, we conclude that the present experiment has supported the various links in our chain of reasoning: specifically, that (a) when a person's freedom is threatened there will occur a motivational state directed toward restoration of the threatened freedom, (b) the greater the number of behavioral freedoms threatened by implication, the greater will be the magnitude of the motivational state and consequent tendency to restore the threatened freedom, and (c) with regard to attitudes, the reestablishment of freedom may take the form of changing one's position away from the position that is implied or forced on one.

REFERENCES

Abelson, R. P., & Miller, J. C. Negative persuasion via personal insult. *Journal of Experimental Social Psychology*, 1967, **3**, 321–333.
Berscheid, E. Opinion change and communicator-communicatee similarity and dissimilarity. *Journal of Personality and Social Psychology*, 1966, **4**, 670–680.
Brehm, J. W. *A theory of psychological reactance.* New York: Academic Press, 1966.
Brehm, J. W., & Sensenig, J. Social influence as a function of attempted and implied usurpation of choice. *Journal of Personality and Social Psychology*, 1966, **4**, 703–707.
Cohen, A. R. A dissonance analysis of the boomerang effect. *Journal of Personality*, 1962, **30**, 75–88.
Hovland, C. I., Janis, I. L., & Kelley, H. H. *Communication and persuasion.* New Haven, Connecticut: Yale University Press, 1953.
McGuire, W. J. Inducing resistance to persuasion. In L. Berkowitz (Ed.), *Advances in experimental social psychology.* Vol. 1. New York: Academic Press, 1964.
Wicklund, R. A., & Brehm, J. W. Attitude change as a function of felt competence and threat to attitudinal freedom. *Journal of Experimental Social Psychology*, 1968, **4**, 64–75.

Part II

INTERPERSONAL PROCESSES

In turning from attitude change to interpersonal processes, we move from what is essentially a one-way process (a source influencing a target person) to a two-way process of interaction. The essence of interaction, as Thibaut and Kelley (1959) have emphasized, is that the consequences for either person in a dyad are a joint function of their own behaviors *and* the behaviors of the partner. Interaction is a process in which one person responds to another as a set of stimuli and himself becomes a stimulus for the other's responses.

The experimental investigation of interaction, however, will rely on the one-way format illustrated in attitude change research. In order to make causal inferences the research will continue to be characterized by the manipulation of at least two values of an independent variable in order to assess effects on a dependent variable. With some notable exceptions, the subjects' responses will not differentially elicit responses from a stimulus person. The content of what a target person says, for example, in a tape recording, will not be altered by a subject's initial reaction of dismay or approval. In natural settings the reactions elicited by a speaker do affect his subsequent responses. The research, however, will often divide the processes of interaction into one-way units, but *the aim of such studies is to generalize to two-way processes.*

This section proceeds from presenting research on the determinants of how one person perceives another, through the determinants of liking for another, and ends with two chapters on mechanisms which control interaction.

Chapter 8

PERSON PERCEPTION AND ATTRIBUTION PROCESSES

Categories and Relationships

Human beings have a strong desire to render their environment as stable, and therefore, as predictable as possible. It is not only the inevitability of death and taxes, but also a myriad of other perceived regularities which guide our daily acts and contribute to our ability to survive. The test for whether or not one has a proper understanding of the physical or social environment is in the accuracy of the predictions one is able to make about the environment. The people who can make the most accurate predictions about the environment stand the best chance of obtaining the best rewards available to them. The desire for stability is sufficiently robust that it is not necessarily constrained by reality. We have already discussed the tendency for a person's cognitions to move to a balanced state—a tendency that can be understood as the creation of stability in the social environment.

It can be instructive to view a person's perception of regularities in terms similar to the scientist's efforts at understanding various features of the environment. The key concept is the construction of hypotheses about how things fit together. We will explicate this similarity with a brief digression and then return to its application in the area of person perception.

A hypothesis specifies a relationship between two or more variables. It can be as elegantly simple as specifying a relationship between the masses and distance of two objects, on the amount of attraction they exert on each other. That is, the amount of attraction between two bodies equals the product of the masses divided by the square of the distance between them and represents one of Newton's contributions to rendering our environment more stable. As Williams (1954) notes, "The elements of the theory . . . did not just float into a mind dazed by a blow from an apple" (p. 6). Newton's theory evolved from a cumulation of centuries of observation of heavenly bodies. Such observations had not only led to working out relationships among heavenly bodies, but also had implicitly detailed the kinds of elements, or attributes, which were of particular importance. Hypotheses require classificatory categories and the specification of relationships among categories. When a person first looks at the night sky he is not likely to perceive much order in what he views. The neophyte observer might notice differences in brightness and size among the objects, but it would require persistent observation to notice that some stars appear to maintain the same relationship to each other or to distinguish suns from planets.

As social perceivers we also use categories. They are culturally given, determined by language and modified by experience. Our understanding of the world is determined by these categories and the relationships we see among them. For example, a person might hold that the categories "football star" and "low grade-point average" are positively related. This is a simple hypothesis which applies whenever we can categorize someone into the class, "football star." Its accuracy can be checked by learning about his grade-point average. A category is useful and will presumably remain viable, to the extent to which it is reliably related to other categories. This is another way of saying that categories which are predictive will be likely to be retained in the language and the cognitive structures of people in a particular culture.

Consider the actuarial method employed by insurance companies. Fees for automobile liability insurance vary with the likelihood of the insured having an accident. Insurance companies begin with age categories. Teenage drivers are more likely to have accidents than middle-aged drivers. This relationship has been established empirically, by past accident records. Knowing a person's age allows predicting the likelihood of an accident; but a finer differentiation can be made. Evidently having passed a driver's education course lowers the accident rate. Insurance companies use both dimensions of age and completion of a driving course to classify people. It should be noted that additional refinements are functional to the extent that they improve predictions. In addition, a particular category is useful in predicting to some other categories, but irrelevant to many more. Frequency of past accidents is a refinement for predicting the probability of future accidents. It is not likely to be useful in predicting grade-point average in college, degree of friendliness, political views, etc.

The linking of one category with another in person perception can be illustrated by reference to a study conducted by Bruner, Shapiro, and Tagiuri (1958). Subjects were asked to imagine a person who was "intelligent" and then rate whether or not such a person possessed other traits, such as "reliable" and "aggressive." Some of the traits on the list were almost always rated as being associated with someone who was intelligent, while others were almost never seen as being associated. Because these connections were similarly rated by most subjects they were termed a "lay theory of personality." Bruner, Shapiro, and Tagiuri also used four additional stimulus words to obtain the inferred connections made by subjects. They were then able to assess what happened when the stimulus words were combined. As one might imagine if each stimulus word was by itself associated with a particular trait, the combination of words would strongly imply the trait. If a person who is either "intelligent" or "industrious" is usually seen to be "thrifty" then an "intelligent and industrious" person will invariably be seen as "thrifty."

The Bruner *et al.* experiment illustrates a way of studying how people combine information to form impressions, that is, how they make attributions about other people. In general, attribution refers to the process of inferring or perceiving properties in one's self and others. It is a way of understanding the stable features of the environment, whether the entities are books, chairs, people, or groups. There are three general problem areas on which research has focused. The first one, already illustrated by the Bruner *et al.* study, concerns the question of how a person combines information about a target person to arrive at attributions about him. The second concerns problems of assessing the accuracy of attributions. The third encompasses attempts to understand the role of causal attributions about a target person's behavior and their effects upon the perceiver.

Combining Cues

PRIMACY EFFECTS

Does the sequence of information received by a person make a difference in the impression he forms? One frequently hears of the importance of making a "good first impression," and thereby has heard a statement of an hypothesis about the occurrence of the primacy effect. There is no general agreement about what cognitive processes determine a primacy effect. In

Chapter 3 we have discussed order effects for serially presented persuasive messages. Miller and Campbell (1959), it will be recalled, interpreted order effects in terms of memory for the communication content. Memory would appear to be an important aspect of impression formation and it has been invoked as an interpretive concept of order effects. Additional explanatory concepts have also been suggested, especially for results obtained in experiments using brief stimulus material and testing intervals of short duration.

Solomon Asch (1946) first reported a primacy effect for impression formation. Subjects were shown a list of six adjectives. Half of them read the list in one order (intelligent, industrious, impulsive, critical, stubborn, and envious) while the other half had the list presented in reverse order. The first group formed more favorable impressions of the target person; for example, they were more likely to see him as happy, humorous, and sociable. It is evident that Asch's adjective list contains three positively valued traits and three negatively valued traits. The order of these adjectives can be seen as either good-bad or bad-good. Asch felt that the primacy effect was caused by the *assimilation of* the *meaning* of the later adjectives toward the meaning established by the earlier ones. This kind of primacy effect depends upon the existence of a polarity in the information contained in the item series. Discrepancies, created by the implications of positive items and negative items, are resolved by retaining the evaluative position initially created.

Luchins (1957a) also demonstrated the existence of a primacy effect in a series of three experiments. He devised two paragraphs describing the activities of a student called Jim. In one paragraph most of Jim's behaviors were "introverted," while in the other they were "extroverted." In the critical conditions subjects read both paragraphs, but some read the "introverted" first and others the "extroverted" first. The content of the first paragraph strongly influenced the subjects' impressions. Luchins offers the following explanations of his results: (1) the material in the second paragraph may have been less well learned because of interference set up by the content being discrepant from the first paragraph; (2) subjects may have been less attentive to the material in the second paragraph; and (3) subjects may have more readily accepted the initial paragraph. Luchins suggests all three of these possibilities can be subsumed under the general hypothesis that initial information produces a set which affects later information.

Other experimenters have also used serial lists of adjectives in order to investigate the way a perceiver processes information. Anderson (e.g., Anderson & Barrios, 1961; Anderson & Hubert, 1963; Anderson, 1965) has extensively investigated the idea that the primacy effect is caused by the assignment of decreased weights to later information, rather than to a change in meaning. Similar to Luchins' second and third explanations, Anderson suggests two mechanisms which could account for perceivers' assigning decreased weight to subsequent information in serial presentations. It could mean that either they discount later discrepant information or they become progressively inattentive. By using adjective lists differing in length and containing different degrees of polarization, Anderson (1968) has shown that discounting seems the more likely process. Hendrick and Costantini (1970), on the other hand, report an experiment favoring an attention-decrement interpretation. Evaluatively opposite groups of adjectives were combined into six-word sets which differed in terms of their judged trait consistency. Trait consistency was defined by judges' ratings of the likelihood that the six traits in any given set would all be possessed by an actual person. For example, from one of the consistent sets, two of the evaluatively opposite adjectives were "energetic" and "dominating." "Self-confident" and "dull" are an example of evaluatively opposite adjectives from a set which was not consistent. The authors deduced that the occurrence of discounting should produce a larger primacy effect for inconsistent sets than for consistent sets. The use of attention decrement, on the other hand, was thought to be insensitive to trait inconsistency and would produce no differences in amount of primacy. Because the results showed that the magnitude of the primacy effect was not changed by the degree of consistency, the authors favored an inattention explanation for primacy effects. It is, of course, entirely possible that discounting and attention decrements occur under different conditions. When attention decrements occur there is little further need or opportunity for discounting.

Anderson's research on the primacy effect was undertaken to clarify the way a perceiver combines separate cues into a single impression. The predictions do not concern the content of the impression, but the degree of favorableness of that impression. Anderson favors an averaging explanation. That is, the final degree of favorableness can be predicted by averaging the favorableness of each separate cue. The averaging model accounts for a primacy effect by assuming later information is discounted before being averaged with prior information. Other people, for example, Fishbein and Hunter (1964), have suggested an additive model. This model assumes that progressive information is added to the existing impression. If two lists of adjectives contain the same number of items, but differ in the proportion of positive cues, both the averaging and the additive model will predict more favorable impressions will be generated by the list containing more favorable adjectives. The models differ, however, in predicting the consequences of additional information. In order to enhance favorableness of an existing impression, the averaging model specifies a new trait must be more favorable than the average of the previous ones. The additive model predicts increments of favorableness by the addition of any favorable item. Neither model adequately accounts for all of the data.

Although the effects of order of stimuli on impression formation have been largely studied with serially presented trait adjectives, many other kinds of information are processed by perceivers. Consider, for example, the way a perceiver combines information about the adequacy of another person's performance over time. Jones, Rock, Shaver, Goethals, and Ward (1968) conducted a series of five studies in which subjects rated the ability of a target person who either gradually improved in his performance (low to high performance) or gradually worsened in his performance (high to low). Each experiment revealed a primacy effect. The subjects' initial opinion of the target person's ability was not offset by changes in subsequent performance. Thibaut and Ross (1969) found that commitment was a crucial variable determining the presence or absence of primacy effects in judgments of serially presented stimuli purporting to be other persons' judgments about the quality of an artist's paintings. The other person's judgments were represented by tables containing different proportions of good and bad ratings. These tables were tachistiscopically presented in ascending (bad-to-good) order or descending (good-to-bad) order. In the commitment condition subjects ranked a set of reproductions of paintings by various artists. Subjects who were to view a bad-to-good order were told that the tables contained others' judgments about paintings done by an artist the subjects had previously ranked low. Subjects who were to view a good-to-bad order were told that the tables contained others' judgments about paintings done by an artist the subjects had previously ranked high. In the noncommitment conditions no initial ranking of paintings was done. Committed subjects presented with a high-to-low sequence made more favorable ratings than subjects presented a low-to-high sequence; that is, a primacy effect was obtained only in the commitment condition.

RECENCY EFFECTS

If the most recent information learned about a target person is given disproportionately large weight in determining the final impression, a recency effect has occurred. The experimental literature also contains examples of recency effects obtained with inconsistent information. There are various experimental manipulations which will induce a perceiver to weigh more heavily the most recent information, but no ready generalization is available about the mechanism (or mechanisms) which most parsimoniously account for the effect. For example, Luchins (1957b), in a study using the same two descriptions of Jim noted above, manipulated the events intervening after subjects had read the first paragraph. When the experimenter either admonished subjects against making snap judgments or required subjects to work on simple arithmetic problems for five minutes, recency effects were found. A recency effect in these circumstances may reflect the effects of forgetting. The interpolated material may also disrupt the set induced by the initial information.

Even when serially presented, inconsistent trait adjectives are used as stimuli, conditions can be created which neutralize the primacy effect or reverse it into a recency effect. These effects have been shown with manipulations which require subjects to do additional cognitive work such as recalling the traits (Anderson & Hubert, 1963), making ratings after each successive trait is presented (Stewart, 1965), or pronouncing the traits out loud (Anderson, 1968; Hendrick & Costantini, 1970). These manipulations are seen by Hendrick and Costantini as inducing the subject to redistribute his attention across the items in the series. A recency effect was obtained by Rosenbaum and Levin (1968) who used a procedure which did not directly require subjects to do additional cognitive work. In this study the positive and negative trait lists were presented as descriptions of the target person given by two different sources, persons who were identified only by their occupation. The presentation of inconsistent information by two communicators is seen by Rosenbaum and Levin as producing a recency effect because it induces a delay of impression formation.

Strong recency effects were found in a face-to-face interaction by Wilson and Insko (1968). Subjects interacted with an experimental confederate who behaved either cooperatively at first and then competitively, or competitively and then cooperatively. The episodes of cooperative and competitive behavior occurred either one immediately after the other or a week apart. Some subjects rated the confederate's interaction style immediately after the second episode and some rated it one week later. In all instances a strong recency effect was found. Although their data provided no basis for interpreting the cause of the recency effect, it is interesting to speculate why it occurred in their experiment while Jones *et al.* found a primacy effect. It may be that perceivers assume abilities are relatively more stable than other personal attributes. Perceivers may also assume that an initial interaction style is less representative of what the person is "truly" like than the styles enacted later in an interaction. Ratings based on information about the course of another's interaction would then exhibit a recency effect, while ability judgments would show a primacy effect. There is another difference between the two experiments which might account for the different findings. Wilson and Insko's subjects were involved in the interaction with the person they were to rate. They may have felt some responsibility for eliciting the change in the confederate's behavior, which could not be the case for the passive observers used by Jones *et al.* or Thibaut and Ross. Recency might serve the ends of maintaining self-esteem for the involved perceiver. It would be uncomfortable to ascribe a partner's change from pleasant to unpleasant behavior to anything but the manifestation of his true traits, whereas a change from unpleasant to pleasant behavior can readily be ascribed to having created a climate where the other's true goodness can flourish. It may be that any involvement in the interaction with the target person will usually produce recency effects, even if ability judgments are at issue. This speculation suggests, for example, that a student who first obtains a grade of F and then an A will receive a higher grade and be seen more favorably by his professor than a student who first obtains an A and then an F.

Jones and Goethals (1971) have surveyed the diverse findings on order effects in impression formation. Their effort to systematize this area includes identifying variables determining order effects. Among other things, they detail the potential importance of distinguishing among the kind of attributes used to manipulate change and the kind of instructions used to obtain final impression measures. Manipulation of stable attributes, such as intelligence or ability, may lead to primacy effects, whereas situationally determined attributes, such as friendliness or involvement, may show recency effects. In addition, if the final impression measures are presented in a context which implies "What is the target person like now?" recency effects will be found. Because the order of receiving information is typically locked with the order in which the behavior was emitted, a current impression of a target person must show recency effects. Finally, Jones and Goethals, following Mettee's (1971a) distinction, point out that separate sequential information about a target person may be independent information or may be replacement information. Most of the research discussed in this section has illustrated independent information, such as lists of traits describing a target person. Discrepancies contained within independent information must be resolved. Replacement information implies that successive information replaces preceding information. A person who has just fallen in love is not likely to gauge his feelings toward the loved one by taking account of his previous, less favorable evaluations. Replacement information means that the most current information is the most accurate and, of course, produces a recency effect.

Summary of Explanations of Primacy and Recency

A primacy effect occurs whenever a perceiver's final impression is determined more by initial information than later information. The three most prominent explanations of primacy are (1) discounting, (2) attention decrements, and (3) altered meaning of later information. A primacy effect is most likely to occur when the initial information leads to the formation of a stable impression which the perceiver protects while processing subsequent, discrepant information. Explanations of a recency effect can be subsumed under two broad headings. One family of explanations invokes processes affecting the recall of the information received. Any conditions which interfere with the recall of initial information, such as information sequences which extend over long time spans, amounts of information which are too large to be memorized, or the occurrence of intervening activity, will produce a tendency toward recency. A second set of explanations relies on specific contextual effects to account for recency. Whenever the sequence of information reflects a process in which later information is more valid than earlier information, recency would be obtained. Replacement information, such as seeing an improving performance as a reflection of the target person's learning or hearing increasingly intimate information reflecting the target person's lessening guardedness, is an example of such contextual effects.

CENTRAL TRAITS

Serial effects are studied by presenting identical information to subjects, but varying the order of presentation. The content of the item series is itself not important. It is, however, obvious that the content of the information is the major source of impressions. While it is evident that different information produces different impressions, one might wonder about the effects of altering only some information, while holding the rest constant. Again, it was Asch (1946) who established a precedent with respect to investigating this broad problem. In one of his studies, subjects were asked to write their impressions of someone who was: intelligent, skillful, industrious, warm, determined, practical, and cautious. They were also asked to rate that target person on a set of traits. A second group received the same materials, but the adjective "cold" was substituted for "warm." The two groups differed markedly in their ratings. The fact that new information alters an impression is rather trivial. What elevates the importance of this finding is Asch's contention that the effect of changing one word has ramifications for the meaning of the entire series—the effect goes beyond the magnitude one might expect to be induced by a single item of information. A warmly intelligent person, in contrast to a coldly intelligent person, was seen as more generous, humorous, and sociable. Not all other traits were judged different between the two types; for example, both were seen as persistent, serious, and honest. The centrality of a trait is determined by how many other attributes are changed when it is altered. Asch substituted polite and blunt for warm and cold in the above list and found fewer differences on trait ratings. The warm-cold dimension had a greater impact than the polite-blunt dimension. This does not mean that warm-cold will always have an important effect regardless of the specific dimensions to which it is to be related. One could easily imagine a set of traits that are irrelevant to warm-cold and quite relevant to polite-blunt. Asch contended that the centrality or peripherality of a trait depended upon the stimulus context in which it was embedded. Some traits, however, were thought to influence more items than others in absolute terms.

What are the ingredients which make one trait more central than another trait? Wishner (1960) thought the answer resided in the extent to which a given trait correlated with the other traits in the stimulus list and with the dependent variable traits. Although he wished to counter Asch's Gestalt interpretation of the interdependence of the stimulus list in determining meaning, he also viewed his work as supplying an operational definition for Asch's findings.

In order to understand Wishner's view it is necessary to discuss the meaning of correlations among traits. Two traits are correlated when variations on one trait are accompanied by variations on the other. Bruner *et al.* showed that a person who is intelligent is also seen as industrious. There is a correlation between attributions of intelligence and industriousness. One could also determine the correlation between two traits by having many subjects make ratings of actual target persons. This is what Wishner did. Presumably the rated intelligence of these target persons would differ and one could determine whether ratings of other traits varied consistently. For example, ratings of "intelligent" and "bright" would be highly correlated. This would be a mundane finding because of the definitional similarity between the two traits. It is reminiscent of Calvin Coolidge's famous insight about unemployment: "When large numbers of people are thrown out of work, unemployment results." One must be careful to distinguish redundancy or denotative similarity between two traits, where high correlations reflect definitional similarities, from the more significant situation of high correlation between denotatively independent traits. It is, of course, this latter condition which provides convincing evidence for the existence of a lay theory of personality. This distinction also adds another reason why the warm-cold dimension was of interest. Its relation to other traits is obviously not a matter of denotative overlap.

By collecting data on the correlations between each trait on Asch's fixed stimulus list and the other, dependent variable traits, as well as the correlations among the traits on the fixed list, Wishner provided evidence for the occurrence of a central trait. Wishner's data indicate that there are three conditions which favor the appearance of a central trait. Centrality occurs for a fixed stimulus trait when (1) it shows large correlations with the traits to be rated, and (2) the other fixed traits on the list show low correlations with the traits to be rated, while (3) there are low correlations between the central trait and the other fixed traits on the list.

EVALUATIVE-DESCRIPTIVE DISTINCTION

By defining centrality in terms of trait intercorrelations, Wishner has clarified some of the conditions which are necessary for a trait to be determinant of an impression. His analysis, however, does not help in understanding how trait correlations, or implicit theories of personality, are formed in the first place. In the previous discussion it was implied that some relationships may be an artifact of the experimenter using two labels for essentially the same trait. The fact that generosity and altruism are highly correlated is not very exciting because both terms summarize identical behaviors of helping others, accepting costs to give others gain, etc. While such a consideration may apply to a limited set of trait correlations, it will not help to explain the numerous other relations not based on such an artifact. One dominant answer to the question of the bases of trait correlations has been given in the attitude section. Positively evaluated traits go together as do negatively valued traits. Osgood (1962) notes how the intercorrelations among trait ratings (by the techniques of factor analyses) predominantly reflect the effects of an evaluative factor.

Recently, Peabody (1967) has taken issue with the balance view of trait correlations. He notes that trait ratings always contain not only an evaluative component but also a descriptive component. By a descriptive component Peabody means the behavioral referents summarized by the trait and, thus, has in mind something comparable to, but broader than, the definitional similarities discussed above. He provides an example of the trait dimension defined by the contrasts kind-cruel. Making a judgment about a person or an action on this dimension combines a descriptive aspect (the action helps or hurts others) and an evaluative aspect (the action is desirable or undesirable). Because two related traits may be similar in both descriptive and evaluative aspects, the separate contribution of each dimension can never be assessed. It is Peabody's contention that much of what passes muster as evaluative similarity is merely a by-product of descriptive similarity.

Peabody's study was designed to determine whether inferences were more likely to follow descriptive or evaluative similarity. The basic technique involved identifying traits that shared a general attribute, such as willingness to take risks. Traits were first categorized according to whether they denoted the presence of the attribute (bold) or its opposite (timid). Forty judges next made evaluative ratings of these traits. Some traits were judged to be favorable (bold, +1.1) and others unfavorable (rash, −1.2). It was then possible to compose sets of traits that shared a common attribute, where the presence of the attribute was either positively or negatively evaluated and the descriptively opposite attribute was either positively or negatively evaluated. An example of a complete set of four such traits for willingness to take risks is bold, cautious, rash, and timid. The evaluatively positive dimension for, respectively, the presence of the attribute and its opposite, is illustrated by the traits, bold (+1.1) and cautious (+.9). The evaluatively negative dimension for, respectively, the presence of the attribute and its opposite is, rash (−1.2) and timid (−1.1). With these categorizations, Peabody could pit descriptive and evaluative similarity against each other. This was accomplished by using one trait as a fixed stimulus and asking subjects whether the occurrence of the evaluatively similar, but descriptively opposite, was more likely than the evaluatively opposite, but descriptively similar. The essence of

the technique required subjects to answer the question: Given that someone is cautious where would he stand with respect to a bold-timid dimension? Cautious is evaluatively similar to bold, but descriptively similar to
timid.

By opposing the descriptive and evaluative aspects of traits, Peabody
was able to demonstrate that the direction of inferences is overwhelmingly
determined by the descriptive dimension. With other data, Peabody calculated the intercorrelations between antecedent and trait terms. He then
used a factor analysis to see what traits clustered together and again found
evidence for descriptive similarity. Peabody suggests that ". . . evaluation
is typically based on a descriptive judgment of the degree of extremeness"
(p. 15). It is his idea that evaluative judgments implicitly take into account the relation between behaviors and the situation. The meaning of a
behavior depends upon its atypicality for that class of circumstances. This
is one type of extremeness. Investing $10,000 may be seen as "bold" or
"rash" depending upon such circumstances as the investor's amount of
resources, the subjective probabilities of gains and losses, etc. A second
kind of extremeness is a location in a distribution of persons on a given
descriptive category. The most extreme persons on a distribution of riskiness would be evaluated negatively, with "timid" at one end and "rash" at
the other. Positive evaluation would apply only to the intermediate ranges.

Peabody's analysis undoubtedly provides an important qualification for
consistency accounts of perceived trait relationships. Subsequent research,
however, has shown that the importance of the descriptive component is
not as pervasive as Peabody initially suggested. Using an improved method
of data analysis, Rosenberg and Olshan (1970) reanalyzed portions of
Peabody's data and collected and analyzed some data of their own. An
evaluative dimension was revealed which was independent of any descriptive dimension. Felipe (1970) also conducted a careful study in this
area. He concluded that both descriptive and evaluative similarities are
important. The sequence the perceiver uses in making trait inferences,
according to Felipe, is to test first for descriptive similarity and then for
evaluative similarity. Peabody (1970) has revised his initial position in
accord with such modifications. It is clear that both evaluative and descriptive components are important determinants of impressions.

IMPRESSION FORMATION AND PERSONALITY

Before leaving this area, it should be mentioned that our impressions
of others typically do not come from learning trait names. We learn about
others through behaviors, or perhaps more accurately, we form impressions by seeing people act, hearing them describe themselves, and learning
what others say about them. An observer, therefore, is faced with the task
of classifying information into categories, drawing relationships from these

categories to those not directly observed and ultimately making predictions. The way people classify and combine information can be a point of entrance for those who are concerned with individual differences. Kelly (1955) and Harvey, Hunt, and Schroder (1961), for example, have had such a concern. They emphasize the kinds of categories a perceiver typically uses and the relationships he forms among categories as defining a crucial aspect of the perceiver's personality. We have focused on the generalities cross-cutting individual differences, but this perspective should not obscure the fact of the existence of cognitive styles which differentiate individuals.

Accuracy of Impressions

It is obviously much easier to study the process of impression formation —to find that people who are intelligent are judged to be industrious—than to study the accuracy of the process—to determine whether people who are intelligent are in fact more industrious than unintelligent people. To study the process requires finding how impressions are systematically affected by changes in information or the circumstances of judgment; to study accuracy requires finding verifiable indices of the content of the impressions. Accuracy is defined by the extent to which the content of impressions matches the actual occurrence of what has been predicted. It is for this reason that this line of research has been very sensitive to the existence of objective indices which are also psychologically relevant.

JUDGMENT OF EMOTION

In the 1920s considerable work was being done on the question of how accurately people could judge the emotions of others from limited cues. One prototype of such research was to show subjects photographs of faces and ask them to make judgments about the emotion being portrayed. In this form, the problem is essentially one of accuracy of categorizing cues— whether subjects could combine the stimulus elements in a photograph and match the emotional category actually represented. When subjects freely responded to photographs, accuracy was typically not very good. It was found that at least three conditions could appreciably increase accuracy: (1) if the subjects were given a fixed list of categories which included the correct one; (2) if the fixed list spanned a wide array of emotions (it is harder to distinguish joy from euphoria than from depression); and (3) if the entire situation in which the target person was involved was known to the subjects. The third point is hardly remarkable. Even the most objective outward manifestations of emotion are sometimes misleading. The properties constituting a smile overlap with a grimace; tears sometimes accompany too much laughter, etc. Such ambiguities are reduced if we know whether the person is involved in an automobile wreck or has just won the Irish Sweepstakes. After all, the experimenter's judgment of what emotion constitutes a correct answer was also based on information about the circumstances. Although the increase in accuracy provided by knowledge of the target person's circumstances is not itself startling, this fact will help in understanding why it is reasonable to suggest that we label our own emotions by knowledge of the circumstances in which they have been elicited. Schachter (1964) makes much of this, and we have already seen how Bem (1967) argues that knowledge of the circumstances eliciting attitude responses in a "dissonance" experiment may be an important determinant of viewing one's own attitude position.

JUDGMENT OF QUESTIONNAIRE RESPONSES

In the late 1940s it was thought that the criteria problems could be solved if subjects were asked to make predictions about the target person's actual responses. This had an intuitive appeal. Establishing the objective facts about an emotional experience is difficult, but there could be no question about whether the target person answered true or false to a particular questionnaire item. The advent of such a methodology induced a subtle shift in the study of accuracy. Research was focused not on whether a particular person was considerate, but on whether he would rate himself as being considerate.

The general thrust of the mushrooming research during this period involved efforts to identify judges who were accurate and those who were not. It looked as if progress might be made on discovering important features of such concepts as "empathy," or "interpersonal sensitivity." It seems reasonable to think that some people are quite good at understanding others, or "putting themselves in someone else's shoes." Such people should then be more accurate in judging a target person's self-description than those persons who do not possess such interpersonal skills. The prototype of such research was to have a target person describe himself on a set of items, for example, ten semantic differential items. Subjects would be given information about the target person and then asked to predict how the target person filled out the questionnaire. Highest accuracy on such a task requires perfect matching of the TP's responses by the subject's responses. The greater the deviation from the TP's patterns the less the accuracy. Formula (8-1) is the general formula for defining accuracy, or its reverse, inaccuracy,

$$\text{Inaccuracy, distance (or } D) = \sqrt{\Sigma(x - y)^2}, \qquad (8\text{-}1)$$

where x is the TP's response on one item and y is the subject's prediction of the TP's response. The difference on each item is squared to remove minus signs and then all the squared differences are summed. The square root transforms the sum back to the original units. The larger the distance score, the less does the subject track the target person and therefore the higher the inaccuracy. It is important to keep these features in mind, because the seeming ease of this format was shown to be highly misleading by Cronbach.

CRONBACH'S ANALYSIS

Cronbach (1955, 1958) left no doubt that the seemingly simple situation was fraught with possibilities for obtaining misleading results. One way of understanding his analysis is to consider what it means to be someone who is very accurate, that is, obtains a low distance score, on this kind of a task. The research on accuracy had equated the ability to be accurate with excellence at understanding other people. Cronbach pointed out that this would be the case if obtaining a low D score resulted only from an ability to distinguish correctly among different patterns of responses of different TPs. The size of the D score, however, is affected by a number of factors other than accuracy. Because none of these additional factors was directly related to the understanding of specific others, Cronbach concluded that extreme caution and care must be taken in designing meaningful studies. Three of the features that alarmed Cronbach relate to response set, stereotypes, and projection. (1) The size of the D score can be a function of the *response set* or *rating style* of the subject. In the extreme case, when one has no information about the TP, subjects who predict the midpoint of the scale are likely to obtain lower D scores than subjects who predict the extremes. Because the midpoint minimizes the maximum possible distance between actual and predicted response, its selection will reduce the size of D, independent of any knowledge about the TP. A subject who always predicts a rating of 3 on a five-point scale can never miss by more than two scale units on any item. (2) Some degree of accuracy can be obtained by knowing a general category to which the TP belongs. If he is a university student, he is very likely to have rated himself on the higher part of the scale for items relating to his intelligence. Such knowledge can produce accuracy, but an accuracy based on *stereotypes,* a topic to be taken up below, rather than on uniquely understanding a specific other. (3) The D score will be small if the TP's responses happen to coincide with how the subject would answer the items for himself and the subject merely uses his own preferences in predicting the TP. Cronbach suggested this would be a proper definition for the process of *projection,* but it hardly is the same as sensitively understanding someone else. Cronbach also detailed the design requirement necessary for removing the contribution of artifacts to the D score. These included the necessity of having TPs that spanned many positions on the variables being rated, having subjects also provide self-ratings on the items, and having subjects make ratings of a typical other.

STEREOTYPES

By understanding the difficulties inherent in assessing accuracy, we are also in a position to understand why most people have no stable sense of their own accuracy about others. While experience tends to modify the kind of categories generated, it is probably difficult to make any major alterations in our construct network. Nowhere is this problem quite as poignant as in relation to stereotypes. From the present view, stereotypes are merely a subset of categories which generate predictions or expectations. In ordinary usage, stereotypes refer to ethnic or occupational categories. They refer to predictions or expectations generated by the knowledge that someone is Irish, Jewish, a used car salesman, etc. It is probably valuable to recognize that stereotypes are any culturally shared beliefs. As such, they represent a great psychic economy because they preclude the necessity for obtaining complete information about each new person one may happen to meet. In the course of an initial meeting with another, as soon as one learns about his occupation, or race, or degree of intelligence, or anything else that permits placing him into a category which generates predictions about matters of interest, one is able to orient oneself to the interaction. The predictions are, of course, probability statements about the likelihood of each of the relations. They should become modified with additional information about the specific other with whom one is interacting. This suggests one of the reasons why stereotypes have enjoyed a bad press. They become dysfunctional when they are not amenable to changing in the face of additional information about a specific other person. Consider the stereotype that used car salesmen are not to be trusted. This is probably a reasonable stereotype to hold if one is about to buy a used car. However, if one happens to meet a used car salesman who gives evidence of trustworthiness, by arguing against his own best interests or maintaining contractual agreements, judgments about that particular salesman's trustworthiness ought to increase. The original stereotype will remain intact. It probably takes more than first-hand experience with any number of exceptions to change a stereotype. While it is not clear what conditions are needed for changing stereotypes, they surely involve something more massive than direct experience. Note that stereotypes of Japanese seemed to change quickly after World War II, when Japan was no longer our enemy but our ally.

Because we view stereotypes as a general way of thinking about others, it is hardly possible to attack them because they lack accuracy. Like all expectations generated from different categories, there will be variation in accuracy. In the long run the most functional stereotypes are the ones that are most accurate. Inaccurate stereotypes, like all other inaccuracies of expectations, bring with them two related problems. First, the initial expectation can be a determinant of how information is interpreted; that is, one is most likely to distort another's actions to fit the stereotype. Second, the expectation itself can be a determinant of eliciting the behavior in another. If one expects redheads to be temperamental, it should not take long to give a specific redhead occasion to display temperamentality. Indeed, once they know this stereotype some redheads may feel an added obligation to behave in a temperamental way. After all, they can attribute their behavior to the color of their hair, whereas a blonde or brunette must discover personal reasons for her or his bad temper.

Causal Attributions

In a general sense, attribution processes refer to the perceiver's efforts at understanding the underlying stabilities in his environment (Heider, 1958). It is in this general sense that attribution has been used to discuss person perception above, as well as being a possible basis for consistency theories, discussed in the attitude change section. The term "attribution process" has also been used in a more specific sense, and it is this narrower meaning which defines the content of this section. This meaning may be stated simply as the process of searching for a sufficient cause for others' behavior or one's own acts. The major impetus to this view was given by Heider (1944, 1958) and has recently been extended by Jones and Davis (1965) and by Kelley (1967).

Attributions About Another Person

Ordinarily, we make judgments about a target person from an information base which contains richer material than a list of trait adjectives which someone else believes to be descriptive of the target person. We usually have observed a sample of the target person's behavior and we know what things he has said, how he has said them, and the circumstances in which it all happened. Although lists of stimulus traits admirably serve the ends of experimental rigor and hypotheses testing, they necessarily exclude many important sources of information. Attribution research typically relies on such other sources of information, especially knowledge of the circumstances surrounding the behavior. One of the main recurring themes of this research is that the meaning attributed to a particular action will depend upon the circumstances in which the action occurs. The specific focus of considerable research has been on attempts to understand the consequences of seeing a target person's acts as caused by factors internal or external to him.

One of the first experimental studies demonstrating the importance of what is referred to as the internal-external dimension was conducted by Thibaut and Riecken (1955). They examined how one determinant of attraction for another person is the kind of attribution made about the other's motives for conforming to a request. Thibaut and Riecken begin their analysis by considering the state of a person who has made a request of another. Compliance to the request is thought to produce greater attraction for the other person than noncompliance because the person making the request obtains an enhanced sense of social control as well as the instrumental value of having the requested act performed. The authors, however, wished to differentiate the attraction felt toward someone who complies depending upon whether his compliance is seen as externally or internally motivated. For this reason, their study required subjects to make identical requests of two other persons, one of whom had high social status and one whose status was low. Thibaut and Riecken's two major hypotheses are interrelated. First, compliance by a high-status other was expected to be attributed to internal motives because a high-status person has sufficient power to resist a request. Compliance by the low-status other was expected to be viewed as externally caused, that is, by the force of the power relationship. Second, internally caused compliance was predicted to enhance attraction more than external compliance. The person who complies for internal reasons not only provides the instrumental values of conforming to the request, but also adds the gratification associated with ". . . the perception of autonomous affection for oneself . . ." (p. 116). In addition, internal compliance implies the existence of spontaneous good will, which has the further benefit of suggesting control of the other in the absence of the application of power. Compliance through external causation provides the instrumental value of conforming to the request, but precludes the other sources of attraction. The person making the request can not determine whether the power relationship or the complier's affection was the major cause of the compliance.

Thibaut and Riecken conducted two separate studies which were similar in form; therefore, it will suffice to describe the details of one of them. Subjects found themselves with two other subjects (actually confederates) whose social status differed. One had high status and was presented as being on the instructional staff, while the other was always a low-status freshman. The subject had to devise a persuasive appeal to induce the other two subjects to donate to a Red Cross blood campaign. After several influence attempts, both high- and low-status confederates always complied by indicating they were persuaded by the messages. The subjects' ratings of internal-external causality and the pre- to post-changes in attractiveness ratings confirmed both predictions. The high-status confederate's motivation to comply was seen as more internal and his attraction ratings increased, relative to the motivation and attractiveness of the low-status confederate.

Thibaut and Riecken's reasoning has been extended in several directions. Strickland (1958), for example, predicted that trust for another would be enhanced if his compliance were obtained seemingly freely (internally) rather than by force of the power relationship (externally). Subjects in the

Strickland experiment were supervisors who desired a high production record from two "workers." Supervisors had the power to punish workers who did not meet an adequate performance standard, but, it turned out, they could actively monitor the performance of only one worker on an initial series of ten trials. At the end of the initial series, the subjects learned that both workers had slightly exceeded the performance standard and their work output was equal. When given a chance to monitor either worker on the next series of trials, the supervisors more frequently monitored the worker who had been under surveillance during the initial series. In addition, as predicted, the initially monitored worker was perceived as less trustworthy than the worker who was not monitored. Strickland draws attention to the relevance of his results to supervisor-subordinate relationships. These will contain "self-perpetuating information loss" if the supervisor's monitoring activity is extensive. Strickland notes, ". . . a supervisor (or any superordinate) cannot know first-hand the nature of the loyalty of his subordinates until he perceives that they had an opportunity to be disloyal" (p. 213). Strickland's results have been recently replicated by Kruglanski (1970), who tested several specific interpretations of this effect. Kruglanski confirms the Strickland hypothesis that attributions of trustworthiness are based on the extent to which another's performance cannot be ascribed to external determinants.

A person whose motivation is attributed to internal causes does not derive benefits in all situations. The Schopler and Matthews (1965) study, which is contained in the Readings section, predicted that someone who is perceived to be dependent for internal causes would receive a lesser amount of help than someone who is dependent for external causes. In their study, subjects always had absolute power over a "partner" who required help. The partner's dependence was manipulated as being internal for some subjects and as being external for others. The subjects' amount of compliance to the dependent partner's request for help was the dependent variable. As predicted, subjects gave more help to externally dependent partners than to internally dependent partners.

Horowitz (1968) has suggested that the Schopler and Matthews format gave subjects limited freedom of choice with respect to the decision to help. Under such conditions, in accordance with Brehm's (1966) theory of reactance, a request from an internally dependent partner may be a greater threat to freedom of action than a request from an externally dependent partner. A person who has complete freedom with respect to helping another was not expected to be affected by the other's locus of dependence. In a choice condition, Horowitz's subjects had complete freedom regarding the amount of help given. In a no-choice condition subjects were forced to give the minimal amount of help, but free to decide about the giving of further help. Choice, no-choice was manipulated in combination with external and internal locus of dependence of the partner. As predicted, similar to the Schopler and Matthews results, within the no-choice condition more help was given to the externally dependent partner than to the internally dependent partner. In the choice condition, unexpectedly, the internally dependent partner was given more help than the externally dependent partner. The powerful person's degree of choice appears to mediate the effects of the other person's internal or external dependence.

The internal-external dimension is also central to the Jones and Davis (1965) analysis of social perception, which is phrased in somewhat different terms. These authors analyzed the conditions affecting the way in which a perceiver makes inferences about a target person's traits by knowing his overt acts. The main intention of the Jones and Davis analysis is to identify the conditions which lead a perceiver to attribute a particular act to a stable disposition of the target person (internal) or to some feature of the environment (external). We have already described some examples. The act of complying to a request, when performed by someone powerful enough to resist, is seen to be internally motivated. Conformity to production standards by a worker who is monitored is attributed externally to the power relationship and not necessarily to the worker's loyalty. Jones and Davis assert that two crucial variables generally determining the direction of attributions are the target person's degree of choice in engaging in the act and the social desirability of the act. The higher the degree of choice and the lower the social desirability of the act, the more certainty will the observer have that the act truly stands for an enduring disposition of the target person, rather than reflecting the evocative potential of a particular circumstance. High choice and low social desirability are indices of internal causes because the former implies a lack of situational pressures, while the latter implies freedom from being determined by the reward value of the act.

This general line of reasoning was tested in a study conducted by Jones and Harris (1967). Instead of traits, the study focused on inferences about another's true opinions. Such inferences were predicted to vary depending upon the perceived degree of choice the other person has had and the social desirability (or typicality) of his opinion. Another's stated opinion will be seen as representing his true opinion if he has had total freedom to state his views and if the content of his views is atypical. In keeping with the Jones and Davis analysis, under these conditions the perceiver's sense of certitude about the inferences he has made should also be high.

Subjects participating in the Jones and Harris experiment learned they were to make judgments of another's attitudes on the basis of limited information. They were given a mimeographed pamphlet containing a 200-word essay on Castro's Cuba written for a political science exam. The pamphlet also contained a final questionnaire which included the crucial items measuring the essay writer's true opinion. Some of the subjects received an essay written in the popular direction (anti-Castro), while the remaining subjects read a pro-Castro essay. Within each of these conditions choice was manipulated. Prior to reading the essay, some subjects were told the essay was written under high choice, that is, the writer could choose whether to write a pro or con essay, while others were told the direction of the content had been specified by the exam question. The major results of this experiment, and two other partial replications, were quite consistent. Attitudes were attributed more in line with behavior under choice than under no-choice conditions. However, even in the no-choice condition, the target person was seen as holding attitudes in line with the content of his essay. The unpopular direction in the no-choice condition produced the greatest variability of opinion attributions in any of the four cells. Given that the content was atypical, some subjects weighted the no-choice directions and assumed true anti-Castro feelings, while others weighted the content as actually reflecting true pro-Castro opinions. In an experiment which expanded the design and refined the manipulations, Jones, Worchel, Goethals, and Grumet (1971) verified the findings reported above.

SELF-ATTRIBUTIONS

How do we know what emotional label to apply to a particular internal state? Schachter (1964) answered this question by contending that the way we construe our own internal state depends upon the cognitions instigated by a particular circumstance. Schachter reviewed the research attempting to establish physiological discriminators of various emotional states and concluded that individuals are able to distinguish among a variety of emotions which have no counterpart in different patterns of physiological arousal. Schachter asserts that labeling of emotions is a joint function of physiological arousal plus a cognition appropriate to this state. A state of physiological arousal sets the occasion for a person to initiate searching for a label or explanation of his state. Much as the circumstances in which an action occurs permit an outside observer to infer a target person's emotions, Schachter implies the actor himself uses the situation for labeling emotions. While there are many potential aspects of one's circumstances that might serve as explanations for a state of physiological arousal (e.g., "the reflection of the moon on the lake," or "this attractive potential spouse," or "something I ate"), Schachter is particularly interested in how a person uses other people as a source of explanatory cognitions. To this end, he used Festinger's (1954) analysis of social comparison processes. Festinger noted that in order for a person to evaluate his own abilities or opinions in the absence of objective criteria, he will turn to other people for confirmation of his views or for estimates of his abilities. In general, it is most informative to make comparisons with someone who is very comparable. The satisfaction one derives from the salary of a starting position will partly be a function of whether it is better or worse than the amount other starting workers are making. It is Schachter's contention that when one is searching for an appropriate cognition about one's own state, information about what other people are feeling will be a determinant of how one labels his own feelings.

Schachter's reasoning was tested in a series of studies reported by Schachter and Singer (1962) and Schachter and Wheeler (1962). If labeling an emotional state requires physiological arousal plus an appropriate cognition, it should be possible to alter self-ratings of emotions either by surreptitiously manipulating physiological arousal or by manipulating the cognitions likely to be entertained by individuals whose bodily state has been aroused. Schachter's experiments incorporated both of these general techniques. They can best be illustrated by reference to one of the experiments reported by Schachter and Singer.

The physiological arousal involved in emotional states is evidently associated with sympathetic nervous system activity. Although any event capable of eliciting emotions would presumably arouse such activity, it can also be obtained by injections of epinephrine. According to Schachter and Singer, "Epinephrine or adrenalin is a sympathomimetic drug whose effects, with minor exceptions, are almost a perfect mimicry of a discharge of the sympathetic nervous system" (p. 382). The experiment was therefore staged in a way which would permit administering injections to subjects. (The records of all potential subjects were cleared with the Student Health Service, prior to the experiment, to insure no one would suffer harmful side effects.) Some subjects were given epinephrine injections and some, the placebo group, were given injections of saline solution. The experimental justification for the injections required deception. If an individual knows he has been injected with epinephrine, according to Schachter's reasoning, the most likely cognition that he will entertain to account for his arousal is: "I have just received an injection." This is a perfectly satisfactory explanation for the arousal and precludes the necessity of searching for other explanatory cognitions. Schachter's solution to this problem was to present the experiment in the guise of a study of the effects of vitamin supplements, "Suproxin," on vision. Subjects received a "Suproxin" injection, which was actually either epinephrine or saline solution, and were immediately introduced to another subject (a confederate) who supposedly had received a shot of Suproxin and would also be taking the vision test. Because it would take about 20 minutes for the Suproxin to be completely absorbed in the bloodstream, the two subjects were asked to wait together for that time. During the waiting period, the confederate enacted a standard routine of increasingly euphoric behaviors. The routine began with doodling on scratch paper and progressed through various activities before terminating with a period of play with a hula hoop. The point of all of this frenzied activity was to provide subjects with clear evidence of the confederate's mood. If the unexplained arousal in the epinephrine subjects induced higher needs for social comparison than existed in the unaroused placebo subjects, the epinephrine subjects should rate their own mood as more euphoric when compared to ratings of placebo subjects. Similarly, they should initiate more euphoric acts than the placebo subjects.

Two other conditions were used in the experiment. Although the epinephrine injection was disguised as a vitamin supplement to preclude subjects' attributing their symptoms to the injection, it was thought likely that some subjects might still attribute their symptoms to the vitamin supplement injection. The other two conditions were intended to manipulate the likelihood of attributing the symptoms to the injection. To increase this likelihood, some subjects were informed of the actual symptoms they would experience, that is, heart-rate increases, tremors, and flushing. This condition was called "epinephrine informed." To decrease the likelihood of attributing the symptoms to the injection, some subjects were misinformed about the symptoms they would experience. In the "epinephrine misinformed" condition, they were told they might experience such side effects as numbness, itching, and a slight headache. Subjects who expected these symptoms from the injection would be least likely to attribute the actual symptoms of palpitations, tremors, and flushing to the injection. These two conditions plus the placebo and epinephrine condition (termed "epinephrine ignorant" because no expectations about symptoms were mentioned) comprised the four experimental conditions. They can be understood as two control and two experimental conditions. The epinephrine-misinformed and the epinephrine-ignorant conditions were expected to produce higher ratings of euphoria than the placebo or epinephrine-informed conditions. Subjects in the placebo group had no arousal to explain, while subjects in the informed group were likely to attribute their arousal to the injection.

The results of this experiment, as well as other experiments involving the emotions of anger and amusement, generally confirmed the predictions. The results for self-ratings of euphoria for the experiment described above are presented in Table 8-1. Higher numbers in the table indicate greater amounts of euphoria. It can be seen that the mean ratings in the misinformed and ignorant conditions are higher than in the informed or placebo conditions. The informed condition is significantly smaller than the misinformed or ignorant condition, but does not differ significantly from the placebo condition. The mean of the placebo group is higher than it should be. Schachter and Singer point out that its magnitude was probably a function of the placebo subjects' physiological arousal induced by the experimental situation. The placebo injection clearly could not prevent physiological arousal. The epinephrine-ignorant manipulation was also recognized as being an imperfect manipulation because there was no guarantee that some of these subjects might not attribute their symptoms to the injection.

TABLE 8-1

Self-Report of Emotional State in the Euphoria Conditions[a]

Condition	N	Self-report scales
Control groups		
Epinephrine informed (Epi Inf)	25	.98
Placebo (Plac)	26	1.61
Experimental groups		
Epinephrine ignorant (Epi Ign)	25	1.78
Epinephrine misinformed (Epi Mis)	25	1.90
Comparisons		p values[b]
Epi Inf vs. Epi Mis		.01
Epi Inf vs. Epi Ign		.02
Plac vs. Epi Mis, Ign or Inf		n.s.

[a] Adapted from Schachter & Singer, 1962, p. 390. Reproduced by permission of the American Psychological Association.

[b] All p values are two-tailed.

Schachter's research has convincingly demonstrated a cognitive component in the labeling of emotions. The cues we use to differentiate among the gamut of possible human emotions are embedded in the environment. Although the characteristics of the stimuli associated with physiological arousal are often the only cue needed to provide an appropriate cognition, the perceived emotional state of other people can also be a basis for such explanatory cognitions.

Valins (1966), in a study contained in the Readings section, has modified the Schachter position. It is his contention that actual physiological arousal is not a necessary component of emotional labeling. As long as someone subjectively feels a physiological change, he will be motivated to make an attribution to account for the change. In his experiment, subjects are led to believe they are experiencing physiological change (rate of heartbeats) in the presence of some stimuli and no change to other stimuli. Valins expected subjects to attribute the perceived changes to the stimuli with which they are associated. Because he employed pictures of attractive, nude females as stimuli (using male subjects), he expected the subjects' ratings of liking of a particular stimulus to be greater when it was associated with a change in heart rate than for those stimuli associated with no change in heart rate. If a class of unpleasant stimuli had been used, for example, pictures of ugly insects, the theory would predict opposite effects. The insects associated with heart rate changes would be expected to produce an attribution of dislike and be rated as less attractive than those associated with no change.

In a subsequent study, Valins and Ray (1967) used similar reasoning to demonstrate that the self-perception of fear aroused by a class of fearful stimuli can be lowered if the stimuli are associated with the perception of *no* physiological change. The perceived heart rate of subjects who had been selected because they expressed a fear of snakes was manipulated to increase in the presence of shock and to remain constant in the presence of pictures of snakes. Control subjects were led to believe the heart-rate sounds were extraneous noise. This procedure was repeated during a second session. At the end of the session, subjects had an opportunity to approach and touch an actual snake, described as "harmless." Subjects who had heard their heart rate remain constant in the presence of snake stimuli and, therefore, presumably attributed less fear arousal to themselves were more willing to approach the snake than were the control subjects. The work on "desensitization" of phobic patients can be interpreted in this framework. By gradually bringing the patient into closer interaction with a feared stimulus, such as a high place, in a supportive and non-fear-producing circumstance, the patient overcomes his phobic fear. The Valins and Ray study suggests that the critical component in such a procedure is that it is started at a sufficient psychological distance to not arouse fear and that each new step is such as not to produce physiological changes. The patient should then attribute lowered fear to himself and be able to approach the previously feared object. It should be recognized that there are definite boundaries to this kind of cognitive control of labeling emotional circumstances. When the circumstances themselves are sufficiently compelling to arouse fear, a cognitive manipulation should not work. As Nisbett and Schachter (1966) point out: "Common sense would indicate that no amount of argument would persuade a man dodging machine-gun bullets that his physiological arousal was due to anything but the exigencies of this situation" (p. 228).

The cognitive account of emotional self-attributions basically assumes individuals are motivated to seek explanations for perceived physiological changes. The phrase "appropriate cognition" indicates a process by which the person attempts to make a causal link between his own affective state and some feature of his environment. We have already discussed how Bem (1967) uses similar reasoning to suggest that a person obtains evidence about his own attitudes by viewing his own acts. The public benchmarks of attitudes are potential evidence for attributions the individual makes about himself. This line of reasoning can be extended to other self-attributions. For example, Schopler and Compere (1971) conducted a study in which subjects praised one confederate for successful responses and criticized a second confederate for incorrect responses. Both confederates always succeeded on half the trials and failed on the other half. As predicted, attraction ratings were significantly more positive for the praised confederate than for the criticized confederate, although both confederates were seen as performing equally well on the task. Behaving kindly or harshly toward another appeared to be translated into the favorableness of feelings toward him.

The Internal-External Dimension

The stress placed in this section on the importance of the internal-external dimension owes a considerable debt to Kelley's (1967) perceptive analysis of attribution processes. He has argued persuasively for the possibility of coordinating a variety of research areas to the internal-external dimension. We have already indicated that the major theme of the Jones and Davis analysis can be stated as the stronger the external pressures upon a person to behave in a given way, the less information his behavior provides to an observer. The extent to which a person's behavior is seen as "free" from such external pressures as high social desirability or lack of choice, the more information would the observer have about the person's true dispositions. Bem's analysis of dissonance effects can be seen in a similar way, with the person doing the observing of his own behavior. The freer the person feels from such external constraints as high reward or forced compliance, the more his behavior represents his true attitudes. Kelley also applies his analysis to other topics such as source credibility. We have previously discussed the evidence documenting the greater persuasiveness of a highly credible source compared to a source of low credibility. Credibility, it will be recalled, consists of trustworthiness and expertness. A trustworthy communicator is one whose responses are determined by the characteristics of his topic and not externally controlled by circumstances. In contrast to the movie stars who appear on television commercials to say positive things about various household products, a trustworthy communicator would hold the same views in different situations, regardless of whether he is paid much or little for stating his views. Expertness can be seen as the ability to differentiate among entities in the environment. The expert's responses about the entities he is discussing are descriptively accurate and not determined by irrelevant external environmental features. In general, internally caused acts or acts lacking external determination increase the persuasiveness of a communication source, permit attributing true attitudes or dispositions, and increase the potency of self-persuasion.

Overview

The way in which a person views other people and events can be understood as being directed toward achieving stability, order, and predictability of the environment. A perceiver construes events in line with the categories he uses for classifying information and the relationships he holds to be true among categories, that is, with his "hypotheses." In order to understand social perception, therefore, it is important to study the content of these hypotheses, their amenability to change, their accuracy and their implications for responding to others. Although each of the areas discussed in this chapter touches on some aspect of any of these issues, research in a particular area tends to have an exclusive focus. Studies of the way perceivers combine cues focus on the content of hypotheses and, to a lesser extent, on how they change. Such studies attempt to discover the implicit rules used by perceivers to combine cues and the variables which are the most important determinants of impressions. Research concerning the accuracy of a perceiver's hypotheses focuses on the perceiver's ability to discriminate among elements in the social environment and to predict their interrelationships. The critical question in this area is how successfully a perceiver can track external events. Accurate perceivers have the ability to make correct predictions. The difficulty of defining objective and psychologically important criteria with which to assess accuracy, as well as other methodological problems, have handicapped this kind of research. Studies involving causal attributions have focused on identification of the situational determinants which shape the meaning of events and, consequently, on the implications that the perceiver's various hypotheses have for his responses to other people. The consequences of whether acts are attributed to internal or external causes has been a major theme of such research. It has also been a way of bridging the areas of perceiving others and self-perceptions by showing that some variables, such as choice, have similar consequences for self-perception and for perception of others.

READINGS

The Influence of the Perceived Causal Locus of Partner's Dependence on the Use of Interpersonal Power[1]

John Schopler and Marjorie Wall Matthews

In recent years a number of studies have examined the conditions affecting the extent to which a powerful person, at some cost to himself, will help a totally dependent partner. This study was conducted to check the hypothesis that a powerful person who perceives his partner's dependence to be caused by "external" (environmental) factors will help more than a powerful person who perceives his partner's dependence to be caused by "internal" (personal) factors. 48 Ss participated in a laboratory study which verified the hypothesis. The results are discussed in terms of the conditions arousing the norm of social responsibility.

It has traditionally been assumed that the person who possesses more power than his partner will enjoy many interpersonal advantages. In a dyad the more powerful person receives deference and flattery, dominates the interaction and, if a conflict arises, is able to resolve it in his own favor. The empirical research documenting such effects has been summarized by Schopler (1965). It has also been assumed that the likelihood of securing these advantages is directly related to the size of the power advantage possessed by one of the participants. In the limiting case, if Person A has absolute power over Person B, A can resolve every conflict to benefit himself maximally, regardless of the consequences to the partner. However, as Berkowitz and Daniels (1963) have suggested a person who has absolute power will not necessarily use it and may even sacrifice some personal benefit in order to help his partner. Berkowitz and Daniels contend the partner's dependence is a cue for arousing the norm of social responsibility in the powerful person. The norm specifies the limits to which self-seeking advantages can be appropriately exploited without regard for the partner. It has been demonstrated that a person with absolute power will work harder for (i.e., give more help to) a partner who is highly dependent on him, compared to one who is only minimally dependent (Berkowitz &

[1] From the *Journal of Personality and Social Psychology*, Volume 2, pages 609–612, 1965 (early publication received May 4, 1965). Reproduced by permission of the American Psychological Association. Authors' affiliation: University of North Carolina. This research was supported in part by Grant GS-182 from the National Science Foundation. The data were collected by the junior author for a senior honors thesis at the University of North Carolina.

Daniels, 1963, 1964; Berkowitz, Klanderman, & Harris, 1964; Daniels & Berkowitz, 1963).

Other conditions impeding or enhancing the help obtained through being dependent have also been studied. Dependence is more effective in eliciting help if the powerful person likes his partner (Daniels & Berkowitz, 1963), has himself received help prior to being in the situation in which he has absolute power (Berkowitz & Daniels, 1964), believes his own behavior is under the partner's immediate surveillance (Berkowitz & Daniels, 1963), and incurs only a small cost for helping (Schopler & Bateson, 1965).

The present study was designed to test another condition affecting yielding to dependence—the perceived causal locus of the partner's dependence. In the tradition of the Thibaut and Riecken (1955) experiment, differences between "internal" and "external" causation were studied. It was expected that someone who chooses to become dependent ("internal" locus) is not likely to arouse the social responsibility norm because he will be seen as responsible for his own fate. The powerful person would be expected to offer him little help. In contrast, the partner who is forced by circumstances to be dependent (a characteristic of every experiment in this area) is more likely to be seen as someone for whom the social responsibility norm is appropriate. His dependence is not of his own making and he may therefore be seen as "deserving" of help. The specific hypothesis to be tested was: an individual who perceives his partner's dependence to be caused by the environment will yield more than an individual who perceives his partner's dependence to be a matter of personal choice.

PROCEDURE

Subjects were recruited from an introductory psychology course in which participation in research was part of the course requirement. Forty-eight male undergraduates were used in the experiment in groups of four. Subjects were escorted to the experimental room and were seated in one of four adjoining booths, separated by 7 foot high partitions, arranged around a semicircle facing a common front. Each booth contained a set of headphones, which were attached to an Ampex tape recorder. Two slots were located in the front of the booth. These permitted the sending and receiving of messages.

Standard Procedure. When all booths were occupied the instructions were played on the tape recorder. The subjects heard that they were taking part in a study of "partnerships, particularly of the different working arrangements and decisions partners make." They heard that two of them would be "directors" and two would be "associates," although every subject was in fact a "director." Both members of the partnership would be working on separate puzzle tasks. Each puzzle represented an abbreviated form of a typical crossword puzzle and consisted of one horizontal and one vertical row. In the director's puzzle the horizontal row contained four boxes and was intersected by a vertical row containing three boxes. Three letters were always placed in the boxes and therefore only three boxes remained blank. The director's turn came first. He would always be given a pool of four letters from which he was to finish his own puzzle. He would be paid at the rate of $.01 for each letter, but only for completed words. The puzzles had of course been pretested to insure their being sufficiently simple for all subjects to complete correctly.

The instructions were then addressed, ostensibly, to the "associates." The associates had similar, but shorter, puzzles. To complete them they would have to request letters from their directors. The independent variable, whether this was seen as an experimental requirement or as an associate's choice, was introduced at this point, and will be described in detail below. On each trial the associates were to receive a carbon copy of the director's letters. They were entitled to request as many as two letters on any given trial. Associates were also to be supplied with message forms on which they would write their requests. (These were prepared beforehand by the experimenter and were standard for all subjects.)

Prior to working on the first item, each subject received a "self-description form" presumably completed by his associate. It contained innocuous background information, along with a reminder of the independent variable manipulation.

This entire scenery was necessary in order to give the subject power over a dependent partner and to control the cost of helping the partner. Out of a total of 15 trials, 12 of the associate's requests included letters which the subject had placed in his own puzzle. Helping the associate therefore cost the subject money, because it destroyed a completed word. On three trials requests were made for nonfunctional letters in order to maintain the credibility of the situation. It was of course essential that all subjects completed every puzzle correctly so that helping the partner incurred the same cost for all subjects. As a check on this requirement, subjects were instructed to write their earnings on the puzzle slips and to pass their completed puzzles to the experimenter. The solution was checked and passed back to the subject along with the partner's request slip. If the subject then destroyed a word, in order to give the partner a letter, he had to cross out the previous total and write in the new amount.

After the 15 trials were completed, subjects filled out a postexperimental questionnaire. It assessed the independent variable manipulation and requested ratings of the partner and of the task. When these had been completed the experiment was finished. The purpose of the experiment was explained to each subject and arrangements for payment were made.

Independent Variable Induction. In order to manipulate the perceived locus of the partner's dependence an "internal locus" (IL) condition and an "external locus" (EL) condition were used. The induction was introduced during the tape recording, repeated in the partner self-description form, and again in the message the subjects received after the fifth trial. Subjects in the EL condition heard that associates could complete their puzzles only by requesting letters from the directors; "the associates have no choice in this matter." The taped instructions for subjects in the IL condition stated that associates had a choice between getting letters from a random pool or requesting letters from their directors. The choice had to be made before the first trial and could not be changed. The induction was repeated when the subjects saw the self-description form their partners had completed. The last item asked, "Are you clear about the partnership arrangement?" In the EL condition the response read,

> I think so the experimenter said I had to ask my director for letters. It's the only way I can complete the puzzles.

In the IL condition it read,

> I think so the experimenter said I could either get letters from a random pool or ask you for some. I figure my best bet is asking you.

Finally, after the fifth trial the associate in the EL condition sent a message which said,

I have no choice—please give me as many letters as you can.

In the IL condition it read,

I decided to ask you—please give me as many letters as you can.

In all other respects subjects in both conditions were treated in identical ways.

RESULTS

In the first item of the postexperimental questionnaire, the subject had to check one of three descriptive statements. In turn, these stated: the partner had no choice in requesting letters, had a choice in requesting letters, or that there was no partner. Each of the 48 subjects endorsed the appropriate statement for his condition.[2]

TABLE 1

Mean Yielding Score by Blocks of Trials and t Values for Between-Condition Comparisons

		Trials		
Condition	1–5	6–10	11–15	Total
Internal locus	.3	1.2	.8	2.3
External locus	1.1	3.3	2.7	7.1
t	2.16*	5.49**	3.57**	5.36**

* $p < .05$.
** $p < .001$.

The mean yielding score for each block of five trials is presented in Table 1.[3] It can be seen that the IL condition produced significantly less yielding than the EL condition. Those subjects who thought their partners had chosen to be dependent yielded significantly less than those who thought their partners had no choice.

In both conditions the yielding scores increased during Trials 6–10, compared to Trials 1–5. In the EL condition 22 subjects yielded more, 1 subject yielded less, and 1 subject the same amount. In the IL condition the frequencies were 16, 6, and 2, respectively. Contrasting the subjects who increased their yielding with those who remained the same or who decreased, produced a highly significant effect for the EL condition and a marginally significant one for the IL condition. This increase undoubtedly

---

[2] Three subjects had to be discarded: one checked the incorrect induction and two said they had no partner.

[3] All probabilities are based on two-tailed tests. The variance in the IL condition were significantly lower than in the EL condition. When two of the tests for unequal population variances recommended by Winer (1962, pp. 36–39) were calculated, the significance levels remained unchanged.

reflects the effect of the note requesting more help, which was sent after the fifth trial.

The postexperimental questionnaire provided additional information consistent with the main hypothesis. The subjects in the EL condition, compared to those in the IL condition, saw their partners as less competitive ($\chi^2 = 9.41$, $df = 1$, $p < .01$), more reasonable ($\chi^2 = 5.37$, $df = 1$, $p < .05$), and as having had more influence ($\chi^2 = 5.33$, $df = 1$, $p < .05$). The two conditions did not differ with respect to ratings of the difficulty of the task or the enjoyment of the experiment.

The postexperimental qeustionnaire also contained one item relevant to the speculation that the social responsibility norm would be aroused less in the IL condition than in the EL condition. This was an open-ended item which asked the subject to state his reasons for whatever actions he had taken toward his partner. On the assumption that the arousal of the social responsibility norm would lead subjects to explaining their behavior by reference to the partner, while an absence of the norm leads to explanations containing only self-references, responses to that item were coded according to whether they made only self-references or whether they also included reference to the partner. In keeping with the speculation, the IL subjects made significantly more self-references and fewer partner references than the EL subjects ($\chi^2 = 10.22$, $df = 1$, $p < .01$).

Perception of the locus of the partner's dependence seems clearly to relate to the extent of help he can obtain. If the partner is seen as a victim of circumstances he will be helped more than if he is seen as being dependent of his own volition. It has been assumed that voluntary dependence lessens the salience of the social responsibility norm. It is likely that this effect has an important counterpart on decisions which are made in such contexts as child rearing or punishing deviant behavior. The criminal who is seen as a victim of circumstances is more likely to elicit sympathetic, helping responses, than one who is judged to have voluntarily committed the deviant act.

References

Berkowitz, L., & Daniels, Louise R. Responsibility and dependency. *Journal of Abnormal and Social Psychology*, 1963, **66**, 429–436.

Berkowitz, L., & Daniels, Louise R. Affecting the salience of the social responsibility norm: Effects of past help on the response to dependency relationships. *Journal of Abnormal and Social Psychology*, 1964, **68**, 275–281.

Berkowitz, L., Klanderman, Sharon, & Harris, R. Effects of experimenter awareness and sex of subject and experimenter on reactions to dependency relationships. *Sociometry*, 1964, **27**, 327–337.

Daniels, Louise R., & Berkowitz, L. Liking and response to dependency relationships. *Human Relations*, 1963, **16**, 141–148.

Schopler, J. Interpersonal power. In L. Berkowitz (Ed.), *Advances in experimental social psychology*. Vol. 2. New York: Academic Press, 1965.

Schopler, J., & Bateson, N. The power of dependence. *Journal of Personality and Social Psychology*, 1965, **2**, 247–254.

Thibaut, J. W., & Riecken, H. W. Some determinants and consequences of the perception of social causality. *Journal of Personality*, 1955, **24**, 113–133.

Winer, B. J. *Statistical principles in experimental design*. New York: McGraw-Hill, 1962.

Cognitive Effects of False Heart-Rate Feedback[1]

Stuart Valins

This experiment was concerned with some of the cognitive effects of internal events. The objective was to ascertain whether the labeling of emotional stimuli would be affected by information concerning internal reactions. Ss viewed 10 slides of seminude females while hearing sounds that were allegedly their heart beats. One group of Ss heard their "heart rates" increase markedly to 5 of the slides and not change to the other 5; a 2nd group of Ss heard a marked decrease in the bogus heart rate to 5 of the slides and no change to the other 5. In comparison with the slides to which Ss did not hear a change in the bogus rate, the slides to which they heard a marked change, whether increased or decreased, were (a) rated significantly more attractive during the experiment proper and during a disguised interview conducted 4–5 weeks later, and (b) chosen significantly more as remuneration for experimental participation.

Although there is considerable evidence that emotional states are accompanied by physiological changes (Duffy, 1962; Woodworth & Schlosberg, 1962), until recently there was little indication that these internal events facilitate the development of emotional behavior. Several experiments have now shown that emotional behavior is affected by the experimental manipulation of sympathetic activity. Emotional behavior is more readily learned when the sympathetic nervous system is intact than when it is surgically enervated (Wynne & Solomon, 1955), and more readily manifested during epinephrine-induced states of sympathetic activation than during states of relative inactivation (Latané & Schachter, 1962; Schachter & Singer, 1962; Schachter & Wheeler, 1962; Singer, 1963).

In an attempt to account for the influence of autonomic arousal on emotional behavior, Schachter (1964) has emphasized the importance of the cognitive effects of internal events. Within his cognitive-physiological theory of emotion, physiological changes are considered to function as stimuli or

[1] From the *Journal of Personality and Social Psychology*, Volume 4, pages 400–408, 1966 (received November 12, 1965). Reproduced by permission of the American Psychological Association. Author's affiliation: University of North Carolina. This research was conducted at Duke University while the author was a National Institutes of Health Postdoctoral Fellow in the Research Training Program in Sciences Related to the Central Nervous System.

cues and are represented cognitively as feelings or sensations. These feelings, in turn, arouse further cognitive activity in the form of attempts to identify the situation that precipitated them. Emotional behavior results when the feeling state is attributed to an emotional stimulus or situation. The optimum conditions for the development of an emotion are thus present when an individual can say, "That stimulus [emotional] has affected me internally." In accord with these notions, it has been found that when subjects are pharmacologically aroused and exposed to stimuli designed to induce emotion, more emotional behavior is manifested when the arousal state is attributed to the emotional situation than when it is attributed to the injection (Schachter & Singer, 1962). Furthermore, the results of a recent experiment suggest that the effects of internal cues on emotional behavior may be mediated by an alteration in the perceived intensity of the emotional stimulus. Nisbett and Schachter (1966) found that when a series of electric shocks were administered to subjects who were in a mild state of fear, the shocks were judged to be more painful by those subjects who correctly attributed their internal symptoms to the shocks than by subjects who incorrectly attributed their symptoms to a pill.

Once it is granted that internal events can function as cues or stimuli then these events can now be considered as a source of cognitive information. They can, for example, result in cognitions such as, "My heart is pounding," or "My face is flushed." As potential cognitive information, however, these events are subject to the same mechanisms that process any stimulus before it is represented cognitively. Such mechanisms can result in their being denied, distorted, or simply not perceived. It is thus plausible that the cognitive representation of an internal event can be nonveridical; a particular reaction can fail to register or can be misperceived, and a nonexistent reaction can be represented cognitively. Mandler (1962) also has questioned the veridicality of internal sensations and suggests that:

> . . . someone may learn to make statements about his internal private events under the control of environmental stimuli or irrelevant internal stimuli. Thus, I could say, "I am blushing," in an embarrassing situation without showing any signs of peripheral vasodilation. Or I may have learned to talk about tenseness in my stomach in a stress situation without stomach events exerting any influence on such a remark [p. 317].

If cognitive representations of internal events are important for emotional behavior, then these nonveridical representations of physiological changes should have the same effects as veridical ones. They will be evaluated by reference to a precipitating situation and result in emotional behavior if the situation is an emotional one. Using Mandler's example, his "symbolic" blusher should be equally embarrassed with or without the presence of peripheral vasodilation. He should be less embarrassed, however, if he now has a mirror at his disposal and observes that he is not blushing. Embarrassment should be greatest only when he *thinks* that he has blushed in response to the situation.

The present experiment represents an attempt to determine the effects of nonveridical cognitive cues concerning internal reactions of the labeling of emotional stimuli. This will be accomplished by manipulating the extent to which a subject believes his heart has reacted to slides of seminude females and by observing the effects on his "liking" for the slides. The research of Schachter and his associates suggests that if a subject were covertly injected with epinephrine and shown a slide of a nude female, he would interpret his internal sensations as due to the nude stimulus and he would label the girl as more attractive than if he had been injected with placebo and he had experienced no internal sensations. If, however, it is the cognitive effect of internal events that influences emotional behavior, then this same influence should be observed when subjects thinks that they have reacted to a given stimulus, regardless of whether they have indeed reacted. As such, it is hypothesized that the cognition, "That girl has affected my heart rate," will induce subjects to consider the girl more attractive or appealing than the cognition, "That girl has not affected my heart rate."

These effects are predicted regardless of whether the heart-rate feedback matches the subjects' stereotyped expectations. Most of us would expect that, if anything, our heart rates would increase in response to photographs of nude females. How would we interpret our heart-rate changes, however, if the rate remained normal to some photographs but decreased substantially to others? If all of the photographs were of attractive females, we could not interpret a decrease as indicating that a girl is a "dog." If we felt it necessary to evaluate these reactions at all, it is likely that we would interpret any change in our heart rates as indicating greater attraction or appeal. Only if all of the photographs were relatively unattractive would we expect that a decrease in heart rate be interpreted as less attraction. Thus, under the appropriate cognitive conditions (highly attractive females), feedback indicating that heart rate has decreased should affect the labeling of emotional stimuli in a manner similar to that of feedback indicating that heart rate has increased.

PROCEDURE

Male introductory psychology students, whose course requirements included 6 hours of participation in experiments, volunteered for a psychophysiological experiment. When the subject arrived at the laboratory, the experiment was described as a study of physiological reactions to sexually oriented stimuli. These reactions were allegedly being recorded while the subjects viewed 10 slides of seminude females. Two groups of subjects were led to believe that they were hearing an amplified version of their hearts beating while watching the slides and heard their "heart rates" change markedly to half of them. Two other groups of subjects heard the identical sounds, but did not associate them with their own heart beats. Several measures of the attractiveness of each slide were subsequently obtained from all subjects and used to evaluate the effects of the heart-rate feedback.

Bogus Heart-Rate Conditions

Subjects in these conditions were told that the experiment was concerned with heart-rate reactions to sexually oriented stimuli. It was explained that:

> Most of our research is conducted over at the Bell Medical Research Building. We have all sorts of electronic wizardry and sound proof chambers over there. Right now there are several experiments being conducted and our facilities at Bell are too overcrowded. Because of this situation, we are doing this experiment here, and are forced to use a fairly crude but adequate measure of heart rate. In our other lab we record heart rate using electrodes which are taped to the chest. They pick up the electrical impulses from the heart which are then recorded on a polygraph. Here we are recording heart rate the way they used to do it 30 years ago. I will be taping this fairly sensitive microphone to your chest. It picks up each major heart sound which is amplified here, and initiates a signal on this signal tracer. This other microphone then picks up the signal and it is recorded on this tape recorder (the signal tracer, amplifier, and tape recorder were on a table next to the subject). By appropriately using a stop watch and this footage indicator, I can later determine exactly where each stimulus occurred and evaluate your heart rate reaction to it.
>
> Unfortunately, this recording method makes it necessary to have audible sounds. They would be a serious problem if we were employing a task which required concentration. Since our procedure does not require concentration, it won't be too much of a problem and it is not likely to affect the results. All that you will be required to do is sit here and look at the slides. Just try to ignore the heart sounds. I will be showing the slides from the next room through this one-way screen. I'll tape this microphone to your chest and after recording your resting heart rate for a while, I will present 10 slides to you at regular intervals. Then I will record your resting heart rate again for several minutes and I will repeat the same slides again in the same order.

After taping the microphone to the subject's chest, the experimenter started the tape recorder and left the room. The sounds which these subjects were hearing were in reality prerecorded. A concealed wire from the tape recorder fed these sounds into the signal tracer speaker. Twenty subjects heard a tape recording which indicated that their heart rates had increased substantially to five slides, but had not changed to five others (heart-rate increase group); 20 other subjects heard a tape recording which indicated that their heart rates had decreased substantially to five of the slides, but had not changed to the other five (heart-rate decrease group).[2]

[2] It should be mentioned that Gerard and Rabbie (1961) and Bramel (1963) have used a similar technique in order to make subjects think that they were more or less frightened or homosexual. They accomplished this by allowing subjects to see dial readings which purportedly indicated internal reactions to experimental stimuli, but which were actually under the control of the experimenter. These investigators, however, were not primarily concerned with the evaluation and labeling of internal states. Their manipulations included detailed explanations of the "meaning" of the dial readings, so that subjects had no choice but to later indicate that they were or were not frightened or homosexual. In contrast, subjects in the present experiment were (a) specifically instructed to ignore the bogus heart sounds, (b) told nothing about the meaning of heart-rate changes, and (c) told that the experimenter could not hear the heart sounds and thus would not know for some time how the subject had reacted. It is the purpose of the present experiment to determine whether subjects will *spontaneously* label their feelings toward a stimulus by reference to their knowledge of how their hearts have reacted.

Extraneous Sound Conditions

Subjects in these conditions thought that the experiment was investigating vasomotor reactions to sexually oriented stimuli. They were told that:

> Most of our research is conducted over at the Bell Medical Research Building. We have all sorts of electronic wizardry and sound proof chambers over there. I am doing this experiment now because of the conflicting results which we have obtained in two other identical experiments which we have done over at Bell. One experiment was done in a completely sound proof chamber. Another one was done in an office in which extraneous sounds could be heard, bells ringing in the hallway, people walking up and down, etc. Well, the results in these two experiments were not the same. We feel that it is possible that the results may have been different due to the extraneous sounds which were heard in the experiment where the subject was in an office. To determine whether extraneous sounds can affect finger temperature reactions to sexual stimuli, throughout this experiment you will hear sounds from this tape recorder, sounds that are completely meaningless but are just our way of controlling and producing extraneous sound. Later I will compare your finger temperature reactions to sexual stimuli with those of subjects who do not hear any sounds. I can then assess the physiological effects of the extraneous sounds and determine whether they were the reason why we obtained directionally different results in the two other experiments.
>
> These sounds have absolutely no meaning for you. Just try to ignore them. I will be showing the slides from the next room through this one-way screen. I'll tape this thermistor to your finger and after recording your resting finger temperature for a while, I will present 10 slides to you at regular intervals. Then I will record your resting finger temperature again for several minutes and I will repeat the same slides again in the same order.

A dummy thermistor was then taped to the subject's finger, the tape recorder started, and the experimenter left the room. Ten of these subjects (sound increase group) heard the same tape recording as the heart-rate increase group, and 10 (sound decrease group) heard the same recording as the heart-rate decrease group. The sounds emanated from the signal tracer as in the experimental conditions, but the subjects were now told that it was just an elaborate speaker.

Tape Recordings

The tape recordings were made by recording square wave pulses produced by a Hewlett-Packard low-frequency signal generator, a signal tracer used as a capacitance network, and an external speaker. Pulses of a given frequency per minute could be varied over a wide range.

Heart Beat and Sound Increase Recording. This recording began with the pulse rate varying every 5 seconds between 66 and 72 beats per minute (BPM). At the start of the third minute the rate increased in 5-second segments from 72 to 84 and then to 90 BPM. It then decreased to 84, 78, and to 72 BPM, and subsequently continued to vary between 66 and 72 BPM. The identical rate increase was recorded at minutes 5, 8, 10, 11, 15, 17, 20, 22, and 23. The rate continued to vary between 66 and 72 BPM at minutes 4, 6, 7, 9, 12, 13, 14, 16, 18, 19, 21, and 24.

Heart Beat and Sound Decrease Recording. This recording was the same as the previous one except for the minutes at which the rate increased. At the start of the third minute for this recording, the rate decreased from 66 to 54 and then to 48 BPM.

It then increased to 54, 60, and to 66 BPM, and subsequently continued to vary between 66 and 72 BPM. This same decrease in rate was recorded whenever an increase had been recorded on the other tape.

Coordination of Slides with Tape Recordings

Ten color slides were made from photographs of seminude females which had been published by *Playboy* magazine. The slides were projected at 1-minute intervals, each for 15 seconds. The first slide was presented approximately 1 minute, 58 seconds after the tape-recorded sounds had begun so that a marked change in the rate of the sounds was evident 2 seconds afterward. Since the remaining nine slides were presented at 1-minute intervals, this same slide-sound change contingency was apparent for slides 3, 6, 8, and 9. Slides 2, 4, 5, 7, and 10 were presented at the minutes when no change in the rate of the sounds occurred. After the tenth slide (Minute 12 on the tape recording), there was a 3-minute break during which the rate of the sounds varied between 66 and 72 BPM. The slides were then repeated in the same manner starting at Minute 15. The slide order was also systematically rotated within conditions so that each slide was followed by a sound change as often as it was not.

To further clarify the procedure, consider the experimental situation as viewed by a subject who thought he was hearing his heart beating. For 2 minutes, he hears it beating at what appears to be a normal and reasonable rate. The first slide is then presented, and shortly afterward he notices a marked change in his heart rate. After 15 seconds of observing the slide, his heart rate gradually returns to what has been established as normal. The second slide is presented, but there is not any noticeable effect on his heart rate. It continues to vary between 66 and 72 BPM. After seeing all 10 slides, it is apparent that 5 of them have affected his heart rate, but the other 5 have not. This conclusion is reinforced when, after a 3-minute period of normal heart rate, the slides are shown again, and the same ones affect his heart rate, while the others have no effect.

Attractiveness Measures

The effects of heart-rate feedback were assessed by determining the extent to which it influenced the subject's opinions of how attractive the girls were. Three measures of these opinions were obtained: (a) attractiveness ratings which were made immediately after the bogus feedback, (b) choice of photographs as remuneration, (c) attractiveness rankings made several weeks after the experiment.

Slide Ratings. After the second presentation of the slides, the experimenter disengaged the apparatus and briefly discussed the slides with the subject. The subject was then told that 12 slides were originally being used but that 2 were eliminated in order to shorten the procedure. It was explained that the experimenter was now considering reducing the number of slides to 7 or 8. He was asking a number of subjects to rate the slides so that only the 7 or 8 most attractive or appealing ones would be included. The slides were quickly shown again to the subject and, using a 100-point scale ranging from "Not at all" to "Extremely," he rated them as to: "How attractive or appealing each girl is to you."

Photograph Choices. The subject then completed a short questionnaire which was followed by an intensive interview to determine whether he had accepted the experimental deceptions. The physiology of sexual arousal was also discussed, but no mention was ever made of the true purpose of the experiment or of the experimental deceptions. The experimenter apologized for being unable to pay the subject and offered to give him some photographs of the girls which had been donated by the publisher. The 10 photographs from which the slides had been made were casually spread on a table, and the subject was told to take 5. The experimenter left the room and thanked the subject before he made his choices. As the subject was leaving, he was intercepted and the photographs taken back. It was explained that the photographs had been offered to the subject only to determine if there were differences in attractiveness estimates relating to slide versus photograph modes of presentation.

Delayed Photograph Rankings. Three weeks after participating in the experiment, the subject received a letter from a fictitious "social scientist." The letter requested the subject's cooperation for an attitude survey and asked him to permit an interviewer to question him. Approximately 1 week later an interviewer arrived at the subject's dormitory room and described the survey as a study of undergraduate attitudes toward the psychological and physical characteristics of members of the opposite sex. The subject first ranked three sets of photographs, each consisting of a model in 12 different dresses, according to how attractive the girl was in each photograph. He then ranked 12 photographs of seminude females on the same dimension. Ten of these photographs were those which he had seen in the experiment proper. After ranking these photographs, the interviewer questioned the subject as to whether he had previously seen them and determined whether he had associated the interview with the original experiment. It should be emphasized that throughout these interviews,[3] the subjects were totally unaware that the feedback in the original experiment was nonveridical.

RESULTS

Adequacy of the Experimental Manipulations

In order to be effective, the manipulation of differential heart-rate feedback must be accurately perceived by the subjects and adequately accepted as a reflection of their internal reactions. Although they were instructed to ignore the bogus heart sounds, the subjects' interest in their reactions and the amplification of the sounds resulted in all subjects being aware of the different slide-sound change contingencies. The bogus heart beats were also accepted as veridical. None of the 40 experimental subjects had substantial suspicions that the sounds might not be their heart beats. Several had what they described as momentary doubts when first hearing the sounds, but these were quickly forgotten or dispelled. The slightly varying sound rate during the first 2 minutes seemed quite reasonable and served, as intended, to convince the subjects of the veridicality of the bogus beats. The bogus heart-rate reactions to the different slides were also accepted as veridical. Although the heart-rate decrease subjects were overwhelmingly surprised by this feedback, they simply considered as wrong their previous expectations of how they react to these stimuli. Suspicions concerning the veridicality of the feedback were also not increased when the subjects were confronted with a marked discordance between their presumed heart-rate reactions and their initial "liking" for a slide. This discordance was apparently reconciled by many subjects in precisely the manner which was predicted. They changed their estimates of how attractive the girls were.

[3] These interviews were skillfully conducted by Joseph Mancusi.

Heart-Rate Feedback and Attractiveness Measures

It was hypothesized that the cue function of internal events affects the labeling of emotional stimuli. A nonveridical cognitive cue which indicates that one has reacted markedly to a slide of a seminude female should, in this situation, be interpreted as indicating that the stimulus object is attractive or appealing.

Slide Ratings. The prerecorded sounds were played throughout the first two presentations of the slides. During the third presentation, the tape recorder was turned off, and the subjects rated the attractiveness or appeal of each girl. If heart-rate feedback has had the predicted effect, the experimental subjects, in comparison to the control subjects, should rate the slides followed by a change in the sound rate (reinforced) as more attractive than the slides not followed by a change (nonreinforced). Table 1 presents

TABLE 1

Mean Slide Attractiveness Ratings[a]

| | Conditions | | |
| | --- | --- | --- |
Slides	Heart-rate increase ($N = 20$)	Heart-rate decrease ($N = 20$)	Sound increase + sound decrease ($N = 10 + 10$)
Reinforced	72.42	69.26	60.86
Nonreinforced	54.11	62.57	63.76
Difference	18.31	6.69	−2.90

[a] All p values reported are 2-tailed, p value of difference score comparisons (t tests): heart-rate increase versus sound increase and decrease, $p < .001$; heart-rate decrease versus sound increase and decrease, $p < .05$; heart-rate increase versus heart-rate decrease, $p < .05$.

the mean ratings of the reinforced and nonreinforced slides for each of the experimental groups and for the combined control groups.[4] When the sounds were not considered heart beats, they had virtually no effect on the subjects' ratings. Since the control groups rated the reinforced and nonreinforced slides similarly, it is evident that the sounds alone did not have any differential excitatory effects.

It can be seen, however, that when subjects thought the sounds were their heart beats, there was a substantial effect of differential feedback on their ratings. Subjects in the heart-rate decrease condition rated the reinforced slides 6.69 points higher than the nonreinforced ones; subjects in the heart-rate increase condition rated the reinforced slides 18.31 points higher

[4] The data of the control groups were combined to facilitate presentation. Their means did not differ significantly on any measure, and both were always in a direction opposite to that of the experimental groups.

TABLE 2

Number of Subjects Rating Reinforced Slides Higher and Number Rating Them Lower than Nonreinforced Slides

Reinforced slides rated	Conditions			
	Heart-rate increase ($N = 20$)	Heart-rate decrease ($N = 19$)[a]	Heart-rate increase + decrease ($N = 20 + 19$)[a]	Sound increase + decrease ($N = 10 + 10$)
Higher	17	15	32	9
Lower	3	4	7	11
p value (sign test)	.002	.02	.001	*ns*

[a] One subject rated the reinforced and nonreinforced stimuli identically.

than the nonreinforced ones. Each of these differences is significantly greater than that of the combined control groups. The heart-rate increase feedback also had a greater effect than the decrease feedback. Subjects in the former condition apparently lowered their ratings of the nonreinforced slides as well as raising their ratings of the reinforced ones. The effects of the manipulations are more clearly portrayed in Table 2 which presents the number of subjects in each condition who rated the reinforced slides higher than the nonreinforced ones. This analysis shows that the bogus feedback affected the ratings of the majority of the subjects in the experimental conditions, whereas extraneous sounds had little effect in the control conditions.

Photograph Choices. Differential heart-rate feedback has obviously affected the subjects' ratings of the slides. It may be asked, however, to what extent these ratings are truly indicative of the way subjects feel about these stimuli. Will they now, for example, choose more photographs of the reinforced nudes than the nonreinforced ones as remuneration for participating in the experiment? It will be recalled that each subject selected five photographs. Table 3 tabulates the number of subjects in each condition

TABLE 3

Number of Subjects Choosing Three or More Reinforced Photographs and Number Choosing Two or Less

No. of reinforced photographs chosen	Conditions			
	Heart-rate increase ($N = 20$)	Heart-rate decrease ($N = 20$)	Heart-rate increase + decrease ($N = 20 + 20$)	Sound increase + sound decrease ($N = 10 + 10$)
3 or more	15	14	29	6
2 or less	5	6	11	14
p value (sign test)	.04	*ns*	.007	*ns*

who chose three or more of the previously reinforced nudes and the number choosing two or less. It can be seen that a significant number of experimental subjects chose more of the photographs that had been reinforced than photographs that had not been reinforced. The data for the heart-rate decrease condition alone are not quite significant, whereas that of the control groups appear just as strong, but in the opposite direction. An analysis of the mean number of reinforced nudes chosen by each group, however, shows that the heart-rate decrease subjects chose significantly more than that expected on a chance basis, but the control groups did not choose significantly less. The control groups chose an average of 2.25 reinforced photographs ($t = 1.55$, ns), whereas the heart-rate decrease subjects chose 3.10 reinforced photographs ($t = 2.41$, $p < .05$), and the heart-rate increase subjects chose 3.20 reinforced photographs ($t = 2.45$, $p < .05$). With the exception that, on this measure the experimental groups did not differ from one another, the analysis of photograph choices clearly supports that of the ratings. A marked change in heart rate which is considered as effected by a nude female is interpreted as attraction and results in greater liking for the stimulus.

Delayed Photograph Rankings. It may also be asked whether the observed effects of the heart-rate feedback are temporary or whether they are sufficiently substantial to result in relatively long-lasting cognitive change. In order to answer this question, interviews were conducted with the subjects 4–5 weeks after the experiment proper. During the course of these interviews, the subjects were asked to rank, from most to least attractive, 12 photographs of seminude females. Since 10 of these photographs were used in the experiment proper, an analysis of these rankings permits an evaluation of the relative permanency of the feedback effects. It should be mentioned that the interviewer made every effort to avoid allowing the subjects to associate the interview procedure with the original experiment. Since the source of the photographs was identified as *Playboy* magazine, the subjects did not think it unusual that two experiments would be using similar stimuli. The subjects were, in fact, quite surprised when subsequently informed of the true purpose of the interview. In addition, most of the subjects appeared to rank the photographs on the basis of how they felt at the moment. They were not aware of, or at least did not verbalize, any tendency to rank them according to their previous attractiveness estimates.

It can be seen in Table 4 that the analysis of the delayed photograph rankings is generally consistent with the previous analyses. In comparison to the control subjects, more of the experimental subjects ranked the reinforced photographs as more attractive than the nonreinforced ones ($\chi^2 = 4.57$, $p < .05$). Thus, differential heart-rate feedback has had effects which are relatively long lasting (mean delay = 31.25 days). Presumed internal reactions have served as cues and have resulted in distinctly different evaluations of emotional stimuli.

TABLE 4

Number of Subjects Ranking Reinforced Photographs Higher and Number Ranking Them Lower than Nonreinforced Photographs

	Conditions			
Reinforced photographs ranked	Heart-rate increase ($N = 20$)	Heart-rate decrease ($N = 20$)	Heart-rate increase + decrease ($N = 20 + 20$)	Sound increase + sound decrease ($N = 10 + 9$)[a]
Higher	14	14	28	7
Lower	6	6	12	12
p value (sign test)	ns	ns	.02	ns

[a] One subject could not be contacted for the interview.

DISCUSSION

The major hypothesis of this study has received considerable experimental support. When a subject thought that his heart had reacted markedly to certain slides of seminude females, he rated these slides as more attractive and chose them more often than slides that he thought had not affected his heart rate. These results are exactly what one would have expected had heart-rate changes and veridical feelings of palpitation been pharmacologically induced to some slides but not to others. The mechanism operating to produce these effects is presumably the same regardless of the veridicality of the feedback. Internal events are a source of cognitive information and, as Schachter has proposed, individuals will want to evaluate and understand this kind of information. When an emotional explanation is prepotent, they will label their reactions accordingly. This process is apparently what has been observed in the present experiment. The subjects did attempt to evaluate their reactions, and, having done so, the conditions were such that it was most appropriate for them to explain their reactions by referring to the slides and to interpret them as indicating varying degrees of attraction.

A given heart-rate reaction, however, was not always evaluated as attraction. Postexperimental interviews revealed that, at times, a particular reaction was attributed to surprise, since the subject was daydreaming, and the presentation of the slide shook him out of his reverie, or to a sudden fit of coughing or sneezing, or to a slight resemblance to a former girl friend. It was often evident that these alternative explanations were sought when subjects could not convince themselves that they liked a particular slide. In such cases, it was apparently necessary for them to explain their reactions by referring to other causes. The subjects' attempts to label their reactions suggest that the attractiveness estimates reflected more than shallow verbal definitions of internal reactions. A number of subjects seemed to actively persuade themselves that a reinforced nude was attractive. They reported looking at the slide more closely, and it was evident that they attempted to justify the feedback by magnifying the girl's positive characteristics. Although these subjects realized that they were looking for an explanation for the feedback, they did not feel that they were distorting the slide. Closer inspection simply showed them what their "subconscious" knew all the time. The girl's breasts or buttocks were indeed nicer than they originally thought. Although there is no systematic evidence available, it would be difficult to explain how the feedback could still have effects after several weeks were it not for a process similar to this active self-persuasion.

It is of some interest to consider whether the heart-rate feedback had a direct physiological excitatory effect. If the bogus heart-rate changes resulted in actual physiological change, the differential attractiveness ratings might be attributed to veridical internal cues rather than nonveridical ones. Although physiological variables were not measured, there is little reason to suspect that the bogus feedback had any direct effects other than cognitive ones. If these auditory stimuli had excitatory effects that were not due to their "meaning," then the extraneous-sound subjects should have manifested differential attractiveness ratings depending upon the slide-sound change contingencies. However, the differences observed for these subjects, between their ratings of the reinforced and nonreinforced stimuli, were slight and in a direction opposite to that which would be expected. Furthermore, when subjects rated their awareness of palpitations or actual *feeling* of heart beating during the experiment (4-point scale, ranging from "Not at all" to "An intense amount"), the experimental subjects reported experiencing *fewer* palpitations than did the control subjects. This effect was significant for the heart-rate increase versus extraneous-sound comparison (.6 versus 1.10, $p < .05$) and has subsequently been replicated ($p < .06$). Analysis of the data of this replication, which include galvanic skin response and heart-rate measurements, also reveals that subjects exposed to the heart-rate increase and sound increase manipulations react alike physiologically.[5] It is thus likely that the observed effects of bogus heart-rate feedback are primarily a result of cognitive factors and not physiological ones. In fact, the bogus feedback appears to mask veridical feedback by diverting the subject's attention from his actual internal reactions.

The cognitive manipulations and processes which have been emphasized in the present experiment bear some similarity to current techniques and theory concerned with the extinction of maladaptive emotional behavior. Using systematic desensitization therapy (Wolpe, 1958) phobic patients have been treated by teaching them to perform responses to phobic objects that are incompatible with the fear responses usually generated. In an experimental study, Lang and Lazovik (1963) trained snake-phobic subjects

[5] S. Valins, unpublished data.

in deep muscle relaxation. The subjects were subsequently hypnotized during each of 11 therapeutic sessions and instructed to relax while imagining a number of situations in which a snake was involved. Subjects participating in this treatment were later observed to be less frightened by snakes, and approximately half of them could even be induced to touch or pick up a live snake. The extinction of these well-established behaviors is presumably due to the resulting incompatibility between the induced muscular relaxation and the physiological changes ordinarily accompanying states of fear. Consider the treatment, however, from a subject's point of view. Whereas in the past he has been physiologically upset when thinking about snakes, he can now think about them without experiencing as many marked internal sensations. His musculature is now completely relaxed and results in his being able to say, "Thinking about snakes no longer affects me internally." Similar cognitions concerning internal events have effectively influenced the labeling of emotional stimuli in the present experiment. It would seem reasonable that such cognitions are also induced during desensitization therapy and might be the primary factor contributing to the successful treatment of phobic patients. If this is so, the rather tedious muscular relaxation procedure could be replaced with another manipulation of the cognitive representation of internal events. It may be possible to eliminate phobic behaviors solely by inducing nonveridical cognitions concerning internal reactions. Such cognitions could be manipulated so that they would be incompatible with the knowledge of how one usually reacts when frightened. Snake-phobic subjects, for example, who are led to believe that thinking about or seeing snakes does not affect them internally, might reevaluate their attitudes toward snakes and become less frightened by them.

REFERENCES

Bramel, D. Selection of a target for defensive projection. *Journal of Abnormal and Social Psychology*, 1963, **66**, 318–324.

Duffy, E. *Activation and behavior.* New York: Wiley, 1962.

Gerard, H., & Rabbie, J. Fear and social comparison. *Journal of Abnormal and Social Psychology*, 1961, **62**, 586–592.

Lang, P. J., & Lazovik, A. D. Experimental desensitization of a phobia. *Journal of Abnormal and Social Psychology*, 1963, **66**, 519–525.

Latané, B., & Schachter, S. Adrenalin and avoidance learning. *Journal of Comparative and Physiological Psychology*, 1962, **65**, 369–372.

Mandler, G. Emotion. *New directions in psychology.* New York: Holt, Rinehart & Winston, 1962. Pp. 267–343.

Nisbett, R., & Schachter, S. Cognitive manipulation of pain. *Journal of Experimental Social Psychology*, 1966, **2**, 227–236.

Schachter, S. The interaction of cognitive and physiological determinants of emotional state. In L. Berkowitz (Ed.), *Advances in experimental social psychology.* Vol. 1. New York: Academic Press, 1964. Pp. 49–80.

Schachter, S., & Singer, J. E. Cognitive, social, and physiological determinants of emotional state. *Psychological Review*, 1962, **69**, 379–399.

Schachter, S., & Wheeler, L. Epinephrine, chlorpromazine, and amusement. *Journal of Abnormal and Social Psychology,* 1962, **65,** 121–128.

Singer, J. E. Sympathetic activation, drugs, and fright. *Journal of Comparative and Physiological Psychology,* 1963, **56,** 612–615.

Wolpe, J. *Psychotherapy by reciprocal inhibition.* Palo Alto, California: Stanford University Press, 1958.

Woodworth, R. S., & Schlosberg, H. *Experimental psychology.* New York: Holt, Rinehart & Winston, 1962.

Wynne, L. C., & Solomon, R. L. Traumatic avoidance learning: Acquisition and extinction in dogs deprived of normal peripheral autonomic function. *Genetic Psychology Monographs,* 1955, **52,** 241–284.

Chapter 9

INTERPERSONAL ATTRACTION

Love and hate, or positive and negative attraction, are very salient and important aspects of our social environment. Interpersonal attraction means the positive or negative affect directed toward one or more persons. Thus the study of interpersonal attraction is the study of attitudes toward persons. Attitudes were previously defined as dispositions to evaluate objects favorably or unfavorably. In the case of interpersonal attraction the objects are persons.

The major purpose of this chapter is to examine possible answers to the question, "What determines one person's degree of interpersonal attraction for another?" One way of answering this question is to focus on the way other people satisfy a self-evaluative need, a matter to which we now turn.

People as Instrumental to the Satisfaction of a Self-Evaluative Need

Why is it that people seek the company of other people? One possibility is that affiliative behavior satisfies some sort of gregarious need. Another possibility is that affiliative behavior is instrumental to the satisfaction of other needs. For example, we may seek out a tennis partner, not because of a gregariousness need, but because the other person is instrumental to the satisfaction of exercise, mastery, or competitiveness needs. Social interaction is replete with instrumental determinants of behavior. For example, a patient may seek a doctor in order to be cured of an illness, a client may seek a lawyer in order to obtain legal advice.

It is important to note, however, that the most immediate effect of such attempted need satisfaction is *affiliative behavior* and not necessarily more positive interpersonal attraction. In order to satisfy certain needs we may affiliate with tennis players, doctors, and lawyers without necessarily increasing our attraction to the persons with whom we have affiliated. Whether or not affiliation leads to increased attraction or liking may at least partially depend upon whether the affiliation successfully results in need satisfaction or positive affect. If playing tennis with a certain individual was successful in satisfying certain needs and was thus a pleasant experience, more positive interpersonal attraction may result. From the perspective of hedonism of the past the other person becomes a secondary reinforcer. (A secondary reinforcer is a previously neutral stimulus which takes on reward properties by virtue of its association with other rewarding stimuli.) From a balance point of view (Heider, 1958) the other person acquires a positive sign since this person was positively instrumental in the achievement of a positive tennis game. Thus a balanced situation of three positive signs results.

What are the needs which affiliative behavior can instrumentally satisfy? Quite possibly there are a sizable number. Most research, however, has concentrated on one single need, the self-evaluative need.

FESTINGER'S THEORY OF SOCIAL COMPARISON PROCESSES

Before his development of dissonance theory, Festinger (1954) had advanced a somewhat different type of theory, a theory of social comparison processes. This theory took as its starting point the notion that people have a self-evaluative drive. (For our purposes the concepts of drive and need can be used synonomously.) This self-evaluative drive is specifically manifested in the individual's motivation to evaluate his *opinions* and *abilities*.

How may opinions and abilities be evaluated? Festinger (1950) had earlier drawn a distinction between *physical reality* and *social reality*. Physical reality is the reality created by empirical observation. Social reality is the reality created by group consensus. If someone believes that a particular surface is fragile he may verify this opinion by taking a hammer and striking the surface. In this instance the opinion is validated through empirical observation. According to Festinger the individual would likely disbelieve information regarding the fragility of the surface that contradicted his own observations. Suppose, on the other hand, it is not possible to validate an opinion through empirical observation. Many of our opinions regarding politics, religion, etc., are of this type. For such opinions validation is sought through social agreement or group consensus. In his social comparison theory Festinger relies on this earlier distinction between physical and social reality when he states that, "To the extent that objective, non-social means are not available, people evaluate their opinions and abilities by comparison respectively with the opinions and abilities of others" (1954, p. 118). Since opinions and abilities frequently cannot be evaluated through empirical observations it often turns out to be the case that one's abilities are good or bad in comparison with the abilities of others and one's opinions are right or wrong in terms of agreement or disagreement with the opinions of others.

Festinger (1954) further states that "The tendency to compare oneself with some other specific person decreases as the difference between his opinion or ability and one's own increases" (p. 120). According to Festinger a student does not evaluate his intelligence by comparison with a group of institutionalized feebleminded nor does someone who believes that blacks and whites are social equals evaluate his opinion by comparison with the opinion of an antiblack group.

The theory is further elaborated with such propositions as "Subjective evaluations of opinions or of abilities are stable when comparison is available with others who are judged to be close to one's opinions or abilities" (p. 122), and "A person will be less attracted to situations where others are very divergent from him than to situations where others are close to him for both abilities and opinions" (p. 123). Since similar others allow for the stable reduction of the self-evaluative drive, people are attracted to such others.

In some instances a minimal amount of dissimilarity may lead to a group conformity effect, "When a discrepancy exists with respect to opinions or abilities there will be tendencies to change one's own position so as to move closer to others in the group" (Festinger, p. 126). The dissimilarity, however, must be minimal, "When a discrepancy exists with respect to opinions or abilities there will be tendencies to cease comparing oneself with those in the group who are very different from oneself" (p. 128).

Social-comparison theory specifies the circumstances under which a person matches his own opinions or abilities with those of another person. When discrepancies occur changes or cessation of comparisons are predicted. It should be evident that social comparison involves the same elements subsequently incorporated in dissonance theory. The social comparison process depends upon cognitions about the self and about another person or group. It is, therefore, interpersonal. Dissonance theory is based on cognitions a person holds about himself. It is, therefore, intrapersonal.

Both formulations attempt to specify the consequences when two kinds of information do not "fit."

SOME RECENT RESEARCH ON SOCIAL COMPARISON THEORY

It is safe to say that Festinger's publication of his theory of social comparison did not stimulate an avalanche of research—possibly because shortly thereafter Festinger himself became involved in dissonance theory. The most notable effect of social-comparison theory was in the stimulation of Schachter's (1959) work on anxiety and birth order, a matter to which we will turn shortly. More recently, however, investigators have begun to take a second look at social comparison theory. A good example of this attention is a study by Byrne, Nelson, and Reeves (1966). Byrne, Nelson, and Reeves found strong evidence for the importance of belief similarity-dissimilarity on attraction and suggestive evidence for the importance of the empirical verifiability of the beliefs in mediating the similarity-dissimilarity effect. Byrne *et al.* initially expected that belief similarity would have the most effect upon attraction when beliefs were not verifiable (e.g., "Racial integration in public schools is a mistake"), an intermediate effect when beliefs were verifiable in the future (e.g., "The amount of integration in Southern schools will sharply decrease over the next five years"), and the least effect when the beliefs were verifiable at present (e.g., "An extremely small percentage of the public schools in the United States are racially integrated"). The experiment was conducted in two sessions. During the first session subjects indicated their beliefs regarding several issues. For some of the subjects the beliefs were not verifiable, for some verifiable in the future, and for some verifiable at present. Several weeks later the subjects were asked to take part in a study of "interpersonal judgment." Their task was to examine the belief responses of a same-sex stranger and then to judge the stranger on a number of dimensions: intelligence, knowledge of current events, morality, adjustment, likability, and desirability as a work partner. Scale values of the last two judgments were summed to form a measure of attraction toward the stranger. The stranger's belief responses were manipulated so as to be completely similar, two-thirds similar, one-half similar, or one-third similar to the subjects' own belief responses.

The results indicated that similarity of unverifiable beliefs did indeed have the most marked effect on attraction, but that the difference between the remaining two types of beliefs was opposite to expectation. Similarity of beliefs verifiable at present had a more marked effect on attraction than similarity of beliefs verifiable in the future. Byrne *et al.* interpret these results in terms of the amount of effort required for empirical verification. For the particular verifiable-at-present beliefs utilized in the experiment, verification required a certain amount of reference and library work. On the other hand, the beliefs that could be verified in the future required only that one wait until the mass media carried the information. Thus Byrne *et al.* go beyond a simple dichotomy of physical and social reality and propose a continuum in terms of the ease of obtaining empirical verification. The most effortful end of the continuum is represented by the unverifiable beliefs.

Shrauger and Jones (1968) have reported an experiment in which purportedly unverifiable beliefs were found to have a greater mediational effect upon attraction than purportedly verifiable beliefs. In three-person groups subjects took turns making predictions concerning how differently described fictitious persons would feel about certain values and then evaluating the predictions made by other subjects. The subjects sat in separate cubicles containing switches and lights allowing them to make evaluations as well as to receive feedback regarding the other subjects' evaluations. Actually this information was falsified by the experimenter so that each subject believed that he received mainly positive evaluations from one subject and mainly negative evaluations from the other subject. In a high social-validation condition the subjects were told that the required predictions were not a test of skill, but only an assessment of their opinions about matters to which there were no right or wrong answers. In the low social-validation condition the subjects were told that the required predictions were a test of skill and that after completing the experiment they would be told how well they had done. Thus, unlike the Byrne *et al.* experiment, the same beliefs were present in all conditions.

The results, as assessed through a measure of interpersonal attraction, were as expected. The subject who supposedly had delivered positive evaluations was liked better than the one who had supposedly delivered negative evaluations and this difference between positive and negative evaluators was greater in the high social-validation condition than in the low.

SCHACHTER'S EXTENSION OF SOCIAL COMPARISON THEORY

In his original statement of social comparison theory Festinger (1954) specifically identified self-evaluation with the evaluation of opinions and abilities. Affiliative behavior was seen as allowing for the evaluation of one's opinions and abilities. Schachter (1959) extended this formulation so as to include the evaluation of anxiety. Affiliative behavior was thus also seen as allowing for the evaluation of one's own anxiety.

Schachter began his research with an investigation of the simple hypothesis that anxiety will lead to an increase in affiliation. His first experiment had two conditions, high anxiety and low anxiety. In the high-anxiety condition female subjects were told by a person wearing a white laboratory coat that the Medical School's Departments of Neurology and Psychiatry were conducting an experiment concerned with the effects of painful electric shock. The importance of research on electric shock was elaborated at some length by reference to electroshock therapy, accidents due to electricity, etc. The room contained a formidable array of electrical equipment. In the low-anxiety condition female subjects were told by a similarly dressed and introduced experimenter that the experiment was concerned with the effects of very mild electric shocks that would ". . . resemble more a tickle or a tingle than anything unpleasant" (p. 14). The room contained no electrical apparatus. Following the introductory statements the subjects in both conditions were asked two things: first, how they felt about taking part in the shock experiment; second, whether they would prefer to wait in a comfortable room with other subjects or alone in an empty classroom while equipment was brought in and set up. It was explained that with so many people in the room it would be difficult to move the equipment.

As expected, the subjects in the high-anxiety condition reported that they were more anxious about the experiment than the subjects in the low-anxiety condition. Furthermore, 63 percent of the subjects in the high-anxiety condition reported that they wished to wait with other subjects while only 33 percent of the subjects in the low-anxiety condition so reported. These significantly differing percentages indicate that anxiety did indeed increase affiliative tendencies. However, as Schachter indicates the obtained results are fairly ambiguous insofar as revealing *why* anxiety should increase affiliative tendencies. In a series of additional experiments Schachter attempted to specify the effect somewhat more exactly. Further research revealed that high-anxiety subjects preferred waiting with subjects from the same experiment rather than with other students who were waiting to see their advisors about the results of an important test. Similarity of the source of anxiety was thus shown to be important in determining affiliation. Also high-anxiety subjects preferred to wait together rather than alone even when they were forbidden either to talk about the experiment or to talk at all. According to Schachter there are two possible interpretations that are consistent with all of the obtained results. First, being together with other people may provide some social reassurance toward a direct reduction of anxiety. Second, being together with other people may provide a framework or social reality for the labeling and identifying or "evaluating" of emotions. Subjects' postexperimental comments gave some indication that both interpretations may have a degree of validity.

The term "evaluation" appears to be used in a slightly different sense as it is applied to opinions, abilities, and emotions. Presumably an opinion is evaluated as correct-incorrect, an ability as superior-inferior, and an emotion as normal-abnormal. Thus Schachter's second interpretation is that anxious subjects preferred to be together in order to ascertain how typical or normal their emotional reactions were. As one of Schachter's subjects stated, "I thought that the others probably had the same feelings toward the experiment that I had, and this thought made me want to be with someone" (p. 41).

An unanticipated aspect of Schachter's work was the discovery that his results were qualified by the subjects' birth order in his or her family. The relationship between anxiety and affiliation held for early born (first and only) and hardly at all for later born. Why should this be the case? Schachter speculates that early born are more likely to have mothers who respond attentively to the child's expression of emotion and furthermore that later born are more likely to have a threatening and anxiety-producing older sibling in their immediate environment. Thus early born more likely than later born would learn to handle their anxiety through affiliation.

Wrightsman (1960) threatened subjects with injections which would cause insulin shock and then let them actually wait together or alone. The results indicated that waiting together resulted in more anxiety reduction than waiting alone for early born, but not for later born. Latané (1969) reported that laboratory rats tested in a circular field are highly gregarious, staying much closer together than expected by chance, and, furthermore, that the rats show less anxiety, as indexed through defecation and freezing, when together than alone. There is thus some evidence that gregariousness or affiliation can serve an anxiety reduction function.

As previously indicated Schachter maintained that the affiliative tendencies of his subjects could be accounted for in two ways: direct anxiety reduction and evaluation of anxiety. In the above-mentioned study by Wrightsman some evidence was found supporting both interpretations. In addition to producing a reduction in anxiety among just early born, waiting together also produced a decrease in the between-subject variability in anxiety—a conformity effect that should have occurred if social comparison tendencies were operating.

Darley and Aronson (1966) designed an experiment which pitted the anxiety-reduction tendency against the evaluation of anxiety tendency. Groups of two female stooges and one female subject received either Schachter's high-fear or low-fear instructions regarding electric shock. Following the instructions the subjects were asked to rate and then report their degree of anxiety. The naive subject was always asked first. One stooge reported her anxiety as one point more than the subject's and one reported her anxiety as two points less. The subject was then given the choice of either waiting alone or with either of the stooges. Darley and Aronson reasoned that the choice of the less anxious, more dissimilar stooge would be motivated by a desire for anxiety reduction while the choice of the more anxious, less dissimilar stooge would be motivated by a desire for self-evaluation. The results indicated a greater tendency to choose the more anxious, less dissimilar stooge in the high-fear than the low-fear condition.

The results thus support the social comparison prediction. Darley and Aronson did not find that birth order was related to the affiliation choice.

Similarity

A second determinant of interpersonal attraction is similarity. According to folk lore it is the case both that "Birds of a feather flock together" and that "Opposites attract." As we shall see there is considerably more evidence supporting the first than the second proposition. We will look first at nonattitudinal similarity and then at attitudinal similarity.

NONATTITUDINAL SIMILARITY

It certainly would be unjustified to expect a correlation between interpersonal attraction and the similarity of two people along every conceivable dimension. Nonetheless there is evidence for such a correlation with regard to a large number of dimensions. For example, interpersonal attraction has been related to similarity of intelligence, education, height, age, deafness, religious affiliation, socioeconomic status, drinking habits, smoking habits, mental health, etc. (cf. Berscheid & Walster, 1969). With regard to personality in general, however, there is some doubt concerning the relationship to attraction. Some investigators (e.g., Izard, 1960) have reported evidence for such a correlation, while others (e.g., Miller, Campbell, Twedt, & O'Connell, 1966) have not. In a review of the early evidence Richardson (1939) noted that the obtained correlations between attraction and personality were generally and markedly lower than the correlations between attraction and attitude—a matter to which we will subsequently turn.

In addition to the idea that similarity of personality and interpersonal attraction are correlated, two additional hypotheses have been advanced, *need complementarity* and *need completion*. Winch and his associates have proposed that individuals with complementary needs will be attracted to each other. Thus the ascendant individual should be attracted to the submissive, the sadistic to the masochistic, the succorant to the nurturant, etc. Winch, Ktsanes, and Ktsanes (1955) examined the need patterns of married couples through interviews and claimed supportive evidence for the need complementarity hypothesis. However, the methodological procedures of this and other studies by Winch have been so severely criticized by Tharp (1963) that there is considerable doubt as to their validity. Furthermore, other investigators (e.g., Banta & Hetherington, 1963) have typically been unable to support the need complementarity hypothesis. However, a variant of the need complementarity hypothesis has been supported by Kerckhoff and Davis (1962). "Pinned" or "seriously attached" couples were given questionnaires assessing the degree of consensus on family values and degree of need complementarity. It was also determined how long they had been going together. The sample was split into couples that had been going together for less than 18 months and couples that had been going together for 18 months or more. Seven months later the couples were contacted for a second time, and it was determined whether or not they had progressed toward a permanent relationship. The results indicated that consensus on family values was the only significant predictor of progress toward permanency for short-term couples, while need complementarity was the only significant predictor of progress toward permanency for long-term couples. Kerckhoff and Davis theorize that a series of "filtering factors" operate in mate selection such that "social status variables (class, religion, etc.) operate in the early stages, consensus on values somewhat later, and need complementarity still later" (p. 303). Since most of their couples were of similar social status, apparently the first "filtering" had occurred before the subjects were contacted.

Cattell and Nesselroade (1967) have advanced a *need completion* hypothesis to the effect that an individual will be attracted to another person who possesses desirable traits that the individual himself lacks. Thus a socially awkward person might be attracted to a socially poised and adroit person. Support for this hypothesis has come mainly from studies in which individuals have been asked to describe their friends. For example, Thompson and Nishimura (1952) found that individuals perceived their friends as more closely approximating their self-ideal than they themselves did. Note that the study did not demonstrate that the friends actually possessed the desired traits, but only that they were perceived as possessing them.

ATTITUDE-BELIEF SIMILARITY

The common-sense observation that we are attracted to others who share our attitudes and beliefs is a very old one. As Byrne (1969) notes, in the fourth century B.C. Aristotle (translated 1932, pp. 103–105) stated:

> And they are friends who have come to regard the same things as good and the same things as evil, they who are friends of the same people, and they who are enemies of the same people. . . . We like those who resemble us, and are engaged in the same pursuits. . . . We like those who desire the same things as we, if the case is such that we and they can share the things together. . . .

First we will consider the nonexperimental research relating attraction and attitude-belief similarity and then the experimental research relating attraction and attitude-belief similarity.

Nonexperimental Research

The literature which has examined the natural relationship between attraction and attitude-belief similarity fairly consistently indicates a positive correlation. For example, Schooley (1936) found that the husband-wife correlations for attitudes toward communism and attitudes toward birth control were .61 and .58, respectively. He also found that the correlations for various scales of the Allport-Vernon Scale of Values (theoretical, economic, aesthetic, political, religious) ranged from .23 to .45. Richardson (1940) found that pairs of friends (college age or adult) showed greater similarity (higher correlations) in their responses to the scales of the Allport-Vernon Scale of Values than did random pairs. Byrne and Blaylock (1963) went one step further when they found that, not only do husbands and wives have similar political attitudes, they overestimate the degree of similarity that in fact exists. When husbands and wives filled out various political attitude assessments according to how they felt and according to how they assumed their spouse would feel, the actual similarity correlations ranged from .30 to .44, while the assumed similarity correlations ranged from .69 to .89, significantly higher. Levinger and Breedlove (1966) obtained similar results with regard to attitudes about family life. They also found that marital satisfaction correlated significantly with assumed similarity but not with actual similarity.

One of the best known nonexperimental, or correlational, studies of similarity and interpersonal attraction is Newcomb's (1961) housing study. For two different groups of male transfer students at the University of Michigan, Newcomb arranged a rent-free semester in a cooperative housing unit in return for spending a few hours a week as subjects. One of the more interesting findings was that preacquaintance agreement on miscellaneous attitude topics and in the rank order of various values predicted attraction after several months. This observed temporal order of the variables suggests in Newcomb's situation, at least, that similarity caused attraction rather than that attraction caused similarity. The latter causal sequence is undoubtedly more typically displayed in the imitative behavior of small children.

Experimental Research

In experimental research on attitude-belief similarity the experimenter manipulates the degree of perceived similarity and examines the effect upon interpersonal attraction. Byrne and his associates have done a whole series of such experimental studies. In one of his early investigations Byrne (1962) studied the effect of the number of similar attitudes upon attraction. Subjects initially responded to six-point favorability scales indicating their attitudes toward seven issues (undergraduate marriages, smoking, integration, drinking, money as one of the most important goals, university grading system, Democratic versus Republican party). Two weeks later the subjects were falsely informed that the attitude scales had also been given to other people and that the experimenter was interested in determining "the extent to which one person can form valid judgments about another person just by knowing a few of his attitudes" (p. 169). Each subject was given a questionnaire supposedly filled out by another subject. Actually the questionnaires were individually tailored for each subject so that the number of similar attitudes varied. For some subjects the number of similar attitudes was seven, for some six, for some five, four, three, two, one, and zero. After examining the questionnaire each subject filled out an interpersonal judgment scale in which he or she indicated guesses as to the intelligence, knowledge of current events, etc., of the person who had filled out the questionnaire. Each subject also indicated the extent to which he or she would like this person and how much he or she would like to work with this person in an experiment. The latter two questions were used as an assessment of attraction. The results indicated a highly significant effect of attitudinal similarity upon attraction. As Byrne (1969) indicates, at each increment in attitudinal similarity there was an increment in attraction.

In an additional study which is contained in the Readings section of this chapter, Byrne and Nelson (1965) demonstrated that interpersonal attraction varies, not with the number of similar attitudes but rather with the proportion of similar attitudes. Byrne and Nelson also found evidence for a straight-line relationship between attraction and proportion of similar attitudes; that is, for every increment of a given size in the proportion of similar attitudes there was a proportional increment in attraction. Subsequent research by Byrne and his associates (e.g., Byrne & Clore, 1966; Byrne & Griffitt, 1966a) has demonstrated the stability and generality of the straight-line relationship. For example, Byrne and Griffitt have demonstrated the relationship holds for children in grades 8 to 12 as well as with children in grades 4 to 8.

From a common-sense point of view the perceived importance or interestingness of the attitude objects or topics utilized in a manipulation of attitude similarity would seem to affect attraction. (Ratings of importance and interestingness tend to be highly correlated.) Research has indicated, however, the situation is not as simple as might initially be thought. Clore and Baldridge (1968) manipulated both the proportion of similar attitudes (.25, .50, .75) and the interestingness of the attitude topics. Interestingness was determined by each subject's previous rating of the topics. The results indicated a striking effect for similarity and no effect for interestingness. In this experiment the attitude topics for a given subject were either all interesting or all uninteresting. In a second experiment each subject received some attitude topics that were interesting and some that were uninteresting. For some subjects the similar attitudes were interesting and the dissimilar uninteresting, and for some subjects the similar attitudes were uninteresting and the dissimilar interesting. As before the proportion of similar attitudes was .25, .50, and .75. This time the results indicated that both similarity and topic interestingness had an effect upon attraction. At all levels of similarity attraction was greater for agreement on interesting topics than for agreement on uninteresting topics.

Four Theoretical Interpretations

There are at least four theoretical interpretations of the effect of attitude-belief similarity upon attraction. Although these various interpretations do overlap to some extent, they nonetheless can be adequately distinguished.

The *first* of these theoretical interpretations is in terms of *balance theory*. As was indicated in Chapter 1 balance theory implies that if p likes x and perceives that o likes x, p should be attracted to x. Also, if p dislikes x, and perceives that o dislikes x, p should be attracted to o. In both of these situations positive attraction allows for a balanced state in which p perceives all of the elements as fitting together harmoniously. The general balance position is thus that p's perceived agreement with o produces attraction for o.

The article by Aronson and Cope (1968), which is contained in the Readings for this chapter, illustrates one attempt to explore the relevance of balance theory to interpersonal attraction. Here the focus of the investigation is to demonstrate how agreement with regard to a common enemy produces attraction that is most easily accounted for in balance terms.

The *second* interpretation of the effect of similarity upon attraction relates to the *anticipated rewards of future interaction*. According to this view the individual is attracted to the similar other because of the anticipation that future interaction with him or her would be rewarding. This interpretation is most plausible when the attitudinal similarity relates to specific activities, like playing tennis, but may possibly apply to all types of attitudinal similarity. The statement of this explanation appears to be an approach to interpersonal attraction based on the hedonistic idea that people are motivated to maximize reward in the future. Note, however, that an alternative account in terms of balance theory is also possible. According to balance theory, an originally neutral other who is assumed to cause or be positively associated with future rewarding (positive) activity should become more attractive (positive). Stated in this way the interpretation differs from the general balance perspective in the emphasis upon future activity rather than the simple effect of agreement on attraction.

The *third* interpretation for the effect of attitudinal similarity upon attraction is in terms of *social comparison theory*. According to social comparison theory people seek out and are attracted to other people with similar beliefs and attitudes because agreement with other people satisfies the self-evaluative need or drive to hold correct opinions. According to Byrne (1969), who is in essential agreement with this interpretation, achieved consensus about one's stimulus world produces positive affect which through simple conditioning becomes associated with similar individuals. Thus the proposed causal sequence is from similarity to need reduction to positive affect to interpersonal attraction. The social-comparison interpretation can be regarded as another variation of the hedonistic or reward perspective on interpersonal attraction. Similarity is rewarding because of the reduction of a particular drive, the self-evaluative drive.

The previously discussed experiment by Byrne, Nelson, & Reeves (1966) represents an attempt to test the applicability of social comparison theory to the present problem. This was the experiment in which beliefs of differing degrees of verifiability were used in the similarity manipulation. Byrne *et al.* interpret their results as indicating that the more effort required to verify a given belief the greater the effect of social agreement (or similarity) upon interpersonal attraction.

The *fourth* and final interpretation of the effect of similarity upon attraction is in terms of *implied evaluation* (Aronson & Worchel, 1966; Byrne & Griffitt, 1966b). According to this interpretation when a subject is informed that he shares similar attitudes with someone else, there is an implicit implication that the other person would like him. Since liking tends to be reciprocated, the subject is attracted to the similar other. The proposed causal sequence is thus from similarity to implied liking to interpersonal attraction.

As previously indicated, the various interpretations differ in detail but still overlap to a considerable degree. This fourth interpretation in terms of implied evaluation is no exception, since it could be regarded as a still different variation of hedonistic, balance, or even social comparison perspectives. From a hedonistic perspective the perception that the similar other will like the subject is rewarding and thus results in attraction for the similar other who produced or is associated with the hedonistic effect. From a balance perspective the perception that the similar o will like p produces a consistent reciprocation of positive sentiment from p to o. When the sentiment relations from o to p and p to o are the same, the dyad is balanced. From a social comparison perspective the perception that the similar other will like the subject reduces the drive for positive self-evaluation and thus results in attraction toward the similar other.

The fact that the four interpretations overlap to some extent should not blur the real distinctions among them. Because the anticipated rewards interpretation and the implied evaluation interpretation, for example, can be expressed in balance terms does not mean that two postulated processes do not differ.

Implied Evaluation

So far we have considered two answers to the question, What determines one person's degree of interpersonal attraction for another? One answer was in terms of the satisfaction of a self-evaluative need, and the other was in terms of similarity. A third determinant of the degree of interpersonal attraction is implied positive or negative evaluation. Information that *o* likes *p* will produce a tendency for *p* to like *o*. In the case in which the individual agrees with the evaluation, implied evaluation becomes another form of attitudinal similarity. Berscheid and Walster (1969) point out that most popular advice on how to win the affection of others is based on the assumption that implied positive evaluation, or implied liking, always evokes reciprocal liking. Even before Dale Carnegie (1937), the philosopher Hecato in the second century B.C. had the same idea, "I will show you a love potion without drug or herb or any witch's spell; if you wish to be loved, love." This theme is also present in Shakespeare's "Much Ado About Nothing."

Backman and Secord (1959) have reported one of the most widely quoted demonstrations of the effect of implied liking. After taking a personality test subjects were told which three members of a group of ten strangers would most likely be attracted to them. Each member of the group was told the three members of the group that would like him. Actually the three members were randomly selected for each subject with the sole restriction that there be no reciprocations; that is, if subject *A* was told that subject *B* would like subject *A*, subject *B* was not told that subject *A* would like subject *B*. There were three same-sex groups which met for a number of sessions over a six-week period. Following each session the subject filled out a sociometric assessment in which he indicated how much he liked each of the other group members. After the first, but not the subsequent, sessions the assessment indicated that subjects liked best the other subjects who had been designated as liking them. Backman and Secord speculated that the effect might have persisted if reciprocal liking relations had been initially established.

There is no doubt that in many situations implied liking does indeed produce reciprocal liking. This does not mean, however, that an increase in implied liking will always have an effect upon attraction. There are at least three qualifications to the general rule: the effect of sequence, the effect of ulterior motives, and the effect of disagreement. We will discuss each of these in turn.

SEQUENCE

Aronson and Linder (1965) designed an experiment to test the effect of differing sequences of implied evaluation upon interpersonal attraction. Female subjects individually interacted with a confederate (who was supposedly another subject) over a series of seven meetings. An elaborate deception was used to allow the subject to overhear an interview between the experimenter and confederate following each of the seven meetings. During each interview the confederate made evaluative remarks about the subject. The major manipulation was the sequence of evaluations over the series of interviews. There were four basic conditions: positive-positive, negative-positive, negative-negative, positive-negative. In the positive-positive conditions the evaluations were uniformly positive throughout the seven interviews. In the negative-negative condition the evaluations were uniformly negative. In the negative-positive condition the evaluations were negative during the first three interviews, began to change on the fourth interview, and grew increasingly positive on the last three interviews. In the positive-negative condition the sequence of information was, of course, opposite to that in the negative-positive condition. Aronson and Linder had initially expected that attraction in the negative-positive condition would be greater than in the positive-positive condition and less in the positive-negative condition than in the negative-negative condition. An assessment of attraction following the seventh interview significantly supported Aronson and Linder's expectation for the positive-positive, negative-positive comparison and nonsignificantly supported Aronson and Linder's expectation for the negative-negative, positive-negative comparison. Evaluations that started negative and became positive resulted in more attraction than evaluations that were uniformly positive.

An alternative way of looking at Aronson and Linder's results is in terms of order effects. Since attraction was obviously greater in the negative-positive sequence than in the positive-negative sequence, Aronson and Linder obtained a recency effect. It is true, however, that the term "recency" does not accurately describe the fact that attraction was greater in the negative-positive sequence than in the positive-positive sequence. Not only was the second information in the sequence more potent than the first, the potency of the second information was increased by evaluatively opposite prior information.

How can we account for the obtained pattern of results? Two explanations mentioned by Aronson and Linder are in terms of contrast and competence. According to the contrast interpretation the later evaluations in the negative-positive sequence appear more positive than the later evaluations in the positive-positive sequence due to perceptual contrast. The heightened favorability or positivity of the later evaluations in turn leads to greater interpersonal attraction. According to the competence interpretation the subjects in the negative-positive condition tried to overcome the initial negative impression by behaving in a more interesting and intelligent fashion during the successive meetings with the confederate. The fact that the confederate's evaluations eventually became positive may thus have led the subject to have a success experience or feeling of increased competence. The affect associated with the feeling of competence may have in turn generalized so as to produce increased attraction to the confederate.

Mettee (1971b) obtained results which he interprets as indicating that attraction is greater following a negative-positive sequence of evaluations than a positive-positive sequence, because in some situations the mixed sequence makes the evaluator appear more discerning or credible. Eighth-grade male subjects worked for two sessions on either the same ability test or on two ability tests. During each session an examiner (evaluator) made three evaluations. Some subjects received three positive evaluations in the first session and three positive evaluations in the second session (positive-positive sequence), and some subjects received three negative evaluations in the first session and three positive evaluations in the second session (negative-positive sequence). The results indicated that when two different ability tests were involved the negative-positive sequence produced significantly greater attraction than the positive-positive sequence. This is, of course, the pattern of results obtained by Aronson and Linder. Mettee, however, found that when the same ability test was worked on during both sessions, there was no significant difference between the negative-positive sequence and the positive-positive sequence. There was, in fact, a nonsignificant tendency for the positive-positive sequence to produce more attraction than the negative-positive. According to Mettee the change in evaluation from negative to positive was more reasonable when the change was associated with a change in the ability being tested. Thus in the two-ability-tests condition the negative-positive sequence produced an increase in the examiner's credibility.

ULTERIOR MOTIVES

An additional qualification of the effect of implied evaluation upon interpersonal attraction has to do with ulterior motives. A study by Dickoff (1961) investigated the effect of varying degrees of implied evaluation in both ulterior motive and "accuracy" conditions. Female subjects were individually interviewed by an observer who was on the opposite side of a one-way mirror. The standard interview questions were designed to reveal a fair amount about the subject's personal history, manner, and values. The subject and observer were then brought together and the subject was given the task of learning the impression she had made on the observer. She did this by attempting to anticipate over a series of 96 trials which of three descriptive traits had been chosen to apply to herself. Each trial consisted of a positive, a neutral, and a negative trait. Implied evaluation was manipulated by the type of traits that the observer had selected a descriptive of the subject. In a positive condition the observer uniformly chose all positive traits; in a self-concept condition the observer chose traits identical to those that the subject had used to describe herself in a previous group testing session; and in a neutral condition the observer chose all neutral traits. The implied evaluation in the self-concept condition was intermediate to that in the neutral and positive conditions. Each of the three implied evaluative conditions was in turn subdivided according to the manner in which the observer's role was described. In the ulterior-motive condition the observer was described as a graduate student in clinical psychology who was temporarily filling in for the usual graduate student assistant. The clinical psychology graduate student was replacing the usual assistant in exchange for use of the subject in a subsequent experiment. The experimenter explained that the observer would be very grateful for the subject's cooperation but that the decision was, of course, up to the subject. In the accuracy condition the subjects were told that the specific purpose of the experiment was to discover "how accurately people form impressions of others." The observer was described as a first-year student in clinical psychology who was participating in the study as part of her training.

An assessment of the subjects' attraction for the observer revealed a strong effect for the implied-evaluation manipulation. For the accuracy condition attraction increased from the neutral to self-concept to positive conditions. For the ulterior-motive condition attraction increased from the neutral to self-concept and positive conditions (which did not differ from each other). The only significant difference between the accuracy and ulterior-motive conditions occurred with positive evaluation. In the ulterior-motive condition positive evaluation produced significantly less attraction than in the accuracy condition. There was no significant difference between the ulterior-motive and accuracy conditions when implied evaluation was either neutral or consistent with self-concept.

Dickoff's results thus indicate that uniformly positive implied evaluation will not be as effective if the source of the liking is perceived to have ulterior motives. Even in this instance, however, the implied evaluation will not necessarily have no effect upon attraction. Even if the implied evaluation is recognized as flattery or ingratiation, there still may be some gain in interpersonal attraction. Jones (1964) has even argued that the target of ingratiation will be less likely to recognize the presence of ulterior motives than a bystander. The target of the ingratiation ". . . has a strong, vain desire to assign credibility to compliments sent his way" (p. 187). Jones, Stires, Shaver, and Harris (1968) present some evidence in support of this hypothesis.

Disagreement

The final qualification of the general effect of implied evaluation upon interpersonal attraction has to do with disagreement. It frequently will be the case that if o compliments p for possessing some virtue, p will agree that he does indeed possess the virtue. What happens, however, if p does not agree? Both social comparison theory and balance theory have the general implication that disagreement leads to negative attraction. However, both theories also imply that the receipt of a compliment should facilitate positive attraction. The case of a disagreed-with compliment thus presents an interesting theoretical dilemma. A critical variable determining whether a disagreed-with compliment leads to an increment or a decrement in attraction may be p's certainty that the compliment is unjustified. If p is not certain that the compliment is unjustified the acceptance of the compliment might lead to a greater degree of balance in his self-concept. If, for example, an average-looking girl is told that she is physically attractive, the acceptance of this compliment would lead to the incorporation of an additional positive element into an already positive self-concept. This would in turn produce an increment in attraction toward the other who had given the compliment. If, on the other hand, p is completely certain that the compliment is unjustified or untrue, it would be less likely that p would incorporate an additional positive element into his or her self-concept. In this situation the disagreed-with compliment would not lead to an increment in attraction, and might even lead to a decrement in attraction. From a balance theory perspective, a disbelieved compliment would thus lead to a decrement in attraction if the compliment were completely and thoroughly disbelieved. Social-comparison theory can be interpreted as similarly making differential predictions depending upon the certainty with which a compliment is regarded as unjustified. With a low degree of certainty, acceptance of the compliment would lead to further validation of belief regarding positive self-worth. With a high degree of certainty, receipt of the compliment would be less likely to lead to belief validation and the lack of consensus, or the disagreement concerning the truth of the compliment, would thus not produce an increment in attraction. In actual fact, however, it may be that instances in which an individual is *completely* certain that he does not possess particular positive traits or aptitudes is rare. People are seemingly very quick to accept flattering statements about their traits and aptitudes. This is particularly true if the complimenter is regarded as a credible or expert source who does not possess any obvious ulterior motives.

One experiment which bears on the effect of disagreement has been described above. Recall that Dickoff created positive implied evaluation by having the observer pick all positive traits, traits that the subject had used to describe herself in a previous group testing session, or all neutral traits. Thus when the observer picked all positive traits she was disagreeing with the subject's own self-description. In the accuracy condition, or condition in which the observer was not described as having ulterior motives, however, this disagreement produced more liking than occurred when the observer agreed with the subject's own self-description.

A further experiment bearing on the general issue of implied evaluation and disagreement was done by Deutsch and Solomon (1959). Groups of eight subjects were tested in a room containing a separate cubicle for each subject. Subjects were told that the group would be divided into two teams, A and B, which would then compete to see which team won two out of three contests. Actually all subjects were told they were members of team A, and only two contests were held. The two contests involved the average team-member performance on the Gottschaldt Embedded Figures Test and the Scrambled Words Test. Following the completion of each test individual subjects were told either that his team had won or lost and that he either had the highest score on both teams or the lowest score on both teams. Thus there was a manipulation of team success or failure and a manipulation of individual success or failure. A third manipulation concerned the evaluation that each subject received from a teammate. Subjects were asked to write a note to some other teammate frankly indicating their feelings about that person and whether or not they would want him or her on the team in the future. These notes were intercepted by the experimenter and others substituted in their place. Half of the subjects received positive evaluations and half negative. After receipt of the note subjects were asked to rate their attraction for the note-sender.

The results indicated that when the subjects were led to believe that they had the highest score on both tests the person sending the positive note was liked much better than the person sending the negative note. When, however, the subjects were led to believe that they had the lowest score on both tests the persons sending the positive and negative notes were liked to an equal and intermediate degree. The manipulation of group success and failure had no significant effect.

In Deutsch and Solomon's experiment implied evaluation had no effect upon attraction when the subjects had the lowest scores on both tests and thus disagreed with the positive notes. Remember, however, that Dickoff did find that in the accuracy condition the ascription of positive traits not in the subject's self-concept produced increased attraction. How can we account for the discrepancy in results? In Deutsch and Solomon's experiment disagreed-with implied liking had no effect on attraction and in Dickoff's experiment disagreed-with implied liking increased attraction. One way to resolve this contradiction is in terms of certainty. Because the subjects in Deutsch and Solomon's experiment had twice received feedback about their inferior performance it is at least possible that Deutsch and Solomon's subjects were more convinced of their failings than Dickoff's subjects were of theirs. If an individual is certain about his failing, contradictory evaluations will not readily be accepted.

Spatial Propinquity and Social Contact

A fourth determinant of interpersonal attraction is spatial propinquity and social contact. Perhaps the best known study of the relationship between spatial propinquity and interpersonal attraction is Festinger, Schachter, and Back's (1950) investigation of two housing projects for married veteran students at Massachusetts Institute of Technology. One of the housing projects, Westgate West, was composed of rectangular-shaped, two-story apartment buildings with five apartments on a floor. Festinger, Schachter, and Back found a direct relationship between interpersonal attraction and the physical distance between apartments on the same floor. The closer the apartments on a given floor of a building the more likely the occupants were to report that they saw each other socially. If walking distance, rather than actual straight-line distance, is used as a measure of distance a similar pattern of results is apparent for the between-floor attraction. The less the walking distance between apartments on different floors the greater the attraction between the occupants. In general, however, same-floor interpersonal attraction was greater than between-floor interpersonal attraction, as would be expected. The general relationship between distance and attraction was also apparent from a comparison of social choices between buildings.

The buildings in the second housing project, Westgate, contained either one or two apartments and were grouped into courts. Festinger, Schachter, and Back found that attraction decreased with an increase in the physical separation of houses in a straight line on any given side of a court and also that attraction decreased from own court to adjacent court to other courts to Westgate West (which was nearby). Festinger *et al.*, however, found some interesting exceptions to the general relationship between physical distance and attraction. Each of the six courts in Westgate had two houses which faced outward to the main street rather than inward to the center of the court. Fewer social choices were directed at the occupants of these houses than at the occupants of any other house positions in the Westgate courts. This finding suggests that not even walking distance, but rather frequency of contact is the important mediator between proximity and attraction. Further support for this hypothesis comes from a closer examination of the physical arrangements in Westgate West. In the Westgate West buildings the stairways to the upper floor passed in front of the doorways to the end apartments on the first floor. Furthermore, all of the second-floor mailboxes were located by one of the end apartments on the first floor. It is thus not surprising that the occupants of the end apartments were more socially oriented toward the upper-floor tenants than the occupants of any other lower-floor apartment. These factors reveal the quite striking, but unintended, effects that can be produced by various architectural arrangements.

Numerous other studies have obtained results in agreement with Festinger, Schachter, and Back's. For example, Deutsch and Collins (1951) found that living in an integrated housing project resulted in decreased outgroup rejection (or "prejudice"). It would undoubtedly be naive to assume, however, that increased contact always leads to increased attraction. As was indicated in Chapter 1, Heider (1958) maintains that social interaction will lead to the formation of a positive sentiment relation only if there is not too great a dissimilarity in attitudes. In this respect it is of interest to note that the subjects in Festinger, Schachter, and Back's study, married veterans attending a technical school with high entrance requirements, undoubtedly had many similar attitudes. Just how much dissimilarity can be overcome is not known. Possibly one important interactive variable is the strength of norms or circumstances requiring cooperative behavior (Sherif, Harvey, White, Hood, & Sherif, 1961). Sherif's research relating to this matter will be discussed in Chapter 15.

Other information bearing on spatial propinquity or social contact comes from crime statistics based on police records (e.g., Hoover, 1966). In the majority of robberies the perpetrator is either related to or acquainted with the victim, and almost a third of all murders occur within the family. Similarly, aggravated assaults tend to occur within the family or among neighbors and acquaintances.

One possible interpretation of the above evidence is that minimal physical distance and resultant social contact provides an opportunity for the exchange of information which may then produce either increased attraction or decreased attraction. Overall, however, there is more evidence for a positive than a negative relation between social contact and attraction.

Physical Attractiveness

A fifth circumstance which has an obvious effect upon interpersonal attraction is physical attractiveness. Perhaps because of this obviousness investigators, until very recently, have avoided study of the effect of physical attractiveness upon interpersonal attraction. Data indicating that the physical attractiveness phenomenon should no longer be ignored, however, have been obtained by Walster, Aronson, Abrahams, and Rottman (1966). The subjects in the experiment were 376 men and 376 women at the University of Minnesota who had purchased tickets to a "computer dance." A computer was supposedly going to match partners for the dance on the basis of questionnaires filled out at the time the tickets were purchased. Immediately after purchasing the tickets each subject was surreptitiously rated by four judges on an eight-point physical attractiveness scale. Subjects were randomly paired for the dance, with the sole exception that a man was never assigned a date taller than himself. During the dance intermission subjects answered a questionnaire which inquired how physically attractive the date was considered to be, how personally attractive the date was considered to be, how much the date seemed to like the subject, whether or not the subject would like to date the partner again, etc. How much couples actually dated was determined with a four to six month follow-up interview.

The results for male subjects indicated that the more physically attractive the female partner the more she was liked, the more desirable she was rated as a future date, and the more actual attempts were made to date her. Similarly for female subjects, the more physically attractive the male partner the more he was liked, and the more desire to date him in the future. As indicated above, physical attractiveness was determined by the ratings of four judges. The intercorrelations among the judges' ratings were not markedly high, ranging from .49 to .58. In view of such low reliability it is surprising that physical attraction should be so potent. The correlation between the average physical attractiveness ratings for females and liking by the male partners was .44, and the correlation between the average physical attractiveness ratings for males and liking by their female partners was .36. When the subject's own rating of the partner's physical attraction, rather than the judges' rating, was used as an index, liking for the partner correlated .78 for male subjects and .69 for female subjects. For these subjects in this situation physical attractiveness was obviously a very important variable.

These latter correlations between perceived physical attractiveness and liking for the partner are somewhat larger for male subjects than for female subjects. This, of course, agrees with the common-sense assumption that physical attractiveness is a more important determiner of the male's attraction to the female than of the female's attraction to the male. Further support for this assumption was obtained by Stroebe, Insko, Thompson, and Layton (1971), particularly when attention was focused on dating preference. The Stroebe *et al.* study followed Byrne's procedure of having subjects judge anonymous strangers on the basis of limited information. In addition to the usual manipulation of similarity there was also a manipulation of the physical attractiveness. Subjects were presented with a picture of the anonymous stranger which was either low, medium, or high in physical attractiveness. In addition to the usual liking ratings there was also a rating of the probability that the stranger was the kind of person who would be considered as a date. Physical attractiveness significantly affected both the liking and dating assessments. More interesting, however, is that on the dating assessment, but not the liking assessment, physical attractiveness had a significantly larger effect for males than for females. Stroebe *et al.* argue that in the computer dance setting used by Walster *et al.* the liking assessment was very much like an indication of dating preference.

An additional study which deals with the importance of physical attractiveness was conducted by Sigall and Aronson (1969). Subjects were met by a departmental assistant who informed them that the psychology department had undertaken a program investigating training in clinical psychology. The subjects' task was simply to fill out a California Psychological Inventory and then wait a few minutes in order to listen to the interpretation of their responses by a first-year graduate student in clinical psychology. It was explained that all first-year graduate students in clinical psychology were involved in the program. After completing the test and waiting for seven minutes the "clinical psychology graduate student" (actually a female stooge) delivered either a positive evaluation (well adjusted, reasonably mature, earnest, frank, insightful, potentially creative, etc.) or a negative evaluation (not neurotic, somewhat immature, shallow, lacking in insight, etc.). Crosscutting this implied-evaluation manipulation was a manipulation of physical attractiveness. In the attractive condition the normally attractive female stooge was tastefully dressed and made-up. In the unattractive condition the female stooge wore no make-up and a "frizzy" blonde wig that "bordered on the grotesque." Following the evaluation the departmental assistant requested that the subject fill out an anonymous questionnaire to provide information for the testing program. This questionnaire, among other things, inquired about the subjects' attraction to the clinical graduate student. The results indicated that attraction was greater when the stooge was physically attractive than physically unattractive, and delivered positive evaluations rather than negative evaluations. Also, however, the differential effectiveness of the positive and negative evaluations was greater when the stooge was physically attractive than physically unattractive. The effect of implied evaluation was magnified when the stooge was physically attractive.

Physical attractiveness is obviously a very important variable in the determination of interpersonal attractiveness. An obvious question, however, is, why? Why should physical attractiveness be of such overwhelming importance? Berscheid and Walster (1969) quote Burgess, Wallin, and Shultz's (1953) report of a college student who, rather plaintively, asks the same question.

> One of the greatest troubles is that men here, as everywhere, I guess are easily overwhelmed by physical beauty. Campus glamor girls have countless beaux flocking around them, whereas many companionable, sympathetic girls who want very much to be companions and, eventually, wives and mothers, but who are not dazzling physically, go without dates and male companionship. Many who could blossom out and be very charming never have the opportunity. Eventually, they decide that they are unattractive and become discouraged to the point that often they will not attend no-date functions where they have their best (and perhaps only) opportunity to meet men. I will never understand why so many men (even, or maybe particularly, those who are the least personally attractive themselves) seem to think they may degrade themselves by dating or even dancing with a girl who does not measure up to their beauty standards [pp. 63–64].

Given that certain physical characteristics are highly valued it is understandable, from a balance perspective, why a person (+) would attempt to associate with (+) a physically attractive other (+). But why are certain physical characteristics valued in the first place? Or, since there is obvious cultural diversity in the specification of attractive physical traits, why are any physical traits selected as attractive? We really don't know the answer to this question. We may speculate that part of the answer relates to the "skin deep" quality of physical traits. Since many physical traits are readily identifiable, the differential evaluation of such traits allows for a relatively effortless categorization of persons as attractive or unattractive. Beyond this, it is not unreasonable that the sex drive or need has something to do with the importance of physical traits. At present, however, we are fairly ignorant about the basis for the powerful effect of physical attractiveness upon interpersonal attraction. Like the student quoted by Burgess, Wallin, and Shultz, we are puzzled as to why physical attractiveness should be of such importance.

Frustration and Aggression

A sixth circumstance or factor affecting interpersonal attraction is frustration. Common sense certainly leads us to expect some sort of a relationship between frustration and negative interpersonal attraction. Some time ago Dollard, Doob, Miller, Mowrer, and Sears (1939) made this common-sense expectation explicit through the formulation of the frustration-aggression hypothesis.

FRUSTRATION-AGGRESSION HYPOTHESIS

According to Dollard *et al.* "the occurrence of aggressive behavior always presupposes the existence of frustration and, contrariwise, . . . the existence of frustration always leads to some form of aggression" (1939, p. 1). Frustration is defined as *"that condition which exists when a goal-response suffers interference,"* and aggression is defined as *"an act whose goal-response is injury to an organism* (or *organism-surrogate)"* (p. 11).

In a later publication one of the authors of the frustration-aggression hypothesis, Neal Miller (1941), maintained that the original statement of the hypothesis was "unclear and misleading." According to Miller the first part of the statement, which asserts that aggression always presupposes frustration is defensible as a working hypothesis. The second part of the statement, however, should be restated as, "Frustration produces instigations to a number of different types of response, one of which is an instigation to some form of aggression" (p. 30). Frustration will have a number of consequences, included among which is the instigation to aggression, but not necessarily actually aggressive behavior. According to Miller the original statement of the theory is inconsistent with the subsequent Dollard *et al.* (1939) statement that punishment can inhibit the occurrence of aggressive behavior.

Dollard *et al.* (1939) elaborate the frustration-aggression hypothesis by theorizing about four groups of factors: (1) those determining the strength of instigation to aggression; (2) those related to the inhibition of aggression; (3) those determining the object of aggression; (4) those related to the reduction of the instigation to aggression.

According to Dollard *et al.* the *strength of the instigation to aggression* varies as a function of three factors: (1) the strength of instigation to the frustrated response; (2) the degree of interference with the frustrated response; (3) the number of frustrated response-sequences. Strength of the instigation to aggression increases with an increase in the strength of instigation to the frustrated response, an increase in the degree of interference with the frustrated response, and the number of frustrated response-sequences. The last point makes explicit Dollard *et al.*'s belief that frustrations have cumulative effects. An individual may tolerate a whole series of frustrations until finally some minor frustration seemingly makes him explode in a fit of anger.

According to Dollard *et al.* the basic variable determining the *inhibition of aggressive behavior* is anticipated punishment. Anticipated punishment, however, is a general category including three specifics: (1) anticipated pain, (2) anticipated injury to a loved object, (3) anticipated failure of the aggressive act. The factors determining whether or not the instigation to aggression will be inhibited are thus whether or not the aggressive act will lead to painful consequences (resulting, for example, from retaliation), whether or not the aggressive act will injure a loved object, and whether or not the aggressive acts will be successful. Dollard *et al.* do not elaborate the latter point, but simply state that failure may be anticipated "either because of a lack of a suitable object or because there are insuperable difficulties involved in carrying out the act" (p. 34).

With regard to determination of the *object of aggression* Dollard *et al.* state that *"the strongest instigation, aroused by a frustration, is to acts of aggression directed against the agent perceived to be the source of the frustration and progressively weaker instigations are aroused to progressively less direct acts of aggression"* (p. 38). In some instances, however, anticipated punishment may prevent aggression from being directed at the frustrating agent. According to Dollard *et al.* *"the greater the degree of inhibition specific to a more direct act of aggression, the more probable will be the occurrence of less direct acts of aggression"* (p. 40). A woman who is, for example, frustrated by her husband may punish or "take it out on" her children. In agreement with Freud, Dollard *et al.* maintain that displaced aggression may even take the extreme form of self-aggression, a particularly dramatic form of which is suicide.

Finally, Dollard *et al.* assert that *"the occurrence of any act of aggression is assumed to reduce the instigation to aggression"* (p. 50). In psychoanalytic terms this is referred to as catharsis. The occurrence of displaced aggression (e.g., kicking a chair) should reduce the tendency to directly attack the frustrating agent and vice versa.

BERKOWITZ'S VIEW

Because of the considerable lapse in time since the original formulation of the frustration-aggression hypothesis it is of interest to consider a more contemporary view of the relation between frustration and aggression. According to Leonard Berkowitz (1962, 1964, 1965, 1969), one of the more active experimenters in the field of aggression, the frustration-aggression hypothesis, if expressed in a less sweeping and all-explanatory fashion, is still viable. First, Berkowitz points out that the original statement that "aggressive behavior always presupposes the existence of frustration" is obviously incorrect. People may learn to be aggressive simply by imitating others; frustration is not a necessary prerequisite for the occurrence of aggression. Second, Berkowitz interprets frustration as the blocking of an anticipation or expectation of making a goal response. Thus frustration is differentiated from deprivation. If an organism has gone without food for some time without expecting to be fed, it is deprived, but not frustrated. Berkowitz notes that this interpretation of frustration is consistent with Davies' (1962) theory of revolution. Davies maintains that the American, French, and Russian Revolutions, as well as other revolutions, occurred, not because of severe hardship and deprivation, but because a sharp socio-economic reverse thwarted or frustrated the expectations that had begun to develop in the course of gradually improving conditions. Third, Berkowitz agrees with Miller (1941) that frustration produces, not aggression, but an instigation to aggression, along with a number of additional response tendencies. Berkowitz, however, states that the instigation to aggression is an emotional reaction which can be labeled "anger." Thus Berkowitz maintains that the blocking of an anticipated goal response produces anger, as well as a number of additional reactions. One of these additional reactions, which Berkowitz considers likely when the frustrating agent is perceived as powerful, is fear. Fourth and finally, Berkowitz emphasizes the importance of environmental cues (such as a gun) in determining whether or not frustration-produced anger will result in aggressive behavior. Berkowitz's initial view was that external cues are necessary before aggression will occur. His more recent view (Berkowitz, 1969), however, is that external cues merely increase the probability of aggression. The anger itself may contain sufficient internal cues to instigate aggression even in the absence of external cues.

SOME RESEARCH EVIDENCE

Research has made it quite evident that in some situations frustration can produce aggression in both animals and humans. Azrin, Hutchinson, and Hake (1966), for example, found that pigeons which had been trained to peck a key in order to receive food, would attack another pigeon in the cage when a correct peck of the key was not rewarded. Furthermore, since the effect occurred for socially isolated birds, it was not due to a history of competition over food. Mallick and McCandless (1966) found that eight- and nine-year-old children who were frustrated in their attempt to complete a simple construction task by a clumsy and sarcastic peer (actually a stooge) made more attempts to interfere with the peer's subsequent work and reported more dislike of him than nonfrustrated controls.

One problem that has attracted the attention of researchers in this area has to do with the arbitrariness of frustrations. Pastore (1952) was the first to call attention to the fact that arbitrary frustrations are more likely to lead to aggression than nonarbitrary frustrations. Subjects described their reactions to a number of hypothetical and supposedly frustrating situations. For some of the subjects the "frustrating" situations were arbitrary [e.g., "You're waiting on the right corner for a bus, and the driver intentionally passes you by" (p. 729)], and for some subjects the "frustrating" situations were nonarbitrary ["You're waiting at the right corner for a bus. You notice it is a special on its way to the garage" (p. 729)]. Pastore found that when judges coded subjects' written reactions more aggressive responses occurred to the arbitrary than to the nonarbitrary situations. These results could be interpreted as indicating that when a frustration is perceived as nonarbitrary either the instigation to aggression is reduced, or there is an increase in the inhibition of aggression.

Burnstein and Worchel (1962) report an experiment in which groups of male undergraduates were prevented from reaching a required unanimous decision on a discussion problem by a fellow group member's continued questions and interruptions. The disruptive member was, of course, a stooge. In the nonarbitrary condition the stooge's interruptions were readily attributable to an obvious hearing defect. In the arbitrary condition the stooge did not represent himself as having a hearing defect. Within each of the frustration conditions were three subconditions of rejection, each containing different groups of subjects. In the public condition the group members had to state publicly if they wished to eliminate any group members from the next discussion, which was presumably to be held at a later date. In the private-punitive condition the group members had to state privately (in writing) if they wished to eliminate any group member. The experimenter explained that if the majority voted to eliminate anyone that person would receive a low "conference skill score." In the private-nonpunitive condition the subjects privately indicated whether any group member should be moved from their group to some other group, after hearing the experimenter explain that no penalties were involved. Following the public or private vote the subjects filled out a questionnaire in which they indicated their feelings toward the experimenter and themselves.

Within the arbitrary condition the percentages of subjects voting to reject the stooge in the public, private-punitive, and private-nonpunitive conditions were 29, 100, and 100. Within the nonarbitrary condition the similar rejection percentages for public, private-punitive, and private-nonpunitive conditions were 0, 27, and 50. Consistent with Pastore's (1952) results there was a greater tendency to reject the stooge in the arbitrary condition than in the nonarbitrary condition. However, within both arbitrary and nonarbitrary conditions rejection increased as the social restraints or inhibitions against expression of aggression were removed. Removal of inhibitions thus can produce rejection even when the frustration is nonarbitrary. Possibly then, there are, in general, greater social inhibitions against aggressing toward a nonarbitrary frustrator than an arbitrary frustrator. If this is the case, what happens to the aggressive tendencies that are evoked by nonarbitrary frustration? One possibility is that they are displaced. Consistent with this line of reasoning, Burnstein and Worchel found that on the postexperimental questionnaire, subjects expressed more hostility toward themselves and the experimenter in the nonarbitrary than in the arbitrary conditions. Furthermore, within the nonarbitrary condition hostility toward the experimenter decreased from the public to the private-punitive to the private-nonpunitive conditions. A similar effect did not occur for hostility toward the self. Except for this latter failure, the intriguing pattern of results is consistent with the hypothesis that social inhibitions produce less aggressive reactions to nonarbitrary frustration than to arbitrary frustration.

Granted that social inhibitions do inhibit aggressive reactions to nonarbitrary frustrations, is this a complete explanation for the difference between arbitrary and nonarbitrary frustrations in evoked aggressiveness? Note that when Burnstein and Worchel minimized the social inhibitions against aggression in their private-nonpunitive conditions, nonarbitrary frustration still produced hostility in fewer subjects (50 percent) than did arbitrary frustration (100 percent). This, at least, suggests that the perceived nonarbitrariness of a frustration, in addition to producing inhibitions against the expression of aggression, reduces or does not produce as much actual instigation to aggression. According to Berkowitz, "Defining a frustration as reasonable or proper, i.e., as nonarbitrary, in essence weakens the frustrater's association with aggression; his aggressive cue value is diminished. As a consequence, he would be less likely to elicit overt aggression from the frustrated individual" (1969, pp. 24–25).

The article by Berkowitz and LePage (1967), which is contained in the Readings section for this chapter, is illustrative of the research in which Berkowitz has demonstrated the importance of cues in the production of aggression following frustration. In the Berkowitz and LePage experiment the aggressive cues were a shotgun and revolver lying on the table in the experimental room.

The Belief in a Just World

A final factor affecting interpersonal attraction is our shared belief in a just world. Melvin Lerner (1965, 1970) has argued that people believe there is an appropriate fit between what they do and the rewards and punishments which they receive; that is., that there is a justice in the world. According to Lerner this belief in justice is universally applied to both self and others. Thus there will be a tendency to assign misdeeds to a suffering victim and competent actions to a successful achiever. Suppose, on the other hand, the suffering victim is clearly innocent and did not engage in any obvious misdeeds. Such a state of affairs would threaten the individual's belief in justice and, under appropriate circumstances, lead to rejection, or dislike, of the victim. Such downgrading of the victim's worth restores the individual's belief in a just world.

Lerner and Simmons (1966) investigated some of the circumstances affecting rejection of an innocent victim. They reasoned that rejection would be relatively great if the victim had suffered for a certain period and, furthermore, was expected to continue suffering for an additional period. On the other hand, if the subject could successfully intervene and prevent the victim's continued suffering, justice would be restored and rejection consequently less necessary. Two of their experimental conditions were designed to test this reasoning. Groups of female subjects volunteered for what was described to them as an experiment on the perception of emotional cues. It was explained to them that they would be watching another experiment in which subjects learned under one of three different conditions: shock, monetary reward, or neither shock nor reward. Accordingly, the curtains on a one-way mirror were opened revealing a room in which an experimenter, "Dr. Stewart," was adjusting the shock apparatus and a technician was working with a television camera. The subjects were informed that previous observers had relied heavily upon skin color to judge emotional state, and that in order to see what other possible cues could be used the observers on that day would watch over a television monitor. The curtains were then closed and the subjects asked to watch the television monitor. At that point Dr. Stewart entered the observation room and asked her subject (the victim) to accompany her. Dr. Stewart stated that she was running subjects in the shock condition.

When the television monitor came on it showed Dr. Stewart entering the next room with the victim who was then strapped into the shock apparatus. During the next 10 minutes the victim's attempted learning of nonsense syllables was accompanied by apparently painful electric shocks. The victim reacted to the shocks with "exclamations and expressions of pain and suffering." She, of course, was not actually shocked, and the subjects, in fact, observed not a live performance but a previously prepared video tape. Following the tape the subjects received differential instructions depending upon the experimental condition. In the midpoint condition the subjects were told that they were at the midpoint of the experiment and there would be another session of equal length after they made their first ratings (of the victim). In the reward condition the subjects were told that they could determine by vote whether the subject (victim) would receive shock, monetary reward, or neither in the second learning session. The group, in fact, voted for reward and were so informed. In neither condition was a second session actually held. The experiment was terminated following the completion of a questionnaire including an assessment of the victim's attractiveness.

Lerner and Simmons expected that the victim would be regarded as less attractive in the midpoint condition in which continued suffering was expected than in the reward condition in which the subjects had successfully intervened to prevent further suffering. This expectation was supported. Mean attraction in the midpoint condition (-25.78) was significantly less than in the reward condition (-5.07).

In two additional conditions Lerner and Simmons created an even more stringent test of the theory. In one of these, the end-point condition, the subjects were told that the experiment was over after the first sequence of shock-motivated learning trials and asked to make their ratings (of the victim). In the other, or martyr, condition the victim appeared to be willing to undergo the dreaded shock for an altruistic purpose, to permit the waiting subjects to get credit for participating in the experiment. When Dr. Stewart arrived at the observation room to obtain her subject, the victim protested that she would not take part in an experiment in which she was shocked. Dr. Stewart then explained that in that case the group of waiting subjects (who were also in the observation room) would not obtain credit for being in the experiment, but, of course, the decision was up to her. After a few minutes of persuasion the victim agreed. Lerner and Simmons report that three psychologists who observed the interchange in rehearsal agreed that the victim appeared to act from altruistic motives. Except for this exchange between Dr. Stewart and the victim, the martyr condition was identical to the end-point condition. Lerner and Simmons expected that the martyr condition would cause a greater violation of the belief in justice than occurred in the end-point condition. Not only was the victim innocent, she suffered for an altruistic, or nonselfish, purpose. The results supported Lerner and Simmons' prediction. Mean attraction in the martyr condition (-34.00) was significantly less than in the end-point condition (-12.85).

Lerner and Simmons had also expected that mean attraction in the above midpoint condition would be less than in the end-point condition. This expectation was based on the idea that the continued suffering in the midpoint condition would cause a greater violation of the belief in justice. Although the attraction ratings differed in the predicted direction (-25.78 versus -12.85), the difference is not significant.

Lerner and Simmons' experiment presents a good case for the belief in justice as a determiner of interpersonal attraction. An alternative explanation in terms of balance theory, however, is at least possible. In the midpoint condition the victim had been and was going to continue being associated with unpleasant-negative circumstances. From a balance perspective it is thus understandable why the victim who had a positive unit relation with the negative circumstances should also become negative $(-+-=+)$. Lerner and Simmons' martyr condition, however, presents a problem for the balance account. If the victim were, in fact, seen as altruistic and positive, balance theory would seem to have trouble accounting for the victim's subsequent negative evaluation. On the other hand, perhaps the victim was really seen as someone who foolishly conformed under pressure and irrationally got herself into a fix. Lerner and Simmons (and also Lerner, 1970) discuss but do not completely resolve the problem. The best evidence that Lerner and Simmons report is that three psychologists who observed the martyr interchange judged the victim's performance as giving the impression of genuine altruism.

Lerner and Matthews (1967) present additional evidence for the belief in justice as a mediator of interpersonal attraction. Pairs of female subjects were informed that they were to participate in a learning experiment in which one of them would receive strong electric shocks for errors. The other would serve as a no-shock control. A memory drum and an imposing apparatus for delivering shocks through wrist electrodes were present in the orientation room. The subjects were then taken to separate waiting rooms and informed that the subject who received the shocks would be determined by drawing slips of paper from a bowl. It was explained that the bowl contained only two slips, one marked "shock" and the other marked "control." There were two basic conditions, self-picks-first and other-picks-first. In the self-picks-first condition the experimenter entered the room with a bowl containing two slips of paper, both marked "control." The subject then selected a slip of paper and discovered her good fortune. In the other-picks-first condition the experimenter entered the room with a bowl containing one slip of paper marked "control," and explained that the other subject had already made her selection. The subject then took the piece of paper and discovered her good fortune. In both conditions the subject thus believed that the other subject was to suffer the misfortune of strong electric shock. Finally, the subjects completed a number of scales which, among other things, assessed their attraction for the other subject and the assigned responsibility for receiving the electric shock.

Lerner and Matthews had expected that the subject would attribute responsibility for assignment to the shock condition to the other in the other-picks-first condition and responsibility to herself in the self-picks-first condition. The ratings, in fact, supported this expectation. Given this assignment of responsibility, what results should then be expected for attraction? Lerner and Matthews argue that whenever possible suffering is ascribed to the victim's misdeeds; that is, the victim is seen as responsible for his or her own fate. When this is not possible, however, the perceiver invents a characterological reason for the misdeeds and, therefore, the victim is regarded as less worthy or less attractive. Such downgrading serves to restore the belief in a just world. The results indicated, consistent with this reasoning, that the other was regarded as less attractive in the self-picks-first condition than in the other-picks-first condition. When the subject regarded herself as responsible for the other's suffering, the other was seen as less attractive. Lerner and Matthews' results thus provide further support for the contention that interpersonal attraction is partially mediated by the belief in a just world.

Overview

At the beginning of this chapter we stated that our major purpose was to examine some answers to the question, "What determines one person's degree of interpersonal attraction for another?" The answers to this question that have been discussed relate to the following: (1) other people as instrumental to the satisfaction of a self-evaluative need; (2) similarity; (3) implied evaluation; (4) spatial propinquity and social contact; (5) physical attractiveness; (6) frustration and aggression; (7) belief in a just world. Each of these matters provides different, although not necessarily unrelated, perspectives on interpersonal attraction. Social psychology does not yet have a complete understanding of the attraction phenomenon, but certainly a provocative beginning has been made.

READINGS

Attraction as a Linear Function of Proportion of Positive Reinforcements[1]

Donn Byrne and Don Nelson

In various investigations of the effects of the similarity of a stranger's attitude on attraction toward him, the proportion of similar attitudes has not been distinguished from the number of similar attitudes. In a 4×3 factorial design, 4 levels of proportion and 3 levels of number were employed. Each of 168 Ss was asked to read an attitude scale purportedly filled out by an anonymous stranger and to evaluate him on a number of variables including attraction toward him. As hypothesized, analysis of variance indicated that attraction was significantly ($p < .001$) affected only by proportion. Utilizing these and other data for a total of 790 Ss, the functional relationship between proportion of similar attitudes and attraction was found to be a linear one. The conceptualization of attitude similarity as constituting positive reinforcement was strengthened by the finding of a linear relationship in McDonald's (1962) data between proportion of high creativity ratings given to 192 Ss and their attraction toward the rater.

It is a well-established finding that the attraction of a subject toward a stranger is a function of the similarity or dissimilarity of the latter's attitudes and values to those of the subject. When similarity is manipulated experimentally, attraction is found to increase as the similarity of the stranger increases (Byrne, 1961a; Jones & Daugherty, 1959; Schachter, 1951; Smith, 1957). In order to proceed beyond these empirical findings to build a genuine theory of attraction, it would be helpful to obtain a clearer identification of the stimulus which evokes differential attraction responses and a more precise specification of the relationship between this stimulus and attraction.

In a series of papers, Newcomb (1953, 1956, 1959, 1961) has dealt with the antecedents of interpersonal relationships. Along with other principles he has proposed that attraction between individuals is a function of the extent to which reciprocal rewards are present in their interaction. As an extension of this conceptualization, it was further suggested (Byrne, 1961a, 1962) that

[1] From the *Journal of Personality and Social Psychology*, Volume 1, pages 659–663, 1965 (received October 9, 1963). Authors' affiliation: University of Texas. This research was supported in part by the United States Air Force under Grant AF-AFOSR 261-63 from the Air Force Office of Scientific Research of the Air Research and Development Command. The authors wish to thank June Goldberg, Rex Golightly, Nancy Johnson, Patricia Yale, and Betsy Young for their assistance on this project. Reprinted by permission of the American Psychological Association.

attraction toward a person is determined by the number of rewards relative to the number of punishments received from him. Various types of reward and punishment have been utilized experimentally, but the major portion of attraction research has utilized similarity and dissimilarity of attitudes, opinions, beliefs, and values as the stimulus. The rationale is that the learned drive to be logical and to interpret incoming information correctly is reinforced by consensual validation and frustrated by consensual invalidation (Dollard & Miller, 1950; Festinger, 1950, 1954; Newcomb, 1953, 1956, 1959, 1961).

Investigations of the effects of varying proportions of similar and dissimilar attitudes have, unfortunately, involved a confounding of the number of positive reinforcements with the proportion of positive reinforcements. For example, Byrne (1962) varied seven items of similarity-dissimilarity in the eight possible combinations ranging from 7-0 to 0-7. The highly significant effects on attraction toward the stranger to whom the attitudes were attributed could have been a function of either the proportion or the number of similar attitudes. The present investigation is designed to test the proposition that attraction toward a stranger is a positive function of the proportion of positive reinforcements received from that stranger.

PROCEDURE

Utilizing attitude similarity-dissimilarity, the design permits the comparison of the effects of number of positive reinforcements (16, 8, and 4) with the effects of proportion of positive reinforcements (1.00, .67, .50, and .33) on attraction in a 4×3 factorial design as shown in Table 1. Each cell contained 14 subjects, divided approximately evenly with respect to sex. Subjects were asked to read an attitude scale supposedly filled out by another student of their same sex and then make several judgments about him or her including the ratings that constitute the measure of attraction.

The subjects consisted of 168 students enrolled in the introductory psychology course at the University of Texas. In their classrooms, each student responded to one of several forms of an attitude scale (ranging in length from 4 to 48 items) in which they indicated their opinions about each topic on a 6-point scale. On the basis of a pilot study with another group of 138 subjects, each scale was balanced with respect to the importance of the topics; in addition, items which yielded extremely uniform

TABLE 1

Number of Items on Which the Stranger Held Similar/Dissimilar Attitudes

Proportion of similar attitudes	Number of similar attitudes		
	4	8	16
1.00	4/0	8/0	16/0
.67	4/2	8/4	16/8
.50	4/4	8/8	16/16
.33	4/8	8/16	16/32

responses in the population were omitted in favor of items yielding as close as possible to 50–50 splits. The latter control was an attempt to avoid the possible confounding of dissimilarity of attitudes with deviancy of attitudes on the part of the stranger. The attitude items covered a variety of topics including fraternities and sororities, integration, science fiction, welfare legislation, tipping, discipline for children, community bomb shelters, and gardening.

In the experiment itself, subjects were brought into a special room in small groups. As has been described previously (Byrne, 1962) they were told that the experiment concerned the accuracy of interpersonal judgments based on limited information. They were to receive an attitude scale filled out by an anonymous stranger, read the responses carefully, and then make several judgments about him or her. Each subject received a spurious scale containing responses which constituted the appropriate number of similar and dissimilar attitudes depending on the cell to which he was assigned.

The stranger was rated on 7-point scales (Byrne & Wong, 1962) with respect to intelligence, knowledge of current events, morality, adjustment, and then on the two attraction scales (probable liking for the stranger and probable enjoyment of working with him). In previous investigations, responses to the latter two scales have been analyzed separately as alternate measures of the dependent variable. It seems advantageous, however, to combine the ratings on the two scales into a single attraction index with a possible range of 2–14. With the two scales conceptualized as forming a two-item measuring device, data from 10 different samples totaling 1,010 subjects yield an average corrected split-half reliability of .85 for the attraction measure.

RESULTS

The means and standard deviations of the attraction scores are shown in Table 2. Before computing the analysis of variance, Hartley's maximum F ratio test for heterogeneity of variance (Walker & Lev, 1953) was employed. The F_{max} of 10.04 indicated a significant departure from homogeneity. Even though it has been found (Young & Veldman, 1963) that heterogeneity of variance has a negligible effect on both the alpha level and the power of the F test, the data were transformed into the square of each number in order to obtain acceptable homogeneity. There was no difference in significance levels between the analysis based on the raw data and that based on the transformed data; the summary shown in Table 3 is based on the raw data. Since the only significant F is that for the proportion of similar attitudes, the hypothesis is confirmed.

TABLE 2

Means and Standard Deviations of Attraction Scores toward Strangers with Varying Numbers and Varying Proportions of Similar Attitudes

| Proportion of similar attitudes | Number of similar attitudes | | | | | | | |
| | 4 | | 8 | | 16 | | Total | |
	M	*SD*	*M*	*SD*	*M*	*SD*	*M*	*SD*
1.00	11.14	1.68	12.79	1.01	10.93	2.28	11.62	1.93
.67	10.79	2.46	9.36	2.64	9.50	2.47	9.88	2.60
.50	9.36	2.52	9.57	2.53	7.93	3.20	8.95	2.86
.33	8.14	3.02	6.64	1.99	6.57	2.02	7.12	2.50
Total	9.86	2.74	9.59	3.05	8.73	3.01		

TABLE 3

Analysis of Variance of Attraction Scores toward Strangers with Varying Numbers and Varying Proportions of Similar Attitudes

Source	df	MS	F
Proportion (A)	3	158.71	23.34*
Number (B)	2	11.11	1.63
A × B	6	8.49	1.25
Within	156	6.80	

* $p < .001$.

DISCUSSION

The positive relationship between proportion of similar attitudes held by a stranger and attraction toward him appears to be a firmly established one. The nature of that relationship can be described somewhat more precisely at this point. Data were available to the author from five published studies (Byrne, 1961a, 1961b, 1962; Byrne & McGraw, 1964; Byrne & Wong, 1962),[2] the present investigation, and two unpublished studies; in each instance attraction was the dependent variable and various proportions of similar attitudes the independent variable. The subjects totaled 790, and 11 different values of the proportion of similar attitudes held by the stranger were represented. A plot of the mean attraction scores for these 11 points suggested linearity, and a straight-line function was fitted to the data by the least-squares method. The solution yielded the formula $Y = 5.44X + 6.62$, and the plot is shown in Fig. 1.

While the linear relationship between proportion of similar attitudes and attraction appears to be a lawful phenomenon, more evidence is needed to support the more general proposition that attraction is a linear function of the proportion of positive reinforcements. Attraction has been found to be influenced by various types of reward and punishment, including high and low ratings of creative productions (McDonald, 1962), facilitation of success at an experimental task (Kleiner, 1960), and insulting and frustrating behavior (Worchel, 1958). Only in McDonald's experiment, however, was proportion of positive reinforcements represented by a series of values. His subjects were asked to create seven stories in response to a set of stimulus cards; a confederate posing as another subject rated each story on a 10-point scale with respect to creativity. Each of the 192 subjects was assigned to one of eight possible conditions (seven high ratings, six high and one low, etc.). Attraction toward the peer who made the ratings was found to increase as a function of the proportion of high ratings. McDonald made his data avail-

---

[2] In two of the studies some of the strangers were identified as Negroes, but for the purpose of the present paper only the data involving white strangers have been utilized.

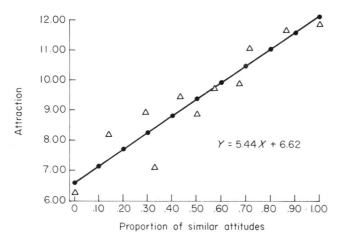

Fig. 1. *Attraction toward stranger as a linear function of proportion of similar attitudes.*

able to the author, and they were plotted as shown in Fig. 2. Again, a linear function was found to fit the data: $Y = 2.98X + 8.47$. Thus, linearity of the relationship is evident across two different experimental conditions but the values of the constants differ. Presumably, the similarity across stimulus conditions is attributable to the common element of positive and negative reinforcements involved. A tentative law of attraction is proposed as $A_x = mPR_x + k$ or attraction toward X is a positive linear function of the proportion of positive reinforcements received from X. The explanation for the differences between the two situations in terms of the slope of the line and the Y intercept must be sought in subsequent research.

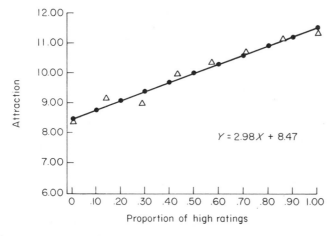

Fig. 2. *Attraction toward stranger as a linear function of proportion of high creativity ratings.*

REFERENCES

Byrne, D. Interpersonal attraction and attitude similarity. *Journal of Abnormal and Social Psychology,* 1961, **62,** 713–715. (a)

Byrne, D. Interpersonal attraction as a function of affiliation need and attitude similarity. *Human Relations,* 1961, **3,** 283–289. (b)

Byrne, D. Response to attitude similarity-dissimilarity as a function of affiliation need. *Journal of Personality,* 1962, **30,** 164–177.

Byrne, D., & McGraw, C. Interpersonal attraction toward Negroes. *Human Relations,* 1964, **17,** 201–213.

Byrne, D., & Wong, T. J. Racial prejudice, interpersonal attraction, and assumed dissimilarity of attitudes. *Journal of Abnormal and Social Psychology,* 1962, **65,** 246–253.

Dollard, J., & Miller, N. E. *Personality and psychotherapy.* New York: McGraw-Hill, 1950.

Festinger, L. Informal social communication. *Psychological Review,* 1950, **57,** 271–282.

Festinger, L. A theory of social comparison processes. *Human Relations,* 1954, **7,** 117–140.

Jones, E. E., & Daugherty, B. N. Political orientation and perceptual effects of an anticipated interaction. *Journal of Abnormal and Social Psychology,* 1959, **59,** 340–349.

Kleiner, R. J. The effects of threat reduction upon interpersonal attractiveness. *Journal of Personality,* 1960, **28,** 145–155.

McDonald, R. D. The effect of reward-punishment and affiliation need on interpersonal attraction. Unpublished doctoral dissertation, University of Texas, 1962.

Newcomb, T. M. An approach to the study of communicative acts. *Psychological Review,* 1953, **60,** 393–404.

Newcomb, T. M. The prediction of interpersonal attraction. *American Psychologist,* 1956, **11,** 575–586.

Newcomb, T. M. Individual systems of orientation. In S. Koch (Ed.), *Psychology: A study of a science.* Vol. 3. *Formulations of the person and the social context.* New York: McGraw-Hill, 1959. Pp. 384–422.

Newcomb, T. M. *The acquaintance process.* New York: Holt, Rinehart, & Winston, 1961.

Schachter, S. Deviation, rejection, and communication. *Journal of Abnormal and Social Psychology,* 1951, **46,** 190–207.

Smith, A. J. Similarity of values and its relation to acceptance and the projection of similarity. *Journal of Psychology,* 1957, **43,** 251–260.

Walker, Helen M., & Lev, J. *Statistical inference* New York: Holt, 1953.

Worchel, P. Personality factors in the readiness to express aggression. *Journal of Clinical Psychology,* 1958, **4,** 355–359.

Young, R. K., & Veldman, D. J. Heterogeneity and skewness in analysis of variance. *Perceptual and Motor Skills,* 1963, **16,** 588.

My Enemy's Enemy Is My Friend[1]

Elliot Aronson and Vernon Cope

An experiment was performed to explore the generality of the proposition that people like those who punish their enemies and reward their friends. Results indicated that the attractiveness of a person who punishes one's enemy or rewards one's friend is not limited to situations which provide indications of attitude similarity, gratitude, or social support. Specifically, the experiment was designed to show that this phenomenon occurs in spite of the fact that the situation was arranged so that: (a) The stimulus person's behavior in no way suggested that his attitudes were similar to those of S; (b) the stimulus person was clearly unaware of S's relationship to the latter's enemy or friend—thus he was not trying to help S; and (c) it was clear that S and the stimulus person would have no opportunity to meet and gain any social benefit from sharing a mutual friend or enemy. Methodologically, the possibility of bias was reduced by using separate Es, who were partially blinded as to treatment, and a 3rd person (similarly blinded) to collect the dependent-variable data.

It makes sense to assume that, all other things being equal, if two people discover that they share a common enemy, their mutual attractiveness will increase. This proposition is a simple derivation from balance theory (Heider, 1958). But such a situation may consist of one or more underlying factors. For example, if I know nothing about the reason why another person dislikes my enemy, I might assume that we dislike him for the same reasons and, therefore, that we share similar beliefs and attitudes. Thus, suppose that Person X's most outstanding characteristic is that he is a pompous ass, and I dislike him for it. If I learn that Person Y also dislikes X, I might assume that Y dislikes X for the same reason. A similarity of beliefs and attitudes has been shown to increase attractiveness (Byrne, 1961; Newcomb, 1961). Accordingly, I might like X because I feel that we both dislike people who exhibit "pompous assiness." Second, I might believe that this other person dislikes my enemy because he knows that I dislike him. This would suggest that my enemy's enemy likes me. Since people generally like those who like them (Aronson & Linder, 1965; Backman & Secord, 1959), I might come to like him. Finally, this relationship

[1] From the *Journal of Personality and Social Psychology*, Volume 8, pages 8–12, 1968 (received February 9, 1967). Authors' affiliation. University of Texas. This experiment was supported by grants from the National Science Foundation (NSF GS 750) and the National Institute of Mental Health (MH 12357-01). We would like to thank Bob Moor and Joe Longley, who served as experimenters, and our secretary, Judith Hilton, who collected the dependent-variable measure. Reprinted by permission of the American Psychological Association.

may have certain concrete practical advantages. Specifically, if I dislike X and I discover that Y dislikes X also, I may feel that it is conceivable that Y and I might band together and beat X up or plot strategy against him or at least engage in some satisfying malicious gossip. Thus, I might like Y purely because he can do me some tangible good.

One may wonder whether the above criteria are essential for the phenomenon to occur. For example, suppose X behaved harshly to me. If Y behaved negatively to X, would I increase my liking for Y even if (a) he were unaware that X had behaved harshly toward me, (b) his nasty behavior toward X was inspired by a totally different set of events, and (c) there was no opportunity for us to socialize and commiserate? For example, if X had insulted me at a cocktail party, and 2 weeks later I noticed a police officer (Y) issuing a summons to X for a traffic violation, would that police officer become dear to my heart? The authors' guess is that he would. It is the authors' contention that Heider's proposition is a general one, not limited to such mediating events; that is, there is something good about seeing one's enemy punished—in and of itself. Consequently, it is predicted that individuals will like their enemy's punisher even if the two events are noncontingent and unrelated, that is, even if the punisher's behavior implies neither attitude similarity nor utility. By the same token, individuals will come to like a person who rewards someone who treated them kindly—even if the two events are noncontingent and related.

METHOD

General Overview

The general procedure involved placing the subject in a situation in which he was treated either harshly or pleasantly by an experimenter and then allowing the subject to overhear the experimenter being treated either harshly or pleasantly by the latter's supervisor. The subject was then given an opportunity to express his feelings for the supervisor. It was obviously essential that the supervisor's evaluation of the experimenter be separate from and unrelated to the experimenter's evaluation of the subject.

Subjects and Design

The subjects were 40 male and 40 female introductory psychology students at the University of Texas. They were randomly assigned to one of four conditions designed to test the hypothesis: pleasant experimenter-pleasant supervisor, pleasant-experimenter-harsh supervisor, harsh experimenter-pleasant supervisor, harsh experimenter-harsh supervisor.[2]

Procedure

The subjects volunteered for participation in a study of creativity. When the subject arrived, the experimenter[3] led him into a cubicle and introduced himself as a

---

[2] In actuality, 86 subjects were run. Because of suspiciousness, 2 subjects were discarded in each of Conditions 2, 3, and 4, respectively.

[3] Two different experiments were used in the experiment. They ran an equal proportion of subjects in all conditions; the results were not influenced by the identity of the experimenter.

graduate student who was assisting Dr. Cope in his creativity project. The experimenter explained that the purpose of the study was to determine the relationship between creativity and college performance. He informed the subject that he would present him with a series of three pictures and that the subject's task would be to write a story about each picture—what the situation is, what led to the situation, what the people are thinking or feeling, and what they will do. The subjects were told that they would have only 4 minutes to write each story.

After the subject had written a story, the experimenter silently read it and marked it with various coded grading signals. During his reading of each story and after the reading of all three stories, the manipulation of either pleasant experimenter or harsh experimenter was put into effect. In order to reduce opportunities for bias, the experimenter was kept ignorant of the condition in which the subject was to be run until this point in the experiment. This was determined randomly. When it was essential to ensure equal numbers of subjects per condition, the senior author determined the condition of each subject in advance and handed the experimenter a folded slip of paper before each subject was run. The slip contained the word "harsh" or "pleasant." After delivering the initial instructions and while the subject was writing the first story, the experimenter simply reached into his pocket, unfolded the paper, and determined the subject's condition. Thus, the initial instructions were delivered in ignorance of the subject's condition. At this point the manipulation commenced.

Harsh Condition. While he read each story, the experimenter occasionally emitted a displeased and condescending grunt, sigh, or grumble. After reading all three stories, the experimenter stated that although the final scoring was not completed and would take more time he would give the subject a tentative evaluation. He then proceeded to tell the subject that his stories were unimaginative and uncreative. The evaluation was given starkly and somewhat brutally, with no punches pulled. The experimenter acted as if he enjoyed making these negative statements.

Pleasant Condition. In this condition the evaluation was essentially the same. The experimenter told the subject that although the final scoring was not completed and would take more time he would give the subject a tentative evaluation. He then told the subject that his stories were uncreative and unimaginative. But in this condition the experimenter treated the subject very gently. Specifically, he told him not to be too worried about it—that although the test was a good measure of creativity, it *was* only one test. In short, although the experimenter told the subject that according to his analysis of the test results the subject was uncreative, he let the subject down gently rather than harshly; he allowed the subject to save face.

A few seconds before the experimenter finished his evaluation, he casually leaned against the door of the testing room and rubbed his foot against the air vent. This served as a signal to the "supervisor" who, although waiting some distance from the door, was able to see it move. After waiting a few seconds, the supervisor knocked on the door, entered, excused himself for interrupting, told the experimenter that he must talk to him for a moment, and asked the experimenter to step into the hall. The experimenter stood up and introduced the supervisor to the subject. The supervisor shook hands with the subject and escorted the experimenter into the corridor.

Although they were careful to close the door behind them (so as not to arouse the subject's suspicions), the situation was such that the subject could easily overhear their conversation through the air vent at the bottom of the door.

At this point the second variable was manipulated: the supervisor's treatment of the experimenter. Half of the subjects were randomly assigned to the pleasant-supervisor condition, half were randomly assigned to the harsh-supervisor condition. The conversations in each condition are presented in that order below:

I read that report you wrote for me, and, well, I think it's one of the finest analyses of the articles I've seen in a long, long time. In particular, I thought you made an excellent selection of references. I don't think I could have done a better job myself—and I know that area pretty well! Also, I think I'll make up another copy of your paper so I can show it to my other research assistants as an example of the sort of work I want from them and just as an example of good, creative work. Uh, I'm on my way to see the department chairman right now and, well, because I'm so impressed with the sort of work you've been doing here, I'm going to ask him if we can get you an increase in salary. Well, I have to run now so you can get back to your subject.

I read that report you wrote for me, and I think it's, well, virtually worthless. It's sloppy and somewhat stupid. I can see no logical reason for using the references you cited. They have absolutely no relevance to the topics you were supposed to write about. I have an idea you were just using those references as filler material. Well, there's a lot of irrelevant material, and the quality and the organization are both very poor. OK, I'm going to give you a couple of days to do it over. As a matter of fact, I'm on my way right now to see the department chairman, and I'm going to ask him if there's anyone else we have who could replace you if you continue to do bad work. OK, I've got to run now so you can get back to your subject.

After he had been "evaluated," the experimenter reentered the room with a gloomy face if he had been negatively evaluated and a smile if positively evaluated. He told the subject that that was all they had time for and instructed him to go upstairs to the psychology office where the secretary would give him credit for the experiment.

It should be noted that at the time the supervisor was acting either harshly or pleasantly to the experimenter, the supervisor was ignorant as to whether the experimenter had been pleasant or harsh to the subject. Similarly, while the experimenter was acting either pleasantly or harshly to the subject, the experimenter was unaware as to whether the supervisor was about to treat him pleasantly or harshly. Thus, since an interaction is being predicted, this technique of "partial ignorance" effectively guards against the systematic bias described by Rosenthal (1966). For a greater elaboration of the applicability of this partial ignorance technique, see Aronson and Carlsmith (1968).

Dependent Variable. The dependent variable was administered by the departmental secretary who was, of course, ignorant of the subject's experimental condition. As she prepared to give the subject credit for participation in the experiment, she said that she had a request to make on behalf of the supervisor of the experiment the subject had just participated in. After ascertaining that the subject recalled having met the supervisor, she proceeded to tell him that he (Dr. Cope) was spending 1 year at the University to do research for the National Science Foundation. In regard to a different project he was directing, she continued, the National Science Foundation had recently informed him that he must use a different body of subjects taken from the local community instead of the college students he had been using as subjects. The result was that the supervisor needed hundreds of nonuniversity people within the next 2 weeks and that the job of contacting people and convincing them to volunteer was enormous. She said that the supervisor did not have the staff to do this work, and he could not afford to pay for it; he was really desperate and needed a favor. Specifically, he had requested that she ask anyone to help him by making phone calls. She said that she had a long list of several thousand phone numbers randomly selected from the Austin telephone directory. She asked:

Would you be willing to help Dr. Cope by making some phone calls and asking people to serve as subjects? Other people have volunteered to call anywhere from 2 to 50 people—would you be willing to help him out?

The number of phone calls served as the dependent variable, being a reflection of the positive feelings the subjects held for the supervisor.

After the subject made his decision, the secretary thanked him. She then handed him a short questionnaire which she introduced as a departmental questionnaire designed to determine the effectiveness and viability of the departmental requirement that all introductory psychology students serve as subjects. The significant item on the questionnaire was an evaluation of the experimenter. The secretary was ignorant of the subject's experimental treatment while she was soliciting his aid in making phone calls and administering the questionnaire. Thus, the inevitable minor variations in her tone and manner could not have had a systematic effect on the results.

After the subject completed the questionnaire, Dr. Cope entered the office and debriefed him. Because all of the subjects had received a rather negative evaluation, they were delighted to learn that the evaluation was preprogrammed rather than an accurate reflection of their creative ability.

RESULTS AND DISCUSSION

Before presenting the primary data, it is necessary to determine if the major manipulation worked: Did the subjects like the harsh experimenter less than the pleasant experimenter? Recall that the subjects were asked to complete a series of rating scales which were introduced as a departmental questionnaire aimed at determining their reaction to the experiment. Included in this questionnaire was a direct evaluation of the experimenter: "How much did you enjoy working with the experimenter?" The results indicate that the manipulation was effective. Subjects were more favorably disposed to the experimenter in the pleasant conditions than in the harsh conditions ($p < .005$).[4]

The hypothesis was that the subject would like his enemy's enemy more than his enemy's friend, and that he would like his friend's friend better than his friend's enemy. Specifically, it was predicted that the subject would volunteer to make the most phone calls as a favor to the supervisor if the latter had acted either harshly to the experimenter who treated the subject harshly or pleasantly to the experimenter who had treated the subject kindly. The results are presented in Table 1. Inspection of the table reveals that the subjects were willing to make more phone calls for a supervisor who was his enemy's enemy than for one who was his enemy's friend. Similarly, subjects were willing to make more phone calls for a friend's friend than for a friend's enemy. The data were analyzed by analysis of variance (Table 2). The prediction is reflected in the interaction between the experimenter's behavior toward the subject and the supervisor's behavior

[4] A rather interesting serendipitous finding should be reported. Specifically, there was an interaction between the sex of the subject and the behavior of the supervisor as it affected the liking of the subject for the experimenter ($p < .005$). Generally, males tended to like the experimenter if he was pleasantly treated by the supervisor; females liked the experimenter better if he was harshly criticized by the supervisor, irrespective of how the experimenter behaved toward the subject. This may reflect a tendency for women to be more nurturant and/or less impressed by success than men.

TABLE 1

Mean Number of Phone Calls Volunteered on Behalf of Supervisor

	Supervisor	
E	Harsh	Pleasant
Harsh	12.1	6.2
Pleasant	6.3	13.5

toward the experimenter. The interaction is highly significant ($p < .005$). Separate contrasts were performed between the harsh supervisor and the pleasant supervisor within the pleasant-experimenter condition and between the harsh supervisor and the pleasant supervisor within the harsh-experimenter condition. Both were significant ($p < .05$). As expected, there were no main effects due to the behavior of the experimenter or the behavior of the supervisor. Likewise, neither sex of the subject nor the identity of the person playing the role of experimenter affected the results to a significant degree.

The results, then, would seem to indicate that a person's hostility toward our enemy or pleasantness toward our friend is, in and of itself, sufficient to bring about an increase in our liking for him. In the present experiment, as far as the subject was concerned, the supervisor was unaware of the fact that the experimenter had been kind or unkind to the

TABLE 2

Analysis of Variance

Source	MS	F
E's evaluation (A)	12.03	.12
Supervisor's evaluation (B)	8.53	.09
Sex of *S* (C)	122.00	1.26
Identity of *E* (D)	1.00	.01
A × B	816.40	8.42*
A × C	4.03	.04
A × D	140.83	1.45
B × C	48.13	.50
B × D	128.13	1.32
C × D	.40	.00
A × B × C	49.40	.51
A × B × D	25.20	.26
A × C × D	17.63	.18
B × C × D	.53	.00
A × B × C × D	143.00	1.47
Error	96.95	

* $p < .005$, $df = 1/64$.

subject. Thus, the supervisor's treatment of the experimenter could in no way be construed as being caused by the experimenter's treatment of the subject. In addition, it was clear that the supervisor's reasons for being nice or nasty to the experimenter were unrelated to the subject's reasons for liking or disliking the experimenter. The subjects liked or disliked the experimenter because he was either kind or harsh during their encounter. On the other hand, the supervisor rewarded or punished the experimenter for his prior performance on a written report which had no relevance to the nature of the experimenter's behavior to the subject. Moreover, the vast difference in status between the subject and the supervisor made it extremely unlikely that the two would ever discuss their mutual feelings about the experimenter.

At the same time, it should be noted that all alternative explanations have not been ruled out. Although the subject and the supervisor clearly dislike the experimenter for different reasons, it is conceivable that the supervisor's negative evaluation of the experimenter could have had an effect on the impact of the experimenter's negative evaluation of the subject; that is, in the harsh-supervisor conditions, the supervisor told the experimenter that he wrote a poor report. This could imply that the experimenter is stupid and incompetent. If the subject had just received harsh criticisim from a person, learning that he (that person) is stupid and incompetent could reduce the impact of this harsh treatment. Consequently, it is possible that the subject came to like the supervisor who treated the unpleasant experimenter harshly, not simply because we like people who punish our enemies, but, more specifically, because we like people who help us believe that a person who judged us harshly may be a stupid and incompetent person, and that, consequently, his harsh judgment may be erroneous. This alternative explanation is unlikely, however, because it is not symmetrical; that is, it does not apply in the pleasant experimenter-pleasant supervisor condition. Recall that, like the harsh experimenter, the pleasant experimenter rated the subject as uncreative—his manner was simply more pleasant as he made this negative evaluation of the subject. Consequently, when the pleasant supervisor implied that the pleasant experimenter was intelligent and competent, he was, in effect, offering support to the experimenter's evaluation of the subject as an uncreative person. In short, if we like someone because he questions the intelligence of someone who has recently judged us as uncreative, then we should have discovered a main effect due to the behavior of the supervisor. The fact that the data show a clear interaction and significant contrasts sharply reduces the plausibility of this alternative explanation.

The results suggest that balance theory applies in a behavioral context even in the absence of specific opinion similarity; that is, the data indicate that: (a) We like someone who likes someone that we like; (b) we like someone who dislikes someone we dislike; (c) we dislike someone who

likes someone we dislike; and (d) we dislike someone who dislikes someone we like. This follows even though it is clear that the respective reasons
for liking or disliking the target person are unrelated. The primary contribution of this experiment, then, is in the demonstration that the basic
proposition of balance theory is true in a very general sense and is not
limited to situations which are mediated by other phenomena, for example,
by specific opinion similarity.

REFERENCES

Aronson, E., & Carlsmith, J. M. Experimentation in social psychology. In G. Lindzey &
    E. Aronson (Eds.), *Handbook of social psychology*. (Rev. ed.) Vol. 2. Reading,
    Massachusetts: Addison-Wesley, 1968.
Aronson, E., & Linder, D. Gain and loss of esteem as determinants of interpersonal
    attractiveness. *Journal of Experimental Social Psychology*, 1965, 1, 156–171.
Backman, C. W., & Secord, P. F. The effect of perceived liking on interpersonal attrac-
    tion. *Human Relations*, 1959, 12, 379–384.
Byrne, D. Interpersonal attraction and attitude similarity. *Journal of Abnormal and
    Social Psychology*, 1961, 62, 713–715.
Heider, F. *The psychology of interpersonal relations*. New York. Wiley, 1958.
Newcomb, T. M. *The acquaintance process*. New York: Holt, Rinehart & Winston, 1961.
Rosenthal, R. *Experimenter effects in behavioral research*. New York: Appleton-Century-
    Crofts, 1966.

Weapons as Aggression-Eliciting Stimuli[1]

Leonard Berkowitz and Anthony LePage

An experiment was conducted to test the hypothesis that stimuli commonly associated with aggression can elicit aggressive responses from people ready to act
aggressively. 100 male university students received either 1 or 7 shocks, supposedly
from a peer, and were then given an opportunity to shock this person. In some cases
a rifle and revolver were on the table near the shock key. These weapons were said
to belong, or not to belong, to the available target person. In other instances there
was nothing on the table near the shock key, while for a control group 2 badminton
racquets were on the table near the key. The greatest number of shocks was given
by the strongly aroused Ss (who had received 7 shocks) when they were in the presence of the weapons. The guns had evidently elicited strong aggressive responses from
the aroused men.

[1] From the *Journal of Personality and Social Psychology*, Volume 7, pages 202–207,
1967 (received October 5, 1966). Reproduced by permission of the American Psychological Association. Authors' affiliation: University of Wisconsin; LePage subsequently
at University of Portland. The present experiment was conducted by Anthony LePage
under Leonard Berkowitz' supervision as part of a research program sponsored by
Grant G-23988 from the National Science Foundation to the senior author.

Human behavior is often goal directed, guided by strategies and influenced by ego defenses and strivings for cognitive consistency. There clearly are situations, however, in which these purposive considerations are relatively unimportant regulators of action. Habitual behavior patterns become dominant on these occasions, and the person responds relatively automatically to the stimuli impinging upon him. Any really complete psychological system must deal with these stimulus-elicited, impulsive reactions as well as with more complex behavior patterns. More than this, we should also be able to specify the conditions under which the various behavior determinants increase or decrease in importance.

The senior author has long contended that many aggressive actions are controlled by the stimulus properties of the available targets rather than by anticipations of ends that might be served (Berkowitz, 1962, 1964, 1965). Perhaps because strong emotion results in an increasing utilization of only the central cues in the immediate situation (Easterbrook, 1959; Walters & Parke, 1964), anger arousal can lead to impulsive, aggressive responses which, for a short time at least may be relatively free of cognitively mediated inhibitions against aggression or, for that matter, purposes and strategic considerations.[2] This impulsive action is not necessarily pushed out by the anger, however. Berkowitz has suggested that appropriate cues must be present in the situation if aggressive responses are actually to occur. While there is still considerable uncertainty as to just what characteristics define aggressive cue properties, the association of a stimulus with aggression evidently can enhance the aggressive cue value of this stimulus. But whatever its exact genesis, the cue (which may be either in the external environment or represented internally) presumably elicits the aggressive response. Anger (or any other conjectured aggressive "drive") increases the person's reactivity to the cue, possibly energizes the response, and may lower the likelihood of competing reactions, but is not necessary for the production of aggressive behavior.[3]

A variety of observations can be cited in support of this reasoning (cf. Berkowitz, 1965). Thus, the senior author has proposed that some of the effects of observed violence can readily be understood in terms of stimulus-elicited aggression. According to several Wisconsin experiments, observed aggression is particularly likely to produce strong attacks against anger instigators who are associated with the victim of the witnessed violence

[2] Cognitive processes can play a part even in impulsive behavior, most notably by influencing the stimulus qualities (or meaning) of the objects in the situation. As only one illustration, in several experiments by the senior author (cf. Berkowitz, 1965) the name applied to the available target person affected the magnitude of the attacks directed against this individual by angered subjects.

[3] Buss (1961) has advanced a somewhat similar conception of the functioning of anger.

(Berkowitz & Geen, 1966, 1967; Geen & Berkowitz, 1966). The frustrater's association with the observed victim presumably enhances his cue value for aggression, causing him to evoke stronger attacks from the person who is ready to act aggressively.

More direct evidence for the present formulation can be found in a study conducted by Loew (1965). His subjects, in being required to learn a concept, either aggressive or nature words, spoke either 20 aggressive or 20 neutral words aloud. Following this "learning task," each subject was to give a peer in an adjacent room an electric shock whenever this person made a mistake in his learning problem. Allowed to vary the intensity of the shocks they administered over a 10-point continuum, the subjects who had uttered the aggressive words gave shocks of significantly greater intensity than did the subjects who had spoken the neutral words. The aggressive words had evidently evoked implicit aggressive responses from the subjects, even though they had not been angered beforehand, which then led to the stronger attacks upon the target person in the next room when he supposedly made errors.

Cultural learning shared by many members of a society can also associate external objects with aggression and thus affect the objects' aggressive cue value. Weapons are a prime example. For many men (and probably women as well) in our society, these objects are closely associated with aggression. Assuming that the weapons do not produce inhibitions that are stronger than the evoked aggressive reactions (as would be the case, e.g., if the weapons were labeled as morally "bad"), the presence of the aggressive objects should generally lead to more intense attacks upon an available target than would occur in the presence of a neutral object.

The present experiment was designed to test this latter hypothesis. At one level, of course, the findings contribute to the current debate as to the desirability of restricting sales of firearms. Many arguments have been raised for such a restriction. Thus, according to recent statistics, Texas communities having virtually no prohibitions against firearms have a much higher homicide rate than other American cities possessing stringent firearm regulations, and J. Edgar Hoover has maintained in *Time* magazine that the availability of firearms is an important factor in murders (Anonymous, 1966). The experiment reported here seeks to determine how this influence may come about. The availability of weapons obviously makes it easier for a person who wants to commit murder to do so. But, in addition, we ask whether weapons can serve as aggression-eliciting stimuli, causing an angered individual to display stronger violence than he would have shown in the absence of such weapons. Social significance aside, and at a more general theoretical level, this research also attempts to demonstrate that situational stimuli can exert "automatic" control over socially relevant human actions.

METHOD

Subjects

The subjects were 100 male undergraduates enrolled in the introductory psychology course at the University of Wisconsin who volunteered for the experiment (without knowing its nature) in order to earn points counting toward their final grade. Thirty-nine other subjects had also been run, but were discarded because they suspected the experimenter's confederate (21), reported receiving fewer electric shocks than was actually given them (7), had not attended to information given them about the procedure (9), or were run while there was equipment malfunctioning (2).

Procedure

General Design. Seven experimental conditions were established, six organized in a 2×3 factorial design, with the seventh group serving essentially as a control. Of the men in the factorial design, half were made to be angry with the confederate, while the other subjects received a friendlier treatment from him. All of the subjects were then given an opportunity to administer electric shocks to the confederate, but for two-thirds of the men there were weapons lying on the table near the shock apparatus. Half of these people were informed the weapons belonged to the confederate in order to test the hypothesis that aggressive stimuli which also were associated with the anger instigator would evoke the strongest aggressive reaction from the subjects. The other people seeing the weapons were told the weapons had been left there by a previous experimenter. There was nothing on the table except the shock key when the last third of the subjects in both the angered and nonangered conditions gave the shocks. Finally, the seventh group consisted of angered men who gave shocks with two badminton racquets and shuttlecocks lying near the shock key. This condition sought to determine whether the presence of *any* object near the shock apparatus would reduce inhibitions against aggression, even if the object were not connected with aggressive behavior.

Experimental Manipulations. When each subject arrived in the laboratory, he was informed that two men were required for the experiment and that they would have to wait for the second subject to appear. After a 5-minute wait, the experimenter, acting annoyed, indicated that they had to begin because of his other commitments. He said he would have to look around outside to see if he could find another person who might serve as a substitute for the missing subject. In a few minutes the experimenter returned with the confederate. Depending upon the condition, this person was introduced as either a psychology student who had been about to sign up for another experiment or as a student who had been running another study.

The subject and confederate were told the experiment was a study of physiological reactions to stress. The stress would be created by mild electric shocks, and the subjects could withdraw, the experimenter said, if they objected to these shocks. (No subjects left.) Each person would have to solve a problem knowing that his performance would be evaluated by his partner. The "evaluations" would be in the form of electric shocks, with one shock signifying a very good rating and 10 shocks meaning the performance was judged as very bad. The men were then told what their problems were. The subject's task was to list ideas a publicity agent might employ in order to better a popular singer's record sales and public image. The other person (the confederate) had to think of things a used-car dealer might do in order to increase sales. The two were given 5 minutes to write their answers, and the papers were then collected by the experimenter who supposedly would exchange them.

Following this, the two were placed in separate rooms, supposedly so that they would not influence each other's galvanic skin response (GSR) reactions. The shock electrodes were placed on the subject's right forearm, and GSR electrodes were attached to fingers on his left hand, with wires trailing from the electrodes to the next room. The subject was told he would be the first to receive electric shocks as the evaluation of his problem solution. The experimenter left the subject's room saying he was going to turn on the GSR apparatus, went to the room containing the shock machine and the waiting confederate, and only then looked at the schedule indicating whether the subject was to be angered or not. He informed the confederate how many shocks the subject was to receive, and 30 seconds later the subject was given seven shocks (angered condition) or one shock (nonangered group). The experimenter then went back to the subject, while the confederate quickly arranged the table holding the shock key in the manner appropriate for the subject's condition. Upon entering the subject's room, the experimenter asked him how many shocks he had received and provided the subject with a brief questionnaire on which he was to rate his mood. As soon as this was completed, the subject was taken to the room holding the shock machine. Here the experimenter told the subject it was his turn to evaluate his partner's work. For one group in both the angered and nonangered conditions the shock key was alone on the table (no-object groups). For two other groups in each of these angered and nonangered conditions, however, a 12-gauge shotgun and a 38-caliber revolver were lying on the table near the key (aggressive-weapon conditions). One group in both the angered and nonangered conditions was informed the weapons belonged to the subject's partner. The subjects given this treatment had been told earlier that their partner was a student who had been conducting an experiment.[5] They now were reminded of this, and the experimenter said the weapons were being used in some way by this person in his research (associated-weapons condition); the guns were to be disregarded. The other men were told simply the weapons "belong to someone else" who "must have been doing an experiment in here" (unassociated-weapons group), and they too were asked to disregard the guns. For the last treatment, one group of angered men found two badminton racquets and shuttlecocks lying on the table near the shock key, and these people were also told the equipment belonged to someone else (badminton-racquets group).

Immediately after this information was provided, the experimenter showed the subject what was supposedly his partner's answer to his assigned problem. The subject was reminded that he was to give the partner shocks as his evaluation and was informed that this was the last time shocks would be administered in the study. A second copy of the mood questionnaire was then completed by the subject after he had delivered the shocks. Following this, the subject was asked a number of oral questions about the experiment, including what, if any, suspicions he had. (No doubts were voiced about the presence of the weapons.) At the conclusion of this interview the experiment was explained, and the subject was asked not to talk about the study.

Dependent Variables

As in nearly all the experiments conducted in the senior author's program, the number of shocks given by the subjects serves as the primary aggression measure. However, we also report here findings obtained with the total duration of each subject's shocks, recorded in thousandths of a minute. Attention is also given to each subject's

[5] This information evidently was the major source of suspicion; some of the subjects doubted that a student running an experiment would be used as a subject in another study, even if he were only an undergraduate. This information was provided only in the associated-weapons conditions, in order to connect the guns with the partner, and, consequently, this ground for suspicion was not present in the unassociated-weapons groups.

rating of his mood, first immediately after receiving the partner's evaluation, and again immediately after administering shocks to the partner. These ratings were made on a series of 10 13-point bipolar scales with an adjective at each end, such as "calm-tense" and "angry-not angry."

RESULTS

Effectiveness of Arousal Treatment

Analyses of variance of the responses to each of the mood scales following the receipt of the partner's evaluation indicate the prior-shock treatment succeeded in creating differences in anger arousal. The subjects getting seven shocks rated themselves as being significantly angrier than the subjects receiving only one shock ($F = 20.65$, $p < .01$). There were no reliable differences among the groups within any one arousal level. Interestingly enough, the only other mood scale to yield a significant effect was the scale "sad-happy." The aroused–seven-shocks men reported a significantly stronger felt sadness than the men getting one shock ($F = 4.63$, $p > .05$).

Aggression toward Partner

A preliminary analysis of variance of the shock data for the six groups in the 3×2 factorial design yielded the findings shown in Table 1. As is indicated by the significant interaction, the presence of the weapons significantly affected the number of shocks given by the subject when the subject had received seven shocks. A Duncan multiple-range test was then made of the differences among the seven conditions means, using the error variance from a seven-group one-way analysis of variance in the error term. The mean number of shocks administered in each experimental condition and the Duncan test results are given in Table 2. The hypothesis guiding the present study receives good support. The strongly provoked men delivered more frequent electrical attacks upon their tormentor in the presence of a weapon than when nonaggressive objects (the badminton racquets and shuttlecocks) were present or when only the shock key was on the table. The angered subjects gave the greatest number of shocks in the presence of the weapons associated with the anger instigator, as pre-

TABLE 1

Analysis of Variance Results for Number of Shocks Given by Subjects in Factorial Design

Source	df	MS	F
No. shocks received (A)	1	182.04	104.62*
Weapons association (B)	2	1.90	1.09
A × B	2	8.73	5.02*
Error	84	1.74	

* $p < .01$.

TABLE 2

*Mean Number of Shocks Given in Each Condition**

Condition	Shocks received	
	1	7
Associated weapons	2.60$_a$	6.07$_d$
Unassociated weapons	2.20$_a$	5.67$_{cd}$
No object	3.07$_a$	4.67$_{bc}$
Badminton racquets	—	4.60$_b$

* Cells having a common subscript are not significantly different at the .05 level by Duncan multiple-range test. There were 10 subjects in the seven-shocks-received–badminton-racquets group and 15 subjects in each of the other conditions.

dicted, but this group was not reliably different from the angered–unassociated-weapons conditions. Both of these groups expressing aggression in the presence of weapons were significantly more aggressive than the angered–neutral-object condition, but only the associated-weapons condition differed significantly from the angered–no-object group.

Some support for the present reasoning is also provided by the shock-duration data summarized in Table 3. (We might note here, before beginning, that the results with duration scores—and this has been a consistent finding in the present research program—are less clear-cut than the findings with number of shocks given.) The results indicate that the presence of weapons resulted in a decreased number of attacks upon the partner, although not significantly so, when the subjects had received only one shock beforehand. The condition differences are in the opposite direction, however, for the men given the stronger provocation. Consequently, even though there are no reliable differences among the groups in this angered condition, the angered men administering shocks in the presence

TABLE 3

*Mean Total Duration of Shocks Given in Each Condition**

Condition	Shocks received	
	1	7
Associated weapons	17.93$_c$	46.93$_a$
Unassociated weapons	17.33$_c$	39.47$_{ab}$
No object	24.47$_{bc}$	34.80$_{ab}$
Badminton racquets	—	34.90$_{ab}$

* The duration scores are in thousandths of a minute. Cells having a common subscript are not significantly different at the .05 level by Duncan multiple-range test. There were 10 subjects in the seven-shocks-received–badminton-racquet group and 15 subjects in each of the other conditions.

of weapons gave significantly longer shocks than the nonangered men also giving shocks with guns lying on the table. The angered–neutral-object and angered–no-object groups, on the other hand, did not differ from the nonangered–no-object condition.

Mood Changes

Analyses of covariance were conducted on each of the mood scales, with the mood ratings made immediately after the subjects received their partners' evaluation held constant in order to determine if there were condition differences in mood changes following the giving of shocks to the partner. Duncan range tests of the adjusted condition means yielded negative results, suggesting that the attacks on the partner did not produce any systematic condition differences. In the case of the felt anger ratings, there were very high correlations between the ratings given before and after the shock administration, with the Pearson rs ranging from .89 in the angered–unassociated-weapons group to .99 in each of the three unangered conditions. The subjects could have felt constrained to repeat their initial responses.

Discussion

Common sense, as well as a good deal of personality theorizing, both influenced to some extent by an egocentric view of human behavior as being caused almost exclusively by motives within the individual, generally neglect the type of weapons effect demonstrated in the present study. If a person holding a gun fires it, we are told either that he wanted to do so (consciously or unconsciously) or that he pulled the trigger "accidentally." The findings summarized here suggest yet another possibility: The presence of the weapon might have elicited an intense aggressive reaction from the person with the gun, assuming his inhibitions against aggression were relatively weak at the moment. Indeed, it is altogether conceivable that many hostile acts which supposedly stem from unconscious motivation really arise because of the operation of aggressive cues. Not realizing how these situational stimuli might elicit aggressive behavior, and not detecting the presence of these cues, the observer tends to locate the source of the action in some conjectured underlying, perhaps repressed, motive. Similarly, if he is a Skinnerian rather than a dynamically oriented clinician, he might also neglect the operation of aggression-eliciting stimuli by invoking the concept of operant behavior, and thus sidestep the issue altogether. The sources of the hostile action, for him, too, rest within the individual, with the behavior only steered or permitted by discriminative stimuli.

Alternative explanations must be ruled out, however, before the present thesis can be regarded as confirmed. One obvious possibility is that the subjects in the weapons condition reacted to the demand characteristics of the situation as they saw them and exhibited the kind of behavior they thought was required of them. ("These guns on the table mean I'm supposed to be aggressive, so I'll give many shocks.") Several considerations appear to negate this explanation. First, there are the subjects' own verbal reports. None of the subjects voiced any suspicions of the weapons and, furthermore, when they were queried generally denied that the weapons had any effect on them. But even those subjects who did express any doubts about the experiment typically acted like the other subjects. Thus, the eight nonangered-weapons subjects who had been rejected gave only 2.50 shocks on the average, while the 18 angered–no-object or neutral-object men who had been discarded had a mean of 4.50 shocks. The 12 angered-weapons subjects who had been rejected, by contrast, delivered an average of 5.83 shocks to their partner. These latter people were evidently also influenced by the presence of weapons.

Setting all this aside, moreover, it is not altogether certain from the notion of demand characteristics that only the angered subjects would be inclined to act in conformity with the experimenter's supposed demands. The nonangered men in the weapons group did not display a heightened number of attacks on their partner. Would this have been predicted beforehand by researchers interested in demand characteristics? The last finding raises one final observation. Recent unpublished research by Allen and Bragg indicates that awareness of the experimenter's purpose does not necessarily result in an increased display of the behavior the experimenter supposedly desires. Dealing with one kind of socially disapproved action (conformity), Allen and Bragg demonstrated that high levels of experimentally induced awareness of the experimenter's interests generally produced a decreased level of the relevant behavior. Thus, if the subjects in our study had known the experimenter was interested in observing their *aggressive* behavior, they might well have given less, rather than more, shocks, since giving shocks is also socially disapproved. This type of phenomenon was also not observed in the weapons conditions.

Nevertheless, any one experiment cannot possibly definitely exclude all of the alternative explanations. Scientific hypotheses are only probability statements, and further research is needed to heighten the likelihood that the present reasoning is correct.

REFERENCES

Anonymous. A gun-toting nation. *Time*, August 12, 1966.
Berkowitz, L. *Aggression: A social psychological analysis.* New York: McGraw-Hill, 1962.
Berkowitz, L. Aggressive cues in aggressive behavior and hostility catharsis. *Psychological Review*, 1964, **71**, 104–122.
Berkowitz, L. The concept of aggressive drive: Some additional considerations. In L. Berkowitz (Ed.), *Advances in experimental social psychology.* Vol. 2. New York: Academic Press, 1965. Pp. 301–329.

Berkowitz, L., & Geen, R. G. Film violence and the cue properties of available targets. *Journal of Personality and Social Psychology*, 1966, 3, 525–530.

Berkowitz, L., & Geen, R. G. Stimulus qualities of the target of aggression: A further study. *Journal of Personality and Social Psychology*, 1967, 5, 364–368.

Buss, A. *The psychology of aggression*. New York: Wiley, 1961.

Easterbrook, J. A. The effect of emotion on cue utilization and the organization of behavior. *Psychological Review*, 1959, 66, 183–201.

Geen, R. G., & Berkowitz, L. Name-mediated aggressive cue properties. *Journal of Personality*, 1966, 34, 456–465.

Loew, C. A. Acquisition of a hostile attitude and its relationship to aggressive behavior. Unpublished doctoral dissertation, State University of Iowa, 1965.

Walters, R. H., & Parke, R. D. Social motivation, dependency, and susceptibility to social influence. In L. Berkowitz (Ed.), *Advances in experimental social psychology*. Vol. 1. New York: Academic Press, 1964. Pp. 231–276.

Chapter 10

CONFORMITY

The study of conformity is obviously closely related to the study of attitude change. Historically, however, conformity and attitude change have represented two quasi-distinct research traditions and, for that reason, are treated separately in this book. But how do the fields of attitude change and conformity differ? There are at least three ways. First, the field of attitude change includes both social and nonsocial influence, while the field of conformity includes only social influence. (An example of nonsocial influence is the choice-produced "spreading apart of the alternatives.") Second, the field of attitude change puts relatively greater emphasis upon affective and cognitive change and relatively less emphasis upon behavioral change, while the field of conformity puts relatively greater emphasis upon behavioral change and relatively less emphasis upon affective and cognitive change. Thus an investigation of the number of people who cross the street against a red light after a confederate crossed the street is considered a study of conformity, not attitude change. In such an investigation be-

315

havioral change is more apparent than is affective and cognitive change. Third and finally, the field of conformity only includes social influence that reduces the total variability among initial positions, while this is not the case for the field of attitude change. An investigation of boomerang effects, or change opposite to the direction of influence, would not be considered an example of conformity.

The historical separation of research on conformity and attitude change should not be taken to mean that the areas are divided by an eternally fixed gulf. It is quite probable that future theoretical developments will result in a merging of these two traditions.

Before discussing some theoretical ideas regarding conformity, we will consider some of the research procedures that have been used to demonstrate the existence of conformity.

Experimental Techniques or Situations for the Demonstration of Conformity

THE SOCIAL FACILITATION TECHNIQUE

One of the earliest problems, if not the earliest, to attract the attention of experimental social psychologists relates to the difference in performance between individuals working alone and in the presence of others. The effect of the group upon the individual's performance has been labeled social facilitation. Floyd Allport (1920) had subjects either work alone or in the presence of two to four other individuals who were seated around the same table. All responses were written and there was no verbal communication among group members regarding the various assigned tasks (making free-associations, writing arguments, cancelling letters, solving multiplication problems, judging odors, etc.). The results were generally interpreted as indicating that "social influence was found to improve the quantity, but not the quality of the mental performance." For example, when working in the presence of others the written arguments contained more words but were of a "lower logical value." Free associations given in the presence of others were more numerous, but also more common and thus less personal or idiosyncratic.

In a well-known further study of the social facilitation phenomenon Dashiell (1930) found that individuals who are not in the actual physical presence of others, but who are working simultaneously with others in different rooms and who are signalled by a buzzer controlled at a common center, show an increase in speed and a decrease in accuracy (on multiplication problems, for example) much as do individuals who are in the actual physical presence of others. Dashiell interpreted his results as indicating that the knowledge that others are also working creates "social attitudes" in the individual.

More contemporary research (Henchy & Glass, 1968) provides evidence that the social facilitation phenomenon may be at least partially a function of evaluation apprehension, that is, the feeling that one's responses are to be evaluated by someone else.

The research on facilitation is concerned with conformity because it has shown how the presence of others decreases variability. Recall that one of the findings of this research is a decrease in the number of idiosyncratic or personal type responses and an increase in more common responses.

SHERIF'S AUTOKINETIC SITUATION

If a pinpoint of light is viewed in an otherwise completely dark room, the light will appear to move. This illusory effect, known as the autokinetic phenomenon, was utilized by Sherif (1935) in an early study of conformity. Subjects were asked to judge the extent of movement in a supposedly moving, but actually stationary, light. On any given trial as soon as movement was perceived the subject pressed a key which turned the light off. When a group of subjects viewed the light together the light was, of course, turned off by the fastest acting subject. After the light was turned off the subjects orally reported the extent of movement in inches. (Subjects evidently adapt to a common time interval for experiencing the movement.) Sherif found that when subjects viewed the light in groups there was a gradual convergence toward an agreed upon extent of movement. Furthermore, when the individuals in the groups were later tested alone they continued giving the group-established judgments. According to Sherif each group formulated a norm regarding the extent of movement.

THE ASCH SITUATION

Perhaps the most influential series of studies on conformity were carried out by Asch (1952). In an initial study a group of eight individuals, all but one of whom were confederates, was instructed to make a series of 18 simple and obvious judgments. On each trial the task was to match the length of a standard line with one of three comparison lines. For each trial, judgments were publicly announced in the order in which the group members sat, and the single naive subjects always sat next to last. On 12 of the trials the seven stooges responded incorrectly. The results indicated that on these 12 critical trials approximately one-third of the subjects' judgments were errors identical with, or in the direction of, the majority and approximately two-thirds of the judgments were correct. At the same time there were rather sizable individual differences. One-fourth of the subjects were completely independent, or not influenced on any of the 12 trials, while one-third were influenced on half or more of the trials.

On the basis of observation and postexperimental interviews Asch distinguished among three types of independent subjects and three types of conforming subjects. The types of independent subjects were: (1) those who responded with confidence and vigor; (2) those who were withdrawn and unemotional; (3) those who manifested considerable tension and doubt. The types of conforming subjects were: (1) those who actually *perceived* the lines in accordance with the erroneous majority; (2) those who did not perceive the lines in accordance with the majority but felt that the *judgment* of their own perceptions was somehow in error; (3) those who did not suffer a distortion in perception or judgment, but who conformed in order not to appear different from the group. As Asch recognized, interview data are not the firmest basis for establishing these various categories, but his suggestions are nonetheless quite provocative. Unfortunately, those suggestions have been ignored by subsequent investigators.

In further research Asch found that the conformity effect was maximized with a majority of three. Further increases in the majority size up to 15 persons did not increase the effect. When the majority was reduced to two, the percentage of errors dropped from 33 to 13, and when the opposition was reduced to one the conformity effect all but disappeared. Asch also reports that when a single stooge responded incorrectly in a large group of naive subjects his judgments created amusement and laughter. Asch notes that the subjects' reactions would radically change if they faced the dissenter alone.

Finally, Asch reports a series of studies in which one of the eight stooges responded correctly on some or all of the trials. This stooge always sat in the fourth position. When the stooge opposed the incorrect majority on all of the trials the amount of conformity dropped dramatically to 6 percent. When the stooge in fourth position changed to responding incorrectly, after initially responding correctly, the amount of conformity increased to 28 percent. When the stooge changed to responding correctly, after initially responding incorrectly, the amount of conformity dropped to 9 percent. These results illustrate the dramatic effect that may be produced in a group's impact by one lone dissenter.

THE CRUTCHFIELD TECHNIQUE

Crutchfield (1955) modified Asch's procedure so that no confederates would be needed. Five naive subjects sat in individual cubicles before separate electrical panels of switches and lights. Instead of verbally announcing judgments, subjects threw an appropriate switch. Each subject was led to believe that the lights which flashed on in succession in his or her panel indicated the judgments of the other subjects. These lights were actually rigged by the experimenter, however, so as to indicate unanimous correct or incorrect judgments. The stimulus material for judging (length of lines, areas of figures, logical completion of number series, vocabulary items, personal preference for line drawings, etc.) was projected on the wall with a slide projector. There were 21 critical slides in which the group consensus was simulated as incorrect. Interpolated among these critical slides or trials were occasional ones in which the group consensus was simulated as correct.

Crutchfield reports that on only two of the critical slides were there insignificant conformity effects; 19 slides showed significant conformity effects. Crutchfield's main orientation, however, was toward the study of individual differences. He reports, for example, that intelligence correlated negatively with conformity and that female college students conformed more than male college students.

In a well-known study Deutsch and Gerard (1955) found that conformity in a "face-to-face" situation, like that used by Asch, is greater than conformity in an "anonymous" situation, like that used by Crutchfield. Deutsch and Gerard distinguished between two types of social influence, *normative* and *informational*. Normative social influence is ". . . influence to conform with the positive expectations of another," and informational social influence is ". . . influence to accept information obtained from another as *evidence* about reality" (1955, p. 629). According to Deutsch and Gerard a face-to-face conformity situation has greater normative social influence than does an anonymous conformity situation. Deutsch and Gerard, however, did demonstrate that conformity in an anonymous situation increases if the group members feel that they are competing with other groups. The group making the fewest errors was to win tickets to a Broadway play. Presumably the competition produced more of a group feeling and hence more normative social influence.

MILGRAM'S CONFORMITY TO AUTHORITY SITUATION

One of the more recent investigations of conformity is the study by Milgram (1965) which is contained in the Readings section of this chapter. Milgram's experiment concerns the punishment of victims in obedience to the directions of an authority figure. In this study influence flowed from a legitimate authority, rather than a group.

NONLABORATORY SITUATIONS

There have been numerous studies demonstrating conformity effects in nonlaboratory situations. Without belaboring the point we can simply regard a nonlaboratory situation as any circumstance in which a subject is not aware that he is in an experiment. Whether the experiment is conducted indoors or outdoors is irrelevant. A whole series of such nonlaboratory studies were conducted in the 1950s by social psychologists at the University of Texas. For example, Lefkowitz, Blake, and Mouton (1955) studied the effect of two independent variables upon violation of a "wait" signal by pedestrians. One variable related to the behavior of a confederate (violation or nonviolation of the signal) and the other to the dress of the confederate (high or low status). The investigators found evidence for conformity to the confederate's violation behavior, particularly when he wore high-status clothes.

In a more recent nonlaboratory study Freedman and Fraser (1966) investigated what they refer to as the "foot-in-the-door" technique. They found that individuals who were initially asked eight innocuous questions regarding the household products that they used were more willing than individuals who were not so asked to agree to a subsequent request that a team of five or six men spend two hours enumerating the contents of their cupboards and storage places. Information was supposedly being collected for a "Guide" by the "California Consumers' Group." In a subsequent study Freedman and Fraser found that the two-request, or foot-in-the-door, technique increased compliance or conformity even if the person making the second request was different from the person making the first request and if the issues and tasks for the two requests were different. Thus individuals who initially received a request from one person to sign a petition urging legislation for keeping California beautiful, relative to individuals who did not receive such a request, were more willing to assent to a request from a second person to put up a large "Drive Carefully" sign in their front yard. Freedman and Fraser suggest that once compliance to the initial request occurred the subjects became in their own eyes ". . . the kind of person who does this sort of thing, who agrees to requests made by strangers, who takes action on things he believes in, who cooperates with good causes" (1966, p. 201). Freedman and Fraser also speculate that when two requests regarding similar issues are made, involvement with the issue may be an additional factor producing compliance.

Why Does Conformity Occur?

The previous discussion of experimental techniques and situations for studying conformity make it abundantly obvious that conformity is a genuine and pervasive aspect of social interaction—if there was ever any doubt about that in the first place. The more fundamental question is thus not "Does conformity occur?" but rather "Why does conformity occur?" The bulk of the conformity research, however, has been directed more toward the first than the second question. Fewer experiments have been directed toward the test of hypotheses or theories concerning why conformity occurs. This does not mean, however, that no theories or hypotheses exist as to why conformity does occur. As a matter of fact, such exist in abundance.

There are two closely related, and yet different, approaches to the problem of why conformity occurs. One approach is to inquire why it is that a group exerts conformity pressures on its members. The other approach is to inquire about the factors, circumstances, or motives within the individual group member that bring about conformity. We will consider these matters in turn.

WHY DOES A GROUP EXERT CONFORMITY PRESSURES UPON ITS MEMBERS

Groups exert real conformity pressures on their members. Such pressures are readily documented in two experiments, one by Schachter (1951) and one by Freedman and Doob (1968).

In Schachter's experiment newly formed clubs were asked to discuss and come to a consensus regarding the treatment of a delinquent boy. Since the case history indicated that the only time the boy had given any indication of improvement was when he was treated decently, the consensus in all groups was for treatment with love and understanding rather than with punishment. Schachter had one confederate in each group take this modal position and another take a deviant, or extreme punishment, position. Following the discussion, each person made written nominations for various committee assignments and also indicated which group members they would like to see remain together and which ones transferred to other clubs. Because the committees differed in desirability the nominations were considered a measure of attraction. The results indicated that the deviant stooge was undernominated for the more prestigious "Executive Committee" and overnominated for the less prestigious "Correspondence Committee," while this was not the case for the modal stooge. The second assessment indicated that the group members were more likely to reject the deviant stooge than the modal stooge. Examination of the communication patterns in the group revealed an interesting tendency for more and more of the communication to be directed toward the deviant stooge, with a tendency to decline during the final period for some groups.

Still more evidence concerning the treatment of deviants comes from some research by Freedman and Doob (1968). Groups of five to six subjects completed a series of five personality tests. During the course of the experiment the group members sat in separate cubicles. Following completion of the first test the second test was distributed. Following completion of the second test the third test along with the results of the first test were distributed. This general procedure was followed through the fifth test. After finishing the fifth test the subjects waited, without talking, until this test could be scored and the results shown to them. Along with the results of the fifth test the subjects were also shown a summary sheet of all five tests. What was actually measured by any of the tests was not revealed to the subjects. The results for any given subject simply pictured the position of each group member along some unlabeled dimension. For "nondeviant" subjects the feedback from all five tests indicated their scores were always near the middle of the dimensions along with the scores of all but one of the remaining group members. One member of the group was consistently described as scoring at the extreme ends of the various personality dimensions, or as being deviant. For "deviant" subjects the feedback from all five tests indicated that their scores, as well as the scores of one other subject, were always extremely deviant from the middle scores of the remaining group members. Thus subjects were made to feel either deviant or nondeviant, and from the perspective of each subject the remaining group members consisted of one deviant and a number of nondeviants. Following the above manipulations the subjects, female high-school students, were told that for the second part of the study one of them would be taking a free-association test. This test was made to appear either pleasant or unpleasant. In the pleasant condition the person taking the test was to receive $2.50; in the unpleasant condition the person taking the test was to receive a moderately painful electric shock every time the group judged a response to be bad. The experimenter explained that he did not care who took the free-association test and therefore he would let the group decide. Each subject thus ranked the group members in terms of order of choice for the job. The results indicated that the nondeviants tended to choose deviants for the unpleasant task and nondeviants for the pleasant task, while deviants tended to choose nondeviants for the unpleasant task and deviants for the pleasant task.

There are at least four possible explanations as to why groups exert conformity pressures on their members.

Frustration-Aggression Hypothesis

According to Dollard *et al.* (1939) frustration-produced aggression may be displaced to weak or defenseless individuals who are unable to retaliate. Since deviants are in a minority, they are thus likely targets or "scapegoats" for such displaced aggression.

Group Locomotion Hypothesis

A second basis for conformity pressure is provided by Festinger's (1950) group locomotion hypothesis. Festinger maintains that one of the factors producing conformity pressures is the facilitation of the group's movement or locomotion toward some goal. There are many situations in which continued deviancy is disruptive of the group's completion of its task.

Social Comparison Theory

A third basis for conformity is the social comparison theory implication (Festinger, 1950, 1954) that group members exert conformity pressures in order to maintain social reality. According to social comparison theory, deviancy destroys the social reality that allows for the validation of opinions and thus the maintenance of a positive self-evaluation.

Balance Theory

A fourth and final basis for conformity pressure is the balance theory implication that consistency, or balance, is created by the directing of negative sentiment toward different, or deviant, individuals and the directing of positive sentiment toward similar, or conforming, individuals.

WHAT ARE THE FACTORS, CIRCUMSTANCES, OR MOTIVES WITHIN THE INDIVIDUAL GROUP MEMBER THAT BRING ABOUT CONFORMITY?

There are at least five possible answers to this question. The first of these flows from three of the theoretical positions (group locomotion hypothesis, social comparison theory, balance theory) used to account for group conformity pressure.

Group Locomotion Hypothesis

To the extent that the individual group member, first, wishes the group to achieve its goal and, second, believes that his conformity will facilitate such achievement, he should be internally motivated to conform.

Social Comparison Theory

Although social comparison theory has mainly been used to explain why a group exerts conformity pressures, it does have implications regarding the group members' internally motivated impetus toward conformity. By conforming an individual may restore the social reality that would then serve to validate his opinions and thus maintain his own positive self-evaluation.

Balance Theory

To the extent that the individual group member is attracted to the group he should be motivated to be similar to, or conform to, the group in order to achieve consistency or balance.

Epistemological Weighting Hypothesis

Campbell (1961) has advanced what we may call an epistemological weighting hypothesis regarding conformity. According to Campbell, knowledge may be acquired through either personal or social modes. The personal mode includes blind trial and error, and perceptual observation of inanimate objects and their relationships. The social mode includes perceptual observations of other people's behavior, and linguistic instruction regarding objects and appropriate responses to these objects. From this perspective conformity experiments, such as the previously described one by Asch (1952), pit the personal mode of knowledge acquisition against the social mode of knowledge acquisition. Campbell thus maintains that *"Differences in the degree of conformity are differences in the degree to which the different modes . . . are weighted in achieving a composite"* (1961, p. 108). From this perspective, then, the factor determining an individual's conformity is the relative weights given to the personal and social modes of knowledge acquisition.

Campbell's epistemological weighting hypothesis in some respects captures the essence of conformity. Campbell argues, however, that not all conformity can be explained as the resolution of the conflict between personal and social modes of knowledge acquisition. In some instances conformity may simply occur because of the rewards of conformity and the costs of nonconformity. Campbell refers to and agrees with Deutsch and Gerard's (1955) above-described distinction between informational and normative influence. Normative social influence is ". . . influence to conform with the positive expectations of another," and informational social influence is ". . . influence to accept information obtained from another as *evidence* about reality" (1955, p. 629). The epistemological weighting hypothesis is, of course, most directly concerned with informational influence.

Allen (1965) has approached the distinction between informational and normative social influence from a somewhat different perspective. He categorizes conformity into four types: (a) public conformity and private agreement, (b) public conformity and private disagreement, (c) public nonconformity and private agreement, (d) public nonconformity and private disagreement. According to Allen ". . . informational influence would be more likely to lead to public conformity with private change than would normative influence" (1965, p. 138). Conversely, a lack of informational influence would, in the absence of any other influence, lead to public nonconformity and private disagreement. Thus Campbell's epistemological weighting hypothesis is more concerned with situations in which public behavior and private acceptance are the same (a, d) rather than different (b, c).

The Hedonistic Hypothesis

According to the hedonistic hypothesis an individual conforms in order to avoid ostracism, censure, or rejection and to achieve acceptance, approval, or positive regard. This hypothesis gains plausibility in view of existing evidence that, in many instances, conformity does, in fact, result in the achievement of benefit and the avoidance of difficulty. The previously described experiments by Schachter (1951) and Freedman and Doob (1968) regarding the treatment of deviants provide good examples.

Thibaut and Kelley (1959) have elaborated the hedonistic hypothesis into what is called an exchange theory of social groups. In Chapter 11 we will consider this theory in detail in an attempt to gain a theoretical grasp of norms. For now we will merely point out that Thibaut and Kelley analyze conformity in terms of the application of negative sanctions (punishments) and positive sanctions (rewards). In order for one person to use negative sanctions to control another person's behavior this behavior must be monitored. Negative sanctions most obviously result in public conformity and minimal private acceptance. The use of positive sanctions, on the other hand, does not require monitoring. The reward is delivered whenever the individual presents evidence of his conformity to the influencing agent. Thibaut and Kelley further imply that positive sanctions are more likely than negative sanctions to result in private acceptance of the influence.

Overview

We have reviewed four possible explanations as to why a group exerts conformity pressures on its members (frustration aggression hypothesis, group locomotion hypothesis, social comparison theory, balance theory), and five explanations as to the factors, circumstances, or motives within the individual group member that bring about conformity (group locomotion hypothesis, social comparison theory, balance theory, epistemological weighting hypothesis, hedonistic hypothesis). Although no claim is made as to the exhaustiveness of the above list, the described theories and hypotheses do represent the more salient explanatory possibilities. Since research has been directed more toward the demonstration of conformity than toward the explanation for its occurrence, it would be premature to select any of these theories or hypotheses as the single, most adequate explanation.

READINGS

Some Conditions of Obedience and Disobedience to Authority

Stanley Milgram[1,2]

The situation in which one agent commands another to hurt a third turns up time and again as a significant theme in human relations. It is powerfully expressed in the story of Abraham, who is commanded by God to kill his son. It is no accident that Kierkegaard, seeking to orient his thought to the central themes of human experience, chose Abraham's conflict as the springboard to his philosophy.

War too moves forward on the triad of an authority which commands a person to destroy the enemy, and perhaps all organized hostility may be viewed as a theme and variation on the three elements of authority, executant, and victim.[3] We describe an experimental program, recently

[1] From *Human Relations,* Volume 18, pages 57–76, 1965. Stanley Milgram conducted cross-national experiments in the Institute for Social Research, Oslo, and the Laboratoire de Psychologie Sociale, Sorbonne, in 1957–59. He spent a year at the Institute for Advanced Study, Princeton, and received a Ph.D. in Social Psychology from Harvard University in 1960. He completed the experiments described here while an assistant professor of psychology at Yale University. Subsequently, he joined the Department of Social Relations faculty at Harvard, where he teaches experimental social psychology.

The present paper was awarded the Socio-Psychological Prize of the American Association for the Advancement of Science in 1964.

[2] This research was supported by two grants from the National Science Foundation: NSF G-17916 and NSF G-24152. Exploratory studies carried out in 1960 were financed by a grant from the Higgins Funds of Yale University. I am grateful to John T. Williams, James J. McDonough, and Emil Elges for the important part they played in the project. Thanks are due to Alan Elms, James Miller, Taketo Murata, and Stephen Stier for their aid as graduate assistants. My wife, Sasha, performed many valuable services. Finally, I owe a profound debt to the many persons in New Haven and Bridgeport who served as subjects.

[3] Consider, for example, J. P. Scott's analysis of war in his monograph on aggression:

> . . . while the actions of key individuals in a war may be explained in terms of direct stimulation to aggression, vast numbers of other people are involved simply by being part of an organized society.
>
> . . . For example, at the beginning of World War I an Austrian archduke was assassinated in Sarajevo. A few days later soldiers from all over Europe were marching toward each other, not because they were stimulated by the archduke's misfortune, but because they had been trained to obey orders. [Slightly rearranged from Scott (1958), *Aggression,* p. 103.]

327

concluded at Yale University, in which a particular expression of this conflict is studied by experimental means.

In its most general form the problem may be defined thus: if X tells Y to hurt Z, under what conditions will Y carry out the command of X and under what conditions will he refuse. In the more limited form possible in laboratory research, the question becomes: if an experimenter tells a subject to hurt another person, under what conditions will the subject go along with this instruction, and under what conditions will he refuse to obey. The laboratory problem is not so much a dilution of the general statement as one concrete expression of the many particular forms this question may assume.

One aim of the research was to study behavior in a strong situation of deep consequence to the participants, for the psychological forces operative in powerful and lifelike forms of the conflict may not be brought into play under diluted conditions.

This approach meant, first, that we had a special obligation to protect the welfare and dignity of the persons who took part in the study; subjects were, of necessity, placed in a difficult predicament, and steps had to be taken to ensure their well-being before they were discharged from the laboratory. Toward this end, a careful, postexperimental treatment was devised and has been carried through for subjects in all conditions.[4]

TERMINOLOGY

If Y follows the command of X we shall say that he has obeyed X; if he fails to carry out the command of X, we shall say that he has disobeyed X. The terms to obey and to disobey, as used here, refer to the subject's overt

---

[4] It consisted of an extended discussion with the experimenter and, of equal importance, a friendly reconciliation with the victim. It is made clear that the victim did not receive painful electric shocks. After the completion of the experimental series, subjects were sent a detailed report of the results and full purposes of the experimental program. A formal assessment of this procedure points to its overall effectiveness. Of the subjects, 83.7 percent indicated that they were glad to have taken part in the study; 15.1 percent reported neutral feelings; and 1.3 percent stated that they were sorry to have participated. A large number of subjects spontaneously requested that they be used in further experimentation. Four-fifths of the subjects felt that more experiments of this sort should be carried out, and 74 percent indicated that they had learned something of personal importance as a result of being in the study. Furthermore, a university psychiatrist, experienced in outpatient treatment, interviewed a sample of experimental subjects with the aim of uncovering possible injurious effects resulting from participation. No such effects were in evidence. Indeed, subjects typically felt that their participation was instructive and enriching. A more detailed discussion of this question can be found in Milgram (1964).

action only, and carry no implication for the motive or experiential states accompanying the action.[5]

To be sure, the everyday use of the word *obedience* is not entirely free from complexities. It refers to action within widely varying situations, and connotes diverse motives within those situations: a child's obedience differs from a soldier's obedience, or the love, honor, and *obey* of the marriage vow. However, a consistent behavioral relationship is indicated in most uses of the term: in the act of obeying, a person does what another person tells him to do. Y obeys X if he carries out the prescription for action which X has addressed to him; the term suggests, moreover, that some form of dominance-subordination, or hierarchical element, is part of the situation in which the transaction between X and Y occurs.

A subject who complies with the entire series of experimental commands will be termed an *obedient* subject; one who at any point in the command series defies the experimenter will be called a *disobedient* or *defiant* subject. As used in this report, the terms refer only to the subject's performance in the experiment, and do not necessarily imply a general personality disposition to submit to or reject authority.

---

[5] *To obey* and *to disobey* are not the only terms one could use in describing the critical action of Y. One could say that Y is cooperating with X, or displays conformity with regard to X's commands. However, *cooperation* suggests that X agrees with Y's ends, and understands the relationship between his own behavior and the attainment of those ends. (But the experimental procedure, and, in particular, the experimenter's command that the subject shock the victim even in the absence of a response from the victim, preclude such understanding.) Moreover, cooperation implies status parity for the co-acting agents, and neglects the asymmetrical, dominance-subordination element prominent in the laboratory relationship between experimenter and subject. *Conformity* has been used in other important contexts in social psychology, and most frequently refers to imitating the judgements or actions of others when no explicit requirement for imitation has been made. Furthermore, in the present study there are two sources of social pressure: pressure from the experimenter issuing the commands, and pressure from the victim to stop the punishment. It is the pitting of a common man (the victim) against an authority (the experimenter) that is the distinctive feature of the conflict. At a point in the experiment the victim demands that he be let free. The experimenter insists that the subject continue to administer shocks. Which act of the subject can be interpreted as conformity? The subject may conform to the wishes of his peer or to the wishes of the experimenter, and conformity in one direction means the absence of conformity in the other. Thus the word has no useful reference in this setting, for the dual and conflicting social pressures cancel out its meaning.

In the final analysis, the linguistic symbol representing the subject's action must take its meaning from the concrete context in which that action occurs; and there is probably no word in everyday language that covers the experimental situation exactly, without omissions or irrelevant connotations. It is partly for convenience, therefore, that the terms *obey* and *disobey* are used to describe the subject's actions. At the same time, our use of the words is highly congruent with dictionary meaning.

SUBJECT POPULATION

The subjects used in all experimental conditions were male adults, residing in the greater New Haven and Bridgeport areas, aged 20 to 50 years, and engaged in a wide variety of occupations. Each experimental condition described in this report employed 40 fresh subjects and was carefully balanced for age and occupational types. The occupational composition for each experiment was: workers, skilled and unskilled: 40 percent; white collar, sales, business: 40 percent; professionals: 20 percent. The occupations were intersected with three age categories (subjects in 20s, 30s, and 40s, assigned to each condition in the proportions of 20, 40, and 40 percent respectively).

THE GENERAL LABORATORY PROCEDURE[6]

The focus of the study concerns the amount of electric shock a subject is willing to administer to another person when ordered by an experimenter to give the "victim" increasingly more severe punishment. The act of administering shock is set in the context of a learning experiment, ostensibly designed to study the effect of punishment on memory. Aside from the experimenter, one naïve subject and one accomplice perform in each session. On arrival each subject is paid $4.50. After a general talk by the experimenter, telling how little scientists know about the effect of punishment on memory, subjects are informed that one member of the pair will serve as teacher and one as learner. A rigged drawing is held so that the naïve subject is always the teacher, and the accomplice becomes the learner. The learner is taken to an adjacent room and strapped into an "electric chair."

The naïve subject is told that it is his task to teach the learner a list of paired associates, to test him on the list, and to administer punishment whenever the learner errs in the test. Punishment takes the form of electric shock, delivered to the learner by means of a shock generator controlled by the naïve subject. The teacher is instructed to increase the intensity of electric shock one step on the generator on each error. The learner, according to plan, provides many wrong answers, so that before long the naïve subject must give him the strongest shock on the generator. Increases in shock level are met by increasingly insistent demands from the learner that the experiment be stopped because of the growing discomfort to him. However, in clear terms the experimenter orders the teacher to continue with the procedure in disregard of the learner's protests. *Thus, the naïve subject*

---

[6] A more detailed account of the laboratory procedure can be found in Milgram (1963). A similar and independently evolved experimental procedure, employing a shock generator, victim, and learning task, was reported by Buss (1961). Buss used the technique for studying aggression, not obedience, and did not make use of the fundamental measure employed in the present study: break-off points. His investigation promises to be a useful complement to the present research.

must resolve a conflict between two mutually incompatible demands from the social field. He may continue to follow the orders of the experimenter and shock the learner with increasing severity, or he may refuse to follow the orders of the experimenter and heed the learner's pleas. The experimenter's authority operates not in a free field, but against ever-mounting countervailing pressures from the person being punished.

A few technical points need to be considered before the findings of the study are described. For the purpose of delivering shock, a simulated shock generator is used, with 30 clearly marked voltage levels that range from 15 to 450 volts (and each activated by one of 30 individual lever switches set in a horizontal line). The naïve subject is given a sample shock of 45 volts to convince him of the authenticity of the instrument. The generator bears verbal designations that range from "Slight shock" to "Danger: Severe Shock."

The responses of the victim are standardized on tape, and each protest is coordinated to a particular voltage level on the shock generator. Starting with 75 volts the learner begins to grunt and moan. At 150 volts he demands to be let out of the experiment. At 180 volts he cries out that he can no longer stand the pain. At 300 volts he refuses to provide any more answers to the memory test, insisting that he is no longer a participant in the experiment and must be freed. In response to this last tactic, the experimenter instructs the naïve subject to treat the absence of an answer as equivalent to a wrong answer, and to follow the usual shock procedure. The experimenter reinforces his demand with the statement: "You have no other choice, you must go on!" (This imperative is used whenever the naïve subject tries to break off the experiment.) If the subject refuses to give the next higher level of shock, the experiment is considered at an end. A quantitative value is assigned to the subject's performance based on the maximum intensity shock he administered before breaking off. Thus any subject's score may range from zero (for a subject unwilling to administer the first shock level) to 30 (for a subject who proceeds to the highest voltage level on the board). For any particular subject and for any particular experimental condition the degree to which participants have followed the experimenter's orders may be specified with a numerical value, corresponding to the metric on the shock generator.

This laboratory situation gives us a framework in which to study the subject's reactions to the principal conflict of the experiment. Again, this conflict is between the experimenter's demands that he continue to administer the electric shock, and the learner's demands, which become increasingly more insistent, that the experiment be stopped. The crux of the study is to vary systematically the factors believed to alter the degree of obedience to the experimental commands, to learn under what conditions submission to authority is most probable, and under what conditions defiance is brought to the fore.

PILOT STUDIES

Pilot studies for the present research were completed in the winter of 1960; they differed from the regular experiments in a few details: for one, the victim was placed behind a silvered glass, with the light balance on the glass such that the victim could be dimly perceived by the subject (Milgram, 1961).

Though essentially qualitative in treatment, these studies pointed to several significant features of the experimental situation. At first no vocal feedback was used from the victim. It was thought that the verbal and voltage designations on the control panel would create sufficient pressure to curtail the subject's obedience. However, this was not the case. In the absence of protests from the learner, virtually all subjects, once commanded, went blithely to the end of the board, seemingly indifferent to the verbal designations ("Extreme Shock" and "Danger: Severe Shock"). This deprived us of an adequate basis for scaling obedient tendencies. A force had to be introduced that would strengthen the subject's resistance to the experimenter's commands, and reveal individual differences in terms of a distribution of break-off points.

This force took the form of protests from the victim. Initially, mild protests were used, but proved inadequate. Subsequently, more vehement protests were inserted into the experimental procedure. To our consternation, even the strongest protests from the victim did not prevent all subjects from administering the harshest punishment ordered by the experimenter; but the protests did lower the mean maximum shock somewhat and created some spread in the subject's performance; therefore, the victim's cries were standardized on tape and incorporated into the regular experimental procedure.

The situation did more than highlight the technical difficulties of finding a workable experimental procedure: it indicated that subjects would obey authority to a greater extent than we had supposed. It also pointed to the importance of feedback from the victim in controlling the subject's behavior.

One further aspect of the pilot study was that subjects frequently averted their eyes from the person they were shocking, often turning their heads in an awkward and conspicuous manner. One subject explained: "I didn't want to see the consequences of what I had done." Observers wrote:

> . . . subjects showed a reluctance to look at the victim, whom they could see through the glass in front of them. When this fact was brought to their attention they indicated that it caused them discomfort to see the victim in agony. We note, however, that although the subject refuses to look at the victim, he continues to administer shocks.

This suggested that the salience of the victim may have, in some degree, regulated the subject's performance. If, in obeying the experimenter, the subject found it necessary to avoid scrutiny of the victim, would the converse be true? If the victim were rendered increasingly more salient to the subject, would obedience diminish? The first set of regular experiments was designed to answer this question.

IMMEDIACY OF THE VICTIM

This series consisted of four experimental conditions. In each condition the victim was brought "psychologically" closer to the subject giving him shocks.

In the first condition (Remote Feedback) the victim was placed in another room and could not be heard or seen by the subject, except that, at 300 volts, he pounded on the wall in protest. After 315 volts he no longer answered or was heard from.

The second condition (Voice Feedback) was identical to the first except that voice protests were introduced. As in the first condition the victim was placed in an adjacent room, but his complaints could be heard clearly through a door left slightly ajar, and through the walls of the laboratory.[7]

---

[7] It is difficult to convey on the printed page the full tenor of the victim's responses, for we have no adequate notation for vocal intensity, timing, and general qualities of delivery. Yet these features are crucial to producing the effect of an increasingly severe reaction to mounting voltage levels. (They can be communicated fully only by sending interested parties the recorded tapes.) In general terms, however, the victim indicates no discomfort until the 75-volt shock is administered, at which time there is a light grunt in response to the punishment. Similar reactions follow the 90- and 105-volt shocks, and at 120 volts the victim shouts to the experimenter that the shocks are becoming painful. Painful groans are heard on administration of the 135-volt shock, and at 150 volts the victim cries out, 'Experimenter, get me out of here! I won't be in the experiment any more! I refuse to go on!' Cries of this type continue with generally rising intensity, so that at 180 volts the victim cries out, 'I can't stand the pain', and by 270 volts his response to the shock is definitely an agonized scream. Throughout, he insists that he be let out of the experiment. At 300 volts the victim shouts in desperation that he will no longer provide answers to the memory test; and at 315 volts, after a violent scream, he reaffirms with vehemence that he is no longer a participant. From this point on, he provides no answers, but shrieks in agony whenever a shock is administered; this continues through 450 volts. Of course, many subjects will have broken off before this point.

A revised and stronger set of protests was used in all experiments outside the Proximity series. Naturally, new baseline measures were established for all comparisons using the new set of protests.

There is overwhelming evidence that the great majority of subjects, both obedient and defiant, accepted the victims' reactions as genuine. The evidence takes the form of: (a) tension created in the subjects (see discussion of tension); (b) scores on "estimated pain" scales filled out by subjects immediately after the experiment; (c) subjects' accounts of their feelings in postexperimental interviews; and (d) quantifiable responses to questionnaires distributed to subjects several months after their participation in the experiments. This matter will be treated fully in a forthcoming monograph.

(The procedure in all experimental conditions was to have the naïve subject announce the voltage level before administering each shock, so that—independently of the victim's responses—he was continually reminded of delivering punishment of ever-increasing severity.)

The third experimental condition (Proximity) was similar to the second, except that the victim was now placed in the same room as the subject, and 1½ feet from him. Thus he was visible as well as audible, and voice cues were provided.

The fourth, and final, condition of this series (Touch-Proximity) was identical to the third, with this exception: the victim received a shock only when his hand rested on a shockplate. At the 150-volt level the victim again demanded to be let free and, in this condition, refused to place his hand on the shockplate. The experimenter ordered the naïve subject to force the victim's hand onto the plate. Thus obedience in this condition required that the subject have physical contact with the victim in order to give him punishment beyond the 150-volt level.

Forty adult subjects were studied in each condition. The data revealed that obedience was significantly reduced as the victim was rendered more immediate to the subject. The mean maximum shock for the conditions is shown in Fig. 1.

Expressed in terms of the proportion of obedient to defiant subjects, the findings are that 34 percent of the subjects defied the experimenter in the Remote condition, 37.5 percent in Voice Feedback, 60 percent in Proximity, and 70 percent in Touch-Proximity.

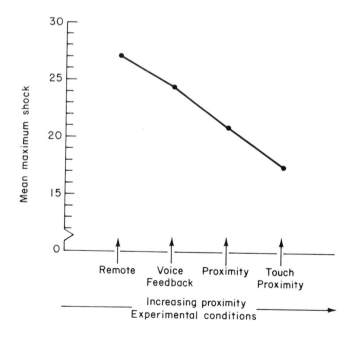

Fig. 1. Mean maxima in proximity series.

How are we to account for this effect? A first conjecture might be that as the victim was brought closer the subject became more aware of the intensity of his suffering and regulated his behavior accordingly. This makes sense, but our evidence does not support the interpretation. There are no consistent differences in the attributed level of pain across the four conditions (i.e., the amount of pain experienced by the victim as estimated by the subject and expressed on a 14-point scale). But it is easy to speculate about alternative mechanisms:

Emphatic Cues. In the Remote and to a lesser extent the Voice Feedback condition, the victim's suffering possesses an abstract, remote quality for the subject. He is aware, but only in a conceptual sense, that his actions cause pain to another person; the fact is apprehended, but not felt. The phenomenon is common enough. The bombardier can reasonably suppose that his weapons will inflict suffering and death, yet this knowledge is divested of affect, and does not move him to a felt, emotional response to the suffering resulting from his actions. Similar observations have been made in wartime. It is possible that the visual cues associated with the victim's suffering trigger emphatic responses in the subject and provide him with a more complete grasp of the victim's experience. Or it is possible that the emphatic responses are themselves unpleasant, possessing drive properties which cause the subject to terminate the arousal situation. Diminishing obedience, then, would be explained by the enrichment of emphatic cues in the successive experimental conditions.

Denial and Narrowing of the Cognitive Field. The Remote condition allows a narrowing of the cognitive field so that the victim is put out of mind. The subject no longer considers the act of depressing a lever relevant to moral judgement, for it is no longer associated with the victim's suffering. When the victim is close it is more difficult to exclude him phenomenologically. He necessarily intrudes on the subject's awareness since he is continuously visible. In the Remote conditions his existence and reactions are made known only after the shock has been administered. The auditory feedback is sporadic and discontinuous. In the Proximity conditions his inclusion in the immediate visual field renders him a continuously salient element for the subject. The mechanism of denial can no longer be brought into play. One subject in the Remote condition said: 'It's funny how you really begin to forget that there's a guy out there, even though you can hear him. For a long time I just concentrated on pressing the switches and reading the words.'

Reciprocal Fields. If in the Proximity condition the subject is in an improved position to observe the victim, the reverse is also true. The actions of the subject now come under proximal scrutiny by the victim. Possibly, it is easier to harm a person when he is unable to observe our actions than when he can see what we are doing. His surveillance of the action directed against him may give rise to shame, or guilt, which may then serve to curtail the action. Many expressions of language refer to the discomfort or inhibitions that arise in face-to-face confrontation. It is often said that it is easier to criticize a man "behind his back" than to "attack him to his face." If we are in the process of lying to a person it is reputedly difficult to "stare him in the eye." We "turn away from others in shame" or in "embarrassment" and this action serves to reduce our discomfort. The manifest function of allowing the victim of a firing squad to be blindfolded is to make the occasion less stressful for him, but it may also serve a latent function of reducing the stress of the executioner. In short, in the Proximity conditions, the subject may sense that he has become more salient in the victim's field of awareness. Possibly he becomes more self-conscious, embarrassed, and inhibited in his punishment of the victim.

Phenomenal Unity of Act. In the Remote conditions it is more difficult for the subject to gain a sense of *relatedness* between his own actions and the consequences of these actions for the victim. There is a physical and spatial separation of the act and its consequences. The subject depresses a lever in one room, and protests and cries are heard from another. The two events are in correlation, yet they lack a compelling phenomenological unity. The structure of a meaningful act—*I am hurting a man*—breaks down because of the spatial arrangements, in a manner somewhat analogous to the disappearance of phi phenomena when the blinking lights are spaced too far apart. The unity is more fully achieved in the Proximity conditions as the victim is brought closer to the action that causes him pain. It is rendered complete in Touch-Proximity.

Incipient Group Formation. Placing the victim in another room not only takes him further from the subject, but the subject and the experimenter are drawn relatively closer. There is incipient group formation between the experimenter and the subject, from which the victim is excluded. The wall between the victim and the others deprives him of an intimacy which the experimenter and subject feel. In the Remote condition, the victim is truly an outsider, who stands alone, physically and psychologically.

When the victim is placed close to the subject, it becomes easier to form an alliance with him against the experimenter. Subjects no longer have to face the experimenter alone. They have an ally who is close at hand and eager to collaborate in a revolt against the experimenter. Thus, the changing set of spatial relations leads to a potentially shifting set of alliances over the several experimental conditions.

Acquired Behavior Dispositions. It is commonly observed that laboratory mice will rarely fight with their litter mates. Scott (1958) explains this in terms of passive inhibition. He writes: "By doing nothing under . . . circumstances [the animal] learns to do nothing, and this may be spoken of as passive inhibition . . . this principle has great importance in teaching an individual to be peaceful, for it means that he can learn not to fight simply by not fighting." Similarly, we may learn not to harm others simply by not harming them in everyday life. Yet this learning occurs in a context of proximal relations with others, and may not be generalized to that situation in which the person is physically removed from us. Or possibly, in the past, aggressive actions against others who were physically close resulted in retaliatory punishment which extinguished the original form of response. In contrast, aggression againt others at a distance may have only sporadically led to retaliation. Thus the organism learns that it is safer to be aggressive toward others at a distance, and precarious to be so when the parties are within arm's reach. Through a pattern of rewards and punishments, he acquires a disposition to avoid aggression at close quarters, a disposition which does not extend to harming others at a distance. And this may account for experimental findings in the remote and proximal experiments.

Proximity as a variable in psychological research has received far less attention than it deserves. If men were sessile it would be easy to understand this neglect. But we move about; our spatial relations shift from one situation to the next, and the fact that we are near or remote may have a powerful effect on the psychological processes that mediate our behavior toward others. In the present situation, as the victim is brought closer to the man ordered to give him shocks, increasing numbers of subjects break off the experiment, refusing to obey. The concrete, visible, and proximal presence of the victim acts in an important way to counteract the experimenter's power and to generate disobedience.[8]

CLOSENESS OF AUTHORITY

If the spatial relationship of the subject and victim is relevant to the degree of obedience, would not the relationship of subject to experimenter also play a part?

There are reasons to feel that, on arrival, the subject is oriented primarily to the experimenter rather than to the victim. He has come to the laboratory to fit into the structure that the experimenter—not the victim— would provide. He has come less to understand his behavior than to *reveal* that behavior to a competent scientist, and he is willing to display himself as the scientist's purposes require. Most subjects seem quite concerned about the appearance they are making before the experimenter, and one could argue that this preoccupation in a relatively new and strange setting makes the subject somewhat insensitive to the triadic nature of the social situation. In other words, the subject is so concerned about the show he is putting on for the experimenter that influences from other parts of the social field do not receive as much weight as they ordinarily would. This overdetermined orientation to the experimenter would account for the relative insensitivity of the subject to the victim, and would also lead us to believe that alterations in the relationship between subject and experimenter would have important consequences for obedience.

In a series of experiments we varied the physical closeness and degree of surveillance of the experimenter. In one condition the experimenter sat just a few feet away from the subject. In a second condition, after giving initial instructions, the experimenter left the laboratory and gave his orders by telephone; in still a third condition the experimenter was never seen, providing instructions by means of a tape recording activated when the subjects entered the laboratory.

Obedience dropped sharply as the experimenter was physically removed from the laboratory. The number of obedient subjects in the first condition (Experimenter Present) was almost three times as great as in the second, where the experimenter gave his orders by telephone. Twenty-six subjects

---

[8] Admittedly, the terms *proximity, immediacy, closeness,* and *salience-of-the-victim* are used in a loose sense, and the experiments themselves represent a very coarse treatment of the variable. Further experiments are needed to refine the notion and tease out such diverse factors as spatial distance, visibility, audibility, barrier interposition, etc.

The Proximity and Touch-Proximity experiments were the only conditions where we were unable to use taped feedback from the victim. Instead, the victim was trained to respond in these conditions as he had in Experiment 2 (which employed taped feedback). Some improvement is possible here, for it should be technically feasible to do a proximity series using taped feedback.

were fully obedient in the first condition, and only 9 in the second (Chi square obedient vs. defiant in the two conditions, 1 d.f. = 14.7; $p < .001$). Subjects seemed able to take a far stronger stand against the experimenter when they did not have to encounter him face to face, and the experimenter's power over the subject was severely curtailed.[9]

Moreover, when the experimenter was absent, subjects displayed an interesting form of behavior that had not occurred under his surveillance. Though continuing with the experiment, several subjects administered lower shocks than were required and never informed the experimenter of their deviation from the correct procedure. (Unknown to the subjects, shock levels were automatically recorded by an Esterline-Angus event recorder wired directly into the shock generator; the instrument provided us with an objective record of the subjects' performance.) Indeed, in telephone conversations some subjects specifically assured the experimenter that they were raising the shock level according to instruction, whereas in fact they were repeatedly using the lowest shock on the board. This form of behavior is particularly interesting: although these subjects acted in a way that clearly undermined the avowed purposes of the experiment, they found it easier to handle the conflict in this manner than to precipitate an open break with authority.

Other conditions were completed in which the experimenter was absent during the first segment of the experiment, but reappeared at the point that the subject definitely refused to give higher shocks when commanded by telephone. Although he had exhausted his power via telephone, the experimenter could frequently force further obedience when he reappeared in the laboratory.

Experiments in this series show that the physical *presence* of an authority is an important force contributing to the subject's obedience or defiance. Taken together with the first experimental series on the proximity of the victim, it would appear that something akin to fields of force, diminishing in effectiveness with increasing psychological distance from their source, have a controlling effect on the subject's performance. As the victim is brought closer, the subject finds it harder to administer shocks to him. When the victim's position is held constant relative to the subject, and the authority is made more remote, the subject finds it easier to break off the experiment. This effect is substantial in both cases, but manipulation of the experimenter's position yielded the more powerful results. Obedience to destructive commands is highly dependent on the proximal relations between authority and subject.

---

[9] The third condition also led to significantly lower obedience than this first situation, in which the experimenter was present, but it contains technical difficulties that require extensive discussion.

TENSIONS

The description of final scores does not fully convey the character of the subjects' performance, and it would be useful to interrupt our reporting of quantitative relationships to remark on the subjects' general reaction to the situation.

One might suppose that a subject would simply break off or continue as his conscience and temperament dictated. Yet this is very far from what happened. There were powerful reactions of tension and emotional strain in a substantial proportion of the participants. Persons were observed to sweat, tremble, stutter, bite their lips, and groan as they found themselves increasingly implicated in the experimental conflict. Some sense of the subjects' mood can be gotten from a transcript of their remarks at break-off point. Here are the remarks of two defiant subjects:

Is he banging? . . . Is he hurt out there? Well, I don't want to be responsible for anything that happens to him. No, I can't go on with it. I don't know whether he's all right or not. I mean he may have a heart condition or something; I wouldn't feel right doing it. He's banging for help. He's evidently in trouble or he wouldn't bang . . . I don't see any sense to this—to knocking him out or something. I just can't see it.
(*Subject refuses to administer shocks*)   [*Subject 0108*]

The man is banging. He wants to get out . . . I'm sorry. If the man wants to get out I'd just as soon stop . . . I don't want to administer any more [extremely excited] . . . I will gladly refund the check, but I will not harm this man . . . I'm sorry, I will not give him any more if he obviously wants to get out. There is no money in the world that will make me hurt another individual.   [*Subject 010X*]

And here is a transcript from an obedient subject. He began the experiment calmly, but became increasingly tense as the experiment proceeded. After administering the 150-volt shock, he began to address the experimenter in agitated tones:

150 volts delivered. You want me to keep going?
165 volts delivered. That guy is hollering in there. There's a lot of them here. He's liable to have heart condition. You want me to go?
180 volts delivered. He can't stand it! I'm not going to kill that man in there! You hear him hollering? He's hollering. He can't stand it. What if something happens to him? . . . I'm not going to get that man sick in there. He's hollering in there. You know what I mean? I mean I refuse to take responsibility. He's getting hurt in there. He's in there hollering. Too many left here. Geez, if he gets them wrong. There's too many of them left. I mean who is going to take responsibility if anything happens to that gentleman?
[*The experimenter accepts responsibility.*] All right.
195 volts delivered. You see he's hollering. Hear that. Gee, I don't know. [*The experimenter says: 'The experiment requires that you go on.'*]—I know it does, sir, but I mean—hugh—he don't know what he's in for. He's up to 195 volts.
210 volts delivered
225 volts delivered

240 volts delivered. Aw, no. You mean I've got to keep going up with the scale? No sir. I'm not going to kill that man! I'm not going to give him 450 volts! [*The experimenter says: 'The experiment requires that you go on.'*]—I know it does, but that man is hollering in there, sir . . .

Despite his numerous, agitated objections, which were constant accompaniments to his actions, the subject unfailingly obeyed the experimenter, proceeding to the highest shock level on the generator. He displayed a curious dissociation between word and action. Although at the verbal level he had resolved not to go on, his actions were fully in accord with the experimenter's commands. This subject did not want to shock the victim, and he found it an extremely disagreeable task, but he was unable to invent a response that would free him from *E*'s authority. Many subjects cannot find the specific verbal formula that would enable them to reject the role assigned to them by the experimenter. Perhaps our culture does not provide adequate models for disobedience.

One puzzling sign of tension was the regular occurrence of nervous laughing fits. In the first four conditions 71 of the 160 subjects showed definite signs of nervous laughter and smiling. The laughter seemed entirely out of place, even bizarre. Full-blown, uncontrollable seizures were observed for 15 of these subjects. One one occasion we observed a seizure so violently convulsive that it was necessary to call a halt to the experiment. In the postexperimental interviews subjects took pains to point out that they were not sadistic types and that the laughter did not mean they enjoyed shocking the victim.

In the interview following the experiment subjects were asked to indicate on a 14-point scale just how nervous or tense they felt at the point of maximum tension (Fig. 2). The scale ranged from "Not at all tense and nervous" to "Extremely tense and nervous." Self-reports of this sort are of limited precision, and at best provide only a rough indication of the subject's emotional response. Still, taking the reports for what they are worth, it can be seen that the distribution of responses spans the entire range of the scale, with the majority of subjects concentrated at the center and upper extreme. A further breakdown showed that obedient subjects reported themselves as having been slightly more tense and nervous than the defiant subjects at the point of maximum tension.

How is the occurrence of tension to be interpreted? First, it points to the presence of conflict. If a tendency to comply with authority were the only psychological force operating in the situation, all subjects would have continued to the end and there would have been no tension. Tension, it is assumed, results from the simultaneous presence of two or more incompatible response tendencies (Miller, 1944). If sympathetic concern for the victim were the exclusive force, all subjects would have calmly defied the experimenter. Instead, there were both obedient and defiant outcomes,

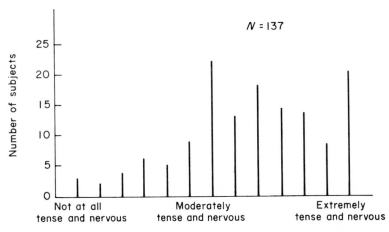

Fig. 2. *Level of tension and nervousness. The self-reports on "tension and nervousness" for 137 subjects in the Proximity experiments are shown. Subjects were given a scale with 14 values ranging from "Not at all tense and nervous" to "Extremely tense and nervous." They were instructed: "Thinking back to that point in the experiment when you felt the most tense and nervous, indicate just how you felt by placing an X at the appropriate point on the scale." The results are shown in terms of mid-point values.*

frequently accompanied by extreme tension. A conflict develops between the deeply ingrained disposition not to harm others and the equally compelling tendency to obey others who are in authority. The subject is quickly drawn into a dilemma of a deeply dynamic character, and the presence of high tension points to the considerable strength of each of the antagonistic vectors.

Moreover, tension defines the strength of the aversive state from which the subject is unable to escape through disobedience. When a person is uncomfortable, tense, or stressed, he tries to take some action that will allow him to terminate this unpleasant state. Thus tension may serve as a drive that leads to escape behavior. But in the present situation, even where tension is extreme, many subjects are unable to perform the response that will bring about relief. Therefore there must be a competing drive, tendency, or inhibition that precludes activation of the disobedient response. The strength of this inhibiting factor must be of greater magnitude than the stress experienced, else the terminating act would occur. Every evidence of extreme tension is at the same time an indication of the strength of the forces that keep the subject in the situation.

Finally, tension may be taken as evidence of the reality of the situations for the subjects. Normal subjects do not tremble and sweat unless they are implicated in a deep and genuinely felt predicament.

BACKGROUND AUTHORITY

In psychophysics, animal learning, and other branches of psychology, the fact that measures are obtained at one institution rather than another is irrelevant to the interpretation of the findings, so long as the technical facilities for measurement are adequate and the operations are carried out with competence.

But it cannot be assumed that this holds true for the present study. The effectiveness of the experimenter's commands may depend in an important way on the larger institutional context in which they are issued. The experiments described thus far were conducted at Yale University, an organization which most subjects regarded with respect and sometimes awe. In postexperimental interviews several participants remarked that the locale and sponsorship of the study gave them confidence in the integrity, competence, and benign purposes of the personnel; many indicated that they would not have shocked the learner if the experiments had been done elsewhere.

This issue of background authority seemed to us important for an interpretation of the results that had been obtained thus far; moreover it is highly relevant to any comprehensive theory of human obedience. Consider, for example, how closely our compliance with the imperatives of others is tied to particular institutions and locales in our day-to-day activities. On request, we expose our throats to a man with a razor blade in the barber shop, but would not do so in a shoe store; in the latter setting we willingly follow the clerk's request to stand in our stockinged feet, but resist the command in a bank. In the laboratory of a great university, subjects may comply with a set of commands that would be resisted if given elsewhere. *One must always question the relationship of obedience to a person's sense of the context in which he is operating.*

To explore the problem we moved our apparatus to an office building in industrial Bridgeport and replicated experimental conditions, without any visible tie to the university.

Bridgeport subjects were invited to the experiment through a mail circular similar to the one used in the Yale study, with appropriate changes in letterhead, etc. As in the earlier study, subjects were paid $4.50 for coming to the laboratory. The same age and occupational distributions used at Yale, and the identical personnel, were employed.

The purpose in relocating in Bridgeport was to assure a complete dissociation from Yale, and in this regard we were fully successful. On the surface, the study appeared to be conducted by Research Associates of Bridgeport, an organization of unknown character (the title had been concocted exclusively for use in this study).

The experiments were conducted in a three-room office suite in a somewhat run-down commercial building located in the downtown shopping area. The laboratory was sparsely furnished, though clean, and marginally respectable in appearance. When subjects inquired about professional affiliations, they were informed only that we were a private firm conducting research for industry.

Some subjects displayed skepticism concerning the motives of the Bridgeport experimenter. One gentleman gave us a written account of the thoughts he experienced at the control board:

> . . . Should I quit this damn test? Maybe he passed out? What dopes we were not to check up on this deal. How do we know that these guys are legit? No furniture, bare walls, no telephone. We could of called the Police up or the Better Business Bureau. I learned a lesson tonight. How do I know that Mr. Williams [the experimenter] is telling the truth . . . I wish I knew how many volts a person could take before lapsing into unconsciousness . . .
>
> [*Subject 2414*]

Another subject stated:

> I questioned on my arrival my own judgment [about coming]. I had doubts as to the legitimacy of the operation and the consequences of participation. I felt it was a heartless way to conduct memory or learning processes on human beings and certainly dangerous without the presence of a medical doctor.
>
> [*Subject 2440*]

There was no noticeable reduction in tension for the Bridgeport subjects. And the subjects' estimation of the amount of pain felt by the victim was slightly, though not significantly, higher than in the Yale study.

A failure to obtain complete obedience in Bridgeport would indicate that the extreme compliance found in New Haven subjects was tied closely to the background authority of Yale University; if a large proportion of the subjects remained fully obedient, very different conclusions would be called for.

As it turned out, the level of obedience in Bridgeport, although somewhat reduced, was not significantly lower than that obtained at Yale. A large proportion of the Bridgeport subjects were fully obedient to the experimenter's commands (48 percent of the Bridgeport subjects delivered the maximum shock vs. 65 percent in the corresponding condition at Yale).

How are these findings to be interpreted? It is possible that if commands of a potentially harmful or destructive sort are to be perceived as legitimate they must occur within some sort of institutional structure. But it is clear from the study that it need not be a particularly reputable or distinguished institution. The Bridgeport experiments were conducted by an unimpressive firm lacking any credentials; the laboratory was set up in a respectable office building with title listed in the building directory. Beyond that, there was no evidence of benevolence or competence. It is possible that the *category* of institution, judged according to its professed function, rather than its qualitative position within that category, wins our compliance. Persons deposit money in elegant, but also in seedy-looking banks, without giving much thought to the differences in security they offer. Similarly, our subjects may consider one laboratory to be as competent as another, so long as it *is* a scientific laboratory.

It would be valuable to study the subjects' performance in other contexts which go even further than the Bridgeport study in denying institutional support to the experimenter. It is possible that, beyond a certain point, obedience disappears completely. But that point had not been reached in the Bridgeport office: almost half the subjects obeyed the experimenter fully.

FURTHER EXPERIMENTS

We may mention briefly some additional experiments undertaken in the Yale series. A considerable amount of obedience and defiance in everyday life occurs in connection with groups. And we had reason to feel in the light of many group studies already done in psychology that group forces would have a profound effect on reactions to authority. A series of experiments was run to examine these effects. In all cases only one naïve subject was studied per hour, but he performed in the midst of actors who, unknown to him, were employed by the experimenter. In one experiment (Groups for Disobedience) two actors broke off in the middle of the experiment. When this happened 90 percent of the subjects followed suit and defied the experimenter. In another condition the actors followed the orders obediently; this strengthened the experimenter's power only slightly. In still a third experiment the job of pushing the switch to shock the learner was given to one of the actors, while the naïve subject performed a subsidiary act. We wanted to see how the teacher would respond if he were involved in the situation but did not actually give the shocks. In this situation only 3 subjects out of 40 broke off. In a final group experiment the subjects themselves determined the shock level they were going to use. Two actors suggested higher and higher shock levels; some subjects insisted, despite group pressure, that the shock level be kept low; others followed along with the group.

Further experiments were completed using women as subjects, as well as a set dealing with the effects of dual, unsanctioned, and conflicting authority. A final experiment concerned the personal relationship between victim and subject. These will have to be described elsewhere, lest the present report be extended to monographic length.

It goes without saying that future research can proceed in many different directions. What kinds of response from the victim are most effective in causing disobedience in the subject? Perhaps passive resistance is more effective than vehement protest. What conditions of entry into an authority system lead to greater or lesser obedience, What is the effect of anonymity and masking on the subject's behavior? What conditions lead to the subject's perception of responsibility for his own actions? Each of these could be a major research topic in itself, and can readily be incorporated into the general experimental procedure described here.

Levels of Obedience and Defiance

One general finding that merits attention is the high level of obedience manifested in the experimental situation. Subjects often expressed deep disapproval of shocking a man in the face of his objections, and others denounced it as senseless and stupid. Yet many subjects complied even while they protested. The proportion of obedient subjects greatly exceeded the expectations of the experimenter and his colleagues. At the outset, we had conjectured that subjects would not, in general, go above the level of "Strong Shock." In practice, many subjects were willing to administer the most extreme shocks available when commanded by the experimenter. For some subjects the experiment provides an occasion for aggressive release. And for others it demonstrates the extent to which obedient dispositions are deeply ingrained, and are engaged irrespective of their consequences for others. Yet this is not the whole story. Somehow, the subject becomes implicated in a situation from which he cannot disengage himself.

The departure of the experimental results from intelligent expectation, to some extent, has been formalized. The procedure was to describe the experimental situation in concrete detail to a group of competent persons, and to ask them to predict the performance of 100 hypothetical subjects. For purposes of indicating the distribution of break-off points judges were provided with a diagram of the shock generator, and recorded their predictions before being informed of the actual results. Judges typically underestimated the amount of obedience demonstrated by subjects.

In Fig. 3, we compare the predictions of forty psychiatrists at a leading medical school with the actual performance of subjects in the experiment. The psychiatrists predicted that most subjects would not go beyond the tenth shock level (150 volts; at this point the victim makes his first explicit demand to be freed). They further predicted that by the twentieth shock level (300 volts; the victim refuses to answer) 3.73 percent of the subjects would still be obedient; and that only a little over one-tenth of one percent of the subjects would administer the highest shock on the board. But, as the graph indicates, the obtained behavior was very different. Sixty-two percent of the subjects obeyed the experimenter's commands fully. Between expectation and occurrence there is a whopping discrepancy.

Why did the psychiatrists underestimate the level of obedience? Possibly, because their predictions were based on an inadequate conception of the determinants of human action, a conception that focuses on motives *in vacuo*. This orientation may be entirely adequate for the repair of bruised impulses as revealed on the psychiatrist's couch, but as soon as

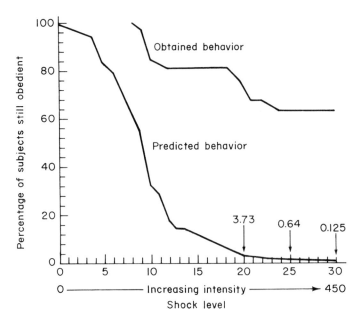

Fig. 3. Predicted and obtained behavior in voice feedback.

our interest turns to action in larger settings, attention must be paid to the situations in which motives are expressed. A situation exerts an important press on the individual. It exercises constraints and may provide push. In certain circumstances it is not so much the kind of person a man is, as the kind of situation in which he is placed, that determines his actions.

Many people, not knowing much about the experiment, claim that subjects who go to the end of the board are sadistic. Nothing could be more foolish as an overall characterization of these persons. It is like saying that a person thrown into a swift-flowing stream is necessarily a fast swimmer, or that he has great stamina because he moves so rapidly relative to the bank. The context of action must always be considered. The individual, upon entering the laboratory, becomes integrated into a situation that carries its own momentum. The subject's problem then is how to become disengaged from a situation which is moving in an altogether ugly direction.

The fact that disengagement is so difficult testifies to the potency of the forces that keep the subject at the control board. Are these forces to be conceptualized as individual motives and expressed in the language of personality dynamics, or are they to be seen as the effects of social structure and pressures arising from the situational field?

A full understanding of the subject's action will, I feel, require that both perspectives be adopted. The person brings to the laboratory enduring dispositions toward authority and aggression, and at the same time he becomes enmeshed in a social structure that is no less an objective fact of the case. From the standpoint of personality theory one may ask: What mechanisms of personality enable a person to transfer responsibility to authority? What are the motives underlying obedient and disobedient performance? Does orientation to authority lead to a short-circuiting of the shame-guilt system? What cognitive and emotional defenses are brought into play in the case of obedient and defiant subjects?

The present experiments are not, however, directed toward an exploration of the motives engaged when the subject obeys the experimenter's commands. Instead, they examine the situational variables responsible for the elicitation of obedience. Elsewhere, we have attempted to spell out some of the structural properties of the experimental situation that account for high obedience, and this analysis need not be repeated here (Milgram, 1963). The experimental variations themselves represent our attempt to probe that structure, by systematically changing it and noting the consequences for behavior. It is clear that some situations produce greater compliance with the experimenter's commands than others. However, this does not necessarily imply an increase or decrease in the strength of any single definable motive. Situations producing the greatest obedience could do so by triggering the most powerful, yet perhaps the most idiosyncratic, of motives in each subject confronted by the setting. Or they may simply recruit a greater number and variety of motives in their service. But whatever the motives involved—and it is far from certain that they can ever be known—action may be studied as a direct function of the situation in which it occurs. This has been the approach of the present study, where we sought to plot behavioral regularities against manipulated properties of the social field. Ultimately, social psychology would like to have a compelling *theory of situations* which will, first, present a language in terms of which situations can be defined; proceed to a typology of situations; and then point to the manner in which definable properties of situations are transformed into psychological forces in the individual.[10]

POSTSCRIPT

Almost a thousand adults were individually studied in the obedience research, and there were many specific conclusions regarding the variables that control obedience and disobedience to authority. Some of these have been discussed briefly in the preceding sections, and more detailed reports will be released subsequently.

There are now some other generalizations I should like to make, which do not derive in any strictly logical fashion from the experiments as carried out, but which, I feel, ought to be made. They are formulations of an

---

[10] My thanks to Professor Howard Leventhal of Yale for strengthening the writing in this paragraph.

intuitive sort that have been forced on me by observation of many subjects responding to the pressures of authority. The assertions represent a painful alteration in my own thinking; and since they were acquired only under the repeated impact of direct observation, I have no illusion that they will be generally accepted by persons who have not had the same experience.

With numbing regularity good people were seen to knuckle under the demands of authority and perform actions that were callous and severe. Men who are in everyday life responsible and decent were seduced by the trappings of authority, by the control of their perceptions, and by the uncritical acceptance of the experimenter's definition of the situation, into performing harsh acts.

What is the limit of such obedience? At many points we attempted to establish a boundary. Cries from the victim were inserted; not good enough. The victim claimed heart trouble; subjects still shocked him on command. The victim pleaded that he be let free, and his answers no longer registered on the signal box; subjects continued to shock him. At the outset we had not conceived that such drastic procedures would be needed to generate disobedience, and each step was added only as the ineffectiveness of the earlier techniques became clear. The final effort to establish a limit was the Touch-Proximity condition. But the very first subject in this condition subdued the victim on command, and proceeded to the highest shock level. A quarter of the subjects in this condition performed similarly.

The results, as seen and felt in the laboratory, are to this author disturbing. They raise the possibility that human nature, or—more specifically—the kind of character produced in American democratic society, cannot be counted on to insulate its citizens from brutality and inhumane treatment at the direction of malevolent authority. A substantial proportion of people do what they are told to do, irrespective of the content of the act and without limitations of conscience, so long as they perceive that the command comes from a legitimate authority. If in this study an anonymous experimenter could successfully command adults to subdue a fifty-year-old man, and force on him painful electric shocks against his protests, one can only wonder what government, with its vastly greater authority and prestige, can command of its subjects. There is, of course, the extremely important question of whether malevolent political institutions could or would arise in American society. The present research contributes nothing to this issue.

In an article titled "The Dangers of Obedience," Harold J. Laski wrote:

> . . . civilization means, above all, an unwillingness to inflict unnecessary pain. Within the ambit of that definition, those of us who heedlessly accept the commands of authority cannot yet claim to be civilized men.
>
> '. . . Our business, if we desire to live a life, not utterly devoid of meaning and significance, is to accept nothing which contradicts our basic experience merely because it comes to us from tradition or convention or authority. It may well be that we shall be wrong; but our self-expression is thwarted at the root unless the certainties we are asked to accept coincide with the certainties we ex-

perience. That is why the condition of freedom in any state is always a widespread and consistent skepticism of the canons upon which power insists.'

REFERENCES

Buss, A. H. *The psychology of aggression.* New York: Wiley, 1961.

Kierkegaard, S. *Fear and trembling.* English edition. Princeton, New Jersey: Princeton University Press, 1941.

Laski, H. J. The dangers of obedience. *Harper's Monthly Magazine,* 1929, **159**, June, 1–10.

Milgram, S. Dynamics of obedience: experiments in social psychology. Mimeographed report, *National Science Foundation,* 1961, January 25.

Milgram, S. Behavioral study of obedience. *Journal of Abnormal & Social Psychology,* 1963, **67**, 371–8.

Milgram, S. Issues in the study of obedience: a reply to Baumrind. *American Psychology,* 1964, **19**, 848–52.

Miller, N. E. Experimental studies of conflict. In J. McV. Hunt (Ed.), *Personality and the behavior disorders.* New York: Ronald Press, 1944.

Scott, J. P. *Aggression.* Chicago, Illinois: University of Chicago Press, 1958.

Chapter 11

NORM FORMATION AND EXCHANGE THEORY

What Is a Norm?

Although social influence is protypically thought of as flowing from a group or another individual, it may also flow from a norm which a group has established. Thus compliance to a norm is an example of conformity. But what is a norm? As the term "norm" is typically used it refers to a set of expectations held by members of a group concerning how one ought to behave. More broadly, though, it would perhaps be best to extend the definition to a set of expectations as to how one ought to feel and believe, as well as behave. It is true, however, that because of behavior's greater publicness norms may place relatively more emphasis upon it than upon feeling or belief.

According to Sherif (1935) the groups of subjects in his autokinetic experiment formulated norms regarding the number of inches which the pinpoint of light moved. Jacobs and Campbell (1961) did an interesting

351

follow-up investigation in the autokinetic situation. In groups of between two and four individuals confederates gave atypically high judgments in order to establish an initial consensus of 15.5 inches. (Ordinarily judgments average around 3.8 inches.) The confederates and other group members were then progressively replaced by new group members for successive blocks of 30 trials. Individual group members stayed in the group from between two to four blocks of trials, or generations. Jacobs and Campbell found that the "tradition" regarding the extent of movement persisted through four or perhaps five successive generations after the last confederate was replaced. By the sixth generation the mean group judgment had decreased to approximately 3.8 inches.

As defined above, norms have an obligatory or ought quality. It is possible that this was the case for the consensus regarding extent of auto-kinetic movement, but there is no way of being certain. Subjects may have conformed to the consensus for reasons other than a feeling of obligation. Only if consensus carries an obligatory quality can it be called a norm by our definition.

Thibaut and Kelley's Exchange Theory

The main intent of the remainder of this chapter is to describe one very influential approach to interpersonal behavior and the formation of norms, Thibaut and Kelley's (1959) exchange theory of social groups. When a customer gives a clerk money and the clerk gives the customer some goods, the interaction is commonly referred to as an *exchange*. Since the customer presumably wanted the goods and the clerk presumably wanted the money, in a general sense rewards were exchanged. Thibaut and Kelley maintain that all social interaction involves the explicit or implicit exchange of rewards or of costs.

REWARDS, COSTS, AND OUTCOMES

By "rewards" Thibaut and Kelley "refer to the pleasures, satisfactions, and gratifications the person enjoys" (p. 12). By "costs" they "refer to any factors that operate to inhibit or deter the performance of a sequence of behavior" (p. 12). Cost is considered high "when great physical or mental effort is required, when embarrassment or anxiety accompany the action, or when there are conflicting forces or competing response tendencies of any sort" (pp. 12–13).

Thibaut and Kelley assume that rewards of all types can be scaled along a single amount-of-reward dimension, and also that costs of all types can be scaled along a single amount-of-cost dimension. For some purposes the two dimensions can be treated separately, but most typically, Thibaut and Kelley refer to a single goodness of outcome dimension. High values on this dimension represent high rewards and low costs, and low values represent low rewards and high costs. "Outcome" is thus a general term for the rewards received and the costs incurred.

COMPARISON LEVELS

Outcomes do not possess absolute values, but rather are judged in relationships to standards. One of these standards is referred to as the *comparison level* and the other as the *comparison level for alternatives.* The comparison level "is the standard against which the member evaluates the 'attractiveness' of the relationship or how satisfactory it is" (p. 21). The comparison level can be conceived of as the neutral point on the goodness of outcome dimension. Outcomes above the comparison level are relatively pleasant and outcomes below the comparison level are relatively unpleasant. The exact location of the comparison level is determined by the outcomes which the individual has experienced or heard about, together with weights for such things as the salience and recency of such information. The outcomes which the individual has experienced in the past establish an expectation about similar outcomes in the future. For example, if these outcomes have been unusually low, the individual's comparison level will be low and the range of outcomes which are judged pleasant will be increased downward. In addition to direct experience, individuals develop expectations by hearing about other people's outcomes. This process will be recognized as Festinger's (1954) social comparison process. If a bachelor's comparison level for the attractiveness of dates is heavily weighted with bathing beauty contestants and actresses appearing on television commercials, his comparison level will be high. When he contemplates dating a girl of average attractiveness, she will be judged below his comparison level and hence as unattractive.

The comparison level for alternatives, like the comparison level, is conceptualized as a reference point on a goodness of outcomes dimension. In distinction to the comparison level, however, the comparison level for alternatives summarizes the quality of the outcomes available in the next best relationship alternative to the existing one. The comparison level for alternatives usually differs for each kind of relationship in which a person is involved. This is because the expected value of the next best date will typically differ from the expected value of the next best tennis opponent. The value of the comparison level for alternatives also includes the value an individual places on being alone. The comparison level for alternatives "is the standard the member uses in deciding whether to remain in or to leave the relationship" (p. 21). It is Thibaut and Kelley's belief that an individual's decision to terminate a relationship does not solely depend upon the poor outcomes obtained in the relationship. The decision will depend upon matching the outcomes in an existing relationship with the outcomes the individual expects to obtain from the next best available alternative relationship. For example, a woman may be quite unsatisfied with her marital relationship and yet not seek a divorce because she believes the outcomes in other possible marriages to be even lower. In this instance, the woman's outcomes are below her comparison level but above her comparison level for alternatives.

MATRIX OF INTERACTIONS AND OUTCOMES

One of the things that makes Thibaut and Kelley's theory distinctive is the use of matrices to represent different interaction and outcome patterns. Table 11-1 is an example matrix for a two-person group, or dyad. One of the members of the dyad is symbolized with an A and the other with a B. The responses in A's repertoire are symbolized a_1, a_2, etc., and the responses in B's repertoire are symbolized b_1, b_2, etc. A's repertoire is represented along the columns, and B's repertoire is represented along the rows. Thus, the upper left-hand cell of the matrix represents the interaction in which A's response is a_1 and B's response is b_1. Each cell of the matrix contains two numbers. For a given cell the number below the diagonal represents the goodness of outcome for B and the number above the diagonal represents the goodness of outcome for A. For the upper left-hand cell A's outcome is 9 and B's is 4.

In the typical dyad, A's repertoire of responses will be quite large, as will B's. In order to simplify matters, however, Thibaut and Kelley restrict

TABLE 11-1

Matrix of Interactions and Outcomes
(Adapted from Thibaut & Kelley, 1959, Table 2-2, p. 15.)

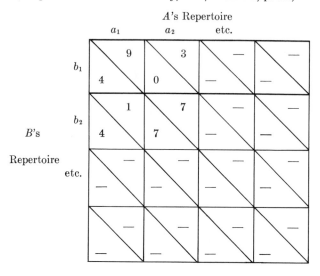

most of their theoretical discussion to the simple situation in which A has only two responses and B has only two responses.

POWER

According to Thibaut and Kelley, A has power over B to the extent that A can affect the quality of B's outcomes. There are two basic types of power, *fate control* and *behavior control*. Fate control is illustrated in matrix I of Table 11-2 and behavior control in matrix II of Table 11-2. In both of these matrices A can reduce B's outcomes from 5 to 0. In the fate-control matrix A can reduce B's outcomes by simply changing his response from a_2 to a_1. It makes no difference which response B makes. This is not the case, however, for the behavior-control matrix. Here B can affect the quality of the outcomes he receives. In order for A to reduce B's outcomes he has to make response a_1 whenever B makes b_1, and a_2 whenever B makes b_2. This, of course, requires that A must monitor B's behavior.

In both of the matrices in Table 11-2 there are no numbers above the diagonals in any of the cells. For a complete description of the situation, however, the quality of A's outcomes should be represented. This has been done in Table 11-3. Here we see that if A exercises his fate control over B, A will reduce his own outcomes. In this type of situation A has high actual power but low *usable power*.

PATTERNS OF INTERDEPENDENCE

There are, of course, a wide number of different patterns of interdependence. Two interesting possibilities are represented in Table 11-4. Matrix I illustrates what are referred to as *correspondent outcomes*, and matrix II illustrates what are referred to as *noncorrespondent outcomes*. In matrix I the cells in which A maximizes his outcomes are the cells in

TABLE 11-2

Two Types of Power
(Adapted from Thibaut & Kelley, 1959, Tables 7-1, 7-2, pp. 102, 103.)

| | I
Fate Control | II
Behavior Control |

TABLE 11-3

High Fate Control but Low Usable Power

(Adapted from Thibaut & Kelley, 1959, Table 7-4, p. 107.)

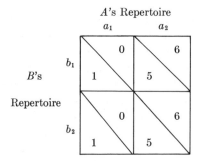

which *B* maximizes his outcomes. The outcomes are correspondent. As long as *A* and *B* cooperate in synchronizing their responses (a_2 with b_1 and a_1 with b_2) mutual benefits accrue. It is the correspondence of outcomes that reduces usable power. In matrix II there are no cells in which *A* and *B* can both maximize their outcomes. The outcomes are noncorrespondent. In this situation conflict will occur and the dyad must evolve norms, such as taking turns, or the relationship may be terminated.

THE HEDONISTIC ASSUMPTION

Thibaut and Kelley make it quite explicit that their theory is social rather than individual in orientation. They are not concerned with characteristics of the individual, but with interactions between or among individuals. As the previous discussion should make clear, Thibaut and Kelley's main orientation is to the patterns of interdependence existing in dyads

TABLE 11-4

Two Patterns of Interdependency
(Adapted from Thibaut & Kelley, 1959, Table 7-6, p. 109.)

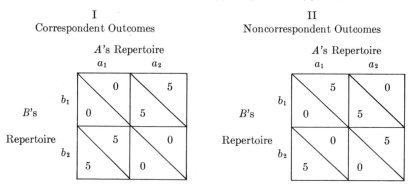

and larger groups. Nonetheless, a basic psychological assumption about individuals is implicitly made. This assumption appears to be that individuals are motivated to maximize rewards and minimize costs. If rewards mean pleasant affect and costs mean unpleasant affect, this basic psychological assumption is a hedonistic one. Hedonism has, of course, been implicitly assumed by many psychologists (e.g., Lewin, 1935). The student, however, should not make the mistake of identifying hedonism with the "pig-in-the-trough" conception of man. This is not what Thibaut and Kelley have in mind. Philosophers have long recognized that if hedonism is taken to mean that individuals are always oriented toward immediate and present gratification, it is obviously untrue.

As pointed out in Chapter 2, there are three varieties of hedonism: *hedonism of the present, hedonism of the future,* and *hedonism of the past.* Hedonism of the present is the view that man is oriented toward the immediate or short-term maximization of pleasant affect and minimization of unpleasant affect. Hedonism of the future is the view that man is oriented toward the long-term maximization of pleasant affect and minimization of unpleasant affect. Such a view tends to be associated with an emphasis upon planfulness and rationality. Hedonism of the past is the view that man makes those responses which in the past have maximized pleasant affect and minimized unpleasant affect. This is the kind of "mindless" hedonism with which stimulus-response psychology has sometimes been associated. According to this perspective when a stimulus-response sequence is followed by reward, subsequent presentation of the stimulus will evoke the response even in the absence of present reward— at least until extinction occurs.

Although Thibaut and Kelley do not use the above terms, their hedonism appears to be mostly a hedonism of the future and present with a very minor emphasis upon hedonism of the past. Thibaut and Kelley make passing reference to persisting, and sometimes inappropriate, habits learned on the basis of past consequences. Their major emphasis, however, is upon present and future consequences. [At one point they refer to the deliberate planning for future consequences (or outcomes) as "purposive hedonism" (1959, p. 29).] Some of the research on the so-called minimal social situation illustrates this dual emphasis upon hedonism of the present and future.

THE MINIMAL SOCIAL SITUATION: AN ILLUSTRATIVE CASE

Sidowski, Wyckoff, and Tabory (1956) began research on what they refer to as the minimal social situation. This research can be used both to illustrate the application of exchange theory and the philosophical problems surrounding such application. In the Sidowski *et al.* experiment subjects were tested in pairs, but individually separated in different rooms. Each subject, in fact, was unaware that another subject was in the adjacent room. Each room contained two buttons. If the subject in room 1 pushed the right-hand button a counter in room 2 registered one point; if the subject in room 1 pushed the left-hand button the subject in room 2 received an electric shock. Room 2 contained two buttons which similarly controlled the outcomes for the subject in room 1. Two shock levels were used: weak (110 percent of absolute threshold) and strong (200 percent of absolute threshold). Half of the subjects were tested with weak shock and half with strong. All subjects received points when their partners pressed the "correct" button.

The results indicated that the points-and-strong-shock group made significantly more "correct" or points-producing button-presses than "incorrect" or shock-producing button-presses, but this was not true for the points-and-weak-shock group; that is, the points-and-strong-shock group learned, but the points-and-weak-shock group did not. Why didn't the points-and-weak-shock group learn? One possibility that immediately comes to mind is that the weak shock was not strong enough to motivate learning. As we shall see, however, this hypothesis is not entirely consistent with the data from subsequent research.

Sidowski (1957) reports a further experiment with three types of outcomes: points-only, strong-shock-only, points-and-strong-shock. In the points-only condition each subject's "partner" received points when one button was pressed and nothing when the other button was pressed. In the strong-shock-only condition each subject's "partner" received a shock when one button was pressed and nothing when the other button was pressed. In the points-and-strong-shock condition each subject's "partner" received points when one button was pressed and shock when the other button was pressed. Each of these three conditions was in turn divided into two subconditions, informed and uninformed. In the informed conditions the subjects were told that their points, or shocks, or points and shocks were controlled by the other subject. In the uninformed conditions the subjects were not informed what controlled their outcomes.

Consistent with Sidowski's prediction, the informed-uninformed manipulation made no difference in the final results. Significant evidence for learning occurred in the points-only and points-and-strong-shock conditions, but not in the strong-shock-only condition. Sidowski offers two possible explanations for the lack of learning in the strong-shock-only condition. First, some minimal rate of responding may be necessary before learning can occur and the overall frequency of button-pressing in the strong-shock-only condition was low. Second, receiving shock and not receiving points may have had equal negative reinforcing effects.

This second experiment makes it appear as if the receipt of points is the crucial factor producing learning. In the two conditions in which points were received, learning occurred. In the previous experiment by Sidowski *et al.* (1956), however, the presence of strong shock would seem to be the crucial factor producing learning. In that experiment the combination of weak shock and points did not produce learning. Something curious apparently happens when weak shock and points are combined that is not adequately explained by the simple hypothesis that weak shock is not strong enough to motivate learning.

The two above experiments began to make clear the strengths and weaknesses of a general hedonistic approach. The hedonistic account in terms of maximized outcomes is a compelling explanation for the shift in responses that occurred when both strong shock and points are used as motivators or when just points are used as a motivator. But why didn't learning occur when only strong shock was used as a motivator? The failure of a prediction doesn't seem to shake one's conviction in the theory. There are too many possible explanations, consistent with the hedonistic point of view, that can account for the results. Translated into hedonistic terms, Sidowski's second explanation for the failure of prediction in the strong-shock-only condition is that receiving shock and not receiving points may be equally unpleasant. This is at least possible. Even more puzzling, however, is the failure of weak shock and points to produce learning when points alone, as well as strong shock and points, produce learning. The proponent of the hedonistic position can still maintain that if he really understood what was going on in the weak-shock-and-points situation he could account for the subject's behavior in terms of attempts to maximize outcomes. And this is indeed possible. Whether such an explanation would be correct or incorrect, however, is another matter.

The weakness of the hedonistic position as currently developed is not that it cannot offer explanations for behavior, but rather that it has failed to specify the behaviors which, if enacted, would disprove the theory. Until such behaviors are specified an adequate test of the theory cannot be carried out. It is such testing which enables researchers to determine the adequacy, correctness, or truth of any theoretical position.

Two further experiments on the minimal social situation have been reported by Kelley, Thibaut, Radloff, and Mundy (1962). Following Thibaut and Kelley (1959), Kelley et al. interpret the minimal social situation as involving mutual fate control. By varying his responses each subject can alter the outcomes of the other subject. According to Thibaut and Kelley (1959), and Kelley et al. (1962) outcomes are maximized in the minimal social situation when the subjects tend to follow a "win-stay, lose-change" sequence of responses. A subject follows this sequence by repeating or staying with a response that produces a positive outcome and altering or changing a response that produces a negative outcome.

One of the main purposes of Kelley et al.'s first experiment was to demonstrate, contrary to Sidowski's (1957) hypothesis and finding, that informed subjects would do better than uninformed. Kelley et al. disputed Sidowski's S-R bias that behavior is automatically controlled by reward and punishment without any mediation of cognition or understanding. Sidowski had informed half of his subjects by telling them that the shocks and points were controlled by another subject. Kelley *et al.* attempted to do a more thorough job of familiarizing the subjects about the nature of the situation. It was explained, for example, that each subject had two responses, that each response affected the point outcomes of the other subject, and that they were to obtain as many points as they could. Each subject could move a switch in one of two directions from a center position, toward or away from himself, and then return the switch to the center position. Movement in one direction produced outcomes (for the other subject) of +10 points (as signalled by a green light), and movement in the other direction produced outcomes (also for the other subject) of −10 points (as signalled by a red light).

The results clearly indicated that learning to maximize outcomes did occur. Furthermore, the effect was more marked in the informed than in the uninformed condition.[1] Postexperimental questioning of the subjects revealed that the subjects in the successful dyads, more than the subjects in the unsuccessful dyads, made the assumption that their partners' responses would be stable if receiving positive outcomes and variable if receiving negative outcomes. According to Kelley *et al.* in order for the subject to discover the exact effect of his responses upon the other subject it is necessary to drop temporarily the outcome-maximization orientation and adopt an information-intake orientation, viewing "payoffs in terms of what they tell about the partner rather than in terms of their favorableness" (p. 7). This statement by Kelley *et al.* illustrates a shift from *hedonism of the present* to *hedonism of the future*. In these terms, the Kelley *et al.* statement is that successful dyads contained subjects who forsook hedonism of the present in order to obtain information that would facilitate future outcome maximization. In order for hedonism of the future to be successful, reasoning and planning are necessary. The assumption that people may adopt the future orientation is thus consistent with Kelley *et al.*'s emphasis upon the importance of being well informed about the nature of the situation.

An emphasis on the importance of rationality and understanding provides another possible explanation as to why subjects may not always act so as to maximize outcomes. A failure to maximize outcomes may be due to an inability to select the appropriate responses. Kelley *et al.*, in fact, evoke such an hypothesis to account for some of the results obtained in their second experiment.

In the second experiment Kelley *et al.* investigated dyads (two-person groups) and quartets (four-person groups). The sequential interdependence in the quartets followed a circular pattern; that is, A determined B's outcomes, B determined C's outcomes, C determined D's outcomes, D deter-

---

[1] This result may partly have resulted from the fact that the informed subjects were explicitly told to maximize points.

mined A's outcomes. All the subjects were uninformed and the outcomes were plus and minus points (referred to as "credits" and "demerits").

The results indicated that learning to maximize outcomes occurred only in the dyads; subjects in the quartets did not maximize their outcomes. Kelley *et al.* account for the failure of outcome maximization with increased group size in terms of the increased probability that some group member will not follow the "win-stay, lose-change" rule, thus "transmitting confusion around the circle" (p. 10).

Thus once again the failure of a prediction flowing from the general hedonistic perspective does not disprove this approach. The quartets did not maximize their outcomes because of the high probability that at least one member of the group was not "smart" enough to figure out the necessary response sequence.

Although Thibaut and Kelley (1959) do not explicitly do so, the possibility of evoking hedonism of the past provides even more flexibility in accounting for prediction failures. Thus an investigator could alternate among the three types of hedonism in accounting for a subject's behavior. If a subject is not responding so as to maximize present outcomes, then perhaps he is attempting to arrange matters so that future outcomes will be maximized. If future outcomes are not maximized, then perhaps the subject made the wrong calculations. And if the subject did not fail to maximize present outcomes in an attempt to maximize future outcomes, then perhaps he was rigidly repeating responses that had maximized outcomes in the past. One of the major factors accounting for hedonism's slippery quality is the lack of explicit principles regarding when hedonism of the present will apply, when hedonism of the future will apply, and when hedonism of the past will apply.

The reader should be aware that our present discussion of the impossibility of testing the hedonistic position, as it is currently formulated, exactly parallels the discussion of hedonism in Chapter 2. In Chapter 2 our concern was the hedonistic approach to attitude change and not the exchange theory approach to interpersonal processes, but we nonetheless arrived at exactly the same general conclusions. We concluded that although a hedonistic orientation focuses our attention on some interesting problems, one should not believe this orientation to be a testable theory; first, because it is not clear when circumstances are to be considered rewarding and when unrewarding (recall the uncertainty regarding the circumstances in which "good" is rewarding in an attitudinal verbal reinforcement setting); and second, because it is not clear what the variables are which determine the shift from past to present to future hedonistic orientations.

The above statement, however, in no way implies that it is impossible to develop a testable hedonistic theory. In a more recent effort Kelley and Thibaut (1969) have emphasized that when present outcomes fall below the comparison level for alternatives the individual will adopt an information-seeking orientation in order to obtain better outcomes; that is, the individual will shift from hedonism of the present to hedonism of the future. Theoretical propositions such as this one are what is needed to change the hedonistic orientation into a testable theory.

One of the interesting problems for which exchange theory appears to be relevant is the process of norm formation—a matter to which we now turn.

The Formation of Norms

Thibaut and Kelley use the relationship represented in Table 11-5 to illustrate the type of situation which may lead to the development of a norm. The wife prefers to go dancing, but only with the husband; and the husband prefers to go to the movies, but only with the wife. Since the husband and wife cannot maximize their outcomes at the same time, they may threaten each other with the possibility of going their separate ways. Such use of personal power, however, will not maximize outcomes for both husband and wife. Outcomes for both husband and wife can only be maximized if some sort of trading rule develops in which going to the movies is alternated with going dancing. For example, the rule might be for the husband and wife to go to the movies on Monday evening and go dancing on Friday evening. Thibaut and Kelley go on to say that after the rule has been followed for some time it takes on the characteristics of a moral obligation—the usual becomes the right. Thibaut and Kelley are not entirely sure how this transformation comes about, but speculate that "It probably has some basis in the fact that conformity to rules and agreements has proven rewarding in past relationships in which some external agent has delivered extrinsic rewards for conformity" (p. 128). Parents, for example, reward children when they conform to rules.

TABLE 11-5

Relationship Leading to a Trading Norm
(Adapted from Thibaut & Kelley, 1959, p. 127.)

In the husband-wife dyad pictured in Table 11-5 both group members have equal power. What happens, however, when there is unequal power? It obviously is to the advantage of a low-person for norms to be established which protect him from the high-power person. But why should the high-power person agree to norms limiting his power? Thibaut and Kelley mention two reasons. First, the high-power person may not wish to exercise his power too freely anyway, because such behavior might reduce the low-power person's outcomes below the comparison level for alternatives and thus force him to leave the group. Second, if the norm specifies correct behavior for both group members the high-power person may be relieved of the necessity of monitoring the low-power person's behavior. A third reason, not mentioned by Thibaut and Kelley, is that it is highly unlikely that one individual will always possess the highest power in all of his interpersonal relations. Norms which generally apply to interpersonal relations may thus be to the long-term benefit of an individual even though they may restrict his power in some particular group.

The Thibaut and Kelley position is that norms develop and continue to exist because they have functional value in maximizing outcomes for all the group members. Such a theoretical position would seemingly provide some support for the conservative, or don't-change-existing-ways-of-doing-things, point of view. This raises an interesting question concerning whether all norms do have functional value for the group. Consider Thibaut and Kelley's husband and wife dyad pictures in Table 11-5. Suppose that the trading norm became so firmly set that it persisted even after the husband became near-sighted and the wife developed painful corns. If the norm, in fact, persisted in this situation, Thibaut and Kelley would seemingly have to maintain that outcomes were still being maximized, perhaps because continued adherence to the norm reassured the husband and wife of their mutual good faith and morality. This is at least possible. It may be, however, that the continued adherence to the trading norm is a type of "cultural lag" in which outcomes are not, in fact, presently maximized, even though they may have been in the past. Thibaut and Kelley could more easily account for such cultural lags if hedonism of the past received greater emphasis in their formulation.

In recent years there has been a fair amount of research on the development of contracts in bargaining situations. Since contracts are norms, albeit very formal ones, this bargaining research is relevant to the general process of norm formation. The article by Thibaut and Faucheux (1965), which is contained in the Readings section of this chapter, is a good example of the bargaining literature. Thibaut and Faucheux demonstrate that bargaining is most likely to lead to contracts when there is both a high noncorrespondence of outcomes (or conflict of interest) and a high comparison level for alternatives.

READINGS

The Development of Contractual Norms in a Bargaining Situation under Two Types of Stress[1]

John Thibaut and Claude Faucheux

The point of view that biological and social systems respond to stress with various adaptive mechanisms, the effects of which often protect the systems from collapse or disruption, has been stated and illustrated by Bertalanffy (1951), Selye (1950), and, with particular reference to psychological systems, by James Miller (1955). Although this conception seems to be an important one for the understanding of group phenomena, its usefulness in predicting social behavior is very limited, and its validity must remain unsupported unless a more detailed theoretical and experimental analysis is made of the processes by which groups respond to various types of stress.

It will be suggested in the following paragraphs that when power differentiation exists in a group whose members have a background of high interdependence and highly convergent interests, the introduction of both external and internal threats to the continued viability of the group creates the conditions for the emergence of norms which to a significant degree reduce the disruptive consequences of the threats.

To present the analysis as simply as possible, let us suppose the existence of a dyad in which the members' interests are highly interdependent and harmonious and in which one member is able potentially to exert more influence on the other than he receives. This situation is strongly favorable to the maintenance of membership. The high degree of interdependence of outcomes means that each member is heavily dependent on the other for positive outcomes and that alternative relationships outside the dyad are relatively unattractive. Motivations to disrupt the dyad by forming mutually

[1] From the *Journal of Experimental Social Psychology*, Volume 1, pages 89–102, 1965. Authors' affiliations: Thibaut, University of North Carolina; Faucheux, Centre National de la Recherche Scientifique, Paris. This research was done while Thibaut was a Special U. S. Public Health Service Fellow at the Sorbonne. Both authors were attached to the Laboratoire de Psychologie Sociale de la Faculté des Lettres et Sciences Humaines de l'Université de Paris. Facilities for the present research were provided by CREDS of Montrouge. The research is also part of the program of the Organization Research Group at the University of North Carolina. The ORG is supported by the Office of Naval Research under contract Nonr-855(04). The assistance of M. W. Doise in the conduct of this research is gratefully acknowledged.

exclusive relationships with external alternatives are likely to be minimal. Hence there is little or no need for policing the loyalty of the members or for developing norms that forbid disloyalty.

Furthermore, in this simplified situation the highly convergent interests of the members means that there is no real problem in the sharing of the outcomes produced by the group's efforts. Thibaut and Kelley (1959, Chapter II) show that when members' outcomes are perfectly correspondent (i.e., where there is a positive correlation of unity between member outcomes over the cells of the matrix describing their joint behaviors), the member holding the higher potential power is unable to use that power to advantage himself at the expense of the other. He cannot help himself without also helping the other, nor hurt the other without hurting himself. Hence, in this situation there is no need for the development of norms governing the sharing of outcomes or protecting the weak from exploitation.

The description of such harmony and mutual dependence suggests two types of stress that might threaten the maintenance of such a dyad[2]:

(1) *Conflict of interest.* This "internal" stress will develop when any factors so reduce the correspondence of member outcomes that they become negatively correlated. As conflict of interest increases so does the degree of "usable" power of the member whose power is greater. The likelihood that this power will be used against his interests constitutes a real threat to the low-power member. In order to protect himself against serious reductions in his share of the outcomes, he will be expected to appeal to norms of "equity" and "fair sharing."

(2) *Improved alternatives outside the group.* This "external" stress will appear whenever outcomes available outside the dyad become attractive enough to compete with those available inside. This stress threatens the interdependence of the group members. Good external alternatives may, of course, be attractive to both group members. However, if there exists in the dyad a degree of conflict of interest, this will create enough potential advantage to the high-power member so that in evaluating his probable share of the outcomes he is likely to remain loyal to the group. It is the low-power member, then, who will respond with greater alacrity to the increasingly attractive external alternative. The potential disloyalty of the low-power member thus constitutes a real threat to the high-power member. In order to preserve the integrity of the group within which he holds the advantage, he will be expected to appeal to norms of "loyalty" and "group spirit."

To make appeals for the invocation of norms is not, of course, a sufficient condition for their realization. The high-power member cannot realistically expect that the low-power one will respond favorably to a contrac-

---

[2] Of course, it is possible for either of these stresses to be sufficiently high so that in fact the group does disrupt. It is assumed in the following that the level of stress, though high, is not overwhelmingly so.

tual restraint on his "disloyalty" unless the eschewing of the temptation to "disloyalty" can be compensated for in some fashion. Nor can the low-power member entertain realistic hopes of a normative approach to "fair sharing" unless he can in some way compensate the high-power member for inhibiting his use of power. How can this compensation be achieved? There is one striking solution which suggests itself.

When *both* external and internal stresses are high, each member is threatened by behaviors which the other is tempted to perform, and each member's appeal is to a rule of behavior, a norm, which will forbid such threatening behaviors. Thus a type of "interdependence" appears in which each member's acceptance of the other's appeal is compensated for by a reduction in threat. The low-power member's agreement to inhibit his "disloyalty" is compensated for by the high-power member's willingness to impose restraint on the use of his power. This argument can be put in another way. Only when both types of stress are high are both members motivated to invoke a norm; furthermore, it is only under these conditions that the low-power member is provided with sufficient "counter power," through the presence of an attractive external alternative, to bargain effectively with the high-power member. If this reasoning is correct, two mutually dependent threats may generate norms of behavior which embody the adaptive mechanisms that support the continued integrity of the group.

Design of the Experiment

To explore the foregoing theoretical formulation, an experiment was designed in which two Ss were confronted with a bargaining task. The situation in which the Ss were placed was one which permitted the manipulation of the attractiveness of the external alternative and the degree of conflict of interest. At a standard point of time in the course of the experiment, an opportunity was introduced for the Ss to regulate their bargaining normatively by forming contracts. The frequency and characteristics of the contracts constituted the main dependent variables.

Preliminary procedure. At the beginning of each experimental session, one member of each dyad was randomly assigned to the high-power position (designated *P*) and the other to the low-power position (designated *X*). The Ss remained in the same power position throughout the experiment. The Ss in each dyad were seated at a table facing one another, with a cardboard screen rising to eye level placed between them. The Ss in each dyad were instructed not to compete with one another in the bargaining game that was to be played, but rather to compete with the other Ss who were in the same power position, i.e., all *P*'s were in competition, and all *X*'s were in competition. In order to facilitate the instruction of the Ss, to provide practice at the bargaining task, and to create the necessary background of uniformly high interdependence and harmony, all dyads were initially confronted with the same simple task. The task consisted of bargaining for points to be won by playing the game summarized in a matrix (Fig. 1) presented to each S. The procedure for playing the game was as follows. By open discussion, the two Ss arrived at a tentative agreement about their joint behavior. When this tentative agreement was reached, *P* recorded it on a printed form provided for this purpose. Each S then recorded privately his actual decision about what he

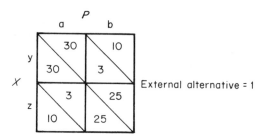

External alternative = 1

Fig. 1. *Matrix summarizing the game played during the preliminary phase of the experiment.*

would play. In this decision he was not obliged to honor the tentative agreement reached earlier; duplicity was thus possible. When the actual decisions were reached, they were announced publicly and recorded by P. The play was repeated with the same matrix for three trials.

In playing the game, each S had three options among which to decide. He could play either of the two columns (or rows) of the matrix or he could play the external alternative. If both Ss played the external alternative, each received one point. However, if one S played the external alternative, while the other played a column (or row) of the matrix, the first received one point while the latter received zero. The alternative was thus a dependable (though in this instance, a paltry) outcome that each S could attain quite independently of the other's behavior, and it also provided a method for threatening one's partner.

The outcomes to be received from playing the columns and rows of the matrix reflect the interdependence of the Ss. For both players to receive the maximum outcomes (30 points) available in the present matrix, P must play a while X plays y. If P played b while X played z, each would receive 25 points.

However, in the remaining two cells of the matrix, by and az, the outcomes accruing to each player depended on the degree to which P exercised his power. It will be recalled from the discussion in the preceding section that "usable" power depends directly on the degree of conflict of interest (noncorrespondence of outcomes) present in the interdependent situation of the group members. Hence, power can be used only when the outcomes to the members form a given joint action are different. This leads to the experimental definition and manipulation of power in this experiment; P was instructed that in any such cells in which the outcomes to the Ss differed, he was empowered to take for himself any number of points from the smaller of the two values *up* to the larger, leaving the remaining points to X. Thus, if *either by* or *az* were played, P was empowered to take any number of points from 3 to 10. If, for example, P took 8 points, X would receive 5. These rules governing the bargaining procedure, the consequences of playing the external alternative, and the use and meaning of power remained invariant throughout the experiment.

Note in this preliminary matrix that the harmonious solution (ay, leading to 30 points apiece) is the obviously dominant solution, that the conflictual solutions (in which power can be exercised) are relatively unattractive, and that the external alternative (1 point) is extremely low and hence mutual dependence on intradyadic cooperation is strongly reinforced.

Experimental treatments. After the three trials of the preliminary phase, the experiment proper began and the experimental manipulations were introduced. The treatments consisted of varying both the level of the external alternative and the degree of conflict of interest in the dyadic situation. The essential characteristics of each of the four experimental conditions can be most succinctly described by the matrix governing the play in each of the conditions. Figure 2 shows the matrices representing high and low conflict of interest and the accompanying external alternatives. Pairing the values of the two variables results in the four conditions: high conflict-high alternative (HH), high conflict-low alternative (HL), low conflict-high alternative (LH), and low conflict-low alternative (LL). It should be observed that, in general, the points to be bargained for are higher in the experimental treatments than in the matrix of the preliminary phase, and that the cells containing the largest total number of points are no longer the harmonious solutions. Note too that the single difference between the matrices for high and low conflict consists in the size of discrepancy between the points contained in the cells of the main diagonal: in all other respects, including the total number of points available, the two matrices are identical. The level of the external alternative when high (35) begins to compete effectively with the matrix values; when low (10) this is not so.

It is perhaps apparent that the HH condition is designed to create high stress from both external and internal sources, the HL and LH conditions to produce mixed degrees of stress, and the LL condition little stress of either sort.

The dyads in each treatment used the same assigned matrix and alternative for the remainder of the experiment. The standard sequence which governed the remaining phases of the experiment was as follows: (1) three trials played with the new matrix and alternative followed by a brief questionnaire; (2) three additional trials with the same matrix and alternative; and finally (3) an opportunity to form contractual agreements which would govern the last three trials on the same matrix and alternative.[3]

Dependent measures. In addition to the tentative agreements, the actual choices in bargaining, and the outcomes received by P and by X on each trial, the dependent measures in the experiment included the interpolated questionnaire and the contractual decisions.

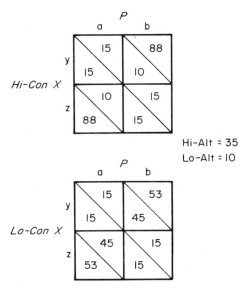

Hi-Alt = 35
Lo-Alt = 10

Fig. 2. *Matrices representing high and low conflict of interest and high and low levels of the external alternative.*

[3] A final questionnaire, also administered, is discussed elsewhere (Faucheux and Thibaut, 1964).

The *questionnaire* which was introduced after the first three trials on the experimental matrices asked each S to indicate on a 100-point scale the degree of his concern or anxiety about the fairness or equity of the division of points and about the likelihood that his partner would play the external alternatives. After each S had made his responses in private, the questionnaires were exchanged between partners. This device thus had two aims: to stimulate oral communication between partners about the variables being manipulated in the experiment and to gain data about the degree to which these variables were apprehended by and mattered to the Ss.

After the sixth trial on the experimental matrices the procedure for forming *contracts* was introduced. The E emphasized that contracts were entirely voluntary and that they need not be formed unless the Ss wanted them. On each of the three following trials each S recorded privately: (1) whether or not he wanted a contract to be formed, and (2) if in fact he wanted a contract to be formed, the single *rule* (among three presented to him) that he would most prefer to have incorporated in the contract and the type and amount of *sanction* that he would like to have applied to violations of any contractual rules.

The three rules among which each S wanting a contract had to choose were as follows:

EA-rule: it is prohibited to play the *external alternative* on this trial if a tentative agreement has been reached to play within the matrix.

D-rule: if on this trial a tentative agreement has been reached concerning the *division and distribution* of points between the partners, it is prohibited in the actual play to change the distribution agreed upon.

RC-rule: if on this trial a tentative agreement has been reached such that each partner is to play a specific *row or column* of the matrix, it is prohibited to shift in the actual play to the other row or column.

It will be apparent that the first two rules are designed to prohibit the kinds of behavior which on theoretical grounds may be expected to threaten differentially the two partners (whose anxiety about specifically these two sources of threat was earlier measured by the brief questionnaire). The third rule, which involves a type of behavior less central to the present research, was introduced primarily as a plausible third alternative which would permit the formation of types of contracts other than those envisaged by our theoretical formulation.

The two types of *sanction* afforded the Ss were indemnities and fines. Indemnities referred to payments (in points) the violator of a rule must make to the injured party. Fines referred to payments (in points) to be made by the violator to E. In the private recording of his preference for aspects of a contract, S could indicate any number of points between zero and 100 to be applied as an indemnity and/or as a fine.

After recording their individual preferences, the partners discussed the matter and decided whether to form a contract, and if a contract were to be formed, the rules and sanctions to be incorporated. The Ss were permitted to include in their contracts as many of the three rules as they liked and either or both types of sanctions. This procedure was repeated for three trials. Adherence to the various provisions of contracts was monitored and enforced by E.

Subjects and administration. Sixteen young adults of both sexes were formed into 8 dyads for the pretest. The experimental treatment was administered separately to each dyad, and the entire proceeding was tape-recorded. The Ss for the experiment proper were 100 14-year-old boys from two public schools in the suburbs of Paris: one at Chatenay and the other at Montrouge.[4] After the elimination from the sample

[4] We wish to thank Mademoiselle Hamel, Inspectrice de l'Enseignement Primaire; M. Forestier, Director of the School of Montrouge; M. Vlaeminkx, Director of the School of Chatenay; Madame Mongroville, directrice, and M. Pechberty (Centre d'Orientation Professionnelle de Montrouge).

of 2 dyads for failure to adhere to the instructions, there remained 24 dyads from each school. Six dyads at each school were assigned to each of the four treatments, making a total of 48 dyads, 12 for each treatment.

At each of the schools, the six dyads assigned to a given treatment were seated at widely separated tables in one large room, and the administration of the experiment thus proceeded simultaneously for all six dyads.[5]

RESULTS

In presenting the experimental findings, we shall proceed by first showing the objective situation confronting the Ss, then moving to the Ss' perception of this situation, and finally inquiring into the process of contract-formation and the characteristics of the contracts adopted.

The Bargaining Situation

There are two main aspects to the situation in which the Ss find themselves. These two aspects can be summarized by referring to the difference between the partners in the numbers of points won in the actual bargaining and to the frequencies with which the Ss chose to play the external alternative.

In presenting the data on points won in bargaining, let us consider the six trials that occurred before the opportunity to form contracts was introduced. (Data from the preliminary trials with the training matrix are, of course, omitted, since the experimental variations had not at that point been introduced.) Total points won in bargaining by dyads during these six trials show no mean differences among the four treatments. Dyads in the various treatments, therefore, were equally successful in their total productivity. On the other hand, the various treatments were not alike with respect to the share of the points won by P and X. Table 1 shows the mean differences between P and X in points received over the six trials before contracts were permitted. Although the variances from condition to condition are not homogeneous, it is plain that the sharing of points is much more nearly equal under low conflict of interest than under high. (High and low conflict of interest are different by analysis of variance: $F = 12.24$, $p < .001$.) A closely related finding is that under high conflict of interest there were 8 dyads in which on 19 occasions P failed to respect the agreement about sharing of points, but when conflict of interest was low, there were only 5 such instances in a total of 2 dyads. Hence, under conditions of high conflict of interest, X's share of the points is far exceeded by P's share, and the reduction of this disparity may pose a major problem for X.

The second aspect of the bargaining situation to be summarized here is the incidence of opting for the external alternative. It was frequently observed that an S would threaten to play the alternative without in fact doing so. Since these threats were not recorded (except in the pretests), the

[5] The assistance of Monique Fichelet, Marie Moscovici, Ferida Rasheed, and W. Doise in administering the experiment is gratefully acknowledged.

TABLE 1

Mean Differences between P and X in Points Received during the Six Trials Preceding the Contract Period

Conflict of interest		Level of external alternative	
		High	Low
High	Mᵃ	61.62	70.96
	SD	62.40	97.90
Low	M	2.79	3.25
	SD	16.71	48.73

ᵃ In all four conditions the mean difference signifies the preponderance of *P*'s share over *X*'s.

present data refer only to actual instances of playing the alternative. Table 2 shows, for all dyads in which either member at any time played the alternative, the number of dyads in which *P* was the first or only member to play the alternative, *X* was the first or only one to do so, or both members did so simultaneously. Note first that a total of 14 (58%) of the dyads in the High-Alternative conditions showed at least one instance of playing the alternative, as against only 4 (17%) of those in the Low-Alternative conditions. This difference yields a χ^2 of 7.20, which is significant at the .01 level. Note also that the initiative in playing the alternative rested mainly with *X*: in 11 dyads *X* was the first or only member to do so, but in only one dyad did *P* show this behavior. Hence, how to prevent *X* from playing the alternative may pose for *P* a major problem.

The Partners' Perception of the Situation

Though it may seem clear that the partners theoretically should have and empirically do have the problems just outlined, it may be important to

TABLE 2

Total Numbers of Dyads in the Various Treatments in which One or Both Members at Any Time Played the Alternative, with Specification of the Order of Doing So

Conflict of interest		Level of external alternative	
		High	Low
High	P first	0	0
	X first	5	3
	Simultaneous	4	0
	Total	9	3
Low	P first	1	0
	X first	2	1
	Simultaneous	2	0
	Total	5	1

assess the degree to which these problems actually are perceived by the partners and matter to them.

It will be recalled that after the first block of three trials on the experimental matrices, a brief questionnaire was administered, partly to stimulate communication between the partners about "fair sharing" and "loyalty" to the dyad, and partly to gain information about the degree to which at that stage the partners were concerned about these two problems. Our theoretical formulation would lead us to expect that P would be more concerned in the High-Alternative than in the Low-Alternative conditions about his partner's playing the alternative, and that X would be more concerned about equitable sharing in the High-Conflict than in the Low-Conflict conditions.

As to the first of these predictions, although P does in fact have a greater degree of concern when the alternative is high than when it is low (the means are 37.30 and 26.58, respectively), this difference does not reach an acceptable level of statistical significance. The second prediction, however, is clearly confirmed. X's concern about fair sharing is greater when conflict of interest is high than when it is low. The means are 38.34 and 25.71, respectively, and the variance analysis yields an F of 4.42, which is significant at the .05 level.

An analysis rather similar to that just summarized can be made from the Ss' preference for various types of rules to be incorporated in contracts. It will be recalled that at the beginning of each of the three trials during which contracts were permitted, each S had the opportunity to record privately his preferences for various aspects of a contract which might be negotiated with his partner. From our formulation it might be expected that, in all conditions, P's preference would exceed that of X for a rule prohibiting the use of the external alternative, and that X's preference would exceed that of P for a rule prohibiting the violation of any agreement reached about the sharing of points between the partners. Both of these expectations are strongly confirmed. In every one of the four conditions P preferred prohibiting the alternative more frequently than did X, the combined probabilities reaching significance at the .01 level. (However, this difference in frequency of preference was not significantly greater under High-Alternative than under Low-Alternative conditions.) Similarly, in every condition X preferred more frequently than did P a rule protecting any agreements about sharing, again with combined probabilities reaching the .01 level. (But again, too, this difference in frequency of preference was not significantly greater when conflict of interest was high than when it was low.)

The Contract

Throughout the following presentation of results, the term contract will be reserved for written agreements specifying at least one rule to be observed and including a sanction for violation in the form of an indemnity.

(Fines were so infrequently attached to contracts that we will omit any consideration of them in this discussion.)

Let us now turn to the various measures which reflect the over-all frequency and intensity of contractual activity in the four conditions. Table 3 summarizes these data. The HH condition shows clear superiority on each of the five measures.

Dyads in the HH condition formed on the average 2.75 contracts (the absolute limit being 3.00), as compared with means of less than two contracts in the other three conditions. An analysis of variance yields an F for interaction of 5.51, which is significant at the .05 level.

Similarly, all 12 of the HH dyads formed at least one contract, while only 64% of the dyads in the remaining conditions did so. This difference between HH and the other conditions combined is significant by χ^2 (4.25) at the .05 level.

The same pattern is revealed by the frequency with which dyads included both rules prohibiting the playing of the external alternative and rules protecting agreements concerning the division of points. In all, 75% of the HH dyads formed such contracts, but only 19% of the remaining dyads did so. This difference yields a χ^2 of 10.13, which is significant at well beyond the .01 level.

The mean size of indemnity for violation of contractual provisions is also atypically high in the HH condition. The F-ratio for interaction resulting from the analysis of variance was 4.93, which is significant at the .05 level.

TABLE 3

Frequency and Intensity of Contractual Activity in the Various Treatments

	Level of external alternative	
Conflict of interest	High	Low
Mean number of contracts	2.75	1.33
Number of dyads forming one or more contracts	12	6
High Number of dyads adopting both EA- and D-rules[a]	9	2
Mean indemnity	65.56	26.39
Index of quantity and intensity	315.83	175.00
Mean number of contracts	1.67	1.92
Number of dyads forming one or more contracts	9	8
Low Number of dyads adopting both EA- and D-rules[a]	2	3
Mean indemnity	35.83	42.22
Index of quantity and intensity	194.17	184.17

[a] EA-rules are prohibitions against playing the alternative; D-rules protect agreements about the division of points.

Finally, an index was constructed to estimate for each dyad the over-all quantity and intensity of its contractual activity by multiplying the number of rules adopted times the magnitude of indemnity to be paid for violations. The shapes of the resulting distributions are markedly different from condition to condition, and hence a variance analysis was not attempted. However, the Mann-Whitney test distinguishes the HH condition from the other conditions combined, yielding a p of exactly .02.

A word about the *effectiveness* of the contracts both from the point of view of the joint profit of the dyads and the division of points between the partners: To make the relevant comparisons, let us consider the joint profit of dyads for the six trials that preceded the contract period. The mean joint profit for these six trials was slightly higher for the 35 dyads that later formed contracts than for the 13 dyads that did not form contracts. Of the dyads forming contracts, 57% achieved the maximum possible joint profit (98 points) on each of the six trials, while only 31% of the "noncontractual" dyads achieved this level of joint profit. In spite of this initially higher level (though it is statistically nonsignificant), 86% of the dyads forming contracts maintained or increased their joint profit over the three trials of the contract period, while only 78% of the "non-contractual" dyads maintained or increased their initial levels of joint profit.

A more crucial test concerns the efficacy of contracts in reducing disparities in points received by the partners. If one compares the disparity in points received by the partners during the initial six trials with that of the three trials of the contract period, the efficacy of contracts becomes clear. In not a single one of the 13 dyads forming no contracts was there a reduction in this inter-partner disparity from the initial trials to the contract trials. However, 15 of the contractual dyads (including 8 from the HH treatment) showed reduced disparities during the contract phase. This difference yields a χ^2 of 6.23, which is significant at the .02 level.

Discussion and Conclusions

Although the task confronting the Ss in the present research was to bargain for points in the context of a game defined by the given matrix, the focus of the study has been not so much on the microscopic analysis of game-playing behavior as on the game situation as a device for studying the development of contractual agreements. The aim of the study, to relate the genesis of contracts to the joint application of external and internal stresses on groups containing members of unequal power, appears to have been realized.

Nevertheless, there are two aspects of the process of game-playing in the present experiment that require comment. The first has to do with the exercise of power in the bargaining process. The reader will have observed that the matrices employed in this research created an interdependence between the players such that neither partner could attain large outcomes without the cooperation of the other. The manipulation of the external alternative set the limit of outcomes that each player could dependably attain by his own efforts alone. From this point of view, then, the partners were equally dependent on one another for any outcomes superior to those of the external alternative.

Hence it may be difficult to see wherein lies the superior power of P. The answer to this question appears to be that both partners accept the E's definition of P's power and find it plausible that the person endowed with superior power should aim for the larger share of the group's rewards. In any case, if P is to compete successfully with other Ps he is forced to strain the upper limits of his possibilities. It is perhaps this aspiration for affluence, activated by E's definition of the possible prerogatives of power, which holds P to the interdependent solution, while at the same time driving X to abandon it. Moreover, both partners apparently felt it in accord with their experience in other groups, that the powerful member will have greater "usable" power as the conflict of interest increases. The present manipulation of P's power, aimed at insuring this relationship of usable power to conflict of interest, was crystallized during the pretests on the basis of reassuring evidence from the comments of Ss.

The second comment on the game-playing process concerns the intensity of the bargaining activity and the involvement of the Ss. There is no doubt that these were maximal in the HH condition and (though this must be said less confidently) that they were minimal in the LL condition. Though precise timing of the bargaining sessions was not attempted, it is worth noting that, both at Chatenay and Montrouge, the order of time taken to complete the experiment was, from greatest to least: HH, HL, LH, and LL.

A word about the LL condition: From the point of view of global theories of cohesiveness, this is the condition which should produce dyads of the greatest cohesiveness. The minimal external stress on such dyads means that, with minimally attractive external alternatives, the resultant motivation to remain in the group should be high. And minimal internal stress should mean that the attractiveness of the group would not be unnecessarily reduced by intermember conflict. It is entirely possible that such dyads would be maximally effective in enforcing conformity to any norms that existed in the group. But from the present research it seems unlikely that such norms, at least of the sort discussed here (of equity and loyalty), will be generated from within the group in the absence of temptations to violate them.

REFERENCES

Bertalanffy, L. von. Theoretical models in biology and psychology. *Journal of Personality*, 1951, **20**, 24–38.

Faucheux, C., and Thibaut, J. L'approche clinique et experimentale de la genèse des normes contractuelles dans differentes conditions de conflit et de menace. *Bulletin C.E.R.P., Paris,* 1964, **13,** 225–243.

Miller, J. G. Toward a general theory for the behavioral sciences. *American Psychology,* 1955, **10,** 513–531.

Seyle, H. The physiology and pathology of exposure to stress: a treatise based on the concepts of the general-adaptation syndrome and the diseases of adaptation. Montreal: Acta, 1950.

Thibaut, J., and Kelley, H. *The social psychology of groups.* New York: Wiley, 1959.

Part III

SMALL GROUPS

The literature in the area of small groups is vast and continues to grow. The proliferation of potentially relevant studies can be seen in the recent bibliography compiled by Raven (1969), which cites 5156 entries. His 1959 bibliography contained only 1314 entries. A discussion of small groups presents two major difficulties. The first is defining the domain of "small groups," while the second is finding a meaningful organization of material within that domain. The first issue will be circumvented by noting the elements most commonly included in definitions. The second issue has been solved by arbitrarily selecting an organization that makes a modicum of sense, but admittedly excludes considerable material.

Defining Small Groups

The area of small groups can be delineated by the following minimal circumstances. At least two or more people must be interacting together to obtain some goal. Ordinarily they share some important values and have agreed upon some norms which will affect their behavior while they act together. Groups, then, are collections of people who have come together for some purpose and who are aware of their interdependence in achieving that purpose. In a more limiting sense, the discussion will also be confined to groups that are small enough to be physically together and to engage in face-to-face interaction.

Problems of Systematization

The taxonomic dilemma has been aptly stated by Gerard and Miller (1967) who assert that: "The problem of organizing the research on group dynamics remains insoluble" (p. 288).

There are four interrelated features of small group research which have contributed to the lack of easy systematization. First the study of interaction means that each person being observed both responds to others and is himself a stimulus for others' responses. Consequently, the causal direction of any observed effect is more ambiguous than in research studying responses to fixed stimuli. Second, the interpretive problem is intensified when the phenomena of interest occur after a considerable time lapse beyond the experimental manipulation. During such intervals a number of processes may arise that could account for a particular consequence. Third, the study of interaction involves dimensions which are used as independent variables in some studies and as dependent variables in others. Fourth, the small group area places little restriction on the dependent variable to be studied. Experimental results, therefore, do not have a necessary relevance for each other. Despite the number of studies in this area, the number addressing themselves to the same problem is often relatively small. There are, nevertheless, numerous important issues in this area and a growing fund of substantive knowledge. The topics covered are intended to provide a grounding in small groups and to provide signposts to more advanced study.

A Working Organization

This section of the book will be organized around the sequential events which occur during group meetings. It begins with the preinteraction variables, such as group size, whose values are set before any interaction takes place. It then moves to group organization or internal variables, such as leadership. In both cases the classification of topics and related research relies on uses of preinteraction or internal variables as independent variables. A discussion of group decisions and intergroup relationships is reserved for the final two chapters. The organization of these chapters will, therefore, focus on the end products of group interaction, rather than on a specific set of independent variables.

Our presentation also will be limited to those studies reporting research on how groups work. This is one of the general orientations investigators have taken. Others have studied small groups because the group is a convenient setting for observing interpersonal problems. In this sense, some of the topics taken up in the previous section could as easily have been located in the present section. Small group research can also be undertaken with an eye to generalizing results to organizations existing in society. Such an approach is most often associated with sociology. Finally, investigators have studied groups in terms of the impact groups have on the environment and the changes they can bring about. While this orientation is an extension of the topics to be discussed, such implications will not be our primary concern.

An Important Distinction

All groups have goals. While these may vary in terms of their explicitness, importance, and content, members have some purpose in coming together as a group. The groups that will be considered are ones that have come together to solve an explicit task. As Schachter (1959) has noted, people can both mediate and be goals for each other. Group goals can include not only the achievement of specific tasks, but also the mere enjoyment of being with others. The end product of group interaction thus has the dual components of task performance and satisfaction with the group.

In considering task-oriented or problem-solving groups, a rough but useful distinction can be made. It involves the extent to which the members' behaviors are controlled by the necessities of task accomplishment versus the extent to which they are controlled by the process of interacting. This distinction has been made in various forms. Homans (1950) distinguished between the "external" and "internal" systems. The external system refers to the environmental prerequisites a group must meet in order to remain functioning and viable. It includes solving such problems as working on the task, adapting to the physical environment, and defining relationships with other groups. The internal system defines the environment the people in a group create for each other and encompasses such features as their feelings for each other, their division of labor, and their patterns of interaction. In a similar way, Bales (1950) has distinguished task activity from maintenance activity. Bales adds the contention that the group organization which is optimal for solving problems associated with task activity is inherently maladaptive for solving problems associated with maintenance activity. Conversely, the group organization which is optimal for solving problems associated with maintenance activity is inherently maladaptive for solving problems associated with task activity. Collins and Guetzkow (1964) also use the distinction between task and maintenance activities to organize various propositions about small groups.

Chapter 12

PREINTERACTION VARIABLES

Preinteraction variables refer to dimensions usually present or established before the beginning of any group meeting, which may affect what happens during the subsequent group interaction. Seating arrangement, group size, and group composition are discussed as three examples of such variables.

Seating Arrangement

The idea that the spatial distance separating people may have an effect on their interactions is not new to the reader. In Chapter 9 we discussed the effects of propinquity on attraction. Although the direct extension of studying the relationship between the physical distance separating group members and amount of attraction has not been made, spatial factors have been studied in two main ways. One of these is to see if a member's location in a particular seating arrangement affects how much he participates. The second is to relate seating arrangements to the direction of communication. Seating arrangements lend themselves more readily to studying group processes than task performance.

PARTICIPATION AND INFLUENCE

A leader of a group is usually physically located in a place where he can maximally influence the events occurring in the group. The speaker in the House of Representatives, as well as a teacher in a classroom, is ordinarily seated in front of the group. The front is the most advantageous position when members are seated in rows. Since there are many other possible seating arrangements, it is probably better to say that the leader is located in the most prominent position, whether or not this happens to be in the front of the group. In discussion groups, where there is no special effort made to institutionalize the leader's location in a prominent position, the effect also holds. Strodtbeck and Hook (1961), for example, reanalyzed data collected in an experimental jury deliberation setting to assess the effect of seating position. Their subjects had been seated around a rectangular table to discuss trial evidence and to reach a verdict. The people who sat at the end or corners of the table, the most prominent places, participated more in the discussion and were rated as having had more influence than the people seated at the sides of the table. Two distinct, yet complementary processes, could contribute to these findings. The first of these is the extent to which the physical location of a member determines his participation. The second is the extent to which the people who are most eager to participate select positions which are prominent. These processes can only be disentangled by randomly assigning members to fixed locations and then measuring amount of participation or influence.

A study by Howells and Becker (1962) is an example of a relatively simple study addressing itself to this point. Five-person groups were randomly seated around a rectangular table and were asked to compose anagrams. Two members were on one side of the table and three on the other side. The two-seat side of the table was predicted to produce more leaders. The prediction was convincingly confirmed. Howells and Becker linked leadership emergence to communication flow, although no data were presented on this point.

Additional verification of the empirical relationship between the prominence of a position and perceived leadership has been provided by Ward (1968). Five-person groups were randomly assigned to predetermined positions in a circle, comprised of eight classroom chairs. Three subjects were always assigned to adjacent chairs, while the remaining two subjects were placed on the opposite side. They were separated by an empty chair from each other and from the three adjacent subjects. The places occupied by the two subjects were most prominent, in terms of their visual accessibility. After reading a case history, each group engaged in a 30 minute discussion. Although the two subjects in the prominent seats were ranked higher on guidance, ideas, and likability than the other three subjects, the differences were not significant. The effect was evidently blunted by the unfortunate happenstance that in about half of the groups some of the subjects knew each other before the experiment. In groups containing only unacquainted members the effect was marginally significant. For these groups the participation rate of the subjects in the prominent seats was also higher than the other three subjects. The mediating mechanism suggested by Howells and Becker was, therefore, given some credence because seating arrangement affected the communication flow.

The use of seating arrangement as an independent variable is usually credited to Steinzor (1950). While observing a training group, Steinzor noted one participant changing seats in order to be directly across from someone with whom he had been arguing. This suggested the hypothesis that communication is more likely to be directed toward persons seated across than toward persons sitting next to each other. The predicted effects were thought to be mediated by the greater physical and expressive stimulus value of those seated opposite each other. Steinzor noted who talked after whom in two different groups. While the data were not completely uniform, the hypothesis was confirmed. Group members did tend to talk immediately after someone opposite them had spoken.

There are limitations to the kind of seating arrangement manipulations which can be made. Sommer (1967), in an excellent review of research related to group ecology, introduced an important caution, especially for designing experiments in natural settings. Despite the virtues of random assignment, Sommer notes, "It must be recognized that these conditions are highly artificial in a society that typically allocates space according to status considerations" (p. 147). Manipulations which severely violate expectations about the concomitant rights of status would not be tolerated by potential subjects.

Normative Distances

One of the most innovative observations about the effect of spatial distance on interactions has been made by Hall (1959). Although these observations led to using distance as a dependent variable it will be discussed briefly because of its general applicability. In attempting to account for why travelers to different cultures feel some anxiety, or cultural shock, Hall noted the possibility that each culture has implicit norms that govern aspects of interaction. The expected spatial distance separating two people interacting is such a norm. Hall claimed that the normative distance between people conversing in our culture is larger than for South American

cultures. If someone from our culture travels to South America, his interactions will produce anxiety because his expectations about proper distance
between conversing pairs will be constantly violated. As he moves back to
establish what is comfortable for him, the people to whom he is talking feel
some discomfort and move closer to reestablish what is normative for them.
There is, of course, no single distance in a given culture which is always
appropriate. The normative distance will depend upon circumstances and
the role relationship linking the participants. For example, the distance
between intimate pairs will be closer than between strangers.

Hall's ideas have inspired various lines of research activity. Lott and
Sommers (1967), for example, have shown that status of the participants is
a determinant of distance. When given a choice of where to sit, their subjects sat further away from someone of higher status than someone of equal
or lower status.

Group Size

The well-worn saying that two is company, but three is a crowd ex-
presses folk wisdom about the effects of group size upon the solidarity of
the group. Although some research on group size has been concerned with
dependent-variable measures such as member satisfaction or group processes, the major focus has been on task performance.

TASK PERFORMANCE

Despite Parkinson's (1957) whimsical arguments about the inevitable
existence of a negative correlation between an organization's size and its
productivity (because people make work for each other), it seems intuitively correct to believe that as the number of members in a problem-
solving group increases, productivity will increase. One of the earlier studies relating group size to productivity was conducted by Gibb (1951), who
sampled group sizes ranging from 1 to 96 members. Each group was asked
to name as many different solutions as possible for three kinds of problems.
One problem, for example, involved how to improve the public relations
policy of the university. As group size increased so did the number of ideas
offered, but the increase in ideas did not keep pace with the increase in
members for the larger groups. Gibb reported performance to be a negatively accelerated increasing function of size. Taylor and Faust (1952) compared the performance of individuals, two-person groups and four-person
groups on the game of "20 questions." This used to be a popular parlor
game played by one person's thinking of an object and revealing only
whether the object is classified as animal, vegetable, or mineral. The participants must identify the object by asking questions which can be answered by a "Yes" or "No." Taylor and Faust permitted each group to use

as many as 30 questions. The major measures of performance were the number of questions used and the total time required for solution. The four-person groups used fewer questions than the two-person groups or than individuals, but four-person groups also required more time. The group experience did not improve the performance of its members when they were subsequently tested in individual sessions.

TAXONOMY OF TASKS

In order to understand the conditions under which a positive relationship between increases in size and performance are likely to hold it will be necessary to make some preliminary distinctions about task characteristics. It is fitting to do this at the outset of the group section because of the general importance of understanding how features of a task determine what happens in a group. Indeed, devising an adequate taxonomy of tasks is among the most critical issues awaiting solution. To date there is no generally accepted taxonomy, but steps in this direction have been taken by several authors. For example, Shaw (1963) has attempted to isolate and scale substantive dimensions contained in a variety of tasks; Roby and Lanzetta (1958) have made a comprehensive analysis relating task features to demands placed on the group. More recently, Roby (1968) has developed a sophisticated framework for analyzing performance functions.

The explanation of group-size effects proposed by Steiner (1966) will be used in the following discussion. He detailed various problem-solving models, each of which implicitly recognized distinctions among tasks. Steiner begins his analysis by noting that group productivity is determined by three classes of variables: task demands, resources, and group process. The fit between available member resources and task requirements determines the potential productivity possible for any group. In principle, it would be possible to specify any group's maximum level of performance from a joint knowledge of the skills required by a particular task and the level of skill possessed by the members. In Steiner's view potential productivity is always greater than actual productivity. When a group works on a task it must assemble its resources, make plans, and generally coordinate its efforts. Thus, such general group processes, as well as motivational losses, detract from potential productivity to determine actual productivity. Because potential productivity is determined by the group's supply of relevant resources, Steiner uses simple principles of sampling theory to estimate the effect the increases in size will have upon available resources. The analysis proceeds by classifying various kinds of task requirements and assumes the requisite task skills can be identified.

The simplest situation is *a task for which the members' responses are added.* Pulling on a rope, or any idea problem in which the greater the number of suggestions the higher the group score, would illustrate such tasks. Because the responses are additive, the potential performance of groups is a linear function of size. A four-person group should accomplish twice as much as a two-person group. The actual performance of groups is not likely, however, to show linear increases because of losses. In the case of rope pulling it is evident that problems of coordination will be critical; for the idea problem it is more likely that motivational losses will occur. As long as the process and/or motivational losses do not exceed the gains made by adding members, larger groups will perform more, even though the relationship will not be linear.

Some tasks (or the rules imposed on the group for working on the task) *require that only one member's response counts as the group's performance.* This can be considered a disjunctive requirement. The potential productivity of a group is then solely determined by the abilities of the most competent member. Steiner points out that as group size increases, the degree of competence of the ablest member is also likely to be greater. A positive relationship between size and performance is therefore expected. This is especially likely for tasks containing feedback about correctness, for example, the "Eureka" class of problems for which the correct insight is readily recognized by all the members, or for tasks whose ability requirements are easy to discern by the group members. Identifying the person who can best pull a rope, in a situation where only one member is allowed to pull, might be easier than finding the person with the best vocabulary skills.

Other tasks (or the rules imposed for working on the task) *require that all members make the correct response* or that group productivity is determined by the least competent member. This can be considered a *conjunctive* requirement. The total work output of an assembly line is determined by the least competent member. A team of mountain climbers, to use Steiner's example, can move no faster than its slowest member. In this instance, increasing group size will make inclusion of someone with greater incompetence more likely and should produce a negative relationship with performance. If one is assembling chains from a population of variable links, the longest chains are more likely to contain the weakest links. When the conjunctive requirement is not absolute, however, the potential productivity may depend upon the ability of the second or third most competent member. This would typically pertain to instances where group size exceeds the number of functions to be performed, for example, when a five-person mountain-climbing group must select two members to make the final ascent. Because the competence of the *ith* most competent person will be greater in larger groups, size and performance should show a positive relationship. According to Steiner, the expected increments of competence are such that potential productivity increases as a negatively accelerated function of group size.

Finally, Steiner discusses *tasks which can be divided into subparts.* Solving such tasks is frequently the most relevant use of groups, because a group can succeed on tasks for which no single member necessarily has all the relevant skills. The "20 questions" game illustrates this type of task. It should be easy to see by now that as group size increases, groups are more likely to include members who jointly have the required skills. In this instance, potential productivity will increase with size. Increased size will produce increased actual productivity except when organizational difficulties occur, or when motivational losses are high. Organizational difficulties occur, for example, when there is a failure to identify or use competent members.

GROUP PROCESSES

At the turn of the century the sociologist Simmel (reprinted 1966) made some insightful observations about the inherent differences between a dyad and a triad. For example, a triad cannot as easily achieve uniformity of mood as a dyad. On the other hand, Simmel also noted that in a triad conflicts between any two members could be mediated by the third person. Members of a dyad must resolve conflicts between themselves. In addition, the triad is the minimum size group which can remain a group after losing one member. The consequences of exercising power, in terms of taking up an alternative relationship, are therefore likely to be more severe in a dyad than in a triad.

Although modern research seems unaffected by Simmel's observations, it has independently corroborated some of them. Two-person groups have consistently been found to have unique process characteristics. Bales and Borgatta (1955), for example, categorized the kind of interpersonal acts occurring in groups varying in size from two to seven members. The frequency of occurrence for each type of act was then transformed to a proportion of the total acts observed for each group. Two-person groups showed a number of distinct features. For example, they evoked relatively fewer expressions of hostility, but more tension. Dyads have also been found to have a lower volume of activity than larger groups. The study by O'Dell (1968), placed in the Readings section, verifies these findings regarding hostility, tension, and activity. He designed one of the few studies in which the time for group discussion corresponded to the number of members in the group. Instead of using a fixed time period during which groups of different sizes must complete a task, the total time allotted to any group of a given size was determined by multiplying nine minutes by the number of persons in the group.

In general, as group size increases a number of consequences for group process follow. As group size increases there is a geometric increase in the number of potential relationships which could be established or maintained. For a fixed time period, to maintain all of them allows less time for each relationship or less time for task activity. In a similar way, as size increases there is less opportunity for any given member to speak. Although the total number of people who speak at least once increases with size, the average amount of time each person speaks decreases. From what has been said previously about spatial arrangements, it should also be evident that groups containing more people must accommodate themselves to different inter-member distances. The exact differences will depend upon the physical arrangement used, but it is likely that members of larger groups will be closer to immediate neighbors and further away from the most distant member than in smaller groups. All of these consequences may contribute to the empirical findings, reviewed by Thomas and Fink (1963), that feelings of intimacy and satisfaction with the group decline with larger sizes, while there is an increase in division of labor and organization, as well as clique formation.

GROUP SIZE AND SPACE

All the research on group size has used locations which are sufficiently spacious to accommodate the largest size group observed. If an experimenter were to use a fixed amount of space that was too small to permit adherence to the expected interpersonal distance norms, he would be studying the phenomenon of crowding. Social psychologists have only recently conducted studies in this area, although interesting findings have been available for some time on research with animals. Calhoun (1962), for example, reports a series of experiments in which the size of groups of domesticated albino rats was permitted to increase to about twice the number judged to be appropriate for the available space. In each series of experiments the stress of overcrowding produced considerable behavioral pathology. Disruption of normal behavior patterns was noted on such indices as courting behavior, eating patterns, and physical activity. The consequences for females were most apparent. Disruption of normal pregnancy and of the ability to care for their young, as well as infant mortality, were extremely high. The strain of crowding did not fall equally on all members of the group. Dominant males, for example, secured large territories which were inhabited by a number of females. These animals showed the lowest indices of pathological behavior. The other animals, who lived in a disproportionately small amount of space, showed the highest indices of pathology. In one series of studies the effects of crowding became especially acute for these animals. The effects were so appalling, the experimenters termed the situation a "behavioral sink." Calhoun believes the major bases for the development of the behavioral sink was the use of food pellets requiring a sustained chewing effort of several minutes. Feeding thus became associated with the presence of others and the animals developed a preference for eating in the presence of others. These preferences magnified the crowding around the food hoppers.

While the Calhoun results are suggestive, it is not evident what mediates the negative effects of crowding or to what extent these results apply
to human groups. Freedman, Klevansky, and Ehrlich (1971) investigated
the effects of crowding upon task performance. They reviewed the available literature, including the work of Calhoun and Hall, and formulated a
simple, working hypothesis to guide their research. Population density, like
any other strong stimulus, at some level of intensity, was predicted to produce stress. Crowding, that is, population density at intense levels, was
expected to induce performance decrements, especially on complex tasks
and on tasks requiring the learning of new material. The authors wished to
study the "pure" effects of density while eliminating or controlling other
factors which are often associated with crowding. Crowding would obviously decrease task performance if there was insufficient space to permit
manipulating task material, too much noise to hear instructions, or uncom-
fortably hot temperatures. Although inadequate space, intense noise, and
hot temperatures may often be concomitants of crowding, they can be
eliminated in the real world in circumstances where crowding remains.

Three separate studies were conducted. The typical procedure was to
test a nine-person group in a small room while a different nine-person group
was being tested in a large room. It is difficult to specify the exact level of
density which defines crowding. Freedman et al. manipulated crowding by
varying the size of the room in which subjects were seated. The small room
could not hold an additional chair and all subjects were seated against a
wall. The large room, on the other hand, provided ample space. Within the
confines of eliminating some of the negative concomitants of crowding, this
appears to be an appropriate manipulation. A variety of tasks, primarily
tasks requiring individual answers, were used. Subjects worked on the tasks
for four hours from two to three successive days. Crowding had no discerni-
ble effects on problem solving for any of the tasks. Although negative results are always difficult to interpret, it is at least clear that crowding per
se does not inevitably interfere with problem solving. The authors speculate
that the harmful effects of crowding are likely to be revealed in the interactions among people. It is perhaps through interference with the ability
of groups to organize and to develop norms that the disruptive effects of
crowding are evoked.

A Note on Group Size and Bystander Intervention

The relation between group size and the likelihood of a bystander intervening in an emergency has been investigated by Latané and Darley
(1970). Bystanders are people who happen to be witnesses to another person's emergency. Because bystanders are unacquainted with each other or
with the victim, as well as having no shared goals which guide their interaction, they are collections of people rather than groups. We will never-

theless discuss this research because it utilizes size as an independent variable and it is interesting.

The general prediction guiding this research was that the likelihood of any given bystander intervening in an emergency would decrease as the number of bystanders present increased. To test this hypothesis it was necessary to stage emergencies which were equally plausible for different numbers of bystanders. Darley and Latané (1968), for example, recruited subjects to participate in an experiment in which they would discuss "personal problems associated with college life." Ostensibly to avoid embarrassment and to preserve anonymity, each subject was seated in an individual room and the discussion was conducted over an intercom system. Subjects were also told the experimenter would not be listening to the discussion, in order to remove possible inhibitions. During the course of the discussion one of the participants underwent what sounded like a severe seizure "similar to epilepsy." The seizure was actually tape-recorded. Because the experimenter was known to be unaware of the events in the discussion, the major dependent variable measure was the speed with which subjects reported the emergency to the experimenter, who was seated in the hall. The number of bystanders the subjects believed to be present was manipulated. Some subjects thought they were alone with the victim, some thought there was one other bystander, and some thought there were four other bystanders. On several indices of speed of helping, the predictions were confirmed. As the number of bystanders increased the speed of helping decreased. For example, 85 percent of the subjects who thought they were alone with the victim reported the emergency within 55 seconds of its onset, whereas only 31 percent of the subjects who thought they were with four others intervened. After four minutes from the onset of the fit no one who had not already decided to intervene did so. By that time all of the alone subjects, but only 62 percent of the subjects who thought they were with four others, intervened. The responses of subjects who thought they were with one other bystander fell between the other two conditions, but were closer to the alone condition.

The results of the "fit" experiment were similar to other experiments in which smoke suddenly puffed into a room while subjects were completing a questionnaire or a female experimenter had a serious fall in a room adjacent to the subjects' room. As the number of bystanders increased the speed and likelihood of any given bystander intervening decreased. Latané and Darley suggested that group size serves to diffuse the personal responsibility felt by any single bystander for deciding to help and diffuses potential self-blame for not helping. A person who is by himself knows he must intervene if any help is to be forthcoming. For five bystanders it is less clear why one of them, rather than another, should step forward to help. In addition, because emergencies are typically ambiguous situations, bystanders may tend to distort emergencies toward seeing them as being harmless.

The quarrel on the street may be an assault or a family disagreement. A bystander who convinces himself it is a family disagreement does not need to decide whether or not to intervene. Such distortions may be facilitated by the presence of other bystanders who remain inactive. Their passivity can be an erroneous cue that the situation is harmless. Latané and Darley suggest the explanations of why bystanders do not help a victim appear to have more to do with the bystander's responses to other observers than with such personality attributes as "apathy" or "indifference."

Group Composition

In many situations it is important to know how to select members in order to constitute an optimum group. What kinds of people should be placed in a particular group in order to produce interpersonal harmony and maximum task effectiveness? This question runs through the mind of a hostess planning a dinner party, a therapist selecting patients for group psychotherapy, the person in charge of selecting astronaut teams for space flights, or anyone having the opportunity selectively to choose group members. Such member attributes as abilities, attitudes, traits, or interaction styles seem to be obvious candidates for predicting the resultant group process and task performance. It seems apparent that group composition research could bring together the wisdom of personality and social psychologists in an arena representing the pinnacle of verification for such integrations. The existing research does not quite match such lofty ideals. The chief difficulty seems to be a lack of theoretical concepts which span the effects of member attributes on group process and subsequent task performance. McGrath and Altman (1966) lament that the theoretical underpinnings of group composition studies, ". . . are often little more than formalizations of such contradictory premises as 'birds of a feather flock together,' 'opposites attract' . . ." (p. 60). (These proverbs have also guided research on the relation between similarity and attraction.) A related difficulty stems from the likelihood that member characteristics do not have simple relationships to particular dependent variables. Increasing amounts of traits such as authoritarianism or dominance will not always decrease harmony or task performance, but are likely to be affected by situational variables. Several studies have shown, for example, that the existence of a clear group structure mitigates member effects found in groups that have not evolved a clear structure.

Ability and Adjustment

Most of the group composition research has attempted to determine how different patterns of member traits affect task performance. In his review of these studies, Heslin (1964) concluded that only two kinds of member characteristics have shown consistent effects on performance. Groups composed of members who have better abilities or who are better adjusted perform better than groups whose members have lesser amounts of these traits. The kind of reasoning detailed for group-size effects pertains to these results. Composition by ability merely increases the probability that a high-ability group will contain members who possess the relevant task competence. This explanation would also account for the positive relation between the members' degree of adjustment and task performance, if adjustment and task competence are positively correlated. A second possibility, which is not mutually exclusive of the first, is that better adjusted persons are able to evolve better group organization. They may use their available resources more efficiently.

A study by Johnson and Torcivia (1967) illustrates the expected effect of composition by member abilities on task performance. At the start of the experiment, subjects, working individually, answered Maier's horse-trading problem.[1] They were then asked to solve the same problem a second time, either individually or in pairs. By using the subjects' initial answers, four types of pairs were formed. These included pairs in which both subjects had been correct, only one had been correct, both gave the same wrong answer, and both gave different wrong answers. Pairs had 15 minutes to agree on a single answer. As would be expected for a single-stage, conjunctive task, pairs who were initially correct performed better than pairs who were initially incorrect. Furthermore, pairs who initially had different wrong answers performed as poorly as pairs with the same wrong answer. The resolutions achieved by the former pairs could not be accounted for by differences between the two members in initial certainty about their own answer. For pairs containing one initially correct subject, however, the joint answer was more often correct than wrong and certainty was related to the joint answer selected.

The horse-trading problem tends to favor males. Hoffman and Maier (1961) demonstrated this in a study composing groups by sex of subject. Subjects were formed into four-person groups and asked to answer the problem individually without prior discussion. Some groups contained only males, some only females, and some two males and two females. Subsequent to an eight-minute discussion, each subject was individually tested again. Members of male groups, who initially had a larger percentage of correct answers (52.3) than did females (21.9), also had a larger percentage the second time (85.6) compared to members of female groups (49.6).

[1] The Maier's horse-trading problem used in this study and by Hoffman and Maier (1961) in the following study has frequently been used as a group task. It is deceptively simple. "A man bought a horse for $60.00 and sold it for $70.00. Then he bought it back again for $80.00 and sold it for $90.00. How much money did he make in the horse business?" (Johnson & Torcivia, 1967, p. 269). Twenty dollars is the correct answer; $10 and $30 are the most frequently occurring incorrect answers.

After group discussion, the percentage of correct responses for males (83.3) and females (80.3) in mixed groups was comparable to the performance of the males. The authors viewed the increased female performance in mixed groups as a joint function of a greater likelihood of exposure to the correct solution and of conformity to the answer favored by a majority. The experimenters also found a marginally significant difference on the percentage of *initially* correct answers between females in mixed groups and in all female groups. More females in the mixed groups obtained correct answers. This is an instance of a composition variable affecting motivation; most likely the effect is due to mixed groups increasing motivation rather than all female groups inducing a motivational loss.

HOMOGENEITY VS. HETEROGENEITY

Composition predictions about task performance have also been made for groups whose members possess similar attitudes or orientations compared to groups whose members differ on these dimensions. Schutz (1966) conducted such a study using a test of interpersonal orientations he had developed. According to Schutz, a stable group structure in a five-person group requires similar interpersonal orientations between the leader and the main supporting member, that is, the two key members. Given such similarity, Schutz defined a compatible group as one in which the other members share the orientation of the two key members. In other words, the group is homogeneous with respect to their interpersonal orientation. An incompatible group is one in which the key members have an orientation opposite to that of the other members. Members with similar orientations are expected to form subgroups, but the two subgroups will be antagonistic towards each other. Task efficiency will then be lowered. The study utilized measures of the subjects' orientation toward "personalness," which involves the individual's orientation toward giving and receiving affection. People scoring at one end of this dimension were labeled "overpersonal," and people scoring at the other end were labeled "underpersonal." Two kinds of compatible groups were formed. In one, all members were homogeneous with respect to being overpersonal, while in the other all members were underpersonal. The incompatible groups consisted of overpersonal key members and underpersonal other members. Four 5-person groups were formed for each of the three composition types. The groups met 14 times over a six-week period and were assigned a variety of tasks. Performance on tasks yielding an objective measure of correctness were summed to form a single score of overall task productivity for each group. On the total score compatible groups did not differ from each other, but their productivity was significantly better than the incompatible groups. The direction of members' orientation did not affect task performance, but the degree of homogeneity of these orientations did affect productivity.

All instances of member homogeneity will not enhance task productivity. Obviously, homogeneity of task incompetence guarantees poor performance. There are, however, many other member characteristics which do not correlate with task ability. What can be said about the consequences of homogeneity on these dimensions? In keeping with the discussion of group-size effects, an answer is suggested. The effects of homogeneity will depend upon the consequences for group processes and member motivation. The task efforts of Schutz' compatible groups were assumed to be unblemished by subgroup antagonisms. Homogeneously underpersonal and homogeneously overpersonal groups did not differ on task competence. Composition based on other dimensions, however, could define member characteristics whose homogeneity would affect group processes and member motivation. The next study to be discussed does not contrast homogeneous with heterogeneous groups, but does illustrate how homogeneity of the members' participation rate produces different task productivity and member satisfaction. These effects appear to be mediated by process and motivational differences.

A person's typical participation rate in class discussions was used by Knutson (1960) to compose groups. After obtaining stable estimates of the participation rate of 31 graduate students in a public health curriculum, Knutson formed four groups. In descending order of the members' amount of participation, these groups were termed very vocal, vocal, quiet, and very quiet. As part of a class assignment, each group had three meetings to write a critique of a health pamphlet. The adequacy of the final written products were judged by two experts. After the last meeting subjects rated how they felt toward their own group and its productivity. The results were striking. In comparison to members of the two quiet groups, members of the two vocal groups consistently rated their own groups more favorably. On task performance, however, the results were exactly opposite. Both experts judged the very quiet group as having produced the best product and the quiet group second best. The experts differed only on whether they ranked the product of the very vocal group as third or fourth best.

There are many factors which could account for the better performance of the quiet groups. The study was not sufficiently controlled to permit specifying the most important variables. Knutson emphasized the process differences between the extreme groups. The homogeneous, high-participators seemed to have engaged in competition for leadership to the neglect of other task roles. The time required for evolving a viable structure may also have detracted from the time available for work. The very quiet group also had process problems, but their difficulties stemmed from the members' unwillingness to participate. This was dramatized at the start of their first meeting, which was spent in silence for the first 15 minutes. The person who broke the silence was looked to as the leader. This kind of process, or perhaps lack of process, may have enhanced the opportunities for working

on the task. It is tempting to think of the quiet people as studiously working through the task at the expense of interpersonal satisfactions. It is also
possible, however, that dissatisfaction with the group induced these persons to work harder outside of the scheduled meetings.

A different relationship between homogeneity and task performance was
found by Tuckman (1967) who composed three-person groups using the
subjects' level of abstract thinking and degree of dominance. Three levels
of homogeneity were manipulated to produce homogeneous, intermediate,
and heterogeneous groups. Each group worked on one structured task and
one unstructured task. The groups of intermediate homogeneity performed
significantly worse than the other two groups on the structured task, but
performed nonsignificantly better on the unstructured task. An observer's
ratings of group process revealed that the intermediate groups evolved
significantly less role differentiation than either the homogeneous or heterogeneous groups. Taken together these results suggest that the effect of
group composition was mediated by the group structure evolved. Groups
who were composed in ways that produced a structure performed better
on the task requiring a structure. Tuckman's study also illustrates how the
effects of group composition can interact with task characteristics, a matter
we will take up next.

COMPOSITION AND TASK INTERACTIONS

An excellent example of how member characteristics can interact with
task features is contained in a study reported by Davis (1969). Although
the study was designed to evaluate problem-solving models as well as
member-task interactions, only the results relevant to the latter issue will
be summarized. Subjects were given an opportunity to state their preference between working individually or with others on "challenging intellectual problems." Half of the subjects were randomly assigned to the condition they preferred and half were not. Three-person groups were
formed, consisting of people who preferred to work in a group or people
who preferred to work individually. Each group worked on two kinds of
problems. One problem (five simple arithmetic questions) could easily be
subdivided. The other problem (number reasoning) was a single-stage task.
Although members could simultaneously work out solutions, the problem
could not be divided into separate parts. Performance was measured by
speed and correctness of solutions. For speed of solution the finding of
relevance to group composition was an interaction between type of group
and task. Groups composed of members preferring groups worked better
on the task permitting division of labor and interaction, while the task
which could not be divided was more effectively solved by groups composed of members preferring to work individually. This effect was shown to
be unrelated to the correlation between subjects' preferences and their task

abilities. Preferences did affect group process as measured by amount of participation. Groups composed of people who preferred groups had an average participation rate significantly greater than the groups whose members wished to work individually.

Overview

Preinteraction variables refer to those factors which are established prior to any group interaction. Three examples of such variables, seating arrangements, group size, and group composition, were discussed. *Seating arrangement* effects can be summarized as showing a positive relationship between the prominence of a position and the perceived leadership of the occupant of that position and a greater communication flow between persons seated across from each other than next to each other. These effects appear to be most pronounced when such variables as prior acquaintance are absent or members' task skills are not salient. These effects probably play a more critical role in the early stages of group formation than during later stages. Whether *group size* helps or hinders task performance depends upon the interrelationship of the level of members' skill, the demands of the task, and the group process. The level of skill possessed by the members of different size groups can be estimated by simple principles of sampling. When these estimates are combined with knowledge of the task demands and estimates of the consequent group process, predictions can be made about the effects of group size on task performance. In general, as group size increases, feelings of intimacy and satisfaction decline, while the degree of organization and clique formation increases. Any discriminable attribute of individuals could serve as the basis for *group composition*. The particular content of the attribute used to compose groups determines whether heterogeneity or homogeneity will help or hinder the group's task accomplishment. It was suggested that the effect on group processes is an important determinant of predicting the consequences of various kinds of composition.

READINGS

Group Size and Emotional Interaction[1]

Jerry W. O'Dell

The discussions of 10 groups each of sizes 2–5 were coded into both the Bales and Leary category systems, and these scores were analyzed across group size. Almost all significant findings occurred in comparing dyads with groups of other sizes. The major finding was that the dyadic groups produced only ¾ as much total interaction as groups of other sizes. Dyadic groups expressed relatively less hostility and more tension than groups of larger sizes. These last 2 findings agreed with a previous study, but appeared more acceptable in the present study because: (a) A larger sample was used; (b) raw data, rather than percentages were analyzed; (c) distorting time pressures on coders were largely eliminated; and (d) time of discussion was increased with group size, thereby controlling for increasing resource input with the size of the group.

Although group size is perhaps the least ambiguous and most precisely measurable characteristic of small groups, the many studies on the topic have not been conducted in the systematic manner that the clarity of the variable would seem to allow. Indeed, group size is often included in a study only as an afterthought, simply because it is such an obvious and available characteristic. As Thomas and Fink (1963) noted, such unsystematic approaches have too often led to the confounding of group-size effects with those of other variables in the experiment. Moreover, few group-size studies concern themselves with group process; most are concerned only with outcome or product.

A notable exception to this is the Bales and Borgatta (1955) study in which problem-solving groups of sizes from two to seven were observed in detail with Bales' (1951) Interaction Process Analysis System. It was found that as group size increased, there were significant increases in showing tension release and giving suggestions; decreases with size occurred in tension expression, agreement, disagreement, and asking for opinion. Dyads also were so different in the following respects that they were termed "unique": they had a very high rate of showing tension, and a very low rate of showing antagonism, asking for orientation, and asking for opinion.

[1] From the *Journal of Personality and Social Psychology*, Volume 8, pages 75–78, 1968 (received January 26, 1967). Author's affiliation: Eastern Michigan University. This paper is based on a dissertation submitted to the Horace H. Rackham School of Graduate Studies of the University of Michigan in partial fulfillment of the requirements for the PhD degree. Reproduced by permission of the American Psychological Association.

In short, dyads were the most strained in their interaction, in contrast to popular belief. In view of the striking nature and potential importance of these findings, it is rather surprising that no one has tried a follow-up study. This is the purpose of the present paper.

In attempting to account for the restraint in the dyads, Slater (1958) hypothesized that experimental dyadic groups, if they are required to continue functioning, cannot tolerate actions (such as hostility of any kind) which could be absorbed in larger groups; this leads to the inhibition that is seen in dyads. Slater constructed an "Inhibition Index" from the Bales scores and showed that it decreased with size.

Unfortunately, there are deficiencies in the Bales and Borgatta (1955) study. Only four groups of each size were studied. Data were analyzed as transformed percentages, destroying the independence of the data and obscuring variations in absolute rates of interaction. Discussion time remained constant during sessions despite differing group size, thus allowing resource input to become a confounding variable. Finally, it is possible that differences found with dyadic groups could merely have been artifacts arising from lesser time pressures placed on Bales coders in smaller groups. As shown in the present study, the pace of interaction is a good deal slower in smaller than in larger groups, so that coders in dyadic groups have more time to think about their coding. If they are trying to code something like anxiety, which takes a bit of reflection, perhaps more of it will be scored in smaller groups simply because there is less time pressure. Also, in larger groups, with more rapid interaction, it is likely that more dramatic actions will receive more attention and be recorded at the expense of the more mundane information-transmission categories.

The present study was designed to correct these deficiencies in, and to expand upon, the Bales and Borgatta study. Note that perhaps the most interesting findings in their study were in the "emotional" categories—10, 11, and 12. However, these Bales categories provide little refinement in the concept of emotion, and consequently it was decided to code the discussions with another coding system in the hope that it would allow a focus on emotional interaction, per se. The system chosen was the one popularly promulgated by Leary (1957), which allows the coding of interaction into 16 categories which could be considered "emotional."

METHOD

Ten groups (cf. Bales & Borgatta's, 1955, four), each of sizes two through five, were formed using male nonpsychiatric patients from the Dearborn Veterans Administration Hospital. All subjects were between 30 and 65. Group discussions were tape-recorded in a large conference room in the hospital, with the microphone in plain view. Also connected to the microphone was the "sound summator," an electromechanical integrating mechanism which indicated the total amount of sound that a group produced during the discussion. An instruction sheet was passed out, specifying that the group should not employ a chairman and describing the discussion problem which concerned the broad issue of reducing automobile accidents. To compensate for increases in resource input with increase in group size, groups were allotted 9 minutes of discussion time per man—two-man groups, 18 minutes; three-man groups, 27 minutes; four-man groups, 36 minutes; and five man groups, 45 minutes.

Typescripts obtained from the tapes were unitized and coded exactly as specified in the Bales and Leary (see Freedman, 1950) coding manuals. The tape recordings were the primary information source for coding; use of recordings eliminated many of the time pressures on the coders. The writer was the primary coder in the study. An independent coder checked 16 of the sessions coded with the Bales method and 20 of those coded with the Leary method, achieving 82% agreement in both cases. The chi-square agreement measure proposed by Bales (1951) was also computed and found satisfactory for all 12 of the Bales-coded groups checked, and for all but 2 of 13 Leary groups.

Since time of discussion varied with the size of the group, all data had to be adjusted to make results obtained from different sized groups comparable. This was done simply by dividing all scores for each group by the size of the group, yielding average scores per 9 minutes of interaction for each group. The data were analyzed as raw data, not percentages, by category and across group size with a simple analysis of variance computer program. The .05 significance level for the F ratio in this case is 2.86.

Results

Volume Measures

The simplest measures to be examined are those for the total volume of interaction for each group; these results are presented in Table 1.

Even a casual examination of this table reveals the most striking effect of the study, namely, that dyadic groups uniformly produced far less volume of interaction than groups of larger sizes. Of 12 possible t's between dyads and groups of other sizes, 10 were significant; no other t ratios were significant. Apparently this effect has not been noted before, and indeed it could not have been demonstrated in a study which did not increase the amount of discussion time with group size, for one could have said that dyadic groups simply did not have sufficient topics to fill out the discussion time, while the five-man groups had more than enough. Similarly, it would not have been noted in a study which dealt only with percentages.

TABLE 1

Mean Volume Measure Results

Variable	Size 2	Size 3	Size 4	Size 5	F
Total typescript pages	4.80	6.37	6.00	5.88	12.530**
Total Bales units	175.60	239.70	234.00	237.50	14.705**
Total Leary units	66.15	94.43	95.10	86.22	5.782**
Sound summator units	77.83	144.27	149.20	140.18	3.253*

* $p < .05$.
** $p < .01$.

Bales and Leary Category Analysis

Table 2 presents the results of the categorization into Bales categories. Significant F ratios were found with regard to Categories 2, 5, 6, 10, 11, and 12. While not presented here, t's were calculated for the groups in these categories, and 14 of the 17 significant t's were between the dyads and groups of other sizes, again supporting a "uniqueness" hypothesis. The laughing and joking behaviors inherent in Category 2 were much less prominent in dyadic groups; indeed, there was not one instance of a joke in all the dyadic discussions. The results of Bales 10 and 12, the hostility categories, show that hostility is much less frequent in dyadic groups. Finally, Category 11 (show tension) became much smaller as group size became larger. Eleven was the only category in the entire study that revealed such a trend. In general, the dyad appears to have less fun, to express much less hostility, and to be very much more tense than groups of other sizes.

The results of the Leary coding will not be presented in detail, since a factor analysis showed that they contributed little that the Bales scoring did not provide. However, the Leary scores, obtained independently of the Bales, do provide a good deal of support for the validity of the Bales measures. For example, Leary Category B (boast, disagree) correlates .85 with Bales 10 (disagree) and .39 with Bales 12 (show antagonism); the parallelism between these hostility measures is apparent. Leary L (cooperate), the agreement category, correlates .87 with Bales 3 (agree). Similar findings were found with respect to other categories.

TABLE 2

Mean Number of Units per Bales Category by Size of Group

Variable	Size 2	Size 3	Size 4	Size 5	F
1. Show solidarity	1.10	1.03	1.10	2.06	.574
2. Show tension release	.65	1.67	8.05	6.42	6.504**
3. Agree	26.90	30.67	25.40	23.82	.842
4. Give suggestion	.65	1.07	.72	1.24	1.202
5. Give opinion	82.40	119.80	92.55	106.04	6.823**
6. Give information	47.65	59.27	82.25	72.76	5.921**
7. Ask for information	2.70	4.57	6.12	5.40	3.557*
8. Ask for opinion	1.35	3.37	1.60	2.28	2.323
9. Ask for suggestion	.20	.13	.02	.20	1.299
10. Disagree	2.10	7.47	7.30	6.52	7.026**
11. Show tension	8.75	6.60	4.85	5.02	6.002**
12. Show antagonism	1.15	3.80	4.00	5.78	5.441**

* $p < .05$.
** $p < .01$.

Discussion

It is puzzling to note that the most striking effect found in the present study, the tendency of dyads to produce far less interaction than larger groups, has not been reported before. However, as mentioned above, previous research has not generally been designed in a manner that would reveal this trend. In this connection, it should be mentioned that there are certain dangers inherent in the practice of increasing discussion time with group size, for any phenomena which might be associated with the initiation of discussion, such as initial silences, "warm-up" effect, etc., would appear to be much stronger in smaller size groups. To check this possibility, the data were analyzed for the first 18 minutes of interaction for all groups; that is, a constant time interval was employed. In spite of the fact that this analysis reduced the data by one-half, the findings were very similar to those produced by the variable-time analysis. Dyads interacted far more slowly than larger groups, and effects in five of the seven Bales categories that were significant in the initial analysis were also noted during the first 18 minutes of interaction. We may feel fairly sure that warm-up effects, though present in some degree, were not primarily responsible for the findings of this study.

There are many correspondences between the results of the present investigation and the Bales and Borgatta (1955) study. Show tension release (2), disagree (Bales 10, Leary B), and show antagonism (Bales 12, Leary F) all increased with the size of the group. At the same time, the finding of the previous study that showing tension (Bales 11) increased as the size of the group *decreased* was also replicated. It is noteworthy that for almost all of the results mentioned the present study obtained significance only when dyads were contrasted with larger groups. However, when Slater's "Inhibition Index" was computed for our groups, the obtained values were: two-man groups, .90; three-man groups, .76; four-man groups, .65; five-man groups, .64.

Thus, although our strongest findings suggest that the dyad is uniquely different from groups of larger size, there is some indication that the inhibition that characterizes the dyad is shared also by the triad, and, to a decreasing degree, by groups of larger size.

References

Bales, R. F. *Interaction process analysis.* Reading, Massachusetts: Addison-Wesley, 1951.

Bales, R. F., & Borgatta, E. F. Size of group as a factor in the interaction profile. In A. P. Hare, E. F. Borgatta, & R. F. Bales (Eds.), *Small groups: Studies in social interaction.* New York: Knopf, 1955. Pp. 396–413.

Freedman, M. The social dimension of personality: Concepts and quantification methods. Unpublished doctoral dissertation, University of California, Berkeley, 1950.

Leary, T. *The interpersonal diagnosis of personality.* New York: Ronald Press, 1957.

Slater, P. E. Contrasting correlates of group size. *Sociometry,* 1958, **21,** 129–139.

Thomas, E. J., & Fink, C. F. Effects of group size. *Psychological Bulletin,* 1963, **60,** 371–384.

Chapter 13

GROUP PROCESSES—STRUCTURE

In order for a group to be able to achieve its goals the group members must interact. The substance and quality of these interactions constitute group processes. One of the main concepts used to abstract these processes is group structure and it is the central theme of this chapter. The term "structure," when applied to groups, refers to the relationships among elements in a group. The elements may be either actual group members or abstractions, such as positions or roles where occupancy by a particular individual is not a necessary feature of the analysis. The term "relationships" refers to various dimensions which connect elements. One such dimension, for example, is that of influence. The familiar organizational charts depicting large bureaucracies typically reflect a hierarchical division of labor in which ascending entities possess increasing influence. Leadership, status, and power are dimensions having an influence referent. Group structure can also be based upon other dimensions. The direction of member participation defines communication networks. The pattern of member to member personal attraction defines an affective structure. The kind of structure revealed by one of these dimensions would often be similar to that shown by another, but they need not necessarily be identical. Some of the research in this area has been concerned with demonstrating the effects of one kind of structure upon a second. For example, do leaders who by definition are high in the influence structure participate more, or rank higher in the communication structure, than nonleaders? In this sense, the research has inquired about maintenance or internal problems. The effects of particular structures upon group productivity and satisfaction have also been investigated. We will discuss group structures based on status, leadership, participation rates, and communication networks.

Status

DEFINITION

For any given group some members will be valued highly, others less so and some very little. The term "status" denotes a ranking of group members on some attribute or set of attributes valued by the group. It describes an asymmetrical structure because if person A is higher than person B, B must be lower than A. Social status in our culture is usually defined by a person's standing on a combination of the attributes of education, occupation, family background, and wealth. The particular attributes which determine status can vary, especially in face-to-face groups. Depending upon the particular group, attributes such as problem-solving skills, physical strength, social competence, or length of membership might be valued.

ASCRIBED AND ACHIEVED ATTRIBUTES

The attributes valued by a group differ with respect to content and also with respect to the basis for a member possessing a particular amount of the attribute. It is useful to distinguish attributes which may be achieved from those that are ascribed, following Parsons' (1951) analysis of role-expectation patterns. Achieved attributes are attributes on which a person's standing is determined by performance criteria, whereas ascribed attributes refer to fixed characteristics of the person, such as sex or family background. As Brown (1965) notes, this distinction does not clearly categorize such traits as age, which is neither a performance nor a fixed attribute. His recommendation to define ascribed attributes as not requiring performance standards, nicely resolves this ambiguity and places age among ascribed attributes.

During the initial meetings of groups composed of previously unacquainted members, the members' interactions serve to establish status rankings. Once a status structure has crystallized, there are two clear implications for the group. In the first place, the group members will have attained general agreement about what particular attributes will define status, although this need not be explicitly stated. Second, the group will be in agreement about any given member's standing with respect to these attributes, although this need not be unanimous. It is likely that a status structure will evolve more quickly if it is based on ascribed attributes rather than on achieved attributes. This is because determining the value of ascribed attributes usually requires simpler information which is immediately visible. In the main, research studies have used a performance criterion for status: the valued attributes are usually those perceived to be related to helping the group attain good outcomes. The processes leading to the formation of a status structure have not been widely studied, although it has been suggested by Bales and Slater (1955) that a group's ability to work on its task is handicapped until the group has reached a consensus about the members' status.

Change in Status

Once a status structure has been formed, any given member's rank need not be permanently fixed. Changes in status can occur either (1) by a member providing evidence of having changed on the amount of the valued attribute he possesses, or (2) by a redefinition of what attributes are to be valued. When status is based on ascribed attributes, the former kind of status changes are not as likely to occur. Achieved attributes, however, permit status changes by performance changes. Some studies have investigated whether the stability or instability of a member's high status will influence how he acts in the group. Berkowitz and Macaulay (1961), for example, view status instability as a source of approach motivation to a group. They therefore predicted that highly accepted members whose status was not secure, compared to highly accepted members whose status was secure, would show greater conformity, greater desire for high status, and more attraction to the group. These predictions were generally confirmed.

Status and Influence

Once a status structure has evolved, several consequences accrue to the group. In general, similar to other structures involving asymmetrical dimensions (power, leadership), status structures provide a basis for minimizing conflicts of interest among the members. The high status members exert more influence and conflicts of interest tend to be resolved in their favor. This point can be illustrated in the ethological work on various animal species. Status in animal groups can be defined in terms of precedence for feeding and mating. As Brown (1965) has noted in discussing Wynne-Edwards' concept of homeostatic mechanisms, conflicts about access to food or mates are typically resolved by a symbolic display of the attribute on which status is based. The animal which has more of the attribute is the winner. It is adaptive for any species to be in "agreement" about the attribute defining status, whether this is the redness of the breast, the ferociousness of cries, or the ability to fill the lung cavity with air. While the validity of the relation between standing on these attributes and actual fighting ability may be tested by combat, it is much more functional for the survival of a particular species to play out the conflict on the symbolic level. Even when actual fighting does occur, it apparently is rarely prolonged and is usually terminated before serious injury has been inflicted. Guhl (1956) reports, for example, that in newly formed flocks of hens a dominance hierarchy is established by a series of single combats. Once a pecking order has been established, such gestures as raising or lowering the head are sufficient to signify dominance or submissiveness and the frequency of actual pecking diminishes.

In human groups it has been shown that, in comparison to low-status members, high-status members have precedence in ability to influence and are more involved in and satisfied with the group. In summarizing the research findings on status, McGrath and Altman (1966) claim there is no necessary conceptual relation either between status and influence or status and involvement. It is nevertheless consistently found that those who have high status exert more influence and are more involved in the group. According to McGrath and Altman, this "implies that status is not only related to power, but also to the individual's commitment to the group and his motivation toward group achievement" (p. 58).

The relationship between a member's status in the wider society and amount of influence in a discussion group was investigated by Strodtbeck, James, and Hawkins (1958). They recognized that a jury situation closely approximates the characteristics of laboratory discussion groups. That is, juries are composed of previously unacquainted members who come together for a brief time to arrive at a unanimous decision. Although it was not feasible to use actual juries deciding real trials, the entire trial proceedings were vividly simulated and subjects were recruited from actual rolls of persons eligible for jury duty. Groups of twelve subjects heard a taped trial, were given instructions by a "judge," elected a foreman and then discussed the case until consensus was reached. Four classes of status were defined (proprietor, clerical, skilled, and laborer) by the occupation of the subject, or the husband's occupation in the case of female subjects. Individuals from each category were represented in every jury group. On such indices of influence as the election of foremen, the correlation of initial opinion with group consensus, and the average number of votes received for "helpful juror," members with higher status had more influence than lower status members. People with the highest status exerted the most influence. Bass (1965) has reported similar results in a study of managers and supervisors attending a training conference. Status in the company and rated influence in the group discussion were positively related.

The consequences of the positive relationship between status and influence on a group's task effectiveness will, of course, depend upon whether the high-status members also possess the abilities required for optimal task solution. The status-influence relationship will be adaptive for the group to the extent to which the valued attribute defining status is positively correlated with the prerequisite task abilities. The relationship will be maladaptive if the attribute and task abilities are negatively correlated. The status-influence relationship shown by Strodtbeck *et al.* is functional to the extent that the attributes determining status in the wider society correlate with the abilities required of jurors. These authors explicitly state that their study does not explain how status differentiation arises, but they apparently assume it to be functional. The existence of status differences is said to ". . . arise in part because the varied requirements of the deliberation recreate within the jury the need for the differential experiences associated with status" (p. 381). This view seems plausible for a jury task, but its validity and generality need to be tested.

STATUS AND COMMUNICATION STRUCTURE

The effects of status upon the kind of communication structure which will evolve in a group has also been studied. Thibaut (1950) and Kelley (1951) demonstrated that low-status members, whose status mobility was experimentally blocked, tended to direct communication to the high-status members of the group. This upward communication on the part of low-status members was seen as a form of substitute locomotion. A different interpretation of this effect has been suggested by Hurwitz, Zander, and Hymovitch (1953). They view the behavior of the low-status members as egodefensive. Because the high-status members have power to help or hurt the low-status members, the lows feel discomfort. They, therefore, should feel more restraint against communicating as frequently as do the high-status members. Furthermore, it was assumed that low-status members have a need to be liked by the highs. When low-status members do communicate, they should more often direct their communications toward highs than lows. The behavior of low-status members can thus be understood in terms of efforts to reduce the uneasiness felt in the presence of high-status members.

The Hurwitz *et al.* study used 42 persons who were invited to attend a one-day conference. All participants were working in the field of mental health; half of the participants had been judged to have high standing and half low standing, with respect to the topic of the conference. During the course of the day each participant was rotated through four different groups. A number of findings emerged. The previously described relationship between status and communication was found. Low-status members directed more comments to highs than to lows. In addition, high-status members initiated more comments than lows and also directed more comments to highs than to lows. Furthermore, participants tended to underrate how much others liked them, but this was less severe for lows rating liking by highs. The authors view this latter result to be in keeping with their assumption that lows have an egodefensive need to see highs as liking them. They also point out that the egodefensive interpretation is not necessarily contradictory to the substitute locomotion explanation.

Aside from the issues raised above, there is an additional aspect to the interactions of high- and low-status members. The study by Alkire *et al.* (1968) contained in the Readings section addresses itself to the question of whether status affects the content of interpersonal communications. They have shown that high-status persons elicit better information, in the sense of information which is more useful for problem solving. Because both high- and low-status subjects had comparable task ability, the effect must be mediated by the interaction between highs and lows. Although it is not clear from the study whether the results are primarily a function of the highs being more active in asking clarifying questions than the lows, the study represents a promising approach to investigating mechanisms which may mediate the influence advantage of the high-status members.

THE FUNCTION OF STATUS DIFFERENCES FOR GROUP MEMBERS

Some of the functional advantages accruing to the various members of a group from the existence of status differences have already been mentioned. First, the high-status members obtain better outcomes—they exert more influence, have better access to group resources, and enjoy a variety of prerogatives. Second, all members benefit from the avoidance of potentially destructive conflicts among members. (An accepted status structure implicitly contains the basis for resolving conflicts of interest among the group members. The resolutions, however, typically favor the high-status members.) Third, if the attribute on which status is based correlates positively with requisite task and maintenance abilities, the entire group receives a further bonus for increased task effectiveness. Fourth, the low-status members gain the advantage of having a stable, and therefore predictable, environment. Fifth, status differences assure that low-status members also have a source of power. Because status is accorded by member consensus about the attribute to be used and the level possessed by any given member, the high status accorded to some can also be withdrawn. The members who do not have high status thereby have a source of power over those who do. The advantages attendant upon high status are likely to be pursued only within the confines set by such a power base.

Leadership

LEADERSHIP AND HEADSHIP

There is no general agreement about a single best definition of leadership. All definitions, however, contain the idea that a leader is the group member who is potentially capable of exercising the most influence in the group. It is undoubtedly useful, as Gibb (1969) points out, to distinguish leadership from domination or headship by reference to the base of the influence. In general, the leader's influence potential is spontaneously granted to him, or is legitimized, by the members. Instances of domination or headship, on the other hand, involve deriving influence from some power external to the group. Such influence is maintained through an organized system. While a teacher exercises influence over students or a corporation president has influence over his subordinates, teachers and corporation presidents are better viewed as heads than as leaders. In practice, however, such distinctions are rarely maintained and investigators of leadership seem to define their domain by the consequences of saying to group members, "Take me to your leader!"

LEADER-NONLEADER DIFFERENCES

The leadership research can best be understood by first presenting a brief overview of the leadership area. From the turn of the century to the 1940s, the dominant theme in leadership research was to discover personal traits which would distinguish leaders from nonleaders. In 1904 Terman (reprinted 1955), for example, reported a study in which leaders among school-age children were shown to be older and were judged by their teachers to be taller than nonleaders. Subsequent studies investigated many other characteristics, such as intelligence, personality dimensions, and attitudes.

As might have been expected, there are few dimensions which differentiate leaders from nonleaders over all kinds of groups. To even speculate about the characteristics the president of a local garden club and the current leader of the Black Panthers have in common, which also distinguish them from their members, staggers the imagination. The single best dimension, according to Mann's (1959) review, is amount of intelligence. Leaders tend to be more intelligent than nonleaders, but the relationship is not strong. For all studies reviewed, Mann reports only a median correlation of .25, and the single highest reported correlation was .50. Indices of personal adjustment run a distant second. Other variables, such as physical attributes or various personality traits, showed little consistency over a variety of settings. It is plain that the kind of persons who become leaders, or remain as leaders, will be determined by the goals, circumstances and composition of particular groups. For example, it is generally thought that a leader's superiority on any given characteristic cannot exceed by too large an amount the level possessed by the members. The predilection for having leaders who are not too discrepant even applies to the characteristic of intelligence, a trait for which it would seem to be maximally functional for the group to obtain the largest discrepancy possible. This paradox of leader selection is aptly stated by Gibb (1969) who wryly comments, "The evidence suggests that every increment of intelligence means wiser government but that the crowd prefers to be ill-governed by people it can understand" (p. 218).

Leadership Characteristics and Leader Acts

The pursuit of personality characteristics distinguishing leaders from nonleaders gave way to two distinct orientations. These orientations differed in terms of the general question guiding the research. One orientation asked whether differences among leader characteristics could affect group processes and productivity. The focus of this orientation remained on leader characteristics, but the comparisons now made were between leaders rather than between leaders and nonleaders. A corollary question asked within this orientation was, "Do effective leaders differ from ineffective leaders?" The earliest expression of this orientation was reflected in two studies initiated by Kurt Lewin and his associates in the late 1930s contrasting "democratic" and "autocratic" leadership styles. Leadership styles are not unitary personality traits, but more global abstractions of interpersonal styles. These studies are of historical importance because they marked the beginning of laboratory experimentation with groups. In addition, their findings have sufficient current relevance that a contemporary account of this research by White and Lippitt (1968) will be summarized below. The second orientation asked whether it was possible to find meaningful ways of categorizing the behaviors occurring during the course of group interaction. Such categorizations again permitted seeking differences between leaders and nonleaders, but in terms of the specific acts performed during a group meeting. More importantly such categorizations could serve as a basis for identifying the acts which facilitate goal achievement and could ascertain whether or not the performance of such acts is the exclusive province of one individual. A leader, or leaders, may thus be identified by the kind or the frequency of acts performed. We will discuss research related to each of these orientations below.

The Effects of Leadership Characteristics

Democratic, Autocratic, and Laissez-Faire Leaders

As has already been mentioned, the research described by White and Lippitt (1968) was the first experimental study of groups. Different leadership styles were created by manipulating the kind of acts the leader performed. In the first study democratic and autocratic styles were used. A laissez-faire style was added to the other two for the second experiment. The autocratic leader determined all policy, dictated activity steps one at a time and the work companions of each member, as well as being personal in his praise or criticism. The democratic leader, on the other hand, referred all policies to group discussion and decision, used the group decisions to link activity steps to group goals, allowed choices of work companions and gave "objective" criticism. It is apparent that the major distinction between these two types of leaders was with respect to the autocratic leader controlling the group's decision-making processes much more than did the democratic leader. The laissez-faire leader was defined, essentially, as being uninvolved and he participated minimally in the group. These manipulations were admittedly extreme, evidently in keeping with Lewin's view that a new research program should begin with the strongest manipulations possible. The pervasiveness of these manipulations is exemplified by the fact that the authors viewed them as creating different "social climates."

In the second, and more comprehensive, study, four adult experimenters were trained to perform each of the three leadership styles. Each experimenter met with a five-member group of ten-year-old boys. The boys were recruited to join recreational clubs engaging in hobby activities after school. All clubs met in the same place and engaged in similar activities. After six weeks the leaders switched clubs and changed their leadership styles. The changes were arranged so that each club experienced all three leadership styles with different adults. The events at each meeting were recorded by observers.

White and Lippitt organized the data of both experiments around a number of generalizations. They noted, for example, that laissez-faire groups differed from democratic groups. Compared to democratic groups, laissez-faire groups were less organized and efficient and were less satisfying to the boys. The most interesting results, however, were based on comparing the democratic and autocratic groups. In autocratic groups there was greater dependence upon the leader. Not only was there a greater frequency of acts classified as "leader-dependent," but also there was a larger decrease of work when the leader left the room. In the autocratic groups there was also considerable more hostility and aggression. Groups under democratic leadership were more cohesive and tended to be more interpersonally satisfying. Although the quantity of work done in democratic groups was somewhat less than in autocratic groups, the autocratic groups spent considerably more time at "adsorption in work." Their productivity was evidently less efficient. The consequences of these two leadership styles can be understood to be primarily mediated by their impact on mobilizing what Lewin called "own" or "induced" forces. The terms distinguish the locus of instigation to engage in behaviors. Own forces originate in the individual and induced forces originate from external circumstances. (Lewin's distinction is an earlier example of what, in Chapter 8, was described as the internal-external dimension.) The democratic style, which induces own forces, should be more interpersonally satisfying and should induce less dependence upon the leader, more cohesiveness, and more relevant work motivation than the autocratic style.

The leadership style experiments had an enormous impact upon subsequent research and application. The results raised the hope in some social psychologists that group productivity could always be increased by training leaders to act more democratically. Even if the productivity of the democratic groups had been superior, this hope was too optimistic because the relationship between leader style and group productivity is mediated by many factors. We will turn next to a model of leadership which attempts to incorporate two such mediating variables.

Fiedler's Concept of ASo

The article by Fiedler (1966) contained in the Readings section presents his model for predicting how a leadership characteristic is expected to interact with a group circumstance and a task dimension in determining group productivity. His current view of leadership can best be understood by summarizing his past work.

In Chapter 9 we have noted the strong relationship between interpersonal similarity and attraction. Fiedler, Warrington, and Blaisdell (1952) found this relationship among fraternity members. Subjects were asked to select their best and least liked fraternity brother. They were then asked to rate their choices, as well as themselves, on a series of descriptive statements. Subjects saw themselves as being significantly more similar to their most liked choice than to their least liked choice. The accuracy of the descriptions was not at issue. It was important that persons *assume* they are more similar to those they like than to those they do not like. Fiedler undertook a series of studies to determine if the perceived similarity among group members was correlated with task effectiveness. The critical variable for the research was the leader's assumptions regarding the similarity existing between himself and the group members.

How can assumed similarity be measured? It is possible to obtain a leader's self-ratings and his ratings of the best and least liked other member on the same set of rating items. One could then obtain a distance score between the self-ratings and each of the other two sets of ratings. Because ratings of self and of best liked other are known to be highly correlated, a final similarity index would probably be unaffected by merely measuring the difference between the most and least liked other and dispensing with the self-ratings. This is the procedure adopted by Fiedler. Leaders were asked to rate their best and least liked co-workers on a number (usually 20) of six-point, bipolar scales. Such antonyms as "friendly-unfriendly" and "cooperative-uncooperative" were used. The assumed distance between the most preferred co-worker (MPC) and the least preferred co-worker (LPC) was obtained by using formula (8-1) with appropriately changed symbols. That is,

$$\text{Distance} = \sqrt{\Sigma(x_{\text{MPC}} - y_{\text{LPC}})^2} \qquad (13\text{-}1)$$

where x_{MPC} is the rating of the MPC on one item and y_{LPC} is the rating of the LPC on the same item. The differences are squared and summed for all items. The larger the distance score the more dissimilarity exists between the two sets of ratings. Fiedler termed this index Assumed Similarity between Opposites, which is abbreviated to ASo. It should be noted that high ASo is reflected by a small distance score, while low ASo is reflected in a large distance score.

Although Fiedler's technique appears to be quite simple, it is vulnerable to some of the same artifacts discussed in Chapter 9 in connection with accuracy of impressions. Cronbach (1958) has suggested that ratings of the MPC have little variation over all raters. Because ratings of MPC are sterotypically positive, the differences in ASo scores are primarily a function of the degree of negativeness assigned to the LPC person. If the LPC ratings are positive they will be similar to the invariantly positive MPC ratings and the distance index will be small. As the LPC ratings become more negative they will become increasingly dissimilar to the MPC ratings. It is for this reason that currently Fiedler uses ratings of the LPC interchangeably with ASo ratings, such that +LPC ratings are equivalent to high assumed similarity between opposites and −LPC ratings are equivalent to low assumed similarity between opposites.

Fiedler's Early Research

In order to assess the relationship between the leader's ASo score and the task productivity of the leader's group, Fiedler needed to search for groups working on identical tasks in circumstances where task performance could be objectively measured. In a series of studies utilizing existing groups, summarized in Fiedler (1960), it was found that the leader's ASo score and his group's productivity were negatively correlated. Because Fiedler correlated ASo scores with group productivity scores (where a 1 was assigned to the most productive group), negative correlations mean low-ASo leaders were more effective than high-ASo leaders. The lower the ASo, that is, the less similarity assumed to exist between MPC and LPC, or simply the more negative the ratings of the LPC, the better was the group's task performance. This relationship held for high-school basketball teams containing informal leaders, as well as in groups with formal organizations such as B-29 bomber crews and work shifts in an open-hearth steel mill. The results for groups with formal organizations were sometimes contradictory, requiring Fiedler to make additional assumptions, but in general, the results were remarkably consistent. Groups with low-ASo leaders performed better than groups with high-ASo leaders.

The Meaning of ASo

Fiedler views ASo as being a test response set that is independent of the particular items used to measure it. Subjects can even be asked to make ratings of a MPC and a LPC they have known, without identifying a particular group. ASo scores reflect an individual's orientation toward interpersonal relationships, particularly the psychological distance he prefers to maintain from other members in a group. High-ASo leaders are thought to prefer close, intimate relationships, while low-ASo leaders prefer distant, formal relationships. Fielder (1960) suggests the effectiveness of the leaders preferring distant relationships might be mediated by their ability to control and discipline group members. High-ASo leaders, on the other hand, may be too involved and interpersonally dependent upon their groups to be sufficiently guided by task requirements. For these reasons the negative correlation between ASo and productivity was expected to be found in groups working on structured, objective tasks, but not necessarily in groups working in settings where a more permissive or "therapeutic" orientation was appropriate.

Although the interpretations Fiedler makes of his results critically depend upon the leadership styles and group processes presumed to be associated with the two kinds of leaders, surprisingly little research has been published on this matter. An example of such a study was conducted by Sample and Wilson (1965). Students enrolled in an experimental psychology course were composed into four-person groups after they completed MPC and LPC ratings. In half of the groups a high-ASo (or +LPC) leader was appointed and a low-ASo (or —LPC) leader was appointed in the other groups. Task performance was measured by the quality of the weekly laboratory assignments completed by each group. One of the later assignments was made stressful by shortening the allotted time and withholding such aides as laboratory manuals. On the regular assignments the task accomplishment of the two kinds of groups did not differ. Performance on the stress assignment, however, did show a difference that was in keeping with Fiedler's concepts. On the stress trial, groups led by low-ASo leaders performed significantly better than those led by high-ASo leaders. By categorizing the leaders' acts during the stress trial, Sampson and Wilson could show that the difference was associated with differences in the leaders' task or maintenance activity during the stages of completing the task. The better performance of the low-ASo leaders was associated with a high proportion of task activity during the planning phase, followed by an increase in positive, supportive statements while the plan was being carried out. The pattern for the high-ASo leaders was just the opposite. They enacted a high proportion of positive statements during the planning phase and increased their task acts only when the plan was being executed. If high-ASo leaders are in fact oriented toward warmer relationships with their members than low-ASo leaders, these results lend themselves to the following speculation. A high-ASo leader responds positively to his members at the expense of task work, while a low-ASo leader's positive responses are determined by the member's task accomplishment. One cannot be certain why these results held for only the stress trial, but it may be that the added pressures of the stress trial converted the weekly tasks from a socially oriented to a task oriented situation.

Fiedler's Current Model

Fiedler devised the contingency model in order more accurately to specify the conditions under which high- and low-ASo leaders will be effective. An article describing the contingency model, Fiedler (1966), is contained in the Readings. Fiedler's current position is that the correlation between the leader's ASo score and group productivity will depend upon three sets of variables: (1) the positiveness of the leader's relationship with his members, (2) the degree of structure present in the task, and (3) the amount of power possessed by the leader. By assigning only two values to each of these three dimensions, eight possible combinations, or cells, emerge. By rank ordering the three dimensions in the order listed above, the eight combinations form a single dimension of "favorableness toward the leader." In general, Fiedler claims that positive correlations between LPC and task effectiveness should exist in the middle ranges of favorableness. Either extremely high or extremely low favorableness to leader will produce negative correlations between LPC and task success, consistent with the relationships found in the early research. The first part of the Fiedler (1966) article describes the research conducted with Belgian naval recruits. This study was aimed at investigating whether heterogeneous or homogeneous group composition would affect task success and whether trained leaders with high position power would produce better group performance scores than untrained leaders with low position power. No evidence for either relationship was found. The intelligence level of the group members, however, was shown to be an important factor for all tasks and homogeneity of language was important for the one task critically involving verbal communication.

The contingency model would seem to be an excellent first step toward evolving a model which will generate accurate predictions about the types of leadership styles which are effective in different circumstances. The weight of additional research evidence will undoubtedly necessitate further modifications, or indeed, a radical change in the dimensions deemed to affect the impact of a leader's style. It is very likely, however, that future models will take the general form currently advocated by Fiedler.

THE CATEGORIZATION OF LEADERSHIP ACTS

One of the earliest, and most extensive, studies attempting to distinguish the acts performed by leaders from those performed by members was conducted by Carter, Haythorn, Shriver, and Lanzetta (1951) at the University of Rochester. The study also sought to discover differences between appointed leaders and leaders who emerged as a consequence of group interaction, as well as whether any differences would be specific to one of three kinds of tasks. Four-person groups were composed and worked under the careful scrutiny of two observers hidden behind one-way mirrors. In half of the groups the leader was appointed by the experimenter and in the other half no leader was appointed. Acts were coded into 53 different categories. Contrasting leader-member differences in appointed and emergent conditions for three kinds of tasks produced a large number of comparisons. Only two kinds of acts always showed higher incidences for leaders regardless of the task. These were "diagnoses situations—makes interpretation," and "gives information on carrying out action." Some other acts showed differences specific to one of the tasks. For example, on the discussion task a leader more often "agrees or approves" than do members. Finally, the emergent leaders were much more active than the appointed leaders. The authors speculate that the high activity of the emergent leaders may have been a function of needing to solidify the bases of their leadership in competition with others. The basis of leadership, of course, was granted at the outset to the appointed leaders.

It should be noted that there is an inherent difficulty in studying leader-member differences in the absence of a prior definition of leadership. If leadership is defined by the behaviors serving as dependent-variable measures, some artifacts may arise. In addition, in the emergent condition two of the ten groups never formed a sufficiently clear structure to permit identification of a single leader.

During this same period, Bales (1950) was also developing a system for categorizing group member behaviors. His interests were not confined to leadership. He wished to find a set of mutually exclusive categories which were capable of coding all the behaviors occurring during a group meeting. After considerable exploration, he settled on the twelve categories of his "Interaction Process Analysis." The categories are coordinated with his equilibrium view of group functioning. In essence, Bales maintains the kind of group organization required for maximum task productivity is opposite to that required for creating maximum solidarity. To effectively proceed with task work a group must create structure through status and role differentiation and a division of labor. Some members, therefore, receive better outcomes than others. These consequences interfere with group maintenance, which can best be achieved through minimizing member differences. When the disruptions caused by the necessities of task work become acute, the group will shift to solving maintenance problems by deemphasizing structure. This, in turn, will interfere with effective work and the cycle begins anew. The attainment of task and maintenance goals requires mutually exclusive structures. In Bales' view a group moves back and forth between giving primacy to one or the other. Half of the observer categories in Bales' "Interaction Process Analysis" refer to task activities, for example, give opinion. The other half refer to maintenance acts, for example, show solidarity. The entire list of Bales' twelve categories is shown in Table 2 of O'Dell's (1968) article, contained in the Readings section of Chapter 12.

The group member who has the highest frequency of task activities is the task leader. Bales and Slater (1955) discovered that the task leader was not usually the best liked member of the group. The best liked member tended to be the person high on positive maintenance acts. It seemed reasonable to postulate the existence of two kinds of leaders (task and maintenance leaders), whose functions in the group served task or maintenance ends. The task leader, by keeping the group working on the task, induces tension and frustration in the other members. It is presumably the function of the maintenance or socioemotional leader to provide support for the task leader, as well as to keep the group intact by providing group members with emotional rewards. Because the skills needed for the two types of leadership were different, it was thought that the two roles would usually be filled by two people.

The generality of Bales' view has been questioned by some authors. Verba (1961) has suggested the sharp distinction between task and maintenance leaders may arise only in groups where the legitimacy of the leader's role is in question. Laboratory groups, the primary source of Bales' data, are ones in which the leader's legitimacy might be questioned by the members. Given that college subjects are similar in many ways, there may be no clear basis for a particular subject in any given group to engage in influence acts. Without such a basis other group members may become resentful and the consequent tension requires a maintenance leader. On the other hand, if some basis for legitimacy for leadership exists no such differentiation would be expected. The critical research testing this hypothesis still needs to be done. Burke (1967) has reported correlational data supportive of Verba's ideas.

In a recent book, Bales (1970) presents modifications of his observer categories and provides detailed scoring criteria (pp. 100–135, 471–491). His current work has a new focus. The observer categories have been extended to personality assessment of individuals. His research, using student groups meeting for an entire academic year, aims to integrate personality types with the emergence of different group processes. Although this interest places it outside the domain of leadership, it should be mentioned that Bales articulates a novel dimension determining structure. His personality types provide an index of each member's characteristic value direction, which guides his participation in the group. Bales suggests, "Each person may be thought of as wishing to maintain his movement, and indeed the movement of all members of the group as far as possible, in his own characteristic value direction. He would like others to perceive, feel, think, act, and evaluate as he himself does" (p. 36). From this view group structure arises among members whose value-direction is similar and who can aid in representing that direction to the rest of the group.

A FINAL WORD ON LEADERSHIP

There are few types of acts which distinguish leaders from nonleaders on the basis of counting the frequency of occurrence of different acts. It is still possible that acts performed by leaders are more important or critical in determining subsequent events in the group. For example, an act categorized as "gives suggestion" may have quite different consequences when initiated by a leader than a nonleader. If a viable system for weighting the importance of acts were found, the differences between leaders and nonleaders might be drawn more sharply. A leader's influence probably resides in one of several bases of power. He may be the most knowledgeable, the most liked, or the one with the most interpersonal skills. Progress on defining these bases should be made for a better understanding of a leader's, or any member's, contribution to the group. Although no particular set of leader characteristics will universally ensure enhancement of group functioning, this is not to say that under certain circumstances some leader characteristics or acts will be no better than others. It is likely that for a group to optimize its efficiency and harmony, the requisite leader characteristics must interact with process features of the group and the nature of the group's goals.

Participation

During a typical day most human beings devote a large proportion of their time to communicating with other people. We talk to people, call them on the telephone, write them letters, etc. It is no wonder that communication has been seen as the core process of social interaction. No group could function without communication among the members. In order to work on any task a group must be able to exchange information, evaluate ideas, and coordinate the activities of members. Communication in a group is usually achieved by people talking to each other. Verbal communication is the most convenient mode of communication, although circumstances can readily be imagined in which written messages are suitable. Experimenters who desire a permanent record, or who want to limit face-to-face interactions, are fond of requiring written messages of their subjects.

PARTICIPATION AND LEADERSHIP

If one observes a number of groups, it is striking how the members' participation rate is usually unequal. It will be recalled that Knutson (1960) used this phenomenon to compose groups. Some people do a great deal of talking, some talk often, and some rarely talk. Knowledge of merely how much each group member talked, without regard to the content of what was said, would provide an important clue about the structure of that group. For example, Bass (1949) formed ten-person groups from members of a class. The members' ratings of leadership and the amount of participation showed an extremely high correlation of .93. Using previously unacquainted persons formed into three-person groups, Kirscht, Lodahl, and Haire (1959) also checked on this relationship. Two groups meeting in separate rooms simultaneously discussed a human relations problem for 20 minutes. They were then required to select one of their members as a representative to meet with a representative from the other group to discuss a related topic. Compared to nonrepresentatives, representatives talked more (44.8 percent vs. 27.6 percent). The authors also report results for the frequency of occurrence of task-related comments (giving suggestions, asking for opinion, and integrating). The selected representatives made significantly more task-related comments than did nonrepresentatives. While it is rare to find as high a relationship between participation and leader choice as did Bass (1949), participation rate is consistently related to influence structure. One can easily think of circumstances that would raise or lower the size of the correlation. For example, groups led by an insistently democratic leadership style would show a lower correlation than those led by an autocratic leader.

AFFECTING PARTICIPATION RATES

Given the positive relationship between participation rate and influence structure, would alteration of the participation rate of a particular member be accompanied by a commensurate change in the perceived influence of that member? It is this question which inspired the series of experiments conducted by Bavelas, Hastorf, Gross, and Kite (1965). Each experiment followed a similar format. Four-person groups were formed to discuss solutions to human relations problems. A green and a red light, shielded from the other three members, were positioned in front of each subject. The experimenter controlled the lights. The onset of the green light represented a positive reinforcement; it signified that whatever the subject had been doing had helped the discussion. The onset of the red light represented a negative reinforcement; it signified that whatever the subject had been doing had hindered the discussion. The discussion was divided into three parts. Reinforcements were administered only during the second part. The subject who ranked third on amount of participation during the first part was chosen as the target person (TP). During the second part the TP's talking was often positively reinforced and his silences were negatively reinforced. The previously high participator, in the first studies, was often negatively reinforced for talking and positively reinforced for being silent. In the first studies the TP's amount of participation increased significantly in the second part and continued to be higher than the initial rate during the third part, when no reinforcements were given. The increases in participation were accompanied by increased ratings of the TP's perceived leadership status. It was subsequently shown that it required the combination of positive reinforcements to the TP and negative reinforcements to the previously high participator to obtain a significant increase in the TP's participation rate. Oakes, who had conducted a series of studies with a similar reinforcement technique, replicated the Hastorf et al. findings (Zdep & Oakes, 1967).

What are the limits within which the reinforcement effect might be produced? In addition to requiring negative reinforcement of the previously high participators, Hastorf et al. pointed out that the effect may be limited to tasks on which the members' abilities are fairly comparable. If the quality of the members' ideas is comparable, the initial differences in participation rate would not reflect different degrees of task competence. Altering the participation rate would then elicit ideas from previously low participators which are equally as good as those already offered by others. Whether or not the reinforcement effect will work if the initial distribution of participation is based on task competence is still to be answered. Finally, Hastorf, Kite, Gross, and Wolfe (1965) have conducted an experiment which suggests the increase in perceived leadership status depends upon the TP's increased participation being seen as internally determined rather than externally induced by the experimenter.

Communication Networks

The process of communication minimally involves one person (a source) sending a message to another person (the receiver). The message is sent via a channel or link connecting the two people. If the channel can only be used by the source to send messages to the receiver it is called a one-way channel. This is the usual circumstance for listening to radio or watching television. A two-way channel between two members would permit the receiver to send messages back to the previous source. The radio programs which are based on audience telephone calls convert the usual one-way channel into a two-way channel for the particular audience member who succeeds in completing a telephone call. The communication structure existing in a group is defined by the pattern of communication channels linking group members.

THE LEAVITT EXPERIMENT

The experimental investigation of communication networks began with two papers by Bavelas (1948, 1950) and an experiment conducted by his student, Leavitt (1951). Bavelas extended Lewin's analysis of differentiation of cognitive structures to communication structures linking persons. Leavitt's experiment, which will be described below, has been the basis for much of the subsequent work in this area. The general question guiding this research was whether imposed communication structures would differentially affect task efficiency and member satisfaction. The dimension distinguishing networks which has received the most attention is degree of centrality. Although the technical definitions of centrality vary, the essential ingredient is the degree to which one or more positions within the network are disproportionately linked with other positions. Figure 13-1 illustrates the networks studied by Leavitt. They progress from the most centralized (wheel) to the least centralized (circle). These four networks, of course, do not exhaust the possible patterns in which five-person groups might be arranged.

The task used by Leavitt was a symbol identification problem. From a pool of six different symbols, each group member was given a card containing five symbols. The cards were constructed so that each person had a different set of symbols and only one symbol was common to all five cards. The task for each group was to identify the common symbol. Partitions screened subjects from each other and they could communicate only by passing messages to the other member with whom they were linked. A conjunctive requirement was imposed on the task in that a trial ended when every person had identified the correct symbol. A new set of cards was then distributed for the next trial. This procedure continued until each group

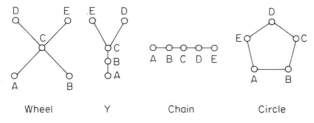

Fig. 13-1. The four communication networks studied by Leavitt (1951).

completed 15 trials. Maximum efficiency on the symbol identification task required a group's obtaining the correct solution in the shortest possible time using the least number of messages. Measures of personal satisfaction with the group and the subjects' perceptions of other features of the experiment were then obtained.

Leavitt's results were generally clear. The centralized networks were more efficient than the decentralized networks. They tended to take less time and to make fewer errors. The members' satisfaction with being in a network, however, was directly opposite. The decentralized networks produced higher member satisfaction ratings than the centralized networks. Within centralized networks, the central member was much more satisfied than the peripheral members. In addition, the centralized networks obtained a clearer picture of the group structure in which they were participating and produced consensus about having a leader. The decentralized networks developed little consensus about structure or the leader position.

SUBSEQUENT RESEARCH AND THE IMPORTANCE OF THE TASK

Once it had been shown how communication networks could be used as an independent variable, a large number of other studies were undertaken. As research accumulated, conflicting results emerged and several controversies were joined. The seemingly simple paradigm of the Leavitt study contained fairly complicated issues. These issues involved not only questions of how best to define the independent-variable dimension on which to array different networks, but also questions about the complications induced by group size, the differential distribution of initial information, and task differences. For example, although Leavitt's performance results were replicated in some experiments, others reported reversals, that is, the decentralized networks were more efficient than the centralized networks. Shaw (1964), in a review of this entire area, suggested the divergent results for group efficiency can be reconciled by taking into account the complexity of the task. For simple tasks, such as Leavitt's symbol identification, centralized networks perform more efficiently. On complex or ambiguous tasks, however, the decentralized networks show superior performance. This is a reasonable generalization which illustrates again the importance of task dimensions in understanding behavior in groups.

PROCESS FEATURES

What are the critical features of the processes producing differences in task efficiency? Several answers have been given to this question. Shaw (1964) argued that performance and satisfaction differences are mediated by two features of network positions, "saturation" and "independence." A position is vulnerable to saturation by an overload of incoming information or by a requirement of sending outgoing messages. In Fig. 13-1, position

C in the wheel, similar to the position of an airport comptroller, is more vulnerable to saturation than the other four positions on the periphery. A position's independence refers to the decision and action freedom it permits. Decentralized networks consist of positions with high independence, whereas the peripheral positions in the centralized networks have low independence. Low-independence positions are thought to frustrate the incumbent's needs for autonomy. In consequence, ". . . lowered independence not only directly limits the possibilities for action (hence performance), but also reduces the person's willingness to perform at his optimum level" (p. 125). The decentralized networks provide greatest autonomy for its members who are willing to work hard on the task. For simple problems, the manifestations of autonomy (each member verifying solutions, etc.) impede efficiency, while for complex problems manifestations of autonomy facilitate efficiency. The centralized networks contain peripheral positions in which potential for having autonomy is low. On simple tasks the peripheral members will not mind accepting the solutions found by the central members. Complex problems are assumed to increase the desire for autonomy, which is likely to be frustrated in the peripheral members, and whose consequent unwillingness to accept solutions will interfere with efficiency. Complex tasks are also likely to increase saturation beyond the critical point where the incumbent of the central position can process information effectively.

Collins and Raven (1969) provide a simpler explanation about the process features accounting for performance differences among network positions. They suggest the solutions to simple tasks are ". . . typically obvious and routine, with relatively little chance for error *if all information is available to a single individual*" (p. 148). The centralized networks are merely the most appropriate arrangements for relaying all the information to one person.

Guetzkow and Simon (1955) believed that communication networks, in principle, do not limit efficiency but do affect the group members' ability to organize. As had been shown by Leavitt (1951), Guetzkow and Simon found that decentralized groups organized more slowly than centralized groups—the circle network had not reached optimal organization by the last (twentieth) trial. The importance of the actual organization evolved by the group as a determinant of efficiency has also been stressed by Mulder (1960). By counting the number of solutions actually sent from each position, Mulder obtained an index of centrality for each position. Achieved centrality, measured by this index, correlated with faster solution times. The achieved structure appeared to be more critical than the actual structure, and problem-solving efficiency was seen to be determined by how rapidly a network can achieve a stable, central structure.

A study by Burgess (1968) demonstrated that differences in problem-solving efficiency between wheel and circle networks disappear if the number of trials is extended and correct solutions are rewarded. Whereas previous experiments had used between 15 to 60 trials, Burgess' groups were required to complete between 900 to 1100 trials over a number of sessions. Four-person groups were assigned to either a circle or wheel network and asked to solve a mechanized version of the common symbol task. Each group worked until their solution rate was not variable from trial to trial, termed by Burgess as reaching a "steady state." They were then switched to the other type of network. For all groups it took an average of 500 trials to reach a steady state. After the groups had worked for a number of sessions, Burgess introduced a mild punishment for errors and a positive reinforcement for correct solutions. The wheel net was significantly faster than the circle net during the initial trials, before the positive reinforcement was introduced. Once a steady state had been reached, however, there was no difference in solution rate between the two networks. In a second experiment reinforcements were used from the beginning. The wheel nets showed a faster optimal organization than the circle nets, but after a steady state was reached there was no difference between the two networks. Burgess' study can serve to emphasize the use of rewards as a way of motivating group members to perform optimally, in line with Shaw, or the development of stable organization regardless of the imposed structure, in keeping with Mulder.

Communication patterns obviously have important significance for determining a group's productivity and its members' satisfaction. The Bavelas-Leavitt approach has instigated thought and research on important issues involving communication networks, but a satisfactory theoretical account detailing the relationships among the prepotent variables has not yet been achieved.

Overview

Group structure refers to the relationships among elements (group members or roles) in a group. Structural features are important determinants of process events and task performance. Group structures based on status, leadership, participation rates, and communication networks were discussed.

Although status differences probably emerge in all groups, the particular attributes determining status can differ among groups. Status structures have general functions both for the group and for the individual members. For the group, they serve to minimize conflicts of interest among the members. Compared to low-status members, high-status members enjoy a number of advantages, such as exerting more influence and receiving better information from other members. Low-status members gain a predictable environment and a source of power from their ability to withdraw the high status accorded to some of the other members. A leader was defined as the group member who is potentially capable of exercising the most influence in the group. Early studies of leadership were primarily concerned with discovering the personal traits which would distinguish leaders from non-leaders. Except for intelligence, and possibly adjustment, no other personal attributes were found which consistently distinguished leaders from non-leaders over a variety of settings. The quest for personal traits was replaced by two different orientations. One orientation attempted to discover whether various leader characteristics, such as autocratic or democratic styles, would differentially affect group processes and productivity. This orientation also led to efforts to distinguish effective leaders from ineffective leaders. The second orientation sought to find meaningful ways to categorize the behavior of group members. With such classification systems it was possible to search for differences between leaders and nonleaders in terms of the kind or frequency of acts performed during a meeting.

Participation rates are defined by each member's amount of talking, while communication networks are defined by the pattern of communication channels linking group members. Amount of participation is positively correlated with perceived influence. Group members tend to see the people who talk the most as the most influential. Alterations in participation rate have been shown to alter influence ratings. Although many different kinds of communication structures can be designed, research has focused on investigating the differences between centralized and decentralized networks. Centralized networks tend to be more efficient with simple tasks and decentralized networks tend to be more efficient with complex tasks. Member satisfaction is higher in decentralized networks. These differences disappear with continued practice in a particular network.

READINGS

Information Exchange and Accuracy of Verbal Communication under Social Power Conditions[1]

Armand A. Alkire, Mary E. Collum, Jaques Kaswan, and Leonore R. Love

This study concerned the concept of communication and the effect of social status on the communication process. High-and low-status members of a sorority were paired into all combinations of senders and receivers. Senders described graphic designs to a receiver who, hidden from view, attempted to choose the design described from 16 alternatives. As predicted, high-status receivers obtained more useful information and asked more clarifying questions than low-status Ss. As a result, high-status Ss made more accurate choices than low status Ss when status differences were made salient. The results indicate that status differences affect the type of information conveyed by senders as well as the level of activity by receivers. Both of these variables interact to affect accuracy.

There has been considerable interest in the study of communication in the past few years. However, it seems that the term has been used in various ways. The term "communication" is sometimes used when studying the function of language and the meaning of words (Brown, 1965; Krech, Crutchfield, & Ballachey, 1962; Osgood, Suci, & Tannenbaum, 1957) or when investigating information processing (Hess, Shipman, & Jackson, 1965; Kagan, 1964; Kagan, Morris, & Sigel, 1963). In each of these frameworks, the major emphasis is upon cognitive variables within given individuals.

From a more interpersonal viewpoint, several investigators have studied persons in face-to-face communication. There is one major difficulty in this approach to interpersonal communication; it stems from the problem of determining who is communicating to whom. If the situation is a natural one involving free interaction, people tend to interchange between these roles until it is difficult to tell who initiated each message, much less whether the other person actually received it or not (Haley, 1962, 1964).

[1] From the *Journal of Personality and Social Psychology*, Volume 9, pages 301–308; 1968 (received June 26, 1967). Reproduced by permission of the American Psychological Association. Authors' affiliation: University of California, Los Angeles. This study was supported by United States Public Health Service Demonstration Grant 1R01-MH-14770. Computing assistance was obtained from the Health Sciences Computing Facility, University of California, Los Angeles, sponsored by National Institutes of Health Grant FR-3. The authors are especially grateful for the assistance of Judy Klusza in programming the data.

In light of this latter problem a more operationally defined concept of interpersonal communication might be formulated. Thus, in a stricter sense, one might speak about communication as a process of information exchange in which one person clearly initiates transmission of some particular unit of information which is received by another person (Krech *et al.*, 1962; Longabaugh, 1962). This manner of conceptualizing communication highlights the notion that there are two clearly defined task roles—that of sending and that of receiving information. Moreover, the notion of a social exchange process of communication emphasizes the interdependent and reciprocal relationship between sender and receiver.

When communication is envisioned as a process of information exchange, another variable emerges which is assumed to have direct consequences on the interaction tendencies between sender and receiver. Several investigators who have attempted to control the sender-receiver variable have observed the effects of social power on the direction and amount of information flow. Most are in agreement in showing that information is directed upward toward high-status persons in a social hierarchy (Back, Festinger, Hymovitch, Kelley, Schachter, & Thibaut, 1950; Thibaut, 1950). Hurwitz, Zander, and Hymovitch (1960) found that when subjects could interact freely with higher, lower, or equal status subjects, the low-status persons talked more frequently to high-status persons than to persons of equal status (low → high > low → low). At the same time, high-status persons talked more frequently to other high-status group members than to low-status persons (high → high > high → low).

There is some question as to how well these investigators have been able to control the experimental situation so that behaviors of the high-status receiver can be completely ruled out as a key factor in inducing this upward flow of information (Cohen, 1958). For instance, Kelley (1951) found evidence for communication downward in the hierarchy. Kelley demonstrated that the high-status receiver is more likely to criticize the task instructions received from a low-status task sender, whereas the low-status receiver is unlikely to criticize the task behavior of his high-status sender. In a natural situation, one would expect such behavior on the part of the high-status receiver to induce further transmission of information by the sender.

Each of these concepts—social power and communication—has been considered important enough to demand attention on its own. If the relationship between the two is as strong as the literature suggests, it would seem of added importance to further investigate the connection between the two variables. In order to explore the connection between social power and communication, the basic task developed by Krauss and Weinheimer (1966) was modified and used in the present study. The task requires the verbal description of a relatively neutral novel graphic design (see Fig. 1) by a sender to a receiver. The receiver, who is hidden from view, has an

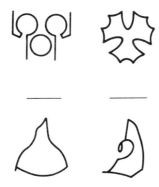

Fig. 1. Novel graphic designs.

array of 16 designs before him and, through a process of asking questions and receiving further information from the sender, attempts to make an accurate selection of the design being transmitted.

Advantages of this task in studying verbal communication are that the designs serve as a neutral bit of information for transmission. The neutral nature of the stimulus objects is important since Longabaugh (1962) pointed out that the vast majority of interpersonal communication consists of neutral, factual, or task-oriented content. Further, in this task there is a clear delineation of sender and receiver roles. Finally, an unambiguous criterion for accuracy of communication is available in the number of correct choices which the receiver is able to make from his array of 16 alternative designs. This procedure, then, operationally parallels the formulation of communication as a process of information exchange as proposed above. It is limited in that it applies only to the verbal mode of communication.

In order to introduce social power variables, initiated members of a sorority were designated as high-status subjects. Pledges who were in a phase in which they were to prove themselves worthy of nonqualified membership in the group were defined as low-status subjects. Thus, the members were in a position which afforded them a pattern of activities, roles, privileges, duties, and powers which, in comparison with the position of the pledges, was generally considered to be more desirable and satisfying. These differences were precisely the critria used by Kelley (1951, p. 39) to separate his high-status from his low-status subjects. The study of a sorority group may seem to be a limited context for studying social power. However, the sorority group has many facets common to most structured groups, which will be discussed in a later section.

While the studies cited above show that social power may strongly affect the direction in which information flows, people often avoid the recognition of existing status differences. In the case of low-status persons, such avoidance may protect self-esteem (Hurwitz *et al.*, 1960). The high-status person may fail to make such differences salient in order to hide the advantages of a powerful position in the hierarchy (Thibaut & Kelley, 1959). It would seem that the effects of social power on communication might be optimized if status similarities and differences were made explicit and salient. This was done in the present study.

The general literature seems consistent enough to generate at least three major hypotheses. It was proposed that:

1. The tendency for upward-directed flow of information would result in more information being sent to high-status receivers in the sorority group.

2. The tendency to question a task partner's behavior would be more probable from the same combination of status and task role as that described by Kelley (1951) above. More specifically, it was felt the high-status sorority member, who was serving as a receiver, would often use opportunities to sharpen and clarify the transmissions of a low-status pledge who was describing a design. Conversely, the pledge should be more inhibited in making interventions into the transmissions of her high-status sender.

3. Accuracy of communication should be a joint function of the information contained in the sender's messages and that resulting from the clarifications by the receiver. Since the high-status members were expected to have more information directed toward them, and to make more interventions than the pledges, it was hypothesized that they would accumulate a greater amount of information about the designs than the low-status receivers. Therefore, it was predicted that the high-status receivers would make significantly more accurate choices than the low-status receivers, in line with the notion of upward-directed flow of information.

METHOD

Subjects

The subjects used in the original task situation were 20 female students who were members of a sorority and 20 pledges of the same sorority.

The subjects were tested in dyads. There were four conditions with five dyads in each. There were two groups in which equal status pairs were tested. One group was comprised of five high-status dyads (the sorority members); the second group contained five low-status dyads (the sorority pledges). Similarly, there were 10 dyads tested in mixed-status conditions. In five of the mixed-status dyads, a low-status pledge began in the sender role with a high-status member in the receiver role. In the other five mixed-status dyads, the high-status member began as the sender paired with a low-status pledge in the receiver role. Subjects were assigned randomly to the same- or mixed-status groups.

Apparatus and Procedure

The basic task required sender-receiver descriptions of novel graphic designs like those shown in Fig. 1. These designs were originally selected by Krauss and Weinheimer (1966) from a larger set of similar designs. The 15 designs selected by these investigators elicited a wide variety of referents from subjects who attempted to describe them. In essence, they are graphic figures for which there are no commonly shared referent concepts. One additional design was selected for the present study using the same criterion, to make a total of 16 designs. Each design was pasted on four faces of a small block. The other two faces of the block were painted red and yellow. A hole was drilled through the block from the red face to the yellow face so the blocks could be placed on a spindle.

The subjects had been asked to participate in a study which dealt with the manner in which sorority girls worked together, and promised a report of the findings as an incentive. These were the only preparatory instructions to the girls. The conditions for testing the dyads were the same for all groups. They were tested in private in a downstairs room of the sorority house. A table was set up with a screen dividing it in half to block subjects' view of one another during the task. All dyads practiced the task with three extra designs to assure that they understood the procedure. The sender had a dispenser in which eight randomly ordered blocks were placed, thus allowing her to pull designs one at a time into view during the experiment. The receiver was required to press a buzzer to indicate that she wanted to question the sender about the design being described. The receiver had a full set of 16 designs in front of her. A separate spindle was provided for the sender and receiver. The receiver made her choice by placing a block with the design which she selected on her own spindle. The sender placed the actual block being described on her spindle. No subject was ever told if she had made a correct choice or not. Thirty seconds were allowed for the description, clarification, and selection of each design. If the receiver made a choice before the time limit was up, the experimenter instructed the subjects to go on to the next block. The verbal interactions of the 20 dyads were tape-recorded for later analysis.

Instructions to Make Status Salient

It was felt that status would not be especially salient to these girls in their general interactions with each other due to a variety of reasons discussed below. In order to make status salient, special instructions were introduced for each of the groups after the first series of eight designs. In the conditions where a high-status person was paired with another high-status member the instructions were as follows:

Member [name], you are going to come over here and become the receiver. And member [name], you are going to come over here and become the sender. As I said before, this is a study to see how people in a sorority house work together. I'm sure you both are aware by now that you are members and know what that is about.

The instructions to subjects in the pledge-pledge group were the same except for the substitution of the term "pledge" for "member." The instructions to the mixed-status pairings were phrased in an analogous manner:

Member [name], you are going to come over here and become the receiver. Pledge [name], you are going to come over here and become the sender. As I said before, this is a study to see how people in a sorority house work together. I'm sure that you know what being a member is about. I'm sure you know what being a pledge is about. [The order for these status labels and names was contingent upon which persons started as sender and receiver in the mixed conditions.]

Procedure for Postsaliency Series

The overall procedure for this second series was identical with that of the base-line series of trials. The sender was given the remaining eight designs in random order. The receiver had the full array of 16 blocks before her.

RESULTS

Accuracy of Communication in the Original Task Situation

The number of correct choices made by each receiver over the eight trials was used as the measure of accuracy. Means and standard deviations of the accuracy before and after the instructions which made status salient are shown in Table 1. A 2 (high-low sender status) $\times$ 2 (high-low receiver status) $\times$ 2 (pre- and poststatus saliency) analysis of variance for the accuracy attained by the four groups yielded a statistically significant interaction between receiver status and the introduction of the saliency instructions ($F = 6.13$, $df = 1/32$, $p < .025$). None of the other effects approached statistical significance. In the presaliency condition, the low receivers tended to be slightly more accurate than the high receivers, although none of the individual group comparisons were close to significance. Table 1 shows that, as predicted, the interaction effect was due to the higher accuracy of high- compared to low-status receivers in the postsalience condition. This finding supports the major hypothesis concerning the outcome of the communication process. In the postsalience condition, the most striking finding was the poor accuracy of low receivers when high subjects were senders. Specific comparisons between groups in this condition show that accuracy in the high $\rightarrow$ low group was significantly poorer than that in the low $\rightarrow$ high group ($F = 5.76$, $df = 1/8$, $p < .05$) and the high $\rightarrow$ high group ($F = 11.66$, $df = 1/8$, $p < .01$).

Objective Measures of Information Exchange

One objective measure of the amount of information sent to another person is simply to count the number of words spoken by the sender. While there was a tendency for the high-status sender to talk more under both the presalience and postsalience conditions than the low-status sender, this result did not approach statistical significance.

TABLE 1

Accuracy of Status Pairings: Pre- and Postsaliency Instructions in the Original Task[a]

| Status pairing | | Accuracy | | | |
| | | M | | SD | |
Sender	Receiver	Pre	Post	Pre	Post
High	High	5.6	6.8	1.14	0.84
Low	High	6.0	6.6	1.87	1.67
High	Low	6.4	4.2	2.07	1.48
Low	Low	6.6	5.8	1.67	1.10

[a] Mean number of accurate choices out of eight possible.

TABLE 2

Means for Type of Concept Sent and Number of Receiver Interventions for Status Pairings: Pre- and Poststatus Saliency[a]

Status pairing		M					
		Referent		Geometric		Receiver intervention	
Sender	Receiver	Pre	Post	Pre	Post	Pre	Post
High	High	9.4	10.2	4.0	5.2	5.4	4.4
Low	High	10.4	8.6	3.8	4.2	5.0	6.2
High	Low	9.2	7.2	4.0	7.2	3.8	2.6
Low	Low	8.6	7.6	3.4	4.4	6.0	5.2

[a] Mean number over eight trials.

The authors' experience with the task suggested that senders tend to use two general types of concepts in the task. One of these is the use of a referent phrase consisting of animate or inanimate noun objects (Krauss & Weinheimer, 1966). Two raters were asked to identify these referent concepts from transcripts. They obtained 92% agreement. A given referent concept was counted only once if it was repeated during the description of any given design. The mean number of referent concepts used in the sender's initial message is shown in Table 2. These results were analyzed in the same three-way analysis of variance as the one used to assess the accuracy data. More referent concepts were sent to the high-status receivers, but the result reached only the .25 level of significance.

The second category of concepts transmitted from the sender to the receiver was termed geometric-descriptive and consisted of phrases referring to lines, circles, curves, enumeration of points, etc. Such a phrase was counted only once for a given design because it was difficult to define where one such description left off and another began. Two raters agreed on 86% of the total messages categorized in this classification. The results are shown in Table 2. The three-way analysis of variance of these results yielded statistically significant main effects for saliency condition ($F = 7.51$, $df = 1/32$, $p < .01$) and status of the sender ($F = 4.72$, $df = 1/32$, $p < .05$).

Table 2 shows that the status effect is due to the high-status subjects sending more geometric message units than the low-status subjects. The Pearson r correlation of $-.51$ ($df = 18$, $p < .05$) between accuracy and mean number of geometric descriptions in the postsalience conditions indicates that these concepts are relatively useless and possibly confusing in affecting decisions about these designs (see Table 3).

Since the receiver was free to ask questions, it is possible that the sender's information could be sharpened considerably by such interventions.

TABLE 3

Correlations between Task-Role Behaviors and Accuracy[a]

	1	2	3	4
		Presaliency		
Accuracy (1)		− .20	− .03	.31
Referents (2)	.27		− .70*	− .39*
		Postsaliency		
Geometric (3)	− .51*	− .59*		.31
Interventions (4)	.37*	− .35	− .61*	

[a] $N = 20$.
* $p < .05$.

Table 2 shows that, as predicted, the high-status receiver intervened more often that the low-status receiver in the mixed-status dyads. The specific comparison of low-high versus high-low status pairings yielded a statistically significant result ($F = 6.48$, $df = 1/8$, $p < .05$). None of the other comparisons reached statistical significance. A Pearson r correlation of .35 ($df = 38$, $p < .05$) between accuracy and number of interventions over the pre- and postsalience series indicates that these questions were helpful in making correct choices of the design.

Qualitative Value of the Sender's Messages

The accuracy attained by the subjects supports the prediction for outcome of the communication process under social power. However, objective measures of the sender's messages do not completely mirror the flow of information presumed to be directed toward the high-status receiver.

In order to determine whether the messages sent toward the high-status receivers were qualitatively superior to those sent toward the low-status receivers, a supplementary study was conducted using 20 female freshman and sophomore students from the general pool of subjects normally used in psychological studies. These subjects did not know any of the girls in the original experiment or anything about the study. They met as a group. Their instructions were to choose the design being described from edited tape recordings of the sender's messages taken from the original task situation. The first two messages, from each of the five senders, in each of the four status pairings following the saliency instructions were presented to these neutral subjects. These 40 messages occurred in random order. All interventions by the original receiver had been eliminated by editing of the tape.

Each neutral subject was provided a 40-page booklet with one set of the 16 novel graphic designs on each page. The tape recorder was stopped after the first message. The subjects were allotted 30 seconds (as in the original task) to make their choice of the design being described by checking one of the designs on the first page of their booklet. Then they were told to turn the page, another message was played, followed by their selection on the new page. This procedure was continued until all 40 messages had been played and selections made.

The following general procedures were also undertaken to make this task as similar to the original situation as possible. The neutral subjects practiced with three extra designs while listening to specially prepared messages to insure that they understood the procedure before they began. They were also told that the person describing the design on the tape recording had the design on a square block and might have it oriented in various ways. The block was illustrated to the neutral subjects, and they were shown that the way the design appeared on their page conformed to the positioning of the block with the red face up. In view of these considerations, they were shown how to turn their booklet upside down, or to turn the page in any way, in order to orient the design. This procedure, then, made the problem of the neutral subjects much like that of the original task receiver in attempting to orient the blocks from the sender's messages.

To make the situation further resemble the original task, it was necessary to provide for random ordering of the array of designs in front of the receiver. Thus, the 16 novel graphic designs were arranged on the page in five random sequences. These five pages were distributed randomly throughout the 40-page booklet. Finally, as in the original task, the neutral subjects were never told whether or not they had made an accurate choice.

In order to analyze how effective the original senders were in providing information that would allow these neutral subjects to make accurate choices, each neutral subject was given four scores. Thus, the accuracy attained for the 10 messages given by (a) highs sending to highs, (b) lows sending to highs, (c) highs sending to lows, and (d) lows sending to lows was tallied for each neutral subject. The scores were used in a repeated-measurements analysis of variance (Lindquist, 1956).

Tables 4 and 5 show that there was a significant difference in the accuracy with which these neutral subjects were able to choose the designs

TABLE 4

Neutral Subject Accuracy when Relying on Information from Original Sender[a]

Status pairing		Neutral accuracy
Sender	Receiver	M
High	High	7.05
Low	High	8.35
High	Low	6.80
Low	Low	6.20

[a] Mean number of accurate choices out of 10 possible.

TABLE 5

Analysis of Variance for Neutral Subject Accuracy

Source	df	MS	F
Pairing	3	16.43	5.61*
S	19	2.38	0.81
Error[a]	57	2.93	

[a] The error term is the interaction mean square for Pairing × Subject as used in Lindquist's (1956) Treatment × Subject design for repeated measurements.

* $p < .01$.

from messages involving the specific pairings of sender and receiver status in the original task ($F = 5.6$, $df = 3/57$, $p < .01$). A comparison (Edwards, 1960) was undertaken to test the hypothesis that the neutral subjects were more accurate in making choices of the designs from information sent toward the high-status receivers than toward the low-status receivers. This was found to be the case, as the means in Table 4 indicate ($\bar{X}$: high receiver, 7.70; low receiver, 6.50; $t = 2.11$, $df = 57$, $p < .05$). A second, orthogonal comparison for status of the sender showed no effect from taking the sender in the original task into account when determining the accuracy of the neutral subject ($\bar{X}$: high sender, 6.93, low sender, 7.28).

Thus, the major trend for accuracy obtained by these neutral subjects is parallel to that found in the original experimental situation and adds support to the notion that information flows upward in a status hierarchy.

DISCUSSION

In general, the results support the hypothesis that social power and task-role considerations combine in such a way that information flows upward in a status hierarchy toward high-powered people. More specifically, following the status-saliency instructions, the high-status receiver became more active in clarifying and sharpening the messages of her low-status sender. This task-role behavior on the part of the receiver correlated with accurate communication. In direct contrast, in the other mixed-status pairing, there was a noted decrease in the number of interventions made by the low-status receiver into the messages of her high-status sender. At the same time, there was a great increase in the number of geometric descriptions sent by the high-status sender to her low-status receiver. Each of these tendencies was especially ineffective and led to a low number of accurate choices of the designs being transmitted.

This observed difference in the task-role behavior of the high- and low-status receiver is of noted importance in itself since there is little attention given to the overt behavior of the receiver in most studies of communication. For instance, the major studies on which these hypotheses were based would lead one to believe that communication is "merely directed toward" the high-status person. The matter is seldom pursued as to whether the high-status person made demands for information, acted like an expert, gave social rewards, or in some other way used his power to initiate the flow of information (Cohen, 1958; Raven, 1965). Kelley's (1951) study and that of Cohen are exceptions to the general lack of interest in the behavior of the receiver, but even there such considerations were investigated in a static sense, not as a process of communication where "the ball is bounced back and forth between the players in the conversational game [Krech et al., 1962, p. 288]."

It should also be noted that the current results came about only after experimental procedures which made formal relationships between the girls salient. On the basis of the literature the authors expected such an eventuality. Even in highly formalized social status organizations one finds a degree of informal interactions that serve the needs of the individual which the formal structure cannot satisfy (Argyris, 1957; Krech et al., 1962). In the present study, the saliency instructions seem to have had the effect proposed by Charters and Newcomb (1958) of "reminding" the individual of her reference point in the formal sorority structure.

Those saliency instructions also led to shifts in the type of information transmitted. There was an increase in the number of geometric descriptions for all four status pairings. The authors speculate that a major reason for this increase in geometrics is that there are only a finite number of abstract referent concepts that a given person can apply to a given design which would be appropriate to transmit to a given receiver. Under inducement to increase transmission of information, the sender would exhaust this available pool of referents. In such conditions the sender might simply describe the details of the readily available concrete stimulus object which he has before him rather than attempt to conceptualize further abstract referents. Thus, any inducement to increase the amount of transmissions would be predicted to lead to a description of details on the part of a sender. In the present case, the details of the novel graphic designs happen to be geometric in nature involving circles, lines, curves, number of points, etc. It is possible, then, that the increase in geometric descriptions by all senders following the saliency procedure was due to increased inducement to transmit more information which was somehow implied by the mere presentation of the procedure itself (e.g., "try harder"). Further, the high-status sender with the low-status receiver may have transmitted an especially great amount of information because she saw it as her duty to assume a more active role and/or because she was induced to do so because of the general failure of her low-status receiver to participate (e.g., few interventions).

Finally, this study indicates that low-status people transmit information efficiently to highs. However, many situations which require the transmission of information are ones which involve a high-status person talking to a person lower in social power. This situation is most obvious in the teacher to pupil, supervisor to employee, directive doctor to patient relationships, and perhaps between certain members of groups like the family. Status differences often become quite salient in these situations. The results of the present study suggest that the accuracy of communication in such interactions might be impaired if conditions do not encourage the low-status receiver to sharpen and clarify what the high-status person is attempting to convey. There is added danger that conditions will also encourage the high-status sender to talk in detailed and detached terms which are ineffectual in communicating with the low-status person. While the population and the task used in the present study can hardly be assumed to sample the total range of interactions under social power variations, the results suggest the importance of this variable to the communication process.

REFERENCES

Argyris, C. *Personality and organization.* New York: Harper & Row, 1957.
Back, K., Festinger, L., Hymovitch, B., Kelley, H. H., Schachter, S., & Thibaut, J. The methodology of studying rumor transmission. *Human Relations,* 1950, 3, 307–312.
Brown, R. *Social psychology.* New York: Free Press of Glencoe, 1965.
Charters, W. W., & Newcomb, T. M. Some attitudinal effects of experimentally increased salience of a membership group. In E. E. Maccoby, T. M. Newcomb, & E. L. Hartley (Eds.), *Readings in social psychology.* (3rd ed.) New York: Holt, Rinehart & Winston, 1958.
Cohen, A. R. Upward communication in experimentally created hierarchies. *Human Relations,* 1958, 11, 41–53.
Edwards, A. *Experimental design in psychological research.* New York: Holt, Rinehart & Winston, 1960.
Haley, J. Family experiments: A new type of experimentation. *Family Process,* 1962, 1, 265–293.
Haley, J. Research on family patterns: An instrument of measurement. *Family Process,* 1964, 3, 41–65.
Hess, R. D., Shipman, V., & Jackson, D. Early experience and the socialization of cognitive modes in children. *Child Development,* 1965, 36, 869–886.
Hurwitz, J. I., Zander, A. F., & Hymovitch, B. Some effects of power on the relations among group members. In D. Cartwright & A. Zander (Eds.), *Group dynamics.* (2nd ed.) New York: Harper & Row, 1960.
Kagan, J., Morris, H. A., & Sigel, I. E. Psychological significance of styles of conceptualization. *Monographs of the Society for Research in Child Development,* 1963, 28(2).
Kagan, J. Information processing in the child: Significance of analysis and reflective attitudes. *Psychological Monographs,* 1964, 78(1, Whole No. 578).
Kelley, H. H. Communication in experimentally created hierarchies. *Human Relations,* 1951, 4, 39–56.
Krauss, R. M., & Weinheimer, S. Concurrent feedback, confirmation, and the encoding of referents in verbal communication. *Journal of Personality and `Social Psychology,* 1966, 4, 343–346.
Krech, D., Crutchfield, R. S., & Ballachey, E. L. *Individual in society.* New York: McGraw-Hill, 1962.

Lindquist, E. F. *Design and analysis of experiments in psychology and education.* Boston, Massachusetts: Houghton Mifflin, 1956.

Longabaugh, R. A category system for coding interpersonal behavior as social exchange. *Sociometry*, 1962, **25**, 319–344.

Osgood, C. E., Suci, G. J., & Tannenbaum, P. H. *The measurement of meaning.* Urbana, Illinois: University of Illinois Press, 1957.

Raven, B. Social influence and power. In I. D. Steiner & M. Fishbein (Eds.), *Readings in contemporary and social psychology.* New York: Holt, Rinehart & Winston, 1965.

Thibaut, J. An experimental study of the cohesiveness of underprivileged groups. *Human Relations*, 1950, 3, 251–278.

Thibaut, J. W., & Kelley, H. H. *The social psychology of groups.* New York: Wiley, 1959.

The Effect of Leadership and Cultural Heterogeneity on Group Performance: A Test of the Contingency Model[1]

Fred E. Fiedler

An experiment was conducted (a) to compare the performance of 96 culturally and linguistically homogeneous and heterogeneous three-man teams under powerful and weak leadership positions and on three types of tasks varying in structure and requirements for verbal interaction, and (b) to test a previously described Contingency Model of Leadership Effectiveness. Homocultural and heterocultural groups differed in performance only on the highly verbal task. Heterogeneous groups, despite obvious communication difficulties and culturally divergent backgrounds, performed about as well on the structured and nonverbal tasks as did homogeneous groups. Groups led by recruit leaders performed as well as groups directed by petty officers. Thus, neither the military leadership training and experience nor the position power of petty officers contributed to the effectiveness of these groups. These findings have considerable potential implications for leadership training programs and evaluation of the communication

[1] From the *Journal of Experimental Social Psychology*, Volume 2, pages 237–264, 1966 (received September 14, 1965). Author's affiliation: University of Illinois. This experiment was conducted while the writer was a Ford Faculty Research Fellow at the University of Louvain, Belgium. The study was funded by a contract with the Advanced Research Projects Agency, through Office of Naval Research Contract NR 177-472, Nonr 1834(36) (F. E. Fiedler, L. M. Stolurow, and H. C. Triandis, Principal Investigators). It was conducted in cooperation with the Center for Social Studies of the Belgian Ministry of Defense (U. Bouvier, Director). The experiment was performed with the assistance of Professor J. M. Nuttin, Jr., and Mrs. Annie Beckers-Janssen, A. van den Hoof, L. Jadot, R. Wathelet, J. P. Cels, and H. Weyns and P. Ninane of the University of Louvain, and S. Shiflett of the University of Illinois. The writer is especially grateful for the active cooperation of Capt. V. Van Laethem, then Commandant of the Naval Training Center, Ste. Croix-Bruges, and his staff, and to Commodore L. Petitjean, then Chief of Staff of the Belgian naval forces, for permission to conduct the study. Many others assisted in the course of this study. These included W. Meuwese, H. C. Triandis, M. Fishbein, P. Knops, H. Noel, and Ping Koo.

variable in affecting group productivity. The experiment clearly supported the hypothesis derived from the Contingency Model that the specific leadership style required for effective group performance is contingent upon the favorableness of the group-task situation. As in previous research, groups under managing, task-controlling (low LPC) leaders performed best in very favorable group-task situations as well as in group-task situations which were relatively unfavorable or very unfavorable. Permissive, considerate, group-oriented leaders performed best in situations intermediate in favorableness.

This experiment, conducted in cooperation with the Belgian Navy, investigated the effects of linguistic and cultural heterogeneity and the leader's position power on team performance under different group-task conditions.

The performance of heterocultural groups is today of considerable importance. It is especially critical in the large number of countries which have culturally and linguistically diverse populations. These include, to mention but a few, Belgium, Canada, Finland, Israel, Italy, Mexico, Spain, Switzerland, Yugoslavia, and the United States, as well as practically all underdeveloped countries in the African and Asian continents. The problem of cultural heterogeneity is likewise a focal concern in international business and governmental organization, and in the increasing number of multilateral military operations which use personnel from different countries in closely cooperating or integrated units. Finally, it has implications for the management of interdisciplinary research and development teams where heterogeneity is due to technical background and training, or to groups where the diversity is due to differences in race and socioeconomic status among members.

This study had two major purposes. First, it tested whether culturally homogeneous task groups perform significantly better than heterogeneous task groups on three types of tasks, and whether such teams will perform better under trained and powerful leadership than under inexperienced and weak leadership.

Second, the study attempted a validation and extension of the recently proposed Contingency Model of Leadership Effectiveness (Fiedler, 1964).

DESIGN AND METHOD

Subjects

The experiment was conducted at the Belgian Naval Training Center in Ste. Croix-Bruges, with 240 recruits and 48 petty officers. Half of these petty officers and recruits were from French-speaking homes, the other half from Dutch-speaking homes. At the time of the study the recruits, ranging in age from 17 to 24 (mean age of 20.17), were expected to serve in the Belgian Navy for a term of 12 months after which most of them would return to civilian life. Petty officers are career men who plan to remain in service for 20 years or more. They typically complete 2 years of petty officer candidate school, which they enter directly after high school or an equivalent technical school. Promotion from the ranks is possible, but unusual. As a result, the Belgian Navy petty officer is highly committed to his career, and enjoys a high status roughly comparable to that of the U. S. Navy's chief petty officer. The 48 petty officers in our sample ranged in age from 19 to 45 years, with a mean of 29.48, and they had, on the average, about 10 years of leadership experience as petty officers in the Navy.

Belgium is sharply divided into two population and geographical sectors. Roughly 55% of the population is Flemish and lives in the northern half of Belgium, with Dutch as the official language. The remaining 45% of the population consists of French-speaking Walloons who live in the southern part of the country. Brussels is primarily French-speaking, although officially bilingual. Only the minority of Belgians speaks both languages well, and relatively few from French-speaking homes are fluent in Dutch.

Since achieving its independence in 1830, the country has been enmeshed in the so-called "linguistic conflict" which has had far-reaching repercussions on its economic, social, and political life. There are considerable cultural and linguistic differences between the Flemish and French-speaking populations, although to a lesser degree than between the populations of Holland and France. The armed services, therefore, have established separate Dutch- and French-speaking units. Officers and petty officers are expected to give orders, training, and instructions in the men's mother tongue, and bilingual units are avoided wherever possible.

Pretests

All available petty officers and men ($N = 546$) at the Naval Training Center were given a series of pretests and questionnaires which served as the basis for the assembly of teams in the main study. All questionnaires were presented in the subject's mother tongue. Those most relevant to the present discussion were:

(a) *Description of Least Preferred Co-Workers* (*LPC*). These scores constituted the major predictors of this study and have been extensively described in other papers (Fiedler, 1962, 1964; Bass and Fiedler, 1962). LPC scores were obtained by asking the men to think of all the co-workers they had ever had and to describe the one individual with whom they could work least well. Thus, the least preferred co-worker would not need to be someone with whom the rater worked at the time of being tested. In fact, these scales were here administered *before the teams were formed*. The LPC scale consisted of eight-point graphic scale items modeled after the Semantic Differential (Osgood *et al.*, 1957), and contained 20 items (in Dutch or French) such as the following:

Pleasant :—8—:—7—:—6—:—5—:—4—:—3—:—2—:—1—: Unpleasant
Friendly :—8—:—7—:—6—:—5—:—4—:—3—:—2—:—1—: Unfriendly[2]

The LPC score is the sum of the twenty item scores, with the most favorable scale position counted 8 and the least favorable scale position counted 1.

The LPC score is best interpreted as a dynamic trait which results in different specific behaviors as the situation changes. The individual who perceives his least preferred co-worker in a relatively favorable manner (high LPC) gains satisfaction and self-esteem from successful interpersonal relations. The person who perceives his least preferred co-worker in a very unfavorable manner (low LPC) gains satisfaction and self-esteem from successful task performance. High and low LPC leaders thus seek to satisfy different needs in the group situation.

This formulation emerges from a number of studies which are giving convergent

[2] Other items on this scale were: accepting-rejecting; helpful-frustrating; enthusiastic-unenthusiastic; lots of fun-serious; relaxed-tense; close-distant; warm-cold; cooperative-uncooperative; supportive-hostile; interesting-boring; harmonious-quarrelsome; self-assured-hesitant; efficient-inefficient; cheerful-gloomy; open-guarded.

results. High LPC leaders are generally described as more considerate of the feelings of group members, less punitive, and more relationship- than task-oriented in their behaviors than are low LPC leaders (Meuwese and Fiedler, 1965; Fiedler, Meuwese, and Oonk, 1961; Morris and Fiedler, 1964). The important clues for the interpretation of the score are to be found, however, in the differences in behavior of high and low LPC persons when they are in anxiety-producing or "difficult" situations as against tension-free, "easy," and nonthreatening situations (Fiedler, 1962).

For example, low LPC persons experienced negotiation groups as considerably and significantly more pleasant when they felt that their side had been successful than when they felt their side had been unsuccessful. In contrast, perceived success did not correlate with perceived pleasantness for high LPC leaders (McGrath and Julian, 1962). In a reanalysis of the rifle teams study by Bishop, low LPC men felt more accepted by their group when they were successful on the task than when their group was unsuccessful, while success again did not influence the feeling of acceptance of high LPC group members. A study by Bishop (1964) showed that group members with high LPC scores improved in adjustment and self-esteem scores if they felt they had been successful in their interpersonal relations (that is, if they felt accepted by the group), but not necessarily if they had been successful on the task. Exactly the reverse was the case for low LPC members, who improved in adjustment and self-esteem scores if they felt successful on the task but not necessarily if they felt successful in their interpersonal relations. Data from the present study, to be reported in a subsequent paper, provide further evidence for this interpretation.

(b) *Verbal Intelligence.* A short verbal intelligence scale, standardized for Belgium in Dutch and French, was administered to assess the level of intellectual functioning.

(c) *Attitude Scale.* A measure of attitude toward Flemish- or French-speaking Belgians (Nuttin, 1960) was administered to assure that the bilingual men who served as subjects would not be systematically more favorable or unfavorable to the other language group than monolingual men.

(d) *Language Comprehension.* A short language comprehension scale was developed to assess the ability of the men to understand and communicate in the second language of their country. Those who passed this test were at least marginally able to communicate in the other national language. Relatively few men were fluently bilingual.

Group Dimensions

Position Power. In 48 of the 96 groups, the leaders were petty officers who, as already mentioned, enjoy considerable prestige in the Belgian Navy. The position power of petty officers was further increased (a) by giving the written task instructions in the leader's language, and (b) by telling the groups that the leader's decision was to be final in all controversial matters.

The 48 groups with low position power had recruits as leaders. Task instructions were given in the language of the group members rather than that of the leader (this, of course, was important only in the case of heterogeneous groups). These groups were instructed that all decisions would have to be unanimous.

Heterogeneity. One of the major aims of this study was the comparison of culturally homogeneous and heterogeneous groups. The 48 homogeneous groups consisted of three French-speaking men or three Dutch-speaking men. The 48 heterogeneous groups consisted either of a French-speaking leader and two Dutch-speaking members, or a Dutch-speaking leader and two French-speaking members.

Construction of Groups. To recapitulate, 120 French- and 120 Dutch-speaking men, as well as 24 petty officers from each language group, participated. Intelligence, LPC, and attitude scores were used in matching, so that the groups were quite similar, man for man, on all control variables.

The men were assigned to 96 three-man teams. The design of the study involved sixteen cells with six groups per cell. Eight cells contained the 48 homogeneous and eight the 48 heterogeneous groups, eight had Flemish and eight French-speaking leaders, eight contained groups with high position power and eight groups with low position power. Three types of tasks (described below) varied in task-structure and in the degree to which they demanded verbal interaction among the men. The presentation of the tasks was counterbalanced so that half the groups started to work with a structured task while the other half began with the unstructured task (a nonverbal, co-acting task was given last). All 96 groups were run on the same day to prevent communication among the men about tasks or procedures. Table 1 presents the experimental design.

TABLE 1

Design of the Experiment[a]

	High position power		Low position power	
	Task sequence		Task sequence	
Leader's language	UT–ST–NVT	ST–UT–NVT	UT–ST–NVT	ST–UT–NVT
Homogeneous				
Dutch	D[b]	H	N	R
French	E	K	O	S
Heterogeneous				
Dutch	F	L	P	T
French	G	M	Q	U

[a] UT = unstructured task; ST = structured task; NVT = nonverbal task.
[b] Letters D through U identify cells in this study.

The six groups within each cell were further subdivided so that three groups were in the upper half and three in the lower half of the intelligence score distribution of our subjects; two groups were high, two medium, and two low in LPC scores. It should be noted that this procedure resulted in groups which were quite homogeneous with respect to intelligence level and LPC scores (Table 2). The cell means on intelligence,

TABLE 2

LPC and Intelligence Distribution of Groups within Each Cell

Intelligence of group	LPC of leader and group members		
	High	Medium	Low
High	One group	One group	One group
Low	One group	One group	One group

LPC, and attitude scores were nearly equal. The men in the heterogeneous groups necessarily had higher scores in comprehension of the second language.

GROUP TASKS

As mentioned, three types of group tasks were used which varied in task structure and in verbal interaction requirements. To assure proper motivation, a prize of 500 Belgian Francs ($10) was offered to each man in the four best groups. These prizes noticeably increased the men's interest in the tasks.

The Unstructured Task. The unstructured task demanded a creative product. The men were told that their committee was to devise a recruiting letter for boys of 16 to 17 years of age, urging them to enlist in the Belgian Naval Forces. The letter, written either in French or in Dutch, was to be completed in 25 minutes (plus 5 minutes for writing it in final form), and it was to be no more than 250 words in length. The men were told that the letters would be judged on style and form as well as on persuasiveness and originality.

Prior studies, using American college students and adult participants in leadership training workshops, required the groups to invent a fable, tell a story for children, or prepare a skit. This was considered unwise by the officers of the Naval Training Center, since they felt that the men would resist working on a completely unstructured task which did not seem related to the military service. For this reason, this task was somewhat more structured than would otherwise be desirable.

Criterion Ratings. Dutch and French letters were rated by separate groups of judges depending upon the language of the letter. The raters were professional psychologists or students with advanced graduate standing. They were given a short training period to acquaint them with the five dimensions on which each letter was to be judged. These dimensions are given below:

1. *Well written versus poorly written, sloppy, awkward.* This scale should gauge the degree to which a product is "good in a literary sense," the extent to which it is well written. High on this scale would be a product which, *independent of its content,* is presented in a readable fashion, with correct sentence structure, grammar, and word use.

2. *Understandably presented versus confused, incomprehensible.* This scale reflects the degree to which the written product can be read and understood easily. There should be no doubt as to the meaning of each sentence, phrase, and paragraph. Lowest on this scale should be products that need to be read several times before the reader can get any meaning from them. The emphasis is on mode of presentation, content *per se* is here irrelevant.

3. *Interesting versus boring.* "How well does this letter capture the reader's attention? To what extent is this "old stuff" and to what extent is this something which is exciting, which is colorful, and which makes you want to hear more?" The emphasis here should be on the colorful language, a sense of excitement, and the interest which the letter evokes.

4. *Persuasive versus unconvincing.* This scale reflects the degree to which the letter evokes the feeling that the Navy life is a desirable, interesting, and worthwhile one. If the letter makes one want to join the Belgian Navy this very moment, it is an excellent one. The letter should be given a low score if it leaves one completely unconvinced or unwilling to join, especially if one would want to discourage others from joining.

5. *Original, creative, versus trite, platitudinous, commonplace.* "Consider here the degree to which the letter is original and new in its approach. Letters which sound trite and 'tried' should get a low score; letters which are new and somewhat offbeat and which show originality of approach and ideas should get a high score."

The ratings for each letter were summed respectively over eight French-speaking and seven Dutch-speaking judges and converted to T scores. The reliability of this criterion, based on inter-rater agreement, was estimated to be .86 for the French-speaking and .92 for the Dutch-speaking judges (Cronbach, Gleser, and Rajaratnam, 1963).

The Structured Tasks. Two structured tasks were administered, always in the same order. These tasks followed the model of the classic salesman's route problem: the groups were required to find the shortest route for a ship which had to touch at ten ports (or twelve in the second task), given certain fuel capacity and required legs of the journey.

The task material was presented on three different sheets, making it impossible for one person to complete the task without help from the other two team-members. The group received a map of the ports which had to be covered. A second sheet contained a matrix of distances between all ports, and a third sheet gave detailed instructions and required the listing of ports and mileages for each leg of the journey. Each of the two structured tasks was to be completed in 20 minutes. The team which computed the shortest mileage was given the best score.

We originally had hoped that the two structured tasks would be highly correlated, and that the scores could be added to increase the reliability of this criterion. However, although these were clearly parallel problems the correlation between the tasks was only .14, and each of the tasks therefore had to be treated separately. The first structured task turned out to be less satisfactory than the second task: nine of the groups obtained a perfect score and, therefore, had tied ranks, and 62 of the 96 groups made a total of 189 routing errors by "running out of fuel," forgetting to make required legs of the journey, and omitting one or more ports, as against 42 groups with 68 errors on the second structured task. The second task would therefore seem to be a methodologically better measure of group performance.

Each of three independent raters[3] devised a method for assessing error penalties which considered the magnitude of the error in terms of the advantage the group would derive from it, and added appropriate additional mileage as correction and penalty. Thus, one method used as the base the average distance to the nearest refueling base; another computed the exact mileage from the nearest refueling port to the ship and back, so that a fuel tanker could go out to refuel the ship. The third method added a penalty which approximated somewhat more than the average mileage that the ship would have gained by its errors. Despite the fact that the three ratings were based on different theories for assessing error penalties, they intercorrelated .86, .93, and .95. These corrected ratings were, therefore, summed as the total score received by the team on the second structured task. As in the unstructured task, the raw scores obtained by the teams were converted to T scores with a mean of 50, and a SD of 10.

The Nonverbal Task. This task was designed to be a completely silent "co-acting" task situation, to determine whether possible differences between homogeneous and heterogeneous groups were due to factors of language alone or to attitudinal factors as well.

The group leaders had previously been given several hours of training in field stripping and reassembling a .45 caliber automatic pistol. They were now asked to imagine that they were in charge of a NATO unit composed of men who presumably did not speak their language. The leader's job was to train his men in field stripping and assembling the hand weapon in a 10-minute period. The group members were then given a blueprint of the various components of the weapon, and they were to indicate the order in which the parts were to be disassembled and reassembled.

The sum of the two members' scores constituted the criterion. Because the correla-

---

[3] We are indebted to Paul Ninane and H. Noel for their assistance. The author was the third rater.

tion between the two members' scores was fairly low (.35), the data could be used only in some of the cruder analyses.

Task Intercorrelations. The median intercorrelation among the four performance scores was only .14, with a range of .03 to .20. The tasks were, therefore, independent. This seems somewhat surprising, especially in the case of the two structured tasks which are essentially identical and which correlated only .14. These findings are, however, quite consistent with the hypothesis of the Contingency Model which is described later.[4]

Post-Session Questionnaires

At the conclusion of each task session all participants completed a number of questionnaires and scales designed to measure the group members' reactions to the tasks, and to permit some inferences about the group processes during the session. A subsequent report will deal with these group process variables. The present paper will discuss only the questionnaires immediately relevant to the understanding of the factors determining group effectiveness.

Of major importance among the post-session questionnaires is the *Group Atmosphere* scale. This is a ten-item questionnaire, similar in form and content to the LPC scale, on which leaders and members were asked to describe the degree to which the group seemed friendly or unfriendly, warm or cold, accepting or rejecting.[5] The internal consistency of the scale was over .90. A group tended to have consistently good or poor group atmosphere, as indicated by the high intercorrelations among the three sessions, namely, .76, .73, and .83.[6]

Additional scales of importance in this report were a 20-item, eight-point *Behavior Description Questionnaire* (BDQ) and a 16-item *Member Reaction Questionnaire* of the same format. The former contained items designed to describe the leader's directive, structuring, and task-oriented actions, as well as person-oriented behavior labeled by Hemphill as "considerate" (1957). The second questionnaire was used to measure the leaders' and group members' reactions to the sessions. It included items on the individual's feelings of interest, motivation, anxiety, and frustration with the task and with his group. Finally, participants were asked to describe each of the other members

[4] On the basis of the Contingency Model we would expect different leader performance depending on whether the group task situation is more or less favorable for the leader. The second task presents an easier situation for the leader, since his previous exposure to the task enables him to direct the group more effectively. Since leadership style and favorableness of the situation interact, the model predicts low group-task intercorrelations.

[5] The remaining items were: satisfying-frustrating; enthusiastic-unenthusiastic; productive-nonproductive; cooperative-uncooperative; supportive-hostile; interesting-boring; successful-unsuccessful.

[6] Group Atmosphere scores are interpreted as conceptually related to good leader-member relations indices derived from sociometric preference questionnaires in real-life groups. However, the correlation between GA and sociometric indices was fairly low in this study. We tentatively interpret this finding as an indication that the leader of the real-life groups experiences the degree of his acceptance by his group as a result of his interaction with his group members. In *ad hoc* groups, which meet at most for a few hours, the leader generally cannot obtain this feedback. He will, therefore, act on the basis of his own feelings toward the group and the group is likely to go along with him for the duration of the experiment.

TABLE 3

Factor Loadings of Scales and Clusters of the Leader Group Climate Factor

	Factor loadings	
Scale or cluster	Unstructured task	Structured task
Leader group atmosphere scale	.80	.81
Leader's esteem for members	.76	.89
Members' satisfaction with group	(− .01)[a]	.77
Leader's description of members as considerate	.69	.73
Leader's satisfaction with group	.66	(− .08)[a]

[a] Parenthesized loadings were not included in the computation of factor scores.

of their group. These *interpersonal perception scales,* identical to those for obtaining LPC scores, yielded esteem scores for leaders and fellow group members.

A factor analysis of the post-meeting scales and questionnaires given after the structured and unstructured task resulted in leader group climate factors, which were used to determine the affective leader-member relations required for the test of the Contingency Model. The items most heavily loaded on the Group Climate Factors are given in Table 3 along with corresponding factor loadings. The group climate factor scores were here utilized to subdivide groups seen by the leader as pleasant and relaxed from those perceived by him as unpleasant and tense. While this *post hoc* method of dividing groups on their leader-member relations is less elegant than would have been an experimental manipulation to assure congenial groups, the design of the study was too complex at this point to permit the introduction of this additional variable.

RESULTS

The Effects of Group Organization and Composition on Performance

One purpose of this study was the comparison of teams in which the leaders and members share the same cultural background and language, with those in which members and leaders differ in language and background. This study also compared teams in which recruits worked under the leadership of trained and experienced petty officers with those in which recruits worked under fellow recruits. The working hypothesis was that homogeneous groups and those led by petty officers would be superior in performance to heterogeneous groups and to groups having recruit leaders.

Analyses of variance, one per task, were computed to compare groups on these variables as well as on three additional factors of leader LPC scores (three levels), group intelligence (two levels), and leader's mother tongue (two levels, i.e., French and Dutch). Table 4 presents the results (in T scores) obtained in the four main conditions. The significant analyses of variance results are summarized in Table 5. The results are shown on Fig. 1.

TABLE 4

Mean Task Performance in Standard Scores for Groups Under Main Experimental Conditions

Group composition	Task	Position power	
		High	Low
Homogeneous	Unstructured	53.10	51.55
	Structured I	53.20	47.32
	Structured II	50.25	49.24
	Nonverbal	51.48	47.89
Heterogeneous	Unstructured	48.52	46.87
	Structured I	46.48	52.05
	Structured II	48.70	51.43
	Nonverbal	50.04	50.60

The differences in the performances of these sets of groups, working under quite diverse experimental treatments, were strikingly small. Only the group's intelligence level emerged as a significant main effect under all four task conditions. Since intelligence level of leader and group members was incorporated into the design as a control variable, these results were anticipated and hardly surprising. These highly significant relations

TABLE 5

Analysis of Significant Variance Results for Performance Scores

	Mean performance scores		F Ratio	P	% Variance
Structured Task I	52.85		10.333	.01	7.2
	47.12				
	Homogeneous	Heterogeneous			
High position power	53.21	46.50			
Low position power	47.33	52.19	11.890	.01	8.4
Structured Task II					
High IQ	52.40				
Low IQ	47.56		4.480	.05	4.5
Unstructured Task					
Homogeneous	52.35				
Heterogeneous		47.71	6.394	.05	4.5
High IQ	54.00				
Low IQ	46.06		18.665	.01	14.8
Nonverbal Task					
High IQ	9.75				
Low IQ	7.38		6.485	.05	5.3
	High IQ	Low IQ			
High position power	8.92	9.00			
Low position power	10.58	5.75	6.948	.05	5.8

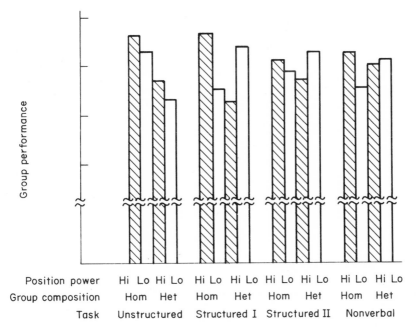

Position power Hi Lo Hi Lo Hi Lo Hi Lo Hi Lo Hi Lo Hi Lo Hi Lo
Group composition   Hom   Het   Hom   Het   Hom   Het   Hom   Het
Task   Unstructured   Structured I   Structured II   Nonverbal

Fig. 1. Performance of homogeneous and heterogeneous groups with high and low position power.

show, however, that the criteria of performance are reliable and meaningful measures.

Three other significant F ratios were obtained:

1. On the unstructured task, which required the group to compose a recruiting letter, the homogeneous teams performed better than did heterogeneous groups. This result again was not surprising since the letter-writing task primarily demanded language and verbal communication skills. These requirements would be more easily met by groups in which all members speak the same language and hold the same cultural values than by groups in which the members are handicapped in communicating with one another.

2. A significant interaction between the leader's position power and group homogeneity occurred in the first structured task (which involved routing a ship through ten ports via the shortest way). Homogeneous groups performed better under the leadership of petty officers than they did under recruit leaders, while heterogeneous groups performed better under recruit leaders than under petty officers.

Two explanations are suggested. (a) This finding may reflect the resentment which men might have felt because they had to work under petty officers from the other ethnic group—mixed teams are uncommon in the Belgian military services. (b) It may reflect the communication barrier between men of different rank which was further exacerbated by linguistic heterogeneity. In heterogeneous groups in which the leader was, himself, a recruit the members may well have assumed more responsibility for the task, and they may have worked extra hard to overcome the communication difficulties which existed. The latter explanation seems more plausible: if the difference in performance had been caused by antagonistic attitudes, these attitudes should have played an even more important part in the second structured task or in the nonverbal task where similar results were not found. This suggests a communication difficulty in the group process that was amenable to learning or practice rather than one caused by deep-seated resentments and antagonistic attitudes.

3. An interaction was also found on the nonverbal task (which required the leader to instruct his men in disassembling and reassembling an automatic pistol). The performance of men trained by dull recruits was substantially poorer than that of men under bright recruits. However, bright recruits and bright petty officers did not differ in their leadership effectiveness. Since this was a fairly simple task, it is easy to see why the relatively dull petty officers would be as effective as the brighter petty officers, since these tasks were quite familiar to all petty officers. The relatively dull recruit leaders, on the other hand, undoubtedly had more difficulty in learning the assembly and disassembly procedures, and they may also have experienced more difficulty in teaching these procedures to their equally dull team members.

The results of this study do not support the conclusion that groups with culturally and linguistically homogeneous membership perform better than culturally and linguistically heterogeneous task groups on all but highly verbal tasks. More importantly, this study fails to support the equally plausible hypothesis that task groups led by trained and experienced leaders with strong position power perform significantly better than teams led by inexperienced and relatively powerless leaders. The implications of these findings will be further considered in the discussion section of this paper.

VALIDATION AND EXTENSION OF THE CONTINGENCY MODEL

The second major concern of this study was a test and extension of the Contingency Model (Fiedler, 1964). This model applies to "interacting" groups, that is, groups in which the members must work together co-operatively, or in which the task cannot be performed by one person alone. It states that the leadership style required for effective performance of these interacting groups is contingent upon the favorableness of the group-task situation: effective performance in very favorable and in very unfavorable group-task situations requires the managing, controlling style of the low LPC leader; situations moderately favorable for the leader require the permissive, considerate, nondirective style of the high LPC leader. The present study tests the Contingency Model and extends the research to heterocultural groups. The nonverbal task in which the work of one individual does not directly affect the performance of another is a "co-acting" group situation, and is, therefore, unsuitable for testing this model. Only the structured and unstructured tests are here considered for purposes of these tests.

Background of the Contingency Hypothesis

There has been considerable controversy in the field of leadership concerning the relative merits of directive, autocratic, versus nondirective, human relations-oriented attitudes and behaviors. The Contingency Model attempts to reconcile these two viewpoints. It postulates that the effectiveness of these particular leadership styles depends upon the degree to which it is "easy" or "difficult" to be a leader of a group under a particular set of circumstances. By the *favorableness of the group situation* is here meant the ease with which the leader is able to influence the group members, that is, the degree to which the group task and group organization facilitates or inhibits the leader's ability to exert influence without incurring resistance.

Our previous research has used the Esteem for the Least Preferred Coworker (LPC) and the Assumed Similarity between Opposites (ASo) score, which are highly correlated (.80 to .90). As already discussed they indicate the degree to which the leader seeks satisfaction from successful interpersonal relations or from successful task performance. These scores have predicted group performance in a wide variety of studies (Fiedler, 1958, 1964). However, the correlations were in the positive direction in some situations and in the negative direction in others. The Contingency Model predicts lawful relations if we classify group-task situations in terms of their favorableness for the leader.

Groups in our previous studies were tentatively classified on the basis of three dimensions. These were, in order of importance, (a) the affective leader-member relation, (b) the task structure, and (c) the power of the leadership position. These dimensions are here briefly described. Detailed operational definitions can be found in a previous paper (Fiedler, 1964).

Affective Leader-Member Relations. These relations were operationally defined either by means of sociometric preference scores which indicate that the leader is the group's most preferred member, or by means of "group-atmosphere scales." The latter are bipolar adjective scales, similar to the Semantic Differential, on which the leader is asked to describe the climate of his group. A recent study by Fishbein *et al.* (1965) shows that approximately one-half the variance is accounted for by this dimension. This dimension seems to represent the most important aspect of the leader-member relationship. A leader having the trust and confidence of his men can do what would be difficult for a disliked or distrusted leader.

Task Structure. The degree to which the job can be spelled out or done "by the numbers," and hence controlled by the leader, was measured on the basis of four scales developed by Shaw (1962). These are (a) the task's goal clarity—the degree to which the desired outcome is specified; (b) its decision verifiability, the objectivity with which the outcome can be measured; (c) its solution specificity, whether there are one or many possible solutions; and (d) its goal path multiplicity, whether there are one or many possible methods for reaching the goal (reverse scoring).

Position Power. The degree to which an organization invests the leader with power to reward and punish, and the degree to which it gives the leader prestige (French, 1956) indicates position power. It is distinct from the power the leader enjoys by virtue of his personal attraction or his ability to inspire loyalty and trust. Rather, position power is here defined as representing the formal power at the leader's disposal, irrespective of his ability or willingness to use it. This dimension can be reliably measured by means of a simple checklist (Fiedler, 1964). Position power was considered to be the least important of these three dimensions in the groups we had previously studied: even low-ranking leaders can control a group if the task is spelled out in detail, and a well-liked leader does not require rank.

The Classification of Group-Task Situations. The three dimensions can be represented in the form of a cube. We can further arbitrarily subdivide each dimension into a high and low half, yielding an eight-celled figure (Fig. 2). Thus, Cell I includes group-task situations in which the leader is, or feels, accepted by his group, in which the task is highly structured, and in which the leader's position power is relatively high compared to that of his members. Cell VIII includes group-task situations in which the leader is not accepted and has little power, and in which the task is ambiguous and unstructured.

A consideration of these eight group-task situations suggested that these cells could be further classified in terms of their favorableness for the leader. Ordering the cells first on the basis of leader-member relations, then on task structure, and finally on position power leads to a continuum indicated by the numbers assigned to the cells, with Cell I being most favorable, Cell II next most favorable, and so on to Cell VIII which is the least favorable pole on this continuum. We have in this manner classified a total of 58 different group-task situations from 15 different studies. A more detailed rationale and description of this procedure can be found in Fiedler (1964).

By ordering the eight cells according to their favorableness and plotting the correlations between leader LPC (or ASo) and group performance within each of the cells, we obtained the curvilinear performance curve shown in Fig. 3. This plot shows negative correlations between leader LPC and group performance in Cells I, II, III and VIII, and positive correlations in Cells IV, V, and VII. In other words, low LPC leaders tended to perform best in very favorable and in very unfavorable group-task

Fig. 2. A model for the classification of group-task situations. (This figure is reproduced by permission from The Harvard Business Review, September–October, 1965, p. 117.)

situations; the high LPC leaders performed best in situations intermediate in difficulty.

Tests of the Contingency Hypothesis

The critical problem of testing the model lies in ordering the group-task situations in this experiment on the basis of their favorableness for the leader. Once this is done, the leader's LPC scores can be correlated with the performance scores of the groups within each of the cells.

Although we had started with the comparatively large sample of 96 groups, the number of cases within each cell shrank rapidly with each variable that had to be incorporated in the design. We obviously had to divide the groups on the basis of the original dimensions, namely, high versus low position power, task structure, and the group climate scores

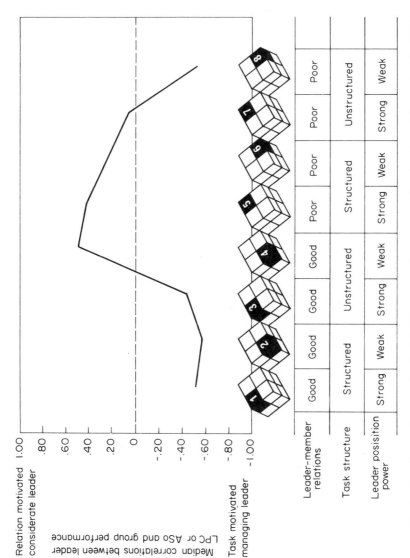

Fig. 3. Correlations between leaders' LPC scores and group effectiveness plotted for each cell. (This figure is reproduced by permission from The Harvard Business Review, September–October, 1965, p. 118.)

that measured affective leader-member relations. A further division was required on the basis of homogeneity versus heterogeneity.

Four other variables in this study also had to be considered or statistically controlled: (a) the intelligence level of the leader and his group members played a major role in affective performance; (b) differences were found between Dutch- and French-speaking groups; (c) the order of presenting the tasks affected the difficulty experienced by the leader (in the "second presentation" tasks the leader had already learned to some extent how to work with his men); and, finally, (d) the second structured task situation was judged less difficult than the first, since some task learning and practice effects had occurred by that time.

Since we would run out of degrees of freedom needed to test the model, it was essential to combine certain cells. For example, although intelligent groups performed better than did dull groups, differences in performance could be statistically controlled by means of covariance adjustments. This procedure involved obtaining the mean difference between performance scores of the relatively bright and dull groups, and adding this difference to the scores of the dull groups. A similar adjustment was needed to equalize mean differences in the performance of French- and Dutch-speaking teams, where such extraneous factors as differences in scoring standards in the two languages and clarity in translating the instructions could have affected the results.

The order of task presentation, as already mentioned, affected the difficulty of the group-task situation, as did the practice effects that occurred on Structured Task II, since the groups had performed an almost identical problem in the immediately preceding Structured Task I. These effects were considered in scaling the group-task situation.

The classification procedure, outlined above, categorized the 96 groups on the basis of (a) homogeneity versus heterogeneity, (b) high versus low leader group climate scores, (c) high versus low leader position power, (d) task presentation order beginning with the structured or with the unstructured task. This classification generated 16 cells with six groups per cell. (Two of the 96 groups had to be discarded for purposes of this analysis because of a clerical error which misclassified two bi-lingual men in terms of their mother tongue, leaving five groups in two of the cells.)

Since the criterion tasks were uncorrelated and, therefore, presumed to be independent, correlations were computed separately for each of the tasks. The resulting 48 correlations (three correlations for each of the 16 cells) constitute the basic data for testing the Contingency Hypothesis.

These data are presented in Table 6. Column 1 of this table indicates the cells which were involved in the analysis, columns 2, 3, 4, and 5 indicate the characteristics of the particular cell. Thus, Cell DE consisted of homogeneous groups (col. 2) with high position power (petty officers) (col. 3), and groups which began the experiment with the unstructured

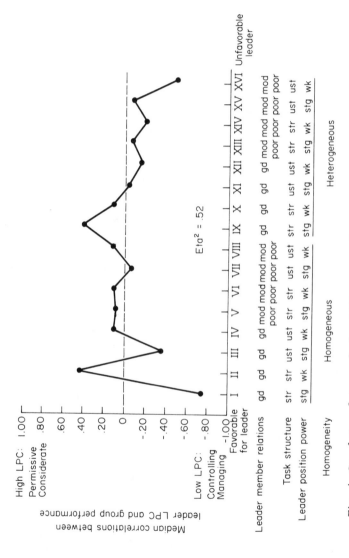

Fig. 4. *Correlations between leader LPC scores and group performance for homogeneous and heterogeneous groups, following the original classification of group-task situations presented in Fiedler (1964).*

task (col. 4). Dutch- (D) and French-speaking (E) groups were merged. The 12 groups were then divided into the six in which the leader had high group climate factor scores and the six in which he had low group climate scores (col. 5). The correlation between LPC of the leader and his performance on the unstructured task are listed in col. 6, those on the first and second structured tasks in columns 7 and 8.

The model requires that we order the group-task situations in terms of their favorableness for the leader. Three tests, each based upon a different method of ordering, are here presented.

Test I: Replication of the original model. The first test follows the method of categorization described in the development of the original model (Fiedler, 1964). It involves the categorization of groups on the basis of group climate scores, task structure (by using the unstructured and second structured task), and position power of the leader, in addition to the main variable of homogeneity versus heterogeneity.

TABLE 6

Correlations between Leader LPC and Group Performance in Different Group-Task Situations[a]
(N = 6)

Cells[b]		PP	Order of task presentation	Leader's group climate	Split on leader group climate			Weights indicating favorableness of the group—task situation		
					UT	STI	STII	UT	STI	STII
DE	Hom.	High	U	High	−16	−20	−77	9	11	12
				Low	26	36	16	6	8	9
HK	Hom.	High	S	High	−54	59	−72	10	10	11
				Low	−27	−03	03	7	7	8
NO	Hom.	Low	U	High	08	67	37	6	8	9
				Low	−37	10	07	3	5	6
RS	Hom.	Low	S	High	13	−43	50	7	7	8
				Low	60	−72	14	4	4	5
FG	Het.	High	U	High	20	−49	03	6	8	9
				Low	−37	54	08	3	5	6
LM	Het.	High	S	High	−26	−09	77	7	7	8
				Low	08	09	−19	4	4	5
PQ	Het.	Low	U	High	−89	−49	77	3	5	6
				Low	−36	−13	53	0	2	3
TU	Het.	Low	S	High[c]	70	−25	−53	4	4	5
				Low[c]	−60	30	−90	1	1	2

[a] UT = unstructured task; STI = first structured task; STII = second structured task. PP = position power. U = task presentation sequence beginning with the unstructured task. S = task presentation beginning with the structured task.

[b] See Table 1 for Cell designation.

[c] *N*'s = 5.

Figure 4 shows the performance curve based upon these data, abstracted for this purpose from Table 6. The curve is drawn through the medians of the correlations representing each cell.

As in Fig. 2, which shows the original performance curve of the Contingency Model, the plot based on the present study is curvilinear. However, the point by point correspondence is far from satisfactory. The curve in the Belgian navy study reaches its highest point in Octant II, while the original curve peaked in Octants IV and V. Octant VIII of the original curve showed high negative correlations between leader LPC and performance, while the corresponding correlations in the present study do not become negative until the much more unfavorable situations presented by heterogeneous groups.

The differences between these two curves may well be due to the special conditions under which this experiment was conducted. The differences in position power between petty officers and men was clearly much greater in the Belgian military teams than in civilian groups or even in the American military crews which we had studied before. On the other hand, the difference between the structured and unstructured tasks seemed to be considerably less important in this experiment than in previous studies. (Tests II and III, contained in the original article, have been omitted.)

DISCUSSION

The first part of this study tested two hypotheses. These were (a) that culturally and linguistically homogeneous teams would perform more effectively on various tasks than would heterogeneous teams, and (b) that groups under powerful as well as experienced and trained leaders would perform better than teams under weak, inexperienced, and untrained leaders. The fact that the results supported neither hypothesis throws doubt on some fundamental assumptions in this area.

Group Heterogeneity

The importance of good communication for group effectiveness has been a keystone in social psychological theories. Shaw (1964), in reviewing research on communication networks, accurately reflects the opinion of writers in the field when he says:

> Communication lies at the heart of the group interaction process. No group, whether an informal or formal organization . . . can function effectively unless its members can communicate with facility. . . . The free flow of information among various members of a group determines to a large extent the efficiency of the group and the satisfaction of its members [pp. 111–112].

According to this widely held assumption, group performance should suffer in teams with poor communication. As indicated before, the men in homogeneous groups shared the same cultural heritage, they shared common attitudes, and they spoke the same language. The men in heterogeneous groups came from one ethnic background while their leader came from another; the men and their leader were raised in different languages, and many men may have had unfavorable attitudes toward each other's ethnic groups. Since most participants were only marginally competent in the other national language, there can be little doubt that the heterogeneous teams were severely handicapped in their verbal interaction. This contention is supported not only by common sense expectation and observer judgments, but also by the questionnaire responses obtained after each session.

While heterogeneous groups had less pleasant group atmosphere and higher anxiety scores, these teams performed as well as homogeneous groups in all but the letter-writing task which demanded a high degree of verbal facility. These results suggest the need for re-evaluating the importance of the communication variable in group interaction.

Leadership Training and Experience

The comparison of petty officers and recruit leaders in this study raises an equally important issue. It is generally assumed that leadership training and experience will increase the effectiveness of leaders (Hare, 1962, p. 390). Trained and experienced leaders should not only be more skillful in handling personnel and administrative problems within their teams but they should also be instrumental in obtaining more effective group performance. Interestingly enough, only a very small number of studies have compared the performance of groups the leaders of which have been given leadership training and those which have not. The majority of studies in this area evaluate the effectiveness of leadership *behavior*, rather than the effectiveness of group performance (Barnlund, 1955; Harris and Fleishman, 1955).

In the present study, as we pointed out before, Belgian petty officers are career men who enjoy considerable prestige and status. The average petty officer in our sample completed 2 years of leadership and technical training in petty officer candidate school, which is comparable in quality and intensity to similar training in the United States. He also had about 10 years of leadership experience behind him. This contrasts with the recruit leaders, most of whom were only 20 years old and therefore untrained and inexperienced in Navy leadership. Moreover, the experimental design gave additional prestige and power to the petty officers by letting them have the final voice on all group decisions, and by giving task instructions for heterogeneous groups in the leader's mother tongue. Petty officers were in fact more highly motivated than were recruit leaders. Despite these advantages favoring the petty officers, neither their training and experience nor their prestige and position power enabled them to perform significantly more effectively than the untrained, inexperienced recruit leaders. Moreover, the correlation between the number of years a man served as petty officer and his group's performance was small and not significant.

A number of questions must be asked before these results can be accepted at face value. First, could the tasks in this study have been unrealistic or unfair to petty officers? This would certainly not be the case for the nonverbal, pistol-assembly task. The training of recruits is one of the main functions of petty officers at Ste. Croix-Bruges. While the pistol-assembly training was to be conducted in silence, this did not seem to handicap the petty officers more than the recruit leaders. The other tasks are also not very far removed from those common in the military services. Petty officers and their clerks are not infrequently called upon to draft reports or letters. The ship-routing task was basically no different from such military tasks as laying out a supply-truck route or a cross-country march, or devising a system which will most efficiently accommodate scarce classroom space for a training program. In any case, not one petty officer or recruit complained that the tasks had been unfair or unreasonable, and most said that they enjoyed the problems. These tasks were also considered fair by the commandant of the Center and by officers of his staff, who, in fact, helped to design the problems.

A related argument could be advanced that petty officers and recruits should not be compared on any but routine Navy problems for which petty officers had received special training. This would imply, however, that leadership skills taught in military schools and acquired through experience are not transferable to new situations. In that case, however, there would be no need for leadership training as it is now conducted by the armed services and most industrial and governmental institutions.

Could it then be that the recruits were overawed by the high-ranking and prestigious petty officers, or unwilling to cooperate with them? Post-meeting data do not support either of these contentions. The men liked to work with petty officers as well as they did with recruits, and communication in groups led by petty officers was rated better than in recruit-led groups. Leadership training and experience may, therefore, improve the men's satisfaction but not their team performance.

Finally, it might be pointed out that the results were obtained on brief tasks given to *ad hoc* groups. This point is valid and limits the generality of our findings. For what it is worth, we may note that the petty officers' performances did not improve proportionately more from the first to the second structured task than did the performances of recruits. Whether the petty officers' performance would have improved over that of recruit leaders in tasks extending over much longer periods of time is a question for further research. However, the petty officers, who already had considerable experience and training, are not likely to gain much, while the untrained recruits would be expected to gain proportionately more. Hence, additional time and experience would be an advantage to recruit leaders, rather than to petty officers. In the meantime, however, the data lead us to question whether extensive training and experience of the leader, at least in *ad hoc* groups, contributes to group effectiveness. These findings point to a pressing need for further research on this problem.

Test of the Contingency Model

The second major purpose of this study was the test and extension of the leadership theory proposed in a recent paper (Fiedler, 1964). The data clearly support the major hypothesis of the Contingency Model, although there are point-by-point discrepancies from the predicted curves. Whether these discrepancies in the shape of the curve are due to the specific peculiarities of the sample and the experimental conditions of the Belgian study, or to the inadequacies of the theory, will need to be determined in future research. The former seems likely in view of the strong position power of Navy petty officers *vis-à-vis* recruits in the Belgian military system, and in view of the relatively small difference between structured and unstructured tasks. That the general hypothesis was supported despite differences in language and population samples, and that it could be extended to heterocultural groups, testifies to the robustness of the theory. Further attempts to generalize the model are now underway.

The model takes on additional significance in view of the fact that we did not find significant differences in leadership performance due to leadership training or experience, or to group heterogeneity. Neither leadership experience nor orthodox leadership training as currently administered is likely to increase the individual's ability to fit his leadership style to the requirements of the group-task situation. Nor is current training designed to assist the leader in modifying the situation so that he will be able to cope with it more effectively.

It is almost always easier to change environmental factors than to change an individual's personality or his style of interpersonal relations. The most eligible solution for increasing leadership effectiveness seems to lie, therefore, in "engineering the group-task situation" so that it will fit the leader's style. This has already been suggested in a recent paper (Fiedler, 1964), and the present data provide further support for this view.

What, then, are the implications of these results for training? As has been demonstrated in this study, we can change the group-task situation in a number of ways. We can modify (a) group homogeneity, (b) leader position power, (c) task structure, (d) the sequencing of tasks and the concomitant learning effects, and (e) the time a group has to work together and to learn how to operate as a team. Our study showed that the groups performed about as well in unfavorable as in favorable group-task situations. It is, apparently, more important that the leader's style fit the group-task situation than that it be favorable for the leader. The Contingency Model, therefore, presents one possible alternative to current practices of leadership training and placement.

REFERENCES

Bass, A. R., & Fiedler, F. E. Interpersonal perception scores and their components as predictors of personal adjustment. *Journal of Abnormal and Social Psychology,* 1961, **62,** 442–445.

Barnlund, D. C. Experiments in leadership training for decision-making groups. *Speech Monographs,* 1955, **22,** 1–14.

Cronbach, L. J., Gleser, Goldene, & Rajaratnam, Nageswari. Theory of generalizeability: A liberalization of reliability theory. *The British Journal of Statistical Psychology,* **16, 2,** 1963.

Fiedler, F. E. *Leader attitudes and group effectiveness.* Urbana, Illinois: University of Illinois Press, 1958.

Fiedler, F. E., Meuwese, W. A. T., & Oonk, Sophie. Performance on laboratory tasks requiring group creativity. *Acta Psychologica,* 1961, **18,** 100–119.

Fiedler, F. E. Leader attitudes, group climate, and group creativity. *Journal of Abnormal and Social Psychology,* 1962, **65,** 308–318.

Fiedler, F. E. A Contingency Model of leadership effectiveness. In L. Berkowitz (Ed.), *Advances in experimental social psychology.* New York: Academic Press, 1964.

Fiedler, F. E. The Contingency Model: A theory of leadership effectiveness. In H. Proshansky and B. Seidenberg (Eds.), *Basic studies in social psychology.* New York: Holt, Rinehart and Winston, 1965.

Fishbein, M., Landy, Eva, & Hatch, Grace. Some determinants of an individual's esteem for his least preferred co-worker: An attitudinal analysis. Urbana, Illinois: Group Effectiveness Research Laboratory, 1965.

French, J. R. P., Jr. A formal theory of social power. *Psychological Review,* 1956, **63,** 181–194.

Hare, A. P. *Handbook of small group research.* New York: Free Press of Glencoe, 1962.

Harris, E. F., & Fleishman, E. A. Human relations training and the stability of leadership patterns. *Journal of Applied Psychology,* 1955, **39,** 20–25.

Hawkins, C. A study of factors mediating a relationship between leader rating behavior and group productivity. Unpublished doctoral dissertation, University of Minnesota, 1962.

Hemphill, J., & Westie, C. M. The measurement of group dimensions. *Journal of Psychology,* 1950, **29,** 325–342.

Maier, N. R. F. An experimental test of the effect of training on discussion leadership. *Human Relations,* 1953, **6,** 161–173.

Meuwese, W., & Fiedler, F. E. Leadership and group creativity under varying conditions of stress. Urbana, Illinois: Group Effectiveness Research Lab., University of Illinois, 1965.

Morris, C. G., & Fiedler, F. E. Application of a new system of interaction analysis to the relationships between leader attitudes and behavior in problem solving groups. Urbana, Illinois: Group Effectiveness Research Lab., 1964.

Nuttin, J. M., Jr. De ontwikkeling van de gezindheid tegenover de Walen en het persoonlijk contact. *Tijdschrift voor Opvoedkunde,* 1960 (5), 315–333.

Osgood, C. E., Suci, G. A., & Tannenbaum, P. H. *The Measurement of meaning.* Urbana, Illinois: University of Illinois Press, 1957.

Stogdill, R. M., & Coons, A. E. Leader behavior, its description and measurement. *Research Monographs, Bureau of Business Research,* Ohio State University, 1957.

Shaw, M. E. Annual Technical Report. Gainesville, Florida: University of Florida, 1962.

Shaw, M. E. Communication networks. In L. Berkowitz (Ed.), *Advances in experimental social psychology.* New York: Academic Press, 1964.

Chapter 14

EXTREMITY SHIFTS

Decisions made in groups require the resolution of initial opinion differences among the members, especially if the group is using a consensus rule. The present chapter reviews the research which has studied the relation of the members' initial opinions to the consensus position. This research began with an interest in group discussion and decisions involving issues of risk taking and was later expanded to decisions about attitude issues. The focus of this research has been on understanding the determinants of the consensus point and the effects of the decision process on the members' postdiscussion opinions.

The Risky Shift

Suppose six subjects are privately asked to read a hypothetical situation about a person, Mr. A, who is faced with a choice between two alternative actions. He can remain in his present, secure position or he can accept a more attractive job with a new company whose future is uncertain. The second alternative, if it proves to be successful, will always provide better outcomes. The six subjects must decide what they consider to be the lowest acceptable probabilities of success for the new company before they would advise Mr. A to change jobs. The initial risk preferences of the subjects will vary. Some will recommend the more attractive alternative only if it has a high likelihood of succeeding, others if it has a moderate likelihood of succeeding, and still others will recommend it even if it has only a small chance of succeeding. Each subject's degree of risk preference is reflected by the smallness of the probability of success he deems acceptable. If the six subjects are then asked to discuss the item with each other until they reach a consensus about the single most acceptable odds, they are very likely to agree on a level of risk which is *more* risky than the average of their individual risk choices. The group will have shifted toward a preference for greater risk.

Such a shift toward greater risk occurs very dependably. Research on this phenomenon has been closely associated with the work of Michael Wallach and Nathan Kogan; the Choice Dilemma questionnaire has been the most frequently used task measuring risk. Wallach and Kogan (1959) devised the items to test individual differences in risk taking. We have summarized this procedure in the preceding paragraph, but the reader may wish to acquaint himself with specific details by consulting the Method section of the Wallach and Kogan (1965) article placed in the Readings section. One of the early reports of a group-induced risky shift was published by Wallach, Kogan, and Bem (1962), who also showed that the group-induced riskiness maintained itself for individual decisions made after the discussion.

If group decisions were characterized by greater conservatism, one would expect a shift toward less risk. If, instead, the effect of the group discussion were solely to reflect conformity pressures, one would expect the group decision to be equal to the average of the individual, prediscussion decisions of the members. Selecting the average of the members' initial positions is probably a very "prominent" solution for any group. It minimizes the maximum change any member needs to make and avoids confronting actual disagreements. Of these three possibilities, a shift toward greater risk was found. Wallach *et al.* thought the shift could be explained by a process they termed "diffusion of responsibility." Presumably the participants' awareness that the decisions are being made jointly with others decreases each of their feelings of personal responsibility for the consequences of the decisions. In a later article, Wallach, Kogan, and Bem (1964) elaborate this explanation by noting that the greater the risk of a decision the more likelihood of failure. Diffusion of responsibility therefore enhances risk taking because no single person can be blamed if things turn out badly.

EXPLANATIONS OF THE RISKY SHIFT

There has been little disagreement about the existence of a group-induced shift to risk, but a great deal of disagreement about the most appropriate explanation for its occurrence. Diffusion of responsibility, as suggested by Wallach and Kogan, has not been the only contender for the most plausible explanation. We will next discuss the research inspired by efforts to establish the best possible explanation for the risky shift.

Unique Effects of Task and Subjects

Any effect which is established in one kind of setting must, sooner or later, be tested in other settings in order to establish the limits of generalization or the appropriate domain to which it may be applied. The risky shift is a particularly apt illustration of this maxim because there was good reason to think it might be confined to the use of the Choice Dilemmas questionnaire or to the use of undergraduate subjects.

The items on the Choice Dilemmas questionnaire require subjects to role-play. They must advise a fictitious person who will not be affected by the advice. The consequences of the decisions are unknowable and, furthermore, have only vague relevance for the group members. If these are the necessary conditions determining the risky shift, there would be no reason to consider other explanations, such as diffusion of responsibility. Will the risky shift occur when the task requires decisions whose consequences will be known and are relevant for the group members? Wallach et al. (1964) demonstrated that the risky shift does indeed occur under such circumstances. College board items, varying in their objective level of difficulty, were used to assess risk preferences. As the item difficulty level increased the amount of money which could be won by correctly answering items also increased. The experiment involved several issues; the major finding was that the average individual risk decision was less risky than the group decision. Unfortunately, the finding held for male groups, but not for female groups; females were thought to be more concerned with the affiliative consequences of their decisions than the monetary consequences. Bem, Wallach, and Kogan (1965), using male subjects, also obtained a risky shift on subjects' choices among various experimental conditions. Larger amounts of money could be earned by selecting experimental conditions associated with higher odds of painful side-effects. The risky shift is clearly not restricted solely to the use of the Choice Dilemmas questionnaire.

It might be argued that college students uniquely value risk and would be less inclined publicly to defend conservative alternatives. The content of the discussion generated by college student groups might, thus, be heavily weighted by arguments favoring risk. Subjects drawn from other categories, especially ones not holding the presumed value for riskiness, might therefore show no shift. Experiments, however, have shown a risky shift with different kinds of subjects. For example, Marquis (1962) replicated the risky shift both with mature, middle-level executives and with first-year graduate students in a School of Industrial Management. It has also been obtained in a psychiatric setting, with three-person groups composed of a psychiatrist, a psychologist, and a social worker (Siegel & Zajonc, 1967). Although male college students are most frequently used as subjects, the risky shift is not confined to this population. The effect occurs in female groups, but not as consistently as in male groups.

Research Related to the Diffusion of Responsibility Interpretation

The diffusion explanation could best be tested by an experiment which directly manipulated amounts of diffusion. Ideally, one condition would require groups to discuss a problem to consensus under maximum diffusion, while the other condition would require a discussion to consensus with minimum diffusion. But, how can this be accomplished? Because diffusion of responsibility is linked with the joint nature of the discussion there appears to be no ready way to manipulate degree of diffusion while leaving the discussion and decision process intact. Marquis (1962) thought diffusion might be manipulated by creating a condition in which each group had an appointed leader who, after discussing the problem with his "board," was told the final decision was his sole responsibility. Five-person groups were formed and the member whose risk preference was closest to the mid-position for that group was the designated leader. Comparison of the pre- and the postdiscussion risk preferences of the appointed leaders, as well as those of the other four members, showed a significant shift toward greater risk. The leaders who had sole responsibility for the final decision shifted toward risk to the same extent as the other members. Furthermore, the magnitude of the shift was comparable to the one Marquis found for groups following the standard procedure. These results, then, cast some doubt about the correctness of the diffusion explanation. By themselves, however, they did not represent an adequate refutation.

Wallach and Kogan (1965) conducted a study designed to disentangle the standard procedure components which were possibly contributing to the risky shift. The experiment is contained in the Readings section. The question of whether the discussion or the consensus requirements were the prepotent aspects determining the shift was answered by results favoring the importance of discussion. The discussion condition, in which subjects discussed each item without having to reach a consensus, showed a risky shift. The consensus only condition, in which subjects balloted to consensus, showed an averaging effect. Discussion, by itself, was thought sufficient to generate diffusion of responsibility which was now also linked to the "emotionally tinged interpersonal connections" which inevitably attend face-to-face discussion.

The preeminence of the diffusion explanation during this period was primarily achieved by demonstrating that other possible explanations were not correct. For example, it could be argued that the shift might occur if those people who are initially most risky are also the persons most influential in the discussion. In the previous chapter we have already noted the consistency with which positive correlations between amount of participation and influence or leadership are obtained. Perhaps the riskier group members are used to participating more in discussions and therefore exert more influence on their less risky colleagues. Wallach et al. (1962), as well as Marquis (1962), found a significant, positive correlation between subjects' initial riskiness and amount of rated influence. The magnitude of the correlations was not sufficiently large to be the sole determinant of the shift. Furthermore, in both studies it was pointed out that such correlations do not reveal the causal direction of the relationship. Higher risk people might be more influential; or, given that diffusion of responsibility causes a shift toward greater risk, people who are initially more risky may only be perceived as being more influential. After all, they happen to advocate a position to which the group will move.

Wallach, Kogan, and Burt (1968) thought to establish the cause of the correlation by conducting a study in which groups, composed by members' initial risk scores, were asked to discuss non-risk-related items. Each same-sex group of five persons contained a maximally heterogeneous set of individuals with respect to risk preferences. In this study, as well as in other risk-composition studies, a subject's risk preference is defined by totalling his responses to all of the risk items. There was no relationship between initial risk preferences and three measures of persuasiveness in the male groups. In the female groups the three persuasiveness measures were positively correlated with riskiness, but the correlations were low and of marginal significance. The persuasiveness of high-risk-taking females may contribute to the risky shift in female groups, but this clearly is not the case for male groups. By composing homogeneous groups with respect to the members' initial risk preference scores, Hoyt and Stoner (1968) sought to neutralize any leadership effects of high risk-takers. Homogeneously composed groups did show a shift whose magnitude was comparable to those obtained in other studies. The risky shift cannot adequately be explained by postulating that high risk-takers exert more influence in the group discussion. The subject with the highest total risk preference score, however, does not necessarily hold the riskiest position on every item. In keeping with a strict situational view of leadership, the possibility still exists that the most extreme risk-taking member on any given item is the most influential participant for that item. He would be expected to be the most influential member on a subsequent item only if he continued to endorse the most extreme risk position. Correlations between judged influence on the entire discussion and total risk preference scores would not reveal such item-to-item changes.

Roger Brown's Value Hypothesis

The most viable interpretation of the risky shift to date was suggested by Brown (1965). Drawing on a number of studies conducted under the direction of Donald Marquis at the Massachusetts Institute of Technology (Stoner, Nordhøy, Hinds; reported in Brown, 1965), Brown argued that the shift must be based on tasks which elicit moderate riskiness as a cultural value. The Choice Dilemmas questionnaire items are examples of such tasks. The first time subjects confront a given item during the individual administration, they will choose a risk preference which is in keeping with the value of risk. As we have already noted, however, the individual responses to any given item show considerable variability. Is it not paradoxical to suggest all persons select a response in keeping with a shared cultural value when it is known their actual choices of recommended degrees of risk will vary? The paradox is resolved if one assumes that acceptance of the value does not translate narrowly into defining the single response, among all the response categories, which best reflects the value. A person who believes that moderate riskiness is the most acceptable course will not necessarily know whether odds of 3/10 or 7/10 indicate moderate riskiness. According to Brown, people believe their own position adequately represents the relevant value they wish to express. Applied to the cultural value of risk this means that subjects will usually see their own response as being somewhat more risky than the average response of their peers. The major function of the group discussion is to provide information about the proper frame of reference to be used for locating the single response which best embodies appropriate riskiness. It is, thus, the social comparison opportunities provided by the discussion which are critical. Information about the other members' choices is the basis for making social comparisons and for establishing that frame of reference. Such information has the most force on the members who initially selected the least risky position. They will realize that their own positions are not as risky as they had thought and that acceptable riskiness is reflected by an answer which is riskier than they initially chose. Brown also suggested that the existence of a cultural value for risk may lead members to raise arguments in the discussion which favor riskiness. Instead of arguments being equally distributed between pro-risk and anti-risk content, a disproportionately large number of pro-risk arguments may be offered. Arguments in keeping with the value may more readily come to mind than arguments opposed to the value. On risk tasks it may be easier to argue for raising the utility of the reward (e.g., the benefits Mr. A would obtain from a new job) or for lowering the perceived cost of the stake (e.g., the lack of harm to Mr. A if the new company fails). Acceptance of new arguments in either of these two categories would logically require greater riskiness.

Brown's ideas were formulated before the publication of the Wallach and Kogan (1965) study, which appears to weaken his argument. It will be recalled that Wallach and Kogan found that group consensus without discussion produced no shift. Yet, if the major determinant of the shift is the establishment of a realistic frame of reference about other members' risk preferences on each item, the balloting procedure used in the consensus condition should have met this requirement. Through the balloting procedure, even without discussion, each member should be keenly aware of the other members' risk position. The least risky members should realize they can keep faith with the value of risk only by shifting their answers toward greater risk.

How can such a puzzle be resolved? The answer is contained in a study conducted by Teger and Pruitt (1967). They thought the value prediction may not have been substantiated by the Wallach and Kogan results because of the wording of the instructions in the consensus condition. The feature deemed critical was the phrase telling subjects in the consensus condition that their recommendations ". . . should consist of what you think the group can agree on and what you think the group should agree on." Teger and Pruitt argued that the most obvious choice on which a group "can" agree is the mean of the members' preferences and therefore, the averaging effect found by Wallach and Kogan should be expected. This idea was tested by Teger and Pruitt through the creation of an information exchange condition which omitted any urging about reaching an expedient consensus. Subjects were asked to compare notes about their private choices on each item by going around the group, in order, displaying their choices. This kind of balloting continued for three rounds. Subjects were encouraged to change their decisions if they wished, but no consensus requirement was made. They were urged to "Always consider your own decision in light of others' decisions" (p. 195). Comparison between this kind of information exchange condition and a control condition showed a significant risky shift in the information condition. The magnitude of that shift was not quite as large as in a discussion condition where consensus was urged, but not required. Teger and Pruitt further showed that the magnitude of shifts over the different items was positively correlated with the members' initial average riskiness on each item. That is, the more the group initially preferred risk on an item, the greater the shift. If the initial item mean is considered to be an index of the value placed on being risky for that item, these positive correlations are in keeping with Brown's hypothesis. Finally, Teger and Pruitt also varied group size. The shift was found in four- and five-person groups, but not in three-person groups. This finding is in keeping with either a diffusion of responsibility or with a value explanation. A three-person group may not be large enough to permit the occurrence of responsibility diffusion. On the other hand, three persons may be too few to establish a clear frame of reference or to generate enough arguments.

The Teger and Pruitt results provided strong support for one aspect of the value interpretation. The mere knowledge of each member's initial risk preference was sufficient to produce the shift. The value interpretation also specifies that individuals mistakenly see themselves as being riskier than their peers. This aspect of the value interpretation has been confirmed by a number of studies. In what is, unfortunately, a rare occurrence in the social sciences, an author who championed one kind of interpretation has subsequently published results favorable to an opposing interpretation. Michael Wallach, who had initially favored the diffusion of responsibility explanation, more recently co-authored a study corroborating the value explanation.

Wallach and Wing (1968) followed a format used in a classroom demonstration by Brown (1965). Male and female freshmen entering Duke University were asked to complete six Choice Dilemma items during the summer before their arrival at school. After recording their own choices to these items, the subjects were asked to reconsider each item in terms of "what you think the majority of your fellow students . . . would mark for each item" (p. 104). In accordance with the value hypothesis, not only did the subjects judge themselves to be significantly more risky on each item than their average fellow, but the magnitude of the overestimation of their own risk positively correlated with the magnitude of shifts found for these items in the usual group discussion paradigm.

Similar results were reported by Levinger and Schneider (1969). Their subjects made three ratings for each Choice Dilemma item. Subjects rated their own risk preferences, the average of their fellows, and the response alternative they most admired. In general, the items showing the risky shift were also the items on which subjects saw themselves as more risky than their fellows and on which the most admired response was *more* risky than their own choice. This latter finding provides direct verification for assuming these items invoke a value for risk.

Further corroboration was provided by Stoner (1968), who asked subjects to guess the average response of 200 other people. By including new items, constructed to elicit caution, Stoner demonstrated both a risky and a conservative shift. An example of the content of one of the new items which showed a shift to caution is summarized by Stoner in the following way: "A couple must choose between allowing a complicated pregnancy to continue, with danger to the mother's life, or having the pregnancy terminated" (p. 447). The risky shift was found for those items where widely held values favored a risky alternative and on which subjects considered themselves relatively risky. A cautious shift, whose average absolute magnitude was considerably less than the risky shift, was found for four of six items where widely held values favored caution and on which subjects considered themselves relatively cautious. Whether a shift toward risk or caution occurs for a particular item evidently is predicted by the location of the average risk preference (the sample mean) of the subjects' initial response. If the mean is in the direction of risk, the expected shift will be toward greater risk. If the direction is toward caution, the expected shift will be toward greater caution.

The value hypothesis also received support from Vidmar's (1970) study, in which groups were composed on the basis of members' risk preferences (the sum of their initial responses to the Choice Dilemmas questionnaire). The total sample was divided into thirds, of high, medium and low risk-takers. In addition to homogeneously high, medium, and low five-person groups, a heterogeneous condition was created by including two highs, one medium, and two lows. The homogeneous groups showed a risky shift. The magnitude of this shift was not significantly different among the three homogeneous conditions. The heterogeneous groups, as would be expected by the value hypothesis, showed a shift to risk which was significantly larger than that of the homogeneous groups. It is in the heterogeneous groups, of course, where the less risky members learn their own responses are most discrepant from the response of the most risky member. The less risky members would thus be expected to shift more in heterogeneous groups than in homogeneous groups.

The major condition for the occurrence of shift in groups, then, is the existence of tasks or settings which invoke a positive cultural value for being risky in the group members. Given such a circumstance, the members who learn they are least risky will shift their risk choices toward higher risk in order to maintain the risk values they erroneously believed they had realized by their initial choices. In addition, it is also likely that these circumstances will generate a disproportionate number of arguments favoring high risk, thereby further enhancing the average shift to risk. Shifts toward increased caution would be expected to be characterized by circumstances which generate a value for caution and for which each person sees himself as more cautious than the average of his peers. Although, to our knowledge, no one has yet explicitly defined the criteria by which items generating a value for risk can be distinguished from those generating a value for caution, the direction of the sample mean of subjects' responses appears to be a reliable index of the kind of value invoked by a given item.

Additional Interpretations

It would be misleading to leave this topic without mentioning the other suggestions which have been offered to account for the risky shift. Bateson (1966) thought that mere familiarization with the problems might be sufficient to account for the risky shift. He included a condition in which subjects were merely asked to reconsider each item on the Choice Dilemmas and to list pro and con arguments. The subjects who had this kind of familiarization showed shifts similar to those engaging in actual discussions. Flanders and Thistlethwaite (1967) reported similar results. On the other hand, neither Teger, Pruitt, St. Jean, and Haaland (1970) nor Rule and Evans (1971) were able to replicate a shift after familiarization. It is therefore not clear when familiarization will or will not produce a shift.

A novel extension of the value hypothesis has been detailed by Jellison and Riskind (1970). They begin with the usual assumption that the group discussion provides social comparison opportunities. They proceed, however, by asserting that the important social comparisons are for comparison of abilities, rather than for opinions. Because in actual situations people who are more able can reasonably take more risky actions than those less able, it might follow that ". . . people make inferences about another's abilities from the level of risk he has chosen" (p. 376). The group discussion, or knowledge of the other members' positions, is then a way of learning how much ability the other members believe they possess. Because comparison of abilities is assumed to contain the desire to see oneself as better than the average of the comparison objects, the group members initially preferring less risk should change toward accepting higher risk. These members change, not in order to embody better the value of risk, but to maintain their perceived ability at an acceptable level. These ideas were tested by Jellison and Riskind in a series of studies. For example, four patterns of risk responses, differing in their average level of risk, were standardly marked in Choice Dilemmas booklets. These booklets were used as the stimuli for an impression formation task. Subjects, who thought an actual person had responded to the items, were essentially asked, "Given these risk preferences, what traits would you infer about the respondent?" As predicted, a higher risk pattern was seen as the responses of someone who had such qualities as creativeness and ingeniousness to a greater degree than someone with a lower risk pattern. Similarly, when another group of subjects was asked to complete the Choice Dilemmas as would either a high- or low-ability person, the average risk endorsement attributed to a high-ability person was greater than to a low-ability person. In another study subjects were asked to imagine themselves and their average fellow in the situations described by the Choice Dilemmas items and to estimate the probability of successfully obtaining the risky alternative. Estimates for their own success were higher than for estimates of the success for their average fellow. This latter experiment was used to reinterpret the studies which have shown that people see themselves as riskier than their fellows. Such misperceptions may be based on attributing more ability to one's self compared to the average of one's fellows, rather than the belief that one's own risk position optimally represents the relevant cultural values.

The lack of shift, or conservative shifts are seen by Jellison and Riskind as occurring on items where the main character's abilities will not determine the success of the risky alternative or where the major trait required in the situation is not related to an ability. Consider the couple who must decide whether or not to let a complicated pregnancy continue—an item which elicits a cautious shift. The outcome of the couple's decision will not depend upon their abilities, but upon the judgment and abilities of a physician. Although these authors have not yet reported on the success of writing actual items based on their criteria, the ability comparison hypothesis may provide an important clue about predicting the direction of a shift.

Clark and Willems (1969) thought that the shift may derive solely from the nature of the instructions. It will be recalled that the standard instructions for the Choice Dilemmas ask subjects to select ". . . the lowest probability that you would consider acceptable . . ." before recommending the alternative which, if successful, always provides better outcomes. The phrase "lowest probability" was thought to cue the discussion in the direction of risk. Clark and Willems created three important conditions which had been used in previous research. In a discussion condition, subjects discussed each item for five minutes; in an information exchange condition they balloted for three rounds; and in a control condition they merely completed the Choice Dilemmas twice. For each of these three conditions two kinds of instructions were used. In addition to the standard instructions, a "neutral" set of instructions was composed. All references to minimum odds were deleted and subjects were instructed to mark the preference they considered "acceptable" for the option in question. As had been true in previous research, the usual instructions produced a shift in the discussion and information exchange conditions, but not in the control condition. The neutral instructions, however, produced no shift in any condition. The lack of shift was not due to the neutral instructions' creating a change in the subjects' initial responses. These did not differ between the two kinds of instruction. It was therefore thought that the risk instructions ". . . somehow cue the process in the direction of risk while the neutral instructions do not" (p. 217). Because the neutral instructions do not affect the initial ratings, they must interact with the discussion or information exchange process. The generality of this effect needs to be investigated. Shifts to caution have also been obtained with the standard instructions. It may be that the standard instructions do not produce an unidirectional cue, but merely sensitize members of the group to extreme positions and facilitate changing responses. Although these instructional features may be important, they cannot account for the risky shifts found on other tasks which do not use "lowest probability" instructions. Jellison and Riskind's (1970) ability comparison hypothesis can also accommodate these results. These authors suggest that the omission of "lowest probability" fails to induce a shift because it eliminates the implications for comparing abilities.

The most parsimonious way to account for the risky (or cautious) shift has not yet been definitively established. The ferment of research activity generated by this area undoubtedly means that new evidence will be quickly accumulated. Indeed, as this is being written a special edition of the *Journal of Personality and Social Psychology* (under the editorship of

Dean Pruitt) devoted exclusively to risk research is being prepared. The material included in the previous section should provide a useful foundation for reading that special edition or for consulting other reviews, such as Kelley and Thibaut (1969, pp. 78–84) or the comprehensive review and analysis published by Dion, Baron, and Miller (1970).

Polarization of Attitudes through Group Discussion

One of the novel facets of the risky shift is the fact that the members' risk preferences become more extreme as a consequence of the discussion. We have already reviewed a number of studies in the conformity chapter, Chapter 10, which convincingly demonstrated that group consensus induces convergence of responses toward an average point of initial views. To the extent that groups were seen as a moderating or a temporizing influence, the risky shift results represented a stark contrast, as did the recent work on cautious shifts. In either case the average risk preference of the members is more extreme, or more polarized, after the discussion than prior to the discussion.

The possibility that group-mediated polarization may extend to attitude issues, as well as to risk preferences, has been suggested by Moscovici and Zavalloni (1969). Their analysis of the risky shift experiments leads them to suggest that the basic process involved is commitment. By commitment they appear to mean an increased involvement with a given attitude-belief position and a greater awareness of the related aspects of this position. Commitment can evidently be increased by involving a person in a discussion which has some relevance for him or by asking him to analyze his own position on some issue. This view nicely accounts for the results of the risk experiments which obtain shifts after discussion or after individual familiarization. These authors see group-mediated averaging effects as being due to a lack of commitment, for example, if the task has little relevance for, or is unknown to, a majority of the members or if the group members feel little involvement in any particular position.

In order to assess whether group discussion induces polarization of attitudes, Moscovici and Zavalloni asked five-person groups to arrive at a consensus about their position on each item of an attitude scale. Similar to the format used in the usual risk experiment, subjects first answered all items individually, discussed each item until a consensus was reached, and then rerated the items individually. The subjects were French, male, secondary school students in their senior year. Two Likert-type attitude scales were developed which measured attitudes toward General de Gaulle (12 items) and toward the Americans (11 items). Each item on a Likert scale is a statement about the attitude issue or object being measured. Subjects respond to each item by marking on a $+3$ to -3 scale their own degree of agreement or disagreement with each item. Agreeing with favorable statements about the attitude issue or disagreeing with unfavorable statements reflects favorableness toward the issue. Disagreeing with favorable statements or agreeing with unfavorable statements indicates unfavorableness toward the issue. A subject's attitude score consists of the sum of his favorableness and unfavorableness ratings.

A third task, which was intended to induce less commitment than the two attitude tasks, was also employed. This task used the items of the General de Gaulle scale, but in the context of a modified Thurstone scaling task. That is, subjects were asked to judge the content of each item, in terms of the item's favorableness or unfavorableness toward de Gaulle, by assigning each item to one of six categories, ranging from extremely unfavorable to extremely favorable. The subjects were not to express their personal degree of agreement with the items, as was required in the two attitude tasks, but were asked to judge the scale value of each item. Direction of polarization was predicted on the basis of the mean scale value for each item. Means in the favorable range $(+)$ predicted a favorable shift; means in the unfavorable range $(-)$ predicted an unfavorable shift.

Before reporting the results it will also be necessary to discuss how Moscovici and Zavalloni predicted the direction of polarization for the attitude tasks. Each subject's favorableness responses were averaged across all items (either toward de Gaulle or toward the Americans). These scores could range from $+3$ (if all responses were extremely favorable) to -3 (if all responses were extremely unfavorable). The mean item score for each subject can, of course, be averaged across *all* subjects in order to obtain the average attitude position of the subjects' in the sample. The arithmetic mean of all the subjects' initial mean item scores indicates the initial direction of favorableness $(+)$ or unfavorableness $(-)$. The sign of the mean also defined the sign of the pole toward which changes were predicted. If the initial direction was favorable, polarization in the $+$, or favorable direction, was predicted.[1] Thus, for the attitude task means were computed first across items for each subject and then across subjects. On the other hand, for the judgment task means were computed across subjects for each item.

The polarization effects predicted by Moscovici and Zavalloni were con-

---

[1] The use of the subjects' prediscussion means to predict the direction of changes is similar to predicting whether a risk item will produce a change toward riskiness or caution. Items which elicit riskiness will show a risky shift while items eliciting caution will show a cautious shift. The major difficulty with all of these procedures is defining the neutral point which separates favorable attitudes from unfavorable attitudes, or riskiness from caution. Whether response distributions for only a single item or summed responses over the scale are used, it is by no means a simple matter to determine an actual neutral point. Arithmetic means of 0 or 5/10 probabilities are convenient midpoints on an attitude or riskiness scale, respectively, but they do not necessarily correspond to neutral points.

firmed by their results. For both the attitude task and the judgment task, group consensus and postdiscussion ratings showed more extremity on various indices of extremity, compared to the individual, prediscussion means. Subjects were initially somewhat favorable toward de Gaulle and became more favorable. Subjects were initially somewhat unfavorable toward Americans and became more unfavorable. On the judgment task, items initially judged to be unfavorable toward de Gaulle, for example, "de Gaulle is too old to carry out such a difficult task," were judged to be even more unfavorable and items initially judged favorable became more favorable. Finally, as predicted, the polarization on the de Gaulle items for the attitude task was greater than for the mean shift on the judgment task.

Moscovici and Zavalloni believe the increased polarization is mediated by commitment. They suggest three consequences of commitment which could induce polarization. The process of commitment could produce increases in the amount of affective involvement, in the meaningfulness of the stimuli, and in the certainty subjects have about the correctness of their own position. These three consequences might be interrelated, but anyone of them might prove to be the variable which can account for polarization.

The commitment interpretation has considerable appeal. Indeed, its appeal is reminiscent of the glow we experienced the first time we learned about diffusion of responsibility. Given the eventual fate of that interpretation, some caution in the present instance may be warranted. The Moscovici and Zavalloni experiment by itself, does not definitely substantiate the role of commitment. Although in their experiment it is probably a minor matter, they did not have a control group and could not assess the amount of shift which would be induced by merely rerating the items. More importantly, they had no validating information about their assumption that the attitude task would induce greater commitment than the judgment task. It might also be mentioned that an expanded version of the value hypothesis could still apply to the polarization results. It is possible that persons believe their own attitude positions to be more extreme in the culturally valued direction than the average position of their peers. Such misperceptions may not be restricted to risk-related material, but may pertain to any attitude issue, or, at least, to those issues where social comparison opportunities have been limited. The lessened polarization found for the judgment task, for example, might then be accounted for by assuming the judgment task does not strongly invoke cultural values.

The polarization effect reported by Moscovici and Zavalloni has been replicated by Myers and Bishop (1970) in a study using racial attitudes. High-school seniors, presumably both males and females, were homogeneously composed by initial prejudice level. Group size varied from four to seven members because all subjects in a given class were placed into an appropriate group at the same time. The usual experimental procedure was used with two-minute discussions for each of eight items. A control group discussed two Choice Dilemma items and then rerated the racial attitude items. In the experimental condition, members in the low-prejudice group shifted toward less prejudice while members in the high and medium groups shifted toward greater prejudice. The low- and high-prejudice *control* groups shifted toward the mean; these shifts are in an opposite direction from the polarization shown in the high and low experimental groups. Second ratings on the same scale often show less extremity. This has been termed "regression toward the mean" and suggests the Moscovici and Zavalloni results would be even more significant if compared to such a control group.

The Myers and Bishop results imply that the initial sample mean of subjects' attitudes does not necessarily specify the direction of polarization. The average prejudice score for all of their subjects would presumably be located in the neutral range. The low- and high-prejudice experimental groups shifted in opposite directions. Changes in opposite directions cannot be predicted from knowledge of the single mean of the entire sample, but only from the initial means of the homogeneous subgroups. Another way of making this point is to compare the Myers and Bishop results with the Vidmar experiment previously discussed. Vidmar found a shift toward greater risk on the Choice Dilemmas items in homogeneous groups composed of high, medium, and low risk-takers. Presumably the content of the risk items, rather than the composition of the group, predicts the shift toward risk. For attitude items, according to the Myers and Bishop results, the composition of the group, rather than the content of the items, predicts the direction of change. This line of reasoning suggests a qualification to the expansion of the value hypothesis mentioned above. For attitude issues, misperceiving the extremity of one's own position may be confined to instances of comparisons with like-minded peers.

Doise (1969), a colleague of Moscovici's, has tested an extension of the polarization phenomena. Doise contends that the presence of a rival group will enhance the amount of polarization induced by group discussion because of an increase in the clarity of the definition of one's own group. For attitude items related to the competition between the two groups, the direction of the polarization is expected to be comparable to that predicted by Moscovici and Zavalloni. That is, for items on which the group feels superior to the rival group, increased favorableness is expected, whereas on items on which the group feels inferior to the rival group, increased negative self-evaluation is expected. Thus, in this experiment the focus is on shifts in individual item means. Doise also predicted that the increased polarization in the presence of a rival group would lead group members to be more accepting of an extremist (group member holding an extreme position in the direction of polarization) than they would be in the absence of a rival group.

In Doise's experiment subjects were French architecture students who had a long-standing rivalry with students at another, more prestigious, school. A ten-item attitude scale about the quality of the professional training at the private school of architecture was constructed. Subjects responded to the items individually and were then formed into four-person groups and asked to discuss each item to consensus. The items were again rerated, and a postexperimental questionnaire was answered. One condition was treated in this usual way. Another condition, which was designed to induce awareness of the rival group, also required subjects to mark the items as they thought students in the rival school would answer them. These responses were recorded each time the attitude items were answered. Ten groups were observed in each condition. The mean shift in both conditions was toward greater polarization, but the awareness-of-rival condition induced significantly greater polarization than the standard condition. Other indices of polarization generally confirmed this finding. The direction of the shift, as in the previously discussed study, was toward the pole on the scale closest to the individual item means. On eight of the items the subjects felt unfavorably toward their own school. Their postdiscussion ratings became even more negative on these items, but became more positive on the other two items. Reactions to the most extreme member were also different between the two conditions. Awareness of the rival group significantly enhanced the member's acceptance of the extremist. This finding seems especially noteworthy. It suggests extremists will be most influential in their own group when the presence of a rival group is made salient.

The results obtained by Doise, in marked contrast to the research we will be presenting in the next chapter, demonstrated that awareness of a rival group induces polarization even when this results in greater negative attitudes toward one's own group. The more typical finding shows an *increase* in positive attitudes toward one's own group in the presence of a rival group. It may be that increased positiveness has been typically found because the only attitude issues investigated were ones on which the group members were initially positive toward their own group. It may also be that Doise's manipulation, responding to the items as subjects thought the other group would respond, does not engage the same processes as the actual presence of the other group.

Extension of the risky shift to polarization on attitude issues is an extremely promising line of research. Not only can it contribute to understanding the processes affecting group decisions but also it has relevance for such diverse topics as attitude change and influence. It can be seen that the evidence is pointing to consequences which would not be expected from knowledge of the conformity literature. The impact of group discussion is not toward creating a compromise at the mean of initial positions, but toward increasing the polarity of an initial direction. To be sure, conformity pressures are a critical part of the process, but their predictable directionality must be explained by any interpretation of the polarization effect.

Overview

An interest in group-induced extremity shifts was sparked by the research findings of a "risky shift." When individuals were placed in groups and asked to discuss risk problems to consensus, both the risk position of that consensus and the postdiscussion position of the individuals were riskier than the average of their prediscussion risk positions. The risky shift was shown to depend upon group discussion or exchange of information about prediscussion positions, rather than upon the requirement to reach consensus. The bulk of the earlier research assumed the discussion of any risk-related material would produce a risky shift, and explanatory mechanisms such as diffusion of responsibility and familiarization were invoked. Subsequent research showed that shifts toward caution could also be obtained. Whether a shift toward risk or caution occurs appears to depend upon the content of the risk material being discussed. Of the various explanations offered to account for risk-related shifts, the most viable interpretation appears to be the value hypothesis. According to the value hypothesis, shifts occur on tasks which invoke shared cultural values about the appropriate degree of riskiness or caution. The group members whose initial position least embody the cultural value will change their position to better realize the value. The function of group discussion is thus seen primarily in terms of providing corrective information to those members whose initial position turns out to be furthest from the value. The discussion may also generate a disproportionate number of arguments supporting the valued direction.

Recently it has also been shown that extremity shifts can occur when groups are discussing attitude issues. Such extremity shifts have been demonstrated with several different attitude issues. It has been suggested that extremity shifts occur when the group members are committed to the topic being discussed.

READINGS

The Roles of Information, Discussion, and Consensus in Group Risk Taking[1]

Michael A. Wallach and Nathan Kogan

If members of a group engage in a discussion and reach a consensus regarding the degree of a risk to accept in the decisions which they make, their conclusion is to pursue a course of action more risky than that represented by the average of the prior decisions of each individual considered separately. Evidence supporting this proposition has been reported in several recent experiments (Bem, Wallach, and Kogan, 1965; Wallach, Kogan, and Bem, 1962; Wallach, Kogan, and Bem, 1964) with decisions involving a wide range of content. Some of the decision contexts have been hypothetical; others have involved risks of monetary gain or loss and risks of intellectual failure; still others, risks of physical pain.

Our initial interest in this phenomenon of a group-induced shift toward increased risk taking arose from the manner in which it flew in the face of two alternative and plausible expectations: the hypothesis of an averaging effect, and the hypothesis of a shift toward increased conservatism. The idea that groups would gravitate toward the average of the individual opinions of their members, when forced to achieve a consensus through discussion, seemed well supported by the experimental finding that attempts to induce judgmental changes in group members are concentrated on those whose individual judgments are most extreme on either side of the central tendency (e.g., Cartwright and Zander, 1960, pp. 165–341). The alternative proposal—groups moving toward greater conservatism when required to arrive at a consensus by means of discussion—appeared likely in the light of the well-known dictum that decision-making by committees leads to a fear of appearing irresponsible through making extreme recommendations (e.g., Whyte, 1956).

[1] From the *Journal of Experimental Social Psychology*, Volume 1, pages 1–19, 1965. Authors' affiliations: Wallach, Duke University; Kogan, Educational Testing Service. This research was supported by a grant (GS-344) from the Division of Social Sciences, National Science Foundation. We are grateful to Roger B. Burt and Jean A. Greenwald for serving as research assistants. Thanks also are due Edward E. Jones for helpful discussions of various points in the paper, and David L. Rosenhan and Lawrence J. Strickler for critical comments.

By contrast, given that group discussion and achievement of a consensus actually enhance the level of risk taking that individual members are willing to endorse, there exists the possibility of a kinship between the apparently "rational" deliberations of our experimentally constituted small groups and the kinds of mass or crowd phenomena that one associates with extreme and violent actions. To speak of such a kinship is to imply that the mechanism at work consists in a diffusion of responsibility such that full participation and involvement in the decision process partially absolves the individual for possible failure. What are the grounds for proposing this interpretation?

Direct support for the hypothesis is provided by two kinds of experimental findings. First, while creation of responsibility for others in itself leads a person to become more conservative, creation of the same responsibility for others in a situation where discussion to consensus ensues with these others leads to a strong shift toward greater risk taking (Bem *et al.*, 1965; Wallach *et al.*, 1964). Second, while group discussion to consensus yields a risky shift when each of the group members is responsible only to himself, the same sort of discussion to consensus results in an even stronger shift toward enhanced risk taking when each group member has been made responsible for the others as well as for himself (Wallach *et al.*, 1964). If group discussion to consensus is present and held constant, then creation of added responsibility leads, paradoxically enough, to greater risk taking.

Indirect support, in turn, accrues from finding other possible explanations of the phenomenon deficient. Several major alternatives have received experimental attention. Each will be stated and the relevant evidence will be considered briefly.

(a) Groups move toward enhanced risk taking because the members are able to pool their cognitive resources toward taking more rational account of the probabilities and desirabilities involved in the various decision alternatives. Two studies address themselves to this issue. In one experiment (Wallach *et al.*, 1964), the decision options available were so designed as to be of equal expected value. In another (Bem *et al.*, 1965), these options were so arranged that greater risk taking was associated with lower expected value. In both cases, the effect of group discussion to a consensus was to enhance risk taking. In the former study, with equal expected values for the decision alternatives, a risky shift can have nothing to do with rationality of choice in the mathematical sense. In the latter, with lower expected values for greater risk taking, a risky shift actually represents a reduction in rationality of decision making.

(b) Risk taking is more socially desirable than conservatism, and hence the publicity present in the group setting generates greater risk taking. We have demonstrated, however, that the expectation that one's individual decisions will be made public to the other group members generates an averaging effect, while the expectation that individual decisions are to serve as one's recommendations in an ensuing group discussion to consensus actually generates a conservative shift (Bem *et al.*, 1965). In both cases, publicity is an active factor. In neither case, however, is there group discussion to a consensus, and, as an apparent consequence, risky shifts do not occur.

(c) Knowing that one will undergo the consequences of one's decisions in the company of others induces a willingness to take greater risks because of the presumed sympathy that these others will provide in the event of negative outcomes. The provision of such knowledge in the absence of discussion with others to consensus, however, leads to a shift in the conservative direction (Bem *et al.*, 1965).

(d) Persons who are greater risk takers exert stronger influence within the group. While this possibility still requires serious consideration (see Marquis, 1962; Wallach *et al.*, 1962), qualitative observations suggest that, at the least, it cannot offer a full explanation of the risky shift phenomenon. In the recent study by Bem *et al.* (1965), group-induced risky shifts took place even though group members sometimes deferred to those who were more conservative, and no one stood out in a group as advocating strong risk taking in general.

THE PRESENT EXPERIMENT

Our search for an understanding of the risky shift phenomenon thus leads to the working assumption that diffusion of responsibility is the process at issue. However, by what means does such a process operate? In all of the work conducted thus far, group discussion to a consensus has constituted the basic experimental operation for inducing the risky shift effect. When we examine group discussion to consensus more closely, we find that is possesses at least three distinguishable components: provision of information about others' judgments, group discussion, and achievement of consensus. Can we dissect these components and study their roles in the production of the basic phenomenon? In specifying more exactly what element within the molar condition of discussion-to-consensus leads to the risky shift effect, we should begin to understand how a mechanism of responsibility diffusion operates.

Let us consider in greater detail the three components just mentioned. In group discussion to a consensus, *information* becomes available to a person concerning the levels of individual risk initially favored by his peers, thereby permitting him to make judgmental comparisons with his own initial level of preferred risk. The presentation of this information concerning the risk-taking levels of others thus may serve to tell the subject that other individuals are willing to accept higher degrees of risk than he might have anticipated. As a result, the subject himself comes to favor greater risk taking. Upon this interpretation, then, the group effect, with its presumed spreading of personal responsibility, arises from the construction of a frame of reference regarding the risk-taking levels favored by others. The active causal ingredient in the situation is the comparison of one's individual decision with those made by the other group members. If this is the case, then neither group discussion nor group consensus is a necessary causal factor; rather, they constitute means for providing each member with information that permits him to compare his decisions with those made by his peers.

It is possible, on the other hand, that the necessary causal element consists of *group discussion* in itself. The fact that such verbal interaction serves as a vehicle for disseminating information may be incidental. Diffusion of responsibility may be carried only or especially by actual discussion, with the affective give-and-take which arises from face-to-face communication. Emotional involvement of the kind that discussion can create may be the precondition of a risky shift on the part of the group. Meaningful psychological contact with others may require such discussion, and diffusion of responsibility from one person to others may be possible only if contact of this kind has been established.

Consider, finally, the possible role of *consensus*. To ask a group to achieve a consensus concerning a matter of risk taking is to provide a request that may influence the type of commitment made by the group members. The requirement that a consensus be reached may engender a feeling of commitment to the group as a unit. Such an increased sense of commitment to the group might well constitute the relevant factor behind the risky shift effect, or at least a contributory factor; that is, diffusion of responsibility might be fostered or even initiated by a recentering which lifts decisional responsibility from the individual and places it squarely upon the group as a whole. A consensus requirement could well be one factor that would operate to increase an individual's degree of involvement with the decision making of other group members relative to his degree of reliance upon personal judgment.

In sum, we have analyzed the situation of group discussion to a consensus into three elements: information about the decisions of others, verbal social interaction, and achievement of consensus. Our purpose in the present research is to examine the relative efficacy of these three elements in producing the phenomenon of a group-induced risky shift. What kinds of experimental manipulations can one design toward accomplishing this end? Three conditions should provide us with the necessary data. The first of these is *discussion and consensus* (DC), the standard situation used in our previous work. Matters of risk taking are discussed by the group and a consensus is reached in each case. The second condition that we shall need to study is *consensus without discussion* (C). Here, we need to arrange a situation such that a group of individuals are required to arrive at a consensus in their decisions regarding matters of risk, but the group members cannot engage in discussion as the means of achieving consensus. Their various recommendations to one another must, nevertheless, be public rather than anonymous, so that a factor of anonymity will not distinguish the C from the DC condition. Finally, it will be necessary to investigate the effects of *discussion without consensus* (D). In the case of this condition, we must permit the processes involved in group interaction to operate, but without the requirement that a consensus be arrived at by the group members.

In each of the foregoing conditions, individual decisions will be made after as well as before the discussion and/or consensus experience. In the case of the discussion-without-consensus condition, these individual decisions furnish all of the data for evaluating the effect of the experimental manipulation. In the case of the other two conditions, we shall be able to examine the consensus decisions as well as the subsequently obtained individual decisions. In all conditions, shifts will be measured relative to the baseline provided by individual decisions made before each experimental manipulation.

Consider now the possible experimental results, and how they might bear upon the questions posed. Our prior findings make it clear that a shift toward greater risk taking is to be expected in condition DC, both for the consensus decisions and for the subsequent individual decisions. What of the other two conditions? If both condition C and condition D yield substantial risky shifts as well, we will have evidence that information about the decisions of others is sufficient to induce the phenomenon, since the provision of such information is common to all three experimental conditions, while neither discussion nor consensus is present in all three. If conditions C and D each yield risky shifts of lesser degree, the implication will be that consensus and discussion make additive contributions to the effect. If neither condition C nor condition D yields a risky shift, such evidence would suggest that *both* discussion and consensus are essential elements in the production of the phenomenon, i.e., that the two must operate jointly in order to be effective. Suppose, on the other hand, that condition C yields the shift, while condition D does not. Such an outcome would imply that pressures toward reaching a consensus provide the necessary and sufficient factor for inducing the phenomenon. Finally, we might discover that a risky shift occurs under condition D but not under condition C. This result would indicate that the element of group discussion, quite apart from the consensus issue, provides the necessary and sufficient ingredient for producing the risky shift effect.

The experiment which follows was designed to provide a basis for choice among the preceding alternatives.

METHOD

Subjects

A total of 360 college students participated in the study, 180 of each sex. The male undergraduates were students at Duke University; the females, at Douglass College.[2] The Ss within sex were randomly assigned to five-person groups, and these groups were randomly assigned to the three experimental conditions. Thus, there were 72 groups of five persons each, 12 groups of each sex in each of three experimental conditions. The Ss received remuneration or credit for experimental participation in the introductory psychology course. A male E worked with the male groups, and a female E with the female groups.

The Measure of Risk Taking

Tendencies toward risk or conservatism were evaluated with an instrument described to Ss as an "opinion questionnaire" and used in several previous studies (see Kogan and Wallach, 1961, 1964; Wallach and Kogan, 1959, 1961; Wallach et al., 1962). Its instructions, read by each S, were:

> On the following pages, you will find a series of situations that are likely to occur in everyday life. The central person in each situation is faced with a choice between two alternative courses of action, which we might call X and Y. Alternative X is more desirable and attractive than alternative Y, but the probability of attaining or achieving X is less than that of attaining or achieving Y.
>
> For each situation on the following pages, you will be asked to indicate the minimum odds of success you would demand before recommending that the more attractive or desirable alternative, X, be chosen.
>
> Read each situation carefully before giving your judgment. Try to place yourself in the position of the central person in each of the situations. There are twelve situations in all. Please do not omit any of them.

The twelve situations described to the S cover a wide range of content with regard to the types of risk involved, extending from risk of loss of prestige, to risk of monetary loss, to risk of death. As an example, item seven is presented:

> Mr. G, a competent chess player, is participating in a national chess tournament. In an early match he draws the top-favored player in the tournament as his opponent. Mr. G has been given a relatively low ranking in view of his performance in previous tournaments. During the course of his play with the top-favored man, Mr. G notes the possibility of a deceptive though risky maneuver which might bring him a quick victory. At the same time, if the attempted maneuver should fail, Mr. G would be left in an exposed position and defeat would almost certainly follow.
>
> Imagine that you are advising Mr. G. Listed below are several probabilities or odds that Mr. G's deceptive play would succeed. PLEASE CHECK THE LOWEST PROBABILITY THAT YOU WOULD CONSIDER ACCEPTABLE FOR THE RISKY PLAY IN QUESTION TO BE ATTEMPTED.
>
> _____The chances are 1 in 10 that the play would succeed.
> _____The chances are 3 in 10 that the play would succeed.
> _____The chances are 5 in 10 that the play would succeed.
> _____The chances are 7 in 10 that the play would succeed.

[2] Thanks are due Donald G. Forgays and the Department of Psychology of Douglass College for facilitating data collection at that institution.

_____The chances are 9 in 10 that the play would succeed.
_____Place a check here if you think Mr. G should *not* attempt the risky play, no matter what the probabilities.

To indicate something of the range of content represented in the other eleven situations, they concern such matters as an electrical engineer with a choice between his present job at a modest salary or a new job offering more money but less security; a man with a heart ailment who must choose between restrictive changes in his way of life or a dangerous surgical operation; a football captain with the choice between a safe play that will yield a tie score or a risky play which might produce victory; a man with an investment choice between secure, low-return stocks and securities of high potential return but high risk; a research physicist who must choose between working on a difficult, long-term problem with the risk of complete failure, or on easier but less important problems of relatively sure solution. The instrument in its entirety may be found in Kogan and Wallach (1964).

An over-all score is obtained by summing the probability levels chosen on the various items. If an S takes the option of refusing to recommend the risky alternative no matter how great its likelihood of success, a score of 10 is assigned. An individual's total score hence can range from 12 to 120, with larger scores reflecting greater conservatism. In order to counterbalance for any order effects in choices of probability levels, the levels are arrayed in ascending order (chances of 1 in 10 upward) for the odd items, and in descending order for the even items.

Previous research with the present procedure provides information concerning its reliability and validity. Thus, Spearman-Brown split-half reliability coefficients have ranged from .53 to .80 for various samples (Kogan and Wallach, 1964; Wallach and Kogan, 1961). In addition, test-retest product-moment correlation coefficients of .78 and .82 have been obtained with 1 week between administrations and under instructions encouraging change (Wallach et al., 1962). With respect to validity, relationships with various other kinds of risk-taking behaviors have been demonstrated (Kogan and Wallach, 1964), and other types of risk-relevant effects have been obtained (Kogan and Wallach, 1961; Wallach and Kogan, 1961). Furthermore, the risky shift phenomenon, first obtained with the present procedure and its hypothetical situations (Wallach et al., 1962), has also been found under various actual risk conditions (Bem et al., 1965; Wallach et al., 1964). In sum, we have much confidence in the present procedure's validity for assessing risk taking.

Initial Individual Decisions

Five Ss were scheduled to appear in the experimental room at a given time. They were seated in chairs spread out around a large table, and were requested to read the instructions to the questionnaire and then to look over the first item. Certain further points then were emphasized by E in standard instructions that were verbally communicated to Ss. Quotations from these further instructions follow:

There are two points I should like to bring to your attention which may seem clear enough at the outset, but are easily overlooked when you become involved in some of the situations. The first is that alternative X—the riskier alternative— is always assumed to be more desirable than the safer course, if X should be successful. . . . The second point concerns the meaning of the odds you are being asked to mark. It is *not* your task to decide what the odds might actually be in a life situation. . . . The odds you mark indicate the lowest odds you would be willing to take and still advise the central figure to give the risky alternative a try. . . . There is no time limit, so take your time and consider the twelve situations carefully. You may return to one if you wish to change your answer after seeing some of the others.

Initial individual decisions were obtained for all twelve situations in each experimental condition. These data provide the baselines for assessing shifts in risk taking as a function of the experimental manipulations. Following this initial assessment of risk-taking levels, the procedures for the different experimental conditions diverged as indicated below.

Experimental Manipulations

Discussion and Consensus. After collecting the booklets containing the Ss' individual decisions, the E handed out new blank copies of the booklets, and said:

> The questionnaire you now have in front of you is the same one which you just finished taking. You have taken it in order to familiarize yourself with all the situations, and to give you some idea where you might stand on each one. What we are really interested in now is having the group discuss each question in turn and arrive at a unanimous decision on each. You will recognize that a unanimous decision is different from a majority vote, by the way. This time you may not return to a question; discuss each one until the group decision is reached and then go on to the next. When the group reaches its decision, you are to mark it on the questionnaire so you have a record of the group's decisions. *I* am not going to participate in the discussion although I will be here to answer any procedural questions which may arise, and I may listen to part of the discussion, although it is only the group's final decision we are interested in.

When the group had reached its consensus decisions for all the situations, E requested them to provide new individual decisions, with instructions that sanctioned deviations from the consensus decisions that had been reached:

> Now we will have some further individual work. I now want you to go back over these situations and indicate your own present personal decision with a "P." In some cases you may feel that the group decision was the best one which could have been made, in which case your "P" would be placed on the same line as the check mark. In other cases you may disagree with the group decision, in which case your "P" will be placed on a different line from the one with the check.

Comparisons in the present condition can be made between the average of the initial individual decisions and the consensus decisions, as well as between the former average and the average of the postconsensus individual decisions. Any change from consensus decisions to postconsensus individual decisions also can be assessed.

Consensus without Discussion. Having collected the individual decision booklets, E distributed new blank copies of the booklets and piles of slips of paper containing places for Ss to record their initials, the item number, the ballot number, and their decision. The E then went to the blackboard and drew a diagram of the table and seating plan, with the Ss' names in their seat locations. In this way, the identity of each S was quite public to the other members of the group. Instructions proceeded as follows:

> I am going to ask you to reach a consensus regarding the first situation, the one concerning the electrical engineer. I would like all of you to reach a consensus concerning the level of risk to advise. I want you to do this in the following way. I want you to write on the first of your slips of paper the decision that

you feel the group of you can and should agree upon. When all of you have written that down, I will collect the slips and write these decisions up on the board next to your names. If all of you have made the same decision, then you will be finished with that item. If not all of you have made the same decision, then I will again ask you to write on a slip of paper the decision that you feel the group can and should agree on, and then I will again write these new decisions on the board next to your names, and so on. We will continue with rounds of balloting until all of you agree on your decision concerning an item. Then we will proceed to the next item.

You may feel free to refer to the description of each situation in the booklet before you as often as you like. When an agreement has been reached on an item, I would like all of you to write this agreed-upon decision down by checking the appropriate place in the new booklet. You are not permitted to talk with each other about these situations. I want each round of balloting to be private, which is why I have asked you to write your recommendations each time on slips of paper. This way, I know that all of you are responding to the information on the board and that only. Finally, remember that the recommendations you make for group adoption should consist of what you think the group *can* agree on and what you think the group *should* agree on. You are to make a recommendation that takes account both of what you believe the group *can* agree on and what you believe the group *should* agree on. Note, by the way, that no deadlock is permitted to occur on an item, since your balloting must take account of what is possible for the group to agree on. As I mentioned, we will continue with rounds of balloting on an item until all of you agree on your decision for that item.

One round of decisions was erased when the next round of decisions was put up on the board. In this condition, then, the group reaches a consensus decision about each situation, but no discussion takes place. Despite the absence of discussion, however, the recommendations of each group member are public in the sense that everyone else knows who is making them. Anonymity is no more present in this condition, therefore, than it is in the condition where consensus decisions are arrived at through discussion.

After all consensus decisions have been reached, postconsensus individual decisions are obtained by means of the same instructions as were described for condition DC. The same kinds of comparisons can be made in the present condition as in condition DC.

Discussion without Consensus. New blank copies of the booklet were distributed after the individual decision booklets had been collected. The E then said:

The questionnaire you now have in front of you is the same one which you just finished taking. We have had each of you fill out the questionnaire so that you would become familiar with all of the situations it contains. What we are really interested in is having you discuss each of the situations as a group. Let me now describe the purpose of these discussions. We are trying to develop a set of case materials for a human relations course. This means that we would like to develop situations for which people are likely to hold many different points of view. We want to see whether the situations we constructed will generate a diversity of opinion, so your discussions will tell us how well the different situations are working out for our purposes. You will have 5 minutes to discuss each situation. I am not going to participate in the discussion although I will be here to answer any procedural questions which may arise. All right, let's begin with the first item. Go right ahead.

Discussion was allowed to ensue for approximately 5 minutes. The E was off to one side, and appeared to be taking notes as the discussion proceeded. He interrupted the group at a natural break in the discussion, and said:

All right. That was a good discussion. Several different points of view were expressed. For some of you, the discussion may have raised issues that you had overlooked when filling out the questionnaire individually. Now, we would like to find out whether the discussion influenced your judgment in any way. When making your decision now, don't feel bound by what you did when filling out the questionnaire the first time. We're not interested in your prior opinion, but rather in just how you feel about the situation now. If you still feel the same way, that's quite all right, but we should like you to consider each situation in the light of the discussion. As I told you before, we're interested in seeing how much diversity of opinion is generated by each situation. Obviously, the expression of such diversity should have some impact on everyone's personal opinions. All right, go ahead and make your decision for the first situation—the one you just discussed.

Then E requested the Ss to discuss the next item, and, after approximately 5 minutes of discussion, once again asked them to arrive at individual decisions. This procedure was repeated for all twelve situations. Note that the instructions were such as to encourage a diversity of opinions.

In the present condition, we can compare the average of the initial individual decisions made by a group and the average of their post-discussion individual decisions.

RESULTS AND DISCUSSION

Comparability of Initial Risk Taking across Experimental Conditions

Before examining the effects of the experimental manipulations upon degree of shift in risk taking, it is necessary to assure ourselves that the random assignment of Ss to conditions did in fact yield comparable initial risk-taking levels for the members of groups in the several conditions. The findings on this question are reported in Table 1. Presented for the 60 persons of each sex in a given condition are the mean over-all risk-taking level exhibited in their initial individual decisions and the associated standard deviation. It is evident that the mean initial risk-taking levels for

TABLE 1

Means and Standard Deviations on Initial Risk-Taking Levels for the Subjects in Each Condition

(N = 60 Ss within sex in each condition)

Condition	Males		Females	
	$\bar{X}$	SD	$\bar{X}$	SD
Discussion and consensus	67.70	12.56	63.60	12.23
Consensus without discussion	68.43	11.99	63.45	12.44
Discussion without consensus	66.55	10.42	62.90	12.25

the three conditions within each sex are highly similar. The Ss assigned to the three conditions within sex clearly represent random samples from the same population with respect to the risk-conservatism measure.[3]

Shifts in Risk Taking as a Function of the Experimental Manipulations

The major findings of the study are reported in Table 2. Of basic interest is the assessment of risk-taking shifts induced by the various experimental conditions. The statistical test evaluates whether the degree of shift obtained is significantly different from a null hypothesis of no shift.

Consider first the nature of the measures used. The measure designated in Table 2 as "Pre — Consensus" consists of the average, for a group, of the five initial over-all individual risk scores, minus that group's consensus decisions as summed over the twelve items. If the latter index is smaller than the former, the difference is positive, and represents a shift toward greater risk taking. This difference score is obtained for each of the twelve groups in a given condition. The mean of these twelve difference scores then is entered as $\bar{D}$, and is tested for deviation from zero by a one-sample

TABLE 2

Shifts in Risk Taking under Each Condition
(N = 12 groups within sex in each condition)

Condition	Males				Females			
	$\bar{D}$	$SE_{\bar{D}}$	t	p^a	$\bar{D}$	$SE_{\bar{D}}$	t	p
1. Discussion and consensus								
a. Pre — Consensus	3.85	1.13	3.40	<.005	6.17	1.28	4.82	<.0005
b. Pre — Post	3.17	1.03	3.07	<.01	4.20	1.06	3.96	<.005
c. Consensus — Post	−0.68	0.52	1.30	n.s.	−2.00	0.41	4.88	<.001
2. Consensus without discussion								
a. Pre — Consensus	−1.13	1.27	0.89	n.s.	1.50	1.02	1.47	n.s.
b. Pre — Post	−0.08	0.80	0.10	n.s.	1.07	0.81	1.32	n.s.
3. Discussion without consensus								
a. Pre — Post	3.05	0.68	4.49	<.001	6.63	1.44	4.60	<.001

[a] In comparisons 1a and 1b, p levels are 1-tailed since direction was predicted; in all other comparisons, p levels are 2-tailed.

[3] We might note in passing that the sexes themselves seem to differ somewhat in risk level, the males showing greater conservatism than the females. Although a trend in the same direction also appeared in the study by Wallach et al. (1962), we hesitate to ascribe such a finding to sex differences, since other data (Kogan and Wallach, 1964; Wallach and Kogan, 1959, 1961) have shown no over-all sex difference on this measure. Results for the two sexes will be reported separately throughout.

t-test (Walker and Lev, 1953, pp. 151–153). The measure designated as "Pre — Post" in Table 2 consists of the average, for a group, of the five initial over-all individual risk scores, minus the average, for that group, of the five postmanipulation over-all individual risk scores. A positive difference once again reflects increased risk taking. The computation just described is repeated for each of the twelve groups in a condition, and the mean of these twelve difference scores once again is represented as $\bar{D}$ and is tested for significance against the null hypothesis of zero. Finally, the measure designated in Table 2 as "Consensus — Post" consists of a group's consensus decisions, summed over the twelve items, minus the average, for that group, of the five postmanipulation over-all individual risk scores. Whereas the former two measures involved comparisons with initial level of individual risk taking, the present measure takes the consensus decisions as the baseline and inquires whether the postmanipulation individual decisions deviate from those consensus decisions. A positive shift indicates enhanced risk taking, and the difference described above is obtained for each of the twelve groups in a condition. With $\bar{D}$ as the mean of these differences, we again test for significance of deviation from zero.

We turn now to the shift findings, and examine first the condition of *discussion and consensus*. Table 2 indicates that a significant shift toward enhanced risk taking is found both for males and females. Furthermore, a risky shift obtains both when comparing consensus decisions with initial individual decisions (row 1a), and when comparing postconsensus individual decisions with initial individual decisions (row 1b). These results define the basic phenomenon and are replications of our earlier findings (Wallach *et al.*, 1962). Turning to the relationship between consensus decisions and postconsensus individual decisions, we find no significant difference in the case of the males, and a significant reversion toward greater conservatism in the case of the females (row 1c). It should be kept in mind, however, that despite this latter reversion, postconsensus individual decisions nevertheless are significantly more risky than initial individual decisions for the females as well as for the males.

Significant risky shifts are found, then, both in terms of the effects exerted upon the group's consensus decisions, and in terms of the effects exerted upon the individual decisions made subsequent to the group encounter. It is appropriate to note that these shifts can be ascribed with confidence to some aspect of the group experience, rather than simply to the effects of a repetition of the risk-taking assessment procedure. In previous work (Wallach *et al.*, 1962), we employed a control condition in which individual risk-taking decisions were obtained a second time 1 week after the original administration of the procedure. Instructions encouraged Ss to reconsider their initial decisions, rather than attempt to remember and reproduce them. No shift was obtained under these conditions for members of either sex.

Since the prediction of a risky shift in the discussion-to-consensus condition has been confirmed, we can now examine the more specific sources of this effect. From rows 2a and 2b of Table 2, we note that *consensus without discussion* yields no systematic shift for males or females in either the risky or the conservative direction. The typical consensus decision closely approximates the average of the group members' initial individual decisions (row 2a). Further, postconsensus individual decisions by a group also are quite similar to the initial individual decisions by the same persons (row 2b). In sum, the imposition of a consensus requirement without opportunity for group discussion evidently results in a type of averaging or compromise effect which minimizes the concessions made by any group member.

Though consensus without discussion yields an averaging effect, it may nevertheless be of interest to note whether any relationship emerges between the degree of difficulty which a group experiences in arriving at consensus decisions without discussion, and the risk or conservatism of the decisions reached. A straightforward index of difficulty is available to us: the number of rounds of balloting required for consensus. We examined, therefore, the relationship between the total number of rounds of balloting in a group and the degree and direction of shift from the average of that group's initial risk-taking levels to their consensus decisions (the Pre — Consensus measure). For males, number of ballots for a group and the group's shift behavior are quite unrelated. For females, there is no strong relationship, but a trend can be detected toward a curvilinear function. A group experiencing greater difficulty in arriving at consensus decisions without discussion tends to show a more extensive shift in either the risky or the conservative direction. On the whole, however, the clearest inference we can make at present is that little relationship exists between degree of difficulty in reaching a consensus without discussion and the nature of the consensus reached.

What of the effect of group discussion per se upon risk taking? Row 3a of Table 2 indicates that the condition of *discussion without consensus* generates a risky shift for the groups of both sexes. The "Pre — Post" measure yields a similar degree of shift toward greater risk taking for conditions DC and D in the case of each sex. Thus, while consensus without discussion yields an averaging effect, discussion without consensus results in a risky shift that is analogous in degree to the shift obtained when discussion takes place with a consensus requirement. Before considering the implications of these findings, let us turn to further analyses of the data.

Direct Comparisons between Pairs of Experimental Manipulations

Thus far, the shift findings for each experimental condition have been subjected to separate statistical tests comparing in each case the obtained shift with a null hypothesis of zero shift. In the present section, we shall

TABLE 3

Comparison of Risk-Taking Shifts between Pairs of Conditions for Males
(N = 12 groups in each condition)

Comparison	X̄	SD	X̄	SD	t	p[a]
DC vs. C						
Pre − Consensus	3.85	3.93	−1.13	4.40	2.93	< .01
Pre − Post	3.17	3.58	−0.08	2.96	2.46	< .05
C vs. D						
Pre − Post	−0.08	2.96	3.05	2.35	2.87	< .01
DC vs. D						
Pre − Post	3.17	3.58	3.05	2.35	0.03	n.s.

[a] All p levels are 2-tailed.

go beyond this indirect type of statistical evaluation to a direct comparison of the degree of shift obtained in one condition with the degree of shift obtained in another. On the basis of the results reported in the previous section, we expect that, for the groups of each sex, condition DC will yield a greater risky shift than condition C, condition D will also yield a greater risky shift than condition C, and conditions DC and D will not differ in their degrees of risky shift. Using a two-sample t-test, we can compare, within sex, the twelve groups in one condition with the twelve groups in another condition on an analogous measure. The results are presented in Tables 3 and 4 for the males and females, respectively.

Conditions DC and C can be compared on two measures, since in the case of each condition both consensus decisions and postconsensus individual decisions are obtained. The difference between the conditions in degree of shift as measured by the Pre — Consensus score is significant (Tables 3 and 4, row 1), and so also is the difference between these conditions as measured by the Pre — Post score (Tables 3 and 4, row 2). On both of these measures, then, condition DC yields a stronger risky shift

TABLE 4

Comparison of Risk-Taking Shifts between Pairs of Conditions for Females
(N = 12 groups in each condition)

Comparison	X̄	SD	X̄	SD	t	p[a]
DC vs. C						
Pre − Consensus	6.17	4.24	1.50	3.40	2.85	< .01
Pre − Post	4.20	8.59	1.07	5.99	2.22	< .05
C vs. D						
Pre − Post	1.07	5.99	6.63	10.65	3.38	< .01
DC vs. D						
Pre − Post	4.20	8.59	6.63	10.65	1.32	n.s.

[a] All p levels are 2-tailed.

than condition C in both male and female groups. Comparing conditions C and D, in turn, we shall use the measure which provides a yardstick common to both conditions: the Pre — Post score. It can be seen that condition D yields a stronger risky shift than condition C in the case of both sexes (Tables 3 and 4, row 3). Finally, row 4 of Tables 3 and 4 compares conditions DC and D. Again, the measure available in common to both conditions for such a comparison is the Pre — Post score. The small nonsignificant differences obtained in the present case indicate that the extent of the risky shifts found in conditions DC and D are of about equal magnitude.

Shifts in Within-Group Variability as a Function of the Experimental Manipulations

Also of interest in the present data is the effect of the experimental manipulations upon the variability of risk-taking levels among the members of a group. In the case of each condition, we can inquire whether the particular type of group experience in question influences the degree of interindividual heterogeneity of risk-conservatism dispositions. As a measure, we shall employ a difference score comparing the variability of the individual risk levels for the five members of a group before and after the experimental manipulation. Table 5 presents the findings. In the case of each group of a given sex within a specific condition, the range of the five postmanipulation over-all individual risk scores is subtracted from the range of the five initial over-all individual risk scores. A positive difference between these two ranges hence indicates a narrowing of variability. The mean of the twelve difference scores obtained for the groups of a given condition and sex is entered as $\bar{D}$ in Table 5, and is tested for deviation

TABLE 5

Shifts in Within-Group Range of Risk-Taking Levels under Each Condition
(N = 12 groups within sex in each condition)

	Males				Females			
Condition	$\bar{D}$	$SE_{\bar{D}}$	t	p^a	$\bar{D}$	$SE_{\bar{D}}$	t	p
1. Discussion and consensus, Pre — Post	12.33	2.27	5.42	< .001	9.08	2.30	3.95	< .01
2. Consensus without discussion, Pre — Post	3.25	2.12	1.53	n.s.	5.50	2.22	2.48	< .05
3. Discussion without consensus, Pre — Post	9.17	2.14	4.29	< .01	10.67	2.30	4.64	< .001

a All *p* levels are 2-tailed.

from zero by a one-sample t-test; i.e., we ask whether the obtained change in variability is significantly different from a null hypothesis of no change.

For five of the six comparisons shown in Table 5, there is a significant reduction of within-group variability following the experimental manipulation. The groups of each sex under either of the discussion conditions —with or without consensus—show particularly strong reductions in variability (Table 5, rows 1 and 3). Recall that these are also the groups which exhibit significant shifts toward greater risk taking. The condition of consensus without discussion yields a significant reduction in variability for the females (Table 5, row 2), but of smaller magnitude than in the case of conditions DC and D. The males in condition C do not show a significant effect.

The evidence indicates, then, a strong tendency toward narrowing of variability in the case of conditions DC and D, and little difference between these conditions in the degree of narrowing. Discussion, with or without a consensus requirement, clearly leads to the operation of influence processes directed toward bringing opinion deviates into line. This conclusion applies even though the postmeasure is obtained under conditions of privacy and anonymity. We know, furthermore, that influence is not directed with equal intensity toward deviates on the risky and on the conservative sides of the central tendency value. Rather, those whose initial attitudes were more conservative are changing to a greater extent than those whose initial attitudes were more disposed toward risk taking. It is of some interest that the reduction of variability is considerable for condition D as well as for condition DC, even though the instructions for condition D encouraged diversity of opinions.

CONCLUSIONS

The findings of the present experiment have led us to the source of the risk-taking shifts emanating from group discussion to a consensus. Of the three elements involved in the group encounter—provision of information about the judgments of others, group discussion, and achievement of consensus—our evidence leads to the conclusion that group discussion provides the necessary and sufficient condition for generating the risky shift effect. Information about judgments given by others is not sufficient to produce the effect. The consensus factor, in turn, is neither sufficient nor necessary. In short, we have learned that the group-induced risky shift phenomenon seems to arise from the experience of discussion per se.

What are the implications of this conclusion? Direct verbal confrontation seems to offer the possibility of affective interdependencies which lead individuals to feel linked, to at least some extent, in a common fate. Such a sense of connectedness seems to depend crucially on the element of discussion, and very little on the factor of consensus. Not only is consensus unable to generate a risky shift without discussion, but consensus adds little to the causal effectiveness of discussion in producing such a shift. Consider too that the variability of individual risk-taking levels undergoes strong reduction under condition D as well as under condition DC. It may well be, therefore, that the process of group interaction carries in itself considerable inducements toward the attainment of consensus. Discussion may of itself produce the operation of interpersonal influence processes, even in the absence of an explicit consensus requirement and even though opinion diversity has been encouraged.

The origin of the risky shift phenomenon seems to lie, therefore, in emotionally tinged interpersonal connections and attempts at influence which inhere in face-to-face discussion. A consensus requirement has little force if it is not rooted in full-fledged discussion, but, on the other hand, seems to emerge as a natural implication of such discussion. Why, however, is the outcome anything other than averaging? Here the concept of diffusion of responsibility again appears to be the most likely explanation. The present experiment's pinpointing of verbal social interaction as the active situational ingredient helps us to understand how this hypothesized process of responsibility diffusion might work. It is the affective bonds formed in discussion that may enable the individual to feel less than proportionally to blame when he entertains the possible failure of a risky decision.

SUMMARY

What situational elements can account for the enhanced risk taking typical of group relative to individual decision making? The three elements investigated were provision of *information* about the risk-taking levels favored by peers, with the implication of judgmental comparison; *group discussion*, with the affective involvement it can generate; and *achievement of consensus*, with its possible centering of commitment upon the group. The Ss were 360 undergraduates, 180 of each sex, randomly assigned within sex to one of three experimental conditions, all involving five-person groups. The group members in the respective conditions reached decisions concerning matters of risk through discussion to a consensus, through achievement of consensus without discussion, or through discusion without the requirement of consensus. For both male and female groups, discussion with or without consensus produced substantial shifts toward greater risk taking, while consensus without discussion yielded an averaging effect. Hence, the occurrence of group discussion is both necessary and sufficient for generating the risky shift effect.

REFERENCES

Bem, D. J., Wallach, M. A., & Kogan, N. Group decisionmaking under risk of aversive consequences. *Journal of Personality and Social Psychology*, 1965, 1, 453–460.

Cartwright, D., & Zander, A. (Eds.) *Group dynamics.* (2nd ed.) Evanston, Illinois: Row, Peterson, 1960.

Kogan, N., & Wallach, M. A. The effect of anxiety on relations between subjective age and caution in an older sample. In P. H. Hoch & J. Zubin (Eds.), *Psychopathology of aging.* New York: Grune and Stratton, 1961. Pp. 123–135.

Kogan, N., & Wallach, M. A. *Risk taking: A study in cognition and personality.* New York: Holt, 1964.

Marquis, D. G. Individual responsibility and group decisions involving risk. *Industrial Management Review,* 1962, **3,** 8–23.

Walker, Helen M., & Lev, J. *Statistical inference.* New York: Holt, 1953.

Wallach, M. A., & Kogan, N. Sex differences and judgment processes. *Journal of Personality,* 1959, **27,** 555–564.

Wallach, M. A., & Kogan, N. Aspects of judgment and decision making: Interrelationships and changes with age. *Behavior Science,* 1961, **6,** 23–36.

Wallach, M. A., Kogan, N., & Bem, D. J. Group influence on individual risk taking. *Journal of Abnormal & Social Psychology,* 1962, **65,** 75–86.

Wallach, M. A., Kogan, N., & Bem, D. J. Diffusion of responsibility and level of risk taking in groups. *Journal of Abnormal & Social Psychology,* 1964, **68,** 263–274.

Whyte, W. H., Jr. *The organization man.* New York: Simon and Schuster, 1956.

Chapter 15

INTERGROUP RELATIONSHIPS: OUTGROUP REJECTION

It is a pervasive human characteristic, perhaps failing, to enjoy more one's membership in a particular group (the ingroup) if there exists another group (the outgroup) which is seen to be in a competitive or rivalrous relationship with the ingroup. The existence of a "common enemy" creates a number of predictable consequences; for example, overevaluation of ingroup products, increased liking for ingroup members, and increased rejection of outgroup members. We will briefly discuss the research on enhancement of own-group products before turning to a lengthier discussion of three theories of outgroup rejection. Because of their applicability to a variety of current social problems, the last two theories to be discussed encompass groups not necessarily composed of interacting members, but merely of members who share a common characteristic such as membership in a university or in an ethnic group.

Overevaluation of Ingroup Products

The evidence documenting the phenomena of overevaluation of ingroup products comes from several sources. For example, Sherif, Harvey, White, Hood, and Sherif (1961), in a study to be discussed at length below, observed overevaluation in groups of boys at a summer camp. Blake and Mouton (1961) used a human relations training setting to examine overevaluation. Adult participants were formed into subgroups to compete with each other in formulating solutions to group relations problems. The subjects' private evaluation of their own group products, compared to their evaluations of other groups' products, was consistently more favorable.

There are at least four processes which might account for such overevaluation. Ferguson and Kelley (1964) suggest the following: (1) involvement in the creation of a product may lead group members to see more of its positive features than individuals who had nothing to do with creating the product; (2) a favorable evaluation of one's own group which is positively linked to the product would require, according to balance principles, a high evaluation of the product; (3) high ratings may have a "propaganda" function in that they are intended to persuade the judges (or experimenter) to decide in favor of the own-group; and (4) members may see the group product objectively, but still make high ratings because they believe they must do so to maintain solidarity with the other members.

Ferguson and Kelley designed a study to provide evidence about the relative merits of the involvement and balance interpretations in an experimental context which minimized the possible propaganda and solidarity functions of group-product ratings. Pairs of groups were placed at opposite ends of a room, decided on a name for their group, and then were told they would each be working on the same three tasks. The tasks were building an original design with blocks, designing a housing development for 100 retired couples, and writing a modern fable. The experimental instructions attempted to avoid any implications about intergroup competition, although the mere presence of another group undoubtedly invoked competitive feelings. Because the groups were clearly temporary and ratings of group products were made in private, there was little instigation for subjects to use these ratings for propaganda purposes or for cementing relationships with their own group. There was thus an attempt to rule out the third and fourth explanations for overevaluation of ingroup products. Prior to working on a given task one member, selected by the group, was taken out of each group to serve as a nonparticipant rater of the finished products for both groups. These nonparticipant subjects were thus not involved with a given task, while the remaining participant subjects were involved. After completing each task all subjects rated the quality of the products for both groups.

The results were quite consistent for several indices of overevaluation.

As a gross index, each subject's ratings of his own-group's product was compared to his ratings of the other group's product for each task. On this comparison, across all three tasks for participant subjects, 55 percent of such scores favored the own-group, 23 percent were equal, and 22 percent favored the other group. Because subjects' ratings were indirectly shown to take into account the objective qualities of the products a more sensitive index was devised. When one group has a product which is clearly inferior to the other group's, overevaluation can still occur if the group with the inferior product rates the difference between the two products as smaller than the group with the superior product. On this index amount of over-evaluation was even greater than on the first index. For both indices, however, participants did not differ from nonparticipants. Thus involvement in the creation of a product had no significant effect. Such results suggest, in accordance with balance theory, that it is a member's attraction to the group which is the basis for overevaluation. This balance interpretation is strengthened by the results from measures of attraction for the group which were obtained just before work began on the first task. Subjects who were initially favorable to the group tended to make greater overevaluations than those subjects who were less attracted to the group. Although propaganda and internal solidarity purposes may be served by overevaluations in some groups, it is clear that positive relationship to the group is by itself a sufficient basis for inducing overevaluations.

Theories of Outgroup Rejection

In addition to the overevaluation of ingroup products the existence of intergroup rivalries produces enhanced ingroup attraction and outgroup rejection. Because these two latter processes tend to occur simultaneously, we will focus mainly on outgroup rejection. Social scientists have advanced numerous theories of outgroup rejection. The most important of these theories are realistic-group-conflict theory, scapegoat theory, and belief-dissimilarity theory. The experiment by Rabbie and Horwitz (1969) contained in the Readings section, sets the stage for considering each of these theories in turn. Rabbie and Horwitz show the minimal conditions which are sufficient for producing the effect. Outgroup rejection is not obtained when unacquainted subjects are merely divided into two groups and assigned a group name. However, even without the expectation of interaction among group members, assignment of a reward to one of the two groups produces the effect in members of both groups.

Realistic-Group-Conflict Theory

Donald Campbell (1965), drawing heavily from the sociological literature (e.g., Coser, 1956) as well as from the writings of certain other social psychologists such as Sherif (1951, 1953), has listed a series of propositions which make explicit what he calls realistic-group-conflict theory. The first proposition is "Real conflict of group interests causes intergroup conflict" (1965, p. 287). Campbell uses the term "real" to emphasize the theory's assumption that ". . . group conflicts are rational in the sense that groups do have incompatible goals and are in competition for scarce resources" (p. 287). Campbell means to differentiate real or realistic conflicts from conflicts that arise when intragroup problems or intraindividual problems lead to displaced aggression. (We will subsequently consider such matters in connection with the scapegoat theory of prejudice.) Real conflict of group interests and subsequent intergroup conflict arise because of competition over scarce resources such as jobs, territorial possessions, or political power.

Some of Campbell's subsequent propositions are: "Real threat causes ingroup solidarity" (p. 288), "Real threat causes increased awareness of own ingroup identity" (p. 289), and "Real threat creates punishment and rejection of deviants" (p. 290). For our purposes, however, the two most important propositions are "Real threat causes hostility toward the source of threat" (p. 288), and "Real threat increases ethnocentricism" (p. 291). Campbell's general position, thus, is that real threat leads to overevaluation of the ingroup and to underevaluation of and hostility toward the outgroup.

According to Campbell, "The observation that outgroup threat to the ingroup increases individual hostility toward the outgroup and individual loyalty to the ingroup is certainly one of the most agreed-upon observations of descriptive, non-experimental social science" (p. 292). One of the more notable examples is the effect of the Japanese attack at Pearl Harbor on the development of ingroup spirit and outgroup rejection. Less dramatic examples are the "football rivalries" that develop between high schools or between colleges. Observation does indeed lend support to the proposition that competition between groups fosters ingroup acceptance and outgroup rejection. Further, the frequently cited relationship between the percentage of blacks in various areas of the country and extent of certain forms of discrimination (Blalock, 1967) roughly fits with this conception. Blalock found a positive relationship between the percentage of blacks in Southern counties and an economic discrimination index. The index is based on educational, income, occupational, homeownership, rental, and overcrowding levels. It is reasonable to suppose that economic competition between blacks and whites becomes more acute as the percentage of blacks increases.

The most noteworthy experimental work relating to realistic-group-conflict theory was done by Sherif and his co-workers (Sherif, 1951; Sherif and Sherif, 1953; Sherif, Harvey, White, Hood, and Sherif, 1961). The settings for the experiments were boys' camps. In each of three separate experiments Sherif was able to use competition as a successful generator of intergroup hostility and intragroup acceptance. The first experiment was conducted in Connecticut, the second in upstate New York, and the third in Robbers Cave, Oklahoma. Of the three experiments the best known is the latter, Robbers Cave experiment—possibly because it had the most successful manipulation of hostility reduction. We will describe this experiment in some detail.

The subjects were 22 twelve-year-old boys of middle class and Protestant background. Subjects were selected only after examination of school records and interviews with teachers had assured the investigators that the boys were normal and well-adjusted. Such precautionary measures make it unlikely that the subsequent development of outgroup rejection was a result of any sort of abnormality. (Written consent from the parents was, of course, obtained for every boy.)

The study had three experimentally controlled stages: (1) formation of ingroups, (2) intergroup conflict and hostility, (3) intergroup cooperation and reduction of hostility. In stage one the boys were assigned to one of two groups which arrived separately at the campsite and settled into cabins a considerable distance apart. During the week-long duration of this stage the boys in each group engaged in various appealing activities which required interdependent activity in order to attain a common goal. These activities included camping out in the woods, cooking, cleaning up a field for athletics, improving a swimming place, transporting canoes over rough terrain to the water. Since the research staff was instructed not to initiate or execute tasks, the boys had to pool their collective efforts in both work and play. During this period the research staff made observations and ratings, and conducted informal interviews. Sherif *et al.* (1961) report that within each group a status hierarchy developed. In addition, there were role differentiations for various tasks (such as cooking), norms for governing behavior, nicknames for the group members, and even names for the groups. One group called itself the "Rattlers" and the other the "Eagles." The Rattlers developed a distinctive norm of toughness ". . . to the point that the adult staff had to watch out for signs of injury, as the boys would not even bother to treat cuts and scratches, much less show signs of hurt" (Sherif & Sherif, 1969, p. 238). The Eagles developed a norm of being "good" in a more conventional sense (e.g., not swearing and being polite). In stage two the differences between the groups were even more evident. Before competing with each other, the Eagles would huddle in prayer while the Rattlers delighted in rowdy behavior and swearing.

The intent of stage two was to create intergroup hostility through competition. Accordingly, the groups were informed of each other's existence and an elaborate four-day tournament arranged. The tournament consisted of a sequence of baseball games, football games, tent-pitching, and tug-of-war contests. In addition, the staff members separately judged the groups on neatness of cabins, skits and songs, and time spent on a treasure hunt.

The latter were included to enable the experimenters to juggle points so as to assure a close contest. Cumulative scores were indicated by rising thermometers on the official score chart. The members of the winning group were to receive medals and four-bladed knives. In addition, there was a winner's trophy. All of these items were displayed at the "tournament exhibit."

On the first day of the tournament the Eagles were defeated in a tug-of-war. After the Rattlers left the playing field the Eagles took down their opponents' flag and burned part of it. The following day, when the Rattlers discovered what had happened, they took the Eagles' flag amid a lot of scuffling and name-calling. Throughout the remaining days of the tournament there were numerous physical encounters and raids on each other's cabins. On the second day of the tournament the Eagles devised a strategy to win the second tug-of-war. On a prearranged signal all of them sat down and dug in their heels while the Rattlers tired themselves by pulling strenuously. When time was called the Rattlers had been pulled slowly toward, but still not across, the line. The contest was declared a tie, much to the relief of the Rattlers who accused the Eagles of employing a dirty strategy. On the following day the boys were individually interviewed in order to obtain their estimates of the duration of the contest after the Rattlers had also sat down and dug in. The Eagles gave estimates ranging from 20 to 45 minutes; the Rattlers gave estimates ranging from 1 to 3½ hours. The actual time was 48 minutes.

In order to document the outgroup hostility and ingroup acceptance the boys were asked individually to rate each other in terms of a number of personal qualities (brave, tough, friendly, sneaky, smart aleck, stinker). Ingroup ratings were 100 percent favorable for the Rattlers and 94.3 percent favorable for the Eagles. Outgroup ratings were 53 percent *un*favorable for the Rattlers and 76.9 percent unfavorable for the Eagles. At the conclusion of the tournament the groups expressed such strong distaste for each other that they voiced a desire for no further contact whatsoever.

Another interesting consequence of the intergroup conflict was an alteration in the status hierarchy. The leadership of the Eagles actually changed when the boy who had initially emerged as leader "proved reluctant in frontline action during the conflict." One of the Rattlers who had initially been reduced to low status because of his bullying became a hero in encounters with the Eagles. It is apparent that the attribute basis defining status and leadership had shifted as a consequence of the group's changed circumstance.

In stage three of the experiment Sherif *et al.* (1961) attempted to reduce the conflict-produced hostility. How was this to be accomplished? Although conferences among leaders may sometimes resolve disputes, Sherif and Sherif (1969) point out that such a procedure was not tried in the Robbers Cave experiment because of some evidence from the first, or Connecticut, experiment. In this experiment a high-status member of one group, on his own initiative, went to the cabin of the opposing group with the intention of negotiating better relations. However, "He was greeted by a hail of green apples, chased down the path, and derided" (Sherif & Sherif, 1969, p. 255). When he returned to his own cabin he was rebuked for his peace-making efforts despite his high status. Sherif and Sherif argue that unless the norms within the group have already begun to change, group leaders are not free to enter into negotiations productive of further change.

In the Robbers Cave experiment the procedure attempted first was the use of "mere contact." A total of seven contact situations were used. These situations included participating in an experiment together, attending a movie together, and having meals together. During these contacts there was always segregated seating, and typically an exchange of insults. The mess hall contacts in fact degenerated into "garbage fights" in which food and other items were thrown from group to group. When leaving the seventh contact, lunch in the mess hall, the Eagles shouted that they would continue the fight at supper. In the opinion of the observers, contact had not reduced the intergroup hostility.

The procedures which were successful in reducing hostility involved what Sherif and his associates called *superordinate goals,* that is, goals which could be most readily obtained through intergroup cooperation. Accordingly, the experimenters engineered a number of problems requiring joint-group cooperation for their solution. The first problem was a failure of the camp water system. The boys were organized into small groups to search out the difficulty. Eventually, all of the groups converged on the water tank, where it was discovered that the valve had been turned off and covered with boulders. A faucet leading directly into the tank had also been stuffed with rags—all supposedly the work of vandals. After some work, and assistance from the staff, the water problem was solved and the thirsty boys achieved the superordinate goal. The second problem was an insufficiency of camp funds for the procuring of a highly desired film, "Treasure Island." After considerable discussion the boys decided to contribute some of their own money so that the movie could be seen by all. The third problem occurred while the boys were on an outing at a considerable distance from the main camp area; the truck which was to go for food supposedly broke down. The same rope which had been used in the tug-of-war was thrown on the ground about 20 feet from the truck. After the boys tried unsuccessfully to push the truck one of them suggested that they "have a tug-of-war against the truck." This suggestion was echoed by the other boys and after two coordinated attempts amid shouts of "heave, heave" the truck started. Sherif *et al.* report that no one of these events was completely successful in breaking down the hostility but that the cumulative effect was nonetheless quite marked. Thus with the solution of still further "problems" strict segregation of groups broke down and relations became quite amicable. The additional problems involved the sharing of equipment so that tents could be erected and a second starting of the obviously unreliable truck. By the end of the problem situations the groups were intermingling, taking turns lining up at the mess hall, desiring and holding joint campfires at which there was further taking of turns in the presenting of skits and songs. A Rattler whom the Eagles had particularly disliked became a "good egg," and individually obtained evaluative ratings indicated that, in fact, outgroup rejection and ingroup preference had broken down. The boys chose to go home in the same rather than different buses, and on the way home one group chose to share its prize money with the other group so that all could have malted milks.

The procedure of using superordinate goals appears to have been markedly successful. This procedure is an obvious extension of the conflict manipulation which initially produced the hostility. It is just that in the conflict situation the superordinate goal was the defeating of the other group. In both stages two and three there was a similar subordination of individual needs for group goals.

The Robbers Cave experiment, and the two earlier experiments, appear to reveal something very pervasive about social interaction. These three experiments all support the realistic-group-conflict theory assertion that real group conflict leads to outgroup rejection and ingroup acceptance. However, we can inquire further concerning why real conflict, in fact, has these effects. In his previously referred to paper Campbell argues that at least some of the effects of real conflict are best explained through the postulation of genetically based group-survival-related needs.

Campbell's paper has the intriguing title, "Ethnocentric and Other Altruistic Motives." He begins by arguing that conflict-produced ethnocentricism (or overevaluation of the group) goes together with altruistic self-sacrificial behavior for the sake of the group. He then states that such self-sacrificial behavior cannot be predicted on the basis of the *"skin-surface-hedonism"* assumption which is dominant in modern-day psychology (learning theory, psychoanalysis, exchange theory, etc.). Campbell describes this assumption as ". . . the notion that all human activity is directed toward the pleasurable activation of taste receptors and other erogenous zones, the reinforcement of food, sex, and pain avoidance" (1965, p. 285). Thus the exchange theorists derive ". . . group processes and structures entirely from the self-centered concern of the actors as to 'What's there in it for me?'—a mutual back scratching on the part of fundamentally selfish organisms" (1965, p. 285).

How then is self-sacrificial behavior for the sake of the group to be explained? Campbell argues that man's various physiologically based motivational states reflect past organism-environment relationships, or "ecological correlations." Organisms in whom certain adaptive mutational changes occurred survived and procreated disproportionately to other organisms.

These adaptive changes were ones which fit the specific requirements of the environment. Thus existing motivational systems have a retrospective validity in that they reflect past ecological correlations or organism-environment relationships. The survival value of language, for example, led to evolutionary changes in the genetic capacity to learn language—though not to inheritance of a specific language. Campbell's main thesis is thus that ". . . any mutations furthering in man a capacity for ingroup identification, outgroup hostility, and ethnocentric self-sacrificial loyalty would have had a past survival value" (1965, p. 301). Campbell admits that his argument goes counter to the existing environmental bias of most contemporary social psychologists, but defends his position with the interesting point that, "The tremendous survival value of being social makes innate social motives as likely on a priori grounds as self-centered ones" (1965, p. 301). Campbell believes that man has both genetically based selfish and altruistic motives.

Although Campbell's argument is an intriguing one, we believe that he has confused two separate issues. One issue relates to whether there is a genetic basis for self-sacrificial behavior that facilitates group survival. The other issue relates to whether hedonic satisfaction can account for such altruistic behavior. Consider maternal behavior, for example. It is quite apparent that the behavior does not obviously follow from the mother's personal, survival-related needs, and does facilitate group survival. The first issue is thus whether or not there is a genetic basis for such behavior. On the other hand, the second issue is whether or not hedonic satisfactions can account for the mother's self-sacrificial behavior. In fact, mothers appear to receive considerable satisfaction from their mothering behavior. It is thus not true that no hedonistic theory can account for such altruistic behavior. There is nothing in Thibaut and Kelley's (1959) statement of exchange theory which requires that the rewards be received from the satisfaction of needs which only facilitate individual, as opposed to group, survival. If there are needs facilitating group survival (whether genetically based or learned), the satisfaction of those needs could still be hedonically rewarding.

As was pointed out in Chapters 2 and 11, the primary difficulty with hedonistic theories is not that they cannot account for behavior, but rather that they can account for all possible behaviors and are thus untestable. Thus it could be argued that the self-sacrificial behavior of the martyr is "really" satisfying, or that the individual anticipates being rewarded in afterlife, or that the individual is afraid of the suffering and pain which would result if the self-sacrificial behavior were not carried out, or that the individual is simply following orders because in the past such obedience was rewarded.

Campbell also states that "cognitive-congruity" theory cannot account for self-sacrificial behavior. At this point he is simply incorrect. A straightforward application of balance theory indicates that to the extent the group is positively evaluated, altruistic behaviors will be positively evaluated if such behaviors are seen as beneficial to the group. It is true that the person would be put in a conflict if the altruistic behaviors were harmful to the self, or self-sacrificial. In this case the final evaluation of the altruistic behaviors would theoretically depend upon the relative evaluation of self and group. The higher the relative evaluation of the group the greater the evaluation of the altruistic behavior. It is for this reason that Campbell is very much on target in the linking of altruism and ethnocentricism.

Scapegoat Theory

The notion that someone may "take out his frustrations" on a defenseless, scapegoat is a very old one. The term "scapegoat" comes from the Hebrew ritual (Lev. 16:20–22) of symbolically transferring iniquities to a goat, which was then driven into the wilderness. For present purposes the scapegoat theory of outgroup hostility can be regarded as one aspect of the frustration-aggression hypothesis, which was discussed in Chapter 9. According to Dollard, Doob, Miller, Mowrer, and Sears (1939) the blocking of goal-directed activity results in frustration which in turn produces aggression. Furthermore, *"the strongest instigation, aroused by a frustration, is to acts of aggression directed against the agent perceived to be the source of the frustration and progressively weaker instigations are aroused to progressively less direct acts of aggression"* (p. 38). In some instances, however, anticipated punishment may prevent aggression from being directed at the frustrating agent. The frustrating agent may appear too powerful for attack. In such cases the aggression is displaced to less powerful agencies or persons who are unable, or less able, to retaliate.

In the present context the less powerful person is a scapegoat. Since minority-group members are frequently in low-power positions they may be selected as the scapegoats. The scapegoat is not a "realistic" target for hostility in the sense that the aggression has no utility in achievement of the blocked goal.

There is some observational data supporting the scapegoat theory. For example, Bettelheim and Janowitz (1949) interviewed a sample of World War II veterans and found an interesting relationship between social mobility and the expression of anti-Semitic and anti-black attitudes. The veterans were classified as having experienced downward mobility, no mobility, or upward mobility from their previous to present civilian employment. Bettelheim and Janowitz found that the percentage of anti-Semitic and anti-black attitudes varied across these three categories. The downwardly mobile veterans had the most negative attitudes and the upwardly mobile veterans had the least negative attitudes. On the assumption that downward mobility is frustrating such results fit the scapegoat theory of outgroup rejection.

The early experimental work on this problem yielded inconsistent results. Some investigators found evidence that frustration increased rejection of minority groups and some that it did not. The first study was by Miller and Bugelski (1948). Eighteen- to twenty-year-old males in a CCC camp had their attitudes assessed before and after a frustrating experience. One group of subjects had their attitudes toward Mexicans assessed in the before-test and their attitudes toward Japanese assessed in the after-test. Another group had their attitudes toward Japanese assessed in the before-test and their attitudes toward Mexicans assessed in the after-test. Attitudes were assessed by asking the subjects to check the traits (in a list of 20) which were descriptive of the average Mexican or the average Japanese. Ten of the traits were favorable (e.g., friendly, smart, clean) and ten were unfavorable (e.g., unfair, selfish, dirty). The frustrating experience had two aspects. First, they took a series of difficult tests on which most all of them failed. Second, the testing period dragged on for two hours so that the subjects were prevented from attending Bank Night at the local movie (the big event of the week). Following the frustrating experience Miller and Bugelski found a significant decrease in the number of favorable traits and a small nonsignificant increase in the number of unfavorable traits ascribed to the two minority groups. Although these results are not completely unambiguous, the study has been widely quoted as demonstrating the effect of frustration upon outgroup rejection.

Stagner and Congdon (1955) were unable to replicate Miller and Bugelski's results with a sample of college students. A series of four aptitude tests were rigged so that the subjects failed all of them or failed none of them. Extent of failure did not produce any before to after change in the ascription of undesirable characteristics to any of four outgroups. How can we account for the failure to find any evidence of displaced hostility? Perhaps the subjects weren't upset by their failure. Stagner and Congdon, however, report that the failure subjects appeared very upset, as evidenced by "verbalization, sweating, and overt movement." On the other hand, Stagner and Congdon do report that their manipulation of frustration may have appeared less arbitrary than Miller and Bugelski's. When Miller and Bugelski's subjects realized that the continuing testing was going to prevent their attendance at the local movie theater for Bank Night, aggressive tendencies may have been more thoroughly aroused. In Chapter 9 we described evidence indicating that arbitrary frustrations are more likely than nonarbitrary frustrations to produce aggression. A second possible explanation for the differing results, also mentioned by Stagner and Congdon, is that their subjects may have displaced the aroused aggression, not toward outgroups, but toward themselves. Such displacement would take the form of self-criticism. Stagner and Congdon, in fact, report that their subjects tended to make self-critical remarks. In Chapter 9 it was pointed out that Dollard *et al.* (1939) regard such "intropunitive" behavior as one form of displacement. When such intropunitiveness is carried to the extreme it may result in suicide. This state of affairs, however, clearly illustrates a major shortcoming of the scapegoat theory. The theory does not specify the group, individual, or object, which will be selected as a target for the displacement reaction. When will the self rather than some individual or group of individuals be selected, and if some group is selected which one will it be? Supposedly, the displacement target should be visible and relatively unable to retaliate, but this leaves many possibilities. Probably, the frustrated individual will have to justify the displacement target in some way.

Cowen, Landes, and Schaet (1959) found that frustration increased rejection of blacks but not of other minority groups. Before and after filling out alternative forms of various attitudinal assessments college students failed to complete two puzzles that were, in fact, insoluble in the allotted time. During administration of the frustrating puzzles the experimenter's attitude was ". . . aloof, nonsupporting, and disbelieving of Ss inability to achieve a correct solution" (p. 35). As indicated above the frustration was found to increase reported rejection of blacks. However, there was no before-after change in Anti-Minority and Patriotism scales. The former measured attitudes toward minority groups in general, and the latter assessed the desirability of a white, Anglo-Saxon, Protestant America. This experiment seems to have demonstrated some displacement, although it is not clear why blacks were selected as the appropriate outgroup for rejection. It is also not clear why Cowen *et al.*'s subjects did not react with self-blame as Stagner and Congdon's subjects may have done.

The above research provides evidence that frustration may indeed lead to displaced aggression. This research, however, also makes it evident that the scapegoat theory in itself is unable sufficiently to specify the target for the displaced aggression. The more recent research, to which we now turn, has made, at least, a beginning in solving this problem.

Weiss and Fine (1956) obtained results indicating that some sort of justification is a necessary prerequisite for the specification of a displacement target. They had two independent variables, presence or absence of frustration and exposure or nonexposure to a written article advocating punitive measures to curb juvenile delinquency. Frustration was manipulated by giving the subjects aptitude tests that were either difficult and thus certain to produce failure or moderately easy and thus certain to produce success. Furthermore, in the frustration condition the experimenter made uncomplimentary remarks about the subjects' performance and in the nonfrustration, or success, condition the experimenter made complimentary remarks about the subjects' performance. For the half of the subjects who read the article advocating punitive treatment of juvenile delinquents, the article was introduced as still another aptitude test. The subjects were to read and evaluate the article in terms of fairness, propagandistic intent, etc., and finally to indicate their agreement with the advocated point of view. Another half of the subjects did not read the article justifying punitive treatment of juvenile delinquents. Change from assessments taken two weeks before to immediately after the appropriate experimental manipulation indicated that acceptance of the more punitive stance toward juvenile delinquents was most apparent when the subjects were both frustrated and read the article. The combination of frustration and exposure to the justifying article produced more punitive attitudes than were produced by either frustration alone or the justifying article alone. A possible alternative explanation for the results is that frustration simply heightened persuasiveness. However, a set of control conditions identical to the above except that the article advocated a certain U. S. foreign-policy position did not show comparable results. Frustration then does not heighten agreement with just any communication. The communication has to advocate or justify punitive action toward some target.

Berkowitz and Green (1962) performed an additional experiment concerned with the general problem of identifying determinants of a displacement target. They obtained evidence consistent with the hypothesis that frustration-aroused hostility will more likely be displaced onto a disliked other than a neutral other. From this perspective then one of the determinants of a displacement target is the degree to which the target is disliked. Berkowitz and Green interpret their results as generally supportive of the position that stimulus cues play an important role in the translation of frustration into aggression or hostility. Berkowitz's general theoretical position regarding the importance of cues was previously discussed in Chapter 9 and is also illustrated in the study by Berkowitz and LePage (1967) contained in the Readings section of the same chapter.

In general, we feel that the scapegoat theory has some utility in explaining the existence of outgroup rejection. The important problem of identifying the displacement target, however, has only begun to be explored.

BELIEF-DISSIMILARITY THEORY

Rokeach, Smith, and Evans (1960) developed a theory of outgroup rejection in terms of belief dissimilarity. From this theoretical perspective outgroup members are rejected not because they belong to certain racial or ethnic categories; rather, they are rejected because of their dissimilar beliefs. It is thus the attribution of dissimilar beliefs which leads to negative attitudes. According to Rokeach *et al.* (1960), ". . . *insofar as psychological processes* are involved, belief is more important than ethnic or racial membership as a determinant of social discrimination" (p. 135). In emphasizing psychological processes Rokeach *et al.* explicitly exclude institutionalized manifestations of rejection, as for example norms against marriage with an outgroup member.

Belief-dissimilarity theory can be regarded as specific application of the general notion that interpersonal attraction varies as a function of similarity —particularly attitudinal similarity. (In the context of the present discussion attitudes and beliefs can be regarded as essentially the same.) In Chapter 9 the extensive literature bearing on the relationship between attitudinal similarity and attraction was discussed at some length.

Rokeach *et al.* reported two studies which provide empirical support for their speculation. The first of these studies was concerned with the black-white distinction and the other with the Jew-gentile distinction. In the first study, students from Michigan State University and the University of Houston were given a questionnaire containing items requiring that they indicate on a nine-point scale whether or not they could see themselves being friends with certain kinds of people. The people were always either blacks or whites who did or did not believe in such things as God, Communism, or segregation. Here are some examples (1960, p. 136):

a. A white person who believes in God
b. A Negro who believes in God

a. A white person who believes in God
b. A white person who is an atheist.

By systematically varying both race and belief it was possible to test for discrimination on the basis of race or of belief. For example, a differential response to the first pair of items above would indicate discrimination on the basis of race, and a differential response to the second pair of items would indicate discrimination on the basis of belief.

The results indicated that for both Northern and Southern subjects belief discrimination was more marked than racial discrimination. Furthermore, a division of subjects into two groups on the basis of an antiblack scale revealed no differences in the relative sizes of the belief and race effects.

In the second study Rokeach *et al.* modified the questionnaire so that it applied to Jew-gentile discrimination and administered it to a sample of Jewish children. Once again it was found that belief discrimination was more marked than racial discrimination.

The bulk of the subsequent research on this specific problem has used an experimental design which differs somewhat from Rokeach *et al.*'s. Some time after subjects initially fill out a belief questionnaire they are presented with four copies of the same questionnaire, each copy supposedly filled out by a different person. The experimenter has prepared these questionnaires so that two of them are similar to the subject's own previous responses and two of them are different from the subject's own previous responses. Responses on the dissimilar questionnaires are arrived at by altering the subject's initial response pattern in accordance with some arbitrary rule. Accompanying each questionnaire is a face sheet containing background information about the subject, for example, sex, year of school, size of family, and *race*. The face sheets are filled out so that two of the questionnaires appear to have been filled out by whites and two by blacks. Thus there are four basic conditions: similar-black, similar-white, dissimilar-black, dissimilar-white. These four conditions are represented in Table 15-1. In the case of ingroup-outgroup distinctions other than black-white, Jew-gentile for example, the information concerning race on the face sheet is altered accordingly. After examining each of the face sheets and questionnaires the subject marks various rating scales indicating his or her reaction to the person who had supposedly made the questionnaire responses.

The bulk of the research using the above design has obtained evidence indicating that belief is indeed a more important determiner than race for dependent variables such as liking and friendship. However, with dependent variables relating to intimate behavioral associations, such as accepting the person as close kin by marriage, race is more important than belief. Since these studies have been conducted with a sizable number of different subject populations we can have considerable faith in the results. A study by Stein, Hardyck, and Smith (1965), which used junior-high school students, is a good example. Stein *et al.* found that belief was more important than race for a friendliness dependent variable, as well as for dependent variables such as willingness to have the person in the same school and willingness to have the person as a member of a social group. However, for three dependent variables: "invite home to dinner," "live in same apartment house," and "date my sister (brother)" race was more important than belief. Stein *et al.* state that these latter three effects possibly relate to institutionalized norms, and hence lie outside of the domain of the theory as Rokeach *et al.* state it. (As was noted earlier, Rokeach *et al.* explicitly limit their theory to noninstitutionalized manifestations of outgroup rejection.) Stein *et al.* point out that the three dependent variables on which race had the greatest effect seem to involve both "intimacy of contact and presence of others—in this case parents—who are the enforcers of social norms" (1965, p. 288).

TABLE 15-1

Four Types of Hypothetical Persons Used in the Study of Belief and Race as Determinants of Outgroup Rejection

	Similar beliefs	Dissimilar beliefs
Black	Similar-black	Dissimilar-black
White	Similar-white	Dissimilar-white

A possible objection to the studies using the design in Table 15-1 relates to the assignment of dissimilar responses. Investigators have created dissimilar responses by altering each subject's own belief responses. Scant attention, however, has been paid to the extent of alteration. Suppose a junior high-school student is asked whether he "strongly feels he should," "feels he should," "doesn't care," "feels he should not," or "strongly feels he should not" have respect for his parents. If he responds "feels he should," then a dissimilar response could be *any* of the remaining four possibilities. When, at a later time, the investigator presents the subject with a dissimilar response to this question, supposedly made by another person, which response should be supplied? Different investigators have used different arbitrary rules.

Robinson and Insko (1969) argued that the "dissimilar responses" should be those that each subject actually attributes to the typical black teenager (or in general the typical outgroup member). Thus if the teenager perceived that the typical black teenager "feels he should not" have respect for his parents then "feels he should not" is the theoretically appropriate "dissimilar response." This would be true even if the white teenager himself "feels he should not" have respect for his parents.

Using this more theoretically appropriate manipulation of belief dissimilarity, Robinson and Insko conducted a study of ninth-grade students from a small North Carolina community. In agreement with the general findings of previous research the results indicated that belief was a more important determiner of general evaluative (or liking) reactions while race was a more important determiner of reactions to such statements as "Eat with this person," and "Accept this person as close kin by marriage." Such results provide a reasonable degree of assurance that belief dissimilarity is important insofar as attention is restricted to overall ratings of goodness, friendship, etc. Obviously, however, this is only part of the total picture. We still need to account for other manifestations of outgroup rejection, such as the reluctance to become intimately associated with outgroup members.

THREE THEORIES OF OUTGROUP REJECTION

We have reviewed three theories of outgroup rejection: realistic-group-conflict theory, scapegoat theory, and belief-dissimilarity theory. Each of these theories has something distinctive to say about outgroup rejection, and each may have a degree of validity. Existing data indicate that this is the case. Certainly, the theories should not be viewed as contradictory. It is even possible that they may be complementary. Scapegoating reactions, for example, may be directed toward minority-group members who are perceived as possessing dissimilar beliefs. And the attribution of dissimilar beliefs may be at least partially facilitated by group conflict.

READINGS

Arousal of Ingroup-Outgroup Bias by a Chance Win or Loss[1]

Jacob M. Rabbie and Murray Horwitz

An experiment conducted with 112 Dutch teenagers formed into pairs of groups, investigated the minimal conditions that produce a more favorable evaluation of the ingroup than the outgroup. Members of each pair of groups, all of whom were strangers, rated first impressions of each other and of the two groups under one of a graded series of experimental treatments. Simply classifying subjects into two distinct groups yielded no difference between the evaluations of ingroups and outgroups. However, flipping a coin to decide which of the two groups would receive a gift produced a significant bias in favor of the ingroup and its members. A proposed interpretation is that the chance win-loss created intergroup bias by leading subjects to anticipate better outcomes from interpersonal encounters with ingroup members than outgroup members

Since the work of Sumner (1906), who coined the term "ethnocentrism," social scientists have speculated about the conditions that lead ingroups to devaluate outgroups. The extent to which this devaluative tendency occurs among natural groups is uncertain. Merton (1957) believed that attitudes toward an outgroup may be positive or neutral as well as negative. Schmidt (1960), on the other hand, contended that the very growth of group consciousness entails rejective attitudes toward outsiders.

Whatever its extent in everyday life, invidiousness between groups is surprisingly easy to evoke in experiments. Sherif, Harvey, White, Hood, and Sherif (1961) worked with children's groups that had developed interdependent roles, a hierarchical status structure, and common norms. By simply placing these groups in competition, they produced severe intergroup antagonism. The same effect was readily obtained with groups of adults competing in a training exercise (Blake & Mouton, 1961). Accord-

[1] From the *Journal of Personality and Social Psychology*, Volume 13, pages 269–277, 1969 (received February 1, 1969). Reproduced by permission of the American Psychological Association. Authors' affiliations: Robbie, University of Utrecht; Horwitz, Boston College. The present research was supported by a grant to the first author from the Institute of Social Psychology, University of Utrecht, and by a Senior Training Fellowship to the second author from the United States Public Health Service supplemented by a grant from the National Science Foundation. We gratefully acknowledge the participation of Sibe Soutendijk throughout the experiment and the research assistance of Sem Everwijn, Wim Fluit, and Ben Schreurs.

ing to Sherif, intergroup hostility will arise where well-developed groups operate in a competitive or reciprocally frustrating situation.

It is doubtful that the two conditions proposed by Sherif *et al.* are necessary to evoke the effect. In pilot experiments, the present authors found that even a newly formed group composed of strangers becomes sharply antagonistic to another group during the course of competition. More surprisingly, we found that well-developed groups working face-to-face on a *cooperative* task also become antagonistic.[2] In the latter experiment, members of each group tended to be suspicious of the other group's intentions, for example viewing offers of assistance as acts of condescension. They also tended to distort the other's communications, for example interpreting proposals for joint action as ultimata. In addition, they tended to attribute hostile motives to the other's ambiguous behavior, for example viewing silence as malevolence. The sheer fact of interaction between groups seemed to produce unstable conditions that erupted into hostility, even on a cooperative task. The question remains an open one as to the source of the antagonism.

The present research aims to isolate the minimal conditions that are sufficient to generate discriminatory ingroup-outgroup attitudes. Our point of departure is that expressed by Lewin (1948). Addressing himself to Jewish adolescents, he wrote, "regardless of whether the Jewish group is a racial, religious, national or cultural one, the fact that it is classified by the majority as a distinct group is what counts . . . the main criterion of belongingness is *interdependence of fate*" (p. 184). In the present experiment, we attempted to separate some of the components of Lewin's formulation and to ascertain their effects.

The experiment was designed to answer the following questions concerning "interdependence of fate." First, will merely classifying persons into two groups lead to discriminatory ingroup-outgroup evaluations? If not, will adding the experience of one group's being rewarded by chance while the other is deprived lead to discriminatory intergroup evaluations? Third, if reward-deprivation by chance is insufficient, will reward-deprivation due to the partiality of some external agent produce the effect? Finally, if neither of these forms of reward-deprivation is sufficient, will reward-deprivation due to action by the ingroup or outgroup suffice for the effect? The questions move from the most rudimentary, concerning the impact of group classification per se, to those which progressively add other possible components of interdependence of group fate.

Corresponding to these questions, the experiment included four conditions, in each of which subjects were classified into two groups. In one

[2] A training exercise in 1963 at the National Training Laboratory conducted in collaboration with Marvin Kaplan, Seymour Levy, Henry Riecken, Leonard Solomon, Robert Tannenbaum, and Eric Trist.

condition, the groups were neither rewarded nor deprived. In these others the groups were either rewarded or deprived by chance alone, by the arbitrary choice of the experimenter, or by the choice of one of the groups. In order to test for possible sex differences in ingroup-outgroup attitudes, we employed male and female groups within each condition.

METHOD

Subjects

Fifty-six girls and 56 boys, average age about 15 years, were recruited as volunteers from junior high schools in or near Utrecht. Eight subjects of the same sex, all from different schools, participated in each experimental session. All subjects present in a given session were strangers.

Classifying Subjects into Groups

The experimenter and an assistant, both Dutch-speaking, introduced the experiment as a study of first impressions. Subjects were divided at random into two groups of four and seated at either side of a screen to prevent their seeing each other. The experimenter publicly designated one group as the blue group and the other as the green. Members of each group wore green or blue identification cards, wrote with green or blue ballpoint pens, used green or blue forms, and were repeatedly addressed by the experimenter and his assistant as "greens" or "blues." In order to diminish any expectation that subjects would interact with one another, the experimenter stated that he had divided them into groups for "administrative reasons only" and that subjects would not work together in any way. The experimenter asked the subjects not to talk with one another "since this would interfere with your task later on—to give unbiased impressions of the personality characteristics of other subjects in this room."

Activities Prior to the First-Impression Ratings

(a) To accustom subjects to working in each other's presence in the laboratory, the experimenter administered a Dutch version of the Hidden Patterns Test (Educational Testing Service, 1962). This brief, 5-minute test was explained as measuring how "you perceive things and figures, rather than people." (b) Each subject then filled out a short Personal Background Form on which he entered his name, address, size of family, and ordinal position. Subjects were told they would use this information in introducing themselves to each other. (c) Subjects next rated two photographs depicting persons of their age and sex. These ratings aimed to give subjects experience with the scales they would later apply to each other. The ratings also provided a base line of subjects' impressions of persons with whom they had no relationship whatsoever.

Experimental Manipulations

The experimenter introduced each of the experimental variations of reward and deprivation with the following common statement:

> We very much appreciate your willingness to cooperate with us and we would like to give you a reward for participating in this research. We have a few transistor radios available and would like to give these to you. Unfortunately, we have only a limited number of these radios. In fact, we have only four available in this session. We are very sorry, but only four of you can get one.

During the statement, the experimenter displayed one of the radios, a pocket transistor model worth about 25 guilders (approximately $7). The procedures then varied according to each experimental treatment as follows:

In the *chance* condition, the experimenter stated:

> Perhaps the best thing we can do is to flip a coin to decide which group gets the radios and which does not. O.K.? Do you want heads or tails? The group whose side is up gets the radios.

The experimenter tossed a coin, announced the winning group, and expressed regrets to the losing group about not having more radios. He proceeded to test the radios, wrap them up, and deliver them to the winning subjects requesting signed receipts.

In the *experimenter* condition, the experimenter arbitrarily designated one of the groups to receive radios, saying, "Let's see—I'll give the radios to this group." Following his decision, the experimenter proceeded to deliver the radios as described above.

In the *group* condition, the experimenter contrived to make the rewarded group appear responsible for the decision. He stated:

> Perhaps the easiest way of deciding who gets the radios is for me to give them to one group rather than the other. However, I feel it would be more fair to give you some voice in the decision. It would take too long and be too much trouble to have all of you vote on this. It would be better if only one group takes the vote. Which group wants to make this decision? . . . Oh, you want to vote. O.K. I'll distribute the ballots to you then.

The experimenter distributed voting forms to one of the groups selected at random in advance of the experiment. As the groups could not see each other, each group could assume that the other had been either faster or slower than itself in attracting the experimenter's attention. Regardless of the actual vote, the experimenter announced after collecting the ballots that the voting group decided "they themselves will receive the radios." The delivery of the radios then proceeded as above.

Finally, the *control* condition dispensed with the prize. Between the steps of rating photographs and rating fellow subjects, the control subjects had no intervening experience of reward or deprivation.

Ratings of First Impressions

Removing the screen so that all subjects could see one another, the experimenter continued:

> You are now ready to give your first impressions of each other. Let's start with introducing yourselves. I would like each of you to stand up in turn and read aloud the personal background information you prepared before—you remember, the form on which you put your name, address, etc. After a person finishes reading this material, you will rate him on the rating scales that I will give you. Don't think too long about your answer. We realize you can't give a considered judgment. It's your first impression that counts.

The experimenter distributed an eight-page booklet of rating scales, one page for each subject. Subjects rated themselves and the others on eight characteristics: responsibility, consideration, fearfulness, cordiality, openness, familiarity, soundness of judgment, and desirability as a friend. The items contained 7-point scales ordered along a favorable-unfavorable dimension. To counteract possible response-set tendencies, some scales ran from favorable to unfavorable while others ran in the reverse direction. Subjects introduced themselves in a random order.

Additional Data Collection

(a) After collecting the group ratings, the experimenter announced that he had "forgotten to pass out some of the photographs" and obtained subjects' ratings of two additional ones. (b) In order to measure possible treatment effects on action as well as on attitude, the experimenter obtained subjects' sociometric choices under the following instructions:

> We said earlier that you would not work together, but we have changed our minds about that. You see, we now have your first impressions about each other. It would be very interesting to know to what extent these impressions change as a result of your getting to know each other a little better. That is why we would like you to work on a group task which I will describe in a moment. But it is important for this task that you like the people you have to work with. Would you please rank in order the three people here with whom you would *most* like to work and the two with whom you would *least* like to work? We need this information to form the new groups in which you'll be working. In this way, we can take account of your preferences.

(c) A final questionnaire, tapping subjects' feelings of belongingness to own and other groups, followed the sociometric measure. The questionnaire checked, too, on various aspects of subjects' experience during the experiment: to whom subjects attributed responsibility for the reward-deprivation, how they felt about the experimenter, his conduct, and the value of the prize,[3] and whether they were acquainted with any other subjects.

After the questionnaire, the experimenter divulged the true purpose of the experiment and stated in the group condition that the announced vote did not necessarily correspond with the actual vote. The experimenter urged subjects not to talk about the experimental procedures with future subjects. We found no subsequent evidence that they did.

In summary, the experimental treatments comprised two overlapping variations. In one variation, half the subjects experienced a reward and half a deprivation. In the second variation, subjects experienced the source of reward or deprivation as chance, the experimenter, or a group, respectively. The term "experimental condition" refers to each of the six cells defined by these twofold variations. Each experimental condition contained equal numbers of males and females and each subject rated both own and other groups. We obtained in consequence a $3 \times 2 \times 2 \times 2$ repeated-measurements design as illustrated in Tables 1 and 2 below. Finally, the control comprised eight girls and eight boys who were neither rewarded nor deprived. In what follows, we examine the effects of the control and experimental conditions separately, and then compare the data from each.

RESULTS

Control Condition

Subjects evaluated own and other groups by rating the personal attributes of members, the attributes of each group as a whole, and by soci-

---

[3] The mean rating of the value of the radio was 6.02 on a 7-point scale. The rating shows an interesting "sour grapes effect" in that deprived subjects rated the radio much lower than rewarded subjects ($p < .025$), suggesting the great potency the prize must have had.

ometric choice, in that order. In this section, we examine whether classifying subjects in the control condition into two groups differentially affected subjects' ingroup and outgroup evaluations.

Excluding self-ratings, each subject rated the personal attributes of three ingroup and four outgroup members. We converted the ratings where necessary so that the more favorable the rating the higher the score, and computed the mean ratings for ingroup and for outgroup members. As we were uncertain whether two of the scales, "wanting to be friends with" and "familiar-unfamiliar," referred directly to personal attributes of the ratee, we excluded these from the computation of means in advance of the analysis. The means of the six remaining scales were 4.37 for ingroup members and 4.41 for outgroup members. Subjects in the control condition appeared to evidence no bias in rating the attributes of own and other members.

A subject's attitude toward each group as a whole is indicated by the mean of his ratings on the eight scales of positive and negative group attributes. For the 16 subjects in the control condition the mean ratings were 4.28 for own group and 4.41 for the other group. No reliable difference appeared between the ratings of ingroup and outgroup attributes.

Finally, each subject ranked the three persons with whom he most liked and the two with whom he least liked to work. By placing each of the two unchosen persons at rank 4½, we obtain a subject's ranking of his seven fellow subjects. An index of the tendency to choose within own group is the sum of ranks for ingroup members. Including ties, this index has 16 possible values whose own rank order has a midrank of 8.5. If subjects discriminated in favor of ingroup members, significantly more of the indexes should be above the midrank than below. Nine indexes in the control condition were above and seven were below, indicating no significant partiality toward working with own members.

In the control condition the experimenter classified subjects into distinct groups whose remaining experiences were identical. With regard to member attributes, group attributes, and sociometric choice, subjects did not differentiate own from other groups. Group classification per se appears to be insufficient to produce discriminatory evaluations.

Experimental Conditions

In the experimental conditions, subjects were not only classified into groups, but were rewarded or deprived by virtue of their membership. Whether the groups were rewarded or deprived depended, according to treatment, on the toss of a coin, the experimenter's decision, or the decision of one of the groups. To check on subjects' awareness of these variations, we obtained ratings on three 7-point scales of the degree to which subjects viewed the outcome as determined by chance, the experimenter, or one of the groups, respectively. Subjects' respective mean ratings were 5.96, 2.11,

1.88 in the chance treatment, 4.46, 6.14, 1.81 in the experimenter treatment, and 2.27, 2.85, 4.70 in the group treatment. All of the expected within and between differences are significant beyond the .01 level. Clearly subjects differed as intended in their perceptions of the source of reward or deprivation in each treatment.

Ratings of Group Attributes

The experience of reward and deprivation markedly affected subjects' combined ratings on the eight scales of positive and negative group attributes. Across treatments, the mean rating of own groups ($M = 4.65$) is significantly more favorable than that of other groups ($M = 4.20$) beyond the .001 level. On individual scales, subjects do not significantly distinguish between the two groups with regard to ratings of goodness-badness, future cohesion, and future performance. However, they view their own group relative to the other as less likely to be hostile ($p < .001$), more desirable to belong to ($p < .001$), more familiar ($p < .005$). None of these perceived differences in group attributes could have been based on the experience of actual differences in group behavior.

Ratings of Personal Attributes

Subjects display the same ingroup-outgroup bias in their ratings of individuals. Table 2 shows the mean ratings of ingroup and outgroup members on the six scales of personal attributes. Across treatments, subjects' mean rating of ingroup members ($M = 4.68$) is significantly more favorable than that of outgroup members ($M = 4.47$) beyond the .001 level. Relative to outgroup members, subjects rate ingroup members as more open ($p < .001$), more responsible ($p < .05$), but no different in fearfulness. On the two personal attribute scales not included in Table 2, subjects rated ingroup members as more familiar ($p < .01$) and more desirable as friends ($p < .001$) than outgroup members.

The ratings of personal attributes are based on a greater number of scores than those of group attributes. Perhaps because of the increased reliability of the personal ratings, three significant effects appear in Table 2 that are not evident in Table 1.

Two of these effects, each significant at the .025 level (Table 3), appear in the analysis of *combined* ingroup-outgroup ratings. These ratings progressively decline from the chance ($M = 4.74$), to experimenter ($M = 4.51$), to group treatments ($M = 4.45$), and they decline primarily among rewarded rather than deprived subjects. The probable explanation is suggested by a surprising fact. When the experimenter delegated the responsibility for awarding the prize to one of the groups in the group treatment, 10 of these 16 subjects unexpectedly voted for the *other* group. The experimenter's subsequent false announcement that the group had voted for itself must have led these "altruistic" subjects to downgrade severely their

TABLE 1

Mean Ratings of Group Attributes[a]

	Chance		Experimenter		Group	
Treatment	Own group	Other group	Own group	Other group	Own group	Other group
Reward						
Boys	5.19	4.71	4.41	4.28	4.20	4.34
Girls	4.84	3.64	4.72	4.21	4.30	3.81
Deprivation						
Boys	4.65	4.58	4.90	4.09	4.84	4.21
Girls	4.71	4.12	4.22	4.40	4.81	4.05
Overall M	4.85	4.26	4.56	4.24	4.54	4.10

[a] Own group versus other group, $F = 25.76$, $df = 1/84$, $p < .001$. All other main effects and interactions are not significant.

fellow members ($M = 4.35$). It would seem likely that subjects viewed their winning in the group treatment as "selfish," in the experimenter treatment as "arbitrary," but in the chance treatment as "fair." In the chance treatment, rewarded subjects produced the highest ingroup ratings ($M = 5.07$), probably reflecting their uncontaminated good fortune. These elevated ratings in the chance treatment and the depressed ones in the group treatment largely account for the two significant effects found among the combined ingroup-outgroup ratings.

The third significant effect ($p < .005$, Table 3) is that among rewarded subjects girls show a stronger ingroup-outgroup bias than boys, but among deprived subjects boys show a stronger bias than girls. A proposed explanation of this finding is presented in the Discussion section.

TABLE 2

Mean Ratings of Personal Attributes

	Chance		Experimenter		Group	
Treatment	Own members	Other members	Own members	Other members	Own members	Other members
Reward						
Boys	5.04	4.93	4.41	4.40	4.31	4.37
Girls	5.10	4.35	4.66	4.71	4.40	4.06
Deprivation						
Boys	4.84	4.57	4.87	4.31	4.76	4.20
Girls	4.63	4.50	4.25	4.55	4.86	4.68
Overall M	4.90	4.58	4.55	4.50	4.58	4.32

TABLE 3

Analysis of Variance of Ratings of Member Attributes

Source	df	MS	F
Between Ss	95		
Chance/Experimenter/Group (B)	2	148.58	4.44*
Reward/Deprivation (C)	1	1.33	<1
Sex (D)	1	4.08	<1
B × C	1	132.52	3.96*
B × D	2	36.58	1.09
C × D	1	.00	<1
B × C × D	2	87.06	2.60
Error between	84	33.48	
Within Ss	96		
Difference own/other group (A)	1	229.69	13.36***
A × B	2	21.94	1.28
A × C	1	6.02	<1
A × D	1	2.52	<1
A × B × C	2	28.58	1.66
A × C × D	1	165.02	9.60**
A × B × D	2	43.27	2.51
A × B × C × D	2	.33	<1
Error within	84	17.20	
Total	191		

$* \ p < .025.$
$** \ p < .005.$
$*** \ p < .001.$

Sociometric Choices

The final measure of intergroup attitudes is that based on subjects' choices of work partners. The index of choice, described above, is the sum of the ranks that each subject assigned to members of his group. Table 4

TABLE 4

Frequency Distribution of Indexes of Ingroup Choice[a]

Treatments	Number	Chance	Experi-menter	Group	Total
Reward	Above midrank	11	8	12	31
	Below midrank	3	6	3	12
Deprivation	Above midrank	11	8	13	32
	Below midrank	4	6	3	13

[a] By the sign test the distributions of the separate total frequencies for reward, deprivation, chance, and group, respectively, are significant beyond the .01 level. The frequencies for reward and for deprivation within chance and group, respectively, are each significant beyond the .05 level.

shows the distribution of these indexes above and below their midrank. The relative frequencies of indexes that are above the midrank for both reward (72%) and deprivation (71%) significantly exceed those that are below ($p < .01$). Since the indexes of ingroup choice cluster above their midrank, the reverse must be true of outgoing choices. The evidence is clear-cut that on measures of sociometric choice, as well as of group and personal attributes, subjects markedly favor the ingroup over the outgroup.

Comparison of Control and Experimental Conditions

While the experimental conditions show a significant bias in favor of ingroups, the control shows none. We ask next whether the tendency to favor own groups is reliably greater in the experimental than in the control conditions.

On the combined ratings of group attributes, the mean ingroup-outgroup differentiation is —.12 in control and .48 in the experimental conditions. The difference is significant ($p < .025$).[4] Considering separate treatments, only the chance treatment significantly exceeds ($p — .025$) control; the experimenter and group treatments do not.

The ratings of personal attributes of members display a similar pattern of results. The mean ingroup-outgroup differentiation for combined personal ratings is —.04 in control and .21 in the experimental conditions, although the difference is only nearly significant ($p < .06$). With regard to separate treatments, again it is only the chance treatment that significantly exceeds ($p < .025$) control.

Finally, we compare the extent to which subjects in the control and experimental treatments differ in sociometrically choosing ingroup rather than outgroup members. By the Mann-Whitney U test, the ranks of indexes of ingroup choice are significantly higher ($p < .03$) in the experimental conditions than in the control, due mainly to the joint effects of the chance and group treatments, although neither considered separately differs significantly from the control.

The consistent differences between experimental conditions and control are due mainly to the chance condition. In the experimenter treatment, ingroup-outgroup differentiation was reduced by the losing girls who favored the outgroup (Tables 1 and 2), which probably reflects their experience that the male experimenter had discriminated against their group. In the group treatment, as noted above, differentiation was again reduced by subjects giving low ratings to fellow members who had been falsely

---

[4] Two-tailed tests would assess probabilities where subjects either favor own or other groups and where either type of bias is greater or less in the experimental than in the control conditions. Since we already know that the experimental conditions showed a significant favoring of ingroups over outgroups and that the control did not, we assess the significance of differences in one direction only by using one-tailed tests in this and the following comparisons.

described as "selfishly" voting to reward themselves. The chance treatment alone is uncontaminated by possible perceptions of experimenter discrimination or ingroup unfairness, which probably accounts for the clear-cut difference between chance and control.

Discussion

The experiment has yielded two statistically reliable facts. First, the act of flipping a coin to award a prize to one of two collections of strangers produces a significant ingroup preference. Second, the strength of this preference is greater among winning girls than winning boys, but greater among losing boys than losing girls.

When the experimenter made the chance award, he changed several components of the subjects' social field. Prior to the flip of the coin, each subject confronted an experimenter, two relatively indistinguishable groups, and several relatively indistinguishable persons within the groups. The flip of the coin changed the subjects' view of each of these units except the experimenter, whose action they saw as dictated by chance. The two groups became distinguishable as winner or loser, and the several persons in these groups became at least distinguishable as satisfied or dissatisfied with their outcomes. We consider next to which of these changes subjects reacted when they developed a bias in favor of their ingroups.

The bias could have been produced if subjects simply reacted with satisfaction or dissatisfaction to their group's winning or losing. According to the theory of group cohesiveness (Cartwright & Zander, 1960), winners should rate their ingroup positively where it mediates a reward. According to the theory of frustration-aggression (Rosenblatt, 1964), losers should rate an outgroup negatively where it mediates a deprivation. The joint occurrence of these processes could account for both winners and losers rating ingroups higher than outgroups. There is evidence, however, that neither process operated in the present experiment. The self-ratings by winning groups were not higher than those by losing groups, the respective means being 4.61 versus 4.69 for own-group attributes, 4.65 versus 4.70 for own-member attributes, and 72% versus 71% for percentages above the mid-rank of ingroup sociometric choice. Nor were the outgroup ratings by losing groups lower than those by winning groups, the respective means being 4.24 versus 4.17 for outgroup attributes and 4.47 in each case for outgroup-member attributes. It is thus unlikely that subjects' ingroup preference stemmed from their satisfaction or dissatisfaction with the changed state of each group.

It is also conceivable that subjects reacted not to the state of each group separately, but to the difference between the groups. According to the theory of cognitive balance, subjects who view themselves as having a common experience with ingroup members should generate positive sentiments toward the ingroup, since "p similar to o induces p likes o [Heider, 1958, p. 184]." Correspondingly, subjects who view themselves as having a contrasting experience with outgroup members should generate negative sentiments toward the outgroup, since a disjunctive relation carries a negative sign. As regards the prize, subjects had contrasting experiences with outgroup members in the experimental conditions, but identical experiences with outgroup members in the control condition. Nevertheless, subjects' ratings of outgroup members were *not* lower in the experimental conditions ($M = 4.47$) than in the control ($M = 4.41$). On this evidence, subjects do not appear to have downgraded groups whose fate differed from that of their own group.

Finally, we consider the possibility that subjects were reacting to the changed emotional states of the persons in the room rather than to the changed states of the groups. After one group won at the other's expense, subjects could readily perceive themselves and others as feeling gratified or disappointed, thereby changing the ease or difficulty of face-to-face encounters. Winners who interacted with losers would need to suppress any display of satisfaction with winning, lest they communicate that they were pleased with the others' loss. Losers who interacted with winners would need to suppress their feelings of dissatisfaction with losing, lest they communicate that they were displeased with the other's gain. By contrast, interaction with members of the subjects' own group would be devoid of conflict and, indeed, offer subjects social support for freely expressing their feelings about winning or losing. Subjects were in visual and sometimes oral communication with each other during the experiment and could anticipate later encounters in the hallway or elevator. A demand characteristic of this, or any psychological experiment, is that subjects respond to their face-to-face encounters. If they perceive that interaction with ingroup members will be easy, but interaction with outgroup members will be difficult, subjects should tend to approach the one and avoid the other, manifesting these approach-avoidance tendencies in their discriminatory ratings of the two groups.

The case for this interpretation is strengthened by its capacity to explain the paradoxical difference between the responses of girls and boys to winning or losing (Table 3). Girls usually show greater compassion than boys (Terman & Miles, 1936) and strive more than boys for fair outcomes rather than to win at another's expense (Bond & Vinacke, 1961; Uesigi & Vinacke, 1963). Yet, where girls and boys were winners in the present study, the supposedly compassionate girls discriminated more strongly than boys against losers; where girls and boys were losers, the supposedly competitive boys favored more strongly than girls their fellow losers. The paradox can be resolved by noting the special conflicts that compassion or competitiveness engenders in encounters between winners and losers. A compassionate winner should desire to express sympathy to a loser although constrained by the method of allocating rewards to be pleased about winning at the other's expense. A competitive loser should desire to avoid the ignominy of facing his conqueror. Thus, winning girls may strongly discriminate against losers because sympathy leads them to avoid those whom they have beaten, while losing boys may strongly discriminate against winners because pride leads them to avoid those who have beaten them.

A testable implication is that under noncompetitive conditions, winning girls will show little ingroup-outgroup bias. By tossing two separate coins instead of a single one, the experimenter could cause one group to win and the other to lose, each independently of the other. Winners should then experience no conflict in interacting with losers since their satisfaction with the prize does not imply satisfaction with the others' loss. If winning girls especially desired to express their sympathy to losers, they might under this non-competitive condition even prefer to interact with the losing outgroup rather than the winning ingroup.[5]

What is striking in the present experiment is how little it evidently takes to move two randomly formed groups of strangers into mutual antipathy. Flipping a coin to decide the allocation of a scarce resource is commonly used in everyday social life in the effort to be fair. Yet this simple act triggered processes within the two groups of strangers that were farreaching enough to affect the perception of personal traits. Although subjects had no prior experience with anyone in the room, the flip of the coin was sufficient to shape their views of outgroup members as less friendly, less familiar, less considerate, and less desirable as associates than ingroup members.

However, the act of awarding a prize by chance is only apparently simple. Viewed as an intervention in the social system of the experiment, this single act ramifies widely into changes in the states of the two groups, of the persons within the groups, and of the interrelations among each of these units. In evincing ingroup-outgroup bias, subjects could have been reacting to any or all of these changes. Our reading of the present evidence is that they were reacting to the perceived emotional changes in themselves and others and to the consequent change in ease or difficulty of face-to-face interaction. Intergroup prejudice can obviously cause difficulties in interpersonal encounters. It is perhaps less obvious that the perceived difficulties of interpersonal encounters can cause intergroup prejudice.

Methodologically, the present experiment was not designed to test a theory, but to determine which, if any, of several experimental interventions suffice to produce a given effect. If the experimental situation is conceived as a social system, the experimental interventions correspond to actions designed to produce social change. There is thus a natural transition from laboratory methodology to the methodology of social action. The present

[5] This experiment has since been run with positive results.

study says to those who intervene in real-life systems that they can use the equitable method of allocating rewards by chance to produce group cohesiveness, rewards by chance to produce group cohesiveness, on the one hand, and intergroup divisiveness, on the other. To reduce divisiveness, we suggest, social practitioners should work to ease the difficulties of here-and-now interaction between the members of two groups. A parallel task for experimental inquiry is to find methods of distributing group rewards that will lessen rather than heighten the difficulties of interpersonal encounters across group lines.

REFERENCES

Blake, R. R., & Mouton, J. S. Reactions to intergroup competition under win-lose conditions. *Management Science*, 1961, **7**, 420–435.

Bond, J. R., & Vinacke, W. E. Coalitions in mixed-sex triads. *Sociometry*, 1961, **24**, 61–75.

Cartwright, D., & Zander, A. (Eds.) *Group dynamics: Research and theory.* Evanston, Illinois: Row, Peterson, 1960.

Educational Testing Service. *The Hidden Patterns Test.* Princeton, New Jersey: Author, 1962.

Heider, R. *The psychology of interpersonal relations.* New York: Wiley, 1958.

Lewin, K. *Resolving social conflicts.* New York: Harper, 1948.

Merton, R. K. *Social theory and social structure.* Glencoe, Illinois: Free Press, 1957.

Rosenblatt, P. C. Origins and effects of group ethnocentrism and nationalism. *Journal of Conflict Resolution*, 1964, **8**, 131–164.

Schmidt, H. D. Bigotry in school children. *Commentary*, 1960, **29**, 253–257.

Sherif, M., Harvey, O. J., White, J., Hood, W. R., & Sherif, C. W. *Intergroup conflict and cooperation: The robbers cave experiment.* Norman, Oklahoma: University Book Exchange, 1961.

Sumner, W. G. *Folkways.* Boston, Massachusetts: Ginn, 1906.

Terman, L. M., & Miles, C. C. *Sex and personality.* New York: McGraw-Hill, 1936.

Uesigi, T. K., & Vinacke, W. E. Strategy in a feminine game. *Sociometry*, 1963, **26**, 75–88.

REFERENCES

Alkire, A. A., Collum, M. E., Kaswan, J., & Love, L. R. Information exchange and accuracy of verbal communication under social power conditions. *Journal of Personality and Social Psychology*, 1968, **9**, 301–308.

Allen, V. L. Uncertainty of outcome and post-decision dissonance reduction. In L. Festinger (Ed.), *Conflict, decision, and dissonance*. Stanford, California: Stanford University Press, 1964. Pp. 34–42.

Allen, V. L. Situational factors in conformity. In L. Berkowitz (Ed.), *Advances in experimental social psychology*. Vol. 2. New York: Academic Press, 1965. Pp. 133–175.

Allport, F. H. The influence of the group upon association and thought. *Journal of Experimental Psychology*, 1920, **3**, 159–182.

Anderson, N. H. Primacy effects in personality impression formation using a generalized order effect paradigm. *Journal of Personality and Social Psychology*, 1965, **2**, 1–9.

Anderson, N. H. Application of a linear-serial model to a personality-impression task using serial presentation. *Journal of Personality and Social Psychology*, 1968, **10**, 354–362.

Anderson, N. H., & Barrios, A. A. Primacy effects in personality impression formation. *Journal of Abnormal and Social Psychology*, 1961, **63**, 346–350.

Anderson, N. H., & Hubert, S. Effects of concomitant verbal recall on order effects in personality impression formation. *Journal of Verbal Learning and Verbal Behavior*, 1963, **2**, 379–391.

Aristotle. *The rhetoric.* New York: Appleton-Century, 1932.

Aronson, E. The effect of effort on the attractiveness of rewarded and unrewarded stimuli. *Journal of Abnormal and Social Psychology,* 1961, **63**, 375–380.

Aronson, E. Dissonance theory: Progress and problems. In R. Abelson, E. Aronson, W. McGuire, T. Newcomb, M. Rosenberg, & P. Tannenbaum (Eds.), *Theories of cognitive consistency: A sourcebook.* Chicago, Illinois: Rand McNally, 1968. Pp. 5–27.

Aronson, E., & Carlsmith, J. M. Effect of the severity of threat on the devaluation of forbidden behavior. *Journal of Abnormal and Social Psychology,* 1963, **66**, 584–588.

Aronson, E., & Cope, V. My enemy's enemy is my friend. *Journal of Personality and Social Psychology,* 1968, **8**, 8–12.

Aronson, E., & Golden, B. The effect of relevant and irrelevant aspects of communicator credibility on opinion change. *Journal of Personality,* 1962, **30**, 135–146.

Aronson, E., & Linder, D. Gain and loss of esteem as determinants of interpersonal attractiveness. *Journal of Experimental Social Psychology,* 1965, **1**, 156–171.

Aronson, E., & Mills, J. The effect of severity of initiation on liking for a group. *Journal of Abnormal and Social Psychology,* 1959, **59**, 177–181.

Aronson, E., Turner, J. A., & Carlsmith, J. M. Communicator credibility and communication discrepancy as determinants of opinion change. *Journal of Abnormal and Social Psychology,* 1963, **67**, 31–36.

Aronson, E., & Worchel, P. Similarity versus liking as determinants of interpersonal attractiveness. *Psychonomic Science,* 1966, **5**, 157–158.

Asch, S. E. Forming impressions of personality. *Journal of Abnormal and Social Psychology,* 1946, **41**, 258–290.

Asch, S. E. *Social psychology.* Englewood Cliffs, New Jersey: Prentice Hall, 1952.

Azrin, N. H., Hutchinson, R. R., & Hake, D. F. Extinction-induced aggression. *Journal of the Experimental Analysis of Behavior,* 1966, **9**, 191–204.

Backman, C. W., & Secord, P. F. The effect of perceived liking on interpersonal attraction. *Human Relations,* 1959, **12**, 379–384.

Bales, R. F. *Interaction process analysis: A method for the study of small groups.* Reading, Massachusetts: Addison-Wesley, 1950.

Bales, R. F. *Personality and interpersonal behavior.* New York: Holt, Rinehart & Winston, 1970.

Bales, R. F., & Borgatta, E. F. Size of group as a factor in the interaction profile. In A. P. Hare, E. F. Borgatta, & R. F. Bales (Eds.), *Small Groups.* New York: Knopf, 1955. Pp. 396–413.

Bales, R. F., & Slater, P. E. Role differentiation in small decision-making groups. In T. Parsons, R. F. Bales, J. Olds, M. Zelditch, Jr., & P. E. Slater (Eds.), *Family socialization and interaction process.* Glencoe, Illinois: Free Press, 1955. Pp. 259–306.

Banta, T. J., & Hetherington, M. Relations between needs of friends and fiancés. *Journal of Abnormal and Social Psychology,* 1963, **66**, 401–404.

Bass, B. M. An analysis of the leaderless group discussion. *Journal of Applied Psychology,* 1949, **33**, 527–533.

Bass, B. M. *Organizational psychology.* Boston, Massachusetts: Allyn and Bacon, 1965.

Bateson, N. Familiarization, group discussion, and risk-taking. *Journal of Experimental Social Psychology,* 1966, **2**, 119–129.

Bavelas, A. A mathematical model for group structure. *Applied Anthropology,* 1948, **7**, 16–30.

Bavelas, A. Communication patterns in task oriented groups. *Journal of the Acoustical Society of America,* 1950, **22**, 725–730.

Bavelas, A., Hastorf, A. H., Gross, A. E., & Kite, W. R. Experiments on the alteration of group structure. *Journal of Experimental Social Psychology,* 1965, **1**, 55–70.

Bem, D. J. An experimental analysis of self-persuasion. *Journal of Experimental Social Psychology*, 1965, **1**, 199–218.

Bem, D. J. Self-perception: An alternative interpretation of cognitive dissonance phenomena. *Psychological Review*, 1967, **74**, 182–200.

Bem, D. J. The epistemological status of interpersonal simulations: A reply to Jones, Linder, Kiesler, Zanna, and Brehm. *Journal of Experimental Social Psychology*, 1968, **4**, 270–274.

Bem, D. J., & McConnell, H. K. Testing the self-perception explanation of dissonance phenomena: On the salience of premanipulation attitudes. *Journal of Personality and Social Psychology*, 1970, **14**, 23–31.

Bem, D. J., Wallach, M. A., & Kogan, N. Group decision making under risk of aversive consequences. *Journal of Personality and Social Psychology*, 1965, **1**, 453–460.

Bergin, A. E. The effect of dissonant persuasive communications upon changes in self-referring attitudes. *Journal of Personality*, 1962, **30**, 423–438.

Berkowitz, L. *Aggression: A social psychological analysis.* New York: McGraw-Hill, 1962.

Berkowitz, L. Aggressive cues in aggressive behavior and hostility catharsis. *Psychological Review*, 1964, **71**, 104–122.

Berkowitz, L. The concept of aggressive drive: Some additional considerations. In L. Berkowitz (Ed.), *Advances in experimental social psychology.* Vol. 2. New York: Academic Press, 1965. Pp. 301–329.

Berkowitz, L. The frustration-aggression hypothesis revisited. In L. Berkowitz (Ed.), *Roots of aggression.* New York: Atherton Press, 1969. Pp. 1–28.

Berkowitz, L., & Green, J. A. The stimulus qualities of the scapegoat. *Journal of Abnormal and Social Psychology*, 1962, **64**, 293–301.

Berkowitz, L., & LePage, A. Weapons as aggression-eliciting stimuli. *Journal of Personality and Social Psychology*, 1967, **7**, 202–207.

Berkowitz, L., & Macaulay, J. R. Some effects of differences in status level and status stability. *Human Relations*, 1961, **14**, 135–147.

Berscheid, E., & Walster, E. H. *Interpersonal Attraction.* Reading, Massachusetts: Addison-Wesley, 1969.

Bettleheim, B., & Janowitz, M. Ethnic tolerance: A function of social and personal control. *American Journal of Sociology*, 1949, **55**, 137–145.

Blake, R. R., & Mouton, J. S. Competition, communication, and conformity. In I. Berg & B. Bass (Eds.), *Conformity and deviation.* New York: Harper, 1961. Pp. 199–229.

Blalock, H. M. *Toward a theory of minority-group relations.* New York: Wiley, 1967.

Bochner, S., & Insko, C. A. Communicator discrepancy, source credibility, and opinion change. *Journal of Personality and Social Psychology*, 1966, **4**, 614–621.

Bostrom, R., Vlandis, J., & Rosenbaum, M. Grades as reinforcing contingencies and attitude change. *Journal of Educational Psychology*, 1961, **52**, 112–115.

Bramel, D. Dissonance, expectation, and the self. In R. Abelson, E. Aronson, W. McGuire, T. Newcomb, M. Rosenberg, & P. Tannenbaum (Eds.), *Theories of cognitive consistency: A sourcebook.* Chicago, Illinois: Rand McNally, 1968. Pp. 355–372.

Brehm, J. W. Post-decision changes in the desirability of alternatives. *Journal of Abnormal and Social Psychology*, 1956, **52**, 384–389.

Brehm, J. W. *A theory of psychological reactance.* New York: Academic Press, 1966.

Brehm, J. W., & Cohen, A. R. *Explorations in cognitive dissonance.* New York: Wiley, 1962.

Brock, T. C. Effects of prior dishonesty on post-decision dissonance. *Journal of Abnormal and Social Psychology*, 1963, **66**, 325–331.

Brock, T. C. Communication discrepancy and intent to persuade as determinants of counterargument production. *Journal of Experimental Social Psychology*, 1967, **3**, 296–309.

Brown, R. Models of attitude change. In R. Brown, E. Galanter, E. Hess, & G. Mandler (Contributors), *New directions in psychology*. New York: Holt, Rinehart and Winston, 1962. Pp. 1–85.

Brown, R. *Social psychology*. New York: Free Press, 1965.

Bruner, J. S., Shapiro, D., & Tagiuri, R. The meaning of traits in isolation and in combination. In R. Tagiuri and L. Petrullo (Eds.), *Person perception and interpersonal behavior*. Stanford, California: Stanford University Press, 1958. Pp. 277–288.

Burgess, E. W., Wallin, P., & Shultz, G. D. *Courtship, engagement and marriage*. Philadelphia, Pennsylvania: Lippincott, 1953.

Burgess, R. L. Communication networks: An experimental reevaluation. *Journal of Experimental Social Psychology*, 1968, 4, 324–337.

Burke, P. J. The development of task and social-emotional role differentiation. *Sociometry*, 1967, 30, 379–392.

Burnstein, E., & Worchel, P. Arbitrariness of frustration and its consequences for aggression in a social situation. *Journal of Personality*, 1962, 30, 528–541.

Byrne, D. Response to attitude similarity-dissimilarity as a function of affiliation need. *Journal of Personality*, 1962, 30, 164–177.

Byrne, D. Attitudes and attraction. In L. Berkowitz (Ed.), *Advances in experimental social psychology*. Vol. 4. New York: Academic Press, 1969. Pp. 35–89.

Byrne, D., & Blaylock, B. Similarity and assumed similarity of attitudes between husbands and wives. *Journal of Abnormal and Social Psychology*, 1963, 67, 636–640.

Byrne, D., & Clore, G. L., Jr. Predicting interpersonal attraction toward strangers presented in three different stimulus modes. *Psychonomic Science*, 1966, 4, 239–240.

Byrne, D., & Griffitt, W. A developmental investigation of the law of attraction. *Journal of Personality and Social Psychology*, 1966, 4, 699–702. (a)

Byrne, D., & Griffitt, W. Similarity versus liking: A clarification. *Psychonomic Science*, 1966, 6, 295–296. (b)

Byrne, D., & Nelson, D. Attraction as a linear function of proportion of positive reinforcements. *Journal of Personality and Social Psychology*, 1965, 1, 659–663.

Byrne, D., Nelson, D., & Reeves, K. Effects of consensual validation and invalidation on attraction as a function of verifiability. *Journal of Experimental Social Psychology*, 1966, 2, 98–107.

Calder, B. J., & Insko, C. A. Two investigations of the relation of cognitive and memorial processes to persuasion. Unpublished manuscript, 1971.

Calhoun, J. B. Population density and social pathology. *Scientific American*, 1962, 206, 139–148.

Campbell, D. T. Factors relevant to the validity of experiments in social settings. *Psychological Bulletin*, 1957, 54, 297–312.

Campbell, D. T. Conformity in psychology's theories of acquired behavioral dispositions. In I. A. Berg & B. M. Bass (Eds.), *Conformity and deviation*. New York: Harper and Row, 1961. Pp. 101–142.

Campbell, D. T. Ethnocentric and other altruistic motives. In D. Levine (Ed.), *Nebraska symposium on motivation*. Vol. 13. Lincoln, Nebraska: University of Nebraska Press, 1965. Pp. 283–311.

Carlson, E. R. Attitude change and attitude structure. *Journal of Abnormal and Social Psychology*, 1956, 52, 256–261.

Carnegie, D. *How to win friends and influence people*. New York: Simon & Schuster, 1937.

Carter, L., Haythorn, W., Shriver, B., & Lanzetta, J. The behavior of leaders and other group members. *Journal of Abnormal and Social Psychology*, 1951, 46, 589–595.

Cartwright, D., & Harary, F. Structural balance: A generalization of Heider's theory. *Psychological Review*, 1956, 63, 277–293.

Cattell, R. B., & Nesselroade, J. R. Likeness and completeness theories examined by 16 personality factor measures on stably and unstably married couples. *Journal of Personality and Social Psychology,* 1967, **7**, 351–361.

Chapanis, N. P., & Chapanis, A. Cognitive dissonance: Five years later. *Psychological Bulletin,* 1964, **61**, 1–22.

Cialdini, R. B., & Insko, C. A. Attitudinal verbal reinforcement as a function of informational consistency: A further test of the two-factor theory. *Journal of Personality and Social Psychology,* 1969, **12**, 342–350.

Clark, R. D., III, & Willems, E. P. Where is the risky shift? Dependence on instructions. *Journal of Personality and Social Psychology,* 1969, **13**, 215–221.

Clore, G. L., & Baldridge, B. Interpersonal attraction: The role of agreement and topic interest. *Journal of Personality and Social Psychology,* 1968, **9**, 340–346.

Collins, B. E. The effect of monetary inducements on the amount of attitude change induced by forced compliance. In A. Elms (Ed.), *Role playing, reward and attitude change.* Princeton, New Jersey: Van Nostrand-Reinhold, 1969. Pp. 209–223.

Collins, B. E., & Guetzkow, H. *A social psychology of group processes for decision-making.* New York: Wiley, 1964.

Collins, B. E., & Raven, B. H. Group structure: Attraction, coalitions, communication, and power. In G. Lindzey & E. Aronson (Eds.), *The handbook of social psychology.* (2nd ed.) Vol. 4. Reading, Massachusetts: Addison-Wesley, 1969. Pp. 102–204.

Cook, T. D., & Insko, C. A. Persistence of attitude change as a function of conclusion reexposure: A laboratory-field experiment. *Journal of Personality and Social Psychology,* 1968, **9**, 322–328.

Cooper, J., & Worchel, S. Role of undesired consequences in arousing cognitive dissonance. *Journal of Personality and Social Psychology,* 1970, **16**, 199–206.

Coser, L. *The functions of social conflict,* New York: Free Press, 1956.

Cowen, E. L., Landes, J., & Schäet, D. E. The effects of mild frustration on the expression of prejudiced attitudes. *Journal of Abnormal and Social Psychology,* 1959, **58**, 33–38.

Cronbach, L. J. Processes affecting scores on "understanding of others" and "assumed similarity." *Psychological Bulletin,* 1955, **52**, 177–193.

Cronbach, L. J. Proposals leading to analytic treatment of social perception scores. In R. Tagiuri & L. Petrullo (Eds.), *Person perception and interpersonal behavior.* Stanford, California: Stanford University Press, 1958. Pp. 353–379.

Crutchfield, R. S. Conformity and character. *American Psychologist,* 1955, **10**, 191–198.

Darley, J. M., & Aronson, E. Self-evaluation vs. direct anxiety reduction as determinants of the fear-affiliation relationship. *Journal of Experimental Social Psychology,* 1966, Supplement 1, 66–79.

Darley, J. M., & Latané, B. Bystander intervention in emergencies: Diffusion of responsibility. *Journal of Personality and Social Psychology,* 1968, **8**, 377–383.

Dashiell, J. F. An experimental analysis of some group effects. *Journal of Abnormal and Social Psychology,* 1930, **15**, 190–199.

Davies, J. C. Toward a theory of revolution. *American Sociological Review,* 1962, **27**, 5–19.

Davis, J. H. Individual-group problem solving, subject preference, and problem type. *Journal of Personality and Social Psychology,* 1969, **13**, 362–374.

Deutsch, M., & Collins, M. E. *Interracial housing: A psychological evaluation of a social experiment.* Minneapolis, Minnesota: University of Minnesota Press, 1951.

Deutsch, M., & Gerard, H. B. A study of normative and informational social influences upon individual judgment. *Journal of Abnormal and Social Psychology,* 1955, **51**, 629–636.

Deutsch, M., & Solomon, L. Reactions to evaluations by others as influenced by self-evaluation. *Sociometry,* 1959, **22**, 93–112.

Dickoff, H. Reactions to evaluations by another person as a function of self-evaluation and the interaction context. Unpublished doctoral dissertation, Duke University, 1961. Also reported in Jones, E. E. *Ingratiation*. New York: Appleton-Century-Crofts, 1964.

Dion, K. L., Baron, R. S., & Miller, N. Why do groups make riskier decisions than individuals? In L. Berkowitz (Ed.), *Advances in experimental social psychology.* Vol. 5. New York: Academic Press, 1970. Pp. 306–377.

Di Vesta, J., & Merwin, J. C. The effects of need-oriented communications on attitude change. *Journal of Abnormal and Social Psychology,* 1960, **60**, 80–85.

Doise, W. Intergroup relations and polarization of individual and collective judgments. *Journal of Personality and Social Psychology,* 1969, **12**, 136–143.

Dollard, J., Doob, L., Miller, N., Mowrer, O., & Sears, R. *Frustration and aggression.* New Haven, Connecticut: Yale University Press, 1939.

Elms, A. C. Influence of fantasy ability on attitude change through role playing. *Journal of Personality and Social Psychology,* 1966, **4**, 36–43.

Felipe, A. I. Evaluative versus descriptive consistency in trait inferences. *Journal of Personality and Social Psychology,* 1970, **16**, 627–638.

Ferguson, C. K., & Kelley, H. H. Significant factors in overevaluation of own-group's product. *Journal of Abnormal and Social Psychology,* 1964, **69**, 223–228.

Festinger, L. Informal social communication. *Psychological Review,* 1950, **57**, 271–282.

Festinger, L. A theory of social comparison processes. *Human Relations,* 1954, **7**, 117–140.

Festinger, L. *A theory of cognitive dissonance.* Stanford, California: Stanford University Press, 1957.

Festinger, L., & Aronson, E. The arousal and reduction of dissonance in social contexts. In D. Cartwright & A. Zander (Eds.), *Group dynamics: Research and theory.* (2nd ed.) New York: Harper & Row, 1960. Pp. 214–231.

Festinger, L., & Carlsmith, J. M. Cognitive consequences of forced compliance. *Journal of Abnormal and Social Psychology,* 1959, **58**, 203–211.

Festinger, L., Schachter, S., & Back, K. *Social pressures in informal groups: A study of human factors in housing.* New York: Harper, 1950.

Fiedler, F. E. The leader's psychological distance and group effectiveness. In D. Cartwright & A. Zander (Eds.), *Group dynamics.* (2nd ed.) Evanston, Illinois: Row, Peterson, 1960. Pp. 586–606.

Fiedler, F. E. The effect of leadership and cultural heterogeneity on group performance: A test of the contingency model. *Journal of Experimental Social Psychology,* 1966, **2**, 237–264.

Fiedler, F. E., Warrington, W. G., & Blaisdell, F. J. Unconscious attitudes as correlates of sociometric choice in a social group. *Journal of Abnormal and Social Psychology,* 1952, **47**, 790–796.

Fishbein, M. An investigation of the relationships between beliefs about an object and the attitude toward that object. *Human Relations,* 1963, **16**, 233–239.

Fishbein, M., & Hunter, R. Summation versus balance in attitude organization and change. *Journal of Abnormal and Social Psychology,* 1964, **69**, 505–510.

Fishbein, M., & Raven, B. H. The AB scales: An operational definition of belief and attitude. *Human Relations,* 1962, **15**, 35–44.

Flanders, J. P., & Thistlethwaite, D. L. Effects of familiarization and group discussion upon risk taking. *Journal of Personality and Social Psychology,* 1967, **5**, 91–97.

Freedman, J. L. Involvement, discrepancy, and change. *Journal of Abnormal and Social Psychology,* 1964, **69**, 290–295.

Freedman, J. L., & Doob, A. N. *Deviancy.* New York: Academic Press, 1968.

Freedman, J. L., & Fraser, S. C. Compliance without pressure: The foot-in-the-door technique. *Journal of Personality and Social Psychology,* 1966, **4**, 195–202.

Freedman, J. L., Klevansky, S., & Ehrlich, P. R. The effect of crowding on human task performance. *Journal of Applied Social Psychology,* 1971, **1,** 7–25.

Gerard, H. B., & Mathewson, G. C. The effects of severity of initiation on liking for a group: A replication. *Journal of Experimental Social Psychology,* 1966, **2,** 278–287.

Gerard, H. B., & Miller, N. Group dynamics. In P. R. Farnsworth (Ed.), *Annual review of psychology.* Vol. 18. Palo Alto, California: Annual Review, 1967. Pp. 287–332.

Gibb, C. A. Leadership. In G. Lindzey & E. Aronson (Eds.), *The handbook of social psychology.* (2nd ed.) Vol. 4. Reading, Massachusetts: Addison-Wesley, 1969. Pp. 205–282.

Gibb, J. R. The effects of group size and of threat reduction upon creativity in a problem-solving situation. *American Psychologist,* 1951, **6,** 324. (Abstract).

Greenbaum, C. W. Effect of situational and personality variables on improvisation and attitude change. *Journal of Personality and Social Psychology,* 1966, **4,** 260–269.

Greenspoon, J. The reinforcing effect of two spoken sounds on the frequency of two responses. *American Journal of Psychology,* 1955, **68,** 409–416.

Greenwald, A. G. Cognitive learning, cognitive responses to persuasion, and attitude change. In A. G. Greenwald, T. C. Brock, & T. M. Ostrom (Eds.), *Psychological foundations of attitudes.* New York: Academic Press, 1968. Pp. 147–170.

Guetzkow, H., & Simon, H. A. The impact of certain communication nets upon organization and performance in task-oriented groups. *Management Science,* 1955, **1,** 233–250.

Guhl, A. M. The social order of chickens. *Scientific American,* 1956, **194,** 42–46.

Hall, E. T. *The silent language.* Garden City, New York: Doubleday, 1959.

Harvey, O. J., Hunt, D. E., & Schroder, H. M. *Conceptual systems and personality organization.* New York: Wiley, 1961.

Hastorf, A. H., Kite, W. R., Gross, A. E., & Wolfe, L. J. The perception and evaluation of behavior change. *Sociometry,* 1965, **28,** 400–410.

Heider, F. Social perception and phenomenal causality. *Psychological Review,* 1944, **51,** 358–374.

Heider, F. Attitudes and cognitive organization. *Journal of Psychology,* 1946, **21,** 107–112.

Heider, F. *The psychology of interpersonal relations.* New York: Wiley, 1958.

Henchy, T., & Glass, D. C. Evaluation apprehension and the social facilitation of dominant and subordinate responses. *Journal of Personality and Social Psychology,* 1968, **10,** 446–454.

Hendrick, C., & Costantini, A. F. Effects of varying trait inconsistency and response requirements on the primacy effect in impression formation. *Journal of Personality and Social Psychology,* 1970, **15,** 158–164.

Heslin, R. Predicting group task effectiveness from member characteristics. *Psychological Bulletin,* 1964, **62,** 248–256.

Higbee, K. L. Fifteen years of fear arousal: Research on threat appeals. *Psychological Bulletin,* 1969, **72,** 426–444.

Hildum, D. C., & Brown, R. W. Verbal reinforcement and interviewer bias. *Journal of Abnormal and Social Psychology,* 1956, **53,** 108–111.

Hoffman, L. R., & Maier, N. R. F. Sex differences, sex composition, and group problem solving. *Journal of Abnormal and Social Psychology,* 1961, **63,** 453–456.

Homans, G. C. *The human group.* New York: Harcourt, Brace, 1950.

Hoover, J. E. Crime in the United States. *Uniform Crime Reports,* August, 1966, U. S. Department of Justice, Washington, D. C.

Horowitz, I. A. Effect of choice and locus of dependence on helping behavior. *Journal of Personality and Social Psychology,* 1968, **8,** 373–376.

Hovland, C. I., & Pritzker, H. A. Extent of opinion change as a function of amount of opinion change advocated. *Journal of Abnormal and Social Psychology*, 1957, **54**, 257–261.

Hovland, C. I., & Weiss, W. The influence of source credibility on communication effectiveness. *Public Opinion Quarterly*, 1952, **15**, 635–650.

Howells, L., & Becker, S. Seating arrangement and leadership emergence. *Journal of Abnormal and Social Psychology*, 1962, **64**, 148–150.

Hoyt, G. C., & Stoner, J. A. F. Leadership and group decisions involving risk. *Journal of Experimental Social Psychology*, 1968, **4**, 275–284.

Hull, C. L. *Principles of behavior*. New York: Appleton-Century-Crofts, 1943.

Hurwitz, J. I., Zander, A. F., & Hymovitch, B. Some effects of power on the relations among group members. In D. Cartwright & A. Zander (Eds.), *Group dynamics: Research and theory*. Evanton, Illinois: Row, Peterson, 1953. Pp. 483–492.

Insko, C. A. Primacy versus recency as a function of the timing of arguments and measures. *Journal of Abnormal and Social Psychology*, 1964, **69**, 381–391.

Insko, C. A. Verbal reinforcement of attitude. *Journal of Personality and Social Psychology*, 1965, **2**, 621–623.

Insko, C. A., & Butzine, K. W. Rapport, awareness, and verbal reinforcement of attitude. *Journal of Personality and Social Psychology*, 1967, **2**, 621–623.

Insko, C. A., & Cialdini, R. B. A test of three interpretations of attitudinal verbal reinforcement. *Journal of Personality and Social Psychology*, 1969, **12**, 333–341.

Insko, C. A., & Melson, W. H. Verbal reinforcement of attitude in laboratory and nonlaboratory contexts. *Journal of Personality*, 1969, **37**, 25–40.

Izard, C. E. Personality similarity and friendship. *Journal of Abnormal and Social Psychology*, 1960, **61**, 47–51.

Jacobs, R. C., & Campbell, D. T. The perpetuation of an arbitrary tradition through several generations of a laboratory microculture. *Journal of Abnormal and Social Psychology*, 1961, **62**, 649–658.

Janis, I. L. Effects of fear arousal on attitude change: Recent developments in theory and experimental research. In L. Berkowitz (Ed.), *Advances in experimental social psychology*. Vol. 3. New York: Academic Press, 1967. Pp. 167–224.

Janis, I. L., & Feshbach, S. Effects of fear-arousing communications. *Journal of Abnormal and Social Psychology*, 1953, **48**, 78–92.

Janis, I. L., & Hoffman, D. Facilitating effects of daily contact between partners who make a decision to cut down on smoking. *Journal of Personality and Social Psychology*, 1971, **17**, 25–35.

Janis, I. L., & King, B. T. The influence of role-playing on opinion change. *Journal of Abnormal and Social Psychology*, 1954, **49**, 211–218.

Janis, I. L., & Mann, L. Effectiveness of emotional role-playing in modifying smoking habits and attitudes. *Journal of Experimental Research in Personality*, 1965, **1**, 84–90.

Janis, I. L., & Mann, L. A. A conflict-theory approach to attitude change and decision making. In A. G. Greenwald, T. C. Brock, & T. M. Ostrom (Eds.), *Psychological foundations of attitudes*. New York: Academic Press, 1968. Pp. 327–360.

Janis, I. L., & Terwilliger, R. F. An experimental study of psychological resistances to fear-arousing communications. *Journal of Abnormal and Social Psychology*, 1962, **65**, 403–410.

Jecker, J. D. The cognitive effects of conflict and dissonance. In L. Festinger (Ed.), *Conflict, decision, and dissonance*. Stanford, California: Stanford University Press, 1964. Pp. 21–30.

Jellison, J. M., & Riskind, J. A social comparison of abilities interpretation of risk-taking behavior. *Journal of Personality and Social Psychology*, 1970, **15**, 375–390.

Johnson, H. H., & Torcivia, J. M. Group and individual performance on a single-stage task as a function of distribution of individual performance. *Journal of Experimental Social Psychology*, 1967, 3, 266–273.

Jones, E. E. *Ingratiation: A social psychological analysis.* New York: Appleton-Century-Crofts, 1964.

Jones, E. E., & Davis, K. E. From acts to dispositions. In L. Berkowitz (Ed.), *Advances in experimental social psychology.* Vol. 2. New York: Academic Press, 1965. Pp. 219–266.

Jones, E. E., & Gerard, H. B. *Foundations of social psychology.* New York: Wiley, 1967.

Jones, E. E., & Goethals, G. R. *Order effects in impression formation: Attribution context and the nature of the entity.* New York: General Learning Press, 1971.

Jones, E. E., & Harris, V. A. The attribution of attitudes. *Journal of Experimental Social Psychology*, 1967, 3, 1–24.

Jones, E. E., Rock, L., Shaver, K., Goethals, G., & Ward, L. Pattern of performance and ability attribution: An unexpected primacy effect. *Journal of Personality and Social Psychology*, 1968, 10, 317–340.

Jones, E. E., Stires, L. K., Shaver, K. G., & Harris, V. A. Evaluation of an ingratiator by target persons and bystanders. *Journal of Personality*, 1968, 36, 349–385.

Jones, E. E., Worchel, S., Goethals, G. R., & Grumet, J. Prior expectancy and behavioral extremity as determinants of attitude attribution. *Journal of Experimental Social Psychology*, 1971, 7, 59–80.

Jones, R. A., Linder, D. E., Kiesler, C. A., Zanna, M., & Brehm, J. W. Internal states or external stimuli: Observers' attitude judgments and the dissonance-theory-self-persuasion controversy. *Journal of Experimental Social Psychology*, 1968, 4, 247–269.

Kelly, G. A. *The psychology of personal constructs.* Vol. 1. New York: Norton, 1955.

Kelley, H. H. Communication in experimentally created hierarchies. *Human Relations*, 1951, 4, 39–56.

Kelley, H. H. Attribution theory in social psychology. In D. Levine (Ed.), *Nebraska symposium on motivation.* Lincoln, Nebraska: University of Nebraska Press, 1967. Pp. 192–238.

Kelley, H. H., & Thibaut, J. W. Group problem solving. In G. Lindzey & E. Aronson (Eds.), *Handbook of social psychology.* Vol. 4. Reading, Massachusetts: Addison-Wesley, 1969. Pp. 1–101.

Kelley, H. H., Thibaut, J. W., Radloff, R., & Mundy, D. The development of cooperation in the "minimal social situation." *Psychological Monographs*, 1962, 76, No. 19.

Kelman, H. C. Compliance, indentification and internalization: Three processes of attitude change. *Journal of Conflict Resolution*, 1958, 2, 51–60.

Kelman, H. C. Effects of role orientation and value orientation on the nature of attitude change. Paper presented at the meeting of the Eastern Psychological Association, New York, April, 1960.

Kelman, H. C., & Hovland, C. I. "Reinstatement" of the communicator in delayed measurement of opinion change. *Journal of Abnormal and Social Psychology*, 1953, 48, 327–335.

Kerckhoff, A. C., & Davis, K. E. Value consensus and need complementarity in mate selection. *American Sociological Review*, 1962, 27, 295–303.

Kerrick, J. S. The effect of relevant and non-relevant sources on attitude change. *Journal of Social Psychology*, 1958, 47, 15–20.

Kerrick, J. S. News pictures, captions and the point of resolution. *Journalism Quarterly*, 1959, 36, 183–188.

Kirscht, J. P., Lodahl, T. M., & Haire, M. Some factors in the selection of leaders by members of small groups. *Journal of Abnormal and Social Psychology*, 1959, 58, 406–408.

Knutson, A. L. Quiet and vocal groups. *Sociometry*, 1960, **23**, 36–49.

Koeske, G. F., & Crano, W. D. The effect of congruous and incongruous source-statement combinations upon the judged credibility of a communication. *Journal of Experimental Social Psychology*, 1968, **4**, 384–399.

Krech, D., & Crutchfield, R. S. *Theory and problems of social psychology.* New York: McGraw-Hill, 1948.

Kruglanski, A. W. Attributing trustworthiness in supervisor-worker relations. *Journal of Experimental Social Psychology*, 1970, **6**, 214–232.

Latané, B. Gregariousness and fear in laboratory rats. *Journal of Experimental Social Psychology*, 1969, **5**, 61–69.

Latané, B., & Darley, J. M. Social determinants of bystander intervention in emergencies. In J. Macauley & L. Berkowitz (Eds.), *Altruism and helping behavior.* New York: Academic Press, 1970. Pp. 13–27.

Leavitt, H. J. Some effects of certain communication patterns on group performance. *Journal of Abnormal and Social Psychology*, 1951, **46**, 38–50.

Lefkowitz, M., Blake, R. R., & Mouton, J. S. Status factors in pedestrian violation of traffic signals. *Journal of Abnormal and Social Psychology*, 1955, **51**, 704–705.

Lerner, M. J. Evaluation of performance as a function of performer's reward and attractiveness. *Journal of Personality and Social Psychology*, 1965, **1**, 355–360.

Lerner, M. J. The desire for justice and reactions to victims. In J. Macaulay & L. Berkowitz (Eds.), *Altruism and helping behavior.* New York: Academic Press, 1970. Pp. 205–230.

Lerner, M. J., & Matthews, G. Reactions to suffering of others under conditions of indirect responsibility. *Journal of Personality and Social Psychology*, 1967, **5**, 319–325.

Lerner, M. J., & Simmons, C. H. Observer's reaction to the "innocent victim": Compassion or rejection? *Journal of Personality and Social Psychology*, 1966, **4**, 203–210.

Leventhal, H., Singer, R., & Jones, S. Effects of fear and specificity of recommendation upon attitudes and behavior. *Journal of Personality and Social Psychology*, 1965, **2**, 20–29.

Levin, S. M. The effect of awareness on verbal conditioning. *Journal of Experimental Psychology*, 1961, **61**, 67–75.

Levinger, G., & Schneider, D. J. Test of the "risk is a value" hypothesis. *Journal of Personality and Social Psychology*, 1969, **11**, 165–169.

Lewin, K. *A dynamic theory of personality.* New York: McGraw-Hill, 1935.

Linder, D. E., Cooper, J., & Wicklund, R. A. Pre-exposure persuasion as a result of commitment to pre-exposure effort. *Journal of Experimental Social Psychology*, 1968, **4**, 470–482.

Lott, D. F., & Sommer, R. Seating arrangement and status. *Journal of Personality and Social Psychology*, 1967, **7**, 90–95.

Luchins, A. S. Primacy-recency in impression formation. In C. I. Hovland (Ed.), *The order of presentation in persuasion.* New Haven, Connecticut: Yale University Press, 1957. Pp. 33–61. (a)

Luchins, A. S. Experimental attempts to minimize the impact of first impressions. In C. I. Hovland (Ed.), *The order of presentation in persuasion.* New Haven, Connecticut: Yale University Press, 1957. Pp. 62–75. (b)

McDougall, W. *An introduction to social psychology.* London: Methuen, 1908.

McGrath, J. E., & Altman, I. *Small group research: A synthesis and critique of the field.* New York: Holt, 1966.

McGuire, W. J. Persistence of the resistance to persuasion induced by various types of prior belief defenses. *Journal of Abnormal and Social Psychology*, 1962, **64**, 241–248.

McGuire, W. J. Inducing resistance to persuasion. In L. Berkowitz (Ed.), *Advances in experimental social psychology.* Vol. I. New York: Academic Press, 1964. Pp. 191–229.

McGuire, W. J. Personality and susceptibility to social influence. In E. F. Borgatta, & W. Lambert (Eds.), *Handbook of personality theory and research.* Chicago, Illinois: Rand McNally, 1968. Pp. 1130–1188.

McGuire, W. J., & Papageorgis, D. The relative efficacy of various types of prior belief-defense in producing immunity against persuasion. *Journal of Abnormal and Social Psychology,* 1961, **62,** 327–337.

Mallick, S. K., & McCandless, B. R. A study of cartharsis of aggression. *Journal of Personality and Social Psychology,* 1966, **4,** 591–596.

Mann, L., Janis, I. L., & Chaplin, R. Effects of anticipation of forthcoming information on predecisional processes. *Journal of Personality and Social Psychology,* 1969, **11,** 10–16.

Mann, R. D. A review of the relationships between personality and performance in small groups. *Psychological Bulletin,* 1959, **56,** 241–270.

Marquis, D. G. Individual responsibility and group decisions involving risk. *Industrial Management Review,* 1962, **3,** 8–23.

Mettee, D. R. Changes in liking as a function of the magnitude and affect of sequential evaluations. *Journal of Experimental Social Psychology,* 1971, **7,** 157–172. (a)

Mettee, D. R. The true discerner as a potent source of positive affect. *Journal of Experimental Social Psychology,* 1971, **7,** 292–303. (b)

Milgram, S. Some conditions of obedience and disobedience to authority. *Human Relations,* 1965, **18,** 57–76.

Miller, N. E. The frustration-aggression hypothesis. *Psychological Review,* 1941, **48,** 337–342.

Miller, N. E., & Bugelski, R. Minor studies in aggression: The influence of frustrations imposed by the in-group on attitudes expressed toward out-groups. *Journal of Psychology,* 1948, **25,** 437–442.

Miller, N., & Campbell, D. T. Recency and primacy in persuasion as a function of the timing of speeches and measurements. *Journal of Abnormal and Social Psychology,* 1959, **59,** 1–9.

Miller, N., Campbell, D. T., Twedt, A., & O'Connell, J. Similarity, contrast, and complementarity in friendship choice. *Journal of Personality and Social Psychology,* 1966, **3,** 3–12.

Moscovici, S., & Zavalloni, M. The group as a polarizer of attitudes. *Journal of Personality and Social Psychology,* 1969, **12,** 125–135.

Mulder, M. Communication structure, decision structure and group performance. *Sociometry,* 1960, **23,** 1–14.

Myers, D. G., & Bishop, G. D. Discussion effects on racial attitudes. *Science,* 1970, **169,** 778–779.

Nel, E., Helmreich, R., & Aronson, E. Opinion change in the advocate as a function of the persuasibility of his audience: A clarification of the meaning of dissonance. *Journal of Personality and Social Psychology,* 1969, **12,** 117–124.

Newcomb, T. M. *The acquaintance process.* New York: Holt, Rinehart and Winston, 1961.

Nisbett, R. E., & Schachter, S. Cognitive manipulation of pain. *Journal of Experimental Social Psychology,* 1966, **2,** 227–236.

O'Dell, J. W. Group size and emotional interaction. *Journal of Personality and Social Psychology,* 1968, **8,** 75–78.

Orne, M. T. On the social psychology of the psychological experiment: With particular reference to demand characteristics and their implications. *American Psychologists,* 1962, **17,** 776–783.

Osgood, C. E. Studies on the generality of affective meaning systems. *American Psychologist*, 1962, **17**, 10–28.

Osgood, C. E., & Tannenbaum, P. H. The principle of congruity in the prediction of attitude change. *Psychological Review*, 1955, **62**, 42–55.

Papageorgis, D., & McGuire, W. J. The generality of immunity to persuasion produced by pre-exposure to weakened counterarguments. *Journal of Abnormal and Social Psychology*, 1961, **62**, 475–481.

Parkinson, C. N. *Parkinson's law, and other studies in administration* (Sentry, ed.). Boston, Massachusetts: Houghton-Mifflin, 1957.

Parsons, T. *The social system.* Glencoe, Illinois: Free Press, 1951.

Pastore, N. The role of arbitrariness in the frustration-aggression hypothesis. *Journal of Abnormal and Social Psychology*, 1952, **47**, 728–731.

Peabody, D. Trait inferences: Evaluative and descriptive aspects. *Journal of Personality and Social Psychology*, 1967, **7**, Monograph, Whole No. 644.

Peabody, D. Evaluative and descriptive aspects in personality perception: A reappraisal. *Journal of Personality and Social Psychology*, 1970, **16**, 639–646.

Peterson, R. C., & Thurstone, L. L. *The effect of motion pictures on the social attitudes of high school children.* New York: Macmillan, 1933.

Rabbie, J. M., & Horwitz, M. Arousal of ingroup-outgroup bias by a chance win or loss. *Journal of Personality and Social Psychology*, 1969, **13**, 269–277.

Raven, B. H. A bibliography of publications relating to the small group. University of California, Los Angeles, 1969 [Supplement to Technical Report No. 24, Contract Nonr-233(54)].

Richardson, H. M. Studies of mental resemblances between husbands and wives and between friends. *Psychological Bulletin*, 1939, **36**, 104–120.

Richardson, H. M. Community of values as a factor in friendships of college and adult women. *Journal of Social Psychology*, 1940, **11**, 303–312.

Robinson, J. E., & Insko, C. A. Attributed belief similarity-dissimilarity versus race as determinants of prejudice: A further test of Rokeach's theory. *Journal of Experimental Research in Personality*, 1969, **4**, 72–77.

Roby, T. B. *Small group performance.* Chicago, Illinois: Rand McNally, 1968.

Roby, T. B., & Lanzetta, J. T. Considerations in the analysis of group tasks. *Psychological Bulletin*, 1958, **55**, 88–101.

Rokeach, M., Smith, P. W., & Evans, R. I. Two kinds of prejudice or one? In M. Rokeach (Ed.), *The open and closed mind.* New York: Basic Books, 1960. Pp. 132–168.

Rosenbaum, M. E., & Levin, I. P. Impression formation as a function of source credibility and order of presentation of contradictory information. *Journal of Personality and Social Psychology*, 1968, **10**, 167–174.

Rosenberg, M. J. Cognitive structure and attitudinal affect. *Journal of Abnormal and Social Psychology*, 1956, **53**, 367–372.

Rosenberg, M. J. An analysis of affective-cognitive consistency. In C. I. Hovland & M. J. Rosenberg (Eds.), *Attitude organization and change.* New Haven, Connecticut: Yale University Press, 1960. Pp. 15–64.

Rosenberg, S., & Olshan, K. Evaluative and descriptive aspects in personality perception. *Journal of Personality and Social Psychology*, 1970, **16**, 619–626.

Ross, E. A. *Social psychology: An outline and source book.* New York: Macmillan, 1908.

Rule, B. G., & Evans, J. F. Familiarization, the presence of others and group discussion effects on risk taking. *Representative Research in Social Psychology*, 1971, **2**, 28–32.

Sample, J. A., & Wilson, T. R. Leader behavior, group productivity, and rating of least preferred co-worker. *Journal of Personality and Social Psychology*, 1965, **1**, 266–270.

Schachter, S. Deviation, rejection, and communication. *Journal of Abnormal and Social Psychology*, 1951, **46**, 190–207.

Schachter, S. *The psychology of affiliation.* Stanford, California: Stanford University Press, 1959.

Schachter, S. The interaction of cognitive and physiological determinants of emotional state. In L. Berkowitz (Ed.), *Advances in experimental social psychology.* Vol. 1. New York: Academic Press, 1964. Pp. 49–80.

Schachter, S., & Singer, J. E. Cognitive, social, and physiological determinants of emotional state. *Psychological Review,* 1962, **69,** 379–399.

Schachter, S., & Wheeler, L. Epinephrine, chlorpromazine, and amusement. *Journal of Abnormal and Social Psychology,* 1962, **65,** 121–128.

Schooley, M. Personality resemblance among married couples. *Journal of Abnormal and Social Psychology,* 1936, **31,** 340–347.

Schopler, J., & Compere, J. S. Effects of being kind or harsh to another on liking. *Journal of Personality and Social Psychology,* 1971, **20,** 155–159.

Schopler, J., & Matthews, M. W. The influence of the perceived causal locus of partner's dependence on the use of interpersonal power. *Journal of Personality and Social Psychology,* 1965, **2,** 609–612.

Schutz, W. C. The harvard compatibility experiment. In A. P. Hare, E. F. Borgatta, & R. F. Bales (Eds.), *Small groups.* (rev. ed.) New York: Knopf, 1966. Pp. 555–562.

Scott, W. A. Attitude change through reward of verbal behavior. *Journal of Abnormal and Social Psychology,* 1957, **55,** 72–75.

Scott, W. A. Attitude change by response reinforcement: Replication and extension. *Sociometry,* 1959, **22,** 328–335.

Sensenig, J., & Brehm, J. W. Attitude change from an implied threat to attitudinal freedom. *Journal of Personality and Social Psychology,* 1968, **8,** 324–330.

Shaw, M. E. Scaling group tasks: A method for dimensional analysis. University of Florida, Gainesville, 1963 [Technical Report No. 1, Contract Nonr 580(11)].

Shaw, M. E. Communication networks. In L. Berkowitz (Ed.), *Advances in experimental social psychology.* Vol. 1. New York: Academic Press, 1964. Pp. 111–147.

Sherif, M. A study of some social factors in perception. *Archives of Psychology,* 1935, **27,** No. 187.

Sherif, M. Experimental study of intergroup relations. In J. H. Rohrer & M. Sherif (Eds.), *Social psychology at the crossroads.* New York: Harper & Row, 1951. Pp. 388–426.

Sherif, M., Harvey, O. J., White, B. J., Hood, W. R., & Sherif, C. *Intergroup conflict and cooperation: The robbers cave experiment.* Norman, Oklahoma: University Book Exchange, 1961.

Sherif, M., & Sherif, C. W. *Groups in harmony and tension.* New York: Harper, 1953.

Sherif, M., & Sherif, C. W. *Social psychology.* New York: Harper & Row, 1969

Shrauger, J. S., & Jones, S. C. Social validation and interpersonal evaluations. *Journal of Experimental Social Psychology,* 1968, **4,** 315–323.

Sidowski, J. B. Reward and punishment in a minimal social situation. *Journal of Experimental Psychology,* 1957, **54,** 318–326.

Sidowski, J. B., Wyckoff, L. B., & Tabory, L. The influence of reinforcement and punishment in a minimal social situation. *Journal of Abnormal and Social Psychology,* 1956, **52,** 115–119.

Siegel, S., & Zajonc, R. B. Group risk-taking in professional decisions. *Sociometry,* 1967, **30,** 339–350.

Sigall, H., & Aronson, E. Liking for an evaluator as a function of her physical attractiveness and nature of the evaluations. *Journal of Experimental Social Psychology,* 1969, **5,** 93–100.

Simmel, G. The significance of numbers for social life. In A. P. Hare, E. F. Borgatta, & R. B. Bales (Eds.), *Small Groups.* (rev. ed.) New York: Knopf, 1966. Pp. 9–15.

Sommer, R. Small group ecology. *Psychological Bulletin,* 1967, **67,** 145–152.

Spielberger, C. D. The role of awareness in verbal conditioning. *Journal of Personality,* 1962, **30,** 73–102.

Stagner, R., & Congdon, C. S. Another failure to demonstrate displacement of aggression. *Journal of Abnormal and Social Psychology,* 1955, **51,** 695–696.

Stein, D. D., Hardyck, J. A., & Smith, M. B. Race and belief: An open and shut case. *Journal of Personality and Social Psychology,* 1965, **1,** 281–289.

Steiner, I. D. Models for inferring relationships between group size and potential group productivity. *Behavioral Science,* 1966, **11,** 273–283.

Steinzor, B. The spatial factor in face to face discussion groups. *Journal of Abnormal and Social Psychology,* 1950, **45,** 552–555.

Stewart, R. H. Effect of continuous responding on the order effect in personality impression formation. *Journal of Personality and Social Psychology,* 1965, **1,** 161–165.

Stoner, J. A. F. Risky and cautious shifts in group decisions: The influence of widely held values. *Journal of Experimental Social Psychology,* 1968, **4,** 442–459.

Strickland, L. H. Surveillance and trust. *Journal of Personality,* 1958, **26,** 200–215.

Strodtbeck, F. L., & Hook, L. H. The social dimensions of a twelve-man jury table. *Sociometry,* 1961, **24,** 397–415.

Strodtbeck, F. L., James, R. M., & Hawkins, C. Social status in jury deliberations. In E. E. Maccoby, T. M. Newcomb, & E. L. Hartley (Eds.), *Readings in social psychology.* (3rd. ed.) New York: Holt, Rinehart and Winston, 1958. Pp. 379–388.

Stroebe, W., Insko, C. A., Thompson, V. D., & Layton, B. D. Effects of physical attractiveness, attitude similarity, and sex on various aspects of interpersonal attraction. *Journal of Personality and Social Psychology,* 1971, **18,** 79–91.

Taffel, C. Anxiety and the conditioning of verbal behavior. *Journal of Abnormal and Social Psychology,* 1955, **51,** 496–501.

Tannenbaum, P. H. Mediated generalization of attitude change via the principle of congruity. *Journal of Personality and Social Psychology,* 1966, 3, 493–499.

Taylor, D. W., & Faust, W. L. Twenty questions: Efficiency in problem solving as a function of size of group. *Journal of Experimental Psychology,* 1952, **44,** 360–368.

Teger, A. I., & Pruitt, D. G. Components of group risk taking. *Journal of Experimental Social Psychology,* 1967, 3, 189–205.

Teger, A. I., Pruitt, D. G., St. Jean, R., & Haaland, G. A. A reexamination of the familiarization hypothesis in group risk taking. *Journal of Experimental Social Psychology,* 1970, **6,** 346–350.

Terman, L. M. A preliminary study of the psychology and pedagogy of leadership. In P. Hare, E. F. Borgatta, & R. F. Bales (Eds.), *Small groups.* New York: Knopf, 1955. Pp. 24–30.

Tharp, R. G. Psychological patterning in marriage. *Psychological Bulletin,* 1963, **60,** 97–117.

Thibaut, J. W. An experimental study of the cohesiveness of underprivileged groups. *Human Relations,* 1950, 3, 251–278.

Thibaut, J., & Faucheux, C. The development of contractual norms in a bargaining situation under two types of stress. *Journal of Experimental Social Psychology,* 1965, **1,** 89–102.

Thibaut, J. W., & Kelley, H. H. *The social psychology of groups.* New York: Wiley, 1959.

Thibaut, J. W., & Riecken, H. W. Some determinants and consequences of the perception of social causality. *Journal of Personality,* 1955, **24,** 113–133.

Thibaut, J., & Ross, M. Commitment and experience as determinants of assimilation and contrast. *Journal of Personality and Social Psychology,* 1969, **13,** 322–329.

Thomas, E. J., & Fink, C. F. Effects of group size. *Psychological Bulletin,* 1963, **60,** 371–384.

Thompson, W. R., & Nishimura, R. Some determinants of friendship. *Journal of Personality*, 1952, **20**, 305–314.

Tuckman, B. W. Group composition and group performance of structured and unstructured tasks. *Journal of Experimental Social Psychology*, 1967, **3**, 25–40.

Valins, S. Cognitive effects of false heart-rate feedback. *Journal of Personality and Social Psychology*, 1966, **4**, 400–408.

Valins, S., & Ray, A. A. Effects of cognitive desensitization on avoidance behavior. *Journal of Personality and Social Psychology*, 1967, **7**, 345–350.

Verba, S. *Groups and political behavior: A study of leadership.* Princeton, New Jersey: Princeton University Press, 1961.

Vidmar, N. Group composition and the risky shift. *Journal of Experimental Social Psychology*, 1970, **6**, 153–166.

Wallace, J. Role reward and dissonance reduction. *Journal of Personality and Social Psychology*, 1966, **3**, 305–312.

Wallach, M. A., & Kogan, N. Sex differences and judgment processes. *Journal of Personality*, 1959, **27**, 555–564.

Wallach, M. A., & Kogan, N. The roles of information, discussion, and concensus in group risk-taking. *Journal of Experimental Social Psychology*, 1965, **1**, 1–19.

Wallach, M. A., Kogan, N., & Bem, D. Group influence on individual risk taking. *Journal of Abnormal and Social Psychology*, 1962, **65**, 75–86.

Wallach, M. A., Kogan, N., & Bem, D. Diffusion of responsibility and level of risk-taking in groups. *Journal of Abnormal and Social Psychology*, 1964, **68**, 263–274.

Wallach, M. A., Kogan, N., & Burt, R. B. Are risk takers more persuasive than conservatives in group discussion? *Journal of Experimental Social Psychology*, 1968, **4**, 76–88.

Wallach, M. A., & Wing, C. W., Jr. Is risk a value? *Journal of Personality and Social Psychology*, 1968, **9**, 101–106.

Walster, E. The temporal sequence of post-decision processes. In L. Festinger (Ed.), *Conflict, decision, and dissonance.* Stanford, California: Stanford University Press, 1964. Pp. 112–127.

Walster, E., Aronson, E., & Abrahams, D. On increasing the persuasiveness of a low prestige communicator. *Journal of Experimental Social Psychology*, 1966, **2**, 325–342.

Walster, E., Aronson, V., Abrahams, D., & Rottman, L. Importance of physical attractiveness in dating behavior. *Journal of Personality and Social Psychology*, 1966, **5**, 508–516.

Ward, C. D. Seating arrangement and leadership emergence in small discussion groups. *Journal of Social Psychology*, 1968, **74**, 83–90.

Watts, W. A. Relative persistence of opinion change induced by active compared to passive participation. *Journal of Personality and Social Psychology*, 1967, **5**, 4–15.

Watts, W. A., & McGuire, W. J. Persistence of induced opinion change and retention of the inducing message contents. *Journal of Abnormal and Social Psychology*, 1964, **68**, 233–241.

Weiss, W., & Fine, B. The effect of induced aggressiveness on opinion change. *Journal of Abnormal and Social Psychology*, 1956, **52**, 109–114.

White, R., & Lippitt, R. Leader behavior and member reaction in three "social climates." In D. Cartwright & A. Zander (Eds.), *Group dynamics.* (3rd ed.) New York: Harper & Row, 1968. Pp. 318–335.

Wicklund, R. A., Cooper, J., & Linder, D. E. Effects of expected effort on attitude change prior to exposure. *Journal of Experimental Social Psychology*, 1967, **3**, 416–428.

Williams, J. D. *The compleat strategyst.* Revised edition. New York. McGraw-Hill, 1954.

Wilson, W., & Insko, C. Recency effects in face-to-face interaction. *Journal of Personality and Social Psychology*, 1968, **9**, 21–23.

Winch, R. F., Ktsanes, T., & Ktsanes, V. Empirical elaboration of the theory of complementary needs in mate selection. *Journal of Abnormal and Social Psychology*, 1955, **51**, 508–513.

Wishner, J. Reanalysis of "impressions of personality." *Psychological Review*, 1960, **67**, 96–112.

Wrightsman, L. S., Jr. Effects of waiting with others on changes in level of felt anxiety. *Journal of Abnormal and Social Psychology*, 1960, **61**, 216–222.

Zajonc, R. B. Cognitive theories in social psychology. In G. Lindzey & E. Aronson (Eds.), *The handbook of social psychology*. (2nd ed.) Vol. 1. Reading, Massachusetts: Addison-Wesley, 1968. Pp. 320–411.

Zanna, M. P., Kiesler, C. A., & Pilkonis, P. A. Positive and negative attitudinal affect established by classical conditioning. *Journal of Personality and Social Psychology*, 1970, **14**, 321–328.

Zdep, S. M., & Oakes, W. F. Reinforcement of leadership behavior in group discussion. *Journal of Experimental Social Psychology*, 1967, **3**, 310–320.

AUTHOR INDEX

Numbers in italics refer to the pages on which the complete references are listed.

SUBJECT INDEX

A

Affective–cognitive consistency theory, *see also* Balance theory
  attitude structure, 10–11
  comparison with congruity and balance theories, 18–19
  fragmentation, 11, *see also* Differentiation
  mathematical index, 11–12
  persistence, 83–84
  sequences of attitude change, 12–14
  summation, 19
After-only design, 3–4
Asch situation, 317–318
ASo, 414–418, *see also* Leadership
Attitude
  behavior, 2–3
  belief, 2–3
  change, xiv
  definition, 1
  opinion, 3
  Rosenberg's definition, 9–10
Attraction, 259–313
  Aronson and Cope experiment, 270, 297–304
  Berkowitz and LePage experiment, 286, 304–313
  Byrne and Nelson experiment, 269, 291–296
  determinants, 259–290
    belief in a just world, 286–290
    frustration and aggression, 282–286
    implied evaluation, 271–277
    physical attractiveness, 279–282
    satisfaction of self-evaluative need, 259–266
    similarity, 266–271
    spacial propinquity and social contact, 277–279
Attribution, *see also* Person perception
  another person, 227–231
  Bem's reinterpretation of dissonance, 139–141
  Kelley, 227–228, 236
  self, 231–236
    Schachter, 231–236, 244–245
Autokinetic situation, 317

B

Averaging, *see also* Summation congruity theory, 17, 19

Balance theory
  affective–cognitive consistency theory, 9–14, *see also* Affective–cognitive consistency theory
  altruism, 511–512
  Aronson and Cope experiment, 297–304
  belief in justice, 288–289
  classical conditioning of attitude, 40
  comparison with congruity and affective–cognitive consistency theories, 18–19
  conformity, 323
  congruity theory, 14–18, *see* Congruity theory
  disagreed with compliment, 276
  Heider's, 5–9
    differentiation, 9
    multiplicative rule, 8–9
    sentiment relation, 6
    unit relation, 6
  overevaluation of ingroup products, 504–505
  similarity and attraction, 270
  verbal reinforcement, 36
Bargaining
  norms, 36
  Thibaut and Faucheux experiment, 365–377
Before-after design, 3–4
Belief, 2–3, *see also* Attitude
Belief–dissimilarity theory, 515–518
Belief in a just world, 286–290
Birth-order, 265–266
Bystander intervention, 391–393

C

Central traits, 219
Choice
  Brehm and Cohen's reinterpretation of dissonance, 137
  dissonance theory, 109–110, 127
  effort, 135–136
Classical conditioning of attitude, 38–40